THE USES OF THE PRESENT

The Uses of the Present

LEONARD WOLF

San Francisco State College

McGraw-Hill Book Company
New York
St. Louis
San Francisco
London
Sydney
Toronto
Mexico
Panama

This book was set in Times Roman by Rocappi, Inc.,
and printed on permanent paper and bound by The Maple Press Company.
The designer was Barbara Ellwood.
The editors were Robert Fry, Cheryl Kupper, and Helen Greenberg.
Peter D. Guilmette supervised the production.

The Uses of the Present

Library of Congress Catalog Card Number 71330

1 2 3 4 5 6 7 8 9 0 **MAMM** 4 3 2 1 0 6 9 8 7 0

ACKNOWLEDGMENTS

PHILIP APPLEMAN, "A Million More Mouths Each Week," "How Does Hunger Feel?" and "The Accelerating Crisis" from *The Silent Explosion* by Philip Appleman. Copyright © 1965, 1966 by Philip Appleman. Reprinted by permission of the Beacon Press.

PETER BERG, excerpts from *Voices of the Love Generation* by Leonard and Deborah Wolf. Copyright © 1968 by Leonard Wolf. Reprinted by permission of Little, Brown and Company.

NORMAN O. BROWN, "Sexuality and Childhood" and "The Resurrection of the Body" from *Life Against Death* by Norman O. Brown. Copyright © 1959 by Wesleyan University and is reprinted by permission of Wesleyan University Press.

ELDRIDGE CLEAVER, "The White Race and Its Heroes" from *Soul on Ice* by Eldridge Cleaver. Copyright © 1968 by Eldridge Cleaver. Used with permission of McGraw-Hill Book Company.

JOHN HOPE FRANKLIN, "The Two Worlds of Race: A Historical View" from *Daedalus,* Fall, 1965. Reprinted by permission from *Daedalus,* Journal of the American Academy of Arts and Sciences, Boston, Massachusetts, Volume 94, Number 4.

TOM GARDNER, "Manpower Unchanneled" by Tom Gardner from *We Won't Go* edited by Alice Lynd. Copyright © 1968 by Alice Lynd. Reprinted by permission of the Beacon Press.

RICHARD GOLDSTEIN, "Theatre of Fear: One on the Aisle." Copyright, international copyright © 1968, The Village Voice, Inc. Reprinted by permission of Richard Goldstein and the Village Voice.

MITCHELL GORDON, "Help, Police!" from *Sick Cities* by Mitchell Gordon. Copyright © 1963 by Mitchell Gordon. Reprinted with permission of The Macmillan Company.

WILLIAM H. GRIER AND PRICE M. COBBS, "Marriage and Love" from *Black Rage* by William H. Grier and Price M. Cobbs. Copyright © 1968 by William H. Grier and Price M. Cobbs. Reprinted by permission of Basic Books, Inc., Publishers, New York.

MICHAEL HARRINGTON, "The Invisible Land" from *The Other America* by Michael Harrington. Copyright © 1962 by Michael Harrington. Reprinted with permission of The Macmillan Company.

IRVING HOWE, "New Styles in Leftism" by Irving Howe from *Dissent,* Summer 1965. Reprinted by permission of the author and *Dissent.*

ALDOUS HUXLEY, excerpt from "The Doors of Perception" from *The Doors of Perception and Heaven and Hell* by Aldous Huxley. Copyright © 1954, 1955, 1956 by Aldous Huxley. Reprinted by permission of Harper and Row, Publishers, Mrs. Laura Huxley, and Chatto and Windus, Ltd.

TO DEBORAH

PREFACE

The Industrial Revolution, whose beginnings are less than two hundred years behind us, did not mark a simple transition from one age to another. Instead, it was the beginning of a radical shift in the quality of human experience, a shift brought about by the incredible change of pace with which motion and communication were accomplished. A long look backward helps to make the point: In the interval between the first ape-men and the last of the French revolutionaries, however mean or noble or bloody history was, it was made by men who moved, within a narrow range of variation, pretty much at the same pace. On land, they could walk or run or hold on to whatever animals they could harness. In water, they waded or swam or floated on contrivances of reeds or hides or wood. The air, except in dreams and myths, was out of bounds.

Now pace is the key and acceleration the central fact. As a species, we evolved through long millennia to the cadence of a slow-motion world. Our senses, our reflexes, our ideas of time, and very likely our unconscious lives have been formed by the bearable speed at which we moved—until the nineteenth century, when, as a result of our own skills, swifter rhythms began to bang in our ears.

Now we move toward and away from each other faster than ever. We communicate or betray sooner than ever. As for killing, we do that so well that the twentieth century is easily the bloodiest in recorded history. And the rate of acceleration, in all areas of endeavor, increases.

Matthew Arnold, worried by the speed with which the nineteenth century moved in the direction of the twentieth, called for "leisure to grow wise." Almost a hundred years later, a shrewd participant in the present must take his leisure with the tense deliberation of the trapeze artist who knows that time is something more than simple duration. He must *use* the arc of his swing, shaping the interval in which he moves with swiftness and grace, treating it as if it were unhurried as eternity. If he fails at being either quick or graceful, he may die.

The Uses of the Present does not claim to teach elegant survival, though there is no reason why it cannot help. Eliot's invocation at the end of *The Waste Land* to "Give . . . Sympathize . . . Control . . ." constitutes the hidden bias on which this book is built and suggests my hope that the lessons herein can help to establish a classical "set" toward the onrushing present.

Meanwhile, its more modest aim is to provide readers with source material in the form of significant essays written within the past decade. The seven section headings under which these essays are grouped call attention to those problems which, particularly in America, have seemed most pressing. The essays themselves, like a handful of snapshots taken in a crisis, are offered as a means of exposing the present, not of explaining or defusing it. There is plenty of material here over which to brood constructively. Plenty to quarrel or write about. Careful readers will get one further point: The best immediate use of these pieces would be to read the whole works from which they have been taken.

This book owes an enormous debt to Daniel Goleman who, as an undergraduate at Amherst and the University of California, and later as a graduate student at Harvard, tested the uses of the present and kept me informed. His energy, his insights, and his wide reading kept me from a variety of errors. For those that I may nevertheless have made, I am entirely responsible.

I have had other generous help from colleagues and friends around the country: at San Francisco State College, Pat Gleeson, Daniel Knapp, James Schevill, and Mark Linenthal gave me better counsel than I was always willing to take. Thanks too are owed to Cheryl Kupper, McGraw-Hill's basic book editor, for guiding me skillfully through this undertaking, and to Bill Orr, who gave me the idea. For important, if informal, conversations, I must thank Michael Rossman, Michael Korman, Sam Blaser, and Jerry Rubin.

To the students it has been my good luck to encounter over the past decade at San Francisco State College, the University of Hawaii, Columbia University, New York University, the University of Shiraz, and Hebrew University in Jerusalem I owe my sense that the present is first of all a hopeful time.

Finally, I must thank Gail Gahagan in San Francisco and Diana Shye in Jerusalem for help with the intricate and wearying details that accompanied the making of this book.

Leonard Wolf

CONTENTS

Introduction

This book begins with shame and ends in prophecy. What lies between is sometimes disturbing, occasionally exalted or angry, and in more than one place, obscene. That may be too bad, but these essays reflect America's preoccupations in the last decade and they are not likely to radiate serenity. It has not been a quiet time, as the roll call of our great assassinations should remind us: John Kennedy, Malcolm X, Martin Luther King, Jr., Robert Kennedy. Not at all quiet. Assassinations, civil disorders, race hatred, sexual confusion, grinding poverty, and war have been the visible signs of our national turmoil. It is as if America has been chosen as the place where the allegory of the present has been pushed to its defining crisis by way of instruction to the world. The American has become the new Everyman whose struggles with the immediate moment are full of meaning for the rest of mankind. Our luck is that we have plunged into the cybernetic, the atomic age. We are not alone, but we were first and our experience is of necessity prototypical. We have stumbled into the future with no better equipment for survival than a cluster of ethical uncertainties and a remarkable competence for creating and using machines.

The essays here do not constitute a history of the last decade, nor do they offer a coherent image of it. They do, however, reflect what a number of activists and thinkers have had to say as they tried to make sense out of their experience.

That these men were not able to arrive at immediately healing wisdom, tomorrow's, not yesterday's, headlines will prove. Still, as they lent their minds to the process of interpretation, they helped to shape the history that had been shaping them.

The first section, The Holocaust: A Heritage of Guilt, must not be read merely as the record of a distant shame. The death camps and the appearance of atomic weaponry marked the beginning, not the end, of an epoch. We now know the answer to the once unasked question: "What are the limits of man's inhumanity to man?" The flames at Auschwitz and at Hiroshima made it clear that those horizons are limitless. To know this is to risk a near-fatal wound to our self-esteem, to begin to despair about our potential for humane behavior. Self-loathing, however, is not an ethically useful form of energy. The proper antidote to such tempting poison is to know more rather than less about what happened. We find as we learn more not merely the evidence of wickedness but also the almost equally terrifying proof that humanity is tenacious enough to survive any number of appalling deaths.

Still, those events *were* too terrible. Robert Lifton says in *Death in Life:*

> Human beings are unable to remain open to experience of this intensity for any length of time. Very quickly—sometimes within minutes or even seconds—*hibakusha* [atomic bomb survivors] began to undergo a process of "psychic closing-off"; that is, they simply ceased to feel. . . .

Psychic closing-off protects an immediate survivor from insanity, but to us, at some distance from all that pain, to close off is to assure a blunted consciousness.This is particularly true since hideous events are so often reported to us in terms of anesthetizing numbers. To a decent man, one death is bad, two are worse, three are dreadful, four appalling, five a tragedy, six a disaster . . . and then . . . and then . . . ? The absurdity of the sequence is clear. Our feelings cannot keep pace with the arithmetic. The emotional difference between five million four hundred thousand as opposed to six million dead is neither imaginable nor expressible. As we read Lifton's report that the deaths at Hiroshima were

> variously estimated from 63,000 to 240,000 or more, the official figure is usually given at 78,000, but the city of Hiroshima estimates 200,000—the total encompassing between 25 and 50 per cent of the city's then daytime population (also a disputed figure, varying from 227,000 to over 400,000) . . .

we run some risk of impatience at what sounds like a bookkeeper's quibble, and we may be sure that psychic closing-off is taking place.

Six million dead *is* worse than five hundred thousand. The point is, and Dostoevsky was not the first to make it, that *one* innocent death is a disaster; but in the presence of such overwhelming numbers, we may lose our sense of outrage for that one. One way to crack through the anonymity of the statistics is to discern in the welter of the burned and the dead for whom we were not responsible, the faces of the living for whom we are.

But to refresh the past in this way is to require an act of love, and that is the reason for including the Holocaust section here. Lifton writes about atomic bomb and concentration camp survivors:

> The survivor cannot formulate from a void. He requires the psychological existence of a past as well as a present, of the dead as well as the living. Without these, neither mastery of his death-encounter nor a place in human society is possible.

Twenty-five years after the two uniquely dreadful events of our time, it is perfectly clear that, in the sense that they are a warning to us, we are all their survivors.

The white, middle-aged, middle-class parents sitting around their swimming pool telling stories of how poor they were in the thirties are acting out their own cartoon. The I-was-poorer-than-you's sound more than a trifle musty at best, but they achieve a comic fatuity when they culminate in self-flattering conclusions about the values of work, frugality, self-discipline, and a variety of other virtues by means of which the parents of the present generation climbed up from the depths. No doubt the young within earshot are expected to take notice.

Such scenes are easy to satirize, but there are somber implications there as well. However mythologized in the telling, the remembered poverty was real. At the height of the Great Depression, twelve million were unemployed. One third of the nation was, as Franklin Roosevelt said, "ill-housed, ill-clothed, and ill-fed." The marks of poverty were widespread *and* they were tangible. Soup kitchens, surplus-food lines, apple vendors, and the WPA were actually and frequently visible. This experience of the Depression had to mark the generation that came to maturity in those years. Ten years of poverty capped by four years of war went a long way toward making a generation interested in stability, security, the comfortable acquisition of things. In the accusing vocabulary of the young, it became a generation of squares who can recognize achievement only when that achievement wears a respectable price tag. Seen through unkind eyes, it is a generation of timorous aspiration, satisfied with mean achievement. More gently observed, its materialism is only one of the dismal marks with which poverty scars the soul.

The old poverty was visible and was shared by much of the nation. As the economy improved, one could better one's lot, one could stop being poor. The new poverty, as Michael Harrington points out in *The Other America*, keeps discreetly out of sight and remains untouched by upward swings in the national income.

> These are the people who are immune to progress . . . The other Americans are the victims of the very inventions and machines that have provided a higher living standard for the rest of society. They are upside down in the economy, and for them greater productivity often means worse jobs; agricultural advance becomes hunger.

Far worse than the old poverty and more dangerous to the health of the nation, the new American poverty presages the fate of increasing numbers of Americans as automation encroaches on higher levels of human skills. More dangerous, however, is the alienation from the center of the American experience that simply being poor produces.

In 1958, Kenneth Galbraith could write:

> An affluent society, that is also both compassionate and rational would, no doubt, secure to all who needed it the minimum income essential for decency and comfort. . . . It can use the forthright remedy of providing for those in want. Nothing requires it to be compassionate. But it has no high philosophical justification for callousness.

Does it, indeed, have any? Or enough to justify even one account such as this of how a black mother of five feeds her children in Tunica County, Mississippi:

> Every morning the first thing I think about is what I can do to feed the kids. I don't have no money coming in. . . . The bossman don't give us much money, but there'll be ten dollars one week and maybe five the next. . . . For breakfast there isn't much, but they know it's not until the middle of the day they can eat. I give them some soup I make—I boil up a bone and some beans and there's the water and I salt it real good. I put some milk flakes [powdered milk] in the children's coffee, that's good for them, I know. They eats their energy from the candy bars, of course. And I gives them grits and once or twice in the year some good bacon. She tells me we get along fine down here and I say yes to her. What else would I be saying, I ask you?

> *"We Need Help," Robert Coles and Harry Huge,* New Republic, *March 8, 1969.*

Forty or fifty million listless, underfed, humiliated people among us raise root questions about the nature of our society. Is it rational? Is it compassionate? If it has the means to provide for those in want, why doesn't it? If it cannot, why not? In 1963, Harrington cried:

> The means are at hand to fulfill the age-old dream: poverty can now be abolished. How long shall we ignore this underdeveloped nation in our midst? How long shall we look the other way while our fellow human beings suffer? How long?

At the end of 1969 Coles and Huge still observed:

> Americans go hungry every day, become malnourished and die because they didn't get enough food and the right kind of food and fall sick and never, never at all see a doctor. . . .

In 1967, Marcus Raskin and Bernard Fall wrote:

> . . . the expanding Vietnamese war, from being the central issue of American foreign policy, has become the central issue of American society. For those of draft age, an increasing number, it is the central issue of their lives. Considering its "ripple effect" on American society in the economic, political and social sphere, this is the first war which will affect the American society radically since the American Civil War a hundred years ago.

If by the time this book reaches its readers the war in Vietnam is over, the inexpressible relief will not do much to heal the wound the war has inflicted on our sense of national decency. Prohibition made hypocrites about law of an entire generation; Vietnam has made another generation cynical about national morality. Years of napalm and saturation bombings, endlessly optimistic military communiqués, and distorted but triumphant body counts have shattered the myths of American invincibility and truthfulness.

Vietnam is the dirty war; its heroes known only to the courageous young men forced to fight it. There were plenty of scenes of individual courage, but none that stood for the aspirations of a nation. The young, who for the most part were either poor or black or both, fought this war. And in a country whose population was approaching two hundred million, only their next of kin seemed to miss the over forty thousand Americans who died in the Vietnamese countryside.

The war produced, however, an upheaval in the national soul. The soldiers fought with a courage and a sense of duty that made it clear how deep is the capacity of the young to be faithful to each other. Their lonely courage widened the gap between their devotion and the cynicism, indifference, or disapproval of the country at large. They were the ones who took seriously an older ethic: "My country right or wrong." But to many others the country was *so* wrong that nothing remained except to condemn the entire venture.

The decline of patriotism as an idea may turn out to be the most terrible price of the war. Without clearly understood national goals, we need not wonder that a scene like the following made a conscientious objector out of a Marine recruit:

> A crew-cut captain greeted us with these words: "What does k-i-l-l spell?"
>
> "Kill," was the obvious, though not too loud, reply of most of the three hundred voices.
>
> "What does k-i-l-l spell?" repeated the man with silver bars on his shoulder.
>
> "Kill!" This time, louder.
>
> "What?"
>
> "Kill!"
>
> "I can't hear you!"
>
> "Kill!" A deafening chant began: "Kill! Kill! Kill! . . ."
>
> I looked around me. Clerks, mechanics, teachers, college students, a few professional men, all were screaming, "Kill!" Who cares who? Just kill. Kill anyone that the President, the Congress, and the generals brand as "evil," "aggressors," "the enemy."
>
> *Stephen Fortunato, Jr., in Alice Lynd,* We Won't Go, *p. 79.*

The war produced a decade of political imprisonment and self-exile. It forced some to make fiery martyrs of themselves.

It may be that if any good comes out of the Vietnam struggle, it will have nothing to do with military victory or defeat. A newly evolving, more responsible definition of what the social contract ought to be between the citizen and his state may develop. For the moment, acquiescence remains the official expectation. But the roll of dissenters continues to grow.

In 1944, Gunnar Myrdal could call the black man's situation in our country "an American dilemma." Twenty years later, Charles Silberman wrote in *Crisis in Black and White:*

> Myrdal was wrong. The tragedy of race relations in the United States is that there is no American Dilemma. White Americans are not torn and tortured by the conflict between their devotion to the American creed and their actual behavior. They are upset by the current state of race relations, to be sure. But what troubles

them is not that justice is being denied but that their peace is being shattered and their business interrupted.

Silberman may in turn be wrong. There *is* a dilemma, and there was one from the moment that the first black man set his shackled foot on America's soil. That moment sealed the guilt of both races: for the black man, the unshakable guilt of being a slave; for the white, the equally unshakable guilt of keeping one. The dilemma was, after that initial crime, how to recognize each other ever again as men. It was a tainted beginning, and that taint has spread. It helped to convulse tha nation in the first of its great modern wars, and it convulses it now. Legal slavery died in America more than a hundred years ago, but the conflict goes on. The new, the necessary dimension is the black man's determination to be guilty no longer.

In another twenty or thirty years, the black revolt of the sixties will be seen for what it is—not nearly so much a movement for social justice as a heroic and occasionally bloody endeavor to achieve psychological and spiritual health. Black power, black consciousness, Negritude, and interest in the African past are not directed against the white man, except as he gets in the way. They are, rather, elements in a struggle to assert manhood, black manhood. The demand for social justice is a consequence of that assertion. It is, in fact, a part of its definition.

Certainly, it is a social justice that not many men, black or white, could have foreseen a couple of decades ago. The black-white struggle of the sixties has effectively ended the myth of our country as the melting pot. The "brown" America envisaged by some liberals as the solution to our race problems has disappeared as a possibility for the future. The painless interfusion of color that was to bring an end to differences is seen now for the puny idea that it was. It was a mask for insufficient courage.

Americans of the future will have to countenance more rather than fewer differences among themselves. Meanwhile, the problem is how to retreat from those programs of integration which, to many blacks, imply the permission to disappear into the white man's world. The situation is more critical than ever because, while there is a palpable new dimension in the black experience, much of white America holds loyally to its usual set of responses. In the natural course of a lifetime, manhood too long suppressed withers into senility. The new black argues that waiting is a fool's game. In the face of black intransigence, the white man may discover that self-doubt, not blackness, constitutes the real threat to manhood. Deprived of the myth of white superiority and facing a fellow American entirely self-confident *and* black, he may finally be ready for an act of recognition.

"Ironically," writes Philip Appleman in *The Silent Explosion,* "the world's poverty and misery are now most heavily concentrated in the lands of dark-skinned peoples. . . ." Irony and paradox, paradox and irony, wherever we turn. The concentration camps and atomic bombs, the persistence of poverty, the Vietnam War, and the dilemma of black and white in America—all reveal or are contained by one or the other. So far, however, implicit in all of these matters has been the possibility that an ethical option for dealing with them does exist. One could hope, momentarily at least, that a decision for good or a recognition of evil might result from putting our minds to the problem. No doubt the same is ultimately true about the problem of crowding, but we must confess that when we consider the population explosion, we seem to be confronted only by a malevolent biology which makes irrelevant all questions of choice. When Appleman tells us that after a fifteen-minute interval

> . . . nearly two thousand more people have been added to this planet. On the other hand, per capita production of food (and of the other necessities and amenities of life) has declined a little more. . . .

the very act of taking thought assumes an aspect of futility. Still, thinking is precisely all that is left to us.

Population pressures threaten the so-called underdeveloped areas of the world with starvation and disease. Yet in the technologically advanced West, one third of the world's people consume two thirds of its food and continue to push life expectancy to new limits. While a compulsively successful science increases both rural and urban productivity, raining material blessings upon us, that very productivity makes the air muddy, our cities unbearable, and our seas malodorous. Here are paradoxes upon paradoxes.

The irritability of animals crowded in cages has already been demonstrated in the laboratory. The effects of crowding on humans are equally clear. If we view America as a place where crowding takes place within the framework of temporarily sufficient resources—though, as we have seen, not always, or for all Americans—we have some clue to a number of social manifestations for which simple wickedness is not an explanation: the mounting crime rate (particularly juvenile crime and crimes of violence), the breakdown in family life, the shift in sexual mores, and the widespread increase in personal distress. As if unconsciously responding to the pressures of population, psychological practice has shifted in the direction of techniques for dealing with patients in clusters instead of one at a time. And it is not entirely farfetched that the growth in recent years of group-reassurance ventures, such as the Esalen Institute, Synanon, and various communal living experiments, involves similar efforts at learning to deal with crowding.

The inescapable picture of America as a technologically advanced but increasingly overpopulated society is dark enough. For the time being, crime, neurosis, sick or eroded cities, and squandered natural resources are the costs we can still afford to pay. Unlike many parts of the Orient where the crowding of human bodies is long past the point of disaster, we still have a breathing space in which to make some choices. India does not have our nervous frenzy. Those who starve there lie down quietly to die.

What are the characteristics of the emerging sensibility in America? It rejects facelessness and the interchangeability of human endeavor; it despises the struggle for personal power and the acquisition of wealth.

> One is instead, encouraged to lend oneself to a life of organic ebb and flow; to be responsive to the natural world; to be aware of one's inner nature, to address one's self to experiences which enrich the quest for ecstatic consciousness. . . . To these, and serving them, we must add several other tenets: the primacy of the immediate moment; the sense of human sexuality as related to the quest for human freedom as well as to the transcendental experience . . . .
>
> *Leonard and Deborah Wolf,* Voices from the Love Generation, *pp. xxv and xxvii.*

This description comes from a book on the hippie movement, but the attitudes it describes are by now diffused through a considerably larger section of our society. Such attitudes can be seen merely as restatements of a Rousseauesque romanticism, but as they are expressed in action, they have taken on peculiarly contemporary characteristics.

The central point is this: The emerging sensibility and the styles of action that express it are the paradoxical result of the cybernetic revolution. The richer sexual freedom envisioned by Norman O. Brown has become instantly possible because of the success of the Pill. And McLuhan tells us in *Understanding Media* that

> as electrically contracted, the globe is no more than a village. Electric speed in bringing all social and political functions together in a sudden implosion has heightened human awareness of responsibility to an intense degree. It is this implosive factor that alters the position of the Negro, the teen-ager, and some other groups. They can no longer be *contained,* in the political sense of limited association. They are now *involved* in our lives, as we in theirs, thanks to the electric media. . . .

Finally, let it be remembered that the mind-expanding drugs praised by Huxley and raised to sacramental heights by Leary—and which have made visionary experience a possibility for the least ecstatic mind—are now the products of assembly-line pharmacology.

In the arts, the new romanticism has moved jubilantly forward. Electricity has merged with eroticism, spontaneity with fantasy, accident with ecstasy. Once more the cry is up to break through the limits of form. A sampling of names suggests what has been taking place: Robert Rauschenberg and Mark di Suvero in painting and sculpture; Merce Cunningham and Ann Halprin in dance; the Living Theater and the San Francisco Mime Troupe in drama; the Beatles, John Cage, and Terry Riley in music; Jean Luc Godard, Kenneth Anger, and Peter Fonda in film.

The emerging sensibility, say its most ardent exponents, is preparing us for the coming of the leisured future when the lion of the machine lies down with the lamb of the spirit. The happy time when we will live in

> . . . a cybernetic ecology
> where we are free of our labors
> and joined back to nature,
> returned to our mammal
> brothers and sisters,
> and all watched over
> by machines of loving grace
>
> *Richard Brautigan in* The Digger Papers, *p. 11.*

Assassinations, civil disorders, race hatred, sexual confusion, grinding poverty, crowding, war. . . . What a decade in which to be alive. What a decade in which to be young. The real wonder is not that youth in the sixties grew agitated, but rather that all of the tumult roiled in the direction of hope.

But to sense what happened with them, we must first consider disillusionment, a disillusionment that went deeper than the response to Vietnam or poverty or racial tension. Those were bad enough, but in addition, what struck young minds made precocious in an age of instantaneous communication was that the frontiers of action which had animated the American myth suddenly began to disappear. If they accepted the world into which they had been born, they could look forward to a lifetime of bland achievement. To be sure, some brilliant prospects for action were still possible: the frontiers of science, the conquest of space. But to the average graduate of an average high school or college, neither the great plains nor the mountains of experience stretched out before him. More realistic was a lifetime as a unit in an automated factory, not quite as productive as the machine he tended; or a white-shirted office worker performing rationalized office routines; or a civil servant checking off the years until his retirement. For the young, the passionate, the energetic, the imaginative, to see the world as a place in which to mark time was already to be in the shadow of a disaster.

For many, the only solution was to reject the world into which they had been born in favor of one that they would have to invent. The result was struggle: against the Vietnam War; against conscription; against poverty; against ROTC; for black freedom; for personal delight; for the expansion of consciousness; for access to power that did not serve personal ambition. The decade was punctuated by energetic dissent and civil disobedience which, for a long while, remained scrupulously nonviolent. However, as the sixties came to their close and the frustration mounted, the call for revolution was more frequently heard and protestors came to demonstrations armed for defense. The new folk heroes were warriors: Che Guevara, Mao Tse-tung, Ho Chi Minh. By the end of 1969, Dave Dellinger, a veteran of nonviolent protest, could worry because, in the aftermath of the Democratic Convention in Chicago, "some people are saying that the time has come when we must fight 'by any means necessary'."

Political activism was one response the young could make to the failures of their society. The hippie movement was another. Both had disillusionment as antecedents, but while the radicals found themselves in action, the hippies, for a brief and brilliant while, seemed, with the aid of LSD, to have stumbled on a contemplative ecstasy which, if all mankind were to share it, might be capable of turning the whole complex and weary struggle for social justice into a simple, innocent, and immediately possible act of love.

The attraction of the movement was immense, not only to the young, and if it is over as a unified force, it has far from disappeared as an emerging element in American life. The clothing and hair styles of the young continue to reflect the pleasure that hippies took in color and in the adornment of their bodies. Rock music and "turned on" sensibilities (whether drug-induced or not) are still inextricably part of the scene. In many parts of the country, experimental life styles continue to be tested in agricultural and urban communes. If students who two or three years ago considered dropping out of college now stay there, it is because so many turned on sensibilities have dropped in. And colleges have changed in the meantime:

> The call for openness in personal relations which the hippies have sounded has had a good effect on this generation of students. They are becoming increasingly willing to speak for themselves and to speak with unabashed feeling. Simple authority in the classroom no longer awes them. . . . College students are not the only ones who have changed under the impact of the hippie movement. There is in the rising generation at large a new and growing interest in the life of the spirit. . . . The hippie insistence on self-awareness and on the transcendental experience has restored vitality in the middle twentieth century to those ideas of feeling and the sublime which many of us thought had glimmered out at the end of the Victorian era.
>
> *Leonard and Deborah Wolf,* Voices from the Love Generation, *pp. 271-272.*

The hippie ideal has even affected the politics of the young. The prophecy that Peter Berg made is being fulfilled. In 1967 he was asked, "What do you foresee?" He replied,

> Civil war. Civil war with some attendant trips . . . hand-holding, candle-watching, high-on-acid-trust-and-hope routine . . . is not the end. Civil war with these things: the life-affirming banners. We're going to view what we're doing as the best we could come up with. It's only the best, scratch it. Scratch '67. Summer in San Francisco '67 First Be-Together for Escapees and Refugees. . . . Our part now coming up [is] to communicate in direct spinal language. Nothing said that can't be done. . . . To push as hard as we can. . . .
>
> Voices from the Love Generation, *pp. 262-263.*

Peter was speaking as a Digger, one of those light-struck, frenzied street people who gave to the hippie movement its instantaneous ethic: "Do your thing and be free." That ethic—although it gave bystanders the feeling that hippies were merely drug-bemused and passive—was dramatically linked to the energetic political activism of many sectors of the New Left and flared up with the appearance of the Youth International Party—the Yippies.

The Yippie movement introduced the politics of rapture to the American scene. It was easy for politicos and the traditional press to be contemptuous of the Yippies. They were too colorful and much too deliberately incoherent to pose a threat to anyone. Still, when Yippie passion was linked with the more purposive energies of the Students for a Democratic Society, the Black Panthers, the War Resisters League, and the Peace and Freedom Party, the clamor they made proved too much for Chicago's Mayor Daley. The ensuing confrontation shook up more than the radical left. McCarthy-and Kennedy-oriented Democrats who were neither ill-dressed nor dissident were swept into, and changed by, the clashes outside the Democratic Convention. It was a murky event in which the subconscious figured more actively than any rational decision taken by either side. That some kind of subtle sexual confrontation would take place was intuited by *Esquire* magazine, which sent Jean Genet, William Burroughs, and

Terry Southern to cover the convention. While the police defended the past, the young people invoked the ecstatic future. The debacle that followed was visible to the entire electronic village of the national electorate. The cost to Hubert Humphrey pales before the cost to the nation.

This book begins with shame and ends in prophecy. It would be mistaken to suppose, however, that ours is an epoch merely of disaster. All ages seem critical to those who live in them, but it seems hard not to believe that our crises surpass in significance those of any previous age. The trouble that pounds at us is an expression of the hunger for an era of fulfillment which, for the first time in history, seems to be within our reach. The confusion, the blood, the babbling, the ferocity, the unparalleled intelligence that assail us are parts of a somatic convulsion—vast tremors induced in the body of the world as it reacts to the news of some intensely human salvation. The new man is furious to set things right. Our immediate troubles come from the clashing visions of what is right offered by men who in previous ages would have had neither voice nor hope. From the vantage point of the present, there is everything to be done.

ONE

The Holocaust...
A Heritage
Of Guilt

Wiesel's *Night* is a poignant act of witnessing.
Cold stars and violin music among the corpses,
hurry, weariness, the attenuation of love
between father and son—the experience itself.
Lifton sifts among the ashes of a different
kind of pain. The scientist moved by science gone
berserk, he calls upon the humanist to endeavor
to see past the *hibakusha* as a victim of an accident
in history. Lifton's book stands against psychic
closing-off. Under his scrutiny the keloid scar
tissue begins to look like the mark of Cain.
But it is Nyszli who, though he suffered less
and understands less, is the greatest mystery:
Nyszli, who could wake at midnight in Auschwitz
and, finding the SS guards were gone,
hurriedly provide himself with food and clothing
and make his way—to where? To the
Birkenau KZ, where the SS was still in charge.
If the persistence of the death wish
were ever in doubt, his act
(and that of the others who went with him)
should put its existence out of all question.

PHOTOGRAPH FROM *Library of Congress.*

From **Night**
ELI WIESEL

An icy wind blew in violent gusts. But we marched without faltering.

The SS made us increase our pace. "Faster, you swine, you filthy sons of bitches!" Why not? The movement warmed us up a little. The blood flowed more easily in our veins. One felt oneself reviving. . . .

"Faster, you filthy sons of bitches!" We were no longer marching; we were running. Like automatons. The SS were running too, their weapons in their hands. We looked as though we were fleeing before them.

Pitch darkness. Every now and then, an explosion in the night. They had orders to fire on any who could not keep up. Their fingers on the triggers, they did not deprive themselves of this pleasure. If one of us stopped for a second, a sharp shot finished off another filthy son of a bitch.

I was putting one foot in front of the other mechanically. I was dragging with me this skeletal body which weighed so much. If only I could have got rid of it! In spite of my efforts not to think about it, I could feel myself as two entities—my body and me. I hated it.

I repeated to myself: "Don't think. Don't stop. Run."

Near me, men were collapsing in the dirty snow. Shots.

At my side marched a young Polish lad called Zalman. He had been working in the electrical warehouse at Buna. They had laughed at him because he was always praying or meditating on some problem of the Talmud. It was his way of escaping from reality, of not feeling the blows. . . .

He was suddenly seized with cramp in the stomach. "I've got stomach ache," he whispered to me. He could not go on. He had to stop for a moment. I begged him:

"Wait a bit, Zalman. We shall all be stopping soon. We're not going to run like this till the end of the world."

But as he ran he began to undo his buttons, crying:

"I can't go on any longer. My stomach's bursting. . . ."

"Make an effort, Zalman. . . . Try. . . ."

"I can't. . . ." he groaned.

His trousers lowered, he let himself sink down.

That is the last picture I have of him. I do not think it can have been the SS who finished him, because no one had noticed. He must have been trampled to death beneath the feet of the thousands of men who followed us.

I quickly forgot him. I began to think of myself again. Because of my painful foot, a shudder went through me at each step. "A few more yards," I thought. "A few more yards, and that will be the end. I shall fall. A spurt of red flame. A shot." Death wrapped itself around me till I was stifled. It stuck to me. I felt that I could touch it. The idea of dying, of no longer being, began to fascinate me. Not to exist any longer. Not to feel the horrible pains in my foot. Not to feel anything, neither weariness, nor cold, nor anything. To break the ranks, to let oneself slide to the edge of the road. . . .

My father's presence was the only thing that stopped me. . . . He was running at my side, out of breath, at the end of his strength, at his wit's end. I had no right to let myself die. What would he do without me? I was his only support.

These thoughts had taken up a brief space of time, during which I had gone on running without feeling my throbbing foot, without realizing that I was running, without being conscious that I owned a body galloping there on the road in the midst of so many thousands of others.

When I came to myself again, I tried to slacken the pace. But there was no way. A great tidal wave of men came rolling onward and would have crushed me like an ant.

I was simply walking in my sleep. I managed to close my eyes and to run like that while asleep. Now and then, someone would push me violently from behind, and I would wake up. The other would shout: "Run faster. If you don't want to go on, let other people come past." All I had to do was to close my eyes for a second to see a whole world passing by, to dream a whole lifetime.

An endless road. Letting oneself be pushed by the mob; letting oneself be dragged along by a blind destiny. When the SS became tired, they were changed. But no one changed us. Our limbs numb with cold despite the running, our throats parched, famished, breathless, on we went.

We were masters of nature, masters of the world. We had forgotten everything—death, fatigue, our natural needs. Stronger than cold or hunger, stronger than the shots and the desire to die, condemned and wandering, mere numbers, we were the only men on earth.

At last, the morning star appeared in the gray sky. A trail of indeterminate light showed on the horizon. We were exhausted. We were without strength, without illusions.

The commandant announced that we had already covered forty-two miles since we left. It was a long time since we had passed beyond the limits of fatigue. Our legs were moving mechanically, in spite of us, without us.

We went through a deserted village. Not a living soul. Not the bark of a dog. Houses with gaping windows. A few slipped out of the ranks to try and hide in some deserted building.

Still one hour's marching more, and at last came the order to rest.

We sank down as one man in the snow. My father shook me.

"Not here. . . . Get up. . . . A little farther on. There's a shed over there . . . come on."

I had neither the will nor the strength to get up. Nevertheless I obeyed. It was not a shed, but a brick factory with a caved-in roof, broken windows, walls filthy with soot. It was not easy to get in. Hundreds of prisoners were crowding at the door.

We at last succeeded in getting inside. There too the snow was thick. I let myself sink down. It was only then that I really felt my weariness. The snow was like a carpet, very gentle, very warm. I fell asleep.

I do not know how long I slept. A few moments or an hour. When I woke up, a frozen hand was patting my cheeks. I forced myself to open my eyes. It was my father.

How old he had grown since the night before! His body was completely twisted, shriveled up into itself. His eyes were petrified, his lips withered, decayed. Everything about him bore witness to extreme exhaustion. His voice was damp with tears and snow:

"Don't let yourself be overcome by sleep, Eliezer. It's dangerous to fall asleep in the snow. You might sleep for good. Come on, come on. Get up."

Get up? How could I? How could I get myself out of this fluffy bed? I could hear what my father said, but it seemed empty of meaning, as though he had told me to lift up the whole building in my arms. . . .

"Come on, son, come on. . . ."

I got up, gritting my teeth. Supporting me with his arm, he led me outside. It was far from easy. It was as difficult to go out as to get in. Under our feet were men crushed, trampled underfoot, dying. No one paid any attention.

We were outside. The icy wind stung my face. I bit my lips continually to prevent them from freezing. Around me everything was dancing a dance of death. It made my head reel. I was walking in a cemetery, among stiffened corpses, logs of wood. Not a cry of distress, not a groan, nothing but a mass agony, in silence. No one asked anyone else for help. You died because you had to die. There was no fuss.

In every stiffened corpse I saw myself. And soon I should not even see them; I should be one of them—a matter of hours.

"Come on, father, let's go back to the shed. . . ."

He did not answer. He was not looking at the dead.

"Come on, father, it's better over there. We can lie down a bit, one after the other. I'll watch over you, and then you can watch over me. We won't let each other fall asleep. We'll look after each other."

He agreed. Trampling over living bodies and corpses, we managed to re-enter the shed. Here we let ourselves sink down.

"Don't be afraid, son. Sleep—you can sleep. I'll look after you myself."

"No, you first, father. Go to sleep."

He refused. I lay down and tried to force myself to sleep, to doze a little, but in vain. God knows what I would not have given for a few moments of sleep. But, deep down, I felt that to sleep would mean to die. And something within me revolted against this death. All round me death was moving in, silently, without violence. It would seize upon some sleeping being, enter into him, and consume him bit by bit. Next to me there was someone trying to wake up his neighbor, his brother, perhaps, or a friend. In vain. Discouraged in the attempt, the man lay down in his turn, next to the corpse, and slept too. Who was there to wake him up? Stretching out an arm, I touched him:

"Wake up. You mustn't sleep here. . . ."

He half opened his eyes.

"No advice," he said in a faint voice. "I'm tired. Leave me alone. Leave me."

My father, too, was gently dozing. I could not see his eyes. His cap had fallen over his face.

"Wake up," I whispered in his ear.

He started up. He sat up and looked round him, bewildered, stupefied—a bereaved stare. He stared all round him in a circle as though he had suddenly decided to draw up an inventory of his universe, to find out exactly where he was, in what place, and why. Then he smiled.

I shall always remember that smile. From which world did it come?

The snow continued to fall in thick flakes over the corpses.

The door of the shed opened. An old man appeared, his moustache covered with frost, his lips blue with cold. It was Rabbi Eliahou, the rabbi of a small Polish community. He was a very good man, well loved by everyone in the camp, even by the Kapos and the heads of the blocks. Despite the trials and privations, his face still shone with his inner purity. He was the only rabbi who was always addressed as "Rabbi" at Buna. He was like one of the old prophets, always in the midst of his people to comfort them. And, strangely, his words of comfort never provoked rebellion; they really brought peace.

He came into the shed and his eyes, brighter than ever, seemed to be looking for someone:

"Perhaps someone has seen my son somewhere?"

He had lost his son in the crowd. He had looked in vain among the dying. Then he had scratched up the snow to find his corpse. Without result.

For three years they had stuck together. Always near each other, for suffering, for blows, for the ration of bread, for prayer. Three years, from camp to camp, from selection to selection. And now—when the end seemed near—fate had separated them. Finding himself near me, Rabbi Eliahou whispered:

"It happened on the road. We lost sight of one another during the journey. I had stayed a little to the rear of the column. I hadn't any strength left for running. And my son didn't notice. That's all I know. Where has he disappeared? Where can I find him? Perhaps you've seen him somewhere?"

"No, Rabbi Eliahou, I haven't seen him."

He left then as he had come: like a wind-swept shadow.

He had already passed through the door when I suddenly remembered seeing his son running by my side. I had forgotten that, and I didn't tell Rabbi Eliahou!

Then I remembered something else: his son had seen him losing ground, limping, staggering back to the rear of the column. He had seen him. And he had continued to run on in front, letting the distance between them grow greater.

A terrible thought loomed up in my mind: he had wanted to get rid of his father! He had felt that his father was growing weak, he had believed that the end was near and had sought this separation in order to get rid of the burden, to free himself from an encumbrance which could lessen his own chances of survival.

I had done well to forget that. And I was glad that Rabbi Eliahou should continue to look for his beloved son.

And, in spite of myself, a prayer rose in my heart, to that God in whom I no longer believed.

My God, Lord of the Universe, give me strength never to do what Rabbi Eliahou's son has done.

Shouts rose outside in the yard, where darkness had fallen. The SS ordered the ranks to form up.

The march began again. The dead stayed in the yard under the snow, like faithful guards assassinated, without burial. No one had said the prayer for the dead over them. Sons abandoned their fathers' remains without a tear.

On the way it snowed, snowed, snowed endlessly. We were marching more slowly. The guards themselves seemed tired. My wounded foot no longer hurt me. It must have been completely frozen. The foot was lost to me. It had detached itself from my body like the wheel of a car. Too bad. I should have to resign myself; I could live with only one leg. The main thing was not to think about it. Above all, not at this moment. Leave thoughts for later.

Our march had lost all semblance of discipline. We went as we wanted, as we could. We heard no more shots. Our guards must have been tired.

But death scarcely needed any help from them. The cold was conscientiously doing its work. At every step someone fell and suffered no more.

From time to time, SS officers on motorcycles would go down the length of the column to try and shake us out of our growing apathy:

"Keep going! We are getting there!"

"Courage! Only a few more hours!"

"We're reaching Gleiwitz."

These words of encouragement, even though they came from the mouths of our assassins, did us a great deal of good. No one wanted to give up now, just before the end, so near to the goal. Our eyes searched the horizon for the barbed wire of Gleiwitz. Our only desire was to reach it as quickly as possible.

The night had now set in. The snow had ceased to fall. We walked for several more hours before arriving.

We did not notice the camp until we were just in front of the gate.

Some Kapos rapidly installed us in the barracks. We pushed and jostled one another as if this were the supreme refuge, the gateway to life. We walked over pain-racked bodies. We trod on wounded faces. No cries. A few groans. My father and I were ourselves thrown to the ground by this rolling tide. Beneath our feet someone let out a rattling cry:

"You're crushing me . . . mercy!"

A voice that was not unknown to me.

"You're crushing me . . . mercy! mercy!"

The same faint voice, the same rattle, heard somewhere before. That voice had spoken to me one day. Where? When? Years ago? No, it could only have been at the camp.

"Mercy!"

I felt that I was crushing him. I was stopping his breath. I wanted to get up. I struggled to disengage myself, so that he could breathe. But I was crushed myself beneath the weight of other bodies. I could hardly breathe. I dug my nails into unknown faces. I was biting all round me, in order to get air. No one cried out.

Suddenly I remembered. Juliek! The boy from Warsaw who played the violin in the band at Buna. . . .

"Juliek, is it you?"

"Eliezer . . . the twenty-five strokes of the whip. Yes . . . I remember."

He was silent. A long moment elapsed.

"Juliek! Can you hear me, Juliek?"

"Yes . . . ," he said, in a feeble voice. "What do you want?"

He was not dead.

"How do you feel, Juliek?" I asked, less to know the answer than to hear that he could speak, that he was alive.

"All right, Eliezer . . . I'm getting on all right . . . hardly any air . . . worn out. My feet are swollen. It's good to rest, but my violin. . . ."

I thought he had gone out of his mind. What use was the violin here?

"What, your violin?"

He gasped.

"I'm afraid . . . I'm afraid . . . that they'll break my violin . . . I've brought it with me."

I could not answer him. Someone was lying full length on top of me, covering my face. I was unable to breathe, through either mouth or nose. Sweat beaded my brow, ran down my spine. This was the end—the end of the road. A silent death, suffocation. No way of crying out, of calling for help.

I tried to get rid of my invisible assassin. My whole will to live was centered in my nails. I scratched. I battled for a mouthful of air. I tore at decaying flesh which did not respond. I could not free myself from this mass weighing down my chest. Was it a dead man I was struggling against? Who knows?

I shall never know. All I can say is that I won. I succeeded in digging a hole through this wall of dying people, a little hole through which I could drink in a small quantity of air.

"Father, how are you?" I asked, as soon as I could utter a word.

I knew he could not be far from me.

"Well!" answered a distant voice, which seemed to come from another world. I tried to sleep.

He tried to sleep. Was he right or wrong? Could one sleep here? Was it not dangerous to allow your vigilance to fail, even for a moment, when at any minute death could pounce upon you?

I was thinking of this when I heard the sound of a violin. The sound of a violin, in this dark shed, where the dead were heaped on the living. What madman could be playing the violin here, at the brink of his own grave? Or was it really an hallucination?

It must have been Juliek.

He played a fragment from Beethoven's concerto. I had never heard sounds so pure. In such a silence.

How had he managed to free himself? To draw his body from under mine without my being aware of it?

It was pitch dark. I could hear only the violin, and it was as though Juliek's soul were the bow. He was playing his life. The whole of his life was gliding on the strings—his lost hopes, his charred past, his extinguished future. He played as he would never play again.

I shall never forget Juliek. How could I forget that concert, given to an audience of dying and dead men! To this day, whenever I hear Beethoven played my eyes close and out of the dark rises the sad, pale face of my Polish friend, as he said farewell on his violin to an audience of dying men.

I do not know for how long he played. I was overcome by sleep. When I awoke, in the daylight, I could see Juliek, opposite me, slumped over, dead. Near him lay his violin, smashed, trampled, a strange overwhelming little corpse.

We stayed at Gleiwitz for three days. Three days without food or drink. We were not allowed to leave the barracks. SS men guarded the door.

I was hungry and thirsty. I must have been very dirty and exhausted, to judge from the appearance of the others. The bread we had brought from Buna had long since been devoured. And who knew when we would be given another ration?

The front was following us. We could hear new gun shots again, very close. But we had neither the strength nor the courage to believe that the Nazis would not have time to evacuate us, and that the Russians would soon be here.

We heard that we were going to be deported into the center of Germany.

On the third day, at dawn, we were driven out of the barracks. We all threw blankets over our shoulders, like prayer shawls. We were directed toward a gate which divided the camp into two. A group of SS officers were standing there. A rumor ran through our ranks—a selection!

The SS officers did the selecting. The weak, to the left; those who could walk well, to the right.

My father was sent to the left. I ran after him. An SS officer shouted at my back:

"Come back here!"

I slipped in among the others. Several SS rushed to bring me back, creating such confusion that many of the people from the left were able to come back to the right—and among them, my father and myself. However, there were some shots and some dead.

We were all made to leave the camp. After half an hour's marching we arrived right in the middle of a field divided by rails. We had to wait for a train to arrive.

The snow fell thickly. We were forbidden to sit down or even to move.

The snow began to form a thick layer over our blankets. They brought us bread—the usual ration. We threw ourselves upon it. Someone had the idea of appeasing his thirst by eating the snow. Soon the others were imitating him. As we were not allowed to bend down, everyone took out his spoon and ate the accumulated snow off his neighbor's back. A mouthful of bread and a spoonful of snow. The SS who were watching laughed at this spectacle.

Hours went by. Our eyes grew weary of scouring the horizon for the liberating train. It did not arrive until much later in the evening. An infinitely long train, composed of cattle wagons, with no roofs. The SS pushed us in, a hundred to a carriage, we were so thin! Our embarkation completed, the convoy set out. . . .

At the gate of the camp, SS officers were waiting for us. They counted us. Then we were directed to the assembly place. Orders were given us through loudspeakers:

"Form fives!" "Form groups of a hundred!" "Five paces forward!"

I held onto my father's hand—the old, familiar fear: not to lose him.

Right next to us the high chimney of the crematory oven rose up. It no longer made any impression on us. It scarcely attracted our attention.

An established inmate of Buchenwald told us that we should have a shower and then we could go into the blocks. The idea of having a hot bath fascinated me. My father was silent. He was breathing heavily beside me.

"Father," I said. "Only another moment more. Soon we can lie down—in a bed. You can rest. . . ."

He did not answer. I was so exhausted myself that his silence left me indifferent. My only wish was to take a bath as quickly as possible and lie down in a bed.

But it was not easy to reach the showers. Hundreds of prisoners were crowding there. The guards were unable to keep any order. They struck out right and left with no apparent result. Others, without the strength to push or even to stand up, had sat down in the snow. My father wanted to do the same. He groaned.

"I can't go on. . . . This is the end. . . . I'm going to die here. . . ."

He dragged me toward a hillock of snow from which emerged human shapes and ragged pieces of blanket.

"Leave me," he said to me. "I can't go on. . . . Have mercy on me. . . . I'll wait here until we can get into the baths. . . . You can come and find me."

I could have wept with rage. Having lived through so much, suffered so much, could I leave my father to die now? Now, when we could have a good hot bath and lie down?

"Father!" I screamed. "Father! Get up from here! Immediately! You're killing yourself. . . ."

I seized him by the arm. He continued to groan.

"Don't shout, son. . . . Take pity on your old father. . . . Leave me to rest here. . . . Just for a bit, I'm so tired. . . at the end of my strength. . . ."

He had become like a child, weak, timid, vulnerable.

"Father," I said. "You can't stay here."

I showed him the corpses all around him; they too had wanted to rest here.

"I can see them, son. I can see them all right. Let them sleep. It's so long since they closed their eyes. . . . They are exhausted . . . exhausted. . . ."

His voice was tender.

I yelled against the wind:

"They'll never wake again! Never! Don't you understand?"

For a long time this argument went on. I felt that I was not arguing with him, but with death itself, with the death that he had already chosen.

The sirens began to wail. An alert. The lights went out throughout the camp. The guards drove us toward the blocks. In a flash, there was no one left on the assembly place. We were only too glad not to have had to stay outside longer in the icy wind. We let ourselves sink down onto the planks. The beds were in several tiers. The cauldrons of soup at the entrance attracted no one. To sleep, that was all that mattered.

It was daytime when I awoke. And then I remembered that I had a father. Since the alert, I had followed the crowd without troubling about him. I had known that he was at the end, on the brink of death, and yet I had abandoned him.

I went to look for him.

But at the same moment this thought came into my mind: "Don't let me find him! If only I could get rid of this dead weight, so that I could use all my strength to struggle for my own survival, and only worry about myself." Immediately I felt ashamed of myself, ashamed forever.

I walked for hours without finding him. Then I came to the block where they were giving out black "coffee." The men were lining up and fighting.

A plaintive, beseeching voice caught me in the spine:

"Eliezer . . . my son . . . bring me . . . a drop of coffee. . . ."

I ran to him.

"Father! I've been looking for you so long. . . . Where were you? Did you sleep? . . . How do you feel?"

He was burning with fever. Like a wild beast, I cleared a way for myself to the coffee cauldron. And I managed to carry back a cupful. I had a sip. The rest was for him. I can't forget the light of thankfulness in his eyes while he gulped it down—an animal gratitude. With those few gulps of hot water, I probably brought him more satisfaction than I had done during my whole childhood.

He was lying on a plank, livid, his lips pale and dried up, shaken by tremors. I could not stay by him for long. Orders had been given to clear the place for cleaning. Only the sick could stay.

We stayed outside for five hours. Soup was given out. As soon as we were allowed to go back to the blocks, I ran to my father.

"Have you had anything to eat?"

"No."

"Why not?"

"They didn't give us anything . . . they said that if we were ill we should

die soon anyway and it would be a pity to waste the food. I can't go on any
more. . . ."

I gave him what was left of my soup. But it was with a heavy heart. I felt
that I was giving it up to him against my will. No better than Rabbi Eliahou's son
had I withstood the test.

He grew weaker day by day, his gaze veiled, his face the color of dead
leaves. On the third day after our arrival at Buchenwald, everyone had to go to
the showers. Even the sick, who had to go through last.

On the way back from the baths, we had to wait outside for a long time.
They had not yet finished cleaning the blocks.

Seeing my father in the distance, I ran to meet him. He went by me like a
ghost, passed me without stopping, without looking at me. I called to him. He did
not come back. I ran after him:

"Father, where are you running to?"

He looked at me for a moment, and his gaze was distant, visionary; it was
the face of someone else. A moment only and on he ran again.

Struck down with dysentery, my father lay in his bunk, five other invalids
with him. I sat by his side, watching him, not daring to believe that he could
escape death again.Nevertheless, I did all I could to give him hope.

Suddenly, he raised himself on his bunk and put his feverish lips to my
ear:

"Eliezer . . . I must tell you where to find the gold and the money I
buried . . . in the cellar. . . . You know. . . ."

He began to talk faster and faster, as though he were afraid he would not
have time to tell me. I tried to explain to him that this was not the end, that we
would go back to the house together, but he would not listen to me. He could no
longer listen to me. He was exhausted. A trickle of saliva, mingled with blood, was
running from between his lips. He had closed his eyes. His breath was coming in
gasps.

For a ration of bread, I managed to change beds with a prisoner in my
father's bunk. In the afternoon the doctor came. I went and told him that my
father was very ill.

"Bring him here!"

I explained that he could not stand up. But the doctor refused to listen to
anything. Somehow, I brought my father to him. He stared at him, then
questioned him in a clipped voice:

"What do you want?"

"My father's ill," I answered for him. "Dysentery. . ."

"Dysentery? That's not my business. I'm a surgeon. Go on! Make room
for the others."

Protests did no good.

"I can't go on, son. . . . Take me back to my bunk. . . ."

I took him back and helped him to lie down. He was shivering.

"Try and sleep a bit, father. Try to go to sleep. . . ."

His breathing was labored, thick. He kept his eyes shut. Yet I was convinced that he could see everything, that now he could see the truth in all things.

Another doctor came to the block. But my father would not get up. He knew that it was useless.

Besides, this doctor had only come to finish off the sick. I could hear him shouting at them that they were lazy and just wanted to stay in bed. I felt like leaping at his throat, strangling him. But I no longer had the courage or the strength. I was riveted to my father's deathbed. My hands hurt, I was clenching them so hard. Oh, to strangle the doctor and the others! To burn the whole world! My father's murderers! But the cry stayed in my throat.

When I came back from the bread distribution, I found my father weeping like a child:

"Son, they keep hitting me!"

"Who?"

I thought he was delirious.

"Him, the Frenchman . . . and the Pole . . . they were hitting me."

Another wound to the heart, another hate, another reason for living lost.

"Eliezer . . . Eliezer . . . tell them not to hit me . . . . I haven't done anything. . . . Why do they keep hitting me?"

I began to abuse his neighbors. They laughed at me. I promised them bread, soup. They laughed. Then they got angry; they could not stand my father any longer, they said, because he was now unable to drag himself outside to relieve himself.

The following day he complained that they had taken his ration of bread.

"While you were asleep?"

"No. I wasn't asleep. They jumped on top of me. They snatched my bread . . . and they hit me . . . again. . . . I can't stand any more, son . . . a drop of water. . . ."

I knew that he must not drink. But he pleaded with me for so long that I gave in. Water was the worst poison he could have, but what else could I do for him? With water, without water, it would all be over soon anyway. . . ."

"You, at least, have some mercy on me. . . ."

Have mercy on him! I, his only son!

A week went by like this.

"This is your father, isn't it?" asked the head of the block.

"Yes."

"He's very ill."

"The doctor won't do anything for him."

"The doctor *can't* do anything for him, now. And neither can you."

He put his great hairy hand on my shoulder and added:

"Listen to me, boy. Don't forget that you're in a concentration camp. Here, every man has to fight for himself and not think of anyone else. Even of his father. Here, there are no fathers, no brothers, no friends. Everyone lives and dies for himself alone. I'll give you a sound piece of advice—don't give your ration of bread and soup to your old father. There's nothing you can do for him. And you're killing yourself. Instead, you ought to be having his ration."

I listened to him without interrupting. He was right, I thought in the most secret region of my heart, but I dared not admit it. It's too late to save your old father, I said to myself. You ought to be having two rations of bread, two rations of soup. . . .

Only a fraction of a second, but I felt guilty. I ran to find a little soup to give my father. But he did not want it. All he wanted was water.

"Don't drink water . . . have some soup. . . ."

"I'm burning . . . why are you being so unkind to me, my son? Some water. . . ."

I brought him some water. Then I left the block for roll call. But I turned around and came back again. I lay down on the top bunk. Invalids were allowed to stay in the block. So I would be an invalid myself. I would not leave my father.

There was silence all round now, broken only by groans. In front of the block, the SS were giving orders. An officer passed by the beds. My father begged me:

"My son, some water. . . . I'm burning. . . . My stomach. . . ."

"Quiet, over there!" yelled the officer.

"Eliezer," went on my father, "some water. . . ."

The officer came up to him and shouted at him to be quiet. But my father did not hear him. He went on calling me. The officer dealt him a violent blow on the head with his truncheon.

I did not move. I was afraid. My body was afraid of also receiving a blow.

Then my father made a rattling noise and it was my name: "Eliezer."

I could see that he was still breathing—spasmodically.

I did not move.

When I got down after roll call, I could see his lips trembling as he murmured something. Bending over him, I stayed gazing at him for over an hour, engraving into myself the picture of his blood-stained face, his shattered skull.

Then I had to go to bed. I climbed into my bunk, above my father, who was still alive. It was January 28, 1945.

I awoke on January 29 at dawn. In my father's place lay another invalid. They must have taken him away before dawn and carried him to the crematory. He may still have been breathing.

There were no prayers at his grave. No candles were lit to his memory. His last word was my name. A summons, to which I did not respond.

I did not weep, and it pained me that I could not weep. But I had no more tears. And, in the depths of my being, in the recesses of my weakened conscience, could I have searched it, I might perhaps have found something like—free at last!

From **Auschwitz**
MIKLOS NYSZLI

For the next three days I had nothing to do. I was still drawing the supplementary rations issued to doctors, but I spent most of my time either stretched out on my bed or seated on the bleachers of the stadium, which was located not far from F Camp. Yes, even Auschwitz had its stadium. But it was reserved exclusively for the use of the German prisoners of the Third Reich, who acted as clerks in various camp sections. On Sundays the stadium was the excited hub of sports activity, but on weekdays the vast field lay quiet and empty. Only a barbed wire fence separated the stadium from number one crematorium. I wanted very much to know just what went on in the shadow of the immense stack, which never ceased spewing tongues of flame. From where I was sitting there was not much one could see. And to approach the barbed wire was unwise, for the watchtower machine guns sprayed the area without warning to frighten away anyone who happened to wander into this No-Man's-Land.

Nevertheless, I saw that a group of men in civilian clothes was lining up in the crematorium courtyard, directly in front of the red-brick building: there were about 200 in all, with an SS guard in front. It looked to me like a roll call, and I assumed that this was the night watch being relieved by the oncoming day watch. For the crematoriums ran on a twenty-four-hour schedule, as I learned from a fellow prisoner, who also informed me that the crematorium personnel were known as the Sonderkommando, which means, merely, kommandos assigned to special work. They were well fed and given civilian clothes. They were never permitted to leave the grounds of the crematorium, and every four months, when they had learned too much about the place for their own good, they were liquidated. Till now such had been the fate of every Sonderkommando since the founding of the KZ; this explains why no one had ever escaped to tell the world what had been taking place inside these grim walls for the past several years.

I returned to Barracks 12 just in time for Dr. Mengele's arrival. He drove up and was received by the barracks guard, then sent for me and asked me to join him in his car. This time there was no guard with us. We were gone before I even had time to say good-bye to my colleagues. He stopped in front of the Camp Office and asked Dr. Sentkeller to get my card, then started off again along the bumpy road.

For about twelve minutes we drove through the labyrinth of barbed wire and entered well-guarded gates, thus passing from one section to another. Only then did I realize how vast the KZ was. Few people had the possibility of verifying that fact, because the majority died at the very place to which they were sent when they first arrived. Later I learned that the Auschwitz KZ had, at certain periods, held more than 100,000 people within its enclosure of electrified barbed wire.[1]

---

[1] Hoess, the camp commander, testified at Nuremberg that the camp held 140,000 prisoners when filled to capacity.—*Tr.*

Dr. Mengele suddenly interrupted my meditations. Without turning, he said: "The place I'm taking you to is no sanatorium, but you'll find that the conditions there are not too bad."

We left the camp and skirted the Jewish unloading ramp for about 300 yards. A large armored gate in the barbed wire opened behind the guard. We went in: before us lay a spacious courtyard, covered with green grass. The gravel paths and the shade of the pine trees would have made the place quite pleasant had there not been, at the end of the courtyard, an enormous red brick building and a chimney spitting flame. We were in one of the crematoriums. We stayed in the car. An SS ran up and saluted Dr. Mengele. Then we got out, crossed the courtyard and went through a large door into the crematorium.

"Is the room ready?" Dr. Mengele asked the guard.

"Yes, sir," the man replied.

We headed towards it, Dr. Mengele leading the way.

The room in question was freshly whitewashed and well lighted by a large window, which, however, was barred. The furnishings, after those of the barracks, surprised me: a white bed; a closet, also white; a large table and some chairs. On the table, a red velvet tablecloth. The concrete floor was covered with handsome rugs. I had the impression I was expected. The Sonderkommando men had painted the room and outfitted it with objects that the preceding convoys had left behind. We then passed through a dark corridor until we reached another room, a very bright, completely modern dissecting room, with two windows. The floor was of red concrete; in the center of the room, mounted on a concrete base, stood a dissecting table of polished marble, equipped with several drainage channels. At the edge of the table a basin with nickel taps had been installed; against the wall, three porcelain sinks. The walls were painted a light green, and large barred windows were covered with green metal screens to keep out flies and mosquitoes.

We left the dissecting room for the next room: the work room. Here there were fancy chairs and paintings; in the middle of the room, a large table covered with a green cloth; all about, comfortable armchairs. I counted three microscopes on the table. In one corner there was a well-stocked library, which contained the most recent editions. In another corner a closet, in which were stowed white smocks, aprons, towels and rubber gloves. In short, the exact replica of any large city's institute of pathology.

I took it all in, paralyzed with fright. As soon as I had come through the main gate I had realized that I was on death's path. A slow death, opening its maddening depths before me. I felt I was lost.

Now I understood why I had been given civilian clothes. This was the uniform of the Sonderkommando—the kommando of the living-dead.

My chief was preparing to leave; he informed the SS guard that as far as "service" was concerned I depended exclusively on him. The crematorium's SS personnel had no jurisdiction over me. The SS kitchen had to provide my food; I could get my linen and supplementary clothing at the SS warehouse. For shaves and haircuts, I had the right to use the SS barbershop in the building. I would not have to be present for the evening or morning roll call.

Besides my laboratory and anatomical work, I was also responsible for the medical care of all the crematorium's SS personnel—about 120 men—as well as the Sonderkommando—about 860 prisoners. Medicines, medical instruments, dressings, all in sufficient quantity, were at my disposal. So that they should receive suitable medical attention, I had to visit all those sick in the crematorium once a day, and sometimes even twice. I could circulate among the four crematoriums without a pass from 7:00 A.M. till 7:00 P.M. I would have to make out a daily report to the SS commandant and to the Sonderkommando Oberschaarführer Mussfeld, listing the number of ill, bed-ridden and ambulatory patients.

I listened, almost paralyzed, to the enumeration of my rights and duties. Under such conditions, I should be the KZ's most important figure, were I not in the Sonderkommando and were all this not taking place in the "Number one Krema."

Dr. Mengele left without a word. Never did an SS, no matter how low in rank, greet a KZ prisoner. I locked the door to the dissecting room; from now on it was my responsibility.

I returned to my room and sat down, wanting to collect my thoughts. It was not easy. I went back to the beginning. The image of my abandoned home came back to me. I could see the neat little house, with its sunny terraces and pleasant rooms, rooms in which I had spent so many long and trying hours with my patients, but with the satisfaction of knowing I had given them comfort and strength. The same house in which I had spent so many hours of happiness with my family.

We had already been separated for a week. Where could they be, lost in this enormous mass, anonymous, like all those swallowed by this gigantic prison? Had my daughter been able to stay with her mother, or had they already been separated? What had happened to my aged parents, whose last years I had tried to make more pleasant? What had become of my beloved younger sister, whom I raised practically as my own child after our father had fallen ill? It had been such a pleasure to love and help them. I had no doubt about their fate. They were certainly en route to one of the forty-car trains that would bring them here to the Jewish ramp of the Auschwitz extermination camp. With one mechanical wave of his hand Dr. Mengele would direct my parents into the left-hand column. And my sister would also join that column, for even if she were ordered into the right-hand column, she would surely beg, on bended knee, for permission to go with our mother. So they would let her go, and she, with tears in her eyes, would shower them with thanks.

The news of my arrival had spread like wildfire throughout the crematorium. Both the SS personnel assigned here and the Sonderkommando came to call on me. The door was first opened by an SS noncom. Two extremely tall, militant looking Schaarführer entered. I knew that the attitude I then assumed would determine their conduct towards me in the future. I recalled Dr. Mengele's order: I was responsible only to him. Consequently I considered this visit merely as a private act of courtesy, and remained seated instead of rising and standing at attention. I greeted them and asked them to sit down.

They stopped in the middle of the room and looked me over. I felt the full importance of this moment: it was the first impression that counted. It seemed to me that my manner was the best one to have adopted, for their rigid face muscles relaxed slightly and, with a gesture of careless indifference, they sat down.

The scope of our conversation was extremely limited. How was my trip? What was I doing in the KZ? These were questions they could not ask, for the answers would embarrass them. Whereas politics, the war, and conditions in the KZ were subjects I could not broach. Still, this did not bother me, for the years I had spent in pre-war Germany furnished plenty of material for discussion. They were much impressed by the fact that I spoke their own language better, or at least in a more cultured manner, than they did. I soon realized that there were even certain expressions they did not understand, although they carefully refrained from letting me know it. I knew their country well, was fully informed about life in their cities and their homes, and about their religious and moral concepts. So conversation was not overly difficult for me. I had a feeling that this examination had also been a success, for they left smiling.

More visitors arrived, men in civilian clothes, clean-shaven and smartly dressed. The Kapo-in-chief[2] and two of his men entered my room. This too was a courtesy call. I learned that they were the ones who had had my room prepared. They had heard of my arrival and invited me to dine with them and meet the other prisoners.

As a matter of fact it was almost dinner time. I followed them up the stairs to the second story of the crematorium where the prisoners lived: an enormous room, with comfortable bunks lining both walls. The bunks were made of unpainted wood, but on each one silk coverlets and embroidered pillows shone. This colorful, expensive bedding was completely out of keeping with the atmosphere of the place. It had not been made here, but left by members of earlier convoys who had brought it with them into captivity. The Sonderkommando was allowed to draw it from the storerooms and use it.

The whole room was bathed in a dazzling light, for here they did not economize on electricity as they did in the barracks. Our way led between the long row of bunks. Only half the kommando was present; the other half, about a hundred men, was on the night shift. Some of those here were already in bed asleep, while others were reading. There were plenty of books to be had, for we Jews are a people who like to read. Each prisoner had brought some books with him, the number and type depending upon his level of intelligence and education.

---

[2] Kapo is the abbreviation of *Kamaradschafts Polizei.* The Kapo-in-chief was generally a German prisoner serving a sentence for some non-political crime. A few of them tried to ease the lot of their fellow sufferers, but most were the faithful servants of the SS.—*Tr.*

To have books and be able to read was yet another privilege granted to the Sonderkommando. In the KZ anyone caught reading was punished with twenty days' solitary confinement, in a sort of sentry box just large enough to stand up in. Unless, of course, the blows dealt him beforehand had already killed him.

The table awaiting us was covered with a heavy silk brocade tablecloth; fine initialled porcelain dishes; and place settings of silver: more objects that had once belonged to the deportees. The table was piled high with choice and varied dishes, everything a deported people could carry with them into the uncertain future: all sorts of preserves, bacon, jellies, several kinds of salami, cakes and chocolate. From the labels I noticed that some of the food had belonged to Hungarian deportees. All perishable foods automatically became the property of the legal heirs, of those who were still alive, that is, the Sonderkommando.

Seated around the table were the Kapo-in-chief, the engineer, the head chauffeur, the kommando leader, the "tooth pullers" and the head of the gold smelters. Their welcome was most cordial. They offered me all they had, and there was an abundance of everything, for the Hungarian convoys continued to arrive at an ever-increasing rate and they brought a great deal of food with them.

I found it difficult to swallow, however. I could not help thinking of my fellow-sufferers who, before starting on their exodus, had gathered and prepared their provisions. They had been hungry, but had refrained from eating during the entire trip in order to save their meager rations for their parents, their children and the more difficult times ahead. Only the more difficult times had never come: in the lobby of the crematorium the food had remained untouched.

I drank some tea spiked with rum. After a few glasses I managed to relax. My mind cleared and freed itself of the unpleasant thoughts that had been plaguing it. A pleasant warmth penetrated me: the voluptuous effects of the alcohol, comforting as the caress of a mother's hand.

The cigarettes we were smoking had also been "Imported from Hungary." In the camp proper a single cigarette was worth a ration of bread: here on the table lay hundreds of packages.

Our conversation grew more and more spirited. Poland, France, Greece, Germany and Italy were represented around the table. Since most of us understood German it served as our common language. From the conversation I learned the history of the crematoriums. Tens of thousands of prisoners had built them of stone and concrete, finishing them in the middle of an extremely rigorous winter. Every stone was stained with their blood. They had worked day and night, often without food or drink, dressed in mere tatters, so that these infernal death-factories, whose first victims they became, might be finished in time.

Since then four years had passed. Countless thousands had since climbed down from the box cars and crossed the thresholds of the crematoriums. The present Sonderkommando was the twelfth to bear the name. I learned the history of each preceding Sonderkommando, when it "reigned" and who its heroes were, and I was reminded of a fact I already knew: that the Sonderkommando's life span was only a few months at the most.

Whoever among them practiced the Jewish faith could thus begin, on the day of his arrival, the purification ceremony in preparation for death. For death would come to him as surely as it had come to every member of all the preceding Sonderkommandos.

It was almost midnight. The company assembled around the table was weary from the day's work and the evening's consumption of alcohol. Our conversation grew more and more listless. An SS making his rounds stopped to remind us that it was high time we were in bed. I took leave of my new companions and returned to my room. Thanks to the rum I had drunk and my tired nerves, I spent a relatively quiet first night. . . .

In number one crematorium's gas chamber 3,000 dead were piled up. The Sonderkommando had already begun to untangle the lattice of flesh. The noise of the elevators and the sound of their clanging doors reached my room. The work moved ahead double-time. The gas chambers had to be cleared, for the arrival of a new convoy had been announced.

The chief of the gas chamber kommando almost tore the hinges off the door to my room as he arrived out of breath, his eyes wide with fear or surprise.

"Doctor," he said, "come quickly. We just found a girl alive at the bottom of the pile of corpses."

I grabbed my instrument case, which was always ready, and dashed to the gas chamber. Against the wall, near the entrance of the immense room, half covered with other bodies, I saw a girl in the throes of a death-rattle, her body seized with convulsions. The gas kommando men around me were in a state of panic. Nothing like this had ever happened in the course of their horrible career.

We removed the still-living body from the corpses pressing against it. I gathered the tiny adolescent body into my arms and carried it back into the room adjoining the gas chamber, where normally the gas kommando men change clothes for work. I laid the body on a bench. A frail young girl, almost a child, she could have been no more than fifteen. I took out my syringe and, taking her arm—she had not yet recovered consciousness and was breathing with difficulty—I administered three intravenous injections. My companions covered her body which was as cold as ice with a heavy overcoat. One ran to the kitchen to fetch some tea and warm broth. Everybody wanted to help, as if she were his own child.

The reaction was swift. The child was seized by a fit of coughing, which brought up a thick globule of phlegm from her lungs. She opened her eyes and looked fixedly at the ceiling. I kept a close watch for every sign of life. Her breathing became deeper and more and more regular. Her lungs, tortured by the gas, inhaled the fresh air avidly. Her pulse became perceptible, the result of the injections. I waited impatiently. The injections had not yet been completely absorbed, but I saw that within a few minutes she was going to regain consciousness: her circulation began to bring color back into her cheeks, and her delicate face became human again.

She looked around her with astonishment, and glanced at us. She still did not realize what was happening to her, and was still incapable of distinguishing the present, of knowing whether she was dreaming or really awake. A veil of mist clouded her consciousness. Perhaps she vaguely remembered a train, a long line of box cars which had brought her here. Then she had lined up for selection and, before she knew what was happening, been swept along by the current of the mass into a large, brilliantly lighted underground room. Everything had happened so quickly. Perhaps she remembered that everyone had had to undress. The impression had been disagreeable, but everybody had yielded resignedly to the order. And so, naked, she had been swept along into another room. Mute anguish had seized them all. The second room had also been lighted by powerful lamps. Completely bewildered, she had let her gaze wander over the mass huddled there, but found none of her family. Pressed close against the wall, she had waited, her heart frozen, for what was going to happen. All of a sudden the lights had gone out, leaving her enveloped in total darkness. Something had stung her eyes, seized her throat, suffocated her. She had fainted. There her memories ceased.

Her movements were becoming more and more animated; she tried to move her hands, her feet, to turn her head left and right. Her face was seized by a fit of convulsions. Suddenly she grasped my coat collar and gripped it convulsively, trying with all her might to raise herself. I laid her back down again several times, but she continued to repeat the same gesture. Little by little, however, she grew calm and remained stretched out, completely exhausted. Large tears shone in her eyes and rolled down her cheeks. She was not crying. I received the first reply to my questions. Not wanting to tire her, I asked only a few. I learned that she was sixteen years old, and that she had come with her parents in a convoy from Transylvania.

The kommando gave her a bowl of hot broth, which she drank voraciously. They kept bringing her all sorts of dishes, but I could not allow them to give her anything. I covered her to her head and told her that she should try and get some sleep.

My thoughts moved at a dizzy pace. I turned towards my companions in the hope of finding a solution. We racked our brains, for we were now face to face with the most difficult problem: what to do with the girl now that she had been restored to life? We knew that she could not remain here for very long.

What could one do with a young girl in the crematorium's Sonderkommando? I knew the past history of the place: no one had ever come out of here alive, either from the convoys or from the Sonderkommando.

Little time remained for reflection. Oberschaarführer Mussfeld arrived to supervise the work, as was his wont. Passing by the open door, he saw us gathered in a group. He came and asked us what was going on. Even before we told him he had seen the girl stretched out on the bench.

I made a sign for my companions to withdraw. I was going to attempt something I knew without saying was doomed to failure. Three months in the same camp and in the same milieu had created, in spite of everything, a certain intimacy between us. Besides, the Germans generally appreciate capable people, and, as long as they need them, respect them to a certain extent, even in the KZ. Such was the case for cobblers, tailors, joiners and locksmiths. From our numerous contacts, I had been able to ascertain that Mussfeld had a high esteem for the medical expert's professional qualities. He knew that my superior was Dr. Mengele, the KZ's most dreaded figure, who, goaded by racial pride, took himself to be one of the most important representatives of German medical science. He considered the dispatch of hundreds of thousands of Jews to the gas chambers as a patriotic duty. The work carried on in the dissecting room was for the furtherance of German medical science. As Dr. Mengele's pathological expert, I also had a hand in this progress, and therein lay the explanation for a certain form of respect that Mussfeld paid me. He often came to see me in the dissecting room, and we conversed on politics, the military situation and various other subjects. It appeared that his respect also arose from the fact that he considered the dissection of bodies and his bloody job of killing to be allied activities. He was the commandant and ace shot of number one crematorium. Three other SS acted as his lieutenants. Together they carried out the "liquidation" by a bullet in the back of the neck. This type of death was reserved for those who had been chosen in the camp, or else sent from another on their way to a so-called "rest camp." When there were merely 500 or less, they were killed by a bullet in the back of the neck, for the large factory of gas chambers was reserved for the annihilation of more important numbers. As much gas was needed to kill 500 as to kill 3,000. Nor was it worthwhile to call out the Red Cross truck to bring the canisters and gas butchers for such a trifling number of victims. Nor was it worth the trouble of having a truck come to collect the clothes, which were scarcely more than rags anyway. Such were the factors which determined whether a group would die by gas or by a bullet in the back of the neck.

And this was the man I had to deal with, the man I had to talk into allowing a single life to be spared. I calmly related the terrible case we found ourselves confronted with. I described for his benefit what pains the child must have suffered in the undressing room, and the horrible scenes that preceded death in the gas chamber. When the room had been plunged into darkness, she had breathed in a few lungfuls of cyclon gas. Only a few, though, for her fragile body had given way under the pushing and shoving of the mass as they fought against death. By chance she had fallen with her face against the wet concrete floor. That bit of humidity had kept her from being asphyxiated, for cyclon gas does not react under humid conditions.

These were my arguments, and I asked him to do something for the child. He listened to me attentively, then asked me exactly what I proposed doing. I saw by his expression that I had put him face to face with a practically impossible problem. It was obvious that the child could not remain in the crematorium. One solution would have been to put her in front of the crematorium gate. A kommando of women always worked there. She could have slipped in among them and accompanied them back to the camp barracks after they had finished work. She would never relate what had happened to her. The presence of one new face among so many thousands would never be detected, for no one in the camp knew all the other inmates.

If she had been three of four years older that might have worked. A girl of twenty would have been able to understand clearly the miraculous circumstances of her survival, and have enough foresight not to tell anyone about them. She would wait for better times, like so many other thousands were waiting, to recount what she had lived through. But Mussfeld thought that a young girl of sixteen would in all naïveté tell the first person she met where she had just come from, what she had seen and what she had lived through. The news would spread like wildfire, and we would all be forced to pay for it with our lives.

"There's no way of getting round it," he said, "the child will have to die."

Half an hour later the young girl was led, or rather carried, into the furnace room hallway, and there Mussfeld sent another in his place to do the job. A bullet in the back of the neck.

"Psychological Effects of the Atomic Bomb in Hiroshima: The Theme of Death"
ROBERT JAY LIFTON

Hiroshima commands our attention now, eighteen years after its exposure to the atomic bomb, perhaps even more insistently than when the event actually occurred.[*][1] We are compelled by the universal threat of nuclear weapons to study the impact of such weapons upon their first human victims, ever mindful of the relevance of this question to our own future and to all of human survival.

Much research has already been done concerning the physical consequences of the Hiroshima and Nagasaki disasters, particularly in relation to their unique feature of delayed radiation effects[2] But little attention has been paid to psychological and social elements, though these might well be said to be at present the most vivid legacies of the first atomic bomb.[3]

My own interest in these problems developed during two years of research, conducted in Tokyo and Kyoto from 1960–1962, on the relationship of individual character and historical change in Japanese youth.[4] I was struck by the significance which the encounter with nuclear weapons had for the Japanese as a whole, even for young Japanese who could hardly remember the event. Also involved in my undertaking a study in Hiroshima was concern with the psychological aspects of war and peace, as well as previous interest in the behavior of individuals and groups under extreme conditions.[5]

---

* References appear at the end of this essay.

I began the work in April of 1962, first through two brief visits to Hiroshima, followed by four and one-half months of residence there. My approach was primarily that of individual interviews with two groups of atomic bomb survivors: thirty-three chosen at random from the more than 90,000 survivors (*hibakusha*),[6] listed at the Hiroshima University Research Institute for Nuclear Medicine and Biology; and an additional group of forty-two survivors specially selected because of their prominence in dealing with A-bomb problems or their capacity to articulate their experiences. Included among the latter were physicians, university professors, city officials, politicians, writers and poets, and leaders of survivor organizations and peace movements. I also sought out all those in Hiroshima (mostly Japanese, but also Americans and Europeans) who could tell me anything about the complex array of group emotions and social problems which had arisen in the city over the seventeen years that had elapsed since the disaster.

I was aware of the delicacy of my situation as an American psychiatrist conducting this study, and I relied heavily upon the continuous support and assistance of Japanese groups within the Hiroshima community, so that all meetings and interviews were arranged through their introductions. In the case of the randomly selected group, my first contact with each survivor was made through a personal visit to the home, in the company of a Japanese social worker from Hiroshima University. My previous experience in Japan—including the ability to speak a certain amount of Japanese—was helpful in eliciting the many forms of cooperation so crucial for the work. Perhaps of greatest importance was my conveying to both colleagues and research subjects a sense of my personal motivation in undertaking the work, the hope that a systematic study of this kind might clarify important problems often spoken about loosely, and thereby in a small way contribute to the mastery of nuclear weapons and the avoidance of their use.

Interviews were generally about two hours long; I tried to see each research subject twice, though I saw some three or four times, and others just once. I tape-recorded all sessions with subjects of the randomly selected group, and did so with many of those in the special group as well, always with the subject's consent. Interviews were conducted in Japanese,[7] and a research assistant was always present to interpret. After making an initial appraisal of the problems involved, I decided to focus my questions upon three general dimensions of the problem: first, the recollection of the experience itself and its inner meaning seventeen years later;[8] second, residual concerns and fears, especially those relating to delayed radiation effects; and third, the survivor's sense of self and society, or of special group identity. Subjects were encouraged to associate freely to these topics and to any feelings or ideas stimulated by them. And in gathering these data I sought always to evaluate to what degree exposure to the atomic bomb in Hiroshima resembles psychological and social patterns common to all disasters, as described in the general literature on disaster, and in what ways it might be a unique experience. What follows is a preliminary statement on work in progress, a composite description of some of the basic trends I have observed.

The Experience Recalled

The degree to which one anticipates a disaster has important bearing upon the way in which one responds, and the predominant tone in the descriptions I heard was that of extreme surprise and unpreparedness. Since it was wartime, people did of course expect conventional bombing; there had been regularly occurring air raid warnings because of planes passing over Hiroshima, though only an occasional stray bomb had actually been dropped on the city. American planes did drop leaflets warning Hiroshima inhabitants that their city was going to be demolished and urging them to evacuate from it. But very few people appear to have seen these leaflets, and those who did tended to ignore them as enemy propaganda. Many wondered at Hiroshima's relatively untouched state, despite its obviously strategic significance as a major staging area for Japan's military operations in China and Southeast Asia. There was general apprehension, the feeling that there was something dangerous about Hiroshima's strangely intact state and that the Americans must be preparing something extraordinarily big for the city (though this latter thought could have been partly a retrospective construction). At 8:15 A.M. on August 6, 1945, the moment the bomb fell, most people were in a particularly relaxed state, since, following a brief air-raid warning, the all-clear had just been sounded. People thus had a false sense of immediate security, as well as a total incapacity to imagine the nature of the weapon that was about to strike them.

It was only those at some distance from the bomb's hypocenter who could clearly distinguish the sequence of the great flash of light in the sky accompanied by the lacerating heat of the fireball, then the sound and force of the blast, and the impressive multicolored "mushroom cloud" rising above the city. Two thousand meters is generally considered to be a critical radius for high mortality (from heat, blast, and radiation), for susceptibility to delayed radiation effects, and for near-total destruction of buildings and other structures. But many were killed outside of this radius, and indeed the number of deaths from the bomb—variously estimated from 63,000 to 240,000 or more—is still unknown. Falling in the center of a flat city made up largely of wooden residential and commercial structures, the bomb is reported to have destroyed or so badly damaged, through blast and fire, more than two-thirds of all buildings within 5000 meters—an area roughly encompassing the city limits—that all of Hiroshima became immediately involved in the atomic disaster.[9] Those within the 2000-meter radius could not clearly recall their initial perceptions: many simply remember what they thought to be a flash—or else a sudden sensation of heat—followed by an indeterminate period of unconsciousness; others recall only being thrown across a room or knocked down, then finding themselves pinned under debris of buildings.

The most striking psychological feature of this immediate experience was the sense of a sudden and absolute shift from normal existence to an overwhelming encounter with death. This is described by a young shopkeeper's assistant, who was thirteen years old at the time the bomb fell, and 1400 meters from the hypocenter:

> I was a little ill . . . so I stayed at home that day. . . . There had been an air-raid
> warning and then an all-clear. I felt relieved and lay down on the bed with my

younger brother. . . . Then it happened. It came very suddenly. . . . It felt something like an electric short—a bluish sparkling light. . . . There was a noise, and I felt great heat—even inside of the house. When I came to, I was underneath the destroyed house. . . . I didn't know anything about the atomic bomb so I thought that some bomb had fallen directly upon me . . . and then when I felt that our house had been directly hit I became furious. . . . There were roof tiles and walls—everything black—entirely covering me. So I screamed for help. . . . And from all around I heard moans and screaming, and then I felt a kind of danger to myself. . . . I thought that I too was going to die in that way. I felt this way at that moment because I was absolutely unable to do anything at all by my own power. . . . I didn't know where I was or what I was under. . . . I couldn't hear voices of my family. I didn't know how I could be rescued. I felt I was going to suffocate and then die, without knowing exactly what had happened to me. This was the kind of expectation I had. . . .

I stress this sudden encounter with death because I believe that it initiates, from this first moment of contact with the atomic bomb, an emotional theme within the victim which remains with him indefinitely: the sense of a more or less permanent encounter with death.

This early impact enveloped the city in an aura of weirdness and unreality, as recalled by an elderly electrician, who at the time of the bomb was in his mid-forties, working at a railroad junction 5000 meters from the hypocenter.

I was setting up a pole . . . near a switch in the railroad tracks. . . . I heard a tremendous noise. There was a flash . . . a kind of flash I had never seen before which I can't describe. . . . My face felt hot and I put my hands over my eyes and rushed under a locomotive that was nearby. I crawled in between the wheels, and then there was an enormous boom and the locomotive shook. I was frightened, so I crawled out. . . . I couldn't tell what happened. . . . For about five minutes I saw nobody, and then I saw someone coming out from an air-raid shelter who told me that the youngest one of our workers had been injured by falling piles . . . so I put the injured man on the back of my bicycle and tried to take him to the dispensary. Then I saw that almost all of the people in that area were crowded into the dispensary, and since there was also a hospital nearby, I went there. But that too was already full. . . . So the only thing to do was to go into [the center of] Hiroshima. But I couldn't move my bicycle because of all the people coming out from Hiroshima and blocking the way. . . . I saw that they were all naked and I wondered what was the matter with them. . . . When we spoke to people they said that they had been hit by something they didn't understand. . . . We were desperately looking for a doctor or a hospital but we couldn't seem to have any success. . . . We walked toward Hiroshima, still carrying our tools. . . . Then in Hiroshima there was no place either—it had become an empty field—so I carried him to a place near our company office where injured people were lying inside, asking for water. But there was no water and there was no way to help them and I myself didn't know what kind of treatment I should give to this man or to the others. I had to let them die right before my eyes. . . . By then we were cut off from escape, because the fire was beginning to spread out and we couldn't move—we were together with the dead people in the building—only we were not really inside of the building because the building itself had been destroyed, so that we were really outdoors, and we spent the night there. . . .

This rote and essentially ineffectual behavior was characteristic of many during the first few hours, in those situations where any attempt at all could be made to maintain a group co-operative effort; people were generally more effective in helping members of their immediate families, or in saving themselves. This same electrician, an unusually conscientious man, kept at his post at the railroad over a period of several weeks, leaving only for brief periods to take care of his family. Again his description of the scene of death and near-death takes on a dreamlike quality:

> There were dead bodies everywhere. . . . There was practically no room for me to put my feet on the floor. . . .At that time I couldn't figure out the reason why all these people were suffering, or what illness it was that had struck them down. . . . I was the only person taking care of the place as all of the rest of the people had gone. . . . Other people came in looking for food or to use the toilet. . . . There was no one to sell tickets in the station, nothing . . . and since trains weren't running I didn't have much work to do. . . . There was no light at all and we were just like sleepwalkers. . . .

And a middle-aged teacher, who was also on the outskirts of the city about 5000 meters from the hypocenter, describes his awe at the destruction he witnessed:

> I climbed Hijiyama Mountain and looked down. I saw that Hiroshima had disappeared. . . . I was shocked by the sight. . . . What I felt then and still feel now I just can't explain with words. Of course I saw many dreadful scenes after that—but that experience, looking down and finding nothing left of Hiroshima—was so shocking that I simply can't express what I felt. I could see Koi [a suburb at the opposite end of the city] and a few buildings standing. . . . But Hiroshima didn't exist—that was mainly what I saw—Hiroshima just didn't exist.

And a young university professor 2500 meters from the hypocenter at the time, sums up these feelings of weird, awesome unreality in a frequently-expressed image of hell:

> Everything I saw made a deep impression—a park nearby covered with dead bodies waiting to be cremated . . . very badly injured people evacuated in my direction. . . . The most impressive thing I saw was some girls, very young girls, not only with their clothes torn off but with their skin peeled off as well. . . . My immediate thought was that this was like the hell I had always read about. . . . I had never seen anything which resembled it before, but I thought that should there be a hell, this was it—the Buddhist hell, where we were taught that people who could not attain salvation always went. . . . And I imagined that all of these people I was seeing were in the hell I had read about.

But human beings are unable to remain open to emotional experience of this intensity for any length of time, and very quickly—sometimes within minutes—there began to occur what we may term *psychological closure;* that is, people simply ceased to feel.

For instance, a male social worker, then in his twenties and in military service in Hiroshima, was temporarily on leave at his home just outside of the city; he rushed back into the city soon after the bomb fell, in accordance with his military duty, only to find that his unit had been entirely wiped out. A certain amount of military order was quickly re-established, and a policy of immediate mass cremation of dead bodies was instituted in order to prevent widespread disease, and in accordance with Japanese custom. As a non-commissioned officer and one of the few able-bodied men left, he was put in charge of this work of disposing of corpses, which he found he could accomplish with little difficulty:

> After awhile they became just like objects or goods that we handled in a very businesslike way. . . . Of course I didn't regard them simply as pieces of wood—they were dead bodies—but if we had been sentimental we couldn't have done the work. . . . We had no emotions. . . . Because of the succession of experiences I had been through I was temporarily without feeling. . . . At times I went about the work with great energy, realizing that no one but myself could do it.

He contrasted his own feelings with the terror experienced by an outsider just entering the disaster area:

> Everything at that time was part of an extraordinary situation. . . . For instance, I remember that on the ninth or tenth of August, it was an extremely dark night. . . . I saw blue phosphorescent flames rising from the dead bodies—and there were plenty of them. These were quite different from the orange flames coming from the burning buildings. . . . These blue phosphorescent flames are what we Japanese look upon as spirits rising from dead bodies—in former days we called them fireballs.[10]—And yet, at that time I had no sense of fear, not a bit, but merely thought, "those dead bodies are still burning". . . . But to people who had just come from the outside, those flames looked very strange. . . . One of those nights I met a soldier who had just returned to the city, and I walked along with him. . . . He noticed these unusual fireballs and asked me what they were. I told him that they were the flames coming from dead bodies. The soldier suddenly became extremely frightened, fell down on the ground, and was unable to move. . . . Yet I at that time had a state of mind in which I feared nothing. Though if I were to see those flames now I might be quite frightened. . . .

Relatively few people were involved in the disposal of dead bodies, but virtually all those I interviewed nonetheless experienced a similar form of psychological closure in response to what they saw and felt, and particularly in response to their overall exposure to death. Thus many told how horrified they were when they first encountered corpses in strange array, or extremely disfigured faces, but how, after a period of time as they saw more and more of these, they felt nothing. Psychological closure would last sometimes for a few hours, and sometimes for days or even months and merge into longer-term feelings of depression and despair.

But even the profound and unconscious psychic defensive maneuvers involved in psychological closure were ultimately unable to afford full protection to the survivor from the painful sights and stimuli impinging upon him. It was, moreover, a defense not devoid of its own psychological cost. Thus the same social worker, in a later interview, questioned his own use of the word "businesslike" to describe his attitude toward dead bodies, and emphasized the pity and sympathy he felt while handling the remains of men from his unit and the pains he took to console family members who came for these remains; he even recalled feeling frightened at night when passing the spot where he worked at cremation by day. He was in effect telling me not only that his psychological closure was imperfect,

but that he was horrified—felt ashamed and guilty—at having behaved in a way
which he now thought callous. For he had indulged in activities which were
ordinarily, for him, strongly taboo, and had done so with an energy, perhaps even
an enthusiasm, which must have mobilized within him primitive emotions of a
frightening nature.

The middle-aged teacher who had expressed such awe at the
disappearance of Hiroshima reveals the way in which feelings of shame and guilt,
and especially shame and guilt toward the dead, break through the defense of
psychological closure and painfully assert themselves:

> I went to look for my family. Somehow I became a pitiless person, because if I
> had pity I would not have been able to walk through the city, to walk over those
> dead bodies. The most impressive thing was the expression in people's
> eyes—bodies badly injured which had turned black—their eyes looking for
> someone to come and help them. They looked at me and knew that I was stronger
> than they. . . . I was looking for my family and looking carefully at everyone I met
> to see if he or she was a family member—but the eyes—the emptiness—the
> helpless expression—were something I will never forget. . . . I often had to go to
> the same place more than once. I would wish that the same family would not still
> be there. . . . I saw disappointment in their eyes. They looked at me with great
> expectation, staring right through me. It was very hard to be stared at by those
> eyes. . . .

He felt, in other words, accused by the eyes of the anonymous dead and
dying, of wrong-doing and transgression (a sense of guilt) for not helping them, for
letting them die, for "selfishly" remaining alive and strong; and "exposed" and
"seen through" by the same eyes for these identical failings (a sense of shame).[11]

There were also many episodes of more focused guilt toward specific
family members whom one was unable to help, and for whose death one felt
responsible. For instance, the shopkeeper's assistant mentioned earlier was finally
rescued from the debris of his destroyed house by his mother, but she was too
weakened by her own injuries to be able to walk very far with him. Soon they
were surrounded by fire, and he (a boy of thirteen) did not feel he had the strength
to sustain her weight, and became convinced that they would both die unless he
took some other action. So he put her down and ran for help, but the neighbor he
summoned could not get through to the woman because of the flames, and the
boy learned shortly afterward that his mother died in precisely the place he had
left her. His lasting sense of guilt was reflected in his frequent experience, from
that time onward, of hearing his mother's voice ringing in his ears calling for help.

A middle-aged businessman related a similarly guilt-stimulating
sequence. His work had taken him briefly to the south of Japan and he had
returned to Hiroshima during the early morning hours of August 6. Having been
up all night, he was not too responsive when his twelve-year-old son came into his
room to ask his father to remove a nail from his shoe so that he could put it on
and go off to school. The father, wishing to get the job quickly over, placed a piece
of leather above the tip of the nail and promised he would take the whole nail out
when the boy returned in the afternoon. As in the case of many youngsters who

were sent to factories to do "voluntary labor" as a substitute for their school work, the boy's body was never found—and the father, after a desperately fruitless search for his son throughout the city, was left with the lingering self-accusation that the nail he had failed to remove might have impeded the boy's escape from the fire.

Most survivors focus upon one incident, one sight, or one particular *ultimate horror* with which they strongly identify themselves, and which left them with a profound sense of pity, guilt, and shame. Thus the social worker describes an event which he feels affected him even more than his crematory activities:

> On the evening of August 6, the city was so hot from the fire that I could not easily enter it, but I finally managed to do so by taking a path along the river. As I walked along the bank near the present Yokogawa Bridge, I saw the bodies of a mother and her child. . . . That is, I thought I saw dead bodies, but the child was still alive—still breathing, though with difficulty. . . . I filled the cover of my lunch box with water and gave it to the child but it was so weak it could not drink. I knew that people were frequently passing that spot . . . and I hoped that one of these people would take the child, as I had to go back to my own unit. Of course I helped many people all through that day . . . but the image of this child stayed on my mind and remains as a strong impression even now. . . . Later when I was again in that same area I hoped that I might be able to find the child . . . and I looked for it among all the dead children collected at a place nearby. . . . Even before the war I had planned to go into social work, but this experience led me to go into my present work with children—as the memory of that mother and child by Yokogawa Bridge has never left me, especially since the child was still alive when I saw it.

These expressions of ultimate horror can be related to direct personal experience of loss (for instance, the businessman who had failed to remove the nail from his son's shoe remained preoccupied with pathetic children staring imploringly at him), as well as to enduring individual emotional themes. Most of them involved women and children, universal symbols of purity and vulnerability, particularly in Japanese culture. And, inevitably, the ultimate horror was directly related to death or dying.

Contamination and Disease

Survivors told me of three rumors which circulated widely in Hiroshima just after the bomb. The first was that for a period of seventy-five years Hiroshima would be uninhabitable—no one would be able to live there. This rumor was a direct expression of the *fear of deadly and protracted contamination from a mysterious poison believed to have been emitted by the frightening new weapon.* (As one survivor put it, "The ordinary people spoke of poison; the intellectuals spoke of radiation.")

Even more frequently expressed, and I believe with greater emotion, was a second rumor: trees and grass would never again grow in Hiroshima; from that day on the city would be unable to sustain vegetation of any kind. This seemed to suggest *an ultimate form of desolation even beyond that of human death:* nature was drying up altogether, the ultimate source of life was being extinguished—a form of symbolism particularly powerful in Japanese culture with its focus upon natural aesthetics and its view of nature as both enveloping and energizing all of human life.

The third rumor, less frequently mentioned to me but one which also had wide currency in various versions, was that all those who had been exposed to the bomb in Hiroshima would be dead within three years. This more naked death symbolism was directly related to the appearance of frightening symptoms of toxic radiation effects. For almost immediately after the bomb and during the following days and weeks, people began to experience, and notice in others, symptoms of a strange form of illness: nausea, vomiting, and loss of appetite; diarrhea with large amounts of blood in the stools; fever and weakness; purple spots on various parts of the body from bleeding into the skin (purpura); inflammation and ulceration of the mouth, throat, and gums (oropharyngeal lesions and gingivitis); bleeding from the mouth, gums, nose, throat, rectum, and urinary tract (hemorrhagic manifestations); loss of hair from the scalp and other parts of the body (epilation); extremely low white blood cell counts when these were taken (leucopenia); and in many cases a progressive course until death.[12] These symptoms and fatalities aroused in the minds of the people of Hiroshima a special terror, *an image of a weapon which not only kills and destroys on a colossal scale but also leaves behind in the bodies of those exposed to it deadly influences which may emerge at any time and strike down their victims.* This image was made particularly vivid by the delayed appearance of these radiation effects, two to four weeks after the bomb fell, sometimes in people who had previously seemed to be in perfect health.

The shopkeeper's assistant, both of whose parents were killed by the bomb, describes his reactions to the death of two additional close family members from these toxic radiation effects:

> My grandmother was taking care of my younger brother on the 14th of August when I left, and when I returned on the 15th she had many spots all over her body. Two or three days later she died. . . . My younger brother, who . . . was just a [five-month-old] baby, was without breast milk—so we fed him thin rice gruel. . . . But on the 10th of October, he suddenly began to look very ill, though I had not then noticed any spots on his body. . . . Then on the next day he began to look a little better, and I thought he was going to survive. I was very pleased, as he was the only family member I had left, and I took him to a doctor—but on the way to the doctor he died. And at that time we found that there were two large spots on his bottom. . . . I heard it said that all these people would die within three years. . . . so I thought, "sooner or later I too will die." . . . I felt very weak and very lonely—with no hope at all . . . and since I had seen so many people's eyebrows falling out, their hair falling out, bleeding from their teeth—I found myself always nervously touching my hair like this [he demonstrated by rubbing his head]. . . . I never knew when some sign of the disease would show itself. . . . And living in the countryside then with my relatives, people who came to visit would tell us these things, and then the villagers also talked about them—telling stories of this man or that man who visited us a few days ago, returned to Hiroshima, and died within a week. . . . I couldn't tell whether these stories were true or not, but I believed them then. And I also heard that when the *hibakusha*

came to evacuate to the village where I was, they died there one by one. . . . This loneliness, and the fear. . . . The physical fear . . . has been with me always. . . . It is not something temporary, as I still have it now. . . .

Here we find a link between this early sense of ubiquitous death from radiation effects, and later anxieties about death and illness.

In a similar tone, a middle-aged writer describes his daughter's sudden illness and death:

My daughter was working with her classmates at a place 1000 meters from the hypocenter. . . . I was able to meet her the next day at a friend's house. She had no burns and only minor external wounds, so I took her with me to my country house. She was quite all right for awhile but on the 4th of September she suddenly became sick. . . . The symptoms of her disease were different from those of a normal disease. . . . She had spots all over her body. . . . Her hair began to fall out. She vomited small clumps of blood many times. Finally she began to bleed all over her mouth. And at times her fever was very high. I felt this was a very strange and horrible disease. . . . We didn't know what it was. I thought it was a kind of epidemic—something like cholera. So I told the rest of my family not to touch her and to disinfect all utensils and everything she used. . . . We were all afraid of it and even the doctor didn't know what it was. . . . After ten days of agony and torture she died on September 14. . . . I thought it was very cruel that my daughter, who had nothing to do with the war, had to be killed in this way. . . .

Survivors were thus affected not only by the fact of people dying around them but by the way in which they died: a gruesome form of rapid bodily deterioration which seemed unrelated to more usual and "decent" forms of death.

We have seen how these initial physical fears could readily turn into lifetime bodily concerns. And during the years that followed, these fears and concerns became greatly magnified by another development: the growing awareness among the people of Hiroshima that medical studies were demonstrating an abnormally high rate of leukemia among survivors of the atomic bomb. The increased incidence was first noted in 1948, and reached a peak between 1950 and 1952; it has been greatest in those exposed closest to the hypocenter so that for those within 1000 meters the increase of leukemia has been between ten and fifty times the normal. Since 1952 the rate has diminished, but it is still higher than in nonexposed populations, and fears which have been aroused remain strong. While symptoms of leukemia are not exactly the same as those of acute radiation effects, the two conditions share enough in common—the dreaded "purple spots" and other forms of hemorrhage, laboratory findings of abnormalities of the blood, progressive weakness and fever and (inevitably in leukemia, and often enough in acute irradiation) ultimate death—that these tend to merge, psychologically speaking, into a diffuse fear of bodily annihilation and death.[13]

Moreover, Hiroshima survivors are aware of the general concern and controversy about genetic effects of the atomic bomb, and most express fear about possible harmful effects upon subsequent generations—a very serious emotional concern anywhere, but particularly so in an East Asian culture which stresses family lineage and the continuity of generations as man's central purpose in life and (at least symbolically) his means of achieving immortality. The Hiroshima people know that radiation *can* produce congenital abnormalities (as has been widely demonstrated in laboratory animals); and abnormalities have frequently been reported among the offspring of survivors—sometimes in very lurid journalistic terms, sometimes in more restrained medical reports. Actually, systematic studies of the problem have so far revealed no higher incidence of abnormalities in survivors' offspring than in those of control populations, so that scientific findings regarding genetic effects have been essentially negative. However, there has been one uncomfortably positive genetic finding, that of disturbances in sex ratio of offspring: men exposed to a significant degree of radiation tend to have relatively fewer daughters, while exposed women tend to have fewer sons, because, it is believed, of sex-linked lethal mutations involving the X chromosome—a finding whose significance is difficult to evaluate. Moreover, there are Japanese physicians who believe that there has been an increase in various forms of internal (and therefore invisible) congenital abnormalities in children of survivors, despite the absence so far of convincing scientific evidence.[14]

Another factor here is the definite damage from radiation experienced by children exposed *in utero,* including many stillbirths and abortions as well as a high incidence of microcephaly with and without mental retardation (occurring almost exclusively in pregnancies which had not advanced beyond four months). This is, of course, a direct effect of radiation upon sensitive, rapidly growing fetal tissues, and, scientifically speaking, has nothing to do with genetic problems. But ordinary people often fail to make this distinction; to them the birth of children with abnormally small heads and retarded minds was often looked upon as still another example of the bomb's awesome capacity to inflict a physical curse upon its victims and their offspring.

There are also other areas of concern regarding delayed radiation effects. There has been a definite increase in cataracts and related eye conditions, which was not stressed to me by survivors as so great a source of emotional concern as the other problems mentioned, but has been nonetheless far from negligible. There has been evidence, though not yet decisive, that the incidence of various forms of cancer has increased among survivors; if confirmed, this could be an extremely serious problem, since it involves fatal disease entities much more frequent in their normal occurrence than leukemia. There has also been evidence of impairment in the growth and development of children, though contested by some on the grounds of inadequately accounting for social and economic factors. And there is a large group of divergent conditions—including anemias and liver and blood diseases, endocrine and skin disorders, impairment of central nervous system (particularly midbrain) function, and premature aging—which have been attributed by various investigators to radiation effects, but have not shown increased incidence in large scale studies involving control populations. Even more difficult to evaluate is a frequently reported borderline condition of general weakness and debilitation also believed—by a very large number of survivors and by some physicians as well—to be caused by delayed radiation effects.

These fears about general health and genetic effects have inevitably affected marriage arrangements (which are usually made in Japan by families with the help of a go-between), in which survivors are frequently thought to encounter discrimination, particularly when involved in arrangements with families outside Hiroshima.

A company employee in his thirties, who was 2000 meters from the bomb's hypocenter when it fell, described to me virtually all of these bodily and genetic concerns in a voice that betrayed considerable anxiety:

> Even when I have an illness which is not at all serious—as for instance when I had very mild liver trouble—I have fears about its cause. Of course if it is just an ordinary condition there is nothing to worry about, but if it has a direct connection to radioactivity, then I might not be able to expect to recover. At such times I feel myself very delicate. . . . This happened two or three years ago. I was working very hard and drinking a great deal of *sake* at night in connection with business appointments and I also had to make many strenuous trips. So my condition might have been partly related to my using up so much energy in all of these things. . . . The whole thing is not fully clear to me. . . . But the results of statistical study show that those who were exposed to the bomb are more likely to have illnesses—not only of the liver, but various kinds of new growths, such as cancer or blood diseases. My blood was examined several times but no special changes were discovered. . . . When my marriage arrangements were made we discussed all these things in a direct fashion. Everyone knows that there are some effects, but in my case it was the eleventh year after the bomb, and I discussed my physical condition during all of that time. From that, and also from the fact that I was exposed to the bomb while inside of a building and taken immediately to the suburbs, and then remained quite a while outside of the city—judging from all of these facts, it was concluded that there was very little to fear concerning my condition. . . . But in general, there is a great concern that people who were exposed to the bomb might become ill five or ten years later or at any time in the future. . . . Also when my children were born, I found myself worrying about things that ordinary people don't worry about, such as the possibility that they might inherit some terrible disease from me. . . . I heard that the likelihood of our giving birth to deformed children is greater than in the case of ordinary people . . . and at that time my white blood cell count was rather low. . . . I felt fatigue in the summertime and had a blood count done three or four times. . . . I was afraid it could be related to the bomb, and was greatly worried. . . . Then after the child was born, even though he wasn't a deformed child, I still worried that something might happen to him afterwards. . . . With the second child too I was not entirely free of such worries. . . . I am still not sure what might happen and I worry that the effects of radioactivity might be lingering in some way. . . .

Here we see a young man carrying on effectively in his life, essentially healthy, with normal children, and yet continually plagued by underlying anxieties—about his general health, then about marriage arrangements, and then in relationship to the birth of each of his children. Each hurdle is passed, but there is little relief; like many survivors, he experiences an inner sense of being doomed for posterity.

And a young clerk, also exposed about 2000 meters from the hypocenter, but having the additional disadvantage of retaining a keloid scar resulting from facial burns, expresses similar emotions in still stronger fashion:

> Frankly speaking, even now I have fear. . . . Even today people die in the hospitals from A-bomb disease, and when I hear about this I worry that I too might sooner or later have the same thing happen to me. . . . I have a special feeling that I am different from ordinary people . . . that I have the mark of wounds—as if I were a cripple. . . . I imagine a person who has an arm or a leg missing might feel the same way. . . . It is not a matter of lacking something externally, but rather something like a handicap—something mental which does not show—the feeling that I am mentally different from ordinary people . . . so when I hear about people who die from A-bomb disease or who have operations because of this illness, then I feel that I am the same kind of person as they. . . .

The survivor's identification with the dead and the maimed initiates a vicious circle on the psychosomatic plane of existence: he is likely to associate the mildest everyday injury or sickness with possible radiation effects; and anything he relates to radiation effects becomes associated with death. The process is accentuated by the strong Japanese cultural focus upon bodily symptoms as expressions of anxiety and conflict. Thus the all-encompassing term "A-bomb sickness" or "A-bomb disease" (*genbakushō*) has evolved, referring on the one hand to such fatal conditions as the early acute radiation effects and later cases of leukemia; and on the other hand to the vague borderline area of fatigue, general weakness, sensitivity to hot weather, suspected anemia, susceptibility to colds or stomach trouble, and general nervousness—all of which are frequent complaints of survivors, and which many associate with radiation effects.[15] Not only does the expression "A-bomb disease" have wide popular currency, but it has frequently been used by local physicians as a convenient category for a condition otherwise hard to classify, and at the same time as a means of making it possible for the patient to derive certain medical and economic benefits.

These benefits also loom large in the picture.[16] Doctors and survivors—as well as politicians and city officials—are caught in a conflict between humanitarian provision for medical need, and the dangers (expressed to me particularly by Japanese physicians) of encouraging the development in survivors of hypochondriasis, general weakness and dependency—or what is sometimes called "A-bomb neurosis." During the years immediately after the war, when medical care was most needed, very little adequate treatment was available, as the national medical law providing for survivors was not enacted until 1957. But since that time a series of laws and amendments have been passed with increasingly comprehensive medical coverage, particularly for those in the "special survivors" group (those nearest the hypocenter at the time of the bomb and those who have shown evidence of medical conditions considered to be related to A-bomb effects). In the last few years the category of "special survivors" has been steadily enlarged: distance from the hypocenter, as a criterion for eligibility, has been extended from 2000 to 3000 meters; and qualifying illnesses—originally limited to such conditions as leukemia, ophthalmic diseases, and various blood and liver disorders, all of which were considered to be related to radiation effects—have been extended to include illnesses not considered to be necessarily directly caused by radiation but possibly aggravated by the overall atomic bomb experience, such as cancer, heart disease, endocrine and kidney disorders, arteriosclerosis, hypertension, and others.

Maximum medical and economic benefits, however, can be obtained only by those "certified" (through a special medical procedure) to have illnesses specifically related to the atomic bomb; but some physicians believe that this "certification"—which can be sometimes given for such minor conditions as ordinary anemia (as well as for more serious illnesses)—tends to stamp one psychologically as a lifetime A-bomb patient. The rationale of these laws is to provide maximum help for survivors and to give them the benefit of the doubt about matters which are not entirely scientifically resolved. But there remains a great deal of controversy over them. In addition to those who feel that the laws foster an exaggerated preoccupation with atomic bomb effects (not only among doctors, but also among city officials, ordinary people, and even survivors themselves), there are other survivors who criticize them as being still insufficiently comprehensive, as having overly complicated categories and sub-categories which in the end deny full care for certain conditions.

My own impression in studying this problem is that, since "A-bomb disease" is at this historical juncture as much a spiritual as a physical condition (as our young clerk made so clear)—and one which touches at every point upon the problem of death—it is difficult for any law or medical program to provide a cure.

The general psychological atmosphere in Hiroshima—and particularly that generated by the effects of the mass media—also has great bearing upon these psychosomatic problems. As one would expect, the whole subject of the atomic bomb and its delayed radiation effects has been continuous front-page news—from 1945-1952 within the limits of the restrictions upon publicizing these matters imposed by the American Occupation,[17] and without such restrictions thereafter. Confronted with a subject so emotionally charged for the people of Hiroshima—its intensity constantly reinforced by world events and particularly by nuclear weapons testing—newspapers in Hiroshima and elsewhere in Japan have dealt with it dramatically, particularly in circulating the concept of "A-bomb disease." Mass media are caught in a moral dilemma in some ways similar to that I have already described for physicians, city officials, and survivors themselves: there is on the one hand the urge to give full publicity to the horrors of nuclear weapons through vivid description of effects and suspected effects of atomic bomb radiation—thereby serving warning to the world and also expressing a form of sympathy to survivors through recognition of their plight—and on the other hand the growing awareness that lurid reports of illness and death have a profoundly disturbing effect upon survivors. Responsible media have struggled to reconcile these conflicting moral pressures and achieve balanced treatment of an unprecedentedly difficult problem; others have been guided mainly by commercial considerations. In any case, the people of Hiroshima have been constantly confronted with frightening descriptions of patients dying in the "A-bomb Hospital" (a medical center built specifically for the treatment of

conditions related to the bomb) of "A-bomb disease." In the majority of cases the
relationship of the fatal condition to delayed radiation effects is equivocal, but this
is usually not made clear, nor does it in any way lessen the enormous impact of
these reports upon individual survivors.[18] Also furthering this impact have been
the activities of peace movements and various ideological and political
groups—ranging from those whose universalistic dedication to peace and
opposition to nuclear weapons testing lead them to circulate the effects of the
bomb on a humanistic basis, to others who seek narrower political goals from the
unique Hiroshima atmosphere.

What I wish to stress is the manner in which these diverse
passions—compounded of moral concern, sympathetic identification, various
forms of fear, hostility, political conviction, personal ambition, and journalistic
sensationalism—interact with the psychosomatic preoccupations of survivors. But
I would also emphasize that these passions are by no means simply manufactured
ones; they are the inevitable expression of the impact of a disaster of this
magnitude upon basic human conflicts and anxieties. And whatever the medical
exaggerations, they are built upon an underlying lethal reality of acute and
delayed radiation effects, and upon the genuine possibility of still-undiscovered
forms of bodily harm.

Yet, in bodily terms or otherwise, human beings vary greatly in their
capacity to absorb an experience of this kind. And one's feelings of health or
invalidism—as well as one's symbolic attitude toward the bomb—have much to
do with individual emotions and life-patterns. This is made clear by a middle-aged
female artist who experienced the bomb just 1500 meters from the hypocenter,
and during subsequent years suffered continuously from a variety of bodily
symptoms of indefinite origin, as well as from general unhappiness in marital and
family relationships:

> It looks as though marriage and the normal life one leads with marriage is good
> for the health. . . . Among A-bomb victims, those that are married and well
> established with their families have fewer complaints. Of course, even those who
> are settled in their families remember the incident. But on the whole they are
> much better off and feel better . . . their attitude is, *"shōganai"* (it can't be helped).
> "It is useless to look back on old memories," they keep saying. They are simply
> interested in their immediate problems of marriage and everyday life. They look
> forward rather than backward. . . . Those without families on the other hand keep
> remembering everything. Clinging to their memories, they keep repeating the
> experience. . . . They curse the whole world—including what happened in the past
> and what is happening now. Some of them even say, "I hope that atomic bombs
> will be dropped again and then the whole world will suffer the same way I am
> suffering now."

This kind of hostility is likely to occur together with psychosomatic
complaints, and particularly in those people who feel that their life has been
blighted by the atomic bomb—those who lost close family members or who in one
way or another feel themselves unable to recover from the experience. The cosmic
nature of the emotion—its curse upon (and in some cases wish for total

annihilation of) the whole world resembles in some ways the retaliatory emotions of hurt children. But it contains additional elements of personal recollection: the experience of "world-destruction" at the time of the bomb. And it is a projection into the future: the even greater world-destruction one can envisage as a consequence of a repetition of the use of nuclear weapons.

Unwanted Identity

It is clear by now that exposure to the atomic bomb changed the survivor's status as a human being, in his own eyes as well as in others'. Both through his immediate experience and its consequences over the years, he became a member of a new group; he assumed the identity of the *hibakusha,* of one who has undergone the atomic bomb. When I asked survivors to associate freely to the word *hibakusha,* and to explain their feelings about it, they invariably conveyed to me the sense of having been compelled to take on this special category of existence, by which they felt permanently bound, however they might wish to free themselves from it. The shopkeeper's assistant expresses this in simple terms characteristic for many:

> Well . . . because I am a *hibakusha* . . . how shall I say it—I wish others would not look at me with special eyes . . . perhaps *hibakusha* are mentally—or both physically and mentally—different from others . . . but I myself do not want to be treated in any special way because I am a *hibakusha.* . . .

To be a *hibakusha* thus separates one from the rest of humankind. It means, as expressed by a young female clerical worker left with a keloid from her atomic bomb exposure at 1600 meters, a sense of having been forsaken.

> I don't like people to use that word [*hibakusha*]. . . . Of course there are some who, through being considered *hibakusha* want to receive special coddling *(amaeru).* . . . But I like to stand up as an individual. When I was younger they used to call us "atomic bomb maidens." . . . More recently they call us *hibakusha.* . . . I don't like this special view of us. . . . Usually when people refer to young girls, they will say girls or daughters, or some person's daughter . . . but to refer to us as atomic bomb maidens is a way of discrimination. . . . It is a way of abandoning us. . . .

What she is saying, and what many said to me in different ways, is that the experience, with all of its consequences, is so profound that it can virtually become the person; others then see one *only* as a *hibakusha* bearing the taint of death, and therefore, in the deepest sense, turn away. And even the special attentions—the various forms of emotional succor—which the survivor may be tempted to seek, cannot be satisfying because such succor is ultimately perceived as unauthentic.

A European priest, one of the relatively few non-Japanese *hibakusha,* expresses these sentiments gently but sardonically:

> I always say—if everyone looks at me because I received the Nobel Prize, that's O.K., but if my only virtue is that I was 1000 meters from the atomic bomb center and I'm still alive—I don't want to be famous for that.

Hibakusha look upon themselves as under-privileged in other ways too. Not only are they literally a minority group (one-fifth of the city's population), but they are generally considered to be at the lower socioeconomic levels of society, and have even at times been compared to the *burakumin,* or outcast group.[19] For once it was realized that Hiroshima was not permanently contaminated after all, not only did the survivors attempt to rebuild their homes, but hordes of outsiders—some from overseas areas, some from the industrial Osaka region, some of them black marketeers and members of gangs who saw special opportunity beckoning: all of them both physically and culturally more vigorous than the atomic-bombed, traditionalistic Hiroshima population—poured into the city, and became perhaps the main beneficiaries of the economic boom which later developed. Survivors have encountered discrimination not only in marriage but also in employment, as it was felt that they could not work as hard as ordinary people and tended to need more time off because of illness and fatigue. Of course, survivors nonetheless regularly work and marry; but they often do so with a sense of having, as *hibakusha,* impaired capacity for both. They strongly resent the popular image of the *hibakusha* which accentuates their limitations, but at the same time accept much of it as their own self-image. Thus, concerning occupational competition, older survivors often feel that they have lacked the over-all energy to assimilate their economic, spiritual, and possibly physical blows sufficiently to be the equal of ordinary people; and young survivors, even if they feel themselves to possess normal energy, often fear that being identified by others as a *hibakusha* might similarly interfere with their occupational standing. Concerning marriage, the sense of impairment can include the need to have one's A-bomb experience more or less "cleared" by a go-between (as we have seen); fears about having abnormal children, or sometimes about the ability to have children at all;[20] and occasionally, in males, diminished sexual potency (thought of as organic but probably psychogenic in origin).

However well or poorly a survivor is functioning in his life, the word *hibakusha* evokes an image of the dead and the dying. The young clerk, for instance, when he hears the word, thinks either of the experience itself (". . . Although I wasn't myself too badly injured I saw many people who were . . . and I think . . . of the look on their faces . . . camps full of these people, their breasts burned and red . . .") or, as we have already heard him describe, of the after-effects: "when I hear about people who die from A-bomb disease or who have operations because of this illness, then I feel that I am the same kind of person as they. . . ."

We are again confronted with the survivor's intimate identification with the dead; we find, in fact, that it tends to pervade the entire *hibakusha* identity. *For survivors seem not only to have experienced the atomic disaster, but to have imbibed it and incorporated it into their beings, including all of its elements of horror, evil, and particularly of death.* They feel compelled virtually to merge with those who died, not only with close family members but with a more anonymous group of "the dead." And they judge, and indeed judge harshly their own behavior and that of other survivors on the basis of the degree of respect it demonstrates toward the dead. They condemn, for instance, the widespread tendency (which, as Japanese, they are at the same time attracted to) of making the anniversary of the bomb an occasion for a gay festival—because they see this as an insult to the dead. Similarly they are extraordinarily suspicious of all individual and group attempts to take any form of action in relationship to the atomic bomb experience, even when done for the apparent purpose of helping survivors or furthering international peace. And they are, if anything, more critical of a survivor prominent in such programs than they are of "outsiders," constantly accusing such a person of "selling his name," "selling the bomb," or "selling Hiroshima." The causes for their suspiciousness are many, including a pervasive Japanese cultural tendency to be critical of the man who shows unconventional initiative (as expressed in the popular saying, "A nail which sticks out will be hammered down"), as well as an awareness of how readily the Hiroshima situation can be "used" by ambitious leaders. But there is an ultimate inner feeling that any such activities and programs are "impure," that they violate the sanctity of the dead. For in relationship to the atomic bomb disaster, it is only the dead who, in the eyes of survivors, remain pure; and any self- or group-assertion can readily be seen as an insult to the dead.

The *hibakusha* identity, then, in a significant symbolic sense, becomes an identity of the dead. Created partly by the particularly intense Japanese capacity for identification, and partly by the special quality of guilt over surviving, it takes shape through the following inner sequence: I almost died; I should have died; I did die, or at least am not really alive; or if I am alive it is impure of me to be so; and anything I do which affirms life is also impure and an insult to the dead, who alone are pure.[21]

Finally, this imposed identity of the atomic bomb survivor is greatly affected by his historical perceptions (whether clear or fragmentary) of the original experience, including its bearing upon the present world situation. The dominant emotion here is the sense of having been made into "guinea pigs," not only because of being studied by research groups (particularly American research groups) interested in determining the effects of delayed radiation, but more fundamentally because of having been victimized by the first "experiment" (a word many of them use in referring to the event) with nuclear weapons. They are affected by a realization, articulated in various ways, that they have experienced something ultimate in man-made disasters; and at the same time by the feeling that the world's continuing development and testing of the offending weapons deprives their experience of meaning. Thus, while frequently suspicious of organized campaigns against nuclear testing, they almost invariably experience anxiety and rage when such testing is conducted, recall the horrors they have been through, and express bitter frustration at the world's unwillingness to heed their warnings. And we have seen how this anger can at times be converted into thoughts of cosmic retaliation. There remains, of course, a residuum of hostility toward America and Americans for having dropped the bomb, but such hostility has been tempered over the years and softened by Japanese cultural restraints—except, as we have also seen, in individuals who experienced personal losses and blows to self-esteem from which they have been unable to recover. More than in relation to the dropping of the bomb itself (which many said they could understand as a product, however horrible, of war), survivors tend to express hostility in response to what they feel to be callousness toward their plight or toward those who died, and also toward nuclear weapons testing. Thus, in singling out President Truman as an object of hatred, as some do, it is not only for his having ordered that the bomb be used but also for being assertively unapologetic about having done so.[22]

Survivors tend to be strongly ambivalent about serving as symbols for the rest of the world, and this ambivalence is expressed in Hiroshima's excruciating conflict about whether or not to tear down the so-called "A-bomb dome" (or "peace dome")—the prominent ruins of a dome-shaped exhibition hall located almost directly at the hypocenter. The dome has so far been permitted to stand as a reminder of the experience and its picture has been featured in countless books and pamphlets dealing, from every point of view, with the A-bomb problem. Three different sets of attitudes on the question were expressed to me. The first: Let it remain permanently so that people (especially outsiders) will remember what we have been through and take steps to prevent repetitions of such disasters. The second: Tear it down for any of the following reasons: it does no good, as no one pays any attention to it; we should adopt the Buddhist attitude of resignation toward the experience; the dome is unauthentic, does not adequately convey what we really experienced, and is not in fact directly, at the hypocenter; it is too painful a reminder for *us (hibakusha)* to have to look at every day (perhaps the most strongly felt objection); and, we should look ahead to the future rather than back to the unpleasant past. And the third: Let it neither be permitted to stand indefinitely nor torn down, but instead left as it is until it begins to crumble of its own, and then simply removed—a rather ingenious (and perhaps characteristically Japanese) compromise solution to the dilemma, which the city administration has proposed. Most survivors simultaneouly feel various conflicting elements of the first and second sets of attitudes, and sometimes of all three. The inner conflict is something like this: For the sake of the dead and of our own sense of worth, we must give our experience significance by enabling it to serve wider moral purposes; but to do so—to be living symbols of massive death—is not only unbearably painful but also tends ultimately to be insincere and to insult, rather than comfort, the dead.

Beyond Hiroshima

We return to the question we raised at the beginning: Does Hiroshima follow the standard patterns delineated for other disasters, or is it—in an experiential sense—a new order of event? We must say first that the usual emotional patterns of disaster[23] are very much present in what I have already described. One can break down the experience into the usual sequence of anticipation, impact, and aftermath; one can recognize such standard individual psychological features as various forms of denial, the "illusion of centrality" (or feeling of each that he was at the very center of the disaster's path),[24] the apathy of the "disaster syndrome" resulting from the sudden loss of the sense of safety and even omnipotence with which we usually conduct our lives, and the conflict between self-preservation and wider human responsibility which culminates in feelings of guilt and shame; even some of the later social and psychological conflicts in the affected population are familiar.[25] Yet we have also seen convincing evidence that the Hiroshima experience,[26] no less in the psychological than in the physical sphere, transcends in many important ways that of the ordinary disaster. I shall try to suggest what I think are some of the important ways in which this is true. And when these special psychological qualities of the experience of the atomic bomb have been more fully elaborated—beyond the preliminary outlines of this paper—I believe that they will, in turn, shed light on general disaster patterns, and, of greater importance, on human nature and its vicissitudes at our present historical juncture. We may then come to see Hiroshima for what it was and is: both a direct continuation of the long and checkered history of human struggle, and at the same time a plunge into a new and tragic dimension.

The first of these psychological elements is one we have already referred to, the continuous encounter with death. When we consider the sequence of this encounter—its turbulent onset at the moment the bomb fell, its shocking reappearance in association with delayed radiation effects, and its prolonged expression in the group identity of the doomed and near-dead—we are struck by the fact that it is an interminable encounter. There is, psychologically speaking, no end point, no resolution. This continuous and unresolvable encounter with death, then, is a unique feature of the atomic bomb disaster. Its significance for the individual survivor varies greatly, according to such factors as previous character traits, distance from the hypocenter at the time the bomb fell, fatalities in his immediate family, and many other features of his bomb experience and subsequent life pattern. There is little doubt that most survivors lead reasonably effective personal, family, and occupational lives. But each retains, in greater or lesser degree, emotional elements of this special relationship to death.

In the light of the Hiroshima experience we should also consider the possibility that in other disasters or extreme situations there may also be more significant inner encounters with death, immediate or longer-term, than we have heretofore supposed. Psychiatrists and social scientists investigating these matters are hampered by the same factors which interfere with everyone else's approach to the subject: first, by our inability to imagine death, which deprives us, as psychiatrists, of our usual reliance upon empathy and leaves us always at several psychological removes from experiential understanding; and second, by the elaborate circle of denial—the profound inner need of human beings to make believe that they will never die—in which we too are enclosed. But these universal psychological barriers to thought about death become much greater in relation to a nuclear disaster, where the enormity of the scale of killing and the impersonal nature of the technology are still further impediments to comprehension. No wonder then that the world resists full knowledge of the Hiroshima and Nagasaki experiences, and expends relatively little energy in comprehending their full significance. And beyond Hiroshima, these same impediments tragically block and distort our perceptions of the general consequences of nuclear weapons. They also raise an important question relevant for the continuous debate about the desirability of preparedness for possible nuclear attacks: If the human imagination is so limited in its capacity to deal with death, and particularly death on a vast scale, can individuals ever be significantly "prepared" for a nuclear disaster?

The Hiroshima experience thus compels us, particularly as psychiatrists, to give more thought to psychic perceptions of death and dying.[27] Here I would particularly stress the psychological importance of identification with the dead—not merely the identification with a particular loved one, as in the case of an ordinary mourning experience, but rather, as we have observed in atomic bomb survivors, a lasting sense of affiliation with death itself. This affiliation creates in turn an enduring element, both within, and standing in judgment of, the self—a process closely related to the experience of shame.[28] Also of great importance is the *style of dying,* real or symbolic, the way in which one anticipates death and the significance with which one can relate oneself to this anticipation. Among those I interviewed in Hiroshima, many found solace in the characteristically Japanese (partially Buddhist) attitude of resignation, but virtually none were able to build a framework of meaning around their overwhelming immersion in death. However philosophically they might accept the horrors of war, they had an underlying sense of having been victimized and experimented upon by a horrible device, all to no avail in a world which has derived no profit from their sufferings.

And this sense of purposeless death suggests the second special feature of the atomic disaster: *a vast breakdown of faith in the larger human matrix supporting each individual life, and therefore a loss of faith (or trust) in the structure of existence.* This is partly due to the original exposure to death and destruction on such an extraordinary scale, an "end-of-the-world" experience resembling the actualization of the wildest psychotic delusion; partly due to the shame and guilt patterns which, initiated during the experience itself, turned into longer-lasting preoccupations with human selfishness (preoccupations expressed to me by a large number of survivors); and partly due to the persisting sense of having encountered an ultimate form of *man-made* destruction. Phrased in another way, the atomic bomb destroyed the complex equilibrium which ordinarily mediates and integrates the great variety of cultural patterns and individual emotions which maintain any society, large or small. One must, of course, take into account here the disruption accompanying the extensive social change which has occurred all over Japan immediately following World War II; and one must also recognize the impressive re-emergence of Hiroshima as an actively functioning city. Nonetheless, this profound loss of confidence in human social ties remains within survivors as a derivative of the atomic bomb experience.

A third psychological feature of particular importance in the Hiroshima disaster is that which I have called *psychological closure*. Resembling the psychological defense of denial, and the behavioral state of apathy, psychological closure is nonetheless a distinctive pattern of response to overwhelmingly threatening stimuli. Within a matter of moments, as we have seen in the examples cited, a person may not only cease to react to these threatening stimuli but in so doing, equally suddenly, violate the most profound values and taboos of his culture and his personal life. Though a highly adaptive response—and indeed very often a means of emotional self-preservation—it can vary in its proportions to the extent at times of almost resembling a psychotic mechanism. Since psychological closure, at least in the form it took in Hiroshima, is specifically related to the problem of death, it raises the question of the degree to which various forms of psychosis might also be responses to the symbolic fear of death or bodily annihilation.

The psychological closure created by the Hiroshima disaster is not limited to the victims themselves, but extends to those who, like myself, attempt to study the event. Thus, although I had had previous research experience with people who had been exposed to extreme situations, I found that at the beginning of my work in Hiroshima the completion of each interview would leave me profoundly shocked and emotionally spent. But as the work progressed and I heard more and more of these accounts, their effects upon me greatly lessened. My awareness of my scientific function—my listening carefully for specific kinds of information and constantly formulating categories of response—enhanced the psychological closure necessary to me for the task of conducting the research (necessary also for a wide variety of human efforts which deal with problems in which death is a factor). It is the vast ramification of psychological closure, rather than the phenomenon itself, that is unique to nuclear disaster, so much so that all who become in any way involved in the problem find themselves facing a near-automatic tendency to close themselves off from what is most disturbing in the evidence at hand.

Finally, there is the question of *psychological mastery of the nuclear disaster experience*. Central to this problem is the task of dealing with feelings of shame and guilt of the most profound nature: the sense that one has, however unwittingly, participated in this total human breakdown which, in Martin Buber's words "the human order of being is injured."[29] That such feelings of self-condemnation—much like those usually termed "existential guilt"—should be experienced by the *victims* of a nuclear disaster is perhaps the most extreme of its many tragic ironies. Faced with the task of dealing with this form of guilt, with the problem of re-establishing trust in the human order, and with the continuing sense of encounter with death, the survivor of a nuclear disaster needs nothing less than a new identity in order to come to terms with his post disaster world. And once more extending the principle beyond the victim's experience, it may not be too much to say that those who permit themselves to confront the consequences of such a disaster, past or future, are also significantly changed in the process. Since these consequences now inhabit our world, more effective approaches to the problem of human survival may well depend upon our ability to grasp the nature of the fundamentally new relationship to existence which we all share.

References

1 Portions of this paper were presented at the Annual Meeting of the American Association for the Advancement of Science in Philadelphia, December, 1962. The work it describes was done in Hiroshima from April to September of 1962, 17 years after the dropping of the atomic bomb. I am profoundly grateful to a large number of friends and colleagues from the various divisions of Hiroshima University (particularly the Research Institute for Nuclear Medicine and Biology), the Hiroshima City Office, and many other groups for their generous assistance in the extensive arrangements necessary for the work; to Mr. Kaoru Ogura and Miss Kyoko Komatsu for their dedicated and skillful research assistance during all of its phases; and to Dr. L. Takeo Doi for stimulating suggestions later on concerning psychological formulations. Responsibility for conclusions is, of course, entirely my own.

2 Studies of the effects of ionizing radiation were instituted by Japanese medical and civilian teams within days after the bomb was dropped, with Dr. Masao Tsuzuki of Toyko Imperial University, playing a leading role. American medical groups began their work in early September of 1945, and became consolidated in the Joint Commission for the Investigation of the Effects of the Atomic Bomb in Japan. Studies of longer-term effects of radiation have been conducted at the medical departments and research institutes of Hiroshima and Nagasaki Universities. The largest research program on delayed radiation effects is being carried out at the Atomic Bomb Casualty Commission, in both Hiroshima and Nagasaki, an affiliate of the United States National Academy of Sciences—National Research Council, under a grant from the U. S. Atomic Energy Commission, administered with the cooperation of the Japanese National Institute of Health of the Ministry of Health and Welfare. Much of the extensive literature on radiation effects has been summarized in the following: Ashley W. Oughterson and Shields Warren, *Medical Effects of the Atomic Bomb in Japan* (New York: McGraw-Hill, 1956); J. W. Hollingsworth, "Delayed Radiation Effects in Survivors of the Atomic Bombings," *New England Journal of Medicine,* Vol. 263 (September 8, 1960), pp. 381-487; "Bibliography of Publications Concerning the Effects of Nuclear Explosions," *Journal of the Hiroshima Medical Association,* Vol. 14, No. 10 (1961); and in the series of Technical Reports of the ABCC and the various issues of the *Proceedings of the Research Institute for Medicine and Biology* of Hiroshima University, and of the *Hiroshima Journal of Medical Sciences.*

3 There has, however, been some preliminary sociological and psychological research in these areas. See S. Nakano, "Genbaku Eikyo no Shakaigakuteki Chōsa" (Sociological Study of Atomic Bomb Effects), *Daigakujinkai Kenkyuronshu I, Betsuzuri* (April, 1954), and "Genbaku to Hiroshima," (The Atomic Bomb and Hiroshima), in *Shinshu Hiroshima Shi-shi (Newly Revised History of Hiroshima City)* Hiroshima Shiyakusho, 1951; Y. Kubo, "Data about the Suffering and Opinion of the A-bomb Sufferers," *Psychologia,* Vol. 4 (March, 1961), pp. 56-59 (in English); and "A Study of A-bomb Sufferers' Behavior in Hiroshima: A Socio-psychological Research on A-bomb and A-energy," *Japanese Journal of Psychology,* Vol. 22 (1952), pp. 103-110 (English abstract); T. Misao, "Characteristics in Abnormalities Observed in Atom-bombed Survivors," *Journal of Radiation Research,* Vol. 2 (September, 1961), pp. 85-97 (in English), in which various psychosomatic factors are dealt with; Irving L. Janis, *Air War and Emotional Stress* (New York: McGraw-Hill, 1951), particularly chapters 1-3. Additional studies of social aspects of the atomic bomb problem, under the direction of

K. Shimizu, are now under way at the Hiroshima University Research Institute for Nuclear Medicine and Biology.

4 Robert J. Lifton, "Youth and History: Individual Change in Postwar Japan," *Daedalus,* Vol. 91 (1962), pp. 172-197; and "Individual Patterns in Historical Change: Imagery of Japanese Youth," presented at the Annual Meeting of the Association for Research in Nervous and Mental Disease, New York, December 8, 1962.

5 Robert J. Lifton, *Thought Reform and the Psychology of Totalism* (New York: W. W. Norton & Company, 1961).

6 *Hibakusha* is a coined word which has no exact English equivalent but means: one (or those) who has (have) experienced, sustained, or undergone the (atomic) bomb. It conveys a little bit more than merely having encountered the bomb, and a little bit less than having experienced definite physical injury from it. *Higaisha,* another word frequently used, means "one who has sustained injury" or simply "victim." But the words are frequently used more or less interchangeably, and both in translation are sometimes rendered as "victim(s)" or "sufferer(s)" from the atomic bomb. Thus, the English word "survivors" is in no sense an exact translation of either *hibakusha* or *higaisha,* but rather a means of designating in a single word persons who fit into the category of *hibakusha.* While *hibakusha* has come to convey many things in popular usage, it also is employed to represent the four groups of people covered by the official legislation on medical benefits for those exposed to the effects of the bomb: those who at the time of the bomb were within the city limits then existing for Hiroshima, an area extending from the bomb's hypocenter to a distance of 4000 (and in some places up to 5000) meters; those who were not in the city at the time, but within 14 days entered a designated area extending to about 2000 meters from the hypocenter; those who were engaged in some form of aid to, or disposal of, bomb victims at various stations then set up; and those who were *in utero,* and whose mothers fit into any of the first three categories (See "Genbaku Iryōhō no Kaise Jishi ni tsuite" [Concerning the Enforcement of the Revision of the Atomic Bomb Medical Treatment Law of August 1, 1960], published by the Hiroshima City Office). For studying physical aspects of delayed radiation effects, such factors as distance from the hypocenter and degree of protection from radiation (by buildings, clothing, etc.) are crucial, and from this standpoint a large number of those designated as *hibakusha* had little or no exposure to significant amounts of radiation. For psychological and social effects, these factors—and particularly that of distance from the hypocenter—are of great importance, but one cannot make the same relatively sharp correlations regarding what is, or is not, significant exposure. I shall deal more with this problem in subsequent publications, and also with some of the special responses of the selected group of survivors; but in this paper I shall emphasize general psychological themes which apply, in greater or lesser degree, to virtually all *hibakusha.*

7 The one exception was an interview with a European priest who had been in Hiroshima at the time of the bomb, my only non-Japanese research subject.

8 It was, of course, inevitable that, after 17 years, elements of selectivity and distortion would enter into these recollections. But I was impressed with the vividness of recall, with the willingness of people, once a reasonable degree of rapport had been established, to express themselves quite freely about painful, and often humiliating, details; and with the over-all agreement contained in these descriptions, with each other and with various published accounts, concerning what took place generally and how people behaved. For corroborating published accounts, see, for instance: M. Hachiya (Warner Wells, ed., trans.), *Hiroshima Diary* (Chapel Hill: University of North Carolina Press, 1955); T. Nagai, *We of Nagaski* (New York: Duell, Sloan and Pearce, 1951): H. Agawa, *Devil's Heritage,* (Tokyo: Hokuseido Press, 1957); A. Osada (compiler), *Children of the A-Bomb* (New York: Putnam, 1963); Robert Yungk, *Children of the Ashes* (New York: Harcourt, Brace & World, 1961); John Hersey, *Hiroshima* (New

York: Bantam Books, 1959); Robert Trumbull, *Nine Who Survived Hiroshima and
Nagasaki* (Tokyo and Rutland, Vermont: Charles E. Tuttle, 1957); S. Imahori,
Gensuibaku Jidai (The Age of the A- and H-bomb) (Hiroshima: 1959); Y. Matsuzaka,
ed. *Hiroshima Genbaku Iryō-shi (Medical History of the Hiroshima A-Bomb)*,
(Hiroshima, 1961); Y. Ota, *Shikabane no Machi* (Town of Corpses) (Tokyo: Kawade
Shobō, 1955); and the large number of back issues of the *Chugoku Shimbun,*
Hiroshima's leading newspaper which include accounts of personal A-bomb
experiences.

 9 For estimates of damage, casualties, and mortality, see Oughterson and Warren, *op. cit.,
Hiroshima Genbaku Iryō-shi, op. cit.,* M. Ishida and I. Matsubayashi, "An Analysis of
Early Mortality Rates Following the Atomic Bomb—Hiroshima," ABCC Technical
Report 20-61, Hiroshima and Nagasaki (undated); S. Nagaoka, *Hiroshima Under
Atomic Bomb Attack* (Peace Memorial Museum, Hiroshima, undated); and "Hiroshima:
Official Brochure Produced by Hiroshima City Hall" (based largely upon previously
mentioned sources). Concerning mortality, Oughterson and Warren estimate 64,000,
believed to be accurate within ± 10 per cent; K. Shimizu (in *Hiroshima Genbaku
Iryō-shi*) estimates "more than 200,000," the figure which is accepted by the City of
Hiroshima; Nagaoka estimates "more than 240,000"; the official estimate is usually
given as 78,150; and one frequently sees estimates of "more than 100,000." Contributing
to this great divergence in figures are such things as varying techniques of calculation,
differing estimates of the number of people in Hiroshima at the moment the bomb fell,
the manner in which military fatalities are included, how long afterward (and after
which census count) the estimate was made, and undoubtedly other human factors
outside the realm of statistical science. The obvious conclusion is that no one really
knows, nor, considering the degree of disorganization interfering with collection of
accurate population data, is the problem ever likely to be fully solved.

10 These "fireballs" have no relationship to the fireball of the atomic bomb previously
mentioned, and are here being compared with ordinary fires caused by the bomb.

11 In such profound emotional experiences, feelings of shame and guilt become intermixed
and virtually indistinguishable. In cases like this one, the guilty inner fantasy is likely to
be "I am responsible for their (his, her) death," or even, "I killed them." The shameful
fantasy is likely to be, "I should have saved them, or at least done more for them." But
these are closely related, and in mentioning either shame or guilt in the remainder of the
paper, I assume that the other is present as well. See reference 28.

12 See Oughterson and Warren, as well as other sources mentioned in reference 2.
Oughterson and Warren demonstrate statistically the relationship between incidence of
radiation effects and distance from the hypocenter—the great majority of cases
occurring within the 2000 meter radius—but these scientific distinctions were, of course,
completely unknown at the time, and even after becoming known they have not
eliminated survivors' fears of later effects.

13 See Hollingsworth, *op cit.,* and other sources mentioned in reference 2 for discussions of
delayed radiation effects and bibliographies of work done on the subject. Concerning
the problem of leukemia, see also A. B. Brill, M. Tomonaga, and R. M. Heyssel,
"Leukemia in Man Following Exposure to Ionizing Radiation," *Annals of Internal
Medicine,* Vol. 56 (1962), pp. 590-609, and S. Watanabe, "On the Incidence of
Leukemias in Hiroshima During the Past Fifteen Years From 1946-1960," *Journal of
Radiation Research,* Vol. 2 (1961), pp. 131-140 (in English).

14 The most extensive work on these genetic problems has been done by James V. Neel
and W. O. Schull. See their "Radiation and Sex Ratio in Man: Sex Ratio among
Children of Atomic Bombings Suggests Induced Sex Linked Lethal Mutations,"
Science, Vol. 128 (1958), pp. 343-348; and *The Effect of Exposure to the Atomic Bomb on
Pregnancy Termination in Hiroshima and Nagasaki,* Washington, D. C., National
Academy of Sciences—National Research Council (Government Printing Office, 1956).

Belief in the possibility of an increase in various forms of congenital malformations in offspring of survivors has been stimulated by the work of I. Hayashi at Nagasaki University, reported in his paper: "Pathological Research on Influences of Atomic Bomb Exposure upon Fetal Development," *Research in the Effects and Influences of the Nuclear Bomb Test Explosions* (in English, undated), though Dr. Hayashi, in summarizing his material, cautions that "one hesitates to give any concrete statement about the effect of the atomic bomb radiation [upon] the growth of fetal life, based on the data available in this paper."

15 These borderline complaints, as detected by the Cornell Medical Index (T. Misao, *op. cit.*) are consistently more frequent in *hibakusha* than in non-*hibakusha*. The cultural concern with bodily symptoms is no more than an intensifying influence, and generally similar psychosomatic anxieties would undoubtedly be manifest in other cultures under similar conditions.

16 The following discussion of the question of medical benefits is based upon regulations published by the Hiroshima City Office (especially "Genbaku Iryōhō no Kaise . . ." *op cit.*) as well as upon extensive discussions of the problems involved with officials responsible for administering the law and physicians who deal with its every day medical and psychological ramifications. My concern here is to point up these problematic areas as reverberations of the atomic bomb experience, rather than to pass judgment on policies or programs.

17 Censorship on matters relating to the atomic bomb and its various effects was imposed almost immediately by the American Occupation; fears of retaliation were undoubtedly an important factor, though it is likely that over the years other concerns and influences affected this policy. Reviewing Japanese perceptions of the censorship (see the later [October 6 to December 7, 1959] series of articles in the *Chugoku Shimbun* on the history of postwar Hiroshima literature; S. Imahori, *Gensuibaku Jidai, op. cit.;* and Robert Jungk, *Children of the Ashes, op. cit*) one gains the impression that its implementation was often inconsistent but sufficient to be felt keenly by writers, and even to interfere with adequate dissemination of much needed medical knowledge about the A-bomb; that descriptions of the A-bomb experience—reportorial, literary, and ideological—nonetheless made their appearance during the early postwar years; that restrictions diminished sufficiently during the last two years of the Occupation for writers to deal freely with the subject; but that the full revelation of the horrors associated with the atomic bomb did not occur for the majority of Japanese until the end of the Occupation in 1952 with the circulation of a now famous issue of the *Asahi Graphic* (a weekly pictorial of Japan's leading newspaper) in which these horrors were vividly depicted.

18 Leukemia, despite its disturbing increase in incidence, remains an infrequent cause of death (Hollingsworth, quoting Heyssel, reports that, up to 1960, 122 cases of leukemia had been discovered in Hiroshima residents); and where death is caused by other conditions it is extremely difficult to assess the influence of radiation effects. But the individual survivor will often automatically associate the A-bomb Hospital with radiation effects, and the situation is further complicated by the medical and legal complexities already mentioned, and by the generally sensitive psychological atmosphere of Hiroshima.

19 Nakano, "Genbaku to Hiroshima," *op. cit.,* gives evidence for the lower socioeconomic position of *hibakusha,* and discusses other social and psychological problems they face. See also Imahori, *op. cit.,* and Jungk, *op. cit.*

20 Survivors often marry each other, and frequently feel that by doing so they are likely to be best understood. But some express a strong preference to marry a non-*hibakusha,* and claim that by marrying one another they increase their possibilities for giving birth to abnormal children; they also here reflect an urge to transcend through marriage, rather than intensify, the *hibakusha* identity.

21 I have in this section barely suggested the Japanese cultural influences—particularly the tendency toward a sense of continuity with the dead—which affect survivors' reactions. These cultural influences are important and I shall attempt to say more about them in later publications. But I believe that the close identification with the dead which I have described, like the psychosomatic patterns discussed in the previous section, should not be thought of as exclusively "Japanese"; rather I would claim that it is also related to the nature of the disaster, although expressed in a particular (Japanese) cultural style. For Japanese attitudes about purity, see Lifton, *Youth and History, op. cit.,* and for relationship of attitudes toward death and purity, see Robert N. Bellah, *Tokugawa Religion* (Glencoe, Ill.: The Free Press, 1957).

22 These attitudes are related to Japanese cultural tendencies to stress human considerations, including apologetic sympathy where this is felt indicated, rather than more abstract determinations of right and wrong or matters of individual conscience. But again it is by no means certain that in similar circumstances, even in cultures with a reverse emphasis, similar hostilities might not occur.

23 Compilations of the general literature on disaster are to be found in: George W. Baker and Dwight W. Chapmen, *Man and Society in Disaster* (New York: Basic Books, 1962); Martha Wolfenstein, *Disaster* (Glencoe, Ill.: The Free Press, 1957); "Human Behavior in Disaster: A New Field of Social Research," *The Journal of Social Issues,* Volume 10, No. 3 (entire issue); *Field Studies of Disaster Behavior, An Inventory* (Disaster Research Group, National Academy of Sciences—National Research Council, Washington, 1961); and L. Bates, C. W. Fogleman and Vernon J. Parenton, *The Social and Psychological Consequences of a National Disaster: A Longitudinal Study of Hurricane Audrey* (National Academy of Sciences—National Research Council, Washington, D. C., 1963).

24 It is to those who were several thousand meters from the hypocenter, including many beyond the outskirts of the city, that the term "illusion of centrality" and its psychological mechanisms (as described in the literature on disaster) apply. Those who were closer, in terms of effects experienced, were sufficiently central to the disaster for the term "illusion" to be inappropriate.

25 As in other recent disaster studies (see, for instance, Bates et al., *op. cit.*) I did not (from discussions with medical, psychiatric, and other authorities) have the impression of a large increase of severe mental illness, such as psychosis, at the time of the disaster or immediately afterwards; in view of the limited available statistical data it would be extremely difficult to study this problem, and I did not attempt to do so. My findings differ, however, from those of other disaster studies in the extent of the psychosocial consequences I encountered which, although emotionally profound, are not of a variety classifiable as "mental illness." This important difference stems mainly, I believe, from special features of the atomic bomb experience, but may also be related to variations in approach and method.

26 I have in this paper dealt only with Hiroshima as it was there that I conducted the research, although I did have the opportunity to make briefer observations in Nagasaki as well. In both cities there is a widely held impression that general reactions to the atomic bomb—mass media dissemination of its effects, peace movements, and even fears and concerns of *hibakusha*—are considerably more intense in Hiroshima than in Nagasaki. I believe this is true, but only in degree, and not in the more or less absolute sense in which it is sometimes depicted. There are a number of factors which have contributed to this difference in intensity, and to Hiroshima's assuming more of a symbolic role for both *hibakusha* and outsiders: Hiroshima was the first to be struck by the new weapon; the bomb fell in the center of Hiroshima, a flat city made up almost entirely of flimsy structures, so that the entire city was virtually devastated, while in Nagasaki the bomb fell at some distance from the center and destruction was limited by the hilly terrain so that the greater part of the city (including a somewhat larger number of concrete structures) was left standing, and casualties and general effects were not so great despite the fact that the Nagasaki bomb was of greater explosive power; Nagasaki could therefore more readily resume some of its previous identity as a city—which included a unique history of having served for several centuries as Japan's main contact with the Western world—while Hiroshima had to recreate itself almost entirely, and without the benefit of a comparable tradition; and Hiroshima is closer to Tokyo and more sensitive to intellectual and ideological currents stemming from Japan's dominant city.

27 The psychiatric and psychological literature leaves much to be desired in its treatment of the subject of death, but recent studies which have made significant contributions to this most difficult of areas include: Herman Feifel, *The Meaning of Death,* (New York: McGraw-Hill, 1959); K. R. Eissler, *The Psychiatrist and the Dying Patient* (New York: International Universities Press, 1955); and Norman O. Brown, *Life Against Death* (Middletown, Connecticut: Wesleyan University Press, 1959). Two interesting reports of work in progress are: Thomas P. Hackett and Avery D. Weisman, "Human Reactions to the Imminence of Death"; and Claus B. Bahnson, "Emotional Reactions to Internally and Externally Derived Threat of Annihilation"—both of which were presented at the Symposium on Human Reactions to the Threat of Impending Disaster at the 1962 Annual Meeting of the American Association for the Advancement of Science in Philadelphia. There has also been an expanding literature on the psychological barriers, mostly concerned with death, which impair approaches to nuclear problems. See, for instance: *Socio-Psychiatric Aspects of the Prevention of Nuclear War,* forthcoming report of the Committee on Social Issues of the Group for the Advancement of Psychiatry; Jerome D. Frank, "Breaking the Thought Barrier: Psychological Challenges of the Nuclear Age," *Psychiatry,* Vol. 23 (1960), pp. 245-266; and Lester Grinspoon, "The Unacceptability of Disquieting Facts," presented at the AAAS Symposium on Human Reactions, etc., Philadelphia, 1962.

28 For discussions of symbolization of the self see Robert E. Nixon, "An Approach to the Dynamics of Growth in Adolescence," *Psychiatry,* Vol. 24 (1961), pp. 18-31; and Susanne Langer, *Philosophy in a New Key* (New York: Mentor Books, 1948), p. 111. For the relevance of shame to this kind of process, see Helen M. Lynd, *On Shame and the Search for Identity* (New York: Harcourt, Brace & Co., 1958).

29 "Guilt and Guilt Feelings," *Psychiatry,* Vol. 20 (1957), p. 120. In attributing guilt feelings to Japanese, here and elsewhere in this article, I am following recent critiques of the concept of "shame cultures" and "guilt cultures": Gerhart Piers and Milton B. Singer, *Shame and Guilt* (Springfield: Charles C. Thomas, 1953); and more specifically in relationship to Japan, George DeVos, "The Relation of Guilt Toward Parents to Achievement and Arranged Marriage Among Japanese," *Psychiatry,* Vol. 23 (1960), pp. 287-301. See also Erik H. Erikson, *Childhood and Society* (W. W. Norton: New York, 1950), pp. 222-226. Feelings of shame and guilt, at their most profound level—their psychological meeting ground—as I suggest below (following Buber, Lynd, Erikson, and my own previous work) can be overcome only though a change in one's relationship to the world, and can be under certain conditions creatively utilized on behalf of achieving such a change. But my impression regarding the atomic bomb experience was that this constructive utilization was the exception rather than the rule, since there was so much that tended to block it and to cause feelings of shame and guilt to be retained in their negative, unresolved form.

TWO

Poverty

Michael Harrington's *The Other America,* it has
been claimed, was the opening shot in what was
later to become Lyndon Johnson's War on Poverty,
a war which, it should be said, is still hardly past
its first skirmish. Michael Reagan's restatement
of the case for a guaranteed annual wage seems

to call into question the American
(some would say Puritan) work ethic.
Adam Walinsky, on the other hand,
raises a more deadly question:
What if the middle class
needs the poor to sustain its self-esteem?

From **The Other America**
MICHAEL HARRINGTON

The Invisible Land

There is a familiar America. It is celebrated in speeches and advertised on television and in the magazines. It has the highest mass standard of living the world has ever known.

In the 1950's this America worried about itself, yet even its anxieties were products of abundance. The title of a brilliant book was widely misinterpreted, and the familiar America began to call itself "the affluent society." There was introspection about Madison Avenue and tail fins; there was discussion of the emotional suffering taking place in the suburbs. In all this, there was an implicit assumption that the basic grinding economic problems had been solved in the United States. In this theory the nation's problems were no longer a matter of basic human needs of food, shelter, and clothing. Now they were seen as qualitative, a question of learning to live decently amid luxury.

While this discussion was carried on, there existed another America. In it dwelt somewhere between 40,000,000 and 50,000,000 citizens of this land. They were poor. They still are.

To be sure, the other America is not impoverished in the same sense as those poor nations where millions cling to hunger as a defense against starvation. This country has escaped such extremes. That does not change the fact that tens of millions of Americans are, at this very moment, maimed in body and spirit, existing at levels beneath those necessary for human decency. If these people are not starving, they are hungry, and sometimes fat with hunger, for that is what cheap foods do. They are without adequate housing and education and medical care.

The government has documented what this means to the bodies of the poor, and the figures will be cited. . . . But even more basic, this poverty twists and deforms the spirit. The American poor are pessimistic and defeated, and they are victimized by mental suffering to a degree unknown in Suburbia.

This is a description of the world in which these people live; it is about the other America. Here are the unskilled workers, the migrant farm workers, the aged, the minorities, and all the others who live in the economic underworld of American life. In all this, there will be statistics, and that offers the opportunity for disagreement among honest and sincere men. I would ask the reader to respond critically to every assertion, but not to allow statistical quibbling to obscure the huge, enormous, and intolerable fact of poverty in America. For, when all is said and done, that fact is unmistakable, whatever its exact dimensions, and the truly human reaction can only be outrage. As W. H. Auden wrote:

> Hunger allows no choice
> To the citizen or the police;
> We must love one another or die.

I

The millions who are poor in the United States tend to become increasingly invisible. Here is a great mass of people, yet it takes an effort of the intellect and will even to see them.

I discovered this personally in a curious way. After I wrote my first article on poverty in America, I had all the statistics down on paper. I had proved to my satisfaction that there were around 50,000,000 poor in this country. Yet, I realized I did not believe my own figures. The poor existed in the Government reports; they were percentages and numbers in long, close columns, but they were not part of my experience. I could prove that the other America existed, but I had never been there.

My response was not accidental. It was typical of what is happening to an entire society, and it reflects profound social changes in this nation. The other America, the America of poverty, is hidden today in a way that it never was before. Its millions are socially invisible to the rest of us. No wonder that so many misinterpreted Galbraith's title and assumed that "the affluent society" meant that everyone had a decent standard of life. The misinterpretation was true as far as the actual day-to-day lives of two-thirds of the nation were concerned. Thus, one must begin a description of the other America by understanding why we do not see it.

There are perennial reasons that make the other America an invisible land.

Poverty is often off the beaten track. It always has been. The ordinary tourist never left the main highway, and today he rides interstate turnpikes. He does not go into the valleys of Pennsylvania where the towns look like movie sets of Wales in the thirties. He does not see the company houses in rows, the rutted roads (the poor always have bad roads whether they live in the city, in towns, or on farms), and everything is black and dirty. And even if he were to pass through such a place by accident, the tourist would not meet the unemployed men in the bar or the women coming home from a runaway sweatshop.

Then, too, beauty and myths are perennial masks of poverty. The traveler comes to the Appalachians in the lovely season. He sees the hills, the streams, the foliage—but not the poor. Or perhaps he looks at a run-down mountain house and, remembering Rousseau rather than seeing with his eyes, decides that "those people" are truly fortunate to be living the way they are and that they are lucky to be exempt from the strains and tensions of the middle class. The only problem is that "those people," the quaint inhabitants of those hills, are undereducated, underprivileged, lack medical care, and are in the process of being forced from the land into a life in the cities, where they are misfits.

These are normal and obvious causes of the invisibility of the poor. They operated a generation ago; they will be functioning a generation hence. It is more important to understand that the very development of American society is creating a new kind of blindness about poverty. The poor are increasingly slipping out of the very experience and consciousness of the nation.

If the middle class never did like ugliness and poverty, it was at least aware of them. "Across the tracks" was not a very long way to go. There were forays into the slums at Christmas time; there were charitable organizations that brought contact with the poor. Occasionally, almost everyone passed through the Negro ghetto or the blocks of tenements, if only to get downtown to work or to entertainment.

Now the American city has been transformed. The poor still inhabit the miserable housing in the central area, but they are increasingly isolated from contact with, or sight of, anybody else. Middle-class women coming in from Suburbia on a rare trip may catch the merest glimpse of the other America on the way to an evening at the theater, but their children are segregated in suburban schools. The business or professional man may drive along the fringes of slums in a car or bus, but it is not an important experience to him. The failures, the unskilled, the disabled, the aged, and the minorities are right there, across the tracks, where they have always been. But hardly anyone else is.

In short, the very development of the American city has removed poverty from the living, emotional experience of millions upon millions of middle-class Americans. Living out in the suburbs, it is easy to assume that ours is, indeed, an affluent society.

This new segregation of poverty is compounded by a well-meaning ignorance. A good many concerned and sympathetic Americans are aware that there is much discussion of urban renewal. Suddenly, driving through the city, they notice that a familiar slum has been torn down and that there are towering, modern buildings where once there had been tenements or hovels. There is a warm feeling of satisfaction, of pride in the way things are working out: the poor, it is obvious are being taken care of.

The irony in this . . . is that the truth is nearly the exact opposite to the impression. The total impact of the various housing programs in postwar America has been to squeeze more and more people into existing slums. More often than not, the modern apartment in a towering building rents at $40 a room or more. For, during the past decade and a half, there has been more subsidization of middle- and upper-income housing than there has been of housing for the poor.

Clothes make the poor invisible too: America has the best-dressed poverty the world has ever known. For a variety of reasons, the benefits of mass production have been spread much more evenly in this area than in many others. It is much easier in the United States to be decently dressed than it is to be decently housed, fed, or doctored. Even people with terribly depressed incomes can look prosperous.

This is an extremely important factor in defining our emotional and existential ignorance of poverty. In Detroit the existence of social classes became much more difficult to discern the day the companies put lockers in the plants. From that moment on, one did not see men in work clothes on the way to the factory, but citizens in slacks and white shirts. This process has been magnified with the poor throughout the country. There are tens of thousands of Americans in the big cities who are wearing shoes, perhaps even a stylishly cut suit or dress, and yet are hungry. It is not a matter of planning, though it almost seems as if the affluent society had given out costumes to the poor so that they would not offend the rest of society with the sight of rags.

Then, many of the poor are the wrong age to be seen. A good number of them (over 8,000,000) are sixty-five years of age or better; an even larger number are under eighteen. The aged members of the other America are often sick, and they cannot move. Another group of them live out their lives in loneliness and frustration: they sit in rented rooms, or else they stay close to a house in a neighborhood that has completely changed from the old days. Indeed, one of the worst aspects of poverty among the aged is that these people are out of sight and out of mind, and alone.

The young are somewhat more visible, yet they too stay close to their neighborhoods. Sometimes they advertise their poverty through a lurid tabloid story about a gang killing. But generally they do not disturb the quiet streets of the middle class.

And finally, the poor are politically invisible. It is one of the cruelest ironies of social life in advanced countries that the dispossessed at the bottom of society are unable to speak for themselves. The people of the other America do not, by far and large, belong to unions, to fraternal organizations, or to political parties. They are without lobbies of their own; they put forward no legislative program. As a group, they are atomized. They have no face; they have no voice.

Thus, there is not even a cynical political motive for caring about the poor, as in the old days. Because the slums are no longer centers of powerful political organizations, the politicians need not really care about their inhabitants. The slums are no longer visible to the middle class, so much of the idealistic urge to fight for those who need help is gone. Only the social agencies have a really direct involvement with the other America, and they are without any great political power.

To the extent that the poor have a spokesman in American life, that role is played by the labor movement. The unions have their own particular idealism, an ideology of concern. More than that, they realize that the existence of a reservoir of cheap, unorganized labor is a menace to wages and working conditions throughout the entire economy. Thus, many union legislative proposals—to extend the coverage of minimum wage and social security, to organize migrant farm laborers—articulate the needs of the poor.

That the poor are invisible is one of the most important things about them. They are not simply neglected and forgotten as in the old rhetoric of reform; what is much worse, they are not seen.

One might take a remark from George Eliot's *Felix Holt* as a basic
statement:

> . . . there is no private life which has not been determined by a wider public life,
> from the time when the primeval milkmaid had to wander with the wanderings of
> her clan, because the cow she milked was one of a herd which had made the
> pasture bare. Even in the conservatory existence where the fair Camellia is sighed
> for by the noble young Pineapple, neither of them needing to care about the frost
> or rain outside, there is a nether apparatus of hot-water pipes liable to cool down
> on a strike of the gardeners or a scarcity of coal.
>
> And the lives we are about to look back upon do not belong to those
> conservatory species; they are rooted in the common earth, having to endure all
> the ordinary chances of past and present weather.

Forty to 50,000,000 people are becoming increasingly invisible. That is a
shocking fact. But there is a second basic irony of poverty that is equally
important: if one is to make the mistake of being born poor, he should choose a
time when the majority of the people are miserable too.

J. K. Galbraith develops this idea in *The Affluent Society,* and in doing so
defines the "newness" of the kind of poverty in contemporary America. The old
poverty, Galbraith notes, was general. It was the condition of life of an entire
society, or at least of that huge majority who were without special skills or the
luck of birth. When the entire economy advanced, a good many of these people
gained higher standards of living. Unlike the poor today, the majority poor of a
generation ago were an immediate (if cynical) concern of political leaders. The old
slums of the immigrants had the votes; they provided the basis for labor
organizations; their very numbers could be a powerful force in political conflict.
At the same time the new technology required higher skills, more education, and
stimulated an upward movement for millions.

Perhaps the most dramatic case of the power of the majority poor took
place in the 1930's. The Congress of Industrial Organizations literally organized
millions in a matter of years. A labor movement that had been declining and
confined to a thin stratum of the highly skilled suddenly embraced masses of men
and women in basic industry. At the same time this acted as a pressure upon the
Government, and the New Deal codified some of the social gains in laws like the
Wagner Act. The result was not a basic transformation of the American system,
but it did transform the lives of an entire section of the population.

In the thirties one of the reasons for these advances was that misery was
general. There was no need then to write books about unemployment and poverty.
That was the decisive social experience of the entire society, and the apple sellers
even invaded Wall Street. There was political sympathy from middle-class
reformers; there were an élan and spirit that grew out of a deep crisis.

Some of those who advanced in the thirties did so because they had
unique and individual personal talents. But for the great mass, it was a question of
being at the right point in the economy at the right time in history, and utilizing
that position for common struggle. Some of those who failed did so because they
did not have the will to take advantage of new opportunities. But for the most part
the poor who were left behind had been at the wrong place in the economy at the
wrong moment in history.

These were the people in the unorganizable jobs, in the South, in the minority groups, in the fly-by-night factories that were low on capital and high on labor. When some of them did break into the economic mainstream—when for instance, the CIO opened up the way for some Negroes to find good industrial jobs—they proved to be as resourceful as anyone else. As a group, the other Americans who stayed behind were not originally composed primarily of individual failures. Rather, they were victims of an impersonal process that selected some for progress and discriminated against others.

Out of the thirties came the welfare state. Its creation had been stimulated by mass impoverishment and misery, yet it helped the poor least of all. Laws like unemployment compensation, the Wagner Act, the various farm programs, all these were designed for the middle third in the cities, for the organized workers, and for the upper third in the country, for the big market farmers. If a man works in an extremely low-paying job, he may not even be covered by social security or other welfare programs. If he receives unemployment compensation, the payment is scaled down according to his low earnings.

One of the major laws that was designed to cover everyone, rich and poor, was social security. But even here the other Americans suffered discrimination. Over the years social security payments have not even provided a subsistence level of life. The middle third have been able to supplement the Federal pension through private plans negotiated by unions, through joining medical insurance schemes like Blue Cross, and so on. The poor have not been able to do so. They lead a bitter life, and then have to pay for that fact in old age.

Indeed, the paradox that the welfare state benefits those least who need help most is but a single instance of a persistent irony in the other America. Even when the money finally trickles down, even when a school is built in a poor neighborhood, for instance, the poor are still deprived. Their entire environment, their life, their values, do not prepare them to take advantage of the new opportunity. The parents are anxious for the children to go to work; the pupils are pent up, waiting for the moment when their education has complied with the law.

Today's poor, in short, missed the political and social gains of the thirties. They are, as Galbraith rightly points out, the first minority poor in history, the first poor not to be seen, the first poor whom the politicians could leave alone.

The first step toward the new poverty was taken when millions of people proved immune to progress. When that happened, the failure was not individual and personal, but a social product. But once the historic accident takes place, it begins to become a personal fate.

The new poor of the other America saw the rest of society move ahead. They went on living in depressed areas, and often they tended to become depressed human beings. In some of the West Virginia towns, for instance, an entire community will become shabby and defeated. The young and the adventurous go to the city, leaving behind those who cannot move and those who lack the will to do so. The entire area becomes permeated with failure, and that is one more reason the big corporations shy away.

Indeed, one of the most important things about the new poverty is that it cannot be defined in simple, statistical terms. [Here] a crucial term is used:

aspiration. If a group has internal vitality, a will—if it has aspiration—it may live in dilapidated housing, it may eat an inadequate diet, and it may suffer poverty, but it is not impoverished. So it was in those ethnic slums of the immigrants that played such a dramatic role in the unfolding of the American dream. The people found themselves in slums, but they were not slum dwellers.

But the new poverty is constructed so as to destroy aspiration; it is a system designed to be impervious to hope. The other America does not contain the adventurous seeking a new life and land. It is populated by the failures, by those driven from the land and bewildered by the city, by old people suddenly confronted with the torments of loneliness and poverty, and by minorities facing a wall of prejudice.

In the past, when poverty was general in the unskilled and semi-skilled work force, the poor were all mixed together. The bright and the dull, those who were going to escape into the great society and those who were to stay behind, all of them lived on the same street. When the middle third rose, this community was destroyed. And the entire invisible land of the other Americans became a ghetto, a modern poor farm for the rejects of society and of the economy.

It is a blow to reform and the political hopes of the poor that the middle class no longer understands that poverty exists. But, perhaps more important, the poor are losing their links with the great world. If statistics and sociology can measure a feeling as delicate as loneliness . . . the other America is becoming increasingly populated by those who do not belong to anybody or anything. They are no longer participants in an ethnic culture from the old country; they are less and less religious; they do not belong to unions or clubs. They are not seen, and because of that they themselves cannot see. Their horizon has become more and more restricted; they see one another, and that means they see little reason to hope.

Galbraith was one of the first writers to begin to describe the newness of contemporary poverty, and that is to his credit. Yet because even he underestimates the problem, it is important to put his definition into perspective.

For Galbraith, there are two main components of the new poverty: case poverty and insular poverty. Case poverty is the plight of those who suffer from some physical or mental disability that is personal and individual and excludes them from the general advance. Insular poverty exists in areas like the Appalachians or the West Virginia coal fields, where an entire section of the country becomes economically obsolete.

Physical and mental disabilities are, to be sure, an important part of poverty in America. The poor are sick in body and in spirit. But this is not an isolated fact about them, an individual "case," a stroke of bad luck. Disease, alcoholism, low IQ's, these express a whole way of life. They are, in the main, the effects of an environment, not the biographies of unlucky individuals. Because of this, the new poverty is something that cannot be dealt with by first aid. If there is to be a lasting assault on the shame of the other America, it must seek to root out of this society an entire environment, and not just the relief of individuals.

But perhaps the idea of "insular" poverty is even more dangerous. To speak of "islands" of the poor (or, in the more popular term, of "pockets of poverty") is to imply that one is confronted by a serious, but relatively minor, problem. This is hardly a description of a misery that extends to 40,000,000 or 50,000,000 people in the United States. They have remained impoverished in spite of increasing productivity and the creation of a welfare state. That fact alone should suggest the dimensions of a serious and basic situation.

And yet, even given these disagreements with Galbraith, his achievement is considerable. He was one of the first to understand that there are enough poor people in the United States to constitute a subculture of misery, but not enough of them to challenge the conscience and the imagination of the nation.

Finally, one might summarize the newness of contemporary poverty by saying: These are the people who are immune to progress. But then the facts are even more cruel. The other Americans are the victims of the very inventions and machines that have provided a higher living standard for the rest of the society. They are upside-down in the economy, and for them greater productivity often means worse jobs; agricultural advance becomes hunger.

In the optimistic theory, technology is an undisguised blessing. A general increase in productivity, the argument goes, generates a higher standard of living for the whole people. And indeed, this has been true for the middle and upper thirds of American society, the people who made such striking gains in the last two decades. It tends to overstate the automatic character of the process, to omit the role of human struggle. (The CIO was organized by men in conflict, not by economic trends.) Yet it states a certain truth—for those who are lucky enough to participate in it.

But the poor, if they were given to theory, might argue the exact opposite. They might say: Progress is misery.

As the society became more technological, more skilled, those who learn to work the machines, who get the expanding education, move up. Those who miss out at the very start find themselves at a new disadvantage. A generation ago in American life, the majority of the working people did not have high-school educations. But at that time industry was organized on a lower level of skill and competence. And there was a sort of continuum in the shop: the youth who left school at sixteen could begin as a laborer, and gradually pick up skill as he went along.

Today the situation is quite different. The good jobs require much more academic preparation, much more skill from the very outset. Those who lack a high-school education tend to be condemned to the economic underworld—to low-paying service industries, to backward factories, to sweeping and janitorial duties. If the fathers and mothers of the contemporary poor were penalized a generation ago for their lack of schooling, their children will suffer all the more. The very rise in productivity that created more money and better working conditions for the rest of the society can be a menace to the poor.

But then this technological revolution might have an even more disastrous consequence: it could increase the ranks of the poor as well as intensify the disabilities of poverty. At this point it is too early to make any final judgment, yet there are obvious danger signals. There are millions of Americans who live just the other side of poverty. When a recession comes, they are pushed onto the relief rolls. (Welfare payments in New York respond almost immediately to any economic decline.) If automation continues to inflict more and more penalties on the unskilled and the semiskilled, it could have the impact of permanently increasing the population of the other America.

Even more explosive is the possibility that people who participated in the gains of the thirties and the forties will be pulled back down into poverty. Today the mass-production industries where unionization made such a difference are contracting. Jobs are being destroyed. In the process, workers who had achieved a certain level of wages, who had won working conditions in the shop, are suddenly confronted with impoverishment. This is particularly true for anyone over forty years of age and for members of minority groups. Once their job is abolished, their chances of ever getting similar work are very slim.

It is too early to say whether or not this phenomenon is temporary, or whether it represents a massive retrogression that will swell the numbers of the poor. To a large extent, the answer to this question will be determined by the political response of the United States in the sixties. If serious and massive action is not undertaken, it may be necessary for statisticians to add some old-fashioned, pre-welfare-state poverty to the misery of the other America.

Poverty in the 1960's is invisible and it is new, and both these factors make it more tenacious. It is more isolated and politically powerless than ever before. It is laced with ironies, not the least of which is that many of the poor view progress upside-down, as a menace and a threat to their lives. And if the nation does not measure up to the challenge of automation, poverty in the 1960's might be on the increase.

II

There are mighty historical and economic forces that keep the poor down; and there are human beings who help out in this grim business, many of them unwittingly. There are sociological and political reasons why poverty is not seen; and there are misconceptions and prejudices that literally blind the eyes. The latter must be understood if anyone is to make the necessary act of intellect and will so that the poor can be noticed.

Here is the most familiar version of social blindness: "The poor are that way because they are afraid of work. And anyway they all have big cars. If they were like me (or my father or my grandfather), they could pay their own way. But they prefer to live on the dole and cheat the taxpayers."

This theory, usually thought of as a virtuous and moral statement, is one of the means of making it impossible for the poor ever to pay their way. There are, one must assume, citizens of the other America who choose impoverishment out of fear of work (though, writing it down, I really do not believe it). But the real explanation of why the poor are where they are is that they made the mistake of being born to the wrong parents, in the wrong section of the country, in the wrong industry, or in the wrong racial or ethnic group. Once that mistake has been made, they could have been paragons of will and morality, but most of them would never even have had a chance to get out of the other America.

There are two important ways of saying this: The poor are caught in a vicious circle; or, The poor live in a culture of poverty.

In a sense, one might define the contemporary poor in the United States as those who, for reasons beyond their control, cannot help themselves. All the most decisive factors making for opportunity and advance are against them. They are born going downward, and most of them stay down. They are victims whose lives are endlessly blown round and round the other America.

Here is one of the most familiar forms of the vicious circle of poverty. The poor get sick more than anyone else in the society. That is because they live in slums, jammed together under unhygienic conditions; they have inadequate diets, and cannot get decent medical care. When they become sick, they are sick longer than any other group in the society. Because they are sick more often and longer than anyone else, they lose wages and work, and find it difficult to hold a steady job. And because of this, they cannot pay for good housing, for a nutritious diet, for doctors. At any given point in the circle, particularly when there is a major illness, their prospect is to move to an even lower level and to begin the cycle, round and round, toward even more suffering.

This is only one example of the vicious circle. Each group in the other America has its own particular version of the experience. . . . But the pattern, whatever its variations, is basic to the other America.

The individual cannot usually break out of this vicious circle. Neither can the group, for it lacks the social energy and political strength to turn its misery into a cause. Only the larger society, with its help and resources, can really make it possible for these people to help themselves. Yet those who could make the difference too often refuse to act because of their ignorant, smug moralisms. They view the effects of poverty—above all, the warping of the will and spirit that is a consequence of being poor—as choices. Understanding the vicious circle is an important step in breaking down this prejudice.

There is an even richer way of describing this same, general idea: Poverty in the United States is a culture, an institution, a way of life.

There is a famous anecdote about Ernest Hemingway and F. Scott Fitzgerald. Fitzgerald is reported to have remarked to Hemingway, "The rich are different." And Hemingway replied, "Yes, they have money." Fitzgerald had much the better of the exchange. He understood that being rich was not a simple fact, like a large bank account, but a way of looking at reality, a series of attitudes, a special type of life. If this is true of the rich, it is ten times truer of the poor. Everything about them, from the condition of their teeth to the way in which they love, is suffused and permeated by the fact of their poverty. And this is sometimes a hard idea for a Hemingway-like middle-class America to comprehend.

The family structure of the poor, for instance, is different from that of the rest of the society. There are more homes without a father, there is less marriage, more early pregnancy and, if Kinsey's statistical findings can be used, markedly different attitudes toward sex. As a result of this, to take but one consequence of the fact, hundreds of thousands, and perhaps millions, of children in the other America never know stability and "normal" affection.

Or perhaps the policeman is an even better example. For the middle class, the police protect property, give directions, and help old ladies. For the urban poor, the police are those who arrest you. In almost any slum there is a vast conspiracy against the forces of law and order. If someone approaches asking for a person, no one there will have heard of him, even if he lives next door. The outsider is "cop," bill collector, investigator (and, in the Negro ghetto, most dramatically, he is "the Man").

While writing this book, I was arrested for participation in a civil-rights demonstration. A brief experience of a night in a cell made an abstraction personal and immediate: the city jail is one of the basic institutions of the other America. Almost everyone whom I encountered in the "tank" was poor: skid-row whites, Negroes, Puerto Ricans. Their poverty was an incitement to arrest in the first place. (A policeman will be much more careful with a well-dressed, obviously educated man who might have political connections than he will with someone who is poor.) They did not have money for bail or for lawyers. And, perhaps most important, they waited their arraignment with stolidity, in a mood of passive acceptance. They expected the worst, and they probably got it.

There is, in short, a language of the poor, a psychology of the poor, a world view of the poor. To be impoverished is to be an internal alien, to grow up in a culture that is radically different from the one that dominates the society. The poor can be described statistically; they can be analyzed as a group. But they need a novelist as well as a sociologist if we are to see them. They need an American Dickens to record the smell and texture and quality of their lives. The cycles and trends, the massive forces, must be seen as affecting persons who talk and think differently.

I am not that novelist. Yet in this book I have attempted to describe the faces behind the statistics, to tell a little of the "thickness" of personal life in the other America. Of necessity, I have begun with large groups: the dispossessed workers, the minorities, the farm poor and the aged. Then, there are three cases of less massive types of poverty, including the only single humorous component in the other America. And finally, there are the slums, and the psychology of the poor.

Throughout, I work on an assumption that cannot be proved by government figures or even documented by impressions of the other America. It is an ethical proposition, and it can be simply stated: In a nation with a technology that could provide every citizen with a decent life, it is an outrage and a scandal that there should be such social misery. Only if one begins with this assumption is it possible to pierce through the invisibility of 40,000,000 to 50,000,000 human beings and to see the other America. We must perceive passionately, if this blindness is to be lifted from us. A fact can be rationalized and explained away; an indignity cannot.

What shall we tell the American poor, once we have seen them? Shall we say to them that they are better off than the Indian poor, the Italian poor, the

Russian poor? That is one answer, but it is heartless. I should put it another way. I want to tell every well-fed and optimistic American that it is intolerable that so many millions should be maimed in body and in spirit when it is not necessary that they should be. My standard of comparison is not how much worse things used to be. It is how much better they could be if only we were stirred.

"Keeping the Poor in Their Place: Notes on the Importance of Being One-Up"
ADAM WALINSKY

No significant shade of political opinion, from I. F. Stone to *Time* magazine, can be found to oppose outright the War on Poverty; the Great Society has thus far been received as an election-year counterpart of the Big Rock Candy Mountain. And yet most of us assume that Congress will not establish the giant public works program for which Gunnar Myrdal calls. Nor will it lower the work week to thirty hours, as Herbert Gans has suggested, nor follow the suggestion of the Ad Hoc Committee on the Triple Revolution and guarantee incomes to all regardless of the work they do. The reasons for Congressional reluctance are familiar; the poor are, by definition, without economic power; except for the Negroes, they are without effective leaders; they are only one fifth of a nation, and the rest of the country is roughly satisfied with things as they are.

The liberals who argue that larger programs are necessary admit readily that the critical barrier is the apathetic or even hostile attitude of the middle-class majority—for present purposes, whites who are not poor—which has been victimized by "myths": that a balanced budget is desirable; that the government economy should be run like a household budget; that free enterprise is inherently superior to government activity; that big government is a bad thing; that tax cuts stimulate economic activity more than government spending; that expenditures result not in a bigger pie, but only a smaller slice for solid taxpayers. If the public is educated in the truth about economics, one hears, these "myths" will disappear.

But the interesting question about a myth is not whether people believe it, but why. Myths are not capricious inventions of storytellers, but ways of organizing and rationalizing group-behavior patterns. They serve real needs; they are less affected by argument than by changes in the conditions to which they are responsive. Viewing these myths as a screen behind which tangible aims are pursued would require a second hypothesis: that the middle-class majority *does not want* to improve significantly the lot of the poor, or—a further step—that the middle-class actively desires to keep the poor where they are.

In present-day America, the middle class is defined largely by the fact that the poor exist. Doctors are middle class, but so are bookkeepers; factory workers vacation with lawyers, drive bigger cars than teachers, live next door to store-owners, and send their children to school with the children of bank tellers. In a middle class so diffuse, with almost no characteristic common to all, middle-class income, education, and housing are what the poor do not have. If the present poor should become middle class, no meaning would remain to that phrase; either it would be a euphemism for the lower part of a bipartite division, or it would cease to apply to those who now boast of their "middle" status. The middle class knows that the economists are right when they say that poverty can be eliminated if we only will it; they simply do not will it.

Such an explanation, of course, seems in direct conflict with American ideals of equality of opportunity and social justice—ideals on which the middle classes themselves insist. But the creed of equal opportunity is a very complex thing. Opportunity to better oneself is usually regarded as self-explanatory, a recognition of the basic human right to fully utilize one's talents and labor. And in part it is recognized as a refusal to admit that others are better than oneself, or (a variant of the last) that others' children are better than one's own. But it has other facets. Virtually everyone who has reached his final life-station must and does believe and say that choice, or more commonly "the breaks," or "the system," prevented him from rising higher. But this same man must and does believe and say that his own abilities are primarily responsible for how far he has risen above others. People above oneself are regarded as no better than equal; people below oneself are regarded as inferior.

It is of course necessary to tinker with the system occasionally. Not only is reform commanded by the ethic; but as long as they pose no threat of basic change, improvements in the opportunity-structure at once reaffirm the existence of the depressed who need help, and serve as further "proof" that their inferior position is the result of inherent inferiority. But since people will not and cannot admit to themselves that the inferior position of others is entirely, or even primarily, caused by an inherently unequal system, they do not support measures that could possibly eliminate all or even most of the inequalities. The result is tokenism.

I suspect that the tension between adherence to democratic ideals and a natural desire to preserve one's relative gains by denying them to others has been heightened by a general loss of middle-class security. One possible reason for such a loss of security is enlargement in the size of the middle class itself; by the social and economic elevation of production and service workers; by the slackening of immigration, which has produced an America 95 per cent native-born and thus eliminated much "native" prestige; by the spread of education, high school and now college; by the general availability of inexpensive goods (especially clothing) virtually identical to those used by the well-to-do. For the old middle class, this has meant a dilution of status, which they have attempted to recapture by shifting the criteria of middle-class membership from income ("mere money") to sophistication of various sorts—education, community service, culture. For the new middle class, the gain in status is precarious; they attempt to reinforce it by appropriating the symbols of the old middle class, especially suburban housing and education for the children. For both old and new middle classes, the problem of preserving status becomes more acute in direct proportion to the technical ease with which poverty can be eliminated from the country.

"Variety of Dingbats"

But the central factor in the loss of security is a general decline in the significance of work. Observers have noted this loss in many different places: among the unemployed and underemployed; among factory hands whose labor is ever more routinized and uncertain; among paper-work employees of great corporations whose only function is the creation of artificial differences between what Pegler called "an ingenious variety of dingbats for the immature"; among craftsmen whose only means of delaying obsolescence is in Luddite strikes, and who are reminded of their uselessness at every well-publicized contract negotiation. Indeed, the meaninglessness of work has become one of the dominant themes of popular culture. But any decline thus far observed in the importance of work is but the start of a potential tobbogan run. The impact of automation on the assembly line is increasingly clear. But white-collar workers are also being replaced by machines; and Donald N. Michael predicts that middle management, whose relatively unsophisticated job is being brought within computer capabilities, is the next threatened class. If present trends in the automation of factory and office continue, there will be fewer jobs, and most of them will be routine.

Understanding the full import of that development requires recognition of the function work has performed in the past. Work everywhere serves the obvious function of enabling men to eat and survive. But work in America has also been the primary source of status in the society. Men have marked out their relation to others through work. The rewards of the society—income, women, power, respect—have gone to men roughly in proportion to their market utility. (Divergences—such as great inherited wealth—have been remarkable chiefly for their tendency to gravitate toward the norm—as in the upper classes' compulsion to enter and subsidize public affairs.) But work has been the organizing principle of American society in more than an economic sense; it has in large part displaced and substituted for ancestry, social class, tradition, and family as bench-marks for men's knowledge of self and their relation to others. Reliance on work as the primary social ethic has been intimately bound up with the growth of a democratic, egalitarian society. For work is alone among our status-givers in its diversity and attendant uniqueness. No man can master all occupations; indeed, few can master more than one. No matter how brilliant a professor may be, he must still call the plumber when his water-pipes freeze, or a mechanic when his car's transmission slips, a butcher when he wants meat, and a laborer when he wants a drain dug. In a diversified economy, so long as a man has a trade or skill, he has something for which people in the community must turn to him—some

claim of importance which is recognized by others. It is not even necessary that
the job be itself intrinsically difficult to learn or perform, so long as it is important
to other people and would not be done except for the labor of those doing it; thus
Michael Harrington reports a striking pride of *metier* among many migrant
fruit-pickers in California. It is the status conferred by work that allows people to
live in reasonable contentment with themselves and others.

The alienation of factory operatives from their work is a story as old as
the assembly line. But technological development continues the spiral.
Automation removes workers from direct contact with the line, and most from the
factory itself; fewer workers remain to do more highly skilled jobs. "Service
industries" are to take up the employment slack of automation, in theory, but
repairmen, for instance, are little more than salesclerks for replacement parts;
consumer goods are built to be sold cheaply and discarded, not repaired when
they fail. Printed electrical circuits, for example, are not, like their more expensive
wired predecessors, repairable by the normal electrician. Other "service"
workers—domestics, waiters, salesclerks, hospital orderlies—are menials easily
replaced by anyone from the growing refuse-heap of the society.

But if work loses its diversity, and hence its importance, for a significant
proportion of the society, we lose our only means for apportioning status on a
roughly equal basis. Other status-givers can confer meaningful prestige only on
those who have *more* than others.

Significance of Housing

The consequences of a decline in the prime importance of work are easily
deduced. One is a rise in the status-importance of consumption, and of all
consumption expenditures, housing has the greatest personal and financial
importance; the one-family house with a plot of ground has always been the ideal
American home. Its possession and quality have always been marks of social
status. By excluding groups of people, communities have appropriated for
themselves a mark of class superiority. In Washington, D.C., as in many other
cities, houses in communities which exclude Jews (or Negroes) bring higher prices
than equivalent houses in otherwise equal areas; the monetary value of such small
differences in neighborhood quality should alert us to the fact that housing status
is essentially predicated on success in excluding social "inferiors." The use of
housing as a symbol of superior status has been increasing. Income-segregation,
abetted by public-housing projects in which no member of the middle class will
live, is well underway. Trends reported by the New York Metropolitan Region
Study are being duplicated elsewhere: luxury apartments will soon house most
older people who can afford them; the exodus of white couples with children from
the large cities will continue, indeed will probably accelerate as fewer remain.
Fair-housing ordinances will be passed in some cities, perhaps even some states;
but the trend will, in general, be toward maintenance of racial segregation. (Surely
it is significant that California will probably repeal this year, by popular
referendum, its established fair-housing law, and that cities like Seattle and

Berkeley have voted down fair-housing ordinances.) In the Philadelphia suburb of Folcroft, a few months ago, residents rioted for weeks to prevent a Negro family from moving in; there is no reason to think that community unique.

Education is a second major heir to the status-giving function once dominated by work. The late ebbing of the Sputnik mentality arises only in part from our missile successes. In larger part, it is a way of raising a new standard of status—"liberal" education pursued for its own sake, which is particularly appropriate as a means of preserving present status-boundaries. First, it is an overexpensive luxury for the lower classes. Thus, Dr. Conant suggests that education for the poor should be vocational training suited to the jobs they can "reasonably" expect to get; a liberal education cannot be cheapened by too-wide distribution. Moreover, stressing the importance of liberal education insures the future position of the present middle class; its children will, by definition, score better on the class-biased tests which are used to determine their eligibility for such education. Lastly, the poor sense the futility of education in an economy where work (especially the kind for which they are trained) is declining, and shun and deprecate it; this phenomenon in turn serves as proof that opportunity is there, but is not taken advantage of by the poor.

A third critical status factor is income, which is important both in itself and as it affects access to other status-givers. In itself, income has been closely connected with work, often measuring the social worth of the work done; when inherited, it also reflects social class. But as work loses significance, income becomes most important as a determinant of consumption and education. To preserve status in these areas, income differentials will probably be preserved—as by making the tax structure more regressive, and keeping doles well below minimum-wage levels. People whose work is meaningless except as it allows them, by earning money, to differentiate themselves from the poor will continue to oppose large-scale employment projects. Instead, they will support transfer payments at a level too low to allow the recipients to compete for status in housing or education.

Two recent proposals, usually thought of as diametric opposites—the President's Poverty program and the Report of the Ad Hoc Committee on the Triple Revolution—are examples of programs which lend themselves to reinforcement of the social hierarchy.

The Kennedy-Johnson program does some excellent things. It attempts to train workers for jobs; to establish community-service programs for unoccupied youth; and to subsidize employment by special loans to municipalities and private employers. It directly will affect about half a million people. Christopher Jencks has stated its essential premise. . . .* The problems of poverty, he noted, will be solved by remedying imperfections in the opportunity-structure—education and jobs (with a side glance at motivation); the measures so far advanced, at any rate, are directed at these imperfections. A rationale advanced for the program's present modest size is that the tax cut will provide more jobs for the economy as a

* Jencks, Christopher, "Johnson vs. Poverty," *The New Republic,* March 28, 1964, pp. 15-18.

whole; some suggest the program will reach its full growth only after arms expenditures are cut as a result of lowered world tensions. It appears from his recent statements that the President plans to expand the government's domestic activities considerably; a program of rebuilding all our cities and countryside would itself be a major step toward the poverty war's expressed goals.

But if my earlier speculations are correct, expansion of the poverty war, or any government activity which tends to lessen class distinctions, will encounter resistance which increases in direct proportion to its size and probable effectiveness. Indeed, I would argue that the program thus far advanced has been received quietly because its fundamentally middle-class principles can be used by the middle class to prevent more significant action. Thus its concentration on opening up the opportunity-structure could be used to justify inaction on government employment programs tailored to large numbers of the un- and underemployed. Similarly, the emphasis on job training could be used to justify class segregation in education à la Dr. Conant and reliance for job expansion on the tax cut could justify regressive taxation as an economic policy to aid the poor.

Guaranteed Incomes

But for all the long-range political dangers of the poverty program's initial direction, it is on far firmer ground than that of the Ad Hoc Committee on the Triple Revolution. Starting from the premise that further increases in worker productivity will make a scarcity-based economy irrelevant, the Ad Hoc Committee sees the vital function of the economy shifted from production to consumption. If machines can produce everything that is within our capacity to consume, and work is available to only a small fraction of the society, then consumption should be separated from labor; manifestly, it is as pointless to deny the products of the automatic machines to those without work as it would be to deny them air or sunlight. Income, therefore, should be guaranteed and paid by the government, regardless of work done in exchange.

In fact, this report is more a projection of the economy in fifty years' time than it is a blueprint for today; in this respect, it is an admirable effort at advanced social planning. But its advanced liberal tone should not blind us to its danger. Of all the devices that have been invented to keep the status-poor in their place, putting them on a dole is by far the most effective. The size of the dole can be controlled so as to keep them always in comparative poverty, and thus unable to compete for higher status in the society; indeed, the fact of being on the dole itself leads to lessened aspiration and pride. Most of the present unemployed continue to covet work because the society's ethic commands it; to make the dole legitimate is to lessen significantly the pressure for reform from below.

The dole, of course, would be extended gradually, in the form of increasing present welfare payments and extending their coverage. The gradual change would start with the present poor; and since the middle class would still have jobs when the dole was extended, a substantial differentiation would be maintained between dole-income and prevailing middle-class wage rates. This differential would then serve as a method for preserving housing and educational segregation and quality differentials. As more of the middle class lose traditional work, however, they would not slip onto the dole and into the ranks of the status-poor. Instead in all probability, they would become social-service workers of an advanced sort—tending, of course, to the needs of the poor. Or they might find large-scale employment overseas, as in a "Management Corps" to aid administration in the poor nations. Means will be found to preserve their status vis-à-vis the poor simply because the middle class is larger and has higher cards.

These developments are not inevitable; they can, and should, be arrested and reversed. But the programs so far suggested, even the most radical, treat symptoms—the poor—and not the illness, which is a loss of meaningful work for most of the society. So long as they treat symptoms which are directed primarily at poverty, they will be restricted by the majority to glorified pilot projects; the existence of these limited projects will salve the conscience and the egos of the middle class.

It cannot be said too often that we are faced with a problem of time, that the resistance of the middle class to change will increase as their own assurance decreases and the lower classes (particularly Negroes) assert themselves more strongly. But neither can it be stressed too much that to castigate the middle class for their resistance to change is both useless and irresponsible. That resistance is based on sound fears that an effective drive on poverty will narrow status-differentials between them and the present poor. Those who criticize middle-class ignorance usually do so from privileged sanctuaries: a Harvard education, a house in an all-white suburb, and a firm position in the academic-political-foundation hierarchy guarantee status which will not be jeopardized no matter what improvement is made in the lot of the poor. But the increasingly useless middle class is being asked to surrender its claims to any superiority of status; even where jobs are insecure and meaningless, simply having one gives status superior to those who cannot support their families without public assistance. The middle class sense this perfectly, and no amount of talk about side effects on consumption and employment will convince them otherwise. A serious program must offer the middle class a new life style in return for the raise in status it would give to the poor; it must deal not only (or even primarily) with pockets of economic poverty, but with the poverty of satisfaction, purpose, and dignity that afflicts us all.

For a "Guaranteed Income"
MICHAEL D. REAGAN

The contrast between America's ability to expand production and her inability to expand employment to keep pace presents a serious problem of public policy, and this is now almost universally conceded. But the solutions enacted and proposed to date—tax cuts, investment incentives, manpower retraining programs, work-study aid for college students, for example—all assume that it still makes sense to work toward the goal of full employment, and that government's major task is to help people prepare themselves for jobs in the private sector of the economy.

One group of publicists, economists, and educators (a group which included this writer) has recently presented a more radical analysis, however. This group, calling itself the Ad Hoc Committee on the Triple Revolution,* explicitly challenges the possibility of *ever* reaching full employment in the face of automation's increasing ability to replace human muscle and skills with machines.

Asserting that automation is creating the capacity to produce all the goods and services our society can use without employing all the men and women who will seek places in the labor force, the Ad Hoc Committee (A.H.C.) fears that "the traditional link between jobs and income is being broken." Its prescription is therefore as radical as its analysis: it proposes that "society, through its appropriate legal and governmental institutions, undertake an unqualified commitment to provide every individual and every family with an adequate income as a matter of right." In short, a guaranteed income.

Why is the A.H.C. so pessimistic about full employment? The first reason is the record of over six consecutive years in which the unemployment rate has not fallen below 5 per cent, despite greatly increased production. Worse still, among unskilled laborers the unemployment rate has been above 12 per cent since 1957; among Negroes, above 10 per cent.

The unprecedented nature of the situation we face is revealed in cold statistical terms in the President's 1964 Manpower Report: in the period 1957-63, 4.3 million new jobs were created—but of these only 300,000 full-time jobs were generated by private demand. Even more startling, for the five years prior to 1963 there was an actual net decline in the number of privately generated positions. Most new jobs were the result of increased governmental employment (especially teachers) and procurement (especially military).

The extent to which automation lies behind the present difficulties is a matter of dispute; that it adds considerably to the problem of cyclical unemployment is hardly debatable. Secretary of Labor Wirtz has characterized the automatic machinery that is being introduced widely today as having, on the

---

* The revolutions: (1) cybernation, or automated machinery; (2) weaponry—the development of weapons capable of obliterating civilization; (3) civil rights.

average, the skills of a high school graduate. The question is, will we ever be able to find jobs for humans whose skills are less developed than those of machines?

How would the guaranteed-income proposal handle the problems? What are the arguments for and against it? Are there any precedents?

The claim that the job-income link is being broken has two levels of meaning, for there are two types of jobs: those arising from production for the market and those—such as teaching, highway construction, public health protection, much of basic research—which are called forth by governmental rather than market demand. As Robert Theobald (in some ways the "father" of the current proposal) says in his book, *Free Men and Free Markets:* "Our scarcity is one of market-supported jobs, not of work that needs to be done."

What Theobald and the A.H.C. mean by a guaranteed income is, in part, that we cannot rely upon privately generated demand to create jobs, but must use government to underwrite income-producing work: to guarantee that public services and public works will take up some of the slack created by the march of automation in the traditional goods-producing industries. This is not too far from the thinking of President Johnson, who said recently that if the tax cut proved to be an insufficient stimulant he would advocate increased public works.

In larger part, and this is the more radical and controversial aspect of the proposal, it is claimed that a guaranteed income—without any work—is needed for the aged, those of low skills and education, those discriminated against by race and those displaced too late in life to learn a new skill and find employment to utilize it—in short, for those who are permanently unemployable, whom the A.H.C. expects to be an increasing number.

Suppose that every family were guaranteed $3,000 a year. What would it cost? A detailed answer cannot be given at this point, yet we have one related estimate that is worth considering. The President's Council of Economic Advisers says that "about $11 billion a year would bring all poor families up to the $3000 income level. . . . The burden—one fifth of the annual defense budget, less than 2 per cent of the gross national product—would certainly not be intolerable."

The economic hope would be that the giving of income which would be spent by its recipients would, by increasing demand for the goods produced in automated plants, elicit higher profits and market-related incomes from which tax returns would help pay the costs. Whether deficits in the national budget would be involved cannot be foretold at this time. What is known from the experience of recent years is that deficits are definite in the absence of a sufficient stimulus to the full use of resources.

Even if costs were not an obstacle, would anyone be willing to work at all, given the availability of nonwork income? How would the necessary dirty jobs get done?

First of all, loosely following Theobald's suggestions, guaranteed income would be used by the permanently unemployable—the coal miner automated out of the only work he knows at age forty-five, the clerk replaced by an inventory computer, and others for whom there is no choice because they lack jobs in any case.

Second, there would be some who simply prefer not to work—perhaps chiefly those already categorized as welfare chiselers. Also, some would use the guaranteed income by preference because they would rather be relatively poor but free to do what they wished than better off financially in jobs alien to their interests. Many creative young people—artists, writers, actors, poets—might make this choice, for our society does little today to provide market or governmental jobs for them.

Third, there would be those workers who earned less than $3000 a year and whose wages would need to be supplemented to bring their income up to that level.

The unpleasant jobs—the dirty ones that still require human muscle power or dull routine—would, of course, still have to be done. Because one could have an income above the poverty level without doing them, they would have to carry much higher wages than at present to attract workers. In the long run the higher costs would lead toward further automation, further reducing the number of jobs. At the other end of the scale, jobs requiring extremely high skill levels or carrying great burdens of managerial responsibility would continue to attract talent because of their intrinsic interest and increasingly higher incomes.

There would thus be a distribution between the job-holders and the workless partly by fate (those who lack the skills called for by any job); partly by economic incentives (most men who can earn $6000 will not be satisfied with an income of $3000—witness the extent of moonlighting); and partly by choice (creative activity that society does not otherwise support, or work because of inner drives).

The crux of the proposal is that jobless income would be absolutely guaranteed: an Office of Guaranteed Income would stand ready to provide the agreed minimum income without question to any jobless applicant. Incentives to work would have to be revolutionized: the threats of poverty, starvation or even a means test would no longer be available as goads. Employers would have to make work more attractive; the bargaining position of employes—even as individuals—would be much stronger. The economy would have a vast new "built-in stabilizer"—along with considerable disruption of the labor market.

The average man would face a unique choice when work became voluntary; his largest problem might be to make satisfying use of new-found leisure. Some would doubtless abandon leisure and return to work after a brief fling. Some would find it an agreeable kind of vegetative existence. Yet others might find liberation, independence and an opportunity for self-development through "serious activity without the pressure of necessity," which Paul Goodman reminds us was one meaning of leisure in ancient Greece.

To set forth this description of the plan and its implications is to raise a host of objections—economic, psychological, and ethical.

The feeling that a man's character is destroyed if he does not work is deeply ingrained. That man should live by the sweat of his brow is an ancient thought, but one which accords with the experience of many modern men who expire through boredom when retired.

Furthermore, there are strong links between work and self-respect. Ours is a society in which success counts, and it is largely measured by job status and income. The leaf-raking of Depression days was no more popular with those who did it than with those whose taxes paid for it. Is human dignity separable from work? Can leisure be respectable?

It may be that, as Robert Theobald has written, "the discovery of the proper uses of freedom is the fundamental task of the remainder of the twentieth century." But many are doubtful that we can make the discovery. Those who will have the most leisure are those with the least education, the most inadequate backgrounds for making effective use of freedom.

Initially at least, it is hard to dispute the contention that most of us are unfit for leisure. Nor is this view confined to economic conservatives. Norman Thomas said at a recent conference that "money without the pressures most of us need to work will make us a poorer and not a richer nation." (However, he is uncertain that we can provide the work.)

And what of those who would make no pretense of useful activity—those who are just plain lazy? The lazy we will always have with us, we might say, and we do not allow them to starve. But does our sense of social ethics require—or even permit—us to support them with some degree of comfort and as a socially guaranteed *right?*

It takes little imagination to picture the response of the Senate Finance Committee or of Congress generally to a bill calling for taxes and expenditures to benefit *voluntary* joblessness with no strings attached. And would the proportion of the population opting for a minimal living without work remain constant, or would it jump so drastically that the economy would come to a grinding halt? No one can answer with certainty.

It could also be argued that the A.H.C. is counseling unwarranted defeatism—gloom and doom. Many will fear that such a proposal would become a self-fulfilling prophecy: that if we assume there cannot be enough jobs to go around, then we will bring about that situation by not trying hard enough to create more jobs.

Finally, would not the guaranteed-income plan lead to a government-created class of hereditary wards of the state? Would not children in this class be condemned to fatalistic apathy? And would not the rest of society too easily shrug off the needs of the poor once its conscience had been salved by having provided minimal income? There are, after all, signs that these unwanted outcomes are already present among at least some second-generation welfare families.

Despite the finality that these objections will have for some readers, there are counterarguments and precedents to be considered before the balance sheet is complete.

Jobless pay is not unknown to us—in the form of unemployment compensation, disability insurance, and old-age and survivors' benefits under the Social Security program that has been part of our system since 1935. Aid to the blind, to dependent children, to the indigent not covered by insured employment—these, too, are forms of guaranteed income without work.

Nor should we forget two important forms of private separation of income from work: inheritance and property income. If a wealthy relative leaves me $100,000, which I invest in tax-free municipal bonds, I can have a workless income of $4000 a year. Or if I buy a swamp in Louisiana and the Space Administration then builds a missile base nearby, I can have a very substantial income—even capital gains—from property ownership without lifting a finger to work.

These ways of breaking the income-job link are not universally admired—though perhaps universally envied—yet they are accepted by our society, especially by those likely to be least sympathetic to the A.H.C. proposal.

To the objection that work and self-respect are inseparable, the major reply is that the real necessity is not for a production job, but for meaningful activity. This may or may not be related to income. Voluntary efforts to improve our communities, pursue the arts, or participate in public affairs are meaningful—sometimes more so than our regular jobs. Ours might be a richer nation in human and esthetic dimensions if more of us were free to direct our skills and energies toward projects not at present supported by the market.

As for the problem of the lazy, it is difficult to believe that a society noted around the world for the frenetic quality even of its recreation would suddenly turn soporific on any large scale. And of course the man with a family will continue to have both conscience and pressures to keep him seeking the higher incomes available through work—where work is available.

One practical advantage of the guaranteed-income plan is that it would greatly simplify the welfare pattern. A thousand administrative requirements and much overseeing expense could be eliminated if income without work were distributed without needing proof of age, blindness, dependency, length of residence, and so on. Also, it would be far more equitable, for existing social-insurance programs—retirement, minimum wage, and so on—leave out many who are most in need simply because they are not in covered types of employment.

Some supplementary action programs would, of course, be required—especially social work and special education to stimulate children of guaranteed-income families and steer them away from apathy, and to aid families in coping with the multiple problems that already beset the unemployed and are not solved simply by the provision of cash. What is necessary is to recognize the need for such programs and their value, and to accord both higher prestige and higher salaries to the enlarged corps of professionals required. One would hope also that the change from grudging welfare to income guaranteed as a right would be accompanied by changes in public attitudes, changes that would lessen the obloquy which underlies the psychological listlessness of some welfare recipients today.

If we learn to educate for life—not just to earn a living—there is no reason, in principle, to assume that we, or at least our children, cannot make productive use of leisure. Let us hope it is possible, because it will have to be. Even without a guaranteed-income plan our working time has on the average been cut to less than half of our waking time. Extended vacations for steelworkers and a twenty-five hour week for New York electricians are but minimal symbols of the revolution already taking place.

It may be easy to scoff at the A.H.C. proposal, but only if we are unwilling to face up to the problem of automation. How else can we handle it? Long-continued unemployment makes it clear that we do not yet have an adequate alternative.

The particular ways by which we will provide income without jobs in the traditional sense remain to be developed, and the plan discussed here is doubtless not the only possibility. But it is clear now that radical revision of our thoughts, our economic institutions and our style of life are the inescapable accompaniments of man's increasing ability to substitute machines for muscles and computers for clerks.

THREE

Vietnam

I. F. Stone and the anonymous author of the State
Department's White Paper of 1965 carry on the
now familiar and wearying dialogue about why
we are in Vietnam. The State Department argues
that we are resisting North Vietnamese aggression,
I. F. Stone that the argument
is biased, inexact, and lacking in frankness.
"Channeling" raises a grim specter. In the
machinelike prose that is dear to bureaucracy,
it describes the techniques—rational,
mechanical, and humanly indifferent—
that are used to modify the free choice
of young Americans regarding their studies

and their professions. Military service,
which is a duty of the citizen, becomes the
unseen electric prod that determines an entire
lifetime's commitment. Tom Gardner's experience
as a young man refusing to be "channeled"
shows how baffling and inconclusive the struggle
against unseen forces can become.
Finally, George Wald's spontaneous, angry grief,
coming as it does from a scientist
and Nobel laureate no longer young,
is a recent indication of the depth
and the persistence
of our country's Vietnam wound.

Department of State White Paper

Aggression from the North

*Hanoi supplies the key personnel for the armed
aggression against South Viet-Nam*

The hard core of the Communist forces attacking South Viet-Nam are men
trained in North Viet-Nam. They are ordered into the South and remain under
the military discipline of the Military High Command in Hanoi. Special training
camps operated by the North Vietnamese army give political and military training
to the infiltrators. Increasingly the forces sent into the South are native North
Vietnamese who have never seen South Viet-Nam. A special infiltration unit, the
70th Transportation Group, is responsible for moving men from North Viet-Nam
into the South via infiltration trails through Laos. Another special unit, the
maritime infiltration group, sends weapons and supplies and agents by sea into
the South.

The infiltration rate has been increasing. From 1959 to 1960, when Hanoi
was establishing its infiltration pipeline, at least 1,800 men, and possibly 2,700
more, moved into South Viet-Nam from the North. The flow increased to a
minimum of 3,700 in 1961 and at least 5,400 in 1962. There was a modest decrease
in 1963 to 4,200 confirmed infiltrators, though later evidence is likely to raise this
figure.

For 1964 the evidence is still incomplete. However, it already shows that
a minimum of 4,400 infiltrators entered the South, and it is estimated more than
3,000 others were sent in.

There is usually a time lag between the entry of infiltrating troops and the
discovery of clear evidence they have entered. This fact, plus collateral evidence of
increased use of the infiltration routes, suggests strongly that 1964 was probably
the year of greatest infiltration so far.

Thus, since 1959, nearly 20,000 VC officers, soldiers, and technicians are
known to have entered South Viet-Nam under orders from Hanoi. Additional
information indicates that an estimated 17,000 more infiltrators were dispatched
to the South by the regime in Hanoi during the past six years. It can reasonably be
assumed that still other infiltration groups have entered the South for which there
is no evidence yet available.

To some the level of infiltration from the North may seem modest in
comparison with the total size of the Armed Forces of the Republic of Viet-Nam.
But one-for-one calculations are totally misleading in the kind of warfare going on
in Viet-Nam. First, a high proportion of infiltrators from the North are
well-trained officers, cadres, and specialists. Second, it has long been realized that
in guerrilla combat the burdens of defense are vastly heavier than those of attack.

In Malaya, the Philippines, and elsewhere a ratio of at least 10-to-1 in favor of the forces of order was required to meet successfully the threat of the guerrillas' hit-and-run tactics.

In the calculus of guerrilla warfare the scale of North Vietnamese infiltration into the South takes on a very different meaning. For the infiltration of 5,000 guerrilla fighters in a given year is the equivalent of marching perhaps 50,000 regular troops across the border, in terms of the burden placed on the defenders.

Above all, the number of proved and probable infiltrators from the North should be seen in relation to the size of the VC forces. It is now estimated that the Viet-Cong number approximately 35,000 so-called hard-core forces, and another 60,000-80,000 local forces. It is thus apparent that infiltrators from the North—allowing for casualties—make up the majority of the so-called hard-core Viet-Cong. Personnel from the North, in short, are now and have always been the backbone of the entire VC operation.

It is true that many of the lower-level elements of the VC forces are recruited within South Viet-Nam. However, the thousands of reported cases of VC kidnapings and terrorism make it abundantly clear that threats and other pressures by the Viet-Cong play a major part in such recruitment.

THE INFILTRATION PROCESS

The infiltration routes supply hard-core units with most of their officers and noncommissioned personnel. This source helps fill the gaps left by battle casualties, illness, and defection and insures continued control by Hanoi. Also, as the nature of the conflict has changed, North Viet-Nam has supplied the Viet-Cong with technical specialists via the infiltration routes. These have included men trained in armor and ordnance, antiaircraft, and communications as well as medical corpsmen and transport experts.

There is no single infiltration route from the North to South Viet-Nam. But by far the biggest percentage of infiltrators follow the same general course. The principal training center for North Vietnamese army men assigned to join the Viet-Cong has been at Xuan Mai near Hanoi. Recently captured Viet-Cong have also reported an infiltration training camp at Thanh Hoa. After completion of their training course—which involves political and propaganda work as well as military subjects—infiltrating units are moved to Vinh on the east coast. Many have made stopovers at a staging area in Dong Hoi where additional training is conducted. From there they go by truck to the Laos border.

Then, usually after several days' rest, infiltrators move southward through Laos. Generally they move along the Laos–South Viet-Nam border. Responsibility for infiltration from North Viet-Nam through Laos belongs to the 70th Transportation Group of the North Vietnamese army. After a time the infiltration groups turn eastward, entering South Viet-Nam in Quang Nam, Quang Tri, Thua Thien, Kontum, or another of the border provinces.

The Communists have established regular lanes for infiltration with way-stations established about one day's march apart. The way-stations are equipped to quarter and feed the Viet-Cong passing through. Infiltrators who suffer from malaria or other illnesses stay at the stations until they recover sufficiently to join another passing group moving south. . . .

Local guides lead the infiltration groups along the secret trails. Generally they direct the infiltrators from halfway between two stations, through their own base station, and on halfway to the next supply base. Thus the guides are kept in ignorance of all but their own way-stations. Only group leaders are permitted to talk with the guides in order to preserve maximum security. The men are discouraged from asking where they are or where they are going.

The same system of trails and guides used along the Lao infiltration routes is used within South Viet-Nam itself. Viet-Cong infiltrators may report directly to a reassignment center in the highlands as soon as they enter South Viet-Nam. But in the past year or more some groups have moved down trails in South Viet-Nam to provinces along the Cambodian border and near Saigon before receiving their unit assignment. Within South Viet-Nam infiltration and supplies are handled by VC units such as the Nam Son Transportation Group.

At the Laos border crossing point infiltrators are re-equipped. Their North Vietnamese army uniforms must be turned in. They must give up all personal papers, letters, notebooks, and photographs that might be incriminating. Document control over the infiltrators has been tightened considerably over the past two years. A number of Vietnamese infiltrators have told of being fitted out with Lao "neutralist" uniforms for their passage through Laos.

Infiltration groups are usually issued a set of black civilian pajama-like clothes, two unmarked uniforms, rubber sandals, a sweater, a hammock, mosquito netting, and waterproof sheeting. They carry a 3–5 day supply of food. A packet of medicines and bandages is usually provided.

The size of infiltration groups varies widely. Prisoners have mentioned units as small as 5 men and as large as 500. Generally the groups number 40–50. When they arrive in South Viet-Nam these groups are usually split up and assigned to various VC units as replacements, although some have remained intact. . . .

Hanoi Supplies Weapons, Ammunition, and Other War Matériel to Its Forces in the South

When Hanoi launched the VC campaign of terror, violence, and subversion in earnest in 1959, the Communist forces relied mainly on stocks of weapons and ammunition left over from the war against the French. Supplies sent in from North Viet-Nam came largely from the same source. As the military campaign progressed, the Viet-Cong depended heavily on weapons captured from the Armed Forces in South Viet-Nam. This remains an important source of weapons and ammunition for the Viet-Cong. But as the pace of the war has quickened, requirements for up-to-date arms and special types of weapons have risen to a point where the Viet-Cong cannot rely on captured stocks. Hanoi has undertaken a program to re-equip its forces in the South with Communist-produced weapons.

Large and increasing quantities of military supplies are entering South Viet-Nam from outside the country. The principal supply point is North Viet-Nam, which provides a convenient channel for matériel that originates in Communist China and other Communist countries.

An increasing number of weapons from external Communist sources have been seized in the South. These include such weapons as 57 mm. and 75 mm. recoilless rifles, dual-purpose machineguns, rocket launchers, large mortars, and antitank mines.

A new group of Chinese Communist-manufactured weapons has recently appeared in VC hands. These include the 7.62 semiautomatic carbine, 7.62 light machinegun, and the 7.62 assault rifle. These weapons and ammunition for them, manufactured in Communist China in 1962, were first captured in December, 1964, in Chuong Thien Province. Similar weapons have since been seized in each of the four Corps areas of South Viet-Nam. Also captured have been Chinese Communist antitank grenade launchers and ammunition made in China in 1963.

One captured Viet-Cong told his captors that his entire company had been supplied recently with modern Chinese weapons. The re-equipping of VC units with a type of weapons that require ammunition and parts from outside South Viet-Nam indicates the growing confidence of the authorities in Hanoi in the effectiveness of their supply lines into the South.

Incontrovertible evidence of Hanoi's elaborate program to supply its forces in the South with weapons, ammunition, and other supplies has accumulated over the years. Dramatic new proof was exposed just as this report was being completed.

On February 16, 1965, an American helicopter pilot flying along the South Vietnamese coast sighted a suspicious vessel. It was a cargo ship of an estimated 100-ton capacity, carefully camouflaged and moored just offshore along the coast of Phu Yen Province. Fighter planes that approached the vessel met machine-gun fire from guns on the deck of the ship and from the shore as well. A Vietnamese Air Force strike was launched against the vessel, and Vietnamese Government troops moved into the area. They seized the ship after a bitter fight with the Viet-Cong.

The ship, which had been sunk in shallow water, had discharged a huge cargo of arms, ammunition, and other supplies. Documents found on the ship and on the bodies of several Viet-Cong aboard identified the vessel as having come from North Viet-Nam. A newspaper in the cabin was from Haiphong and was dated January 23, 1965. The supplies delivered by the ship—thousands of weapons and more than a million rounds of ammunition—were almost all of Communist origin, largely from Communist China and Czechoslovakia, as well as North Viet-Nam. At least 100 tons of military supplies were discovered near the ship.

A preliminary survey of the cache near the sunken vessel from Hanoi listed the following supplies and weapons:

approximately 1 million rounds of small-arms ammunition;

more than 1,000 stick grenades;

500 pounds of TNT in prepared charges;

2,000 rounds of 82 mm. mortar ammunition;

500 antitank grenades;

500 rounds of 57 mm. recoilless rifle ammunition;

more than 1,000 rounds of 75 mm. recoilless rifle ammunition;

one 57 mm. recoilless rifle;

2 heavy machine guns;

2,000, 7.95 Mauser rifles;

more than 100, 7.62 carbines;

1,000 submachine guns;

15 light machine guns;

500 rifles;

500 pounds of medical supplies (with labels from North Viet-Nam, Communist China, Czechoslovakia, East Germany, Soviet Union, and other sources). . . .

North Viet-Nam: Base for Conquest of the South

The Third Lao Dong Party Congress in Hanoi in September, 1960, set forth two tasks for its members: "to carry out the socialist revolution in North Viet-Nam" and "to liberate South Viet-Nam."

The resolutions of the congress described the effort to destroy the legal Government in South Viet-Nam as follows: "The revolution in the South is a protracted, hard, and complex process of struggle, combining many forms of struggle of great activity and flexibility, ranging from lower to higher, and taking as its basis the building, consolidation, and development of the revolutionary power of the masses."

At the September meeting the Communist leaders in the North called for formation of "a broad national united front." Three months later Hanoi announced creation of the "Front for Liberation of the South." This is the organization that Communist propaganda now credits with guiding the forces of subversion in the South; it is pictured as an organization established and run by the people in the South themselves. At the 1960 Lao Dong Party Congress the tone was different. Then, even before the front existed, the Communist leaders were issuing orders for the group that was being organized behind the scenes in Hanoi. "This front must rally . . ."; "The aims of its struggle are . . ."; "The front must carry out . . ."—this is the way Hanoi and the Communist Party addressed the "Liberation Front" even before its founding.

The Liberation Front is Hanoi's creation; it is neither independent nor southern, and what it seeks is not liberation but subjugation of the South. . . .

Organization, Direction, Command, and Control of the
Attack on South Viet-Nam Are Centered in Hanoi

The VC military and political apparatus in South Viet-Nam is an extension of an elaborate military and political structure in North Viet-Nam which directs and supplies it with the tools for conquest. The Ho Chi Minh regime has shown that it is ready to allocate every resource that can be spared—whether it be personnel, funds, or equipment—to the cause of overthrowing the legitimate Government in South Viet-Nam and of bringing all Viet-Nam under Communist rule.

POLITICAL ORGANIZATION

Political direction and control of the Viet-Cong is supplied by the Lao Dong Party, i.e., the Communist Party, led by Ho Chi Minh. Party agents are responsible for indoctrination, recruitment, political training, propaganda, anti-Government demonstrations, and other activities of a political nature. The considerable intelligence-gathering facilities of the party are also at the disposal of the Viet-Cong.

Over-all direction of the VC movement is the responsibility of the Central Committee of the Lao Dong Party. Within the Central Committee a special Reunification Department has been established. This has replaced the "Committee for Supervision of the South" mentioned in intelligence reports two years ago. It lays down broad strategy for the movement to conquer South Viet-Nam.

Until March, 1962, there were two principal administrative divisions in the VC structure in the South. One was the Inter-zone of South-Central Viet-Nam (sometimes called Interzone 5); the other was the Nambo Region. In a 1962 reorganization these were merged into one, called the Central Office for South Viet-Nam. The Central Committee, through its Reunification Department, issues directives to the Central Office, which translates them into specific orders for the appropriate subordinate command.

Under the Central Office are six regional units (V through IX) plus the special zone of Saigon/Cholon/Gia Dinh. A regional committee responsible to the Central Office directs VC activities in each region. Each regional committee has specialized units responsible for liaison, propaganda, training, personnel, subversive activities, espionage, military bases, and the like.

Below each regional committee are similarly structured units at the province and district levels. At the base of the Communist pyramid are the individual party cells, which may be organized on a geographic base or within social or occupational groups. The elaborateness of the party unit and the extent to which it operates openly or underground is determined mainly by the extent of VC control over the area concerned. . . .

A Brief History of Hanoi's Campaign of Aggression Against South Viet-Nam

While negotiating an end to the Indochina War at Geneva in 1954, the Communists were making plans to take over all former French territory in Southeast Asia. When Viet-Nam was partitioned, thousands of carefully selected party members were ordered to remain in place in the South and keep their secret apparatus intact to help promote Hanoi's cause. Arms and ammunition were stored away for future use. Guerrilla fighters rejoined their families to await the party's call. Others withdrew to remote jungle and mountain hideouts. The majority—an estimated 90,000—were moved to North Viet-Nam.

Hanoi's original calculation was that all of Viet-Nam would fall under its control without resort to force. For this purpose, Communist cadres were ordered to penetrate official and non-official agencies, to propagandize and sow confusion, and generally to use all means short of open violence to aggravate war-torn conditions and to weaken South Viet-Nam's Government and social fabric.

South Viet-Nam's refusal to fall in with Hanoi's scheme for peaceful takeover came as a heavy blow to the Communists. Meantime, the Government had stepped up efforts to blunt Viet-Cong subversion and to expose Communist agents. Morale in the Communist organization in the South dropped sharply. Defections were numerous.

Among South Vietnamese, hope rose that their nation could have a peaceful and independent future, free of Communist domination. The country went to work. The years after 1955 were a period of steady progress and growing prosperity.

Food production levels of the prewar years were reached and surpassed. While per capita food output was dropping 10 per cent in the North from 1956 to 1960, it rose 20 per cent in the South. By 1963, it had risen 30 per cent—despite the disruption in the countryside caused by intensified Viet-Cong military attacks and terrorism. The authorities in the North admitted openly to continuing annual failures to achieve food production goals.

Production of textiles increased in the South more than 20 per cent in one year (1958). In the same year, South Viet-Nam's sugar crop increased more than 100 percent. Despite North Viet-Nam's vastly larger industrial complex, South Viet-Nam's per capita gross national product in 1960 was estimated at $110 a person while it was only $70 in the North.

More than 900,000 refugees who had fled from Communist rule in the North were successfully settled in South Viet-Nam. An agrarian reform program was instituted. The elementary school population nearly quadrupled between 1956 and 1960. And so it went—a record of steady improvement in the lives of the people. It was intolerable for the rulers in Hanoi; under peaceful conditions, the South was outstripping the North. They were losing the battle of peaceful competition and decided to use violence and terror to gain their ends.

After 1956 Hanoi rebuilt, reorganized, and expanded its covert political and military machinery in the South. Defectors were replaced by trained personnel from party ranks in the North. Military units and political cells were enlarged and were given new leaders, equipment, and intensified training. Recruitment was pushed. In short, Hanoi and its forces in the South prepared to take by force and violence what they had failed to achieve by other means.

By 1958 the use of terror by the Viet-Cong increased appreciably. It was used both to win prestige and to back up demands for support from the people, support that political and propaganda appeals had failed to produce. It was also designed to embarrass the Government in Saigon and raise doubts about its ability to maintain internal order and to assure the personal security of its people. From 1959 through 1961, the pace of Viet-Cong terrorism and armed attacks accelerated substantially.

The situation at the end of 1961 was so grave that the Government of the Republic of Viet-Nam asked the United States for increased military assistance. That request was met. Meantime, the program of strategic hamlets, designed to improve the peasant's livelihood and give him some protection against Viet-Cong harassment and pressure, was pushed energetically.

But the Viet-Cong did not stand still. To meet the changing situation, they tightened their organization and adopted new tactics, with increasing emphasis on terrorism, sabotage, and armed attacks by small groups. They also introduced from the North technicians in fields such as armor and antiaircraft. Heavier weapons were sent in to the regular guerrilla forces.

The military and insurgency situation was complicated by a quite separate internal political struggle in South Viet-Nam, which led in November, 1963, to the removal of the Diem government and its replacement with a new one. Effective power was placed in the hands of a Military Revolutionary Council. There have been a number of changes in the leadership and composition of the Government in Saigon in the ensuing period.

These internal developments and distractions gave the Viet-Cong an invaluable opportunity, and they took advantage of it. . . .

Conclusion

The evidence presented in this report could be multiplied many times with similar examples of the drive of the Hanoi regime to extend its rule over South Viet-Nam.

The record is conclusive. It establishes beyond question that North Viet-Nam is carrying out a carefully conceived plan of aggression against the South. It shows that North Viet-Nam has intensified its efforts in the years since it was condemned by the International Control Commission. It proves that Hanoi continues to press its systematic program of armed aggression into South

Viet-Nam. This aggression violates the United Nations Charter. It is directly contrary to the Geneva Accords of 1954 and of 1962 to which North Viet-Nam is a party. It shatters the peace of Southeast Asia. It is a fundamental threat to the freedom and security of South Viet-Nam.

The people of South Viet-Nam have chosen to resist this threat. At their request, the United States has taken its place beside them in their defensive struggle.

The United States seeks no territory, no military bases, no favored position. But we have learned the meaning of aggression elsewhere in the postwar world, and we have met it.

If peace can be restored in South Viet-Nam, the United States will be ready at once to reduce its military involvement. But it will not abandon friends who want to remain free. It will do what must be done to help them. The choice now between peace and continued and increasingly destructive conflict is one for the authorities in Hanoi to make.

"A Reply to the White Paper"
I. F. STONE

That North Viet-Nam supports the guerrillas in South Viet-Nam is no more a secret than that the United States supports the South Vietnamese government against them. The striking thing about the State Department's new White Paper is how little support it can prove. "Incontrovertible evidence of Hanoi's elaborate program to supply its forces in the South with weapons, ammunition and other supplies," the White Paper says, "has accumulated over the years." A detailed presentation of this evidence is in Appendix D; unfortunately few will see the appendices since even the *New York Times* did not reprint them, though these are more revealing than the report. Appendix D provides a list of weapons, ammunition, and other supplies of Chinese Communist, Soviet, Czech, and North Vietnamese manufacture, with the dates and place of capture from the Viet-Cong guerrillas, over the eighteen-month period from June, 1962, to January 29 last year when it was presented to the International Control Commission. The Commission was set up by the Geneva agreement of 1954. This list provides a good point at which to begin an analysis of the White Paper.

The Pentagon's Figures

To put the figures in perspective, we called the Pentagon press office and obtained some figures the White Paper does not supply—the number of weapons captured from the guerrillas and the number lost to them in recent years:

	Captured from guerrillas	*Lost to them*
1962	4,800	5,200
1963	5,400	8,500
1964	4,900	13,700
3-year total	15,100	27,400

In three years, the guerrillas captured from our side 12,300 more weapons than they lost to us.

What interests us at the moment is not this favorable balance but the number of guerrilla weapons our side captured during the past three years. The grand total was 15,100. If Hanoi has indeed engaged in an "elaborate program" to supply the Viet-Cong, one would expect a substantial number of enemy-produced weapons to turn up. Here is the sum total of enemy-produced weapons and supplies in that eighteen-month tally to the Control Commission—

    72 rifles (46 Soviet, 26 Czech)

    64 submachine guns (40 Czech, 24 French but "modified" in North Vietnam)

    15 carbines (Soviet)

     8 machine guns (6 Chinese, 2 North Vietnamese)

     5 pistols (4 Soviet, 1 Czech)

     4 mortars (Chinese)

     3 recoilless 75 mm. rifles (Chinese)

     3 recoilless 57 mm. guns (Chinese)

     2 bazookas (1 Chinese, 1 Czech)

     2 rocket launchers (Chinese)

     1 grenade launcher (Czech)

   179 total

This is not a very impressive total. According to the Pentagon figures, we captured on the average 7,500 weapons each eighteen months in the past three years. If only 179 Communist-made weapons turned up in eighteen months, that is less than 2½ per cent of the total. Judging by these White Paper figures, our military are wrong in estimating, as they have in recent months, that 80 per cent of the weapons used by the guerrillas are captured from us. It looks as if the proportion is considerably higher. The material of North Vietnamese origin included only those 24 French submachine guns "modified" in North Viet-Nam, 2 machine guns made in North Viet-Nam, 16 helmets, a uniform and an undisclosed number of mess kits, belts, sweaters and socks. Judging by this tally, the main retaliatory blow should be at North Viet-Nam's clothing factories.

Not Enough for a Battalion

There is another way to judge this tally of captured Communist weapons. A Communist battalion has about 450 men. It needs 500 rifles, four 80 mm. mortars, eight 60 mm. mortars and at least four recoilless rifles. The weapons of Communist origin captured in eighteen months would not adequately outfit one battalion. The figures in the appendix on ammunition captured provides another index. We captured 183 (Chinese) shells for a 60 mm. mortar. This fires about twenty shells a minute, so that was hardly enough ammunition for ten minutes of firing. There were 100,000 (Chinese) cartridges for 7.26 mm. machine guns. That looks impressive until one discovers on checking with knowledgeable military sources that these machine guns fire 600 rounds a minute. A machine gun platoon normally has four machine guns. This was enough ammunition for about forty minutes of firing by one platoon. Indeed, if the ratio of Communist-made weapons captured is the same for weapons used, then only twelve and a half days of those eighteen months were fought by the guerrillas on the basis of Communist-made supplies.

If these figures were being presented in a court of law, they would run up against a further difficulty: one would have to prove the arms actually came from the Communist side. There is a world-wide market in second-hand weapons. One can buy Soviet, Czech, and Chinese Communist weapons of all kinds only two miles or so from the Pentagon at Interarmco, Ltd., 7 Prince Street, Alexandria, Virginia. Interarmco, one of the world's foremost dealers, can provide more Communist weapons than we picked up in eighteen months on Vietnamese battlefields. Interarmco's East European Communist weapons come in large part from the huge stocks of Soviet and Czech arms captured by the Israelis in the Suez campaign. It has Chinese Communist weapons captured by our side in the Korean war. It also has, of course, a wide selection of our own military surplus. This has turned up in strange places.

For example, a book on the Algerian war, *Les Algériens en guerre,* by Dominique Darbois and Philippe Vingneau, was published in Milan in 1960 by Feltrinelli. It shows pictures of FLN (National Liberation Front) Algerian rebels wearing U.S. Marine Corps uniforms from which the "USMC" and the eagle and globe insignia have not even been removed. It shows Algerians carrying U.S. 81 mm. mortars and U.S. 50-calibre machine guns. Such photos could have been used by France to accuse the U.S. of supplying the Algerian rebels.

The State Department's White Paper says "dramatic new proof was exposed just as this report was being completed" in the discovery of a suspected Viet-Cong arms cargo ship on February 16. The *New York Times* commented astringently on this in an editorial February 28—

> Apparently, the major new evidence of a need for escalating the war, with all the
> hazard that this entails, was provided by the sinking in a South Vietnamese cove

earlier this month of a 100-ton cargo ship loaded with Communist-made small arms and ammunition. A ship of that size is not much above the Oriental junk class. The standard Liberty or Victory ship of World War II had a capacity of 7,150 to 7,650 tons.

The affair of the cargo ship is curious. Until now there has been little evidence of arms coming in by ship. A huge fleet of small vessels patrols the coast and there have been glowing stories in the past of its efficiency. "About 12,000 vessels," the AP reported from Saigon (*New York Times,* February 22), "are searched each month by the South Vietnamese coastal junk patrol force but arrests are rare and no significant amounts of incriminating goods or weapons ever have been found." This lone case of a whole shipload of arms is puzzling.

Few Northern Infiltrees Cited

The White Paper's story on the influx of men from the North also deserves a closer analysis than the newspapers have given it. Appendix C provides an elaborate table from 1959–60 to 1964 inclusive, showing the number of "confirmed" military infiltrees per year from the North. The total is given as 19,550. One way to measure this number is against that of the military we have assigned to South Viet-Nam in the same years. These now total 23,500, or 25 per cent more, and 1,000 are to be added in the near future. The number of North Vietnamese infiltrees is "based on information . . . from at least two independent sources." *Nowhere are we told how many men who infiltrated from the North have actually been captured.* There is reason to wonder whether the count of infiltrees may be as bloated as the count of Viet-Cong dead; in both cases the numbers used are estimates rather than actual bodies.

The White Paper calls the war an invasion and claims "that as many as 75 per cent of the more than 4,400 Viet-Cong who are known to have entered the South in the first eight months of 1964 were natives of North Viet-Nam." But a careful reading of the text and the appendices turns up the names of only six North Vietnamese infiltrees. In Part I of the White Paper, Section B gives "individual case histories of North Vietnamese soldiers" sent South by Hanoi but all nine of these are of South Vietnamese origin. The next Section, C, is headed "Infiltration of Native North Vietnamese." It names five infiltrees but one of these is also from the South. That leaves four North Vietnamese natives. Then, in Appendix C, we are given the case histories and photographs of nine other Viet-Cong sent south by Hanoi. The report does not explain which ones were originally from the South but it does give the names of the provinces in which they were born. When these are checked, it turns out that only two of the nine were born in North Viet-Nam. This gives us a total of six northern infiltrees. It is strange that after five years of fighting, the White Paper can cite so few.

None of this is discussed frankly in the White Paper. To do so would be to bring the war into focus as a rebellion in the South, which may owe some men and matériel to the North but is largely dependent on popular indigenous support for its manpower, as it is on captured U.S. weapons for its supply. The White

Paper withholds all evidence which points to a civil war. It also fails to tell the full story of the July, 1962, Special Report by the International Control Commission. Appendix A quotes that portion in which the Commission 2-to-1 (Poland dissenting) declared that the North had in specific instances sent men and material south in violation of the Geneva Accords. But nowhere does the State Department mention that the same report also condemned South Viet-Nam and the U.S., declaring that they had entered into a military alliance in violation of the Geneva Agreements. The U.S. was criticized because it then had about 5,000 military advisers in South Viet-Nam. The Geneva Accords limited the U.S. military mission to the 684 in Viet-Nam at the time of the 1954 cease-fire. The U.S. and South Viet-Nam were also criticized by the I.C.C. for hamstringing the Commission's efforts to check on imports of arms in violation of the Geneva Accords.

The reader would never guess from the White Paper that the Geneva Accords promised that elections would be held in 1956 to reunify the country. The 1961 Blue Book at least mentioned the elections, though somehow managing to make them seem a plot. "It was the Communists' calculation," the Blue Book put it, "that nationwide elections scheduled in the accords for 1956 would turn all of South Viet-Nam over to them. . . . The authorities in South Viet-Nam refused to fall into this well-laid trap." The White Paper omits mention of the elections altogether and says, "South Viet-Nam's refusal to fall in with Hanoi's scheme for peaceful takeover came as a heavy blow to the Communists." This is not the most candid and objective presentation. From the Viet-Minh point of view, the failure to hold the elections promised them when they laid down their arms was the second broken promise of the West. The earlier one was in 1946 when they made an agreement to accept limited autonomy within the French union, and welcomed the returning French troops as comrades of the liberation. Most of the French military did not want to recognize even this limited form of independence, and chose instead the road which led after eight years of war to Dien Bien Phu.[1]

That "Economic Miracle" Again

The most disingenuous part of the White Paper is that in which it discusses the origins of the present war. It pictures the war as an attack from the North, launched in desperation because the "economic miracle" in the South under Diem had destroyed Communist hopes of a peaceful takeover from within. Even the strategic hamlets are described as "designed to improve the peasant's livelihood" and we are asked to believe that for the first time in history a guerrilla war spread not because the people were discontented but because their lot was improving!

The true story is a story of lost opportunities. The Communist countries acquiesced in the failure to hold elections. Diem had a chance to make his part of the country a democratic showcase. The year 1956 was a bad one in the North.

[1] See Jean Saintény's *Histoire d'une paix manquée* (Paris, 1953) and Ellen Hammer's *The Struggle for Indochina* (Stanford, 1954).

There was a peasant uprising and widespread resentment among the intellectuals over the Communist Party's heavy-handed thought control. But Diem on the other side of the 17th Parallel was busy erecting a dictatorship of his own. In 1956 he abolished elections even for village councils. In 1957 his mobs smashed the press of the one legal opposition party, the Democratic Bloc, when it dared criticize the government. That was the beginning of a campaign to wipe out every form of opposition. It was this campaign and the oppressive exactions imposed on the peasantry, the fake land reform and the concentration camps Diem set up for political opponents of all kinds, which stirred ever wider rebellion from 1958 onward in the grass roots *before* North Viet-Nam gave support. It was this which drove oppositionists of all kinds into alliance with the Communists in the National Liberation Front.

Long before the North was accused of interference, its government was complaining to the Control Commission of "border and air-space violations by the south and infringements of the Geneva Agreement by the introduction of arms and U.S. servicemen." For four years after Geneva, both North Viet-Nam and China followed the "peaceful coexistence" policy while the U.S. turned South Viet-Nam into a military base and a military dictatorship. It is in this story the White Paper does not tell, and the popular discontent it does not mention, that the rebellion and the aid from the North had their origins.

Selective Service Orientation Kit "Channeling"

One of the major products of the Selective Service classification process is the channeling of manpower into many endeavors, occupations, and activities that are in the national interest. This function is a counterpart and amplification of the System's responsibility to deliver manpower to the armed forces in such a manner as to reduce to a minimum any adverse effect upon the national health, safety, interest, and progress. By identifying and applying this process intelligently, the System is able not only to minimize any adverse effect but to exert an effect beneficial to the national health, safety, and interest.

The line dividing the primary function of armed forces manpower procurement from the process of channeling manpower into civilian support is often finely drawn. The process of channeling by not taking men from certain activities who are otherwise liable for service, or by giving deferment to qualified men in certain occupations, is actual procurement by inducement of manpower for civilian activities which are manifestly in the national interest.

While the best known purpose of Selective Service is to procure manpower for the armed forces, a variety of related processes takes place outside delivery of manpower to the active armed forces. Many of these may be put under the heading of "channeling manpower." Many young men would not have pursued a higher education if there had not been a program of student deferment. Many young scientists, engineers, tool and die makers, and other possessors of scarce skills would not remain in their jobs in the defense effort if it were not for a program of occupational deferments. Even though the salary of a teacher has historically been meager, many young men remain in that job, seeking the reward of a deferment. The process of channeling manpower by deferment is entitled to much credit for the large number of graduate students in technical fields and for the fact that there is not a greater shortage of teachers, engineers, and other scientists working in activities which are essential to the national interest.

More than ten years ago, it became evident that something additional had to be done to permit and encourage development of young scientists and trained people in all fields. A million and a half registrants are now deferred as students. One reason the Nation is not in shorter supply of engineers today is that they were among the students deferred by Selective Service in previous years. Similarly, Selective Service student deferments reduced what otherwise would have developed into more serious shortages in teaching, medicine, dentistry, and every field requiring advanced study. The System has also induced needed people to remain in these professions and in industry engaged in defense activities or in the support of national health, safety, or interest.

The opportunity to enhance the national well being by inducing more registrants to participate in fields which relate directly to the national interest came about as a consequence, soon after the close of the Korean episode, of the knowledge within the System that there was enough registrant personnel to allow stringent deferment practices employed during war time to be relaxed or tightened as the situation might require. Circumstances had become favorable to induce registrants, by the attraction of deferment, to matriculate in schools and pursue subjects in which there was beginning to be a national shortage of personnel. These were particularly in the engineering, scientific, and teaching professions.

This was coupled with a growing public recognition that the complexities of future wars would diminish further the distinction between what constitutes military service in uniform and a comparable contribution to the national interest out of uniform. Wars have always been conducted in various ways but appreciation of this fact and its relationship to preparation for war has never been so sharp in the public mind as it is now becoming. The meaning of the word "service," with its former restricted application to the armed forces, is certain to become widened much more in the future. This brings with it the ever increasing problems of how to control effectively the service of individuals who are not in the armed forces.

In the Selective Service System the term "deferment" has been used millions of times to describe the method and means used to attract to the kind of service considered to be most important, the individuals who were not compelled to do it. The club of induction has been used to drive out of areas considered to be less important to the areas of greater importance in which deferments were given, the individuals who did not or could not participate in activities which were considered essential to the defense of the Nation. The Selective Service System anticipates further in this area. It is promoting the process by the granting of deferments in liberal numbers where the national need clearly would benefit.

Soon after Sputnik I was launched it became popular to reappraise critically our educational, scientific, and technicological inventory. Many deplored our shortage of scientific and technical personnel, inadequacies of our schools, and shortage of teachers. Since any analysis having any connection with manpower and its relation to the Nation's survival vitally involves the Selective Service System, it is well to point out that for quite some time the System has been following a policy of deferring instructors who were engaged in the teaching of mathematics and physical and biological sciences. It is appropriate also to recall the System's previously invoked practice of deferring students to prepare themselves for work in some essential activity and the established program of deferring engineers, scientists, and other critically skilled persons who were working in essential fields.

The Congress, in enacting the Universal Military Training and Service legislation declared that adequate provisions for national security required maximum effort in the fields of scientific research and development, and the fullest possible utilization of the Nation's technicological, scientific, and other critical manpower resources. To give effect to this philosophy, the classifying boards of the Selective Service System defer registrants determined by them to be necessary in the national health, safety, or interest. This is accomplished on the basis of evidence of record in each individual case. No group deferments are permitted. Deferments are granted, however, in a realistic atmosphere so that the fullest effect of channeling will be felt, rather than be terminated by military service at too early a time.

Registrants and their employers are encouraged and required to make available to the classifying authorities detailed evidence as to the occupations and activities in which the registrants are engaged. It is not necessary for any registrant to specifically request deferment, but his Selective Service file must contain sufficient current evidence on which can be based a proper determination as to whether he should remain where he is or be made available for service. Since occupational deferments are granted for no more than one year at a time, a process of periodically receiving current information and repeated review assures that every deferred registrant continues to contribute to the overall national good. This reminds him of the basis for his deferment. The skills as well as the activities are periodically reevaluated. A critical skill that is not employed in an essential activity does not qualify for deferment.

Patriotism is defined as "devotion to the welfare of one's country." It has been interpreted to mean many different things. Men have always been exhorted to do their duty. But what that duty is depends upon a variety of variables, most important being the nature of the threat to national welfare and the capacity and opportunity of the individual. Take, for example, the boy who saved the Netherlands by plugging the dike with his finger.

At the time of the American Revolution the patriot was the so-called "embattled farmer" who joined General Washington to fight the British. The concept that patriotism is best exemplified by service in uniform has always been under some degree of challenge, but never to the extent that it is today. In today's complicated warfare when the men in uniform may be suffering far less than the civilians at home, patriotism must be interpreted far more broadly than ever before.

This is not a new thought, but it has had new emphasis since the development of nuclear and rocket warfare. Educators, scientists, engineers, and their professional organizations, during the last ten years particularly, have been convincing the American public that for the mentally qualified man there is a special order of patriotism other than service in uniform—that for the man having the capacity, dedicated service as a civilian in such fields as engineering, the sciences, and teaching constitute the ultimate in their expression of patriotism. A large segment of the American public has been convinced that this is true.

It is in this atmosphere that the young man registers at age 18 and pressure begins to force his choice. He does not have the inhibitions that a philosophy of universal service in uniform would engender. The door is open for him as a student to qualify if capable in a skill badly needed by his nation. He has many choices and he is prodded to make a decision.

The psychological effect of this circumstantial climate depends upon the individual, his sense of good citizenship, his love of country and its way of life. He can obtain a sense of well being and satisfaction that he is doing as a civilian what will help his country most. This process encourages him to put forth his best effort and removes to some extent the stigma that has been attached to being out of uniform.

In the less patriotic and more selfish individual it engenders a sense of fear, uncertainty, and dissatisfaction which motivates him, nevertheless, in the same direction. He complains of the uncertainty which he must endure; he would like to be able to do as he pleases; he would appreciate a certain future with no prospect of military service or civilian contribution, but he complies with the needs of the national health, safety, or interest—or he is denied deferment.

Throughout his career as a student, the pressure—the threat of loss of deferment—continues. It continues with equal intensity after graduation. His local board requires periodic reports to find out what he is up to. He is impelled to pursue his skill rather than embark upon some less important enterprise and is encouraged to apply his skill in an essential activity in the national interest. The loss of deferred status is the consequence for the individual who has acquired the skill and either does not use it or uses it in a nonessential activity.

The psychology of granting wide choice under pressure to take action is the American or indirect way of achieving what is done by direction in foreign countries where choice is not permitted. Here, choice is limited but not denied, and it is fundamental that an individual generally applies himself better to something he has decided to do rather than something he has been told to do.

The effects of channeling are manifested among student physicians. They are deferred to complete their education through school and internship. This permits them to serve in the armed forces in their skills rather than in an unskilled capacity as enlisted men.

The device of pressurized guidance, or channeling, is employed on Standby Reservists of which more than 2½ million have been referred by all services for availability determinations. The appeal to the Reservist who knows he is subject to recall to active duty unless he is determined to be unavailable is virtually identical to that extended to other registrants.

The psychological impact of being rejected for service in uniform is severe. The earlier this occurs in a young man's life, the sooner the beneficial effects of pressured motivation by the Selective Service System are lost. He is labeled unwanted. His patriotism is not desired. Once the label of "rejectee" is upon him all efforts at guidance by persuasion are futile. If he attempts to enlist at 17 or 18 and is rejected, then he receives virtually none of the impulsion the System is capable of giving him. If he makes no effort to enlist and as a result is not rejected until delivered for examination by Selective Service System at about the age 23, he has felt some of the pressure but thereafter is a free agent.

This contributed to establishment of a new classification of I-Y (registrant qualified for military service only in time of war or national emergency). That classification reminds the registrant of his ultimate qualification to serve and preserves some of the benefit of what we call channeling. Without it or any other similar method of categorizing men in degrees of acceptability, men rejected for military service would be left with the understanding that they are unfit to defend their country, even in war time.

An unprejudiced choice between alternative routes in civilian skills can be offered only by an agency which is not a user of manpower and is, therefore, not a competitor. In the absence of such an agency, bright young men would be importuned with bounties and pirated like potential college football players until eventually a system of arbitration would have to be established.

From the individual's viewpoint, he is standing in a room which has been made uncomfortably warm. Several doors are open, but they all lead to various forms of recognized, patriotic service to the Nation. Some accept the alternatives gladly—some with reluctance. The consequence is approximately the same.

The so-called Doctor Draft was set up during the Korean episode to insure sufficient physicians, dentists, and veterinarians in the armed forces as officers. The objective of that law was to exert sufficient pressure to furnish an incentive for application for commission. However, the indirect effect was to induce many physicians, dentists, and veterinarians to specialize in areas of medical personnel shortages and to seek outlets for their skills in areas of greatest demand and national need rather than of greatest financial return.

Selective Service processes do not compel people by edict as in foreign systems to enter pursuits having to do with essentiality and progress. They go because they know that by going they will be deferred.

The application of direct methods to effect the policy of every man doing his duty in support of national interest involves considerably more capacity than the current use of indirection as a method of allocation of personnel. The problem, however, of what is every man's duty when each individual case is approached is not simple. The question of whether he can do one duty better than another is a problem of considerable proportions and the complications of logistics in attempting to control parts of an operation without controlling all of it (in other words, to control allocation of personnel without controlling where people eat, where they live, and how they are to be transported) adds to the administrative difficulties of direct administration. The organization necessary to make the decisions, even poor decisions, would extract a large segment of population from productive work. If the members of the organization are conceived to be reasonably qualified to exercise judgment and control over skilled personnel, the impact of their withdrawal from war production work would be severe. The number of decisions would extend into billions.

A quarter billion classification actions were needed in World War II for the comparatively limited function of the Selective Service System at that time. Deciding what people should do, rather than letting them do something of national importance of their own choosing, introduces many problems that are at least partially avoided when indirect methods, the kind currently invoked by the Selective Service System, are used.

Delivery of manpower for induction, the process of providing a few thousand men with transportation to a reception center, is not much of an administrative or financial challenge. It is in dealing with the other millions of registrants that the System is heavily occupied, developing more effective human beings in the national interest. If there is to be any survival after disaster, it will take people, and not machines, to restore the Nation.

July 1, 1965

"Manpower Unchanneled"
TOM GARDNER

With the maintenance of the "Peacetime" draft, the government outlines for young men certain alternatives (such as, kill or go to prison), and to most the ultimatum is a compelling one. But the final decision still rests with us. It is wrong to say that we are "forced" into the army or "forced" to fight in a war. Many of us, at one point or another, are saying "No."

It is not even enough to say "I won't go." There are many different ways to refuse to join the military or fight in a war. Among those of us who have made the basic decision not to go, there is a constant debate concerning which method of refusal is the most moral, effective, or successful.

I have found it impossible to formulate a position in relation to the Selective Service System without considering much broader questions. Is the singular, moral witness the best way personally to affect history? Should effectiveness be considered at all? In light of the present war and pending disaster, don't we have a moral duty to be effective? How can we act most effectively to end the war, abolish the draft, and change the American system that breeds imperialism? Should I go out of my way to help Uncle Sam lock me up? Is that "resistance"? What personal course will contribute the most toward building a popular resistance movement? Am I personally ready to act on the basis of my political and moral decisions? To what extent are my decisions political and moral decisions? To what extent are my decisions political and to what extent are they rationalizations for personal shortcomings?

I don't pretend to have the answers to these questions, nor will I attempt to deal with all of them here. In the hope that my experience may assist at least one other person, I would like to review some of the decisions I have made and discuss how and why my position has changed.

I have, until recently, lived a fairly normal, middle-class life. My father is a career dental officer in the Navy, and most of my nomadic life has been spent in the South. A Kennedy-Peace Corps admirer, I enrolled at the University of Virginia, planning to enter the foreign service and enrolled in Air Force ROTC. I quickly dropped out of ROTC. Through contact with activists in the civil rights and campus reform movements, and after discovering some facts about our foreign policy, I became active in anti-war organizing. The comparative emptiness of the "education" I was receiving in college, and a desire to do something significant compelled me toward my first confrontation with the selective slavery system. I call it a confrontation not because I received any orders from my local board, but because the probable threat of induction if I were to drop out of school forced me to consider the draft while deciding whether or not to drop out. The obvious conflict was between what I wanted to do and what the Selective Service System would want me to do.

There were three main factors that influenced me to drop out in spite of the draft. One factor was that a best friend had withdrawn from the University of Virginia in order to work with the Virginia Students' Civil Rights Committee in southside Virginia, while I was still in school. His example affected me for two reasons: one, I respected his courage and commitment; and, two, he was living testimony to the fact that it was possible to drop out of school and still avoid or delay induction.

The second factor was my exposure to the moral absolutist position. When we organized a state-wide demonstration in support of Beardall, Keith, and Rodd, who were imprisoned at Petersburg Federal Reformatory, I publicly read Tom Rodd's statement to Judge Rosenberg. That gave me a stronger feeling of identity with the noncooperators. John Buenfil of Charlottesville, Virginia; was the first person to ever articulate the non-cooperator position to me. At that time, I didn't completely agree with the absolutists' position, but their witness would have made me ashamed to stay in college rather than risk prison.

The third factor, probably the decisive one, was my strong personal resentment and rebellion against the idea of some distant group of old men presuming to control my life. I grew up believing in democracy and the sanctity of the individual conscience—you know, Thomas Paine, Jefferson, Adams, Thoreau, Jesus Christ, etc. (or, by antithetical example, Adolph Eichmann)—and it was just too late for all those old people who taught me those things to reverse themselves and tell me: "Forget all that conscience stuff, don't think, just follow orders—kill, kill, kill!!" Not only was I so much of a Christian, American, "democrat" that I wouldn't let them order me to kill a stranger, but I also didn't think that they should be able to force me to go to college.

So, I decided that regardless of the eventual consequences, I would leave college because I wanted to—period. I also intended to use whatever semi-legitimate evasive tactics I could, so that I could continue to work in the movement. Being by now a convinced pacifist, I felt I would eventually apply for conscientious objector status. If possible, I wanted to avoid a direct confrontation while doing the organizing work that I wanted to do. To stay in college to avoid that confrontation would not have been evasive; for me, it would have been total prostitution and humiliation.

After leaving the University, working with the Virginia Students' Civil Rights Committee, and then coming on the staff of the USNSA [National Student Association] Southern Project, I began to question whether I could accept certain deferments or exemptions or whether I should be a total noncooperator. During this period of indecision, I was what the SSS calls a delinquent, i.e., I ignored the draft board, not informing them of my work or address. I could have applied for an occupational deferment (II-A), since NSA was, as is now obvious, "essential to the national safety." Since I didn't consider myself to be part of NSA's national defense scheme, the very thought of being classified as essential to Johnson's definition of "the national safety or interest" was too repugnant to consider. Also, at an early meeting of the advisory committee of the Southern Project, the National Affairs Vice-President of NSA was asked what NSA is doing on the draft. His reply was, "To be honest with you, we (the officers and staff) all have occupational deferments and we don't want to do anything too drastic because we're afraid we'll lose them." That was the kind of statement that pushed me closer toward noncooperation.

In September of 1966, in an effort to think through my position, I wrote myself a short diatribe. Part of it follows:

> The draft—to take a purely moral stand, or to be effective? It's difficult to divide those two satisfactorily so that you can actually choose one from the other. For instance, I tend to have more respect for those who take a seemingly moral stand rather than thinking primarily of effectiveness. On the other hand, I also begin to get the feeling that wanting just to wipe one's own moral slate clean is a rather selfish goal when you consider the moral imperative of needing to end the war. In other words, you can't divide "moral" from "effective" when you consider that with thousands of people being killed, you have a moral duty to be effective. But then, what is "being effective"? How the hell are we going to end this war-drunk world's spiral toward disaster? How can we just end the war in Vietnam? If I feel

that the only way I can work toward that is by urging others not to fight, and if I feel that the best way to protest the draft is for myself and others to refuse allegiance even to its alternative service, then how can I continue to pussy-foot around about my own status? And if I rationalize staying out of jail so that I can build a larger draft resistance movement, what the hell am I doing working for NSA which, like the schools it wants to change, is more responsive to its ownership, foundations, and government, than to its constituency—students? Should I burn my card? Apply for I-O? Ask for asylum in Cuba? Go to Canada? What?

　　I want to work full-time on learning and talking with people about relating to other people, about love and peace, hate and war, freedom and FREEDOM. I want to help people overcome what the system is doing to them. I want to love and help build bridges between people and maybe nations. Is that so evil or dangerous? Well, I guess it may be to those who have a vested interest in keeping people hating and killing each other. But, I'm going to do it anyway; I'm tired of that word "later." I'm tired of allowing my life to be ruled by a machine which I have no influence over. To quote Mrs. Fannie Lou Hamer, "All my life I've been sick and tired, and now I'm sick and tired of being sick and tired!" All of us have so many chains wrapped around us, we're slaves; but most of us are cringing inside those chains, trying to roll ourselves into insignificant little balls of flesh so that we won't even be touched by the cold iron that surrounds us. Other people have been in that situation; most of them also cringed frightened, but some have stood up and pushed against the chains that bound them—with their whole bodies, with their feet, with their songs, with their lives. Whether the chains broke or remained, those men and women were declaring themselves free and were, in fact, close to FREEDOM, by virtue of having lost their fear of the consequences and standing up and asserting their manhood or womanhood. Through that kind of involvement, one *can* declare his own freedom, and only by doing so can he be maximally and individually both effective and moral. It is the persons who have taken that kind of stand who have had a stronger effect on history than those who have compromised their principles as a price for effectiveness. Now, how about me?

Sounds good doesn't it, but before I attended the Noncooperators' Conference in New York [October 1966], I still had two major reservations about noncooperation: one, how effective would it be?; and two, is the fact of my nominal affiliation, registration, or classification with the SSS so immoral in itself that I am willing to go to prison in an attempt to sever it? At the conference, I don't really think I resolved those questions, but I was overwhelmingly impressed with the courage and moral clarity of the men who had chosen noncooperation. They were beautiful people and I wanted to be part of them. But even as I joined, two lingering impressions bothered me (slightly, then, but more later); considering the dominant air of self-righteousness (which is possibly inherent in martyrdom), many of the noncooperators seemed disproportionately politically naïve, especially about the probably short-range effect of their own act of refusal. It was to me a convincing point that for a person to live an effective life he must have a consistent record of having stood up for what he believes in. However, that appraisal of one's lifelong effectiveness should not lead one to an unrealistic overestimation of the immediate political effect of burning or returning a draft card, or, as some see it, volunteering for prison. Anyone deciding to risk prison should distinguish between the long and the short range effectiveness arguments, and decide for himself how each of them relates specifically to him.

I then decided to join the long line of revolutionary zealots and sign the statement: "Saying No to Military Conscription."

> We, the undersigned men of draft age (18–35), believe that all war is immoral and ultimately self-defeating. We believe that military conscription is evil and unjust. Therefore, we will not cooperate in any way with the Selective Service System.
>
> We will not register for the draft.
>
> If we have registered, we will sever all relations with the Selective Service System.
>
> We will carry no draft cards or other Selective Service certificates.
>
> We will not accept any deferment, such as 2-S.
>
> We will not accept any exemption, such as 1-O or 4-D.
>
> We will refuse induction into the armed forces.
>
> We urge and advocate that other young men join us in non-cooperating with the Selective Service System.
>
> We are in full knowledge that these actions are violations of the Selective Service laws punishable by up to 5 years imprisonment and/or a fine of $10,000.

On my way back South, I went by my home at Camp Lejeune, North Carolina, and found waiting for me a I-A classification card. I immediately wrote the following letter, carried it around for a couple of weeks, and finally dropped it in the mailbox, along with my draft card.

> Dear Board Members,
>
> I recently received a card from you indicating my classification as I-A. In recent months, I have spent much time considering my relation to the system of conscription. . . .
>
> I have decided to refuse cooperation with conscription for several reasons. . . . I know of the alternatives within the System, and I imagine I could avoid having to kill by asking for alternative "service." I also realize, however, that I would have a chance of qualifying for one of the alternatives: I've had a formal education; I've been exposed to the varying philosophies of pacifism and can articulate my beliefs; I could afford appeals and lawyers; and I'm white. I realize also that there are a lot of men who couldn't avoid military service because their environment makes the military look to them like a positive step by comparison; or because they lack the same financial resources; or, regardless of other qualifications, because they are Black. Am I going to work with my brothers in a common struggle, and then at the danger point step "up" and use my "privileged" position? If I were to accept a privileged position under the draft law, I would, in a very real sense, be recognizing the right of the regime to gobble up my brethren, and I don't recognize that right. I feel that in order to be of service to my "country," which is Humanity, and to be loyal to my god, whom I call Love, and to participate in my religion, which I define as action, I must sever all connections with the system of destruction which wishes to induct me into its services. I hereby consider myself no longer connected with the system of military conscription, and under no circumstances will I accept induction.

I received no reply other than an order to report for my physical on December 14. I didn't intend to report (I discovered later that the Justice Department had been notified so that they could arrest me when I failed to show), but on December 8, I was sentenced by a kind North Carolina judge to thirty days in jail for criminal contempt, thereby making it impossible for me to report for my physical, even if I had wanted to.

I was in Greensboro, North Carolina, helping a recently indicted nonregistrant find a lawyer. While attending the court sessions, I met two other fellows who were charged with refusing induction. The one with whom I had a chance to speak had withdrawn from Appalachian State Teachers College. He had never read any of the standard peace literature or heard of any of the peace organizations. He said he wasn't a conscientious objector—he was "just sick of the whole mess"; he was just a calm, ordinary guy who had decided he wasn't going. In court, this registrant refused to make a statement. He had written his board: "I don't feel a need to justify my action in anyone's mind." Nobody in the courtroom, not the D.A., the FBI agent, nor the judge could figure out what possible reason this young man could have for not wanting to kill people. So the judge, scratching his head and saying, "I wish there were something else I could do," sentenced him to two years in prison. The other draft refuser was also sentenced to two years.

At recess, when the command was given, "Everyone rise," having little respect for that court to indicate by rising, I remained seated. When the court reconvened, the judge declared that I had been "disrespectful and contemptuous of the court" and that I had planned to "disrupt the order and decorum of the court and obstruct the administration of justice." I was then hauled off to Forsyth County jail in Winston-Salem, North Carolina, without being given a chance to speak. I was released after sixteen days so that I could enjoy Christmas at home.

My jail term in North Carolina was the first chance I had to just read and think. I learned as much about myself as I did about our "just society." It was in jail where my position regarding the SSS began to modify itself toward a more personally realistic one. The following excerpt out of my thick file of prison notes relates a couple of my most important realizations.

> I was thinking, in regards to noncooperation, that one of the valuable things would be to confront the Judge and other officials with the burden of having to imprison me, etc. After watching Judge Gordon throw two guys away for two years and imprison me, as I sit here in jail, I can't help but give more pensive thought to the possibility of a two- to five-year term. Judge Gordon was not affected in the slightest, nor were any of the spectators. I am just now seeing more vividly that they . . . have absolute power, and that it's somewhat ridiculous to let them put me away for four damn years (that's forty-eight times as long as I'm serving now). . . . I'm just not sure it's worth it.
>
> Secondly, I'm just not sure that with the doubts I have, I could fabricate the daily consolation that going to prison for conscience sake requires. Going to jail for absolutism means that if one expects to maintain his sanity, one must be an absolutist in his decision. That means that one has to be able to look at the entire world and domestic situation—at everything that's happening socially, politically, economically, technologically—at the way people think, at the alternatives available and then decide that the best place for him is jail for 5 yrs. I don't think I can say that now, I just don't think I can.
>
> . . . What this means practically, I guess, is that I would be willing to apply for CO and take alternative service . . . Goddamn, Gardner, don't be so defensive, everyone has a right to grow or change his mind.

More specifically, with the world spiraling toward destruction and America marching toward fascism . . . I felt a lot more pessimistic about the possible short-range effectiveness of my noncooperation. I wanted to be outside, talking to people, organizing with them where they are *at*. What could I do in prison? Who would understand? Who is going to join a "Go to Prison" movement? Why should I help the enemy take me out of commission for several years? Perhaps I also learned about myself (as Thomas More says in *A Man for All Seasons*), that, "This is not the stuff from which martyrs are made." I decided to apply for conscientious objector status—at least to give me more time to think, although I didn't rule out the possibility of doing alternative service. Since receiving a I-O from the state appeal board, I have not received an order to report for alternative service, as of this writing.

So, what conclusions have I drawn and what is my present position? One point is that a guy may be influenced to drop out of school and/or resist the draft just as much by the example of someone escaping both the draft and prison as by the example of an imprisoned noncooperator. Another point is that it would be a good idea for everyone contemplating noncooperation to spend just a few days in the pokey so that they could make a more realistic appraisal of the consequences of their act. A decision to noncooperate after one has experienced imprisonment is likely to be more personally realistic.

I think that the major weakness of my original act of noncooperation was that it was not real enough for me to stand on. I wasn't yet really refusing or responding to any final orders from Selective Service, nor had I exhausted all the possibilities for delaying or completely avoiding induction. I was waging an offensive against the SSS, the major issue being whether or not I was registered with them. When pressed on the point, I decided that it really didn't make any difference what my board thought my status was or whether or not they considered me to be a registrant. (It is impossible in that sense to be "unregistered," since even if you go to prison, the warden can register you with the SSS.) What really mattered was whether in the end *I* would grant the draft system any influence over the direction of my life.

Perhaps the issue of disaffiliation is not the best issue around which to organize a resistance movement; although, acts of total noncooperation do help add to a general sense of rebellion and thus contribute toward building a resistance movement. Essentially, though, the point at which guys will more readily resist is the point at which the draft comes into their lives and attempts to coerce their bodies into slavery. There are basically two ways that the SSS attempts to enter our lives. One way is through induction into the military—hopefully more and more young men will at this point say "No." The other way, which is just as much an essential function of the SSS as the former one, is through the granting of various deferments and exemptions (II-S, II-A, I-O, IV-D, etc.) that are designed "to channel people into the occupations that are defined by those in government as critical" and to buy off potential resisters. The important point here for me has been to decide what I want to do, not considering the draft, and then go ahead and do it.

The question arises, what if what I really want to do would entitle me to a deferment anyway? This, of course, must be resolved personally. I haven't completely resolved it for myself, but if I *really* wanted to return to college, I would probably accept a II-S. What would be important would be not to let that II-S be the decisive factor for keeping me in school. And if I *really* wanted to work for the American Friends Service Committee, or work in a hospital for two years, then I would probably let the draft board call it "alternative service." However, since I plan to keep working with the Southern Student Organizing Committee for at least the next several years, and since SSOC is not recognized as alternative service, I am reaching a point at which I will have to decide whether I will do what I want to do or what "they" want me to do. If I were to state here and now exactly what I intend to do, that would only indicate that I have learned nothing from my past experience. I do not know what I am going to do. How far can one bend and still call himself a man? For myself, I suspect, not much further.

"A Generation in Search of a Future"
GEORGE WALD

All of you know that in the last couple of years there has been student unrest breaking at times into violence in many parts of the world: in England, Germany, Italy, Spain, Mexico and needless to say, in many parts of this country. There has been a great deal of discussion as to what it all means. Perfectly clearly it means something different in Mexico from what it does in France, and something different in France from what it does in Tokyo, and something different in Tokyo from what it does in this country. Yet unless we are to assume that students have gone crazy all over the world, or that they just decided that it's the thing to do, there must be some common meaning.

I don't need to go so far afield to look for that meaning. I am a teacher, and at Harvard, I have a class of about 350 students—men and women—most of them freshmen and sophomores. Over these past few years I have felt increasingly that something is terribly wrong—and this year ever so much more than last. Something has gone sour, in teaching and in learning. It's almost as though there were a widespread feeling that education has become irrelevant.

A lecture is much more of a dialogue than many of you probably appreciate. As you lecture, you keep watching the faces; and information keeps coming back to you all the time. I began to feel, particularly this year, that I was missing much of what was coming back. I tried asking the students, but they didn't or couldn't help me very much.

But I think I know what's the matter, even a little better than they do. I think that this whole generation of students is beset with a profound uneasiness. I don't think that they have yet quite defined its source, I think I understand the reasons for their uneasiness even better than they do. What is more, I share their uneasiness.

What's bothering those students? Some of them tell you it's the Vietnam War. I think the Vietnam War is the most shameful episode in the whole of American history. The concept of War Crimes is an American invention. We've committed many War Crimes in Vietnam; but I'll tell you something interesting about that. We were committing War Crimes in World War II, even before Nuremburg trials were held and the principle of war crimes started. The saturation bombing of German cities was a War Crime. Dropping atom bombs on Hiroshima and Nagasaki was a War Crime. If we had lost the war, some of our leaders might have had to answer for those actions.

I've gone through all of that history lately, and I find that there's a gimmick in it. It isn't written out, but I think we established it by precedent. That gimmick is that if one can allege that one is repelling or retaliating for an aggression—after that everything goes. And you see we are living in a world in which all wars are wars of defense. All War Departments are now Defense Departments. This is all part of the double talk of our time. The aggressor is always on the other side. And I suppose this is why our ex-Secretary of State, Dean Rusk—a man in whom repetition takes the place of reason, and stubbornness takes the place of character—went to such pains to insist, as he still insists, that in Vietnam we are repelling an agression. And if that's what we are doing—so runs the doctrine—anything goes. If the concept of war crimes is ever to mean anything, they will have to be defined as categories of acts, regardless of alleged provocation. But that isn't so now.

I think we've lost that war, as a lot of other people think, too. The Vietnamese have a secret weapon. It's their willingness to die, beyond our willingness to kill. In effect they've been saying, you can kill us, but you'll have to kill a lot of us, you may have to kill all of us. And thank heavens, we are not yet ready to do that.

Yet we have come a long way—far enough to sicken many Americans, far enough even to sicken our fighting men. Far enough so that our national symbols have gone sour. How many of you can sing about "the rockets' red glare, bombs bursting in air" without thinking those are *our* bombs and *our* rockets bursting over South Vietnamese villages? When those words were written, we were a people struggling for freedom against oppression. Now we are supporting real or thinly disguised military dictatorships all over the world, helping them to control and repress peoples struggling for their freedom.

But that Vietnam War, shameful and terrible as it is, seems to me only an immediate incident in a much larger and more stubborn situation.

Part of my trouble with students is that almost all the students I teach were born since World War II. Just after World War II, a series of new and abnormal procedures came into American life. We regarded them at the time as temporary aberrations. We thought we would get back to normal American life some day. But those procedures have stayed with us now for more than 20 years, and those students of mine have never known anything else. They think those things are normal. They think we've always had a Pentagon, that we have always had a big army, and that we always had a draft. But those are all new things in American life; and I think that they are incompatible with what America meant before.

How many of you realize that just before World War II the entire American army including the Air Force numbered 139,000 men? Then World War II started, but we weren't yet in it: and seeing that there was great trouble in the world, we doubled this army to 268,000 men. Then in World War II it got to be 8 million. And then World War II came to an end, and we prepared to go back to a peacetime army somewhat as the American army had always been before. And indeed in 1950—you think about 1950, our international commitments, the Cold War, the Truman Doctrine, and all the rest of it—in 1950 we got down to 600,000 men.

Now we have 3.5 million men under arms: about 600,000 in Vietnam, about 300,000 more in "support areas" elsewhere in the Pacific, about 250,000 in Germany. And there are a lot at home. Some months ago we were told that 300,000 National Guardsmen and 200,000 reservists—so half a million men—had been specially trained for riot duty in the cities.

I say the Vietnam War is just an immediate incident, because so long as we keep that big an army, it will always find things to do. If the Vietnam War stopped tomorrow, with that big a military establishment, the chances are that we would be in another such adventure abroad or at home before you knew it.

As for the draft: Don't reform the draft—get rid of it.

A peacetime draft is the most un-American thing I know. All the time I was growing up I was told about oppressive Central European countries and Russia, where young men were forced into the army; and I was told what they did about it. They chopped off a finger, or shot off a couple of toes; or better still, if they could manage it, they came to this country. And we understood that, and sympathized, and were glad to welcome them.

Now by present estimates four to six thousand Americans of draft age have left this country for Canada, another two or three thousand have gone to Europe, and it looks as though many more are preparing to emigrate.

A few months ago I received a letter from the Harvard Alumni Bulletin posing a series of questions that students might ask a professor involving what to do about the draft. I was asked to write what I would tell those students. All I had to say to those students was this: If any of them had decided to evade the draft and asked my help, I would help him in any way I could. I would feel as I suppose members of the underground railway felt in pre-Civil War days, helping runaway slaves to get to Canada. It wasn't altogether a popular position then; but what do you think of it now?

A bill to stop the draft was recently introduced in the Senate (S. 503), sponsored by a group of senators that ran the gamut from McGovern and

Hatfield to Barry Goldwater. I hope it goes through; but any time I find that Barry Goldwater and I are in agreement, that makes me take another look.

And indeed there are choices in getting rid of the draft. I think that when we get rid of the draft we must also cut back the size of the armed forces. It seems to me that in peacetime a total of one million men is surely enough. If there is an argument for American military forces of more than one million men in peacetime, I should like to hear that argument debated.

There is another thing being said closely connected with this: that to keep an adequate volunteer army, one would have to raise the pay considerably. That's said so positively and often that people believe it. I don't think it is true.

The great bulk of our present armed forces are genuine volunteers. Among first-term enlistments, 49 percent are true volunteers. Another 30 percent are so-called "reluctant volunteers," persons who volunteer under pressure of the draft. Only 21 percent are draftees. All re-enlistments, of course, are true volunteers.

So the great majority of our present armed forces are true volunteers. Whole services are composed entirely of volunteers: the Air Force for example, the Navy, almost all the Marines. That seems like proof to me that present pay rates are adequate. One must add that an Act of Congress in 1967 raised the base pay throughout the services in three installments, the third installment still to come, on April 1, 1969. So it is hard to understand why we are being told that to maintain adequate armed services on a volunteer basis will require large increases in pay; that they will cost an extra $17 billion per year. It seems plain to me that we can get all the armed forces we need as volunteers, and at present rates of pay.

But there is something ever so much bigger and more important than the draft. That bigger thing, of course, is the militarization of our country. Ex-President Eisenhower warned us of what he called the military-industrial complex. I am sad to say that we must begin to think of it now as the military-industrial-labor union complex. What happened under the plea of the Cold War was not alone that we built up the first big peace time army in our history, but we institutionalized it. We built, I suppose, the biggest government building in our history to run it, and we institutionalized it.

I don't think we can live with the present military establishment and its $80 billion a year budget, and keep America anything like we have known it in the past. It is corrupting the life of the whole country. It is buying up everything in sight: time to greatly increase our nuclear armaments so that we can disarm from a position of strength.

The Defense Department is always broke: but some of the things they do with that $80 billion a year would make Buck Rogers envious. For example: the Rocky Mountain Arsenal on the outskirts of Denver was manufacturing a deadly nerve poison on such a scale that there was a problem of waste disposal. Nothing daunted, they dug a tunnel two miles deep under Denver, into which they have injected so much poisoned water that beginning a couple of years ago Denver began to experience a series of earth tremors of increasing severity. Now there is a grave fear of a major earthquake. An interesting debate is in progress as to whether Denver will be safer if that lake of poisoned water is removed or left in place. (*N.Y. Times,* July 4, 1968; *Science,* Sept. 27, 1968).

Perhaps you have read also of those 6000 sheep that suddenly died in Skull Valley, Utah, killed by another nerve poison—a strange and, I believe, still unexplained accident, since the nearest testing seems to have been 30 miles away.

As for Vietnam, the expenditure of fire power has been frightening. Some of you may still remember Khe Sanh, a hamlet just south of the Demilitarized Zone, where a force of U.S. Marines was beleaguered for a time. During that period we dropped on the perimeter of Khe Sanh more explosives than fell on Japan throughout World War II, and more than fell on the whole of Europe during the years 1942 and 1943.

One of the officers there was quoted as having said afterward, "It looks like the world caught smallpox and died." (*N.Y. Times,* Mar. 28, 1968).

The only point of government is to safeguard and foster life. Our government has become preoccupied with death, with the business of killing and being killed. So-called Defense now absorbs 60 percent of the national budget, and about 12 percent of the Gross National Product.

A lively debate is beginning again on whether or not we should deploy antiballistic missiles, the ABM. I don't have to talk about them, everyone else here is doing that. But I should like to mention a curious circumstance. In September, 1967, or about 1½ years ago, we had a meeting of M.I.T. and Harvard people, including experts on these matters, to talk about whether anything could be done to block the Sentinel system, the deployment of ABM's. Everyone present thought them undesirable; but a few of the most knowledgeable persons took what seemed to be the practical view, "Why fight about a dead issue? It has been decided, the funds have been appropriated. Let's go on from there."

Well, fortunately, it's not a dead issue.

An ABM is a nuclear weapon. It takes a nuclear weapon to stop a nuclear weapon. And our concern must be with the whole issue of nuclear weapons.

There is an entire semantics ready to deal with the sort of thing I am about to say. It involves such phrases as "those are the facts of life." No—these are the facts of death. I don't accept them, and I advise you not to accept them. We are under repeated pressures to accept things that are presented to us as settled—decisions that have been made. Always there is the thought: let's go on from there! But this time we don't see how to go on. We will have to stick with those issues.

We are told that the United States and Russia between them have by now stockpiled in nuclear weapons approximately the explosive power of 15 tons of TNT for every man, woman and child on earth. And now it is suggested that we must make more. All very regrettable, of course; but those are "the facts of life." We really would like to disarm; but our new Secretary of Defense has made the ingenious proposal that now is the time to greatly increase our nuclear armaments so that we can disarm from a position of strength.

I think all of you know there is no adequate defense against massive nuclear attack. It is both easier and cheaper to circumvent any known nuclear defense system than to provide it. It's all pretty crazy. At the very moment we talk of deploying ABM's, we are also building the MIRV, the weapon to circumvent ABM's

So far as I know, the most conservative estimates of Americans killed in a major nuclear attack, with everything working as well as can be hoped and all foreseeable precautions taken, run to about 50 millions. We have become callous to gruesome statistics, and this seems at first to be only another gruesome statistic. You think, Bang!—and next morning, if you're still there, you read in the newspapers that 50 million people were killed.

But that isn't the way it happens. When we killed close to 200,000 people with those first little, old-fashioned uranium bombs that we dropped on Hiroshima and Nagasaki, about the same number of persons was maimed, blinded, burned, poisoned and otherwise doomed. A lot of them took a long time to die.

That's the way it would be. Not a bang, and a certain number of corpses to bury; but a nation filled with millions of helpless, maimed, tortured and doomed persons, and the survivors huddled with their families in shelters, with guns ready to fight off their neighbors, trying to get some uncontaminated food and water.

A few months ago Sen. Richard Russell of Georgia ended a speech in the Senate with the words: "If we have to start over again with another Adam and Eve, I want them to be Americans; and I want them on this continent and not in Europe." That was a United States senator holding a patriotic speech. Well, here is a Nobel Laureate who thinks that those words are criminally insane. (Prolonged applause.)

How real is the threat of full scale nuclear war? I have my own very inexpert idea, but realizing how little I know and fearful that I may be a little paranoid on this subject, I take every opportunity to ask reputed experts. I asked that question of a very distinguished professor of government at Harvard about a month ago. I asked him what sort of odds he would lay on the possibility of full-scale nuclear war within the foreseeable future. "Oh," he said comfortably, "I think I can give you a pretty good answer to that question. I estimate the probability of full-scale nuclear war, provided that the situation remains about as it is now, at 2 percent per year." Anybody can do the simple calculation that shows that 2 percent per years means that the chance of having that full-scale nuclear war by 1990 is about one in three, and by 2000 it is about 50-50.

I think I know what is bothering the students. I think that what we are up against is a generation that is by no means sure that it has a future.

I am growing old, and my future so to speak is already behind me. But there are those students of mine who are in my mind always; and there are my children, two of them now 7 and 9, whose future is infinitely more precious to me than my own. So it isn't just their generation; it's mine too. We're all in it together.

Are we to have a chance to live? We don't ask for prosperity, or security; only for a reasonable chance to live, to work out our destiny in peace and decency. Not to go down in history as the apocalyptic generation.

And it isn't only nuclear war. Another overwhelming threat is in the population explosion. That has not yet even begun to come under control. There is every indication that the world population will double before the year 2000; and there is a widespread expectation of famine on an unprecedented scale in many parts of the world. The experts tend to differ only in their estimates of when those famines will begin. Some think by 1980, others think they can be staved off until 1990, very few expect that they will not occur by the year 2000.

That is the problem. Unless we can be surer than we now are that this generation has a future, nothing else matters. It's not good enough to give it tender loving care, to supply it with breakfast foods, to buy it expensive educations. Those things don't mean anything unless this generation has a future. And we're not sure that it does.

I don't think that there are problems of youth, or student problems. All the real problems I know are grown-up problems.

Perhaps you will think me altogether absurd, or "academic", or hopelessly innocent—that is, until you think of the alternatives—if I say as I do to you now: we have to get rid of those nuclear weapons. There is nothing worth having that can be obtained by nuclear war: nothing material or ideological, no tradition that it can defend. It is utterly self-defeating. Those atom bombs represent an unusable weapon. The only use for an atom bomb is to keep somebody else from using it. It can give us no protection, but only the doubtful satisfaction of retaliation. Nuclear weapons offer us nothing but a balance of terror; and a balance of terror is still terror.

We have to get rid of those atomic weapons, here and everywhere. We cannot live with them.

I think we've reached a point of great decision, not just for our nation, not only for all humanity, but for life upon the Earth. I tell my students, with a feeling of pride that I hope they will share, that the carbon, nitrogen and oxygen that make up 99 percent of our living substance, were cooked in the deep interiors of earlier generations of dying stars. Gathered up from the ends of the universe, over billions of years, eventually they came to form in part the substance of our sun, its planets and ourselves. Three billion years ago life arose upon the Earth. It seems to be the only life in the solar system. Many a star has since been born and died.

About two million years ago, man appeared. He has become the dominant species on the Earth. All other living things, animal and plant, live by his sufferance. He is the custodian of life on Earth. It's a big responsibility.

The thought that we're in competition with Russians or with Chinese is all a mistake, and trivial. Only mutual destruction lies that way. We are one species, with a world to win. There's life all over this universe, but in all the universe we are the only men.

Our business is with life, not death. Our challenge is to give what account we can of what becomes of life in the solar system, this corner of the universe that is our home and, most of all, what becomes of men—all men of all nations, colors and creeds. It has become one world, a world for all men. It is only such a world that now can offer us life and the chance to go on.

PHOTOGRAPH BY *Benedict J. Fernandez.*

The Black Revolt

John Hope Franklin's survey of the black man's American experience exemplifies a fairly traditional view of race relations in our country: the problem is defined as separation, and the implied solution is integration.
Martin Luther King, Jr.'s gentle and extraordinarily Christian chiding of his fellow clergymen already sounds as if it came from a distant past. He spoke—sadly—from within the

precincts of Christian fellowship and pleaded—softly—for an end to white patience with injustice. Since his tragic death, the validity of impatience is being tested in the streets.

Malcolm X, another martyr to an assassin's bullet, had all the marks of greatness: a flexible mind, a perceptive imagination, a leader's charisma, and a compassion based on an intimate experience of poverty and degradation. Anyone who still does not understand the black man's desire to be himself should read and reread Malcolm's account of his first "conk." In Cleaver's "The White Race and Its Heroes," we hear the still harsher voice of the new black consciousness. Cleaver has been identified with violence, but his selection should remind us that change, not brutality, is his hope. Whether the one can come without the other is one of the grim questions for the next decade.

The selection from William Grier and Price Cobbs' *Black Rage* is a painful example of special pleading. No doubt being black affects every experience a black man has in America, including his sexual and family life. But all failures, and even all successes, cannot be referred to a single crux; that leads to a determinism that can freeze the instincts and the will. Precisely the point of the black man's present struggle is that he has seen the fallacy of such determinism: his instincts are human, and his will is to break out of a pattern imposed on him by someone else. Finally, interracial sexuality is not always and forever symptomatic. Ordinary and abiding attraction often plays its color-blind part.

In Candice Van Ellison's Introduction to "Harlem on My Mind," we have one more in the necessary series of witnessings about life in the worst of America's ghettos. At the present moment, candor about race relations is received so uneasily that it is not entirely surprising that Miss Ellison's essay has touched off controversy even while it intended to clear the air.

"The Two Worlds of Race: A Historical View"
JOHN HOPE FRANKLIN

I

Measured by universal standards the history of the United States is indeed brief. But during the brief span of three and one-half centuries of colonial and national history Americans developed traditions and prejudices which created the two worlds of race in modern America. From the time that Africans were brought as indentured servants to the mainland of English America in 1619, the enormous task of rationalizing and justifying the forced labor of peoples on the basis of racial differences was begun; and even after legal slavery was ended, the notion of racial differences persisted as a basis for maintaining segregation and discrimination. At the same time, the effort to establish a more healthy basis for the new world social order was begun, thus launching the continuing battle between the two worlds of race, on the one hand, and the world of equality and complete human fellowship, on the other.

For a century before the American Revolution the status of Negroes in the English colonies had become fixed at a low point that distinguished them from all other persons who had been held in temporary bondage. By the middle of the eighteenth century, laws governing Negroes denied to them certain basic rights that were conceded to others. They were permitted no independence of thought, no opportunity to improve their minds or their talents or to worship freely, no right to marry and enjoy the conventional family relationships, no right to own or dispose of property, and no protection against miscarriages of justice or cruel and unreasonable punishments. They were outside the pale of the laws that protected ordinary humans. In most places they were to be governed, as the South Carolina code of 1712 expressed it, by special laws "as may restrain the disorders, rapines, and inhumanity to which they are naturally prone and inclined. . . ." A separate world for them had been established by law and custom. Its dimensions and the conduct of its inhabitants were determined by those living in a quite different world.

By the time that the colonists took up arms against their mother country in order to secure their independence, the world of Negro slavery had become deeply entrenched and the idea of Negro inferiority well established. But the dilemmas inherent in such a situation were a source of constant embarrassment. "It always appeared a most iniquitous scheme to me," Mrs. John Adams wrote her husband in 1774, "to fight ourselves for what we are daily robbing and plundering from those who have as good a right to freedom as we have." There were others who shared her views, but they were unable to wield much influence. When the fighting began General George Washington issued an order to recruiting officers that they were not to enlist "any deserter from the ministerial army, nor any stroller, negro, or vagabond, or person suspected of being an enemy to the liberty of America nor any under eighteen years of age." In classifying Negroes with the dregs of society, traitors, and children, Washington made it clear that Negroes, slave or free, were not to enjoy the high privilege of fighting for political independence. He would change that order later, but only after it became clear that Negroes were enlisting with the "ministerial army" in droves in order to secure their own freedom. In changing his policy if not his views, Washington availed himself of the services of more than 5,000 Negroes who took up arms against England.* [1]

Many Americans besides Mrs. Adams were struck by the inconsistency of their stand during the War for Independence, and they were not averse to making moves to emancipate the slaves. Quakers and other religious groups organized antislavery societies, while numerous individuals manumitted their slaves. In the years following the close of the war most of the states of the East made provisions for the gradual emancipation of slaves. In the South, meanwhile, the antislavery societies were unable to effect programs of state-wide emancipation. When the Southerners came to the Constitutional Convention in 1787 they succeeded in winning some representation on the basis of slavery, in securing federal support of the capture and rendition of fugitive slaves, and in preventing the closing of the slave trade before 1808.

Even where the sentiment favoring emancipation was pronounced, it was seldom accompanied by a view that Negroes were the equals of whites and should become a part of one family of Americans. Jefferson, for example, was opposed to slavery; and if he could have had his way, he would have condemned it in the Declaration of Independence. It did not follow, however, that he believed Negroes to be the equals of whites. He did not want to "degrade a whole race of men from the work in the scale of beings which their Creator may *perhaps* have given them. . . . I advance it therefore, as a suspicion only, that the blacks, whether originally a distinct race, or made distinct by time and circumstance, are inferior to the whites in the endowment both of body and mind." It is entirely possible that Jefferson's later association with the extraordinarily able Negro astronomer and mathematician, Benjamin Banneker, resulted in some modification of his views. After reading a copy of Banneker's almanac, Jefferson told him that it was "a document to which your whole race had a right for its justifications against the doubts which have been entertained of them." [2]

In communities such as Philadelphia and New York, where the climate was more favorably disposed to the idea of Negro equality than in Jefferson's Virginia, few concessions were made, except by a limited number of Quakers and their associates. Indeed, the white citizens in the City of Brotherly Love contributed substantially to the perpetuation of two distinct worlds of race. In the 1780's, the white Methodists permitted Negroes to worship with them, provided the Negroes sat in a designated place in the balcony. On one occasion, when the

* References appear at the end of this selection.

Negro worshippers occupied the front rows of the balcony, from which they had been excluded, the officials pulled them from their knees during prayer and evicted them from the church. Thus, in the early days of the Republic and in the place where the Republic was founded, Negroes had a definite "place" in which they were expected at all times to remain. The white Methodists of New York had much the same attitude toward their Negro fellows. Soon, there were separate Negro churches in these and other communities. Baptists were very much the same. In 1809 thirteen Negro members of a white Baptist church in Philadelphia were dismissed, and they formed a church of their own. Thus, the earliest Negro religious institutions emerged as the result of the rejection by white communicants of their darker fellow worshippers. Soon there would be other institutions—schools, newspapers, benevolent societies—to serve those who lived in a world apart.

Those Americans who conceded the importance of education for Negroes tended to favor some particular type of education that would be in keeping with their lowly station in life. In 1794, for example, the American Convention of Abolition Societies recommended that Negroes be instructed in "those mechanic arts which will keep them most constantly employed and, of course, which will less subject them to idleness and debauchery, and thus prepare them for becoming good citizens of the United States." When Anthony Benezet, a dedicated Pennsylvania abolitionist, died in 1784 his will provided that on the death of his wife the proceeds of his estate should be used to assist in the establishment of a school for Negroes. In 1787 the school of which Benezet had dreamed was opened in Philadelphia, where the pupils studied reading, writing, arithmetic, plain accounts, and sewing.

Americans who were at all interested in the education of Negroes regarded it as both natural and normal that Negroes should receive their training in separate schools. As early as 1773 Newport, Rhode Island, had a colored school, maintained by a society of benevolent clergymen of the Anglican Church. In 1798 a separate private school for Negro children was established in Boston; and two decades later the city opened its first public primary school for the education of Negro children. Meanwhile, New York had established separate schools, the first one opening its doors in 1790. By 1814 there were several such institutions that were generally designated as the New York African Free Schools.[3]

Thus, in the most liberal section of the country, the general view was that Negroes should be kept out of the main stream of American life. They were forced to establish and maintain their own religious institutions, which were frequently followed by the establishment of separate benevolent societies. Likewise, if Negroes were to receive any education, it should be special education provided in separate educational institutions. This principle prevailed in most places in the North throughout the period before the Civil War. In some Massachusetts towns, however, Negroes gained admission to schools that had been maintained for whites. But the School Committee of Boston refused to admit Negroes, arguing that the natural distinction of the races, which "no legislature, no social customs, can efface renders a promiscuous intermingling in the public schools disadvantageous both to them and to the whites." Separate schools remained in Boston until the Massachusetts legislature in 1855 enacted a law providing that in determining the qualifications of students to be admitted to any public school no distinction should be made on account of the race, color, or religious opinion of the applicant.

Meanwhile, in the Southern states, where the vast majority of the Negroes lived, there were no concessions suggesting equal treatment, even among the most liberal elements. One group that would doubtless have regarded itself as liberal on the race question advocated the deportation of Negroes to Africa, especially those who had become free. Since free Negroes "neither enjoyed the immunities of freemen, nor were they subject to the incapacities of slaves," their condition and "unconquerable prejudices" prevented amalgamation with whites, one colonization leader argued. There was, therefore, a "peculiar moral fitness" in restoring them to "the land of their fathers." Men like Henry Clay, Judge Bushrod Washington, and President James Monroe thought that separation—expatriation—was the best thing for Negroes who were or who would become free.[4]

While the colonization scheme was primarily for Negroes who were already free, it won, for a time, a considerable number of sincere enemies of slavery. From the beginning Negroes were bitterly opposed to it, and only infrequently did certain Negro leaders, such as Dr. Martin Delany and the Reverend Henry M. Turner, support the idea. Colonization, however, retained considerable support in the most responsible quarters. As late as the Civil War, President Lincoln urged Congress to adopt a plan to colonize Negroes, as the only workable solution to the race problem in the United States. Whether the advocates of colonization wanted merely to prevent the contamination of slavery by free Negroes or whether they actually regarded it as the just and honorable thing to do, they represented an important element in the population that rejected the idea of the Negro's assimilation into the main stream of American life.

Thus, within fifty years after the Declaration of Independence was written, the institution of slavery, which received only a temporary reversal during the Revolutionary era, contributed greatly to the emergence of the two worlds of race in the United States. The natural rights philosophy appeared to have little effect on those who became committed, more and more, to seeking a rationalization for slavery. The search was apparently so successful that even in areas where slavery was declining, the support for maintaining two worlds of race was strong. Since the Negro church and school emerged in Northern communities where slavery was dying, it may be said that the free society believed almost as strongly in racial separation as it did in racial freedom.

II

The generation preceding the outbreak of the Civil War witnessed the development of a set of defenses of slavery that became the basis for much of the racist doctrine to which some Americans have subscribed from then to the present time. The idea of the inferiority of the Negro enjoyed wide acceptance among

Southerners of all classes and among many Northerners. It was an important ingredient in the theory of society promulgated by Southern thinkers and leaders. It was organized into a body of systematic thought by the scientists and social scientists of the South, out of which emerged a doctrine of racial superiority that justified any kind of control over the slave. In 1826 Dr. Thomas Cooper said that he had not the slightest doubt that Negroes were an "inferior variety of the human species; and not capable of the same improvement as the whites." Dr. S. C. Cartwright of the University of Louisiana insisted that the capacities of the Negro adult for learning were equal to those of a white infant; and the Negro could properly perform certain physiological functions only when under the control of white men. Because of the Negro's inferiority, liberty and republican institutions were not only unsuited to his temperament, but actually inimical to his well-being and happiness.

Like racists in other parts of the world, Southerners sought support for their ideology by developing a common bond with the less privileged. The obvious basis was race; and outside the white race there was to be found no favor from God, no honor or respect from man. By the time that Europeans were reading Gobineau's *Inequality of Races,* Southerners were reading Cartwright's *Slavery in the Light of Ethnology.* In admitting all whites into the pseudo-nobility of race, Cartwright won their enthusiastic support in the struggle to preserve the integrity and honor of *the* race. Professor Thomas R. Dew of the College of William and Mary comforted the lower-class whites by indicating that they could identify with the most privileged and affluent of the community. In the South, he said, "no white man feels such inferiority of rank as to be unworthy of association with those around him. Color alone is here the badge of distinction, the true mark of aristocracy, and all who are white are equal in spite of the variety of occupation." [5]

Many Northerners were not without their own racist views and policies in the turbulent decades before the Civil War. Some, as Professor Louis Filler has observed, displayed a hatred of Negroes that gave them a sense of superiority and an outlet for their frustrations. Others cared nothing one way or the other about Negroes and demanded only that they be kept separate.[6] Even some of the abolitionists themselves were ambivalent on the question of Negro equality. More than one antislavery society was agitated by the suggestion that Negroes be invited to join. Some members thought it reasonable for them to attend, but not to be put on an "equality with ourselves." The New York abolitionist, Lewis Tappan, admitted "that when the subject of acting out our profound principles in treating men irrespective of color is discussed heat is always produced."[7]

In the final years before the beginning of the Civil War, the view that the Negro was different, even inferior, was widely held in the United States. Leaders in both major parties subscribed to the view, while the more extreme racists deplored any suggestion that the Negro could ever prosper as a free man. At Peoria, Illinois, in October 1854, Abraham Lincoln asked what stand the opponents of slavery should take regarding Negroes. "Free them, and make them politically and socially, our equals? My own feelings will not admit of this; and if mine would, we well know that those of the great mass of white people will not.

Whether this feeling accords with justice and sound judgment, is not the sole question, if indeed, it is any part of it. A universal feeling, whether well or ill founded, cannot be safely disregarded. We cannot, then, make them equals."

The Lincoln statement was forthright, and it doubtless represented the views of most Americans in the 1850's. Most of those who heard him or read his speech were of the same opinion as he. In later years, the Peoria pronouncement would be used by those who sought to detract from Lincoln's reputation as a champion of the rights of the Negro. In 1964, the White Citizens' Councils reprinted portions of the speech in large advertisements in the daily press and insisted that Lincoln shared their views on the desirability of maintaining two distinct worlds of race.

Lincoln could not have overcome the nation's strong predisposition toward racial separation if he had tried. And he did not try very hard. When he called for the enlistment of Negro troops, after issuing the Emancipation Proclamation, he was content not only to set Negroes apart in a unit called "U. S. Colored Troops," but also to have Negro privates receive $10 per month including clothing, while whites of the same rank received $13 per month plus clothing. Only the stubborn refusal of many Negro troops to accept discriminatory pay finally forced Congress to equalize compensation for white and Negro soldiers.[8] The fight for union that became also a fight for freedom never became a fight for equality or for the creation of one racial world.

The Lincoln and Johnson plans for settling the problems of peace and freedom never seriously touched on the concomitant problem of equality. To be sure, in 1864 President Lincoln privately raised with the governor of Louisiana the question of the franchise for a limited number of Negroes, but when the governor ignored the question the President let the matter drop. Johnson raised a similar question in 1866, but he admitted that it was merely to frustrate the design of radical reformers who sought a wider franchise for Negroes. During the two years following Appomattox Southern leaders gave not the slightest consideration to permitting any Negroes, regardless of their service to the Union or their education or their property, to share in the political life of their communities. Not only did every Southern state refuse to permit Negroes to vote, but they also refused to provide Negroes with any of the educational opportunities that they were providing for the whites.

The early practice of political disfranchisement and of exclusion from public educational facilities helped to determine subsequent policies that the South adopted regarding Negroes. While a few leaders raised their voices against these policies and practices, it was Negroes themselves who made the most eloquent attacks on such discriminations. As early as May 1865, a group of North Carolina Negroes told President Johnson that some of them had been soldiers and were doing everything possible to learn how to discharge the higher duties of citizenship. "It seems to us that men who are willing on the field of battle to carry the muskets of the Republic, in the days of peace ought to be permitted to carry the ballots; and certainly we cannot understand the justice of denying the elective franchise to men who have been fighting *for* the country, while it is freely given to men who have just returned from *four* years fighting against it." Such pleas fell on deaf ears, however; and it was not until 1867, when Congress was sufficiently outraged by the inhuman black codes, widespread discriminations in the South, and unspeakable forms of violence against Negroes, that new federal legislation sought to correct the evils of the first period of Reconstruction.

The period that we know as Radical Reconstruction had no significant or permanent effect on the status of the Negro in American life. For a period of time, varying from one year to fifteen or twenty years, some Negroes enjoyed the privileges of voting. They gained political ascendancy in a very few communities only temporarily, and they never even began to achieve the status of a ruling class. They made no meaningful steps toward economic independence or even stability; and in no time at all, because of the pressures of the local community and the neglect of the federal government, they were brought under the complete economic subservience of the old ruling class. Organizations such as the Ku Klux Klan were committed to violent action to keep Negroes "in their place" and, having gained respectability through sponsorship by Confederate generals and the like, they proceeded to wreak havoc in the name of white supremacy and protection of white womanhood.[9]

Meanwhile, various forms of segregation and discrimination, developed in the years before the Civil War in order to degrade the half million free Negroes in the United States, were now applied to the four million Negroes who had become free in 1865. Already the churches and the military were completely segregated. For the most part the schools, even in the North, were separate. In the South segregated schools persisted, even in the places where the radicals made a half-hearted attempt to desegregate them. In 1875 Congress enacted a Civil Rights Act to guarantee the enjoyment of equal rights in carriers and all places of public accommodation and amusement. Even before it became law Northern philanthropists succeeded in forcing the deletion of the provision calling for desegregated schools. Soon, because of the massive resistance in the North as well as in the South and the indifferent manner in which the federal government enforced the law, it soon became a dead letter everywhere. When it was declared unconstitutional by the Supreme Court in 1883, there was universal rejoicing, except among the Negroes, one of whom declared that they had been "baptized in ice water."

Neither the Civil War nor the era of Reconstruction made any significant step toward the permanent elimination of racial barriers. The radicals of the post-Civil War years came no closer to the creation of one racial world than the patriots of the Revolutionary years. When Negroes were, for the first time, enrolled in the standing army of the United States, they were placed in separate Negro units. Most of the liberals of the Reconstruction era called for and worked for separate schools for Negroes. Nowhere was there any extensive effort to involve Negroes in the churches and other social institutions of the dominant group. Whatever remained of the old abolitionist fervor, which can hardly be described as unequivocal on the question of true racial equality, was rapidly disappearing. In its place were the sentiments of the business men who wanted peace at any price. Those having common railroad interests or crop-marketing interests or investment interests could and did extend their hands across sectional lines and joined in the task of working together for the common good. In such an atmosphere the practice was to accept the realities of two separate worlds of race. Some even subscribed to the view that there were significant economic advantages in maintaining the two worlds of race.

III

The post-Reconstruction years witnessed a steady deterioration in the status of Negro Americans. These were the years that Professor Rayford Logan has called the "nadir" of the Negro in American life and thought. They were the years when Americans, weary of the crusade that had, for the most part, ended with the outbreak of the Civil War, displayed almost no interest in helping the Negro to achieve equality. The social Darwinists decried the very notion of equality for Negroes, arguing that the lowly place they occupied was natural and normal. The leading literary journals vied with each other in describing Negroes as lazy, idle, improvident, immoral, and criminal.[10] Thomas Dixon's novels, *The Klansman* and *The Leopard's Spots,* and D. W. Griffith's motion picture, "The Birth of A Nation," helped to give Americans a view of the Negro's role in American history that "proved" that he was unfit for citizenship, to say nothing of equality. The dictum of William Graham Sumner and his followers that "stateways cannot change folkways" convinced many Americans that legislating equality and creating one great society where race was irrelevant was out of the question.

But many Americans believed that they *could* legislate inequality; and they proceeded to do precisely that. Beginning in 1890, one Southern state after another revised the suffrage provisions of its constitution in a manner that made it virtually impossible for Negroes to qualify to vote. The new literacy and "understanding" provisions permitted local registrars to disqualify Negroes while permitting white citizens to qualify. Several states, including Louisiana, North Carolina, and Oklahoma, inserted "grandfather clauses" in their constitutions in order to permit persons, who could not otherwise qualify, to vote if their fathers or grandfathers could vote in 1866. (This was such a flagrant discrimination against Negroes, whose ancestors could not vote in 1866, that the United States Supreme Court in 1915 declared the "grandfather clause" unconstitutional.) Then came the Democratic white primary in 1900 that made it impossible for Negroes to participate in local elections in the South, where, by this time, only the Democratic party had any appreciable strength. (After more than a generation of assaults on it, the white primary was finally declared unconstitutional in 1944.)

Inequality was legislated in still another way. Beginning in the 1880's, many states, especially but not exclusively in the South, enacted statutes designed to separate the races. After the Civil Rights Act was declared unconstitutional in

1883 state legislatures were emboldened to enact numerous segregation statutes. When the United States Supreme Court, in the case of Plessy *v.* Ferguson, set forth the "separate but equal" doctrine in 1896, the decision provided a new stimulus for laws to separate the races and, of course, to discriminate against Negroes. In time, Negroes and whites were separated in the use of schools, churches, cemeteries, drinking fountains, restaurants, and all places of public accommodation and amusement. One state enacted a law providing for the separate warehousing of books used by white and Negro children. Another required the telephone company to provide separate telephone booths for white and Negro customers. In most communities housing was racially separated by law or practice.[11]

Where there was no legislation requiring segregation, local practices filled the void. Contradictions and inconsistencies seemed not to disturb those who sought to maintain racial distinctions at all costs. It mattered not that one drive-in snack bar served Negroes only on the inside, while its competitor across the street served Negroes only on the outside. Both were committed to making racial distinctions; and in communities where practices and mores had the force of law, the distinction was everything. Such practices were greatly strengthened when, in 1913, the federal government adopted policies that segregated the races in its offices as well as in its eating and rest-room facilities.

By the time of World War I, Negroes and whites in the South and in parts of the North lived in separate worlds, and the apparatus for keeping the worlds separate was elaborate and complex. Negroes were segregated by law in the public schools of the Southern states, while those in the Northern ghettos were sent to predominantly Negro schools, except where their numbers were insufficient. Scores of Negro newspapers sprang up to provide news of Negroes that the white press consistently ignored. Negroes were as unwanted in the white churches as they had been in the late eighteenth century; and Negro churches of virtually every denomination were the answer for a people who had accepted the white man's religion even as the white man rejected his religious fellowship.

Taking note of the fact that they had been omitted from any serious consideration by the white historians, Negroes began in earnest to write the history of their own experiences as Americans. There had been Negro historians before the Civil War, but none of them had challenged the white historians' efforts to relegate Negroes to a separate, degraded world. In 1882, however, George Washington Williams published his *History of the Negro Race in America* in order to "give the world more correct ideas about the colored people." He wrote, he said, not "as a partisan apologist, but from a love for the truth of history." [12] Soon there were other historical works by Negroes describing their progress and their contributions and arguing that they deserved to be received into the full fellowship of American citizens.

It was in these post-Reconstruction years that some of the most vigorous efforts were made to destroy the two worlds of race. The desperate pleas of Negro historians were merely the more articulate attempts of Negroes to gain complete acceptance in American life. Scores of Negro organizations joined in the struggle to gain protection and recognition of their rights and to eliminate the more sordid practices that characterized the treatment of the Negro world by the white world. Unhappily, the small number of whites who were committed to racial equality dwindled in the post-Reconstruction years, while government at every level showed no interest in eliminating racial separatism. It seemed that Negro voices were indeed crying in the wilderness, but they carried on their attempts to be heard. In 1890 Negroes from twenty-one states and the District of Columbia met in Chicago and organized the Afro-American League of the United States. They called for more equitable distribution of school funds, fair and impartial trial for accused Negroes, resistance "by all legal and reasonable means" to mob and lynch law, and enjoyment of the franchise by all qualified voters. When a group of young Negro intellectuals, led by W. E. B. Du Bois, met at Niagara Falls, Ontario, in 1905, they made a similar call as they launched their Niagara Movement.

However eloquent their pleas, Negroes alone could make no successful assault on the two worlds of race. They needed help—a great deal of help. It was the bloody race riots in the early years of the twentieth century that shocked civic minded and socially conscious whites into answering the Negro's pleas for support. Some whites began to take the view that the existence of two societies whose distinction was based solely on race was inimical to the best interests of the entire nation. Soon, they were taking the initiative and in 1909 organized the National Association for the Advancement of Colored People. They assisted the following year in establishing the National Urban League. White attorneys began to stand with Negroes before the United States Supreme Court to challenge the "grandfather clause," local segregation ordinances, and flagrant miscarriages of justice in which Negroes were the victims. The patterns of attack developed during these years were to become invaluable later. Legal action was soon supplemented by picketing, demonstrating, and boycotting, with telling effect particularly in selected Northern communities.[13]

IV

The two world wars had a profound effect on the status of Negroes in the United States and did much to mount the attack on the two worlds of race. The decade of World War I witnessed a very significant migration of Negroes. They went in large numbers—perhaps a half million—from the rural areas of the South to the towns and cities of the South and North. They were especially attracted to the industrial centers of the North. By the thousands they poured into Pittsburgh, Cleveland, and Chicago. Although many were unable to secure employment, others were successful and achieved a standard of living they could not have imagined only a few years earlier. Northern communities were not altogether friendly and hospitable to the newcomers, but the opportunities for education and the enjoyment of political self-respect were the greatest they had ever seen. Many of them felt that they were entirely justified in their renewed hope that the war would bring about a complete merger of the two worlds of race.

Those who held such high hopes, however, were naive in the extreme. Already the Ku Klux Klan was being revived—this time in the North as well as in the South. Its leaders were determined to develop a broad program to unite "native-born white Christians for concerted action in the preservation of American institutions and the supremacy of the white race." By the time that the war was over, the Klan was in a position to make capital of the racial animosities that had developed during the conflict itself. Racial conflicts had broken out in many places during the war; and before the conference at Versailles was over race riots in the United States had brought about what can accurately be described as the "long, hot summer" of 1919.

If anything, the military operations which aimed to save the world for democracy merely fixed more permanently the racial separation in the United States. Negro soldiers not only constituted entirely separate fighting units in the United States Army, but, once overseas, were assigned to fighting units with the French Army. Negroes who sought service with the United States Marines or the Air Force were rejected, while the Navy relegated them to menial duties. The reaction of many Negroes was bitter, but most of the leaders, including Du Bois, counseled patience and loyalty. They continued to hope that their show of patriotism would win for them a secure place of acceptance as Americans.

Few Negro Americans could have anticipated the wholesale rejection they experienced at the conclusion of World War I. Returning Negro soldiers were lynched by hanging and burning, even while still in their military uniforms. The Klan warned Negroes that they must respect the rights of the white race "in whose country they are permitted to reside." Racial conflicts swept the country, and neither federal nor state governments seemed interested in effective intervention. The worlds of race were growing further apart in the postwar decade. Nothing indicated this more clearly than the growth of the Universal Negro Improvement Association, led by Marcus Garvey. From a mere handful of members at the end of the war, the Garvey movement rapidly became the largest secular Negro group ever organized in the United States. Although few Negroes were interested in settling in Africa—the expressed aim of Garvey—they joined the movement by the hundreds of thousands to indicate their resentment of the racial duality that seemed to them to be the central feature of the American social order.[14]

More realistic and hardheaded were the Negroes who were more determined than ever to engage in the most desperate fight of their lives to destroy racism in the United States. As the editor of the *Crisis* said in 1919, "We return from fighting. We return fighting. Make way for Democracy! We saved it in France, and by the Great Jehovah, we will save it in the U.S.A., or know the reason why." This was the spirit of what Alain Locke called "The New Negro." He fought the Democratic white primary, made war on the whites who consigned him to the ghetto, attacked racial discrimination in employment, and pressed for legislation to protect his rights. If he was seldom successful during the postwar decade and the depression, he made it quite clear that he was unalterably opposed to the un-American character of the two worlds of race.

Hope for a new assault on racism was kindled by some of the New Deal policies of Franklin D. Roosevelt. As members of the economically disadvantaged group, Negroes benefited from relief and recovery legislation. Most of it, however, recognized the existence of the two worlds of race and accommodated itself to it. Frequently bread lines and soup kitchens were separated on the basis of race. There was segregation in the employment services, while many new agencies recognized and bowed to Jim Crow. Whenever agencies, such as the Farm Security Administration, fought segregation and sought to deal with people on the basis of their needs rather than race they came under the withering fire of the racist critics and seldom escaped alive. Winds of change, however slight, were discernible, and nowhere was this in greater evidence than in the new labor unions. Groups like the Congress of Industrial Organizations, encouraged by the support of the Wagner Labor Relations Act, began to look at manpower resources as a whole and to attack the old racial policies that viewed labor in terms of race.

As World War II approached, Negroes schooled in the experiences of the nineteen-twenties and thirties were unwilling to see the fight against Nazism carried on in the context of an American racist ideology. Some white Americans were likewise uncomfortable in the role of freeing Europe of a racism which still permeated the United States; but it was the Negroes who dramatized American inconsistency by demanding an end to discrimination in employment in defense industries. By threatening to march on Washington in 1941 they forced the President to issue an order forbidding such discrimination. The opposition was loud and strong. Some state governors denounced the order, and some manufacturers skillfully evaded it. But it was a significant step toward the elimination of the two worlds.

During World War II the assault on racism continued. Negroes, more than a million of whom were enlisted in the armed services, bitterly fought discrimination and segregation. The armed services were, for the most part, two quite distinct racial worlds. Some Negro units had white officers, and much of the officer training was desegregated. But it was not until the final months of the war that a deliberate experiment was undertaken to involve Negro and white enlisted men in the same fighting unit. With the success of the experiment and with the warm glow of victory over Nazism as a backdrop, there was greater inclination to recognize the absurdity of maintaining a racially separate military force to protect the freedoms of the country.[15]

During the war there began the greatest migration in the history of Negro Americans. Hundreds of thousands left the South for the industrial centers of the North and West. In those places they met hostility, but they also secured employment in aviation plants, automobile factories, steel mills, and numerous other industries. Their difficulties persisted as they faced problems of housing and adjustment. But they continued to move out of the South in such large numbers that by 1965 one third of the twenty million Negroes in the United States lived in twelve metropolitan centers of the North and West. The ramifications of such large-scale migration were numerous. The concentration of Negroes in communities where they suffered no political disabilities placed in their hands an enormous amount of political power. Consequently, some of them went to the legislatures, to Congress, and to positions on the judiciary. In turn, this won for them political respect as well as legislation that greatly strengthened their position as citizens.

V

Following World War II there was a marked acceleration in the war against the two worlds of race in the United States. In 1944 the Supreme Court ruled against segregation in interstate transportation, and three years later it wrote the final chapter in the war against the Democratic white primary. In 1947 the President's Committee on Civil Rights called for the "elimination of segregation, based on race, color, creed, or national origin, from American life." [16] In the following year President Truman asked Congress to establish a permanent Fair Employment Practices Commission. At the same time he took steps to eliminate segregation in the armed services. These moves on the part of the judicial and executive branches of the federal government by no means destroyed the two worlds of race, but they created a more healthy climate in which the government and others could launch an attack on racial separatism.

The attack was greatly strengthened by the new position of world leadership that the United States assumed at the close of the war. Critics of the United States were quick to point to the inconsistencies of an American position that spoke against racism abroad and countenanced it at home. New nations, brown and black, seemed reluctant to follow the lead of a country that adhered to its policy of maintaining two worlds of race—the one identified with the old colonial ruling powers and the other with the colonies now emerging as independent nations. Responsible leaders in the United States saw the weakness of their position, and some of them made new moves to repair it.

Civic and religious groups, some labor organizations, and many individuals from the white community began to join in the effort to destroy segregation and discrimination in American life. There was no danger, after World War II, that Negroes would ever again stand alone in their fight. The older interracial organizations continued, but they were joined by new ones. In addition to the numerous groups that included racial equality in their over-all programs, there were others that made the creation of one racial world their principal objective. Among them were the Congress of Racial Equality, the Southern Christian Leadership Conference, and the Student Non-Violent Coordinating Committee. Those in existence in the 1950's supported the court action that brought about the decision against segregated schools. The more recent ones have taken the lead in pressing for new legislation and in developing new techniques to be used in the war on segregation.

V I

The most powerful direct force in the maintenance of the two worlds of race has been the state and its political subdivisions. In states and communities where racial separation and discrimination are basic to the way of life, the elected officials invariably pledge themselves to the perpetuation of the duality. Indeed, candidates frequently vie with one another in their effort to occupy the most extreme segregationist position possible on the race question. Appointed officials, including the constabulary and, not infrequently, the teachers and school administrators, become auxiliary guardians of the system of racial separation. In such communities Negroes occupy no policy-making positions, exercise no influence over the determination of policy, and are seldom even on the police force. State and local resources, including tax funds, are at the disposal of those who guard the system of segregation and discrimination; and such funds are used to enforce customs as well as laws and to disseminate information in support of the system.

The white community itself acts as a guardian of the segregated system. Schooled in the specious arguments that assert the supremacy of the white race and fearful that a destruction of the system would be harmful to their own position, they not only "go along" with it but, in many cases, enthusiastically support it. Community sanctions are so powerful, moreover, that the independent citizen who would defy the established order would find himself not only ostracized but, worse, the target of economic and political reprisals.

Within the community many self-appointed guardians of white supremacy have emerged at various times. After the Civil War and after World War I it was the Ku Klux Klan, which has shown surprising strength in recent years. After the desegregation decision of the Supreme Court in 1954 it was the White Citizens' Council, which one Southern editor has called the "uptown Ku Klux Klan." From time to time since 1865, it has been the political demagogue, who has not only made capital by urging his election as a sure way to maintain the system but has also encouraged the less responsible elements of the community to take the law into their own hands.

Violence, so much a part of American history and particularly of Southern history, has been an important factor in maintaining the two worlds of race. Intimidation, terror, lynchings, and riots have, in succession, been the handmaiden of political entities whose officials have been unwilling or unable to put an end to it. Violence drove Negroes from the polls in the 1870's and has kept them away in droves since that time. Lynchings, the spectacular rope and faggot kind or the quiet kind of merely "doing away" with some insubordinate Negro, have served their special purpose in terrorizing whole communities of Negroes. Riots, confined to no section of the country, have demonstrated how explosive the racial situation can be in urban communities burdened with the strain of racial strife.

The heavy hand of history has been a powerful force in the maintenance of a segregated society and, conversely, in the resistance to change. Americans, especially Southerners whose devotion to the past is unmatched by that of any others, have summoned history to support their arguments that age-old practices and institutions cannot be changed overnight, that social practices cannot be changed by legislation. Southerners have argued that desegregation would break down long-established customs and bring instability to a social order that, if left alone, would have no serious racial or social disorders. After all, Southern whites "know" Negroes; and their knowledge has come from many generations of intimate association and observation, they insist.

White Southerners have also summoned history to support them in their resistance to federal legislation designed to secure the civil rights of Negroes. At every level—in local groups, state governments, and in Congress—white Southerners have asserted that federal civil rights legislation is an attempt to turn back the clock to the Reconstruction era, when federal intervention, they claim, imposed a harsh and unjust peace.[17] To make effective their argument, they use such emotion-laden phrases as "military occupation," "Negro rule," and "black-out of honest government." Americans other than Southerners have been frightened by the Southerners' claim that civil rights for Negroes would cause a return to the "evils" of Reconstruction. Insecure in their own knowledge of history, they have accepted the erroneous assertions about the "disaster" of radical rule after the Civil War and the vengeful punishment meted out to the South by the Negro and his white allies. Regardless of the merits of these arguments that seem specious on the face of them—to say nothing of their historical inaccuracy—they have served as effective brakes on the drive to destroy the two worlds of race.

One suspects, however, that racial bigotry has become more expensive in recent years. It is not so easy now as it once was to make political capital out of the race problem, even in the deep South. Local citizens—farmers, laborers, manufacturers—have become a bit weary of the promises of the demagogue that he will preserve the integrity of the races if he is, at the same time, unable to persuade investors to build factories and bring capital to their communities. Some Southerners, dependent on tourists, are not certain that their vaunted racial pride is so dear, if it keeps visitors away and brings depression to their economy. The cities that see themselves bypassed by a prospective manufacturer because of their reputation in the field of race relations might have some sober second thoughts about the importance of maintaining their two worlds. In a word, the economics of segregation and discrimination is forcing, in some quarters, a reconsideration of the problem.

It must be added that the existence of the two worlds of race has created forces that cause some Negroes to seek its perpetuation. Some Negro institutions, the product of a dual society, have vested interests in the perpetuation of that society. And Negroes who fear the destruction of their own institutions by desegregation are encouraged by white racists to fight for their maintenance. Even where Negroes have a desire to maintain their institutions because of their honest commitment to the merits of cultural pluralism, the desire becomes a strident struggle for survival in the context of racist forces that seek with a vengeance to destroy such institutions. The firing of a few hundred Negro school teachers by a zealous, racially-oriented school board forces some second thoughts on the part of the Negroes regarding the merits of desegregation.

VII

The drive to destroy the two worlds of race has reached a new, dramatic, and somewhat explosive stage in recent years. The forces arrayed in behalf of maintaining these two worlds have been subjected to ceaseless and powerful attacks by the increasing numbers committed to the elimination of racism in American life. Through techniques of demonstrating, picketing, sitting-in, and boycotting they have not only harassed their foes but marshaled their forces. Realizing that another ingredient was needed, they have pressed for new and better laws and the active support of government. At the local and state levels they began to secure legislation in the 1940's to guarantee the civil rights of all, eliminate discrimination in employment, and achieve decent public and private housing for all.

While it is not possible to measure the influence of public opinion in the drive for equality, it can hardly be denied that over the past five or six years public opinion has shown a marked shift toward vigorous support of the civil rights movement. This can be seen in the manner in which the mass-circulation magazines as well as influential newspapers, even in the South, have stepped up their support of specific measures that have as their objective the elimination of at least the worst features of racism. The discussion of the problem of race over radio and television and the use of these media in reporting newsworthy and dramatic events in the world of race undoubtedly have had some impact. If such activities have not brought about the enactment of civil rights legislation, they have doubtless stimulated the public discussion that culminated in such legislation.

The models of city ordinances and state laws and the increased political influence of civil rights advocates stimulated new action on the federal level. Civil rights acts were passed in 1957, 1960, and 1964—after almost complete federal inactivity in this sphere for more than three quarters of a century. Strong leadership on the part of the executive and favorable judicial interpretations of old as well as new laws have made it clear that the war against the two worlds of race now enjoys the sanction of the law and its interpreters. In many respects this constitutes the most significant development in the struggle against racism in the present century.

The reading of American history over the past two centuries impresses one with the fact that ambivalence on the crucial question of equality has persisted almost from the beginning. If the term "equal rights for all" has not always meant what it appeared to mean, the inconsistencies and the paradoxes have become increasingly apparent. This is not to say that the view that "equal rights for some" has disappeared or has even ceased to be a threat to the concept of real equality. It is to say, however, that the voices supporting inequality, while no less strident, have been significantly weakened by the very force of the numbers and elements now seeking to eliminate the two worlds of race.

References

1 Benjamin Quarles, *The Negro in the American Revolution* (Chapel Hill, N.C., 1961), pp. 15-18.

2 John Hope Franklin, *From Slavery to Freedom: A History of American Negroes* (New York, 1956), pp. 156-157.

3 Carter G. Woodson, *The Education of the Negro Prior to 1861* (Washington, D.C., 1919), pp. 93-97.

4 P. J. Staudenraus, *The African Colonization Movement, 1816-1865* (New York, 1961), pp. 22-32.

5 John Hope Franklin, *The Militant South, 1800-1861* (Cambridge, Mass., 1956), pp. 83-86.

6 Louis Filler, *The Crusade Against Slavery, 1830-1860* (New York, 1960), pp. 142-145.

7 Leon F. Litwack, *North of Slavery; The Negro in the Free States, 1790-1860* (Chicago, 1961), pp. 216-217.

8 Benjamin Quarles, *The Negro in the Civil War* (Boston, 1953), p. 200.

9 John Hope Franklin, *Reconstruction After the Civil War* (Chicago, 1961), pp. 154-158.

10 Rayford W. Logan, *The Negro in American Life and Thought: The Nadir, 1877-1901* (New York, 1954), pp. 239-274.

11 John Hope Franklin, "History of Racial Segregation in the United States," *Annals of the Academy of Political and Social Science,* Vol. 304 (March 1956), pp. 1-9.

12 George W. Williams, *History of the Negro Race in America from 1619 to 1880* (New York, 1882), p. x.

13 Franklin, *From Slavery to Freedom,* pp. 437-443.

14 Edmund David Cronon, *Black Moses, The Story of Marcus Garvey and the Universal Negro Improvement Association* (Madison, Wis., 1955), pp. 202-206.

15 Lee Nichols, *Breakthrough on the Color Front* (New York, 1954), pp. 221-226.

16 *To Secure These Rights, The Report of the President's Committee on Civil Rights* (New York, 1947), p. 166.

17 John Hope Franklin, "As For Our History," in Charles G. Sellers (ed.), *The Southerner as American* (Chapel Hill, N.C., 1960), pp. 1-18.

Letter from Birmingham Jail*
MARTIN LUTHER KING, JR.

April 16, 1963

My *Dear Fellow Clergymen:*

While confined here in the Birmingham city jail, I came across your recent statement calling my present activities "unwise and untimely." Seldom do I pause to answer criticism of my work and ideas. If I sought to answer all the criticisms that cross my desk, my secretaries would have little time for anything other than such correspondence in the course of the day, and I would have no time for constructive work. But since I feel that you are men of genuine good will and that your criticisms are sincerely set forth, I want to try to answer your statement in what I hope will be patient and reasonable terms.

I think I should indicate why I am here in Birmingham, since you have been influenced by the view which argues against "outsiders coming in." I have the honor of serving as president of the Southern Christian Leadership Conference, an organization operating in every southern state, with headquarters in Atlanta, Georgia. We have some eighty-five affiliated organizations across the South, and one of them is the Alabama Christian Movement for Human Rights. Frequently we share staff, educational and financial resources with our affiliates. Several months ago the affiliate here in Birmingham asked us to be on call to engage in a nonviolent direct-action program if such were deemed necessary. We readily consented, and when the hour came we lived up to our promise. So I, along with several members of my staff, am here because I was invited here. I am here because I have organizational ties here.

But more basically, I am in Birmingham because injustice is here. Just as the prophets of the eighth century B.C. left their villages and carried their "thus saith the Lord" far beyond the boundaries of their home towns, and just as the Apostle Paul left his village of Tarsus and carried the gospel of Jesus Christ to the far corners of the Greco-Roman world, so am I compelled to carry the gospel of freedom beyond my own home town. Like Paul, I must constantly respond to the Macedonian call for aid.

Moreover, I am cognizant of the interrelatedness of all communities and states. I cannot sit idly by in Atlanta and not be concerned about what happens in Birmingham. Injustice anywhere is a threat to justice everywhere. We are caught in an inescapable network of mutuality, tied in a single garment of destiny.

---

* AUTHOR'S NOTE: This response to a published statement by eight fellow clergymen from Alabama (Bishop C. C. J. Carpenter, Bishop Joseph A. Durick, Rabbi Hilton L. Grafman, Bishop Paul Hardin, Bishop Holan B. Harmon, the Reverend George M. Murray, the Reverend Edward V. Ramage and the Reverend Earl Stallings) was composed under somewhat constricting circumstances. Begun on the margins of the newspaper in which the statement appeared while I was in jail, the letter was continued on scraps of writing paper supplied by a friendly Negro trusty, and concluded on a pad my attorneys were eventually permitted to leave me. Although the text remains in substance unaltered, I have indulged in the author's prerogative of polishing it for publication.

Whatever affects one directly, affects all indirectly. Never again can we afford to live with the narrow, provincial "outside agitator" idea. Anyone who lives inside the United States can never be considered an outsider anywhere within its bounds.

You deplore the demonstrations taking place in Birmingham. But your statement, I am sorry to say, fails to express a similar concern for the conditions that brought about the demonstrations. I am sure that none of you would want to rest content with the superficial kind of social analysis that deals merely with effects and does not grapple with underlying causes. It is unfortunate that demonstrations are taking place in Birmingham, but it is even more unfortunate that the city's white power structure left the Negro community with no alternative.

In any nonviolent campaign there are four basic steps: collection of the facts to determine whether injustices exist; negotiation; self-purification; and direct action. We have gone through all these steps in Birmingham. There can be no gainsaying the fact that racial injustice engulfs this community. Birmingham is probably the most thoroughly segregated city in the United States. Its ugly record of brutality is widely known. Negroes have experienced grossly unjust treatment in the courts. There have been more unsolved bombings of Negro homes and churches in Birmingham than in any other city in the nation. These are the hard, brutal facts of the case. On the basis of these conditions, Negro leaders sought to negotiate with the city fathers. But the latter consistently refused to engage in good-faith negotiation.

Then, last September, came the opportunity to talk with leaders of Birmingham's economic community. In the course of the negotiations, certain promises were made by the merchants—for example, to remove the stores' humiliating racial signs. On the basis of these promises, the Reverend Fred Shuttlesworth and the leaders of the Alabama Christian Movement for Human Rights agreed to a moratorium on all demonstrations. As the weeks and months went by, we realized that we were the victims of a broken promise. A few signs, briefly removed, returned; the others remained.

As in so many past experiences, our hopes had been blasted, and the shadow of deep disappointment settled upon us. We had no alternative except to prepare for direct action, whereby we would present our very bodies as a means of laying our case before the conscience of the local and the national community. Mindful of the difficulties involved, we decided to undertake a process of self-purification. We began a series of workshops on nonviolence, and we repeatedly asked ourselves: "Are you able to accept blows without retaliating?" "Are you able to endure the ordeal of jail?" We decided to schedule our direct-action program for the Easter season, realizing that except for Christmas, this is the main shopping period of the year. Knowing that a strong economic-withdrawal program would be the by-product of direct action, we felt that this would be the best time to bring pressure to bear on the merchants for the needed change.

Then it occurred to us that Birmingham's mayoralty election was coming up in March, and we speedily decided to postpone action until after election day.

When we discovered that the Commissioner of Public Safety, Eugene "Bull" Connor, had piled up enough votes to be in the run-off, we decided again to postpone action until the day after the run-off so that the demonstrations could not be used to cloud the issues. Like many others, we waited to see Mr. Connor defeated, and to this end we endured postponement after postponement. Having aided in this community need, we felt that our direct-action program could be delayed no longer.

You may well ask: "Why direct action? Why sit-ins, marches and so forth? Isn't negotiation a better path?" You are quite right in calling for negotiation. Indeed, this is the very purpose of direct action. Nonviolent direct action seeks to create such a crisis and foster such a tension that a community which has constantly refused to negotiate is forced to confront the issue. It seeks so to dramatize the issue that it can no longer be ignored. My citing the creation of tension as part of the work of the nonviolent-resister may sound rather shocking. But I must confess that I am not afraid of the word "tension." I have earnestly opposed violent tension, but there is a type of constructive, nonviolent tension which is necessary for growth. Just as Socrates felt that it was necessary to create a tension in the mind so that individuals could rise from the bondage of myths and half-truths to the unfettered realm of creative analysis and objective appraisal, so must we see the need for nonviolent gadflies to create the kind of tension in society that will help men rise from the dark depths of prejudice and racism to the majestic heights of understanding and brotherhood.

The purpose of our direct-action program is to create a situation so crisis-packed that it will inevitably open the door to negotiation. I therefore concur with you in your call for negotiation. Too long has our beloved Southland been bogged down in a tragic effort to live in monologue rather than dialogue.

One of the basic points in your statement is that the action that I and my associates have taken in Birmingham is untimely. Some have asked: "Why didn't you give the new city administration time to act?" The only answer that I can give to this query is that the new Birmingham administration must be prodded about as much as the outgoing one, before it will act. We are sadly mistaken if we feel that the election of Albert Boutwell as mayor will bring the millennium to Birmingham. While Mr. Boutwell is a much more gentle person than Mr. Connor, they are both segregationists, dedicated to maintenance of the status quo. I have hope that Mr. Boutwell will be reasonable enough to see the futility of massive resistance to desegregation. But he will not see this without pressure from devotees of civil rights. My friends, I must say to you that we have not made a single gain in civil rights without determined legal and nonviolent pressure. Lamentably, it is an historical fact that privileged groups seldom give up their privileges voluntarily. Individuals may see the moral light and voluntarily give up their unjust posture; but, as Reinhold Niebuhr has reminded us, groups tend to be more immoral than individuals.

We know through painful experience that freedom is never voluntarily given by the oppressor; it must be demanded by the oppressed. Frankly, I have yet to engage in a direct-action campaign that was "well timed" in the view of those who have not suffered unduly from the disease of segregation. For years now I have heard the word "Wait!" It rings in the ear of every Negro with piercing familiarity. This "Wait" has almost always meant "Never." We must come to see, with one of our distinguished jurists, that "justice too long delayed is justice denied."

We have waited for more than 340 years for our constitutional and God-given rights. The nations of Asia and Africa are moving with jetlike speed toward gaining political independence, but we still creep at horse-and-buggy pace toward gaining a cup of coffee at a lunch counter. Perhaps it is easy for those who have never felt the stinging darts of segregation to say, "Wait." But when you have seen vicious mobs lynch your mothers and fathers at will and drown your sisters and brothers at whim; when you have seen hate-filled policemen curse, kick and even kill your black brothers and sisters; when you see the vast majority of your twenty million Negro brothers smothering in an airtight cage of poverty in the midst of an affluent society; when you suddenly find your tongue twisted and your speech stammering as you seek to explain to your six-year-old daughter why she can't go to the public amusement park that has just been advertised on television, and see tears welling up in her eyes when she is told that Funtown is closed to colored children, and see ominous clouds of inferiority beginning to form in her little mental sky, and see her beginning to distort her personality by developing an unconscious bitterness toward white people; when you have to concoct an answer for a five-year-old son who is asking: "Daddy, why do white people treat colored people so mean?"; when you take a cross-country drive and find it necessary to sleep night after night in the uncomfortable corners of your automobile because no motel will accept you; when you are humiliated day in and day out by nagging signs reading "white" and "colored"; when your first name becomes "nigger," your middle name becomes "boy" (however old you are) and your last name becomes "John," and your wife and mother are never given the respected title "Mrs."; when you are harried by day and haunted by night by the fact that you are a Negro, living constantly at tiptoe stance, never quite knowing what to expect next, and are plagued with inner fears and outer resentments; when you are forever fighting a degenerating sense of "nobodiness"—then you will understand why we find it difficult to wait. There comes a time when the cup of endurance runs over, and men are no longer willing to be plunged into the abyss of despair. I hope, sirs, you can understand our legitimate and unavoidable impatience.

You express a great deal of anxiety over our willingness to break laws. This is certainly a legitimate concern. Since we so diligently urge people to obey the Supreme Court's decision of 1954 outlawing segregation in the public schools, at first glance it may seem rather paradoxical for us consciously to break laws. One may well ask: "How can you advocate breaking some laws and obeying others?" The answer lies in the fact that there are two types of laws: just and unjust. I would be the first to advocate obeying just laws. One has not only a legal but a moral responsibility to obey just laws. Conversely, one has a moral responsibility to disobey unjust laws. I would agree with St. Augustine that "an unjust law is no law at all."

Now, what is the difference between the two? How does one determine whether a law is just or unjust? A just law is a man-made code that squares with the moral law or the law of God. An unjust law is a code that is out of harmony with the moral law. To put it in the terms of St. Thomas Aquinas: An unjust law is a human law that is not rooted in eternal law and natural law. Any law that uplifts human personality is just. Any law that degrades human personality is unjust. All segregation statutes are unjust because segregation distorts the soul and damages the personality. It gives the segregator a false sense of superiority and the segregated a false sense of inferiority. Segregation, to use the terminology of the Jewish philosopher Martin Buber, substitutes an "I-it" relationship for an "I-thou" relationship and ends up relegating persons to the status of things. Hence segregation is not only politically, economically and sociologically unsound, it is morally wrong and sinful. Paul Tillich has said that sin is separation. Is not segregation an existential expression of man's tragic separation, his awful estrangement, his terrible sinfulness? Thus it is that I can urge men to obey the 1954 decision of the Supreme Court, for it is morally right; and I can urge them to disobey segregation ordinances, for they are morally wrong.

Let us consider a more concrete example of just and unjust laws. An unjust law is a code that a numerical or power majority group compels a minority group to obey but does not make binding on itself. This is *difference* made legal. By the same token, a just law is a code that a majority compels a minority to follow and that it is willing to follow itself. This is *sameness* made legal.

Let me give another explanation. A law is unjust if it is inflicted on a minority that, as a result of being denied the right to vote, had no part in enacting or devising the law. Who can say that the legislature of Alabama which set up that state's segregation laws was democratically elected? Throughout Alabama all sorts of devious methods are used to prevent Negroes from becoming registered voters, and there are some counties in which, even though Negroes constitute a majority of the population, not a single Negro is registered. Can any law enacted under such circumstances be considered democratically structured?

Sometimes a law is just on its face and unjust in its application. For instance, I have been arrested on a charge of parading without a permit. Now, there is nothing wrong in having an ordinance which requires a permit for a parade. But such an ordinance becomes unjust when it is used to maintain segregation and to deny citizens the First-Amendment privilege of peaceful assembly and protest.

I hope you are able to see the distinction I am trying to point out. In no sense do I advocate evading or defying the law, as would the rabid segregationist. That would lead to anarchy. One who breaks an unjust law must do so openly, lovingly, and with a willingness to accept the penalty. I submit that an individual who breaks a law that conscience tells him is unjust, and who willingly accepts the penalty of imprisonment in order to arouse the conscience of the community over its injustice, is in reality expressing the highest respect for law.

Of course, there is nothing new about this kind of civil disobedience. It was evidenced sublimely in the refusal of Shadrach, Meshach and Abednego to obey the laws of Nebuchadnezzar, on the ground that a higher moral law was at stake. It was practiced superbly by the early Christians, who were willing to face hungry lions and the excruciating pain of chopping blocks rather than submit to certain unjust laws of the Roman Empire. To a degree, academic freedom is a reality today because Socrates practiced civil disobedience. In our own nation, the Boston Tea Party represented a massive act of civil disobedience.

We should never forget that everything Adolf Hitler did in Germany was "legal" and everything the Hungarian freedom fighters did in Hungary was "illegal." It was "illegal" to aid and comfort a Jew in Hitler's Germany. Even so, I am sure that, had I lived in Germany at the time, I would have aided and comforted my Jewish brothers. If today I lived in a Communist country where certain principles dear to the Christian faith are suppressed, I would openly advocate disobeying that country's antireligious laws.

I must make two honest confessions to you, my Christian and Jewish brothers. First, I must confess that over the past few years I have been gravely disappointed with the white moderate. I have almost reached the regrettable conclusion that the Negro's great stumbling block in his stride toward freedom is not the White Citizen's Counciler or the Ku Klux Klanner, but the white moderate, who is more devoted to "order" than to justice; who prefers a negative peace which is the absence of tension to a positive peace which is the presence of justice; who constantly says: "I agree with you in the goal you seek, but I cannot agree with your methods of direct action"; who paternalistically believes he can set the timetable for another man's freedom; who lives by a mythical concept of time and who constantly advises the Negro to wait for a "more convenient season." Shallow understanding from people of good will is more frustrating than absolute misunderstanding from people of ill will. Lukewarm acceptance is much more bewildering than outright rejection.

I had hoped that the white moderate would understand that law and order exist for the purpose of establishing justice and that when they fail in this purpose they become the dangerously structured dams that block the flow of social progress. I had hoped that the white moderate would understand that the present tension in the South is a necessary phase of the transition from an obnoxious negative peace, in which the Negro passively accepted his unjust plight, to a substantive and positive peace, in which all men will respect the dignity and worth of human personality. Actually, we who engage in nonviolent direct action are not the creators of tension. We merely bring to the surface the hidden tension that is already alive. We bring it out in the open, where it can be seen and dealt with. Like a boil that can never be cured so long as it is covered up but must be opened with all its ugliness to the natural medicines of air and light, injustice must be exposed, with all the tension its exposure creates, to the light of human conscience and the air of national opinion before it can be cured.

In your statement you assert that our actions, even though peaceful, must be condemned because they precipitate violence. But is this a logical assertion? Isn't this like condemning a robbed man because his possession of money precipitated the evil act of robbery? Isn't this like condemning Socrates because his unswerving commitment to truth and his philosophical inquiries precipitated the act by the misguided populace in which they made him drink hemlock? Isn't this like condemning Jesus because his unique God-consciousness and never-ceasing devotion to God's will precipitated the evil act of crucifixion? We must come to see that, as the federal courts have consistently affirmed, it is wrong to urge an individual to cease his efforts to gain his basic constitutional rights because the quest may precipitate violence. Society must protect the robbed and punish the robber.

I had also hoped that the white moderate would reject the myth concerning time in relation to the struggle for freedom. I have just received a letter from a white brother in Texas. He writes: "All Christians know that the colored people will receive equal rights eventually, but it is possible that you are in too great a religious hurry. It has taken Christianity almost two thousand years to accomplish what it has. The teachings of Christ take time to come to earth." Such an attitude stems from a tragic misconception of time, from the strangely irrational notion that there is something in the very flow of time that will inevitably cure all ills. Actually, time itself is neutral; it can be used either destructively or constructively. More and more I feel that the people of ill will have used time much more effectively than have the people of good will. We will have to repent in this generation not merely for the hateful words and actions of the bad people but for the appalling silence of the good people. Human progress never rolls in on wheels of inevitability; it comes through the tireless efforts of men willing to be co-workers with God, and without this hard work, time itself becomes an ally of the forces of social stagnation. We must use time creatively, in the knowledge that the time is always ripe to do right. Now is the time to make real the promise of democracy and transform our pending national elegy into a creative psalm of brotherhood. Now is the time to lift our national policy from the quicksand of racial injustice to the solid rock of human dignity.

You speak of our activity in Birmingham as extreme. At first I was rather disappointed that fellow clergymen would see my nonviolent efforts as those of an extremist. I began thinking about the fact that I stand in the middle of two opposing forces in the Negro community. One is a force of complacency, made up in part of Negroes who, as a result of long years of oppression, are so drained of self-respect and a sense of "somebodiness" that they have adjusted to segregation; and in part of a few middle-class Negroes who, because of a degree of academic and economic security and because in some ways they profit by segregation, have become insensitive to the problems of the masses. The other force is one of bitterness and hatred, and it comes perilously close to advocating violence. It is expressed in the various black nationalist groups that are springing up across the nation, the largest and best-known being Elijah Muhammad's Muslim movement. Nourished by the Negro's frustration over the continued existence of racial discrimination, this movement is made up of people who have lost faith in America, who have absolutely repudiated Christianity, and who have concluded that the white man is an incorrigible "devil."

I have tried to stand between these two forces, saying that we need emulate neither the "do-nothingism" of the complacent nor the hatred and despair of the black nationalist. For there is the more excellent way of love and nonviolent protest. I am grateful to God that, through the influence of the Negro church, the way of nonviolence became an integral part of our struggle.

If this philosophy had not emerged, by now many streets of the South would, I am convinced, be flowing with blood. And I am further convinced that if our white brothers dismiss as "rabble-rousers" and "outside agitators" those of us who employ nonviolent direct action, and if they refuse to support our nonviolent efforts, millions of Negroes will, out of frustration and despair, seek solace and security in black-nationalist ideologies—a development that would inevitably lead to a frightening racial nightmare.

Oppressed people cannot remain oppressed forever. The yearning for freedom eventually manifests itself, and that is what has happened to the American Negro. Something within has reminded him of his birthright of freedom, and something without has reminded him that it can be gained. Consciously or unconsciously, he has been caught up by the *Zeitgeist,* and with his black brothers of Africa and his brown and yellow brothers of Asia, South America and the Caribbean, the United States Negro is moving with a sense of great urgency toward the promised land of racial justice. If one recognizes this vital urge that has engulfed the Negro community, one should readily understand why public demonstrations are taking place. The Negro has many pent-up resentments and latent frustrations, and he must release them. So let him march; let him make prayer pilgrimages to the city hall; let him go on freedom rides—and try to understand why he must do so. If his repressed emotions are not released in nonviolent ways, they will seek expression through violence; this is not a threat but a fact of history. So I have not said to my people: "Get rid of your discontent." Rather, I have tried to say that this normal and healthy discontent can be channeled into the creative outlet of nonviolent direct action. And now this approach is being termed extremist.

But though I was initially disappointed at being categorized as an extremist, as I continued to think about the matter I gradually gained a measure of satisfaction from the label. Was not Jesus an extremist for love: "Love your enemies, bless them that curse you, do good to them that hate you, and pray for them which despitefully use you, and persecute you." Was not Amos an extremist for justice: "Let justice roll down like waters and righteousness like an ever-flowing stream." Was not Paul an extremist for the Christian gospel: "I bear in my body the marks of the Lord Jesus." Was not Martin Luther an extremist: "Here I stand; I cannot do otherwise, so help me God." And John Bunyan: "I will stay in jail to the end of my days before I make a butchery of my conscience." And Abraham Lincoln: "This nation cannot survive half slave and half free." And Thomas Jefferson: "We hold these truths to be self-evident, that all men are created equal . . ." So the question is not whether we will be extremists, but what kind of extremists we will be. Will we be extremists for hate or for love? Will we be extremists for the preservation of injustice or for the extension of justice? In that dramatic scene on Calvary's hill three men were crucified. We must never forget that all three were crucified for the same crime—the crime of extremism.

Two were extremists for immorality, and thus fell below their environment. The other, Jesus Christ, was an extremist for love, truth and goodness, and thereby rose above his environment. Perhaps the South, the nation and the world are in dire need of creative extremists.

I had hoped that the white moderate would see this need. Perhaps I was too optimistic; perhaps I expected too much. I suppose I should have realized that few members of the oppressor race can understand the deep groans and passionate yearnings of the oppressed race, and still fewer have the vision to see that injustice must be rooted out by strong, persistent and determined action. I am thankful, however, that some of our white brothers in the South have grasped the meaning of this social revolution and committed themselves to it. They are still all too few in quantity, but they are big in quality. Some—such as Ralph McGill, Lillian Smith, Harry Golden, James McBride Dabbs, Ann Braden and Sarah Patton Boyle—have written about our struggle in eloquent and prophetic terms. Others have marched with us down nameless streets of the South. They have languished in filthy, roach-infested jails, suffering the abuse and brutality of policemen who view them as "dirty nigger-lovers." Unlike so many of their moderate brothers and sisters, they have recognized the urgency of the moment and sensed the need for powerful "action" antidotes to combat the disease of segregation.

Let me take note of my other major disappointment. I have been so greatly disappointed with the white church and its leadership. Of course, there are some notable exceptions. I am not unmindful of the fact that each of you has taken some significant stands on this issue. I commend you, Reverend Stallings, for your Christian stand on this past Sunday, in welcoming Negroes to your worship service on a nonsegregated basis. I commend the Catholic leaders of this state for integrating Spring Hill College several years ago.

But despite these notable exceptions, I must honestly reiterate that I have been disappointed with the church. I do not say this as one of those negative critics who can always find something wrong with the church. I say this as a minister of the gospel, who loves the church; who was nurtured in its bosom; who has been sustained by its spiritual blessings and who will remain true to it as long as the cord of life shall lengthen.

When I was suddenly catapulted into the leadership of the bus protest in Montgomery, Alabama, a few years ago, I felt we would be supported by the white church. I felt that the white ministers, priests and rabbis of the South would be among our strongest allies. Instead, some have been outright opponents, refusing to understand the freedom movement and misrepresenting its leaders; all too many others have been more cautious than courageous and have remained silent behind the anesthetizing security of stained-glass windows.

In spite of my shattered dreams, I came to Birmingham with the hope that the white religious leadership of this community would see the justice of our cause and, with deep moral concern, would serve as the channel through which our just grievances could reach the power structure. I had hoped that each of you would understand. But again I have been disappointed.

I have heard numerous southern religious leaders admonish their worshipers to comply with a desegregation decision because it is the law, but I have longed to hear white ministers declare: "Follow this decree because integration is morally right and because the Negro is your brother." In the midst of blatant injustices inflicted upon the Negro, I have watched white churchmen stand on the sideline and mouth pious irrelevancies and sanctimonious trivialities. In the midst of a mighty struggle to rid our nation of racial and economic injustice, I have heard many ministers say: "Those are social issues, with which the gospel has no real concern." And I have watched many churches commit themselves to a completely other-worldly religion which makes a strange, un-Biblical distinction between body and soul, between the sacred and the secular.

I have traveled the length and breadth of Alabama, Mississippi and all the other southern states. On sweltering summer days and crisp autumn mornings I have looked at the South's beautiful churches with their lofty spires pointing heavenward. I have beheld the impressive outlines of her massive religious-education buildings. Over and over I have found myself asking: "What kind of people worship here? Who is their God? Where were their voices when the lips of Governor Barnett dripped with words of interposition and nullification? Where were they when Governor Wallace gave a clarion call for defiance and hatred? Where were their voices of support when bruised and weary Negro men and women decided to rise from the dark dungeons of complacency to the bright hills of creative protest?"

Yes, these questions are still in my mind. In deep disappointment I have wept over the laxity of the church. But be assured that my tears have been tears of love. There can be no deep disappointment where there is not deep love. Yes, I love the church. How could I do otherwise? I am in the rather unique position of being the son, the grandson and the great-grandson of preachers. Yes, I see the church as the body of Christ. But, oh! How we have blemished and scarred that body through social neglect and through fear of being nonconformists.

There was a time when the church was very powerful—in the time when the early Christians rejoiced at being deemed worthy to suffer for what they believed. In those days the church was not merely a thermometer that recorded the ideas and principles of popular opinion; it was a thermostat that transformed the mores of society. Whenever the early Christians entered a town, the people in power became disturbed and immediately sought to convict the Christians for being "disturbers of the peace" and "outside agitators." But the Christians pressed on, in the conviction that they were "a colony of heaven," called to obey God rather than man. Small in number, they were big in commitment. They were too God-intoxicated to be "astronomically intimidated." By their effort and example they brought an end to such ancient evils as infanticide and gladiatorial contests.

Things are different now. So often the contemporary church is a weak, ineffectual voice with an uncertain sound. So often it is an archdefender of the status quo. Far from being disturbed by the presence of the church, the power structure of the average community is consoled by the church's silent—and often even vocal—sanction of things as they are.

But the judgment of God is upon the church as never before. If today's church does not recapture the sacrificial spirit of the early church, it will lose its authenticity, forfeit the loyalty of millions, and be dismissed as an irrelevant social club with no meaning for the twentieth century. Every day I meet young people whose disappointment with the church has turned into outright disgust.

Perhaps I have once again been too optimistic. Is organized religion too inextricably bound to the status quo to save our nation and the world? Perhaps I must turn my faith to the inner spiritual church, the church within the church, as the true *ekklesia* and the hope of the world. But again I am thankful to God that some noble souls from the ranks of organized religion have broken loose from the paralyzing chains of conformity and joined us as active partners in the struggle for freedom. They have left their secure congregations and walked the streets of Albany, Georgia, with us. They have gone down the highways of the South on tortuous rides for freedom. Yes, they have gone to jail with us. Some have been dismissed from their churches, have lost the support of their bishops and fellow ministers. But they have acted in the faith that right defeated is stronger than evil triumphant. Their witness has been the spiritual salt that has preserved the true meaning of the gospel in these troubled times. They have carved a tunnel of hope through the dark mountain of disappointment.

I hope the church as a whole will meet the challenge of this decisive hour. But even if the church does not come to the aid of justice, I have no despair about the future. I have no fear about the outcome of our struggle in Birmingham, even if our motives are at present misunderstood. We will reach the goal of freedom in Birmingham and all over the nation, because the goal of America is freedom. Abused and scorned though we may be, our destiny is tied up with America's destiny. Before the pilgrims landed at Plymouth, we were here. Before the pen of Jefferson etched the majestic words of the Declaration of Independence across the pages of history, we were here. For more than two centuries our forebears labored in this country without wages; they made cotton king; they built the homes of their masters while suffering gross injustice and shameful humiliation—and yet out of a bottomless vitality they continued to thrive and develop. If the inexpressible cruelties of slavery could not stop us, the opposition we now face will surely fail. We will win our freedom because the sacred heritage of our nation and the eternal will of God are embodied in our echoing demands.

Before closing I feel impelled to mention one other point in your statement that has troubled me profoundly. You warmly commended the Birmingham police force for keeping "order" and "preventing violence." I doubt that you would have so warmly commended the police force if you had seen its dogs sinking their teeth into unarmed, nonviolent Negroes. I doubt that you would so quickly commend the policemen if you were to observe their ugly and inhumane treatment of Negroes here in the city jail; if you were to watch them push and curse old Negro women and young Negro girls; if you were to see them slap and kick old Negro men and young boys; if you were to observe them, as they did on two occasions, refuse to give us food because we wanted to sing our grace together. I cannot join you in your praise of the Birmingham police department.

It is true that the police have exercised a degree of discipline in handling the demonstrators. In this sense they have conducted themselves rather "nonviolently" in public. But for what purpose? To preserve the evil system of segregation. Over the past few years I have consistently preached that nonviolence demands that the means we use must be as pure as the ends we seek. I have tried to make clear that it is wrong to use immoral means to attain moral ends. But now I must affirm that it is just as wrong, or perhaps even more so, to use moral means to preserve immoral ends. Perhaps Mr. Connor and his policemen have been rather nonviolent in public, as was Chief Pritchett in Albany, Georgia, but they have used the moral means of nonviolence to maintain the immoral end of racial injustice. As T. S. Eliot has said: "The last temptation is the greatest treason: To do the right deed for the wrong reason."

I wish you had commended the Negro sit-inners and demonstrators of Birmingham for their sublime courage, their willingness to suffer and their amazing discipline in the midst of great provocation. One day the South will recognize its real heroes. They will be the James Merediths, with the noble sense of purpose that enables them to face jeering and hostile mobs, and with the agonizing loneliness that characterizes the life of the pioneer. They will be old, oppressed, battered Negro women, symbolized in a seventy-two-year-old woman in Montgomery, Alabama, who rose up with a sense of dignity and with her people decided not to ride segregated buses, and who responded with ungrammatical profundity to one who inquired about her weariness: "My feets is tired, but my soul is at rest." They will be the young high school and college students, the young ministers of the gospel and a host of their elders, courageously and nonviolently sitting in at lunch counters and willingly going to jail for conscience' sake. One day the South will know that when these disinherited children of God sat down at lunch counters, they were in reality standing up for what is best in the American dream and for the most sacred values in our Judaeo-Christian heritage, thereby bringing our nation back to those great wells of democracy which were dug deep by the founding fathers in their formulation of the Constitution and the Declaration of Independence.

Never before have I written so long a letter. I'm afraid it is much too long to take your precious time. I can assure you that it would have been much shorter if I had been writing from a comfortable desk, but what else can one do when he is alone in a narrow jail cell, other than write long letters, think long thoughts and pray long prayers?

If I have said anything in this letter that overstates the truth and indicates an unreasonable impatience, I beg you to forgive me. If I have said anything that understates the truth and indicates my having a patience that allows me to settle for anything less than brotherhood, I beg God to forgive me.

I hope this letter finds you strong in the faith. I also hope that circumstances will soon make it possible for me to meet each of you, not as an integrationist or a civil-rights leader but as a fellow clergyman and a Christian brother. Let us all hope that the dark clouds of racial prejudice will soon pass away and the deep fog of misunderstanding will be lifted from our fear-drenched communities, and in some not too distant tomorrow the radiant stars of love and brotherhood will shine over our great nation with all their scintillating beauty.

Yours for the cause of Peace and Brotherhood,

Martin Luther King, Jr.

From **The Autobiography of Malcolm X**
MALCOLM X

Homeboy

I looked like Li'l Abner. Mason, Michigan, was written all over me. My kinky, reddish hair was cut hick style, and I didn't even use grease in it. My green suit's coat sleeves stopped above my wrists, the pants legs showed three inches of socks. Just a shade lighter green than the suit was my narrow-collared, three-quarter length Lansing department store topcoat. My appearance was too much for even Ella. But she told me later she had seen countrified members of the Little family come up from Georgia in even worse shape than I was.

Ella had fixed up a nice little upstairs room for me. And she was truly a Georgia Negro woman when she got into the kitchen with her pots and pans. She was the kind of cook who would heap up your plate with such as ham hock, greens, black-eyed peas, fried fish, cabbage, sweet potatoes, grits and gravy, and cornbread. And the more you put away, the better she felt. I worked out at Ella's kitchen table like there was no tomorrow.

Ella still seemed to be as big, black, outspoken and impressive a woman as she had been in Mason and Lansing. Only about two weeks before I arrived, she had split up with her second husband—the soldier, Frank, whom I had met there the previous summer; but she was taking it right in stride. I could see, though I didn't say, how any average man would find it almost impossible to live for very long with a woman whose every instinct was to run everything and everybody she had anything to do with—including me. About my second day there in Roxbury, Ella told me that she didn't want me to start hunting for a job right away, like most newcomer Negroes did. She said that she had told all those she'd brought North to take their time, to walk around, to travel the buses and the subway, and get the feel of Boston, before they tied themselves down working somewhere, because they would never again have the time to really see and get to know anything about the city they were living in. Ella said she'd help me find a job when it was time for me to go to work.

So I went gawking around the neighborhood—the Waumbeck and Humboldt Avenue Hill section of Roxbury, which is something like Harlem's Sugar Hill, where I'd later live. I saw those Roxbury Negroes acting and living

differently from any black people I'd ever dreamed of in my life. This was the
snooty-black neighborhood; they called themselves the "Four Hundred," and
looked down their noses at the Negroes of the black ghetto, or so-called "town"
section where Mary, my other half-sister, lived.

What I thought I was seeing there in Roxbury were high-class, educated,
important Negroes, living well, working in big jobs and positions. Their quiet
homes sat back in their mowed yards. These Negroes walked along the sidewalks
looking haughty and dignified, on their way to work, to shop, to visit, to church. I
know now, of course, that what I was really seeing was only a big-city version of
those "successful" Negro bootblacks and janitors back in Lansing. The only
difference was that the ones in Boston had been brainwashed even more
thoroughly. They prided themselves on being incomparably more "cultured,"
"cultivated," "dignified," and better off than their black brethren down in the
ghetto, which was no further away than you could throw a rock. Under the pitiful
misapprehension that it would make them "better," these Hill Negroes were
breaking their backs trying to imitate white people.

Any black family that had been around Boston long enough to own the
home they lived in was considered among the Hill elite. It didn't make any
difference that they had to rent out rooms to make ends meet. Then the
native-born New Englanders among them looked down upon recently migrated
Southern home-owners who lived next door, like Ella. And a big percentage of the
Hill dwellers were in Ella's category—Southern strivers and scramblers, and West
Indian Negroes, whom both the New Englanders and the Southerners called
"Black Jews." Usually it was the Southerners and the West Indians who not only
managed to own the places where they lived, but also at least one other house
which they rented as income property. The snooty New Englanders usually owned
less than they.

In those days on the Hill, any who could claim "professional"
status—teachers, preachers, practical nurses—also considered themselves
superior. Foreign diplomats could have modeled their conduct on the way the
Negro postmen, Pullman porters, and dining car waiters of Roxbury acted,
striding around as if they were wearing top hats and cut-aways.

I'd guess that eight out of ten of the Hill Negroes of Roxbury, despite the
impressive-sounding job titles they affected, actually worked as menials and
servants. "He's in banking," or "He's in securities." It sounded as though they
were discussing a Rockefeller or a Mellon—and not some gray-headed,
dignity-posturing bank janitor, or bond-house messenger. "I'm with an old
family" was the euphemism used to dignify the professions of white folks' cooks
and maids who talked so affectedly among their own kind in Roxbury that you
couldn't even understand them. I don't know how many forty- and fifty-year-old
errand boys went down the Hill dressed like ambassadors in black suits and white
collars, to downtown jobs "in government," "in finance," or "in law." It has never
ceased to amaze me how so many Negroes, then and now, could stand the
indignity of that kind of self-delusion.

Soon I ranged out of Roxbury and began to explore Boston proper. Historic buildings everywhere I turned, and plaques and markers and statues for famous events and men. One statue in the Boston Commons astonished me: a Negro named Crispus Attucks, who had been the first man to fall in the Boston Massacre. I had never known anything like that.

I roamed everywhere. In one direction, I walked as far as Boston University. Another day, I took my first subway ride. When most of the people got off, I followed. It was Cambridge, and I circled all around in the Harvard University campus. Somewhere, I had already heard of Harvard—though I didn't know much more about it. Nobody that day could have told me I would give an address before the Harvard Law School Forum some twenty years later.

I also did a lot of exploring downtown. Why a city would have *two* big railroad stations—North Station and South Station—I couldn't understand. At both of the stations, I stood around and watched people arrive and leave. And I did the same thing at the bus station where Ella had met me. My wanderings even led me down along the piers and docks where I read plaques telling about the old sailing ships that used to put into port there.

In a letter to Wilfred, Hilda, Philbert, and Reginald back in Lansing, I told them about all this, and about the winding, narrow, cobblestoned streets, and the houses that jammed up against each other. Downtown Boston, I wrote them, had the biggest stores I'd ever seen, and white people's restaurants and hotels. I made up my mind that I was going to see every movie that came to the fine, air-conditioned theaters.

On Massachusetts Avenue, next door to one of them, the Loew's State Theater, was the huge, exciting Roseland State Ballroom. Big posters out in front advertised the nationally famous bands, white and Negro, that had played there. "COMING NEXT WEEK," when I went by that first time, was Glenn Miller. I remember thinking how nearly the whole evening's music at Mason High School dances had been Glenn Miller's records. What wouldn't that crowd have given, I wondered, to be standing where Glenn Miller's band was actually going to play? I didn't know how familiar with Roseland I was going to become.

Ella began to grow concerned, because even when I had finally had enough sight-seeing, I didn't stick around very much on the Hill. She kept dropping hints that I ought to mingle with the "nice young people my age" who were to be seen in the Townsend Drugstore two blocks from her house, and a couple of other places. But even before I came to Boston, I had always felt and acted toward anyone my age as if they were in the "kid" class, like my younger brother Reginald. They had always looked up to me as if I were considerably older. On weekends back in Lansing where I'd go to get away from the white people in Mason, I'd hung around in the Negro part of town with Wilfred's and Philbert's set. Though all of them were several years older than me, I was bigger, and I actually looked older than most of them.

I didn't want to disappoint or upset Ella, but despite her advice, I began going down into the town ghetto section. That world of grocery stores, walk-up flats, cheap restaurants, poolrooms, bars, storefront churches, and pawnshops seemed to hold a natural lure for me.

Not only was this part of Roxbury much more exciting, but I felt more relaxed among Negroes who were being their natural selves and not putting on airs. Even though I did live on the Hill, my instincts were never—and still aren't—to feel myself any better than any other Negro.

I spent my first month in town with my mouth hanging open. The sharp-dressed young "cats" who hung on the corners and in the poolrooms, bars and restaurants, and who obviously didn't work anywhere, completely entranced me. I couldn't get over marveling at how their hair was straight and shiny like white men's hair; Ella told me this was called a "conk." I had never tasted a sip of liquor, never even smoked a cigarette, and here I saw little black children, ten and twelve years old, shooting craps, playing cards, fighting, getting grown-ups to put a penny or a nickel on their number for them, things like that. And these children threw around swear words I'd never heard before, even, and slang expressions that were just as new to me, such as "stud" and "cat" and "chick" and "cool" and "hip." Every night as I lay in bed I turned these new words over in my mind. It was shocking to me that in town, especially after dark, you'd occasionally see a white girl and a Negro man strolling arm in arm along the sidewalk, and mixed couples drinking in the neon-lighted bars—not slipping off to some dark corner, as in Lansing. I wrote Wilfred and Philbert about that, too.

I wanted to find a job myself, to surprise Ella. One afternoon, something told me to go inside a poolroom whose window I was looking through. I had looked through that window many times. I wasn't yearning to play pool; in fact, I had never held a cue stick. But I was drawn by the sight of the cool-looking "cats" standing around inside, bending over the big, green, felt-topped tables, making bets and shooting the bright-colored balls into the holes. As I stared through the window this particular afternoon, something made me decide to venture inside and talk to a dark, stubby, conk-headed fellow who racked up balls for the pool-players, whom I'd heard called "Shorty." One day he had come outside and seen me standing there and said "Hi, Red," so that made me figure he was friendly.

As inconspicuously as I could, I slipped inside the door and around the side of the poolroom, avoiding people, and on to the back, where Shorty was filling an aluminum can with the powder that pool players dust on their hands. He looked up at me. Later on, Shorty would enjoy teasing me about how with that first glance he knew my whole story. "Man, that cat still *smelled* country!" he'd say, laughing. "Cat's legs was so long and his pants so short his knees showed—an' his head looked like a briar patch!"

But that afternoon Shorty didn't let it show in his face how "country" I appeared when I told him I'd appreciate it if he'd tell me how could somebody go about getting a job like his.

"If you mean racking up balls," said Shorty, "I don't know of no pool joints around here needing anybody. You mean you just want any slave you can find?" A "slave" meant work, a job.

He asked what kind of work I had done. I told him that I'd washed restaurant dishes in Mason, Michigan. He nearly dropped the powder can. "My homeboy! Man, gimme some skin! I'm from Lansing!"

I never told Shorty—and he never suspected—that he was about ten years older than I. He took us to be about the same age. At first I would have been embarrassed to tell him, later I just never bothered. Shorty had dropped out of first-year high school in Lansing, lived a while with an uncle and aunt in Detroit, and had spent the last six years living with his cousin in Roxbury. But when I mentioned the names of Lansing people and places, he remembered many, and pretty soon we sounded as if we had been raised in the same block. I could sense Shorty's genuine gladness, and I don't have to say how lucky I felt to find a friend as hip as he obviously was.

"Man, this is a swinging town if you dig it," Shorty said. "You're my homeboy—I'm going to school you to the happenings." I stood there and grinned like a fool. "You got to go anywhere now? Well, stick around until I get off."

One thing I liked immediately about Shorty was his frankness. When I told him where I lived, he said what I already knew—that nobody in town could stand the Hill Negroes. But he thought a sister who gave me a "pad," not charging me rent, not even running me out to find "some slave," couldn't be all bad. Shorty's slave in the poolroom, he said, was just to keep ends together while he learned his horn. A couple of years before, he'd hit the numbers and bought a saxophone. "Got it right in there in the closet now, for my lesson tonight." Shorty was taking lessons "with some other studs," and he intended one day to organize his own small band. "There's a lot of bread to be made gigging right around here in Roxbury," Shorty explained to me. "I don't dig joining some big band, one-nighting all over just to say I played with Count or Duke or somebody." I thought that was smart. I wished I had studied a horn; but I never had been exposed to one.

All afternoon, between trips up front to rack balls, Shorty talked to me out of the corner of his mouth: which hustlers—standing around, or playing at this or that table—sold "reefers," or had just come out of prison, or were "second-story men." Shorty told me that he played at least a dollar a day on the numbers. He said as soon as he hit a number, he would use the winnings to organize his band.

I was ashamed to have to admit that I had never played the numbers. "Well, you ain't never had nothing to play with," he said, excusing me, "but you start when you get a slave, and if you hit, you got a stake for something."

He pointed out some gamblers and some pimps. Some of them had white whores, he whispered. "I ain't going to lie—I dig them two-dollar white chicks," Shorty said. "There's a lot of that action around here, nights: you'll see it." I said I already had seen some. "You ever had one?" he asked.

My embarrassment at my inexperience showed. "Hell, man," he said, "don't be ashamed. I had a few before I left Lansing—them Polack chicks that used to come over the bridge. Here, they're mostly Italians and Irish. But it don't matter what kind, they're something else! Ain't no different nowhere—there's nothing they love better than a black stud."

Through the afternoon, Shorty introduced me to players and loungers.

"My homeboy," he'd say, "he's looking for a slave if you hear anything." They all said they'd look out.

At seven o'clock, when the night ball-racker came on, Shorty told me he had to hurry to his saxophone lesson. But before he left, he held out to me the six or seven dollars he had collected that day in nickel and dime tips. "You got enough bread, homeboy?"

I was okay, I told him—I had two dollars. But Shorty made me take three more. "Little fattening for your pocket," he said. Before we went out, he opened his saxophone case and showed me the horn. It was gleaming brass against the green velvet, an alto sax. He said, "Keep cool, homeboy, and come back tomorrow. Some of the cats will turn you up a slave."

When I got home, Ella said there had been a telephone call from somebody named Shorty. He had left a message that over at the Roseland State Ballroom, the shoeshine boy was quitting that night, and Shorty had told him to hold the job for me.

"Malcolm, you haven't had any experience shining shoes," Ella said. Her expression and tone of voice told me she wasn't happy about my taking that job. I didn't particularly care, because I was already speechless thinking about being somewhere close to the greatest bands in the world. I didn't even wait to eat any dinner.

The ballroom was all lighted when I got there. A man at the front door was letting in members of Benny Goodman's band. I told him I wanted to see the shoeshine boy, Freddie.

"You're going to be the new one?" he asked. I said I thought I was, and he laughed, "Well, maybe you'll hit the numbers and get a Cadillac, too." He told me that I'd find Freddie upstairs in the men's room on the second floor.

But downstairs before I went up, I stepped over and snatched a glimpse inside the ballroom. I just couldn't believe the size of that waxed floor! At the far end, under the soft, rose-colored lights, was the bandstand with the Benny Goodman musicians moving around, laughing and talking, arranging their horns and stands.

A wiry, brown-skinned, conked fellow upstairs in the men's room greeted me. "You Shorty's homeboy?" I said I was, and he said he was Freddie. "Good old boy," he said. "He called me, he just heard I hit the big number, and he figured right I'd be quitting." I told Freddie what the man at the front door had said about a Cadillac. He laughed and said, "Burns them white cats up when you get yourself something. Yeah, I told them I was going to get me one—just to bug them."

Freddie then said for me to pay close attention, that he was going to be busy and for me to watch but not get in the way, and he'd try to get me ready to take over at the next dance, a couple of nights later.

As Freddie busied himself setting up the shoeshine stand, he told me, "Get here early . . . your shoeshine rags and brushes by this footstand . . . your polish bottles, paste wax, suede brushes over here . . . everything in place, you get rushed, you never need to waste motion. . . ."

While you shined shoes, I learned, you also kept watch on customers inside, leaving the urinals. You darted over and offered a small white hand towel. "A lot of cats who ain't planning to wash their hands, sometimes you can run up with a towel and shame them. Your towels are really your best hustle in here. Cost you a penny apiece to launder—you always get at least a nickel tip."

The shoeshine customers, and any from the inside rest room who took a towel, you whiskbroomed a couple of licks. "A nickel or a dime tip, just give 'em that," Freddie said. "But for two bits, Uncle Tom a little—white cats especially like that. I've had them to come back two, three times a dance."

From down below, the sound of the music had begun floating up. I guess I stood transfixed. "You never seen a big dance?" asked Freddie. "Run on awhile, and watch."

There were a few couples already dancing under the rose-colored lights. But even more exciting to me was the crowd thronging in. The most glamorous-looking white women I'd ever seen—young ones, old ones, white cats buying tickets at the window, sticking big wads of green bills back into their pockets, checking the women's coats, and taking their arms and squiring them inside.

Freddie had some early customers when I got back upstairs. Between the shoeshine stand and thrusting towels to me just as they approached the wash basin, Freddie seemed to be doing four things at once. "Here, you can take over the whiskbroom," he said, "just two or three licks—but let 'em feel it."

When things slowed a little, he said, "You ain't seen nothing tonight. You wait until you see a spooks' dance! Man, our own people carry *on!*" Whenever he had a moment, he kept schooling me. "Shoelaces, this drawer here. You just starting out, I'm going to make these to you as a present. Buy them for a nickel a pair, tell cats they need laces if they do, and charge two bits."

Every Benny Goodman record I'd ever heard in my life, it seemed, was filtering faintly into where we were. During another customer lull, Freddie let me slip back outside again to listen. Peggy Lee was at the mike singing. Beautiful! She had just joined the band and she was from North Dakota and had been singing with a group in Chicago when Mrs. Benny Goodman discovered her, we had heard some customers say. She finished the song and the crowd burst into applause. She was a big hit.

"It knocked me out, too, when I first broke in here," Freddie said, grinning, when I went back in there. "But, look, you ever shined any shoes?" He laughed when I said I hadn't, excepting my own. "Well, let's get to work. I never had neither." Freddie got on the stand and went to work on his own shoes. Brush, liquid polish, brush, paste wax, shine rag, lacquer sole dressing . . . step by step, Freddie showed me what to do.

"But you got to get a whole lot faster. You can't waste time!" Freddie showed me how fast on my own shoes. Then, because business was tapering off, he had time to give me a demonstration of how to make the shine rag pop like a firecracker. "Dig the action?" he asked. He did it in slow motion. I got down and tried it on his shoes. I had the principle of it. "Just got to do it faster," Freddie said. "It's a jive noise, that's all. Cats tip better, they figure you're knocking yourself out!"

By the end of the dance, Freddie had let me shine the shoes of three or four stray drunks he talked into having shines, and I had practiced picking up my speed on Freddie's shoes until they looked like mirrors. After we had helped the janitors to clean up the ballroom after the dance, throwing out all the paper and cigarette butts and empty liquor bottles, Freddie was nice enough to drive me all the way home to Ella's on the Hill in the second-hand maroon Buick he said he was going to trade in on his Cadillac. He talked to me all the way. "I guess it's all right if I tell you, pick up a couple of dozen packs of rubbers, two-bits apiece. You notice some of those cats that came up to me around the end of the dance? Well, when some have new chicks going right, they'll come asking you for rubbers. Charge a dollar, generally you'll get an extra tip."

He looked across at me. "Some hustles you're too new for. Cats will ask you for liquor, some will want reefers. But you don't need to have nothing except rubbers—until you can dig who's a cop.

"You can make ten, twelve dollars a dance for yourself if you work everything right," Freddie said, before I got out of the car in front of Ella's. "The main thing you got to remember is that everything in the world is a hustle. So long, Red."

The next time I ran into Freddie I was downtown one night a few weeks later. He was parked in his pearl gray Cadillac, sharp as a tack, "cooling it."

"Man, you sure schooled me!" I said, and he laughed; he knew what I meant. It hadn't taken me long on the job to find out that Freddie had done less shoeshining and towel-hustling than selling liquor and reefers, and putting white "Johns" in touch with Negro whores. I also learned that white girls always flocked to the Negro dances—some of them whores whose pimps brought them to mix business and pleasure, others who came with their black boy friends, and some who came in alone, for a little freelance lusting among a plentiful availability of enthusiastic Negro men.

At the white dances, of course, nothing black was allowed, and that's where the black whores' pimps soon showed a new shoeshine boy what he could pick up on the side by slipping a phone number or address to the white Johns who came around the end of the dance looking for "black chicks."

Most of Roseland's dances were for whites only, and they had white bands only. But the only white band ever to play there at a Negro dance to my recollection, was Charlie Barnet's. The fact is that very few white bands could have satisfied the Negro dancers. But I know that Charlie Barnet's "Cherokee" and his "Redskin Rhumba" drove those Negroes wild. They'd jampack that ballroom, the black girls in way-out silk and satin dresses and shoes, their hair done in all kinds of styles, the men sharp in their zoot suits and crazy conks, and everybody grinning and greased and gassed.

Some of the bandsmen would come up to the men's room at about eight o'clock and get shoeshines before they went to work. Duke Ellington, Count

Basie, Lionel Hampton, Cootie Williams, Jimmie Lunceford were just a few of those who sat in my chair. I would really make my shine rag sound like someone had set off Chinese firecrackers. Duke's great alto saxman, Johnny Hodges—he was Shorty's idol—still owes me for a shoeshine I gave him. He was in the chair one night, having a friendly argument with the drummer, Sonny Greer, who was standing there, when I tapped the bottom of his shoes to signal that I was finished. Hodges stepped down, reaching his hand in his pocket to pay me, but then snatched his hand out to gesture, and just forgot me, and walked away. I wouldn't have dared to bother the man who could do what he did with "Daydream" by asking him for fifteen cents.

I remember that I struck up a little shoeshine-stand conversation with Count Basie's great blues singer, Jimmie Rushing. (He's the one famous for "Sent For You Yesterday, Here You Come Today" and things like that.) Rushing's feet, I remember, were big and funny-shaped—not long like most big feet, but they were round and roly-poly like Rushing. Anyhow, he even introduced me to some of the other Basie cats, like Lester Young, Harry Edison, Buddy Tate, Don Byas, Dickie Wells, and Buck Clayton. They'd walk in the rest room later, by themselves. "Hi, Red." They'd be up there in my chair, and my shine rag was popping to the beat of all of their records, spinning in my head. Musicians never have had, anywhere, a greater shoeshine-boy fan than I was. I would write to Wilfred and Hilda and Philbert and Reginald back in Lansing, trying to describe it.

I never got any decent tips until the middle of the Negro dances, which is when the dancers started feeling good and getting generous. After the white dances, when I helped to clean out the ballroom, we would throw out perhaps a dozen empty liquor bottles. But after the Negro dances, we would have to throw out cartons full of empty fifth bottles—not rotgut, either, but the best brands, and especially Scotch.

During lulls up there in the men's room, sometimes I'd get in five minutes of watching the dancing. The white people danced as though somebody had trained them—left, one, two; right, three, four—the same steps and patterns over and over, as though somebody had wound them up. But those Negroes—nobody in the world could have choreographed the way they did whatever they felt—just grabbing partners, even the white chicks who came to the Negro dances. And my black brethren today may hate me for saying it, but a lot of black girls nearly got run over by some of those Negro males scrambling to get at those white women; you would have thought God had lowered some of his angels. Times have sure changed; if it happened today, those same black girls would go after those Negro men—and the white women, too.

Anyway, some couples were so abandoned—flinging high and wide, improvising steps and movements—that you couldn't believe it. I could feel the beat in my bones, even though I had never danced.

"Showtime!" people would start hollering about the last hour of the dance. Then a couple of dozen really wild couples would stay on the floor, the

girls changing to low white sneakers. The band now would really be blasting, and all the other dancers would form a clapping, shouting circle to watch that wild competition as it began, covering only a quarter or so of the ballroom floor. The band, the spectators and the dancers, would be making the Roseland Ballroom feel like a big rocking ship. The spotlight would be turning, pink, yellow, green, and blue, picking up the couples lindy-hopping as if they had gone mad. *"Wail, man, wail!"* people would be shouting at the band; and it *would* be wailing, until first one and then another couple just ran out of strength and stumbled off toward the crowd, exhausted and soaked with sweat. Sometimes I would be down there standing inside the door jumping up and down in my gray jacket with the whiskbroom in the pocket, and the manager would have to come and shout at me that I had customers upstairs.

The first liquor I drank, my first cigarettes, even my first reefers, I can't specifically remember. But I know they were all mixed together with my first shooting craps, playing cards, and betting my dollar a day on the numbers, as I started hanging out at night with Shorty and his friends. Shorty's jokes about how country I had been made us all laugh. I still was country, I know now, but it all felt so great because I was accepted. All of us would be in somebody's place, usually one of the girls', and we'd be turning on, the reefers making everybody's head light, or the whisky aglow in our middles. Everybody understood that my head had to stay kinky a while longer, to grow long enough for Shorty to conk it for me. One of these nights, I remarked that I had saved about half enough to get a zoot.

"Save?" Shorty couldn't believe it. "Homeboy, you never heard of credit?" He told me he'd call a neighborhood clothing store the first thing in the morning, and that I should be there early.

A salesman, a young Jew, met me when I came in. "You're Shorty's friend?" I said I was; it amazed me—all of Shorty's contacts. The salesman wrote my name on a form, and the Roseland as where I worked, and Ella's address as where I lived. Shorty's name was put down as recommending me. The salesman said, "Shorty's one of our best customers."

I was measured, and the young salesman picked off a rack a zoot suit that was just wild: sky-blue pants thirty inches in the knee and angle-narrowed down to twelve inches at the bottom, and a long coat that pinched my waist and flared out below my knees.

As a gift, the salesman said, the store would give me a narrow leather belt with my initial "L" on it. Then he said I ought to also buy a hat, and I did—blue, with a feather in the four-inch brim. Then the store gave me another present: a long, thick-linked, gold-plated chain that swung down lower than my coat hem. I was sold forever on credit.

When I modeled the zoot for Ella, she took a long look and said, "Well, I guess it had to happen." I took three of those twenty-five-cent sepia-toned, while-you-wait pictures of myself, posed the way "hipsters" wearing their zoots would "cool it"—hat dangled, knees drawn close together, feet wide apart, both index fingers jabbed toward the floor. The long coat and swinging chain and the

Punjab pants were much more dramatic if you stood that way. One picture, I autographed and airmailed to my brothers and sisters in Lansing, to let them see how well I was doing. I gave another one to Ella, and the third to Shorty, who was really moved: I could tell by the way he said, "Thanks, homeboy." It was part of our "hip" code not to show that kind of affection.

Shorty soon decided that my hair was finally long enough to be conked. He had promised to school me in how to beat the barbershops' three- and four-dollar price by making up congolene, and then conking ourselves.

I took the little list of ingredients he had printed out for me, and went to a grocery store, where I got a can of Red Devil lye, two eggs, and two medium-sized white potatoes. Then at a drugstore near the poolroom, I asked for a large jar of vaseline, a large bar of soap, a large-toothed comb and a fine-toothed comb, one of those rubber hoses with a metal spray-head, a rubber apron and a pair of gloves.

"Going to lay on that first conk?" the drugstore man asked me. I proudly told him, grinning, "Right!"

Shorty paid six dollars a week for a room in his cousin's shabby apartment. His cousin wasn't at home. "It's like the pad's mine, he spends so much time with his woman," Shorty said. "Now, you watch me—"

He peeled the potatoes and thin-sliced them into a quart-sized Mason fruit jar, then started stirring them with a wooden spoon as he gradually poured in a little over half the can of lye. "Never use a metal spoon; the lye will turn it black," he told me.

A jelly-like, starchy-looking glop resulted from the lye and potatoes, and Shorty broke in the two eggs, stirring real fast—his own conk and dark face bent down close. The congolene turned pale-yellowish. "Feel the jar," Shorty said. I cupped my hand against the outside, and snatched it away. "Damn right, it's hot, that's the lye," he said. "So you know it's going to burn when I comb it in—it burns *bad*. But the longer you can stand it, the straighter the hair."

He made me sit down, and he tied the string of the new rubber apron tightly around my neck, and combed up my bush of hair. Then, from the big vaseline jar, he took a handful and massaged it hard all through my hair and into the scalp. He also thickly vaselined my neck, ears and forehead. "When I get to washing out your head, be sure to tell me anywhere you feel any little stinging." Shorty warned me, washing his hands, then pulling on the rubber gloves, and tying on his own rubber apron. "You always got to remember that any congolene left in burns a sore into your head."

The congolene just felt warm when Shorty started combing it in. But then my head caught fire.

I gritted my teeth and tried to pull the sides of the kitchen table together. The comb felt as if it was raking my skin off.

My eyes watered, my nose was running. I couldn't stand it any longer; I bolted to the washbasin. I was cursing Shorty with every name I could think of when he got the spray going and started soap-lathering my head.

He lathered and spray-rinsed, lathered and spray-rinsed, maybe ten or twelve times, each time gradually closing the hot-water faucet, until the rinse was cold, and that helped some.

"You feel any stinging spots?"

"No," I managed to say. My knees were trembling.

"Sit back down, then. I think we got it all out okay."

The flame came back as Shorty, with a thick towel, started drying my head, rubbing hard. *"Easy, man, easy!"* I kept shouting.

"The first time's always worst. You get used to it better before long. You took it real good, homeboy. You got a good conk."

When Shorty let me stand up and see in the mirror, my hair hung down in limp, damp strings. My scalp still flamed, but not as badly; I could bear it. He draped the towel around my shoulders, over my rubber apron, and began again vaselining my hair.

I could feel him combing, straight back, first the big comb, then the fine-tooth one.

Then, he was using a razor, very delicately, on the back of my neck. Then, finally, shaping the sideburns.

My first view in the mirror blotted out the hurting. I'd seen some pretty conks, but when it's the first time, on your *own* head, the transformation, after the lifetime of kinks, is staggering.

The mirror reflected Shorty behind me. We both were grinning and sweating. And on top of my head was this thick, smooth sheen of shining red hair—real red—as straight as any white man's.

How ridiculous I was! Stupid enough to stand there simply lost in admiration of my hair now looking "white," reflected in the mirror in Shorty's room. I vowed that I'd never again be without a conk, and I never was for many years.

This was my first really big step toward self-degradation: when I endured all of that pain, literally burning my flesh to have it look like a white man's hair. I had joined that multitude of Negro men and women in America who are brainwashed into believing that the black people are "inferior"—and white people "superior"—that they will even violate and mutilate their God-created bodies to try to look "pretty" by white standards.

Look around today, in every small town and big city, from two-bit catfish and soda-pop joints into the "integrated" lobby of the Waldorf-Astoria, and you'll see conks on black men. And you'll see black women wearing these green and pink and purple and red and platinum-blonde wigs. They're all more ridiculous than a slapstick comedy. It makes you wonder if the Negro has completely lost his sense of identity, lost touch with himself.

You'll see the conk worn by many, many so-called "upper class" Negroes, and, as much as I hate to say it about them, on all too many Negro entertainers. One of the reasons that I've especially admired some of them, like Lionel Hampton and Sidney Poitier, among others, is that they have kept their natural hair and fought to the top. I admire any Negro man who has never had himself conked, or who has had the sense to get rid of it—as I finally did.

I don't know which kind of self-defacing conk is the greater shame—the one you'll see on the heads of the black so-called "middle class" and "upper class," who ought to know better, or the one you'll see on the heads of the poorest, most downtrodden, ignorant black men. I mean the legal-minimum-wage ghetto-dwelling kind of Negro, as I was when I got my first one. It's generally among these poor fools that you'll see a black kerchief over the man's head, like Aunt Jemima; he's trying to make his conk last longer, between trips to the barbershop. Only for special occasions is this kerchief-protected conk exposed—to show off how "sharp" and "hip" its owner is. The ironic thing is that I have never heard any woman, white or black, express any admiration for a conk. Of course, any white woman with a black man isn't thinking about his hair. But I don't see how on earth a black woman with any race pride could walk down the street with any black man wearing a conk—the emblem of his shame that he is black.

To my own shame, when I say all of this I'm talking first of all about myself—because you can't show me any Negro who ever conked more faithfully than I did. I'm speaking from personal experience when I say of any black man who conks today, or any white-wigged black woman, that if they gave the brains in their heads just half as much attention as they do their hair, they would be a thousand times better off.

From **"The Ballot or the Bullet"**
MALCOLM X

Mr. Moderator, Brother Lomax, brothers and sisters, friends and enemies: I just can't believe everyone in here is a friend and I don't want to leave anybody out. The question tonight, as I understand it, is "The Negro Revolt, and Where Do We Go From Here?" or "What Next?" In my little humble way of understanding it, it points toward either the ballot or the bullet.

Before we try and explain what is meant by the ballot or the bullet, I would like to clarify something concerning myself. I'm still a Muslim, my religion is still Islam. That's my personal belief. Just as Adam Clayton Powell is a Christian minister who heads the Abyssinian Baptist Church in New York, but at the same time takes part in the political struggles to try and bring about rights to the black people in this country; and Dr. Martin Luther King is a Christian minister down in Atlanta, Georgia, who heads another organization fighting for the civil rights of black people in this country; and Rev. Galamison, I guess you've heard of him, is another Christian minister in New York who has been deeply involved in the school boycotts to eliminate segregated education; well, I myself am a minister, not a Christian minister, but a Muslim minister; and I believe in action on all fronts by whatever means necessary.

Although I'm still a Muslim, I'm not here tonight to discuss my religion.
I'm not here to try and change your religion. I'm not here to argue or discuss
anything that we differ about, because it's time for us to submerge our differences
and realize that it is best for us to first see that we have the same problem, a
common problem—a problem that will make you catch hell whether you're a
Baptist, or a Methodist, or a Muslim, or a nationalist. Whether you're educated or
illiterate, whether you live on the boulevard or in the alley, you're going to catch
hell just like I am. We're all in the same boat and we all are going to catch the
same hell from the same man. He just happens to be a white man. All of us have
suffered here, in this country, political oppression at the hands of the white man,
economic exploitation at the hands of the white man, and social degradation at
the hands of the white man.

Now in speaking like this, it doesn't mean that we're anti-white, but it
does mean we're anti-exploitation, we're anti-degradation, we're anti-oppression.
And if the white man doesn't want us to be anti-him, let him stop oppressing and
exploiting and degrading us. Whether we are Christians or Muslims or nationalists
or agnostics or atheists, we must first learn to forget our differences. If we have
differences, let us differ in the closet; when we come out in front, let us not have
anything to argue about until we get finished arguing with the man. If the late
President Kennedy could get together with Khrushchev and exchange some
wheat, we certainly have more in common with each other than Kennedy and
Khrushchev had with each other.

If we don't do something real soon, I think you'll have to agree that we're
going to be forced either to use the ballot or the bullet. It's one or the other in
1964. It isn't that time is running out—time has run out! 1964 threatens to be the
most explosive year America has ever witnessed. The most explosive year. Why?
It's also a political year. It's the year when all of the white politicians will be back
in the so-called Negro community jiving you and me for some votes. The year
when all of the white political crooks will be right back in your and my
community with their false promises, building up our hopes for a letdown, with
their trickery and their treachery, with their false promises which they don't
intend to keep. As they nourish these dissatisfactions, it can only lead to one thing,
an explosion; and now we have the type of black man on the scene in America
today—I'm sorry, Brother Lomax—who just doesn't intend to turn the other
cheek any longer.

Don't let anybody tell you anything about the odds are against you. If
they draft you, they send you to Korea and make you face 800 million Chinese. If
you can be brave over there, you can be brave right here. These odds aren't as
great as those odds. And if you fight here, you will at least know what you're
fighting for.

I'm not a politician, not even a student of politics; in fact, I'm not a
student of much of anything. I'm not a Democrat, I'm not a Republican, and I
don't even consider myself an American. If you and I were Americans, there'd be
no problem. Those Hunkies that just got off the boat, they're already Americans;

Polacks are already Americans; the Italian refugees are already Americans. Everything that came out of Europe, every blue-eyed thing, is already an American. And as long as you and I have been over here, we aren't Americans yet.

Well, I am one who doesn't believe in deluding myself. I'm not going to sit at your table and watch you eat, with nothing on my plate, and call myself a diner. Sitting at the table doesn't make you a diner, unless you eat some of what's on that plate. Being here in America doesn't make you an American. Being born here in America doesn't make you an American. Why, if birth made you American, you wouldn't need any legislation, you wouldn't need any amendments to the Constitution, you wouldn't be faced with civil-rights filibustering in Washington, D.C., right now. They don't have to pass civil-rights legislation to make a Polack an American.

No, I'm not an American. I'm one of the 22 million black people who are the victims of Americanism. One of the 22 million black people who are the victims of democracy, nothing but disguised hypocrisy. So, I'm not standing here speaking to you as an American, or a patriot, or a flag-saluter, or a flag-waver—no, not I. I'm speaking as a victim of this American system. And I see America through the eyes of the victim. I don't see any American dream; I see an American nightmare.

These 22 million victims are waking up. Their eyes are coming open. They're beginning to see what they used to only look at. They're becoming politically mature. They are realizing that there are new political trends from coast to coast. As they see these new political trends, it's possible for them to see that every time there's an election the races are so close that they have to have a recount. They had to recount in Massachusetts to see who was going to be governor, it was so close. It was the same way in Rhode Island, in Minnesota, and in many other parts of the country. And the same with Kennedy and Nixon when they ran for President. It was so close they had to count all over again. Well, what does this mean? It means that when white people are evenly divided, and black people have a bloc of votes of their own, it is left up to them to determine who's going to sit in the White House and who's going to be in the dog house.

It was the black man's vote that put the present administration in Washington, D.C. Your vote, your dumb vote, your ignorant vote, your wasted vote put in an administration in Washington, D.C., that has seen fit to pass every kind of legislation imaginable, saving you until last, then filibustering on top of that. And your and my leaders have the audacity to run around clapping their hands and talk about how much progress we're making. And what a good President we have. If he wasn't good in Texas, he sure can't be good in Washington, D.C. Because Texas is a lynch state. It is in the same breath as Mississippi, no different; only they lynch you in Texas with a Texas accent and lynch you in Mississippi with a Mississippi accent. And these Negro leaders have the audacity to go and have some coffee in the White House with a Texan, a Southern cracker—that's all he is—and then come out and tell you and me that he's going to be better for us because, since he's from the South, he knows how to deal with the Southerners. What kind of logic is that? Let Eastland be President, he's from the South too. He should be better able to deal with them than Johnson.

In this present administration they have in the House of Representatives 257 Democrats to only 177 Republicans. They control two-thirds of the House vote. Why can't they pass something that will help you and me? In the Senate, there are 67 Senators who are of the Democratic Party. Only 33 of them are Republicans. Why, the Democrats have got the government sewed up, and you're the one who sewed it up for them. And what have they given you for it? Four years in office, and just now getting around to some civil-rights legislation. Just now, after everything else is gone, out of the way, they're going to sit down now and play with you all summer long—the same old giant con game that they call filibuster. All those are in cahoots together. Don't you ever think they're not in cahoots together, for the man that is heading the civil-rights filibuster is a man from Georgia named Richard Russell. When Johnson became President, the first man he asked for when he got back to Washington, D.C., was "Dicky"—that's how tight they are. That's his boy, that's his pal, that's his buddy. But they're playing that old con game. One of them makes believe he's for you, and he's got it fixed where the other one is so tight against you, he never has to keep his promise.

So it's time in 1964 to wake up. And when you see them coming up with that kind of conspiracy, let them know your eyes are open. And let them know you got something else that's wide open too. It's got to be the ballot or the bullet. The ballot or the bullet. If you're afraid to use an expression like that, you should get on out of the country, you should get back in the cotton patch, you should get back in the alley. They get all the Negro vote, and after they get it, the Negro gets nothing in return. All they did when they got to Washington was give a few big Negroes big jobs. Those big Negroes didn't need big jobs, they already had jobs. That's camouflage, that's trickery, that's treachery, window-dressing. I'm not trying to knock out the Democrats for the Republicans, we'll get to them in a minute. But it is true—you put the Democrats first and the Democrats put you last.

Look at it the way it is. What alibis do they use, since they control Congress and the Senate? What alibi do they use when you and I ask, "Well, when are you going to keep your promise?" They blame the Dixiecrats. What is a Dixiecrat? A Democrat. A Dixiecrat is nothing but a Democrat in disguise. The titular head of the Democrats is also the head of the Dixiecrats, because the Dixiecrats are a part of the Democratic Party. The Democrats have never kicked the Dixiecrats out of the party. The Dixiecrats bolted themselves once, but the Democrats didn't put them out. Imagine, these lowdown Southern segregationists put the Northern Democrats down. But the Northern Democrats have never put the Dixiecrats down. No, look at that thing the way it is. They have got a con game going on, a political con game, and you and I are in the middle. It's time for you and me to wake up and start looking at it like it is, and trying to understand it like it is; and then we can deal with it like it is.

The Dixiecrats in Washington, D.C., control the key committees that run the government. The only reason the Dixiecrats control these committees is because they have seniority. The only reason they have seniority is because they come from states where Negroes can't vote. This is not even a government that's based on democracy. It is not a government that is made up of representatives of the people. Half of the people in the South can't even vote. Eastland is not even supposed to be in Washington. Half of the senators and congressmen who occupy these key positions in Washington, D.C., are there illegally, are there unconstitutionally.

I was in Washington, D.C., a week ago Thursday, when they were debating whether or not they should let the bill come onto the floor. And in the back of the room where the Senate meets, there's a huge map of the United States, and on that map it shows the location of Negroes throughout the country. And it shows that the Southern section of the country, the states that are most heavily concentrated with Negroes, are the ones that have senators and congressmen standing up filibustering and doing all other kinds of trickery to keep the Negro from being able to vote. This is pitiful. But it's not pitiful for us any longer; it's actually pitiful for the white man, because soon now, as the Negro awakens a little more and sees the vise that he's in, sees the bag that he's in, sees the real game that he's in, then the Negro's going to develop a new tactic.

These senators and congressmen actually violate the constitutional amendments that guarantee the people of that particular state or county the right to vote. And the Constitution itself has within it the machinery to expel any representative from a state where the voting rights of the people are violated. You don't even need new legislation. Any person in Congress right now, who is there from a state or a district where the voting rights of the people are violated, that particular person should be expelled from Congress. And when you expel him, you've removed one of the obstacles in the path of any real meaningful legislation in this country. In fact, when you expel them, you don't need new legislation, because they will be replaced by black representatives from counties and districts where the black man is in the majority, not in the minority.

If the black man in these Southern states had his full voting rights, the key Dixiecrats in Washington, D.C., which means the key Democrats in Washington, D.C., would lose their seats. The Democratic Party itself would lose its power. It would cease to be powerful as a party. When you see the amount of power that would be lost by the Democratic Party if it were to lose the Dixiecrat wing, or branch, or element, you can see where it's against the interests of the Democrats to give voting rights to Negroes in states where the Democrats have been in complete power and authority ever since the Civil War. You just can't belong to that party without analyzing it.

I say again, I'm not anti-Democrat, I'm not anti-Republican, I'm not anti-anything. I'm just questioning their sincerity, and some of the strategy that they've been using on our people by promising them promises that they don't intend to keep. When you keep the Democrats in power, you're keeping the

Dixiecrats in power. I doubt that my good Brother Lomax will deny that. A vote for a Democrat is a vote for a Dixiecrat. That's why, in 1964, it's time now for you and me to become more politically mature and realize what the ballot is for; what we're supposed to get when we cast a ballot; and that if we don't cast a ballot, it's going to end up in a situation where we're going to have to cast a bullet. It's either a ballot or a bullet.

In the North, they do it a different way. They have a system that's known as gerrymandering, whatever that means. It means when Negroes become too heavily concentrated in a certain area, and begin to gain too much political power, the white man comes along and changes the district lines. You may say, "Why do you keep saying white man?" Because it's the white man who does it. I haven't ever seen any Negro changing any lines. They don't let him get near the line. It's the white man who does this. And usually, it's the white man who grins at you the most, and pats you on the back, and is supposed to be your friend. He may be friendly, but he's not your friend.

So, what I'm trying to impress upon you, in essence, is this: You and I in America are faced not with a segregationist conspiracy, we're faced with a government conspiracy. Everyone who's filibustering is a senator—that's the government. Everyone who's finagling in Washington, D.C., is a congressman—that's the government. You don't have anybody putting blocks in your path but people who are a part of the government. The same government that you go abroad to fight for and die for is the government that is in a conspiracy to deprive you of your voting rights, deprive you of your economic opportunities, deprive you of decent housing, deprive you of decent education. You don't need to go to the employer alone, it is the government itself, the government of America, that is responsible for the oppression and exploitation and degradation of black people in this country. And you should drop it in their lap. This government has failed the Negro. This so-called democracy has failed the Negro. And all these white liberals have definitely failed the Negro.

So, where do we go from here? First, we need some friends. We need some new allies. The entire civil-rights struggle needs a new interpretation, a broader interpretation. We need to look at this civil-rights thing from another angle—from the inside as well as from the outside. To those of us whose philosophy is black nationalism, the only way you can get involved in the civil-rights struggle is give it a new interpretation. That old interpretation excluded us. It kept us out. So, we're giving a new interpretation to the civil-rights struggle, an interpretation that will enable us to come into it, take part in it. And these handkerchief-heads who have been dillydallying and pussyfooting and compromising—we don't intend to let them pussyfoot and dillydally and compromise any longer.

How can you thank a man for giving you what's already yours? How then can you thank him for giving you only part of what's already yours? You haven't even made progress, if what's being given to you, you should have had already. That's not progress. And I love my Brother Lomax, the way he pointed out we're right back where we were in 1954. We're not even as far up as we were in 1954.

We're behind where we were in 1954. There's more segregation now than there was in 1954. There's more racial animosity, more racial hatred, more racial violence today in 1964, than there was in 1954. Where is the progress?

And now you're facing a situation where the young Negro's coming up. They don't want to hear that "turn-the-other-cheek" stuff, no. In Jacksonville, those were teenagers, they were throwing Molotov cocktails. Negroes have never done that before. But it shows you there's a new deal coming in. There's new thinking coming in. There's new strategy coming in. It'll be Molotov cocktails this month, hand grenades next month, and something else next month. It'll be ballots, or it'll be bullets. It'll be liberty, or it will be death. The only difference about this kind of death—it'll be reciprocal. You know what is meant by "reciprocal"? That's one of Brother Lomax's words, I stole it from him. I don't usually deal with those big words because I don't usually deal with big people. I deal with small people. I find you can get a whole lot of small people and whip hell out of a whole lot of big people. They haven't got anything to lose, and they've got everything to gain. And they'll let you know in a minute: "It takes two to tango; when I go, you go."

The black nationalists, those whose philosophy is black nationalism, in bringing about this new interpretation of the entire meaning of civil rights, look upon it as meaning, as Brother Lomax has pointed out, equality of opportunity. Well, we're justified in seeking civil rights, if it means equality of opportunity, because all we're doing there is trying to collect for our investment. Our mothers and fathers invested sweat and blood. Three hundred and ten years we worked in this country without a dime in return—I mean without a *dime* in return. You let the white man walk around here talking about how rich this country is, but you never stop to think how it got rich so quick. It got rich because you made it rich.

You take the people who are in this audience right now. They're poor, we're all poor as individuals. Our weekly salary individually amounts to hardly anything. But if you take the salary of everyone in here collectively it'll fill up a whole lot of baskets. It's a lot of wealth. If you can collect the wages of just these people right here for a year, you'll be rich—richer than rich. When you look at it like that, think how rich Uncle Sam had to become, not with this handful, but millions of black people. Your and my mother and father, who didn't work an eight-hour shift, but worked from "can't see" in the morning until "can't see" at night, and worked for nothing, making the white man rich, making Uncle Sam rich.

This is our investment. This is our contribution—our blood. Not only did we give of our free labor, we gave of our blood. Every time he had a call to arms, we were the first ones in uniform. We died on every battlefield the white man had. We have made a greater sacrifice than anybody who's standing up in America today. We have made a greater contribution and have collected less. Civil rights, for those of us whose philosophy is black nationalism, means: "Give it to us now. Don't wait for next year. Give it to us yesterday, and that's not fast enough."

I might stop right here to point out one thing. Whenever you're going after something that belongs to you, anyone who's depriving you of the right to have it is a criminal. Understand that. Whenever you are going after something that is yours, you are within your legal rights to lay claim to it. And anyone who puts forth any effort to deprive you of that which is yours, is breaking the law, is a criminal. And this was pointed out by the Supreme Court decision. It outlawed segregation. Which means segregation is against the law. Which means a segregationist is breaking the law. A segregationist is a criminal. You can't label him as anything other than that. And when you demonstrate against segregation, the law is on your side. The Surpeme Court is on your side.

Now, who is it that opposes you in carrying out the law? The police department itself. With police dogs and clubs. Whenever you demonstrate against segregation, whether it is segregated education, segregated housing, or anything else, the law is on your side, and anyone who stands in the way is not the law any longer. They are breaking the law, they are not representatives of the law. Any time you demonstrate against segregation and a man has the audacity to put a police dog on you, kill that dog, kill him, I'm telling you, kill that dog. I say it, if they put me in jail tomorrow, kill—that—dog. Then you'll put a stop to it. Now, if these white people in here don't want to see that kind of action, get down and tell the mayor to tell the police department to pull the dogs in. That's all you have to do. If you don't do it, someone else will.

If you don't take this kind of stand, your little children will grow up and look at you and think "shame." If you don't take an uncompromising stand—I don't mean go out and get violent; but at the same time you should never be nonviolent unless you run into some nonviolence. I'm nonviolent with those who are nonviolent with me. But when you drop that violence on me, then you've made me go insane, and I'm not responsible for what I do. And that's the way every Negro should get. Any time you know you're within the law, within your legal rights, within your moral rights, in accord with justice, then die for what you believe in. But don't die alone. Let your dying be reciprocal. This is what is meant by equality. What's good for the goose is good for the gander.

When we begin to get in this area, we need new friends, we need new allies. We need to expand the civil-rights struggle to a higher level—to the level of human rights. Whenever you are in a civil-rights struggle, whether you know it or not, you are confining yourself to the jurisdiction of Uncle Sam. No one from the outside world can speak out in your behalf as long as your struggle is a civil-rights struggle. Civil rights comes within the domestic affairs of this country. All of our African brothers and our Asian brothers and our Latin-American brothers cannot open their mouths and interfere in the domestic affairs of the United States. And as long as it's civil rights, this comes under the jurisdiction of Uncle Sam.

But the United Nations has what's known as the charter of human rights, it has a committee that deals in human rights. You may wonder why all of the atrocities that have been committed in Africa and in Hungary and in Asia and in Latin America are brought before the UN, and the Negro problem is never brought before the UN. This is part of the conspiracy. This old, tricky, blue-eyed liberal who is supposed to be your and my friend, supposed to be in our corner, supposed to be subsidizing our struggle, and supposed to be acting in the capacity of an adviser, never tells you anything about human rights. They keep you wrapped up in civil rights. And you spend so much time barking up the civil-rights tree, you don't even know there's a human-rights tree on the same floor.

When you expand the civil-rights struggle to the level of human rights, you can then take the case of the black man in this country before the nations in the UN. You can take it before the General Assembly. You can take Uncle Sam before a world court. But the only level you can do it on is the level of human rights. Civil rights keeps you under his restrictions, under his jurisdiction. Civil rights keeps you in his pocket. Civil rights means you're asking Uncle Sam to treat you right. Human rights are something you were born with. Human rights are your God-given rights. Human rights are the rights that are recognized by all nations of this earth. And any time any one violates your human rights, you can take them to the world court. Uncle Sam's hands are dripping with blood, dripping with the blood of the black man in this country. He's the earth's number-one hypocrite. He has the audacity—yes, he has—imagine him posing as the leader of the free world. The free world!—and you over here singing "We Shall Overcome." Expand the civil-rights struggle to the level of human rights, take it into the United Nations, where our African brothers can throw their weight on our side, where our Asian brothers can throw their weight on our side, where our Latin-American brothers can throw their weight on our side, and where 800 million Chinamen are sitting there waiting to throw their weight on our side.

Let the world know how bloody his hands are. Let the world know the hypocrisy that's practiced over here. Let it be the ballot or the bullet. Let him know that it must be the ballot or the bullet.

When you take your case to Washington, D.C., you're taking it to the criminal who's responsible; it's like running from the wolf to the fox. They're all in cahoots together. They all work political chicanery and make you look like a chump before the eyes of the world. Here you are walking around in America, getting ready to be drafted and sent abroad, like a tin soldier, and when you get over there, people ask you what are you fighting for, and you have to stick your tongue in your cheek. No, take Uncle Sam to court, take him before the world.

By ballot I only mean freedom. Don't you know—I disagree with Lomax on this issue—that the ballot is more important than the dollar? Can I prove it? Yes. Look in the UN. There are poor nations in the UN; yet those poor nations can get together with their voting power and keep the rich nations from making a move. They have one nation—one vote, everyone has an equal vote. And when those brothers from Asia, and Africa and the darker parts of this earth get together, their voting power is sufficient to hold Sam in check. Or Russia in check. Or some other section of the earth in check. So, the ballot is most important.

Right now, in this country, if you and I, 22 million African-Americans—that's what we are—Africans who are in America. You're nothing but Africans. Nothing but Africans. In fact, you'd get farther calling yourself African instead of Negro. Africans don't catch hell. You're the only one catching hell. They don't have to pass civil-rights bills for Africans. An African

can go anywhere he wants right now. All you've got to do is tie your head up. That's right, go anywhere you want. Just stop being a Negro. Change your name to Hoogagagooba. That'll show you how silly the white man is. You're dealing with a silly man. A friend of mine who's very dark put a turban on his head and went into a restaurant in Atlanta before they called themselves desegregated. He went into a white restaurant, he sat down, they served him, and he said, "What would happen if a Negro came in here?" And there he's sitting, black as night, but because he had his head wrapped up the waitress looked back at him and says, "Why, there wouldn't no nigger dare come in here."

So, you're dealing with a man whose bias and prejudice are making him lose his mind, his intelligence, every day. He's frightened. He looks around and sees what's taking place on this earth, and he sees that the pendulum of time is swinging in your direction. The dark people are waking up. They're losing their fear of the white man. No place where he's fighting right now is he winning. Everywhere he's fighting, he's fighting someone your and my complexion. And they're beating him. He can't win any more. He's won his last battle. He failed to win the Korean War. He couldn't win it. He had to sign a truce. That's a loss. Any time Uncle Sam, with all his machinery for warfare, is held to a draw by some rice-eaters, he's lost the battle. He had to sign a truce. America's not supposed to sign a truce. She's supposed to be bad. But she's not bad any more. She's bad as long as she can use her hydrogen bomb, but she can't use hers for fear Russia might use hers. Russia can't use hers, for fear that Sam might use his. So, both of them are weaponless. They can't use the weapon because each's weapon nullifies the other's. So the only place where action can take place is on the ground. And the white man can't win another war fighting on the ground. Those days are over. The black man knows it, the brown man knows it, the red man knows it, and the yellow man knows it. So they engage him in guerrilla warfare. That's not his style. You've got to have heart to be a guerrilla warrior, and he hasn't got any heart. I'm telling you now.

I just want to give you a little briefing on guerrilla warfare because, before you know it, before you know it—It takes heart to be a guerrilla warrior because you're on your own. In conventional warfare you have tanks and a whole lot of other people with you to back you up, planes over your head and all that kind of stuff. But a guerrilla is on his own. All you have is a rifle, some sneakers and a bowl of rice, and that's all you need—and a lot of heart. The Japanese on some of those islands in the Pacific, when the American soldiers landed, one Japanese sometimes could hold the whole army off. He'd just wait until the sun went down, and when the sun went down they were all equal. He would take his little blade and slip from bush to bush, and from American to American. The white soldiers couldn't cope with that. Whenever you see a white soldier that fought in the Pacific, he has the shakes, he has a nervous condition, because they scared him to death.

The same thing happened to the French up in French Indochina. People who just a few years previously were rice farmers got together and ran the heavily-mechanized French army out of Indochina. You don't need it—modern warfare today won't work. This is the day of the guerrilla. They did the same thing in Algeria. Algerians, who were nothing but Bedouins, took a rifle and sneaked off to the hills, and de Gaulle and all of his highfalutin' war machinery couldn't defeat those guerrillas. Nowhere on this earth does the white man win in a guerrilla warfare. It's not his speed. Just as guerrilla warfare is prevailing in Asia and in parts of Africa and in parts of Latin America, you've got to be mighty naive, or you've got to play the black man cheap, if you don't think some day he's going to wake up and find that it's got to be the ballot or the bullet.

I would like to say, in closing, a few things concerning the Muslim Mosque, Inc., which we established recently in New York City. It's true we're Muslims and our religion is Islam, but we don't mix our religion with our politics and our economics and our social and civil activities—not any more. We keep our religion in our mosque. After our religious services are over, then as Muslims we become involved in political action, economic action and social and civic action. We become involved with anybody, anywhere, any time and in any manner that's designed to eliminate the evils, the political, economic and social evils that are afflicting the people of our community.

The political philosophy of black nationalism means that the black man should control the politics and the politicians in his own community; no more. The black man in the black community has to be re-educated into the science of politics so he will know what politics is supposed to bring him in return. Don't be throwing out any ballots. A ballot is like a bullet. You don't throw your ballots until you see a target, and if that target is not within your reach, keep your ballot in your pocket. The political philosophy of black nationalism is being taught in the Christian church. It's being taught in the NAACP. It's being taught in CORE meetings. It's being taught in SNCC [Student Nonviolent Coordinating Committee] meetings. It's being taught in Muslim meetings. It's being taught where nothing but atheists and agnostics come together. It's being taught everywhere. Black people are fed up with the dillydallying, pussyfooting, compromising approach that we've been using toward getting our freedom. We want freedom *now,* but we're not going to get it saying "We Shall Overcome." We've got to fight until we overcome.

The economic philosophy of black nationalism is pure and simple. It only means that we should control the economy of our community. Why should white people be running all the stores in our community? Why should white people be running the banks of our community? Why should the economy of our community be in the hands of the white man? Why? If a black man can't move his store into a white community, you tell me why a white man should move his store into a black community. The philosophy of black nationalism involves a re-education program in the black community in regards to economics. Our people have to be made to see that any time you take your dollar out of your community and spend it in a community where you don't live, the community where you live will get poorer and poorer, and the community where you spend your money will get richer and richer. Then you wonder why where you live is always a ghetto or a slum area. And where you and I are concerned, not only do we lose it when we spend it out of the community, but the white man has got all our stores in the community tied up; so that though we spend it in the community, at sundown the man who runs the store takes it over across town somewhere. He's got us in a vise.

So the economic philosophy of black nationalism means in every church, in every civic organization, in every fraternal order, it's time now for our people to become conscious of the importance of controlling the economy of our community. If we own the stores, if we operate the businesses, if we try and establish some industry in our own community, then we're developing to the position where we are creating employment for our own kind. Once you gain control of the economy of your own community, then you don't have to picket and boycott and beg some cracker downtown for a job in his business.

The social philosophy of black nationalism only means that we have to get together and remove the evils, the vices, alcoholism, drug addiction, and other evils that are destroying the moral fiber of our community. We ourselves have to lift the level of our community, the standard of our community to a higher level, make our own society beautiful so that we will be satisfied in our own social circles and won't be running around here trying to knock our way into a social circle where we're not wanted.

So I say, in spreading a gospel such as black nationalism, it is not designed to make the black man re-evaluate the white man—you know him already—but to make the black man re-evaluate himself. Don't change the white man's mind—you can't change his mind, and that whole thing about appealing to the moral conscience of America—America's conscience is bankrupt. She lost all conscience a long time ago. Uncle Sam has no conscience. They don't know what morals are. They don't try and eliminate an evil because it's evil, or because it's illegal, or because it's immoral; they eliminate it only when it threatens their existence. So you're wasting your time appealing to the moral conscience of a bankrupt man like Uncle Sam. If he had a conscience, he'd straighten this thing out with no more pressure being put upon him. So it is not necessary to change the white man's mind. We have to change our own mind. You can't change his mind about us. We've got to change our own minds about each other. We have to see each other with new eyes. We have to see each other as brothers and sisters. We have to come together with warmth so we can develop unity and harmony that's necessary to get this problem solved ourselves. How can we do this? How can we avoid jealousy? How can we avoid the suspicion and the divisions that exist in the community? I'll tell you how.

I have watched how Billy Graham comes into a city, spreading what he calls the gospel of Christ, which is only white nationalism. That's what he is. Billy Graham is a white nationalist; I'm a black nationalist. But since it's the natural tendency for leaders to be jealous and look upon a powerful figure like Graham with suspicion and envy, how is it possible for him to come into a city and get all the cooperation of the church leaders? Don't think because they're church leaders that they don't have weaknesses that make them envious and jealous—no, everybody's got it. It's not an accident that when they want to choose a cardinal [as Pope] over there in Rome, they get in a closet so you can't hear them cussing and fighting and carrying on.

Billy Graham comes in preaching the gospel of Christ, he evangelizes the gospel, he stirs everybody up, but he never tries to start a church. If he came in trying to start a church, all the churches would be against him. So, he just comes in talking about Christ and tells everybody who gets Christ to go to any church where Christ is; and in this way the church cooperates with him. So we're going to take a page from his book.

Our gospel is black nationalism. We're not trying to threaten the existence of any organization, but we're spreading the gospel of black nationalism. Anywhere there's a church that is also preaching and practicing the gospel of black nationalism, join that church. If the NAACP is preaching and practicing the gospel of black nationalism, join the NAACP. If CORE is spreading and practicing the gospel of black nationalism, join CORE. Join any organization that has a gospel that's for the uplift of the black man. And when you get into it and see them pussyfooting or compromising, pull out of it because that's not black nationalism. We'll find another one.

And in this manner, the organizations will increase in number and in quantity and in quality, and by August, it is then our intention to have a black nationalist convention which will consist of delegates from all over the country who are interested in the political, economic and social philosophy of black nationalism. After these delegates convene, we will hold a seminar, we will hold discussions, we will listen to everyone. We want to hear new ideas and new solutions and new answers. And at that time, if we see fit then to form a black nationalist party, we'll form a black nationalist party. If it's necessary to form a black nationalist army, we'll form a black nationalist army. It'll be the ballot or the bullet. It'll be liberty or it'll be death.

It's time for you and me to stop sitting in this country, letting some cracker senators, Northern crackers and Southern crackers, sit there in Washington, D.C., and come to a conclusion in their mind that you and I are supposed to have civil rights. There's no white man going to tell me anything about *my* rights. Brothers and sisters, always remember, if it doesn't take senators and congressmen and presidential proclamations to give freedom to the white man, it is not necessary for legislation or proclamation or Supreme Court decisions to give freedom to the black man. You let that white man know, if this is a country of freedom, let it be a country of freedom; and if it's not a country of freedom, change it.

We will work with anybody, anywhere, at any time, who is genuinely interested in tackling the problem head-on, nonviolently as long as the enemy is nonviolent, but violent when the enemy gets violent. We'll work with you on the voter-registration drive, we'll work with you on rent strikes, we'll work with you on school boycotts—I don't believe in any kind of integration; I'm not even worried about it because I know you're not going to get it anyway; you're not going to get it because you're afraid to die; you've got to be ready to die if you try and force yourself on the white man, because he'll get just as violent as those crackers in Mississippi, right here in Cleveland. But we will still work with you on the school boycotts because we're against a segregated school system. A segregated school system produces children who, when they graduate, graduate with crippled minds. But this does not mean that a school is segregated because it's all black. A segregated school means a school that is controlled by people who have no real interest in it whatsoever.

Let me explain what I mean. A segregated district or community is a community in which people live, but outsiders control the politics and the economy of that community. They never refer to the white section as a segregated community. It's the all-Negro section that's a segregated community. Why? The white man controls his own school, his own bank, his own economy, his own politics, his own everything, his own community—but he also controls yours. When you're under someone else's control, you're segregated. They'll always give you the lowest or the worst that there is to offer, but it doesn't mean you're segregated just because you have your own. You've got to *control* your own. Just like the white man has control of his, you need to control yours.

You know the best way to get rid of segregation? The white man is more afraid of separation than he is of integration. Segregation means that he puts you away from him, but not far enough for you to be out of his jurisdiction; separation means you're gone. And the white man will integrate faster than he'll let you separate. So we will work with you against the segregated school system because it's criminal, because it is absolutely destructive, in every way imaginable, to the minds of the children who have to be exposed to that type of crippling education.

Last but not least, I must say this concerning the great controversy over rifles and shotguns. The only thing that I've ever said is that in areas where the government has proven itself either unwilling or unable to defend the lives and the property of Negroes, it's time for Negroes to defend themselves. Article number two of the constitutional amendments provides you and me the right to own a rifle or a shotgun. It is constitutionally legal to own a shotgun or a rifle. This doesn't mean you're going to get a rifle and form battalions and go out looking for white folks, although you'd be within your rights—I mean, you'd be justified; but that would be illegal and we don't do anything illegal. If the white man doesn't want the black man buying rifles and shotguns, then let the government do its job. That's all. And don't let the white man come to you and ask you what you think about what Malcolm says—why, you old Uncle Tom. He would never ask you if he thought you were going to say, "Amen!" No, he is making a Tom out of you.

So, this doesn't mean forming rifle clubs and going out looking for people, but it is time, in 1964, if you are a man, to let that man know. If he's not going to do his job in running the government and providing you and me with the protection that our taxes are supposed to be for, since he spends all those billions for his defense budget, he certainly can't begrudge you and me spending $12 or $15 for a single-shot, or double-action. I hope you understand. Don't go out shooting people, but any time, brothers and sisters, and especially the men in this audience—some of you wearing Congressional Medals of Honor, with shoulders this wide, chests this big, muscles that big—any time you and I sit around and read where they bomb a church and murder in cold blood, not some grownups, but four little girls while they were praying to the same god the white man taught them to pray to, and you and I see the government go down and can't find who did it.

Why, this man—he can find Eichmann hiding down in Argentina somewhere. Let two or three American soldiers, who are minding somebody else's business way over in South Vietnam, get killed, and he'll send battleships, sticking his nose in their business. He wanted to send troops down to Cuba and make them have what he calls free elections—this old cracker who doesn't have free elections in his own country. No, if you never see me another time in your life, if I die in the morning, I'll die saying one thing: the ballot or the bullet, the ballot or the bullet.

If a Negro in 1964 has to sit around and wait for some cracker senator to filibuster when it comes to the rights of black people, why, you and I should hang our heads in shame. You talk about a march on Washington in 1963, you haven't seen anything. There's some more going down in '64. And this time they're not going like they went last year. They're not going singing "We Shall Overcome." They're not going with white friends. They're not going with placards already painted for them. They're not going with round-trip tickets. They're going with one-way tickets.

And if they don't want that non-nonviolent army going down there, tell them to bring the filibuster to a halt. The black nationalists aren't going to wait. Lyndon B. Johnson is the head of the Democratic Party. If he's for civil rights, let him go into the Senate next week and declare himself. Let him go in there right now and declare himself. Let him go in there and denounce the Southern branch of his party. Let him go in there right now and take a moral stand—right now, not later. Tell him, don't wait until election time. If he waits too long, brothers and sisters, he will be responsible for letting a condition develop in this country which will create a climate that will bring seeds up out of the ground with vegetation on the end of them looking like something these people never dreamed of. In 1964, it's the ballot or the bullet. Thank you.

From **Soul on Ice**
ELDRIDGE CLEAVER

The White Race and Its Heroes

> White people cannot, in the generality, be taken as models of how to live.
> Rather, the white man is himself in sore need of new standards, which will release
> him from his confusion and place him once again in fruitful communion with the
> depths of his own being.
> *James Baldwin*—The Fire Next Time

Right from the go, let me make one thing absolutely clear: I am not now, nor have
I ever been, a white man. Nor, I hasten to add, am I now a Black
Muslim—although I used to be. But I *am* an Ofay Watcher, a member of that
unchartered, amorphous league which has members on all continents and the
islands of the seas. Ofay Watchers Anonymous, we might be called, because we
exist concealed in the shadows wherever colored people have known oppression
by whites, by white enslavers, colonizers, imperialists, and neo-colonialists.

Did it irritate you, compatriot, for me to string those epithets out like
that? Tolerate me. My intention was not necessarily to sprinkle salt over anyone's
wounds. I did it primarily to relieve a certain pressure on my brain. Do you cop
that? If not, then we're in trouble, because we Ofay Watchers have a pronounced
tendency to slip into that mood. If it is bothersome to you, it is quite a task for me
because not too long ago it was my way of life to preach, as ardently as I could,
that the white race is a race of devils, created by their maker to do evil, and make
evil appear as good; that the white race is the natural, unchangeable enemy of the
black man, who is the original man, owner, maker, cream of the planet Earth; that
the white race was soon to be destroyed by Allah, and that the black man would
then inherit the earth, which has always, in fact, been his.

I have, so to speak, washed my hands in the blood of the martyr,
Malcolm X, whose retreat from the precipice of madness created new room for
others to turn about in, and I am now caught up in that tiny space, attempting a
maneuver of my own. Having renounced the teachings of Elijah Muhammad, I
find that a rebirth does not follow automatically, of its own accord, that a void is
left in one's vision, and this void seeks constantly to obliterate itself by pulling one
back to one's former outlook. I have tried a tentative compromise by adopting a
select vocabulary, so that now when I see the whites of *their* eyes, instead of saying
"devil" or "beast" I say "imperialist" or "colonialist," and everyone seems to be
happier.

In silence, we have spent our years watching the ofays, trying to
understand them, on the principle that you have a better chance coping with the
known than with the unknown. Some of us have been, and some still are,
interested in learning whether it is *ultimately* possible to live in the same territory
with people who seem so disagreeable to live with; still others want to get as far
away from ofays as possible. What we share in common is the desire to break the
ofays' power over us.

At times of fundamental social change, such as the era in which we live, it is easy to be deceived by the onrush of events, beguiled by the craving for social stability into mistaking transitory phenomena for enduring reality. The strength and permanence of "white backlash" in America is just such an illusion. However much this rear-guard action might seem to grow in strength, the initiative, and the future, rest with those whites and blacks who have liberated themselves from the master/slave syndrome. And these are to be found mainly among the youth.

Over the past twelve years there has surfaced a political conflict between the generations that is deeper, even, than the struggle between the races. Its first dramatic manifestation was within the ranks of the Negro people, when college students in the South, fed up with Uncle Tom's hat-in-hand approach to revolution, threw off the yoke of the NAACP. When these students initiated the first sit-ins, their spirit spread like a raging fire across the nation, and the technique of non-violent direct action, constantly refined and honed into a sharp cutting tool, swiftly matured. The older Negro "leaders," who are now all die-hard advocates of this tactic, scolded the students for sitting-in. The students rained down contempt upon their hoary heads. In the pre-sit-in days, these conservative leaders had always succeeded in putting down insurgent elements among the Negro people. (A measure of their power, prior to the students' rebellion, is shown by their success in isolating such great black men as the late W. E. B. DuBois and Paul Robeson, when these stalwarts, refusing to bite their tongues, lost favor with the U.S. government by their unstinting efforts to link up the Negro revolution with national liberation movements around the world.)

The "Negro leaders," and the whites who depended upon them to control their people, were outraged by the impudence of the students. Calling for a moratorium on student initiative, they were greeted instead by an encore of sit-ins, and retired to their ivory towers to contemplate the new phenomenon. Others, less prudent because held on a tighter leash by the whites, had their careers brought to an abrupt end because they thought they could lead a black/white backlash against the students, only to find themselves in a kind of Bay of Pigs. Negro college presidents, who expelled students from all-Negro colleges in an attempt to quash the demonstrations, ended up losing their jobs; the victorious students would no longer allow them to preside over the campuses. The spontaneous protests on southern campuses over the repressive measures of their college administrations were an earnest of the Free Speech upheaval which years later was to shake the UC campus at Berkeley. In countless ways, the rebellion of the black students served as catalyst for the brewing revolt of the whites.

What has suddenly happened is that the white race has lost its heroes. Worse, its heroes have been revealed as villains and its greatest heroes as the arch-villains. The new generations of whites, appalled by the sanguine and despicable record carved over the face of the globe by their race in the last five hundred years, are rejecting the panoply of white heroes, whose heroism consisted in erecting the inglorious edifice of colonialism and imperialism; heroes whose careers rested on a system of foreign and domestic exploitation, rooted in the myth of white supremacy and the manifest destiny of the white race. The emerging shape of a new world order, and the requisites for survival in such a world, are fostering in young whites a new outlook. They recoil in shame from the spectacle of cowboys and pioneers—their heroic forefathers whose exploits filled earlier generations with pride—galloping across a movie screen shooting down Indians like Coke bottles. Even Winston Churchill, who is looked upon by older whites as perhaps the greatest hero of the twentieth century—even he, because of the system of which he was a creature and which he served, is an arch-villain in the eyes of the young white rebels.

At the close of World War Two, national liberation movements in the colonized world picked up new momentum and audacity, seeking to cash in on the democratic promises made by the Allies during the war. The Atlantic Charter, signed by President Roosevelt and Prime Minister Churchill in 1941, affirming "the right of all people to choose the form of government under which they may live," established the principle, although it took years of postwar struggle to give this piece of rhetoric even the appearance of reality. And just as world revolution has prompted the oppressed to re-evaluate their self-image in terms of the changing conditions, to slough off the servile attitudes inculcated by long years of subordination, the same dynamics of change have prompted the white people of the world to re-evaluate their self-image as well, to disabuse themselves of the Master Race psychology developed over centuries of imperial hegemony.

It is among the white youth of the world that the greatest change is taking place. It is they who are experiencing the great psychic pain of waking into consciousness to find their inherited heroes turned by events into villains. Communication and understanding between the older and younger generations of whites has entered a crisis. The elders, who, in the tradition of privileged classes or races, genuinely do not understand the youth, trapped by old ways of thinking and blind to the future, have only just begun to be vexed—because the youth have only just begun to rebel. So thoroughgoing is the revolution in the psyches of white youth that the traditional tolerance which every older generation has found it necessary to display is quickly exhausted, leaving a gulf of fear, hostility, mutual misunderstanding, and contempt.

The rebellion of the oppressed peoples of the world, along with the Negro revolution in America, have opened the way to a new evaluation of history, a re-examination of the role played by the white race since the beginning of European expansion. The positive achievements are also there in the record, and future generations will applaud them. But there can be no applause now, not while the master still holds the whip in his hand! Not even the master's own children can find it possible to applaud him—he cannot even applaud himself! The negative rings too loudly. Slave-catchers, slaveowners, murderers, butchers, invaders, oppressors—the white heroes have acquired new names. The great white statesmen whom school children are taught to revere are revealed as the architects of systems of human exploitation and slavery. Religious leaders are exposed as condoners and justifiers of all these evil deeds. Schoolteachers and college professors are seen as a clique of brainwashers and whitewashers.

The white youth of today are coming to see, intuitively, that to escape the onus of the history their fathers made they must face and admit the moral truth concerning the works of their fathers. That such venerated figures as George Washington and Thomas Jefferson owned hundreds of black slaves, that all of the Presidents up to Lincoln presided over a slave state, and that every President since Lincoln connived politically and cynically with the issues affecting the human rights and general welfare of the broad masses of the American people—these facts weigh heavily upon the hearts of these young people.

The elders do not like to give these youngsters credit for being able to understand what is going on and what has gone on. When speaking of juvenile delinquency, or the rebellious attitude of today's youth, the elders employ a glib rhetoric. They speak of the "alienation of youth," the desire of the young to be independent, the problems of "the father image" and "the mother image" and their effect upon growing children who lack sound models upon which to pattern themselves. But they consider it bad form to connect the problems of the youth with the central event of our era—the national liberation movements abroad and the Negro revolution at home. The foundations of authority have been blasted to bits in America because the whole society has been indicted, tried, and convicted of injustice. To the youth, the elders are Ugly Americans; to the elders, the youth have gone mad.

The rebellion of the white youth has gone through four broadly discernible stages. First there was an initial recoiling away, a rejection of the conformity which America expected, and had always received, sooner or later, from its youth. The disaffected youth were refusing to participate in the system, having discovered that America, far from helping the underdog, was up to its ears in the mud trying to hold the dog down. Because of the publicity and self-advertisements of the more vocal rebels, this period has come to be known as the beatnik era, although not all of the youth affected by these changes thought of themselves as beatniks. The howl of the beatniks and their scathing, outraged denunciation of the system—characterized by Ginsberg as Moloch, a bloodthirsty Semitic deity to which the ancient tribes sacrificed their firstborn children—was a serious, irrevocable declaration of war. It is revealing that the elders looked upon the beatniks as mere obscene misfits who were too lazy to take baths and too stingy to buy a haircut. The elders had eyes but couldn't see, ears but couldn't hear—not even when the message came through as clearly as in this remarkable passage from Jack Kerouac's *On the Road:*

> At lilac evening I walked with every muscle aching among the lights of 27th and Welton in the Denver colored section, wishing I were a Negro, feeling that the best the white world had offered was not enough ecstasy for me, not enough life, joy, kicks, darkness, music, not enough night. I wished I were a Denver Mexican, or even a poor overworked Jap, anything but what I so drearily was, a "white man" disillusioned. All my life I'd had white ambitions. . . . I passed the dark porches of Mexican and Negro homes; soft voices were there, occasionally the dusky knee of some mysterious sensuous gal; the dark faces of the men behind rose arbors. Little children sat like sages in ancient rocking chairs.

The second stage arrived when these young people, having decided emphatically that the world, and particularly the U.S.A., was unacceptable to them in its present form, began an active search for roles they could play in changing the society. If many of these young people were content to lay up in their cool beat pads, smoking pot and listening to jazz in a perpetual orgy of esoteric bliss, there were others, less crushed by the system, who recognized the need for positive action. Moloch could not ask for anything more than to have its disaffected victims withdraw into safe, passive, apolitical little nonparticipatory islands, in an economy less and less able to provide jobs for the growing pool of unemployed. If all the unemployed had followed the lead of the beatniks, Moloch would gladly have legalized the use of euphoric drugs and marijuana, passed out free jazz albums and sleeping bags to all those willing to sign affidavits promising to remain "beat." The non-beat disenchanted white youth were attracted magnetically to the Negro revolution, which had begun to take on a mass, insurrectionary tone. But they had difficulty understanding their relationship to the Negro, and what role "whites" could play in a "Negro revolution." For the time being they watched the Negro activists from afar.

The third stage, which is rapidly drawing to a close, emerged when white youth started joining Negro demonstrations in large numbers. The presence of whites among the demonstrators emboldened the Negro leaders and allowed them to use tactics they never would have been able to employ with all-black troops. The racist conscience of America is such that murder does not register as murder, really, unless the victim is white. And it was only when the newspapers and magazines started carrying pictures and stories of white demonstrators being beaten and maimed by mobs and police that the public began to protest. Negroes have become so used to this double standard that they, too, react differently to the death of a white. When white freedom riders were brutalized along with blacks, a sigh of relief went up from the black masses, because the blacks knew that white blood is the coin of freedom in a land where for four hundred years black blood has been shed unremarked and with impunity. America has never truly been outraged by the murder of a black man, woman, or child. White politicians may, if Negroes are aroused by a particular murder, say with their lips what they know with their minds they should feel with their hearts—but don't.

It is a measure of what the Negro feels that when the two white and one black civil rights workers were murdered in Mississippi in 1964, the event was welcomed by Negroes on a level of understanding beyond and deeper than the grief they felt for the victims and their families. This welcoming of violence and death to whites can almost be heard—indeed it can be heard—in the inevitable words, oft repeated by Negroes, that those whites, and blacks, do not die in vain. So it was with Mrs. Viola Liuzzo. And much of the anger which Negroes felt toward Martin Luther King during the Battle of Selma stemmed from the fact that he denied history a great moment, never to be recaptured, when he turned tail on the Edmund Pettus Bridge and refused to all those whites behind him what they had traveled thousands of miles to receive. If the police had turned them back by force, all those nuns, priests, rabbis, preachers, and distinguished ladies and gentlemen old and young—as they had done the Negroes a week earlier—the violence and brutality of the system would have been ruthlessly exposed. Or if, seeing King determined to lead them on to Montgomery, the troopers had stepped aside to avoid precisely the confrontation that Washington would not have tolerated, it would have signaled the capitulation of the militant white South. As it turned out, the March on Montgomery was a show of somewhat dim luster, stage-managed by the Establishment. But by this time the young whites were already active participants in the Negro revolution. In fact they had begun to transform it into something broader, with the potential of encompassing the whole of America in a radical reordering of society.

The fourth stage, now in its infancy, sees these white youth taking the initiative, using techniques learned in the Negro struggle to attack problems in the general society. The classic example of this new energy in action was the student battle on the UC campus at Berkeley, California—the Free Speech Movement. Leading the revolt were veterans of the civil rights movement, some of whom spent time on the firing line in the wilderness of Mississippi/Alabama. Flowing from the same momentum were student demonstrations against U.S. interference in the internal affairs of Vietnam, Cuba, the Dominican Republic, and the Congo and U.S. aid to apartheid in South Africa. The students even aroused the intellectual community to actions and positions unthinkable a few years ago: witness the teach-ins. But their revolt is deeper than single-issue protest. The characteristics of the white rebels which most alarm their elders—the long hair, the new dances, their love for Negro music, their use of marijuana, their mystical attitude toward sex—are all tools of their rebellion. They have turned these tools against the totalitarian fabric of American society—and they mean to change it.

From the beginning, America has been a schizophrenic nation. Its two conflicting images of itself were never reconciled, because never before has the survival of its most cherished myths made a reconciliation mandatory. Once before, during the bitter struggle between North and South climaxed by the Civil War, the two images of America came into conflict, although whites North and South scarcely understood it. The image of America held by its most alienated citizens was advanced neither by the North nor by the South; it was perhaps best expressed by Frederick Douglass, who was born into slavery in 1817, escaped to the North, and became the greatest leader-spokesman for the blacks of his era. In words that can still, years later, arouse an audience of black Americans, Frederick Douglass delivered, in 1852, a scorching indictment in his Fourth of July oration in Rochester:

> What to the American slave is your Fourth of July? I answer: a day that reveals to him, more than all other days in the year, the gross injustice and cruelty to which he is the constant victim. To him your celebration is a sham; your boasted liberty, an unholy licence; your national greatness, swelling vanity; your sounds of rejoicing are empty and heartless; your denunciation of tyrants, brass-fronted impudence; your shouts of liberty and equality, hollow mockery; your prayers and hymns, your sermons and thanksgivings, with all your religious parade and solemnity, are, to him, more bombast, fraud, deception, impiety and hypocrisy—a thin veil to cover up crimes which would disgrace a nation of savages. . . .

> You boast of your love of liberty, your superior civilization, and your pure Christianity, while the whole political power of the nation (as embodied in the two great political parties) is solemnly pledged to support and perpetuate the enslavement of three millions of your countrymen. You hurl your anathemas at the crown-headed tyrants of Russia and Austria and pride yourselves on your democratic institutions, while you yourselves consent to be the mere *tools* and *bodyguards* of the tyrants of Virginia and Carolina.
>
> You invite to your shores fugitives of oppression from abroad, honor them with banquets, greet them with ovations, cheer them, toast them, salute them, protect them, and pour out your money to them like water; but the fugitive from your own land you advertise, hunt, arrest, shoot, and kill. You glory in your refinement and your universal education; yet you maintain a system as barbarous and dreadful as ever stained the character of a nation—a system begun in avarice, supported in pride, and perpetuated in cruelty.
>
> You shed tears over fallen Hungary, and make the sad story of her wrongs the theme of your poets, statesmen and orators, till your gallant sons are ready to fly to arms to vindicate her cause against the oppressor; but, in regard to the ten thousand wrongs of the American slave, you would enforce the strictest silence, and would hail him as an enemy of the nation who dares to make these wrongs the subject of public discourse!

This most alienated view of America was preached by the Abolitionists, and by Harriet Beecher Stowe in her *Uncle Tom's Cabin.* But such a view of America was too distasteful to receive wide attention, and serious debate about America's image and her reality was engaged in only on the fringes of society. Even when confronted with overwhelming evidence to the contrary, most white Americans have found it possible, after steadying their rattled nerves, to settle comfortably back into their vaunted belief that America is dedicated to the proposition that all men are created equal and endowed by their Creator with certain inalienable rights—life, liberty and the pursuit of happiness. With the Constitution for a rudder and the Declaration of Independence as its guiding star, the ship of state is sailing always toward a brighter vision of freedom and justice for all.

Because there is no common ground between these two contradictory images of America, they had to be kept apart. But the moment the blacks were let into the white world—let out of the voiceless and faceless cages of their ghettos, singing, walking, talking, dancing, writing, and orating *their* image of America and of Americans—the white world was suddenly challenged to match its practice to its preachments. And this is why those whites who abandon the *white* image of America and adopt the *black* are greeted with such unmitigated hostility by their elders.

For all these years whites have been taught to believe in the myth they preached, while Negroes have had to face the bitter reality of what America practiced. But without the lies and distortions, white Americans would not have been able to do the things they have done. When whites are forced to look honestly upon the objective proof of their deeds, the cement of mendacity holding white society together swiftly disintegrates. On the other hand. the core of the black world's vision remains intact, and in fact begins to expand and spread into the psychological territory vacated by the non-viable white lies, i.e., into the minds of young whites. It is remarkable how the system worked for so many years, how the majority of whites remained effectively unaware of any contradiction between their view of the world and that world itself. The mechanism by which this was rendered possible requires examination at this point.

Let us recall that the white man, in order to justify slavery and, later on, to justify segregation, elaborated a complex, all-pervasive myth which at one time classified the black man as a subhuman beast of burden. The myth was progressively modified, gradually elevating the blacks on the scale of evolution, following their slowly changing status, until the plateau of separate-but-equal was reached at the close of the nineteenth century. During slavery, the black was seen as a mindless Supermasculine Menial. Forced to do the backbreaking work, he was conceived in terms of his ability to do such work—"field niggers," etc. The white man administered the plantation, doing all the thinking, exercising omnipotent power over the slaves. He had little difficulty dissociating himself from the black slaves, and he could not conceive of their positions being reversed or even reversible.

Blacks and whites being conceived as mutually exclusive types, those attributes imputed to the blacks could not also be imputed to the whites—at least not in equal degree—without blurring the line separating the races. These images were based upon the social function of the two races, the work they performed. The ideal white man was one who knew how to use his head, who knew how to manage and control things and get things done. Those whites who were not in a position to perform these functions nevertheless aspired to them. The ideal black man was one who did exactly as he was told, and did it efficiently and cheerfully. "Slaves," said Frederick Douglass, "are generally expected to sing as well as to work." As the black man's position and function became more varied, the images of white and black, having become stereotypes, lagged behind.

The separate-but-equal doctrine was promulgated by the Supreme Court in 1896. It had the same purpose domestically as the Open Door Policy toward China in the international arena: to stabilize a situation and subordinate a non-white population so that racist exploiters could manipulate those people according to their own selfish interests. These doctrines were foisted off as *the epitome of enlightened justice, the highest expression of morality.* Sanctified by religion, justified by philosophy and legalized by the Supreme Court, separate-but-equal was enforced by day by agencies of the law, and by the KKK & Co. under cover of night. Booker T. Washington, the Martin Luther King of his day, accepted separate-but-equal in the name of all Negroes. W. E. B. DuBois denounced it.

Separate-but-equal marked the last stage of the white man's flight into cultural neurosis, and the beginning of the black man's frantic striving to assert his humanity and equalize his position with the white. Blacks ventured into all fields of endeavor to which they could gain entrance. Their goal was to present in all fields a performance that would equal or surpass that of the whites. It was long axiomatic among blacks that a black had to be twice as competent as a white in any field in order to win grudging recognition from the whites. This produced a pathological motivation in the blacks to equal or surpass the whites, and a pathological motivation in the whites to maintain a distance from the blacks. This is the rack on which black and white Americans receive their delicious torture! At first there was the color bar, flatly denying the blacks entrance to certain spheres of activity. When this no longer worked, and blacks invaded sector after sector of American life and economy, the whites evolved other methods of keeping their distance. The illusion of the Negro's inferior nature had to be maintained.

One device evolved by the whites was to tab whatever the blacks did with the prefix "Negro." We had *Negro* literature, *Negro* athletes, *Negro* music, *Negro* doctors, *Negro* politicians, *Negro* workers. The malignant ingeniousness of this device is that although it accurately describes an objective biological fact—or, at least, a sociological fact in America—it concealed the paramount psychological fact: that to the white mind, prefixing anything with "Negro" automatically consigned it to an inferior category. A well-known example of the white necessity to deny due credit to blacks is in the realm of music. White musicians were famous for going to Harlem and other Negro cultural centers literally to steal the black man's music, carrying it back across the color line into the Great White World and passing off the watered-down loot as their own original creations. Blacks, meanwhile, were ridiculed as *Negro* musicians playing inferior coon music.

The Negro revolution at home and national liberation movements abroad have unceremoniously shattered the world of fantasy in which the whites have been living. It is painful that many do not yet see that their fantasy world has been rendered uninhabitable in the last half of the twentieth century. But it is away from this world that the white youth of today are turning. The "paper tiger" hero, James Bond, offering the whites a triumphant image of themselves, is saying what many whites want desperately to hear reaffirmed: *I am still the White Man, lord of the land, licensed to kill, and the world is still an empire at my feet.* James Bond feeds on that secret little anxiety, the psychological white backlash, felt in some degree by most whites alive. It is exasperating to see little brown men and little yellow men from the mysterious Orient, and the opaque black men of Africa (to say nothing of these impudent American Negroes!) who come to the UN and talk smart to us, who are scurrying all over *our* globe in their strange modes of dress—much as if they were new, unpleasant arrivals from another planet. Many whites believe in their ulcers that it is only a matter of time before the Marines get the signal to round up these truants and put them back securely in their cages. But it is away from this fantasy world that the white youth of today are turning.

In the world revolution now under way, the initiative rests with people of color. That growing numbers of white youth are repudiating their heritage of blood and taking people of color as their heroes and models is a tribute not only to their insight but to the resilience of the human spirit. For today the heroes of the initiative are people not usually thought of as white: Fidel Castro, Che Guevara, Kwame Nkrumah, Mao Tse-tung, Gamal Abdel Nasser, Robert F. Williams, Malcolm X, Ben Bella, John Lewis, Martin Luther King, Jr., Robert Parris Moses,

Ho Chi Minh, Stokeley Carmichael, W. E. B. DuBois, James Forman, Chou En-lai.

The white youth of today have begun to react to the fact that the "American Way of Life" is a fossil of history. What do they care if their old baldheaded and crew-cut elders don't dig their caveman mops? They couldn't care less about the old, stiffassed honkies who don't like their new dances: Frug, Monkey, Jerk, Swim, Watusi. All they know is that it feels good to swing to way-out body-rhythms instead of dragassing across the dance floor like zombies to the dead beat of mind-smothered Mickey Mouse music. Is it any wonder that the youth have lost all respect for their elders, for law and order, when for as long as they can remember all they've witnessed is a monumental bickering over the Negro's place in American society and the right of people around the world to be left alone by outside powers? They have witnessed the law, both domestic and international, being spat upon by those who do not like its terms. Is it any wonder, then, that they feel justified, by sitting-in and freedom riding, in breaking laws made by lawless men? Old funny-styled, zipper-mouthed political night riders know nothing but to haul out an investigating committee *to look into the disturbance* to find the cause of the unrest among the youth. Look into a mirror! The cause is you, Mr. and Mrs. Yesterday, you with your forked tongues.

A young white today cannot help but recoil from the base deeds of his people. On every side, on every continent, he sees racial arrogance, savage brutality toward the conquered and subjugated people, genocide; he sees the human cargo of the slave trade; he sees the systematic extermination of American Indians; he sees the civilized nations of Europe fighting in imperial depravity over the lands of other people—and over possession of the very people themselves. There seems to be no end to the ghastly deeds of which his people are guilty. *GUILTY*. The slaughter of the Jews by the Germans, the dropping of atomic bombs on the Japanese people—these deeds weigh heavily upon the prostrate souls and tumultuous consciences of the white youth. The white heroes, their hands dripping with blood, are dead.

The young whites know that the colored people of the world, Afro-Americans included, do not seek revenge for their suffering. They seek the same things the white rebel wants: an end to war and exploitation. Black and white, the young rebels are free people, free in a way that Americans have never been before in the history of their country. And they are outraged.

There is in America today a generation of white youth that is truly worthy of a black man's respect, and this is a rare event in the foul annals of American history. From the beginning of the contact between blacks and whites, there has been very little reason for a black man to respect a white, with such exceptions as John Brown and others lesser known. But respect commands itself and it can neither be given nor withheld when it is due. If a man like Malcolm X could change and repudiate racism, if I myself and other former Muslims can change, if young whites can change, then there is hope for America. It was certainly strange to find myself, while steeped in the doctrine that all whites were devils by nature, commanded by the heart to applaud and acknowledge respect for these young whites—despite the fact that they are descendants of the masters and I the descendant of slave. The sins of the fathers are visited upon the heads of the children—but only if the children continue in the evil deeds of the fathers.

From **Black Rage**
WILLIAM H. GRIER
and PRICE M. COBBS

Marriage and Love

> A schoolteacher married a laborer. They worked hard and with economy and planning managed to acquire a home and a car. Children came as planned, but conflict came and grew. The wife wanted a larger home with a yard. The husband resented her demands. He felt that she had no respect for him, that to her he was merely a provider for her endless wishes. She was embarrassed by his poor education. He felt that she and her friends were "phony" and that she was preoccupied with maintaining senseless appearances. Their mutual hostility led to verbal and later physical assaults. Divorce was the result.

This pattern is so common in Negro marriages that it deserves special study, which might shed light on the broader problems of how in America choice of mate and marriage in general is influenced by a person's blackness.

There are voluminous studies describing the economic and social function of Negroes and we feel no necessity to duplicate this work. Rather we shall link the psychological functioning of the individual to his role as a discrete citizen, as an American, as a black man, and as a member of a family. All his possible roles are in a vital way related to his position as a member of a family: as a son, husband, and father. The family is the matrix out of which the inner, uniquely individual man grows; it is this which first offers him vital information about his world. And later it is the source of comfort which will heal him on his return from the wars it prepared him for.

To understand marriage and choice of mate we must understand childhood. Children develop psychologically within the framework supplied by parents and family. For example, if religion occupies a central position in a family, then each child in that family must develop at least partly in response to religion. It must occupy a certain space within his psychological body. He may adopt a pious posture and at least give the appearance of being a devout and faithful believer in the gods of his fathers. Or he may become irreverent and be actively against religion, presenting himself as diametrically opposed to his religious parents. But while differing from them in this important respect he will resemble them in the amount of psychic energy he devotes to religious matters. Or he may ignore religion and to all intents and purposes disengage himself from it altogether. An inspection will reveal, however, that he has displaced his religious concerns onto some seemingly innocuous area where it escapes recognition. He may even have denied himself that displacement, but in his silence one will sense a significant silent area of his psychic life. There will seem to be a vacuum, a hole, and one later may wonder what had been there.

We want to show that issues which were important in childhood, and important to people who in turn were important to the child, must of necessity show themselves as issues which must be taken into account in the child's later adult life.

A minor point may be illustrative. The racial mixture in the background of black people is so varied that it is extremely rare to find two Negroes who have exactly the same brown tones to their skin. There is usually a bit more yellow or red or black that distinguishes seemingly identical skin colors from one another. But these are minor variations on a brown theme and their least deviations are generally of small moment to adults.

The infant's world is so very different in this regard. His mother's body is a vitally important part of his world. Her breasts, her hands, arms, face, are the most important things he sees and touches. She is the first human he recognizes and for a long time in his small life she is the bringer of life.

As he plays with her breast or face, he looks intently, with the myopic vision of a child, at her skin. Its color becomes to him the color of all loving people's skin, and in fact the particular skin tones he sees as a child will ever after evoke emotional overtones based on that intimacy. It is no wonder then that men choose women whose skin tones are closely matched to their mother's, or that in multiple marriages all the wives will have the identical color.

> A woman so fair that one had to take her word for it that she was Negro chose a series of deep-black lovers. She clearly seemed first attracted by their color and, although she gave any number of reasons for her choices, there seemed a deeper cause. A dream reminded her of a deep-black "relative," a gentle kindly man with whom she had no kin, but who had befriended her as a fatherless child and toward whom she ever after maintained a deep attachment. As a matter of fact, tracing this relationship brought her to question her conviction that she was "Negro." There was no proof, but there was much to suggest that she was actually a white girl who had been adopted by Negro foster parents and that her natural father had not been a black man as she had grown up believing. Very possibly, her attachment to the dark man not only had determined the color of her lovers but had in fact determined the racial identity she later assumed.

Thus, with women as well, the color of the father or father surrogate may be so intimately linked with the positive aspects of their attachment to him as to determine the color of all future lovers.

At times, the theme "Black is the color of my true love's skin" might become the credo of several generations of a family.

> A fair-skinned girl was the first child of a black mother. The father was white. The parents did not marry, however, and the black mother subsequently married a black man. The dark-skinned children who followed made the fair child's life miserable with taunts about her "yellowness." She came to hate her color and indeed to dislike all fair-skinned people. She married a very dark man and warned her daughters that fair-skinned men were deceptive and not to be trusted. They,

in turn, married dark men. And though it is not known what message they conveyed to their daughters, the daughters also chose dark husbands.

Color may be significant for one's own deep emotional responses or may come to symbolize virtue or perfidy, but by far the most universal significance color has had among black Americans has been as a symbol of status.

If you're white, you're right.
If you're brown, hang around.
If you're black, get back.

Sadly, even now there is too much truth in this doggerel. Mothers have wanted fair girls for their sons and fair husbands for their daughters. Until very recent times, beauty among Negro girls has been synonymous with fair skin and a minimum of Negroid features. A "good-looking" Negro man has traditionally been a fair-skinned or light-brown man. The issue has been of less importance to men, since male beauty is of less significance in this country. It has played a part, however, in opportunities available for masculine achievement. In many vocational and academic settings opportunities have come more rapidly for the Negro with a lighter hue and straighter hair.

Thus those Negro families which have placed such a premium on light color have had some meager reality to justify their attitude. We should emphasize the meagerness of the justification, however, for the preponderant sources of their desperate dread of blackness have been their own unreasoning self-hatred and their pitiful wish to be white. Such families can often trace their origins back to a slaveowner who gave land to his children by black mothers or who allowed these children to obtain an education that provided them with economic advantages. As a result, the fair-skinned aristocracy among Negroes are families with money, position, and influence—advantages counterbalanced by the terrible burden of a self-hatred so powerful that they can exercise the greatest cruelties on people who remind them that they too are black.

Such families are becoming anomalous and, more important, they are becoming irrelevant. The grand encounter with which this nation is occupied is between the black masses and the white power holders. Fair-skinned dilettantes have earned little consideration.

But permeating the thinking of all Negroes remains the connection between status and beauty and fair skin. If she were typical, the schoolteacher with whose story this chapter opened is probably fairer than her husband, and in fact most Negro couples are likely to show this color difference. The man pursues the woman, the beauty; and the frequency with which Negro men choose women fairer than they attests at least in part to the connection in the mind of the black man between fair skin and beauty. If in affairs of love women were the aggressors, the color relationship might be reversed.

These are some of the additional considerations that enter into a relationship betweeen a black man and a black woman. Their love and their union produce a family, a new entity. Central to the new union is their adulthood. A marriage signifies the maturity of the partners and, importantly as well, their autonomy. Small wonder that young black married couples are likely to guard their dignity. Honor becomes more important and humiliation more unbearable, not only because the people are young and new at marriage but because it is precisely the perquisites of maturity that are so mindlessly made difficult for black people to enjoy. In such a cruel way it is necessary for each young black man to find his own variety of manhood with which he can live and which does not jeopardize his own safety or that of his now extended self, his wife and children. And the woman must find a way for a flowering of her womanhood which complements her mate and at the same time can bloom in spite of the economic burden she must bear—and in such a way that it does not spur her mate to challenges which jeopardize the family.

The tragedy and complexity of the situation become more apparent when we remember that a family is a functional unit designed for one primary purpose—the protection of the young; and while it serves other vital social purposes, none is more important than the function of *protection.*

But the black family cannot protect its members. Nowhere in the United States can the black family extend an umbrella of protection over its members in the way that a white family can. In every part of the nation its members are subjected to physical and verbal abuse, humiliation, unlawful search and seizure, and harassment by authorities. Its members are jailed, beaten, robbed, killed, and raped, and exposed to this kind of jeopardy to a degree unheard of in white families. Thus the black family is prevented from performing its most essential function—its *raison d'être*—protection of its members.

Marriage among slaves was a farce, but not because of their low station or ignorance of the ways of the nation. It was so because there could be no marriage where the nation moved monolithically and institutionally to keep all slaves exposed to capricious punishment and when by law no man in the nation could protect a slave, least of all the members of his family. By law no slave husband could protect his wife from physical or sexual abuse at the hands of a white man. By law no slave mother could protect her child against physical or sexual abuse at the hands of a white man. These were the reasons why marriage among slaves was meaningless. There could be no functioning family.

All black families in the United States face the task of establishing a family in a nation that is institutionally opposed to this fundamental function of the family. Black husbands cannot provide their wives with as much protection as can white husbands. This can be seen with great clarity in many parts of the South and as one observes the relationship between blacks and policemen in any part of the country. Mothers cannot protect their children from exposure to criminal elements in their neighborhoods because white law-enforcement authorities show little enthusiasm and even less capability for the suppression of crime in Negro neighborhoods. Their actions accentuate the attitude they often express: Negro neighborhoods produce a superabundance of crime, so why should the residents object? When white mothers seek to improve the environment in which their children grow up, they find a more responsive and helpful police department.

Black parents have faced a virtual stone wall as they have tried to improve the educational experience of their children. In spite of heavy taxes, often

paid many times over, these parents are in the main unable to bring about
·improvement in the quality of the education their children receive. White parents
have generally found a more responsive Board of Education, and in fact the
quality of instruction available to white children in this country is significantly
higher than that available to black children.

Black parents are forced to pay fantastic amounts of money for decent
housing and are barred by law and custom (restrictive covenants, real estate
discrimination condoned by courts) from decent housing at a decent price. And
the black parents are absolutely helpless in the face of this collusion among real
estate men, landlords, and the courts of law. When a black child notices that a
white man with the same job as his father can provide good housing for his family
while his father provides him with a slum, that child may draw conclusions about
his father's ability to look after his own. But the father may not be incompetent at
all; it may simply be that he lives in a smooth-running community where black
folk are being contained and are helpless.

The Negro family is in deep trouble. It is coming apart and it is failing to
provide the nurturing that black children need. In its failure the resulting isolated
men and women fail generally to make a whole life for themselves in a nation
designed for families and for white families besides.

A great many of the problems of black people in America can be traced
back to the widespread crumbling of the family structure.

But in spite of the many simplistic half-truths that have been uttered, as
in Daniel P. Moynihan's celebrated report on the Negro family, the cause of the
sickness in black families is not primarily the attack on manhood that
discrimination relentlessly carries out. Men have borne that and remained men. It
is not urbanization and the demand that the family adjust itself to a new world.
Families have done that successfully since the beginning of time. Nor could it be
poverty alone, if men were allowed the rights and privileges, the opportunities and
assistance which citizens of any nation call their due.

No! No! No! The problem of the Negro family is not these challenges.
The problem is a latter-day version of the problem faced by the slave family. How
does one build a family, make it strong, and breed from it strong men and women
when the institutional structures of the nation make it impossible for the family to
serve its primary purpose—the protection of its members?

The Negro family is weak and relatively ineffective because the United
States sets its hand against black people and by the strength of wealth, size, and
number *prevents* black families from protecting their members.

Moynihan's argument seemed to have been developed in reverse. Starting
with the task of providing a sociological basis in theory for a federal program of
jobs for Negroes, he was obviously limited to a few concepts which would support
his argument.

A program for strengthening black families would have to include a
change in the fabric of the nation so that a black man could extend physical
protection to his family everywhere, throughout the country. Such a program
would include a change in the working of governments so that black people could
command that officials serve them, not humiliate them; that policemen protect

them, not prey on them. Such a program would see to it that officialdom generally and courts of law in particular occupy themselves with grander matters than keeping black families huddled together in a ghetto for the enrichment of real estate interests.

If to these changes in national life is added a program of jobs for Negroes, then we would agree that substantive aid will have been given the ailing black family.

But in spite of the problems facing them, black couples continue to marry, establish families, and try to make a worthwhile contribution to the stream of life. The husband works as best he can, the wife mothers as best she can, and they love each other as best they can. As they mold their lives together and form a matrix from which children grow, the next most important function of a family, second only to protection and survival, comes into focus: to provide an accurate interpretation of the world to its children. Children must above all be taught what the world is like, how it functions, and how *they* must function if they are to survive and eventually establish their own families. If the family does not convey an accurate image of the world, the children will either succumb or fail to prosper sufficiently to allow them to start their own families. So important is this interpretive function that the natural relationship between children and parents makes it certain that the children will first see the world through the eyes of their parents.

The intimacy, the love, and above all the identification with the parents, not to mention the absence of competing models, all make certain that the child will view the world with the eyes of the parents.

Is it not conceivable that many of the dismal consequences of Negro family life might be related to the world the children first view? The family, we can be certain, has given them an accurate view of the world. If this view is bleak and dismaying, may not the family say to its young:

> It is a terrible place you come to;
> I'm not sure I can hearten you in any way,
> Although I would like to.
> I can only say I have survived—
> I honestly don't know how—
> And you must also survive.

If such a message is indeed conveyed by black families, and surely it must be, then this may account for the fragmenting of the family structure. The family is in fact saying that it has no skills of mastery to pass on, that it has found no way to reliably "make it" in society. It says that one must fight to live; one can only survive, and one *must* survive. This would seem quite enough to shake any young generation.

But families continue to form, to function, and to grow old. The bond which makes it all possible is that between men and women. It is the bedrock, the solace which makes so many darknesses bearable. And even here, in the love relation which makes the family possible, we find the contaminating influence of racial hatred.

A black couple, describing their love-making, said that much of the bantering between them involved invidious comparisons between the wife's sexual desirability and that of any hypothetical white woman. The joking would extend to the idea that white people generally are more attractive, more refined, more natural objects of desire, whereas blacks are deformed, repugnant, and debased. In this polarization of black and white, they would become aroused by the fantasy which made them animal-like and the ensuing sexual experience would be enhanced.

It should be no surprise to find racial issues accompanying a black man to bed. The black man occupies a very special sexual role in American society. He is seen as the ultimate in virility and masculine vigor. But at the same time he is regarded as socially, economically, and politically castrated, and he is gravely handicapped in performing every other masculine role. It is difficult for him to acquire goods for his family, to achieve power in the councils of his fellow men, and, in fact, to fulfill the fundamental role of providing protection for his family.

His society has barred him from white women. However much love and passion he feels for his black partner, he cannot help bringing the idea to his bed that only here, and only with her, is he granted the opportunity to function in a truly manly way. Such attitudes carry with them feelings of rage, depression, futility, and, not unexpectedly, sometimes a heightening of sexual excitement. However much he may love his partner, he cannot help seeing, reflected in her, the narrowed range of his own world. She is his black counterpart and is depreciated as much as he. The natural male inclination to obtain and possess a highly valued woman, to compete with other men for her favor, and to win out because of his own strength—none of this does he fulfill with his beloved. He sees her as a depreciated object and this reinforces his own perception of himself as a depreciated man. The enhancement of the sexual act which comes to the male who feels he has laid hold of a prize is absent. Moreover, his depreciation of her and his hostility toward her cannot help being perceived by the woman, and likewise cannot but contribute to her own feeling of degradation.

As mentioned previously, a device may be brought into play which seems an ingenious solution to an otherwise impossible psychological impasse. Because in this society our defenses are set firmly in opposition to sexual impulses, such impulses are experienced as degrading aspects of ourselves and the full drive and power of human sexuality is linked to a feeling of debasement. Thus insofar as the black man sees himself as a cornered, debased, and castrated sexual object, this very perception of himself allows him to circumvent the inhibition of sexual desire. In his degradation he lays hold of a fuller range of sexual powers. It is as if he says: "If I am beast and animal, then let me show you how this animal makes love!"

With this enhancement of his sexual powers his self-esteem rises. Out of his feelings of devaluation come an increase in his feelings as a man and, no doubt, a strengthening of his resolution to enter again into outside competition, that competition which in every other way is so heavily weighted against him.

It is in the nature of women to experience sex as an interplay between narcissism and masochism. As the black woman enters the embrace of her black lover, many of the same ghosts which haunt him now also haunt her, but in a characteristically feminine way. All her life her narcissism has been deeply wounded and impaired. She finds it difficult to experience herself as a highly valued object to whom any man would be drawn. Rather she sees herself as a depreciated, unwanted instrument of no inherent value, to be used by men and society at their pleasure. The bitterness that grows out of such a self-perception augments her already established self-hatred, her feelings of being used, and her feelings of worthlessness.

Under the circumstances she feels hatred and scorn for the man who embraces her, since she sees in him the evidence of her own degradation. Where a woman would otherwise find narcissistic enhancement in being possessed by a powerful lover, she cannot regard the man as either powerful or loving. Instead of narcissistic enhancement, she experiences narcissistic depletion. She hates him for his being castrated in society at large and unable to bring that special increment of power to their loving. She finds herself progressively degraded in the course of the sexual relationship. But again, as happens to her lover, she finds her own erotic feelings strengthened by the feelings of degradation. In the feminine sexual mode these feelings of masochism have a strong erotic component, so that she finds herself not only degraded but masochistically submitting to a man she views as depreciated and participating in an act which further depletes her slender narcissistic resources. She finds a sexual reinforcement and strengthening which brings a heightening of erotic pleasure out of the very circumstances which might have initially blunted it.

While this phenomenon of degradation and masochistic submission ultimately serves to strengthen the sexual experience, beyond the world of the black woman it is in large measure a commentary upon the repressive attitudes generally held toward sexual functioning in the Western world. It speaks as much for the adaptability of the human organism as for man's apparently infinite ability to make life difficult for himself.

Sexual union, then, requires a synthesis of real life and fantasy in a way that will make for a vigorous coming together. The fact that their real life is often an oppressed life can impose an additional psychological burden on the black lovers, which serves as a divisive element in the black family and in a significant way contributes to the fragility of that union.

Black men and women have this complex of problems in large measure because they have always been regarded by white Americans as sexual objects, exotic people living close to instinct and primitivism. The fascination black people have for white people in the sexual area can hardly be exaggerated, and this factor alone makes a major contribution to the charged quality of racial relationships in this country.

One result of this sexual tension between the races is a preoccupation with interracial sexual liaisons. The black lover fears that his partner will be tempted by a white seducer. And conversely, his white counterparts feel impotent if challenged by a black rival. One could make a case for mutual lust and jealousy as the basis for racial conflict in America.

But since interracial sexual unions have so infatuated Americans, black and white, and form so large a part of their secret fantasies, some study of these relationships is in order.

When a black man and a white woman unite, one can assume that unnumbered racially connected issues will arise. For the black man, the white woman represents the *socially identified* female ideal and thus an intensely exciting object for his sexual possession. She has been identified as precisely the individual to whom access is barred by every social institution. The forbiddenness and desirableness of the white woman make her a natural recipient of his projected oedipal fantasies. He sees himself as finally possessing the maternal object under circumstances which reproduce the dangerous, defiant quality of oedipal interest as experienced by the child. He feels a sense of power at having acquired this highly valuable woman and a sense of power that she finds him desirable and indeed that she finds him *more* desirable than a white lover. But at the same time he perceives her as white and as a representative of all the white oppressors who have made his life so wretched. In a sense then, she becomes the target for a hatred which far transcends the encounter between this man and this woman.

The sexual act itself carries aggressive overtones, and in the fantasy of all men there is a likening of male aggression in the sexual act to murderous aggression and a likening of the female partner to the victim of murder. The black man then has an opportunity to live out murderous fantasies of revenge. In possessing the white woman he sees himself as degrading her (a function of his own feelings of degradation), in this instance sharing the community's feeling that a white woman who submits to a black lover becomes as debased as he. In this way he may feel the gratification of turning the tables on his white oppressor and thus becoming the instrument through which a white person is degraded.

Finally, and perhaps most importantly, he sees himself as having vanquished the white man in the field of love and of having rendered him impotent and castrated, for the white woman, in fantasy at least, has embraced a white lover and then chosen a black one. While in every other area of life the black man may feel emasculated and humiliated by the white man, here he can reverse the roles and, because of the central importance of the sexual function in human affairs, may feel that the scales are almost balanced.

His fantasies find reinforcement in the keen delight his partner takes in his embrace. Her delight may rest on her own set of fantasies, but they both know that, whatever the causes may be, she finds more intense gratification from her black lover than she does from her white one.

Should the relationship progress to marriage, the problems increase exponentially, since in this culture marriage progressively downgrades the importance of the sexual act and lays increasing emphasis on the economic and social functioning of the partners. The black man married to a white woman is hounded by the knowledge that outside the bedroom his manhood is compromised. In fact, both the initial delight of his partner and his own intense satisfaction may pall under the certain knowledge that in the outside world he is an emasculated half-man. This places a grave strain on the relationship. The greatest stress seems to come, however, from the perception by the partners of the nature of the world in which they live, a perception which is sufficiently tied to reality to change in response to a change in that external world. The evidence for this is seen in the happy marriages between blacks and whites which flourish outside this country and which emphasize that the love relationship, given half a chance by society, can flourish between people of disparate origins.

The white woman who seeks a black lover finds him to be an intensely exciting sexual partner because of his forbiddenness and because of the ease with which she can project onto him her own oedipal fantasies. Since black people are a minority, representing less than one-tenth of the population, they may not find the physical appearance of the Caucasian so exotic. This is not true for the Caucasian. A white woman finds her black lover sufficiently strange, and she is able to experience the excitement of having a forbidden sexual object as well as a lover who is so different-looking as to allow her to see him as a different kind of human being or even a subhuman animal. She is thus able to experience herself as different or subhuman along with her partner and in that way to participate in sexuality of an intensity and quality forbidden her as "herself," with all of the strictures and inhibitions that go along with that self-perception. Though she may view her black lover as a degraded object, she also views him as a sexual master.

As she submits to him, her own masochistic strivings feed her excitement at being possessed by such a being. These feelings contribute in a major way to her gratification. In his arms she merges with him and abandons her previous identity. In so doing she finds it easy to isolate the experience as a unique, intensely gratifying moment which has no relationship to the rest of her life. The emasculation of her black lover in the outside world makes it easier for her to feel separated and different from him and, in fact, safe from the invasion of her own forbidden fantasies into everyday life.

In fact, her attraction to him may rest in large measure specifically on these grounds. The relationship allows her uninhibited enjoyment of otherwise forbidden sexual impulses without experiencing any threat to her life generally. Should such a union eventuate in marriage, she would likely be concerned primarily with his ability to bring home the bacon, and if she found him lacking in this respect, her resulting bitterness might well cause her latent hostility toward all black people to emerge.

If, on the other hand, she experienced no disadvantages economically, her primary concern would surely focus on the social problems they met as a couple. The contempt she would encounter from the majority of white people would be a constant burden and the contempt she would feel when they saw her with her brown children would cause even greater pain.

A white woman had enjoyed a happy marriage to a black man for six years. During this time she rarely saw her mother. But when her mother became seriously ill, she sat by her bedside and promised God that if her mother survived she would never again cause her pain.

Her mother recovered and the patient developed severe anxiety, phobias, and in fact a pan-neurosis. She became hypersensitive to the stares of white people when she appeared in public with her brown children. She refused to go out in public with her husband and discouraged physical intimacy. At the same time she sought to reestablish a close relationship with her mother.

What had been to all appearances a happy marriage dissolved as this woman required a great sacrifice of herself. She had to undo the greatest pain she had caused her mother, marriage to a black man.

The white woman who is married to a black man feels her most intense discomfort in the relationship when she considers her children, the contempt in which they may be held, and the difficulties they may encounter as a result of mixed parentage. Her misery will subside only when they are married and she no longer suffers with them for every rebuff they receive.

The relationship which has the longest history and the most complex psychological structure is the relationship between the white man and the black woman. From the very first introduction of black slaves into America, black women have been used sexually by their white owners. In contrast to the male slaves they had a threefold use—their labor was economically valuable, their bodies had a marketable value as sexual objects, and their potential as breeders of additional slaves was also a source of wealth to their owners.

Even now in many areas a black woman has no protection from the sexual appetites of white men. In the raw circumstance of power and the imposition of the will of the powerful on the weak, the most significant aspect of the woman's position is her helplessness against sexual assault. She cannot protect herself against sexual use by a powerful male. Her only protection lies in binding herself sexually to a powerful man who can in turn protect her from other men. It would seem that both the erotic component of a woman's masochism and her tendency to gain narcissistic gratification from being chosen by a powerful man make it easy for her to yield herself to a powerful man and to gain special gratification out of such submission. In addition, a woman need feel no qualms of conscience if she is taken sexually against her will and must submit to the sexual act under pain of violence. Under such circumstances her own conscience, moral code, and inhibitions stand in suspension.

All these factors are important in the manner in which a black woman relates herself to a white lover. However weak in fact he may be, however ineffective and poor, he is potentially more powerful than any black lover. He is a part of and a representative of the powerful white majority—a representative of the wealth and prestige accrued in the United States and throughout the Western world over the past two thousand years.

In a historical sense, she, on the other hand, stands in the position of all the black people who have been exploited and dominated by white men since the beginning of recorded time. In a historical sense and in a very real contemporary sense, she faces a powerful lover. The prospect of sexually submitting to him evokes excitement in her. In addition to the explicit pleasure involved in masochistic submission, she gains some of the strength and power of the white man.

An attractive black wife and mother sought out a highly recommended white professional man and in his consultation room began describing in a very businesslike manner the relevant issues which had brought her to his office. After listening to her briefly he got up from his desk, came around, kissed her, took off her clothes, and made love to her. He then told her he would look after her problems and dismissed her.

What is of special interest here is the frame of mind of the woman during the episode in the white professional's office. In treatment later she recounted that she had been chaste as a single woman and faithful as a wife but found herself strangely submissive and yielding to this man. In fact she was intensely aroused by the experience. Her associations were of his impressive office, his wide reputation, his apparent wealth and power. While there were other determinants to her behavior, the relation of her passivity to his power and the aggressive manner in which he thrust himself on her are instructive.

This type of passive submission, strongly colored by eroticism, has historically characterized the relationship between black women and white men. It is the converse of the relationship between black men and white women. The black man is highly excited by possessing the valuable ideal female and the black woman is intensely aroused at being subdued and possessed by the powerful white man. His power, desirability, and forbiddenness evoke her own oedipal fantasies and she finds herself particularly gratified that this powerful man chooses her in preference to a white woman.

In her relationship with a white man, the black woman can partake of his power and masculinity and can for once free herself of her degraded self-perception. In his embrace she is whole again and can experience the sexual act as simply a woman submitting to a desirable man. Her own thwarted narcissistic strivings can for once find embodiment in a lover whose possibilities for living them out are apparently limitless—an experience she cannot have with a black lover.

To the extent that she sees her own blackness as ugly and repellent, her possession of a white lover and her identification with him allow her to view herself as white and therefore beautiful. The problem arises, however, when she must leave his bed and face the real world again. However much her white lover protests his devotion to her, she is beset with feelings of self-depreciation, depression, and futility. She sees herself as having been used and debased for the satisfaction of a powerful man who only took advantage of her weakness and susceptibility. She perceives herself as having striven for something beyond her, and her remorse is her "punishment" for "reaching above her station." Should she return to a black lover, she might well feel herself all the more degraded and oppressed.

If her relationship with the white man leads to marriage, the prospect is that as the bloom of romance fades she will find herself dreading that he will abandon her. Past experiences make her feel truly worthless and undesirable. It is only in his arms that she feels a whole woman, sexually desirable to men. Away from him she is again potentially the ugly, despised black woman. She is convinced that he has a false perception of her which makes her seem beautiful and desirable to him, and she dreads the moment when he sees her as she sees herself and, in revulsion, thrusts her away from him. Her position is a wretched one.

On the other side of the coin, the white man, by taking to himself a black woman, acts in defiance of all socially accepted norms. Our society allows a white man to surreptitiously experiment with black women sexually but never to take one into a love relationship. As a prostitute or as a casual mistress, a black woman can be a meaningless sexual toy and involvement with her need have no profound effect on his life. Psychologically, he can look upon her as a debased human animal who finds pleasure in a sexual life no decent woman would tolerate. The uninhibited pleasures he shares with her might serve to further dichotomize his emotional life, and his relationship with his white wife might suffer. But beyond this there need be no grave disruption of his functioning.

If, on the other hand, the black woman assumes some emotional importance for him, his problems are compounded. It is likely that he would enter into a relationship only in response to feelings of defiance toward the social order generally, and perhaps his family or parents specifically. Under these circumstances the black woman serves a *specific* psychological purpose for him because of her general unacceptability as a mate.

Whatever gratification the two of them might share in their union, her role as evidence of his defiance and her functioning as a social curiosity will clearly limit the richness of their relationship and dull their satisfaction. In any event, in the United States, the psychological truth is that when a white man chooses a black woman, both in his own eyes and in the eyes of his confreres, he has chosen a depreciated sexual object rather than a highly valued one. This factor is obviously of greater social importance than the desirability of the black woman as an exotic and forbidden representative of his inner desires. Such fantasies and strivings allow him to act out unconscious wishes which intensify his pleasure. The social value set on each of the partners reverses their roles, making him the highly valued object whom the woman has been fortunate enough to obtain.

His own narcissism is enhanced thereby and he finds a special gratification in their relationship. He feels constantly inferior to black men, however, feeling that sexually he is less satisfying as a partner than *any* black man. He is the victim of the stereotype which played such an important part in his choosing a black woman in the first place.

If their relationship develops into marriage, his fantasies inevitably lead him into doubts about his wife's fidelity. It is easy for him to become dissatisfied with her and feel the lack of a *desirable* woman whose *desirability* would enhance his own self-esteem. His role as the more desirable of the pair fades in importance.

Again, the evidence is clear that however much misery the black woman and white man experience in their relationship, their suffering is remarkably alleviated by living in a community which does not contain the intense social hostility of communities in the United States. If they moved to Europe or Latin

America, they would have a better chance of operating in terms of their individual compatibility, much as any other couple, and of finding fulfillment in their union without special reference to their racial difference. The factor which militates heavily against such unions is the society rather than the racial origins of the pair.

However troubled his mating and however fragile his union with his woman, the black man has found sufficient nourishment to endure and bring forth issue, to exploit his strengths, and to relentlessly attack the social order which limits the expanse of this most precious place.

Introduction to **"Harlem on My Mind"**
CANDICE VAN ELLISON

History of Harlem

To fully understand the Harlem ghetto, one must examine the history of Afro-American settlement in New York. During the years preceding World War I, a slow but steady migration of Blacks from the Southern countryside to the Northern cities began. This period is generally referred to as the advance guard of the "Great Migration," which occurred during World War I. It is during this era that we find "the migration of the talented tenth"—the Blacks who came to the big cities to become lawyers, doctors, businessmen and politicians. Actually, these people represented only a small portion of the Southern migrants. The rest were young inexperienced "boys and girls," fresh off the farm.

These young people had lived on the sharecropper and tenant farms of their parents, they had been subjected to the initiation of a score of Jim Crow laws and the Ku Klux Klan. But worst of all, they saw their parents, who were content to submit to the abuses of a Southern caste society. In order not to lose all hope, they fled the land in which they were born, and sought the "freedom" of the Northern cities. The migrants' pet phrase, "I came North to better my condition," expresses simply the attitude of the Southern Black at this time. Now was the time for them to move, as the country's industrial expansion created economic opportunity for the rural people. So they began leaving the South in great numbers, and as they did, Southern cities reflected on their migration. In the minds of most Southerners, Negroes seemed racially adapted to agricultural life, permanently tied to the soil. To forsake farm life would necessarily lead to their degradation. This was their only "proper calling," their "proper place." Instead of creating conditions which would encourage Blacks to remain in the South, Southerners took the opposite view and made it almost impossible for Blacks to leave the farm.

Unfortunately, these Black migrants did not find their "promised land" in the Northern cities. Instead, they found the alienation and the "evil temptations" of the big city. In New York, Blacks made their way to the "Tenderloin" (Seventh

Avenue and 34th Street area), and "San Juan Hill" (Columbus Circle area). These
Black concentrations were overcrowded, dirty and expensive to live in.

Faced with so many perils in the big city, Blacks banded together to
protect themselves. They established benevolent, fraternal and protective societies,
and insurance pools and church groups (since they weren't allowed to worship in
the city's white churches). It was quite natural, therefore, for the Black migrants
to search for a place to form their own social community. This was the pattern of
almost all immigrant groups in New York City. Form your own community and
put another "crack" in the melting pot. Thus, the Black social community in New
York City became Harlem.

At this time Harlem was a white upper-middle-class residential
community—Manhattan's first suburb. Speculators were buying up land in
Harlem every hour and becoming millionaires overnight.

"On the outskirts of this Utopian community, one would be amazed to
see the dark marshlands inhabited by the Irish gangs of Canary Island, the 'Italian
Colony' of East Harlem filled with marionette shows, organ grinders and garbage
dumps, and 'a large colony of the poorest colored people' in Harlem's Darktown."
In the latter part of the nineteenth century the construction of new subway routes
in Harlem set off a second wave of speculation. It was this second wave of
over-speculation which created the final "bust" in 1904 and 1905. Financial
institutions no longer made loans to Harlem speculators, mortgages were
foreclosed, the land depreciated, and prices lowered. These conditions of ruin
created the proper atmosphere for Black settlement in Harlem. This was the start
of the Black ghetto called Harlem.

Housing

Today, one of the city's biggest "sore thumbs" is housing in Harlem. The problem
is simple—the annual average income of Harlem residents is not high enough to
support competitive private housing. Greedy slumlords control the maze of
Harlem's tenements. The City Building Department receives some 500 complaints
a day about falling plaster, holes in walls, rats, hazardous plumbing and
unsanitary facilities. Housing Court can do little more than levy fines against
apathetic slumlords. Very often a slumlord will accept a fine one day, merely to
continue to rake high profits from substandard tenements for the rest of the year.
There are many cases of "absentee" landlords who have agents which collect the
rent. The most frightening danger of these crumbling tenements is fire. Fires occur
so frequently in Harlem that only the most spectacular are reported in the
newspapers.

The city's only answer to this age-old problem is the Housing Authority.
In 1962, more than 450,000 people were housed in city projects. City projects are
such popular environments for the poor that they have become a worthy
competitor for the slum. The kind of life created by these project complexes is a
prime example of city planning. The Housing Authority not only builds
apartment houses, it also attempts to create integrated housing communities

among lower-income families. This isn't easy. In Harlem's city projects, such groups as poor Italians, Irish, Puerto Ricans and Blacks are huddled together in "planned communities" which are surrounded by familiar slums. A large portion of these tenants are on welfare. Fear and suspicion are widespread, and there is constantly the feeling of isolation. The project community is permeated by surrounding slums and eventually begins to look like them. Street gangs begin in order to strengthen ethnic ties. Although incinerators are present, garbage is constantly thrown in the hallways. Apartment walls are so thin than one cannot sleep for the noise in the next apartment. Project apartments number from one to three bedrooms. What happens to the Puerto Rican family of twelve?

The city housing system cannot be considered a complete failure when viewed in the light of the city tenements. City projects are considerably cleaner, cheaper and more attractive than any city tenement. They also represent a kind of equalizer for all the lower-socioeconomic groups in the city.

Education

It has been said that "Afro-Americans do place a high value on education." In Harlem there are many elementary schools, a few Junior high schools and one high school. The major qualm about "the area's" elementary schools is lack of integration, both in the staff and student body. The junior high schools also suffer from lack of integration and modern facilities. In the community's one high school, Benjamin Franklin, the 1966 senior class contained approximately 2,000 seniors, 1,000 June graduates, and 38 graduating academic diplomas.

The city's answer to this problem was "free transfer" programs, community cultural programs, after-school study programs and vocational training programs. In February 1961, the first enactment of the city's new transfer program began. "P.S. 197, a new school surrounded by middle-class housing projects in the Harlem area—Riverton and Lenox Terrace showed the highest percentage of requests." It was in this year that my best friend, Deborah Whittington, was granted a transfer from P.S. 197 to the all-girls finishing school—Elizabeth Barrett Browning Junior High School. One year later I was also transferred, on a two-year "S.P." program. We found the predominantly Jewish school quite different from our own "cozy" elementary school in Harlem. Competition was keen and we were no longer the "teacher's pet." The widest "gaps" between elementary and junior high school appeared in math and language. Fortunately, we managed to keep up. As we were leaving the school in 1964, it was rumored that a large influx of Lower East Bronx and Harlem students would be coming in in the next year. Some of the teachers complained that "the school is going to the dogs."

Today, Harlem civic groups have organized to "prod" city education. They have managed to establish a busing system for elementary students. They have also managed to incur the wrath of many of the community's educators by making a number of unreasonable demands. Many of the community's middle-class families still prefer to send their children to private or parochial schools—"they'd rather switch than fight."

Politics and the Church

What are the political objectives of Harlem voters? The basic problems considered in national Black protests do not always apply to New York's Afro-Americans. In New York there are already laws against discrimination in employment and housing (although their administration has proved wholly inadequate). The Board of Education actively tries to integrate the city's schools, and in higher education there is practically no discrimination at all. There is probably little or no discrimination in hotels and restaurants. In other words, there are no easy problems left for Blacks in New York City, nor easy solutions. Improvement of the Afro-American's economic position in the city requires radical changes in the nation's power structure. It is evident that this can only be attained through more political positions for Afro-Americans. Congressman Powell in 1960 demanded that Blacks should get 21 per cent of the jobs in a Democratic city administration, since 21 per cent of the enrolled Democrats in Manhattan are Black. At present, Blacks hold only 6 per cent of the high political posts, and yet they are still doing considerably better than Blacks in other large cities. It is easy to demand political positions, but not quite as easy to find capable Black political leaders to fill these positions.

In Harlem the history of political leadership leads directly to the church, in which the Black minister was projected as both the political and spiritual leader of the Black community. Harlem ministers have a long tradition of political involvement. In the past it has always been the Black minister who acted as a political liaison between the downtown bosses and the Black people. These political ministers are no longer dependent upon the downtown bosses for orders. It is true that many ministers still need the financial support of the city's white community, but it is also evident that those politicians (or ministers) who are most popular in Harlem are those who advocate Black exclusivism and nationalism. This is a highly emotional concept, which advocates the advancement of Black people through the efforts and actions of Black people, excluding all white liberals. These political leaders call for unity of the Black community from the pulpit of their church. This combination of religion and politics serves several important purposes. First, large numbers of the Black community can be reached, influenced and educated through the church. Second, these secular gains attained by political ministers help strengthen the belief in religion and the moral codes advocated by it. Yet there are religions which advocate the advantages of unified self-defense. For example, at the height of Malcolm X's career, he could be seen on almost any Sunday afternoon preaching Black unity and self-defense on the corner of 125th Street in Harlem.

Depending upon the era and area of Harlem in which they preach, self-defense or peaceful demonstration will be the slogan of the Harlem politician. It has been said that in this second stage of the Black civil rights movement, peaceful demonstration is no longer the answer. If this is the case, then Harlem's political voices may be preaching street riots from the pulpits.

Intergroup Relations

Black-white relationships in Harlem are poor, to say the least. This of course is part of a much larger national problem. We would do well to examine the specific factors which have influenced racial tensions in Harlem.

First, consider the racial tensions between the Blacks and the Irish in Harlem. It is true that only a small portion of Harlem's population is Irish, yet a strong Irish influence is exerted on Harlem through the city's police force. As early as 1900, when the city's main poverty concentration was in the Tenderloin, a bloody three-day riot was sparked when an Afro-American named Arthur Harris knifed and killed an Irish policeman who was manhandling his girl. This incident was just the spark needed to set off the already strained Irish—Afro-American relations. The numerous tales of police brutality in the riot ranged from policemen merely looking the other way while mobs attacked Blacks, to the arresting of Negroes and beating them senseless inside the precinct. This incident was only one indication of an underlying attitude between Afro-Americans and Irish. The Irish at that time were immigrants in the city. Yet it is amazing how quickly they caught on to white America's tradition of hatred for Blacks. It was also disconcerting that Blacks, who were actually American citizens, could never have gotten the jobs on the city's police force as the Irish immigrants so easily managed to do. Harlem riots between Afro-Americans and policemen have reoccurred in 1935, 1943 and 1964. Although the Irish no longer hold a complete monopoly over New York's police force, it is definite that damage created by them in past riots will not soon be forgotten.

The next intergroup relationship to be examined is that between the Afro-Americans and Jews of Harlem. Anti-Jewish feeling is a natural result of the Black Northern migration. Afro-Americans in Northeastern industrial cities are constantly coming in contact with Jews. Pouring into lower-income areas in the city, the Afro-American invariably pushes out the Jew. Behind every hurdle that the Afro-American has yet to jump stands the Jew who has already cleared it. Jewish shopkeepers are the only remaining "survivors" in the expanding Black ghettoes. This is especially true in Harlem, where almost all of the high-priced delicatessens and other small food stores are run by Jews. The lack of competition in this area allows the already badly exploited Black to be further exploited by Jews.

Another major area of contact involves the Jewish landlord and the Black tenant. A large portion of Harlem's Black women serve as domestics in middle-class Jewish homes. Perhaps this would explain the higher rate of anti-Semitism among Black women than men. Even the middle-class Harlem Black who has managed to work his way up the ladder in government jobs come in contact with Jews who have already climbed the same ladder and now maintain the higher government positions. One other important factor worth noting is that, psychologically, Blacks may find that anti-Jewish sentiments place them, for once, within a majority. Thus, our contempt for the Jew makes us feel more completely American in sharing a national prejudice.

The third major group of racial relations in Harlem are those between Afro-Americans and Puerto Ricans. If Blacks invariably find themselves bumping into Jews ahead of them, they just as invariably find themselves bumping into Puerto Ricans behind them. In all of the major areas in which Blacks have fought so hard to prevent discrimination, newly arrived Puerto Ricans are now benefiting. In the city's great housing complexes, Puerto Ricans command a large proportion of the apartments. With so great an influx of Puerto Ricans into the Harlem community, Blacks are left with only three choices—fight them, ignore them or welcome them.

Employment

Prior to the mass unemployment of the late 1950's and early 1960's, Black men found it much easier to obtain jobs in the Midwest than in New York. Still, it was easier for the Black woman, who did not have to depend on manual labor for an income. Working conditions in New York were much better for women because they were ideal employees for the city's non-unionized banks, insurance companies, "communications" industries, and retail stores. This resulted in better jobs for women than men at the lower levels of skill. According to statistics compiled in 1960, the median income for Black women was 93 per cent of the median for white women; for Black men it was only 68 per cent of the white median.

Oddly enough, the problem of Black employment in America is a problem of the Black male, rather than the female. In the past Black women were always the first to be taken into the white man's house to work as maids and cooks. It was easy for the white world to accept a Black woman because she offered no physical threat and could always be kept in her "proper" place. It was always the Black woman who was exposed to the white world and received the favors from them whenever they were forthcoming. It is this particular problem of Black employment, which has been of primary concern to the present Afro-American community. The creation of a somewhat matriarchal society in Harlem is largely the result of Black employment patterns in New York City.

In the past, Blacks emerging from slavery found themselves devoid of both money and business experience. Thus, even after the destruction of slavery the Afro-American became basically a hired laborer or servant. These positions offered little chance for business experience. Unlike the other immigrant groups who came to New York with some particular skill or trade, the migrant Afro-Americans from the South had nothing to sell but themselves. They tended to depend on themselves, and therefore did not form many close business ties. Thus, Afro-Americans have attained a history of unskilled labor since they arrived in the New World. Even today, those young people who do manage to go on to higher education reject wholly the idea of skilled labor. Yet so few do complete the college and graduate level that there are thousands left to the mercy of that rapidly disappearing market of unskilled labor.

At present Harlem's principal anti-poverty program is Haryou-Act. Whatever its purposes and failures, Haryou-Act has managed to do one important thing—that is, to employ a large number of Harlem residents in an area that is sorely in need of economic stability.

Harlem is not an isolated Black ghetto; it is connected by the bonds of poverty, filth, illiteracy and unemployment to all the other Black ghettoes throughout the United States. In order to understand the problem of the Afro-American in America it is necessary to understand the environment in which he lives. Harlem is one such environment, and its problems have too long been ignored.

FIVE

Crowding

The act of love makes babies, whether or not that
is what is intended. These selections from
Philip Appleman, Lewis Mumford, and
Mitchell Gordon give a sardonic twist to the injunction
of the young to "Make love, not war." Appleman
sees the population clock as furiously ticking.
Mumford examines the problem of hardware—
machines as they redefine people in crowded cities.
Gordon gives a dispiriting account of the decline
of police authority in population-swollen centers.
In the meantime, religious convictions,
persistent traditions, financial considerations,
and, of course, the intrinsic pleasure of
love itself continue to stand in the way of rational
programs for easing up on crowding—and,
perhaps, for saving humanity from self-annihilation.

PHOTOGRAPH BY *The New York Times.*

From **The Silent Explosion**
PHILIP APPLEMAN

A Million More Mouths Each Week

> Are there not thousands in the world . . .
> Who love their fellows even to the death,
> And feel the giant agony of the world . . . ?

John Keats

At Sealdah Station, Calcutta, misery radiates outward. In the station, displaced families from East Pakistan hover around little piles of possessions. Outside, dusty streets straggle away in every direction, lined with tiny shacks built of metal scraps, pieces of old baskets, strips of wood, and gunny sacks. In the dark interiors of the shacks, small fires glow through the smoke, and dark faces gaze out at children playing in the urinous-smelling, fly-infested streets. In a few years the children who survive these conditions will stop playing and become adults; that is, they will grow taller and thinner and stand in the streets like ragged skeletons, barefoot, hollow-eyed, blinking their apathetic stares out of gray, dusty faces. That is not a bright future, but it is the only one many of these children can expect.

A visiting American student described his response to this sight: "I thought I was prepared for poverty. But to see men, women, and children sleeping on the sidewalks, looking like little bundles of rags, to see thousands of people living in shacks, like animals . . ." Another student finished his thought: "Once when I was stopped by a woman begging, I gathered all my courage and looked straight into her eyes, and it hit me then—these are *people*, like ourselves, and they have a right to live better than this." "About Asia," a third student reflected, "What I'll remember best is not its history but its misery."

Misery: traveling in Asia, you see it everywhere—in Jericho, Bangkok, Delhi, and Cairo; in Hong Kong in the thousands of squatters' shacks, without water or sanitation, or in the miles of tenements where dozens of people live in a single room; and in the acres of sampans and junks crowded together to form the strange floating cities of the Orient, dark, dense aquatic jungles of bamboo and fluttering rags and people. Dr. Johnson's verdict still applies to those parts of the world: "Human life is everywhere a state in which much is to be endured, and little to be enjoyed."

The agony of the world has a long pedigree. "Man that is born of woman is of few days, and full of trouble," Job complained; "He cometh forth like a flower, and is cut down." "Nothing that hurts," cried Aeschylus' Prometheus, "can come with a new face." "Birth is suffering, decay is suffering, death is suffering," said the Buddha in his first sermon. Man's pilgrimage through this valley of tears has characteristically been weary, stale, flat, and unprofitable, nasty, brutish, and short.

Ironically, the world's poverty and misery are now most heavily concentrated in the lands of dark-skinned peoples whose ancestors had raised brilliant civilizations when the light-skinned Europeans were still comparatively barbarous. The Egyptians developed a complex and viable society thousands of years before the ancient Greeks. The splendid Gupta dynasty in India flourished five hundred years before Charlemagne. The Khmers developed a sophisticated civilization in Southeast Asia before William the Conqueror invaded England. The sumptuous Chinese cultures of the T'ang and Sung dynasties stretched over six centuries before the discovery of the New World. The Mayas, Toltecs, Aztecs, and Incas built brilliant empires in Latin America long before Europeans came.

Time, the great destroyer, eventually leveled all this ancient grandeur. Exhausted by wars, retrenched in traditional forms and customs, skeptical of the European Renaissance and Industrial Revolution, dominated and exploited by colonial Powers, the dark-skinned people did not "develop"; and their poverty-stricken lands gradually became, as Kipling once called them, "the dark places of the earth," seeming to have been "created by Providence in order to supply picturesque scenery."

That, unfortunately, is how Americans too often continue to think of them. I do not mean only that a few thoughtless tourists can look upon half-starved "natives" and pronounce them "picturesque." What is worse is that from our land of refrigerators, television, automobiles, and air conditioning, even people of good will cannot conceive of Asian poverty and misery.

There are poor people in the United States, of course; thirty million Americans live in varying degrees of poverty. We have our slums and shantytowns, our run-down marginal farms, our half-deserted mining areas, our disadvantaged groups: minorities, the very young workers, the very old, the chronically ill, the dropouts, the migrants. All of these share some degree of discomfort, some of them a steady and terrible misery. But without minimizing the cruel suffering of many of our own poor, it ought to be recognized that standards of poverty vary. An American family of four is considered poor if it has an annual income of less than three thousand dollars. The *average* (not the "poor") family in underdeveloped countries gets about one-tenth of that. Even an out-of-work American may take home more money in unemployment compensation in a month than many working men in the underdeveloped countries earn in a whole year. Our relief and charitable organizations (unlike those in the underdeveloped countries) are not only well financed but also able to draw upon vast stores of surplus commodities. During the Great Depression itself we in this country were surrounded by the paradox of badly distributed abundance.

In Latin America, Asia, and Africa, on the other hand, poverty has a grim and simple meaning: there is just not enough to go around. An Indian eats about half as much food as an American does, partly because that is all he can afford and partly for the compelling reason that that is all there is for him. It is this perpetual scarcity, this fact of having *nowhere to turn,* that is so hard for Americans to understand—but until we do understand it, we will remain hopelessly out of touch with most of the world.

If we could somehow come to understand the meaning of this "giant agony," we would never again be complacent about it. When you walk the streets of Calcutta, you see gaunt and half-naked men bathing at public water taps; women huddling over little piles of manure, patting it into cakes for fuel; children competing with dogs for refuse; hundreds of thousands of homeless people living in the streets, shaving in the streets, having their teeth pulled in the streets, and sleeping in the streets. Seeing this scene for the first time, Westerners react with shock, shame, and revulsion. American students told me:

> I wanted to run away, to weep. I was disgusted, horrified, saddened. How I wished I were back in my secure and satisfying home. My heart and thoughts were thrown into turmoil and confusion.

> The first emotion this poverty evoked from me was shame—shame that I had so much, that I have been so lucky, that I could board a plane and leave all this. I felt I should be in the streets with them, begging.

> To associate with these slum-dwellers is to go insane from pity and frustration; to ignore them is not only inhumane, it's impossible. Day after day this "life" goes on. What hope is there?

"What hope is there?" The unhappy answer is that, as of now, there can be very little hope for improvement.

The reasons for the poverty of the underdeveloped countries are complicated; they stretch back into obscure pre-history and out into the jigsaw relations of religion, law, education, politics, economics, and social custom. But one reason conditions are *staying* so persistently bad is that the populations of these countries are growing much too rapidly. Demands—for everything—are increasing so fast that supplies cannot keep pace. It takes only simple arithmetic to show that when a country's population increases faster than its production, there are less and less goods per consumer. The late Prime Minister Nehru of India once wrote, "We can never plan for the nation . . . if the population grows at this rate." Each year, growing at a rate of 2.2 per cent, India adds a population greater than Sweden's to the masses it already has. In many other parts of the underdeveloped world, populations are growing at an even faster rate. The "population explosion" is not a vague menace of the distant future. It is here and now.

In 1960 the population of the earth reached three billion. It took tens of thousands of years for mankind to produce this number; yet in about thirty-five more years—while most of the children born in 1960 are still alive—there will almost certainly be an *additional* three billion people on the earth. This incredible acceleration is unmanageable and malignant—more like cancer than like healthy growth. It will intensify the misery in the underdeveloped countries, for nations that cannot even now feed, clothe, house, and educate their people surely will not be able to satisfy so many more, so soon. Calcutta today, still swollen by millions of refugees until the streets are spotted with their sleeping bodies, seems a unique problem; but, for the underdeveloped countries at least, it may very well represent the City of the Future.

How to Cause an Explosion

> I've been in Mongolian villages where people can remember syphilis epidemics when, of 2,000 families, only one baby survived. Now syphilis is eradicated.

> *Edgar Snow*

Ironically, this threatening bulge of population has come about because man has recently been so successful in his age-old battle with nature. In the past, "natural" deaths have always approximately equaled births. Famines and devastating epidemics have often claimed hundreds of thousands of lives at a stroke, and the non-epidemic diseases were, in the long run, even more destructive. "Against the plague," Boccaccio wrote,

> all human wisdom and foresight were vain. . . . No doctor's advice, no medicine would overcome or alleviate this disease. . . . Either the disease was such that no treatment was possible or the doctors were so ignorant that they did not know what caused it, and consequently could not administer the proper remedy. In any case, very few recovered . . .

Now, with remarkable suddenness, all that has been changed. People still starve all too often, but famine relief has become more systematic and efficient. People still die of "unnecessary" diseases, but governments all over the world, armed with new insecticides, drugs, and vaccines, have undertaken the mass control of disease. The U.N. World Health Organization has introduced a dramatic concept of public health, resolving to *eradicate* diseases—to cause them simply to pass out of existence. Vast campaigns have scored spectacular gains against malaria, smallpox, cholera, yellow fever, typhus—all the old mass killers. In Ceylon, for instance, deaths from malaria were reduced almost by half in three years. Cholera now exists only in parts of Asia; deaths from cholera were reduced from 130,000 in 1950 to 12,800 in 1960. There has not been a major pandemic, a U.N. publication reports, since 1919, when influenza caused 25 million deaths around the world. Man has seemed to be conquering nature.

But nature is a tricky opponent. It had been keeping a kind of balance, a tragic balance, between births and deaths. The potential of human reproduction is tremendous. In 1798 Thomas Malthus, an English parson-economist, first brought serious attention to the now familiar predicament: population tends to increase faster than the means of subsistence. Under good health conditions it is possible for the human race to multiply itself sixty times in less than a century. Nature (among other things) has never yet let this happen; but nature, as we have seen, has recently been deprived of some of its power to destroy, and population is therefore increasing explosively. The world now has one million more mouths to feed every week.

"Overpopulation" is not an easy word to define, because it is relative to economic and social conditions in a given society. But some illustrations will help. For instance:

> It took mankind the whole period of recorded time until the early nineteenth century to achieve a population of *one* billion. It took only a century to add the *second* billion. It took somewhat over 30 years to raise the world population to *three* billion. And, at the present rate of increase, only 15 years will be required to bring the figure to *four* billion.

Not only is world population growing, but the *rate* of population growth keeps going up. Over the last eighty years, the rate of *doubling* has doubled.

To put it another way: in 1900, world population increased by about 40,000 people every day; now it is increasing by 180,000 every day. And the rate is going up.

To put it another way: the world is now *adding* to its population about 125 people every minute, 7,500 every hour, more than a million every week, 65 million every year. And the rate is going up.

Overpopulation occurs whenever there are so many people or such a rapid growth of people that the skills and resources of a given area cannot provide them a decent standard of living. It is a biological form of living beyond one's means. This condition has already been reached in many of the underdeveloped countries. We sometimes hear people discussing World War I "as if it were yesterday"; but world population will probably double before the year 2000, which is not as far in the future as World War I is in the past. By then conditions in the underdeveloped countries will almost certainly be worse, not better, than they are now. And whereas two-thirds of the world's people lived in the underdeveloped countries in 1950, three-quarters of them will be there in the year 2000.

Population, we need to be constantly and forcefully reminded, means people: human beings, who will be hungry if they are not fed, cold if they are not clothed, wretched if they are not housed, and mentally stunted if they are not educated. Yet, of the millions of babies being born into our world this year, most will be ill-fed, ill-clothed, ill-housed, and ill-educated. The world offers them more frustration than fulfillment, more pain than pleasure. This is not prophecy but a present fact.

How Does Hunger Feel?

> Hunger is a curious thing: at first it is with you all the time, waking and sleeping and in your dreams, and your belly cries out insistently, and there is a gnawing and a pain as if your very vitals were being devoured, and you must stop it at any cost . . . Then the pain is no longer sharp but dull, and this too is with you always . . .
>
> *Kamala Markandaya*

The majority of the world's people are inadequately fed. In Hong Kong, lean Chinese women with nervous, taut-skinned faces (their children strapped to their backs and clinging to their hands) stand in block-long lines waiting for American surplus food. In the agricultural villages of India (where 80 per cent of that country's people live), the fields are worn out from centuries of use and misuse, and subdivided among unnumbered successions of male heirs until many of them are so small it would be uneconomical to work them with large modern machinery, even if it were available. Instead, skinny gray humped oxen endlessly circle ancient wells in an inefficient attempt to irrigate the crops, or pull wooden plows, scratching out shallow furrows in the earth. Manure that should fertilize the soil is burnt for fuel. So it is not surprising to notice people's lethargy—an inertia born of hunger and reinforced by generations of fatalistic acceptance of a system that has never yielded them much except disappointment.

How does it feel to be constantly hungry? Few of us in the land of the supermarket really know. In the 1940's, Ancel Keys and his colleagues at the University of Minnesota carried out an important experiment in semi-starvation. One of the subjects reported:

> I'm hungry. I'm always hungry—not like the hunger that comes when you miss lunch, but a continual cry from the body for food. At times I can almost forget about it but there is nothing that can hold my interest for long. . . . I'm cold. In July I walk downtown on a sunny day with a shirt and sweater on to keep me warm. . . . I'm weak. . . . I trip on cracks in the sidewalk. To open a heavy door it is necessary to brace myself and push or pull with all my might. . . . When I tried to smile it was a grimace and I didn't feel like smiling and never laughed.

The American journalist Dickey Chapelle was once imprisoned by Hungarian Communists as a spy and put on a severely limited diet for an indefinite period. Later she wrote:

> Within ten days on this diet I learned something about hunger I had never known . . . It was a local pain as big as my hand, sharp or dull but never still. More important, under the impact of hunger, I watched myself become another person. . . . There was just one mood of which I was capable. Sullen and terrible ugliness. After a time, I thought I probably had forgotten how to weep or curse. I knew I could not laugh.

The fortunate *one-third* of the world's people who do have enough to eat are consuming *two-thirds* of the world's total food production. That is why Americans, members of the lucky one-third, rarely have to experience the pain and lassitude that many of the world's people suffer constantly, and why we can hardly grasp the importance of Gandhi's remark that to a hungry people the only form God dare appear in is the form of food.

The problem of food shortage is closely linked to the problem of bad health. With Western help, American surplus food, and improved transportation, the devastating famines of a few decades ago are currently being thwarted, but although fewer people are actually starving to death, the health of millions is nevertheless still being impaired. In Turkey, for instance, there is now little outright starvation, but people's health suffers because most of them are on a "bread, rice, and beans" diet. When all food is in chronically short supply, as it often is in the underdeveloped countries, the quality of the diet is inevitably low.

Foods rich in vitamins are generally expensive, beyond the reach of the great masses of people. The Asian staple of polished rice is also deficient in fat, protein, and minerals; most Asians, Africans, and Latin Americans get far too little meat, fish, and eggs, too little milk, and too few fruits and vegetables to maintain good health.

It is not only that the people cannot afford better foods; in most of the underdeveloped countries these foods simply do not exist in anything like sufficient quantities to supply their expanding populations. Thus, ironically, the eradication of the contagious diseases has tended to increase the diseases of malnutrition; I noticed the symptoms of these everywhere—eyes inflamed with trachoma, bones bent from rickets, thin bodies exhausted from anemia, beriberi, and pellagra. Sickly, tired people do not work well, so the production of food suffers—and a vicious circle is created.

Houses, Schools, Morals

Say, for instance, that a proud new housing project is begun in a crowded area. All too often by the time the buildings are completed, so many people have moved into, or so many babies have been born into, the area that the number living in poorer, overcrowded homes remains the same.

Report on Latin America

Another problem caused by explosively growing populations is the shortage of proper housing. Hong Kong, for instance, has jumped from a million and a half to more than three million since World War II. Some of the growth was caused by an influx of refugees from the mainland, but a million babies have also been born in the city in the last fifteen years. Whole families live in little sampans and in makeshift shacks. Some of the lucky ones will eventually move into the comparative luxury of government resettlement buildings—but even there families of seven live in the standard cubicles, about ten feet square.

The situation is little better in many other cities and villages. Two hundred and fifty new families move into Bangkok every day, causing further complications in a country where the national population will double in the next twenty years. This overcrowding of urban areas is going on in most of the underdeveloped countries, with unhappy results. In Indian cities such as Bombay and Calcutta, about one-half of the families live in housing that amounts to one room or less.

Under such conditions, the problem of ill health takes a new form. In Bangkok, people bathe in and drink from the same canals that serve them as open sewers. Bangkok is a city of water and sometimes called the Venice of the East, but its back streets—where houses are built directly over little ditches used for the disposal of garbage and sewage—are as ugly as anything in the world. In other cities, lack of water causes trouble: half the city dwellers in India must carry their water from ponds and reservoirs, and people who have to carry heavy water jars for many blocks simply cannot use it in great quantities for general cleanliness. Also, cities trying to supply more and more water to exploding populations cannot always manage to assure its purity. Over these crowded masses, therefore, hovers the constant threat of tuberculosis.

If the population explosion continues, it will not be easy—perhaps not even possible—to improve these conditions significantly. An Indian economic expert estimated in 1963 that to give Indians barely adequate housing, twice as much money would be required as is contemplated for all investment in the country's whole economy in the current economic plan. Because of rapid population growth, low-cost housing never keeps up with demand. For example, a recent Inter-American Development Bank loan of one million dollars to the capital of Honduras will supply houses for 4,300 people. But the city is growing by 6,000 people *each year.* This same dismal mathematics is in force throughout the underdeveloped world.

Throughout Asia, the hope of rising from misery is closely linked with the magic of education. From peasants in muddy villages to executives in the centers of government, I found an enthusiasm for education perhaps greater than our own. Yet this simply presents another problem, for less than half the children of these countries are in school.

In Hong Kong it is only one-fourth of the children. The Executive Secretary of the Hong Kong Teacher's Association was deeply concerned. "We cannot keep up with them," he told me. "We have the teachers working in shifts, and the government is constantly building classrooms—but there is another baby born here every four minutes." Furthermore, he said that the schoolwork of the lucky ones who get into the classroom often suffers because the children are undernourished. And the quality of the instruction suffers even more. In the cities and villages of Asia, great crowds of children sit on the ground around their teachers and recite, at the tops of their voices, their rote lessons; in Bangkok, university professors have to waste class time reading homework aloud from textbooks that the students can't afford to buy. Unsatisfactory as all this is, at least these students are better off than the majority of Asian children, who wander about the streets with still smaller children strapped to their backs, and whose minds and lives will always be stunted by illiteracy. The story is the same in all of the underdeveloped countries; only the percentages vary. Brazil quadrupled its schools between 1933 and 1959, but still only half the children between the ages of seven and fourteen are in school there. In Venezuela, despite heavy investment in school facilities, the national literacy level has dropped from 57 per cent to 51 per cent since World War II. Education is legally compulsory in Thailand, in India, in Egypt, and in Turkey, but in none of these places can this law be enforced, because exploding populations have created such masses of children that there are neither teachers nor classrooms enough to go around.

One of the most sinister problems connected with rapid population growth is a crisis in morals. There is an ancient Chinese saying: "It is difficult to tell the difference between right and wrong when the stomach is empty." People driven by constant hunger, by joblessness, by insecurity; huddled together in overcrowded cities and villages; unaided by education; and with nowhere to turn in their misery—can such people honestly be expected to develop respect for the ethical niceties which admonish them not to covet, not to steal, not even to envy? In poverty-stricken, underdeveloped Sicily, one group of outlaws is known to have spent, collectively, seven hundred and fifty years in school—and more than three thousand years in prison. While I was in New Delhi, Tara Ali Baig, General Secretary of the Indian Council for Child Welfare, wrote about the slum dwellers of Delhi in the *Hindustan Times:*

> They live in tiny sheds made from flattened oil tins and gunny sacking. Almost any slum scene is that of a woman with two or three tiny immobile children squatting beside her while she feeds the one in her arms . . . Desperation and insecurity become, for a family like this, a second nature, blighting their entire lives.

This "blight" is both physical and moral, and it will doubtless spread right along with the growth of the misery-ridden people.

This suggests another, subtler moral problem, and one that concerns us all directly: the present growth of world population may seem so overwhelming, so inevitable, as to cause us, the comparatively well-to-do peoples of the world, simply to throw up our hands—to disclaim responsibility for helping those less well off than we. That is a particularly tempting corruption, simply because it is so easy, and seems so "sensible." Repelled as I was by the first sight of Asian misery, I could not help remarking on the psychological defense mechanism that gradually dulled my shock at the sight of old women carrying heavy loads on bamboo poles through the streets of Hong Kong, or that somehow permitted visiting Americans to lie comfortably in the overstaffed luxury of the Grand Hotel of Calcutta, while outside thousands of half-starved human beings were sleeping in the streets under thin rags. Everyone who has lived in Asia knows why this defense mechanism operates: it is the only way the mind can keep its sanity in an insane situation. It does not always work perfectly; I saw one well-to-do Indian who, when accosted by a beggar, lectured him severely—and then burst into tears. Personal compassion notwithstanding, however, the basic, unhappy situation remains, and it is now a familiar story: overpopulation reinforces poverty, poverty generates desperation, and desperation leads to immorality. It is perhaps worth reminding ourselves that the immorality of the envious poor who rebel against their painful lot is no worse than the immorality of the comfortable rich who too easily accept such intolerable conditions.

What Can Be Done?

> So long as we are concerned with the quality of life, we have no choice but to be concerned with the quantity of life.
>
> *Richard N. Gardner*

The problems of the underdeveloped, overpopulated countries are extremely difficult ones. What can be done about them? Loans and gifts from the wealthier countries are, for the time being, essential; but they are only a stopgap. A proper solution must begin by creating more food—not in the nations that already have enough, but in those where people desperately need it. Ambitious moves are being made in this direction. In India, in Egypt, in Turkey, and elsewhere, irrigation is being extended, production of fertilizer is being stepped up, acreage is being increased, and better crop plants are being produced. But in many of the underdeveloped countries, domestic food supplies are nevertheless still falling behind population growth. A gigantic agricultural effort will be necessary simply to keep greater and greater numbers of people in their present malnourished condition.

Industrial development in the underdeveloped countries is also imperative, and attempts are being made to build strong local industries. But industrial growth depends upon capital investment, and capital is scarce in these needy areas. Furthermore, merely to keep per capita incomes at their present low levels through the next few decades, huge annual investments—from 6 to 10 per cent of national incomes—will be necessary. To permit a noticeable and encouraging growth in per capita incomes, investment would have to reach 12 or 15 per cent or more—rates that are not likely to materialize in the underdeveloped areas. Thus, in industrial production as well as in food production, the future looks dim indeed: instead of relieving people's misery, enormous and well-intentioned agricultural and industrial efforts may end up simply maintaining more people in greater misery. Rapid population growth is saying to the underdeveloped economies, in effect, what the Red Queen said to Alice: "It takes all the running *you* can do to keep in the same place. If you want to get somewhere else, you must run at least twice as fast as that!"

Then what *is* to be done? I asked the question everywhere in Asia. There were no easy answers, but I often heard the rather wistful remark: "If only the population were not growing so fast!" And, just as often: "Medical science has lowered our death rate; if only it would help to lower our birth rate!" This was not an attempt to reduce all problems to a matter of birth control, but a realization that without regulation of births, the other problems are insoluble.

Some effort is already being made in the underdeveloped countries to encourage limitation of births. The governments of India, Pakistan, Egypt, Ceylon, South Korea, and other countries are officially sponsoring family planning programs. Unfortunately, though, none of these has yet reached far enough into the villages to have had a significant effect on national growth rates.

One drawback to such programs is that peasant peoples are generally motivated to want more, not fewer, children. This is partly because of the age-old approval of fertility as such. For example, in Benares I once saw women tying rocks to temple trees in the pious belief that this would bring more sons; in Greece, according to Margaret Mead, childlessness is considered a "terrible calamity"; in Latin America, newlywed husbands feel they must produce children quickly to prove they are "real men"; and in Mexico, writes one scholar, "a large family is . . . the supreme cultural and religious value . . . mothers are surrounded by an emotional veneration second only to that of the Virgin Mother herself. Partly, too, large families are a kind of substitute for social security. Few of the underdeveloped countries have, or are planning to have soon, a social security system, and a large number of sons seems the only protection against the hazards of old age.

Among upper-class people in the cities, these ideas are beginning to disappear. I was in New Delhi on India's national Family Planning Day in 1960. A considerable amount of excitement seemed to have been generated: debates, displays, newspaper articles, and so on. But most of this interest, I was told by Lt. Col. B. L. Raina, Director of Family Planning for the Indian Government, is limited to the cities, where it is least needed. Massive education, he said, has to be undertaken in the villages, where the great bulk of the people live. There, many people do not even know that family size is controllable. Too often, an Indian demographer told me, it is supposed that a propaganda poster (in English!) will solve the problem; whereas what is really needed is a large staff of trained and sympathetic people who will go into the villages and advise the people about family planning.

"Motivation," then, is an important part of the whole problem of population limitation, and it is a complex one. What sort of motivation for family limitation is needed, for instance, given presently available contraceptives? The expense, the relative inconvenience, and the unreliability of these devices make a high degree of motivation necessary. Considerably less motivation would be required if a simpler, cheaper, more reliable contraceptive were available. "What we really need in India today," says M. C. Chagla, formerly India's ambassador to the United States, "is a cheap oral contraceptive." Ayub Khan, the president of Pakistan, calls the rapidly growing population Pakistan's "Problem Number One" and has asked Americans "to apply your mind and your resources to be able to combat this problem." But so far, the simple contraceptive that both these nations need and want does not exist.

Contraceptive pills are now widely used in some countries. They are effective and safe under medical supervision, but they are still too expensive and too complicated to be of any use to poor, illiterate peasants. (The directions for Enovid, the first of the pills, read, in part: "One 5-mg. tablet should be prescribed daily for twenty days beginning on day 5 of the cycle, counting the first day of menstruation as day 1.") Furthermore, the fact that they require any medical supervision at all makes them impracticable for areas where people have rarely or never seen a doctor. (In India there is only one doctor for every six thousand people, and most of them are in the cities.) More research is needed to develop an ideal oral or immunological contraceptive. Experts in the field are confident that this problem could be solved in less than ten years if funds, facilities, and technicians were available. . . .

The Accelerating Crisis:
A Postscript to the 1966 Edition

Every honest writer with a "message" hopes that his work will soon become obsolete: that the problems he describes will be publicly recognized, that his suggested solutions (or better ones) will be vigorously prosecuted, and that threatening crises will therefore be averted. In the year and a half since *The Silent Explosion* first went to press, there have indeed been some encouraging developments, but on the whole, the population problem seems to have worsened. At the end of the last chapter of this book, I reminded the reader of the hundreds of thousands of people in the streets of Calcutta, with little food, no homes, no jobs, and no future: huddled in their ragged, dusty brown blankets, looking like little lumps of earth, waiting out one more day of their miserable existence. Those people, I said, are still there. Today they are *still* there—more and more of them—and the whole underdeveloped world is full of such human suffering, less spectacular, perhaps, but just as real.

Population growth rates in the poorest countries have continued to climb, and the United Nations demographers are now predicting a possible world population of seven and a half billion by the end of the century. India alone, where the growth rate has risen to 2.4 per cent, is adding twelve million people each year to the total. In the single minute that it has taken the average reader to read this much of the Postscript, two hundred and fifty babies have been born and one hundred and twenty-five people have died, leaving a net gain of one hundred and twenty-five people. Tomorrow at this time there will be almost two hundred thousand more; next year, about seventy million more: seventy million more mouths to feed, more bodies to clothe and make shelter for, more people to build schools for and to provide with the whole range of public services—power, water, roads, hospitals, police protection, and so on. And seventy million people, one would hope, who will want something more than mere sustenance and a meager borderline existence; seventy million people who would like to have some kind of challenge, interest, meaning, and purpose in their lives. Of course, most of them will not have any of these things; many of them, in fact, will be very lucky if they don't starve.

Food production in the last half-dozen years has simply not increased as fast as population growth. World agricultural output in 1965 grew by 1.5 per cent over 1964, but population went up by more than 2 per cent. On a country-by-country basis, the situation is even worse than those grim figures indicate, for in most of the poorer countries the agricultural output is lower than the average and the population growth higher. That is what I meant when I wrote that the population explosion is not a vague menace of the distant future; it is here and now.

For all of these reasons, the silent explosion gets less and less silent every month. In India, where severe drought is causing the worst harvest in many years, members of Parliament have reported that hundreds of people have already starved to death. The Indian government has instituted food rationing, and there have been widespread food riots, sometimes involving tens of thousands of people; many of the protestors have been killed or wounded. The unhappy prospect is that things will probably get still worse in the foreseeable future. Experts think it likely that serious and persistent famines will sweep southern and eastern Asia in the next few years and most of Asia, Africa, and Latin America within the next decade. "In ten years' time," President Ayub of Pakistan has said, "human beings will eat human beings in Pakistan." *

The more things change, the more they are the same: the population crisis has worsened, but it is still the same problem. I have therefore not revised this edition of *The Silent Explosion.* Population statistics are constantly being superseded by newer and more depressing ones. The statistics in this book are correct as of the date of first publication; revised figures added now would soon be out of date. A reader who wants current statistics should consult the most recent publications of the United States Census Bureau and the United Nations demographic, economic, and agricultural organizations, available in many libraries.

In Chapter 2 of this book [not included here] I discussed the "Cornucopian" economists. Those theoreticians are still with us, but their numbers seem to be dwindling, and one hears less and less about economic miracles. Some former economic "optimists" (like David Lilienthal, who had been hopeful about the prospect of feeding the world's expanding population) have recently changed their minds and admit that increased agricultural yields, however desirable, cannot be considered independent alternatives to population control.

It is always instructive to use India as a vast microcosm, representing the problems of the whole underdeveloped world. Through the 1960's, India has only once been able to produce more than the usual eighty million tons of food per year. This year the crop will be much smaller because of the drought. The United States has had to step in (as it has in other countries) and try to save the situation with our surplus food. Last year thirty million Indians lived on United States surplus wheat. About three shiploads (amounting to thirty thousand tons) of American grain now reach India every day. This means that one in every four American grain farmers is now producing food for India. If India's population goes on increasing at its present rate for only ten more years, India's food deficit will require the production of *every* grain producer in America. And, of course, India won't get it.

In the face of this tragic situation, there is now talk in Washington about reversing our domestic farm policy and encouraging, rather than limiting, food production. Even so, few experts think that our production could continue to meet the mounting world food deficit for more than another ten or fifteen years, at best.

What about the Communists, in the meantime? Have the Soviets and the Chinese finally shown that their agricultural theories are right, that their collective and communal farms can provide sufficiently for the people of the U.S.S.R. and China? Have they now proved the Marxist contention that under communism it is not necessary to worry about rapid population growth? Not at all: in 1965, once

---

* Karachi *Leader,* Oct. 7, 1964; reported in *International Planned Parenthood News,* Jan., 1965.

again, Canada and other Western food exporters had to supply wheat not only to the U.S.S.R. and China, but also to Czechoslovakia, Bulgaria, and Poland. The Soviet Union alone bought 330 million bushels of wheat from Western agriculturists. It is hardly surprising, therefore, that government-sponsored family planning is now proceeding rapidly in the Communist countries.

Nevertheless, the Soviet delegate to the U.N. World Health Organization continued to insist, in 1965, that the World Health Organization should not concern itself with regulating the growth of population but rather with developing the world's food resources. So we are still confronted with that darkly intriguing Communist contradiction: population control at home, but encouragement of population pressures (and therefore mounting chaos) abroad. This contradiction puts a sinister emphasis on Dean Rusk's testimony before the U.S. Senate Agriculture Committee in 1966: "There is a very real relationship between hunger and political instability."

Chapters 4 and 5 of *The Silent Explosion* [not included here] analyze various Roman Catholic attitudes toward birth control. Catholic influence has been the main barrier to proposals for population control; because of this, many people permitted their hopes to rise when the Vatican Ecumenical Council undertook a full review of the Catholic position on birth control. Subsequently, of course, Pope Paul withdrew the subject from the Council's competence and placed it in the hands of a special commission, which, according to the Pope, was to study the problem "in complete objectivity and liberty of spirit." The liberal Catholics on the commission, however, were soon complaining that they were being harassed by lack of funds, by deliberately misplaced documents, by tampered texts, and by inability to communicate with their superiors. These obstructions were invariably traced back to the powerful Doctrinal Congregation (formerly the Holy Office), presided over by the arch-conservative Cardinal Ottaviani. Ottaviani is seventy-five years old and is fond of reminding the world that he is the eleventh of twelve children. He often invokes the primitive command to "increase and multiply," and he recently insisted that "To try to change the [birth control] situation simply because the population is increasing or because there are economic problems cannot be a valid reason in view of the great doctrinal principles based in great part on natural law." He has also said, "The freedom granted to married couples to determine for themselves the number of their children cannot possibly be approved."

There was understandable concern, then, among liberal Catholics and concerned non-Catholics alike, when Pope Paul recently reorganized the "birth control commission" and appointed, as its new chairman, none other than Cardinal Ottaviani. One wonders how the Pope can expect "complete objectivity and liberty of spirit" from a committee headed by a man whose mind is so obviously closed. How can the Church expect to achieve "aggiornamento," or modernizing, if it sets about it by putting still more power in the hands of conservatives who will undoubtedly do their best to prevent any changes at all? How long, in these circumstances, can the Catholic Church expect to keep the respect of its more enlightened members? Polls in this country show about four out of five Catholics in favor of freedom of conscience regarding birth control, and study groups of important American and European Catholic theologians and intellectuals have recommended a whole new stand on the subject.

Unfortunately, this modern and responsible Catholic opinion is persistently ignored by the conservative prelates who are still in charge in Rome. Pope Paul himself seems to be at one with these conservatives, having repeatedly spoken against birth control. At the United Nations General Assembly in 1965, for instance, in an astonishing speech to delegates from hunger-plagued countries, he denounced population control and called for more and more babies to join us at the "banquet of life." The unconscious irony of that phrase was underscored a month later when he called for a "war against world hunger."

At this writing, then, it seems unlikely that there will be any major change in the Church's stand on birth control. That means that if there is to be any action in the field of population control—which almost all informed people now consider mandatory—that action will have to be taken despite the Catholic Church's official objections. It will therefore be slower and more cautious than the situation warrants, but there is little doubt now that it must come. Catholic representatives to the United Nations will no doubt continue to suppress debate on this issue and will continue to throw road blocks in the way of action by the World Health Organization and other United Nation bodies, as Argentina, Brazil, Ireland, and others recently have done, but eventually those organizations will act. With the welfare of most of the world at stake, there is no other choice. Thus, as time goes on, it will become more and more clear that on this crucial matter, the Roman Catholic Church, powerfully influenced by its most conservative members, has simply withdrawn from the twentieth century. That is a great pity, chiefly because it means delay and therefore massive and unnecessary suffering on the part of hundreds of millions of people; but it is also a pity because the Catholic Church, which has taken enlightened and progressive stands on so many controversial issues in our time, will have branded itself as officially close-minded and repressive on one of the most important problems of all time. It is more than a pity; it is a tragedy.

As public awareness of the dangers of overpopulation has grown and continues to grow, an American consensus has gradually evolved on the issue of birth control, and this has been reflected in a whole new set of official attitudes and actions on the part of the United States government. President Johnson has spoken up frequently and forcefully since his State of the Union message in 1965, when he proposed "new ways to use our knowledge to help deal with the explosion in world population and the growing scarcity in world resources." Next to the search for peace, he has said, the population crisis "is humanity's greatest challenge."

Concurrently, the Agency for International Development has become increasingly involved in population problems, collecting and analyzing data, training family planning workers, and providing various supplies for family planning units. And a special White House advisory panel in 1965 made two very important recommendations to the President: (1) that we set an international example by making birth control information and services readily available in this country; and (2) that we substantially increase our aid to other countries in developing and implementing population control programs; specifically, that we make available 100 million dollars a year for the next three years to help foreign governments carry out their family planning programs.

Despite these hopeful signs, there is still considerable debate over the degree of commitment that governmental bodies should make. The United States government is *not* providing the recommended 100 million dollars annually to this critically important field; currently it allows only about five and a half million. The Administration seems reluctant to commit itself fully in other ways, too. In 1965, identical bills were introduced in the House and the Senate, calling for Assistant Secretaries in the Department of State and the Department of Health, Education, and Welfare, to be in charge of coordinating and disseminating information on population and birth control. In the subsequent Congressional hearings, scores of experts testified to the necessity of such legislation, but at this writing, a conflict has developed between the Congressional supporters of the bill and Administration officials. Retiring Undersecretary of State Thomas C. Mann has created an office to "serve as a focal point for policy matters" on birth control and population policies; but the job was given to a special assistant to Mr. Mann, not to an Assistant Secretary. Similarly, the head of the Agency for International Development, David E. Bell, has testified against a bill to earmark American-held foreign currencies for birth control and family planning programs in the underdeveloped countries. Senator Ernest Gruening, who introduced the "birth control bill" in the Senate, has called this an "evasion." Clearly, the evolving American consensus has not yet produced a really purposeful approach to the enormous population problems the world is facing.

Not only is there a lack of clarity in our attempts to deal with the population explosion; there is a genuine uncertainty whether any such attempts will have a real chance of success. Few people concerned with population studies expect that even a crash program of fertility control would have any profound effect on population growth rates for the next few years, or possibly for the next decade; and of course no such program has been started yet. Even if a major program got under way, its effectiveness would be questionable, since most of our contraceptive methods are still antiquated and awkward and (worst of all) not 100 per cent effective. There are constant reports of newer methods, but so far only the oral contraceptives and the intra-uterine devices, among the recently developed methods, have had wide and prolonged testing and are known to be nearly 100 per cent effective, as well as safe. Former Senator Kenneth Keating, Chairman of the Population Crisis Committee, recently pointed out that of its vast research budget, the United States spends less than seven one-hundredths of one per cent for research on birth control. The total funds available for birth-control research, public and private, were reviewed by John D. Rockefeller III before Senator Gruening's subcommittee; and Mr. Rockefeller concluded that they were "totally inadequate in terms of the magnitude of the population problem and the urgency of its solution."

The population explosion is most crucial in the underdeveloped countries, but nothing that has happened in the last year and a half has indicated that it can be overlooked in our own country, either. The post-World War II "baby boom" has lasted longer here than in any of the developed, Western nations, and although there has been a falling-off in our birth rate since 1957, our growth rate remains much higher than in Japan or most of Europe.

We can take some comfort in the decline of our birth rate, but we should at the same time be aware of certain complications. In the first place, the United States is adding almost two and a half million people a year to its population. Thus the base figure on which the birth rate is calculated has swollen considerably over the last twenty years, so that lower birth rates now can still mean higher absolute increases of population than before. This demonstrates the geometric nature of population increase. The "baby boom" babies are now reaching adulthood. And even if this very numerous generation of young people, now in their teens, elect to have comparatively small families (which is not at all certain), the absolute net increase of such a large crop of new reproducers is going to be enormous. So even at best, our population is going to continue to grow very rapidly, in absolute terms; we have just passed the 195 million mark, and will probably top 200 million by May, 1967. If we continue to grow at the present rate, it will be only sixty years before we have as many people as India now has.

Sixty years—are we going to be prepared for such a huge population, so soon? Are we even now solving the problems, for our own comparatively modest population, of water shortages, water pollution, soil depletion, air pollution, urban sprawl, urban blight, peacetime unemployment, juvenile delinquency, and infringements on our personal liberties? All of these difficult problems, and others, are aggravated by too-rapid population growth. What evidence do we have that America is preparing to cope, on a really practical basis, with a doubling or tripling of these problems?

The average reader would take about fifteen minutes to read this brief Postscript; in that time, nearly two thousand more people have been added to this planet. On the other hand, per capita production of food (and of the other necessities and amenities of life) has declined a little more. That is a somber picture; insofar as there is any bright side to it, it is that today, to a degree that would have been unthinkable a few years ago, people in all walks of life—including government—are at last recognizing the problem, studying it, and (although slowly) facing up to it. If this continues to happen, there may yet be a happy ending to the depressing story of the silent explosion. For the sake of billions of people now alive, and more billions soon to be born, I hope it does.

From **The City In History**
LEWIS MUMFORD

Railroad Line, Greenbelt, Motor Sprawl

The suburbs built between 1850 and 1920 owed their existence primarily to the railroad, though those nearer the central city were, after 1895, likewise indebted to the electric trolley car (tramway) and the underground. Sometimes land speculators promoted rapid transit, but as often as not electric power and transit magnates—like the van Sweringens in Cleveland (Shaker Heights) and Insull in Chicago (Niles Center)—promoted the suburbs. The bold initiative of Frank Pick, as head of the London Underground, played no small part in London's twentieth-century suburban development.

The earlier type of suburb, which was most dependent on the railroad, had a special advantage that could be fully appreciated only after it had disappeared. These suburbs, strung along a railroad line, were discontinuous and properly spaced; and without the aid of legislation they were limited in population as well as area; for the biggest rarely held as many as ten thousand people, and under five thousand was more usual. In 1950, for example, Bronxville, New York, a typical upper-class suburb, had 6,778 people, while Riverside, Illinois, founded as early as 1869, had only 9,153.

The size and scale of the suburb, that of a neighborhood unit, was not entirely the result of its open planning, which favored low densities. Being served by a railroad line, with station stops from three to five miles apart, there was a natural limit to the spread of any particular community. Houses had to be sited "within easy walking distance of the railroad station," as the advertising prospectus would point out; and only those wealthy enough to afford a horse and carriage dared to penetrate farther into the open country.

Through its spaced station stops, the railroad suburb was at first kept from spreading or unduly increasing in numbers, for a natural greenbelt, often still under cultivation as market gardens, remained between the suburbs and increased the available recreation area. Occasionally, in a few happy areas like Westchester, between 1915 and 1935, a parkway, like the Bronx River Parkway, accompanied by a continuous strip of park for pedestrian use, not yet over-run by a constant stream of metropolitan traffic, added to the perfection of the whole suburban pattern. Whatever one might say of the social disadvantages, this was in many ways an idyllic physical environment. But it lasted less than a generation.

Probably it was the very existence of these natural greenbelts, insulating the small, self-contained, but closely linked suburban communities, that prompted the economist, Alfred Marshall, to suggest in 1899, a "national fresh air tax," in England, as a means of securing permanent green belts between towns. "We need," he observed, "to increase the playgrounds in the midst of our towns. We need also to prevent one town from growing into another, or into a neighboring village; we need to keep intermediate stretches of country in dairy farms, etc. as well as public pleasure grounds."

More timely and perspicuous advice could not have been offered to municipal governments: indeed more than half a century later, it is still timely and far more urgent. That it was not at once followed up by city planners and municipal officials, that it is still far from being appreciated and acted upon in most growing urban centers, is a disgrace to these professions and a blot on our common civic intelligence. (The New Towns movement in England and the far-sighted policies of a few notable cities, such as Rotterdam, Amsterdam, and Stockholm, contrast with the dismal failure of New York to protect Westchester and Long Island, or of San Francisco to protect the Bay Region, and even more the vineyards and orchards of Santa Clara Valley: to choose but two sorry examples out of scores.)

Had Marshall's advice been promptly heeded, by introducing appropriate zoning and land-use legislation, and providing for the large-scale acquisition of public land for settlement with every fresh highway development, a radical change in the urban pattern could have been introduced. Not merely would it have been possible to prevent the consolidation and extension of vast masses of suburban and sub-suburban housing, but we could have taken positive steps to build up a more organic form, on a regional scale, in keeping with our modern facilities for transportation and communication.

Instead of creating the Regional City, the forces that automatically pumped highways and motor cars and real estate developments into the open country have produced the formless urban exudation. Those who are using verbal magic to turn this conglomeration into an organic entity are only fooling themselves. To call the resulting mass Megalopolis, or to suggest that the change in spatial scale, with swift transportation, in itself is sufficient to produce a new and better urban form, is to overlook the complex nature of the city. The actual coalescence of urban tissue that is now taken by many sociologists to be a final stage in city development, is not in fact a new sort of city, but an anti-city. As in the concept of anti-matter, the anti-city annihilates the city whenever it collides with it.

What has happened to the suburb is now a matter of historic record. As soon as the motor car became common, the pedestrian scale of the suburb disappeared, and with it, most of its individuality and charm. The suburb ceased to be a neighborhood unit: it became a diffused low-density mass, enveloped by the conurbation and then further enveloping it. The suburb needed its very smallness, as it needed its rural background, to achieve its own kind of semi-rural perfection. Once that limit was overpassed, the suburb ceased to be a refuge from the city and became part of the inescapable metropolis, "la ville tentaculaire," whose distant outlying open spaces and public parks were themselves further manifestations of the crowded city. This fact that will not cease to be true even if jet transportation brings an area twelve hundred miles away as near as one sixty miles distant today. For when one conquers space one also increases the populations to whom that distant space is accessible. The prospective net gain is considerably less than zero.

As long as the railroad stop and walking distances controlled suburban growth, the suburb had a form. The very concentration of shops and parking facilities around the railroad station in the better suburbs even promoted a new kind of market area, more concentrated than the linear market along an avenue. This was a spontaneous prototype of the suburban shopping center, whose easy facilities for parking gave it advantages over more central urban establishments, once the private motor car became the chief mode of transportation. But the motor car had done something more than remove the early limits and destroy the pedestrian scale. It either doubled the number of cars needed per family, or it turned the suburban housewife into a full time chauffeur.

These duties became even more imperative because the advent of the motor car was accompanied by the deliberate dismantling of the electric (rail) transportation system. In the more urbanized parts of America, electric transportation, often on its own private right of way, like the steam railroad, achieved far higher rates of speed than the present motor bus. Far from supplementing public rail transportation, the private motor car became largely a clumsy substitute for it. Instead of maintaining a complex transportation system, offering alternative choices of route and speed to fit the occasion, the new suburban sprawl has become abjectly dependent upon a single form, the private motor car, whose extension has devoured the one commodity the suburb could rightly boast: space. Instead of buildings set in a park, we now have buildings set in a parking lot.

Whilst the suburb served only a favored minority it neither spoiled the countryside nor threatened the city. But now that the drift to the outer ring has become a mass movement, it tends to destroy the value of both environments without producing anything but a dreary substitute, devoid of form and even more devoid of the original suburban values. We are faced by a curious paradox: the new suburban form has now produced an anti-urban pattern. With the destruction of walking distances has gone the destruction of walking as a normal means of human circulation: the motor car has made it unsafe and the extension of the suburb has made it impossible.

As a result, Unwin's salutary demonstration, "Nothing Gained by Overcrowding," must now be countered with a qualifying admonition: "Something Lost by Overspacing." This applies to every feature of the suburban conglomerate. The once modest highway whose Roman width of fifteen feet remained standard almost until the Parkway was invented, now demands thousands of acres, with rights of way broader than mainline railroads required in the height of their expansion.

To ensure the continuous flow of traffic, even in rural areas, immense clover leaves and jug-handles are designed, demolishing still more open space. And instead of freight yards and marshalling yards at the far terminals of a railroad system, the very dispersion of motor traffic demands similar facilities around every individual building where people congregate. Thus, each new factory or office, each new department store or shopping center, established in the midst of the open country, demands parking lots so ample that those who park on the rim have a far longer walk to the shop than they would have in a densely crowded city after leaving their bus or their subway train, though they still obstinately retain the illusionist image of the motor car's taking them from "door to door."

All this is a far cry from the aristocratic enjoyment of visual space that provided the late baroque city with open squares and circles and long vistas for carriage drives down tree-lined avenues. In the new suburban dispensation, wasteful spacing has become a substitute for intelligent civic design, far-seeing municipal organization, or rational economy. Each separate building sprawls in lazy, one-story plans over the maximum possible building area, insulated from its neighbors, if any, by an ever-enlarging parking lot, the latter again increasing steadily in size as mass transportation falls into completer disuse. Yet when the dispersed plant releases it workers at the end of the day, the time-wasting congestion at the exit may fully equal that in the big city.

Under the present suburban regime, every urban function follows the example of the motor road: it devours space and consumes time with increasing friction and frustration, while, under the plausible pretext of increasing the range of speed and communication, it actually obstructs it and denies the possibility of easy meetings and encounters by scattering the fragments of a city at random over a whole region.

At the bottom of this miscarriage of modern technics lies a fallacy that goes to the very heart of the whole underlying ideology: the notion that power and speed are desirable for their own sake, and that the latest type of fast-moving vehicle must replace every other form of transportation. The fact is that speed in locomotion should be a function of human purpose. If one wants to meet and chat with people on an urban promenade, three miles an hour will be too fast; if a surgeon is being rushed to a patient a thousand miles away, three hundred miles an hour may be too slow. But what our experts in transportation are kept by their own stultifying axioms from realizing is that an adequate transportation system cannot be created in terms of any single limited means of locomotion however fast its theoretic speed.

What an effective network requires is the largest number of alternative modes of transportation, at varying speeds and volumes, for different functions and purposes. The fastest way to move a hundred thousand people within a limited urban area, say a half mile radius, is on foot: the slowest way of moving them would be to put them all into motor cars. The entire daytime population of historic Boston could assemble by foot on Boston Common, probably in less than an hour if the streets were clear of motor traffic. If they were transported by motor car, they would take many hours, and unless they abandoned their unparkable vehicles would never reach their destination.

Our highway engineers and our municipal authorities, hypnotized by the popularity of the private motor car, feeling an obligation to help General Motors to flourish, even if General Chaos results, have been in an open conspiracy to dismantle all the varied forms of transportation necessary to a good system, and have reduced our facilities to the private motor car (for pleasure, convenience, or trucking) and the airplane. They have even duplicated railroad routes and repeated all the errors of the early railroad engineers, while piling up in the terminal cities a population the private motor car cannot handle unless the city itself is wrecked to permit movement and storage of automobiles.

If technical experts and administrators had known their business, they would have taken special measures to safeguard more efficient methods of mass transportation, in order to maintain both the city's existence and the least time-wasting use of other forms of transportation. To have a complete urban structure capable of functioning fully, it is necessary to find appropriate channels for every form of transportation: it is the deliberate articulation of the pedestrian, the mass transit system, the street, the avenue, the expressway, and the airfield that alone can care for the needs of a modern community. Nothing less will do.

By favoring the truck over the railroad for long-distance traffic, we have replaced a safe and efficient service by a more dangerous and inefficient one. If we want to improve our highway system, we should be zealous to keep as large a part of goods haulage as possible on the rails. Not the least reason for saving the passenger and freight railroad service and mass transportation is to ensure free movement by private vehicles on highways. Similarly, if the expressways that we have built around our cities are to function as such, mass transit must be improved and widened, not permitted to go out of existence.

The only effective cure for urban congestion is to so relate industrial and business zones to residential areas that a large part of their personnel can either walk or cycle to work, or use a public bus, or take a railroad train. By pushing all forms of traffic onto high speed motor ways, we burden them with a load guaranteed to slow down peak traffic to a crawl; and if we try to correct this by multiplying motor ways, we only add to the total urban wreckage by flinging the parts of the city ever farther away in a formless mass of thinly spread semi-urban tissue. The spatial dissociation of functions in suburbia results in an extreme specialization of the individual parts: segregated residence areas without local shops: segregated shopping centers without industries: segregated industrial plants without eating facilities unless provided by the management. In escaping the complex co-operations of the city Suburbia recovers the original vices of overspecialization and rigid control.

Good urban planning must provide a place for the motor car: that goes without saying. But this does not in the least mean that the motor car must be permitted to penetrate every part of the city and stay there, even though it disrupts all other activities. Neither does it mean that the auto shall dictate the whole scheme of living; nor yet does it mean that its manufacturers should be permitted to flout the requirements of the city by designing ever broader and longer vehicles. Quite the contrary, the time has come to discriminate between two functions of the motor car—urban movement and countrywide movement. For the latter, a big car with plenty of room to house a family and hold their baggage is admirable. In the city, however, such cars should be encouraged to stay on the outskirts, and be heavily taxed for the privilege of parking within it; while special favors should be given to the design and distribution of small cars, electric powered, for ordinary intra-urban movement, to supplement rather than replace mass transportation. Moderate speed, quiet, ease and compactness of parking—these are the characteristics of a town car.

It is an absurdly impoverished technology that has only one answer to the problem of transportation; and it is a poor form of city planning that permits that answer to dominate its entire scheme of existence.

Mass Suburbia As Anti-city

Under the present dispensation we have sold our urban birthright for a sorry mess of motor cars. As poor a bargain as Esau's pottage. Future generations will perhaps wonder at our willingness, indeed our eagerness, to sacrifice the education of our children, the care of the ill and the aged, the development of the arts, to say nothing of ready access to nature, for the lopsided system of mono-transportation, going through low density areas at sixty miles an hour, but reduced in high density areas to a bare six. But our descendants will perhaps understand our curious willingness to expend billions of dollars to shoot a sacrificial victim into planetary orbit, if they realize that our cities are being destroyed for the same superstitious religious ritual: the worship of speed and empty space. Lacking sufficient municipal budgets to deal adequately with all of life's requirements that can be concentrated in the city, we have settled for a single function, transportation, or rather for a single part of an adequate transportation system, locomotion by private motor car.

By allowing mass transportation to deteriorate and by building expressways out of the city and parking garages within, in order to encourage the maximum use of the private car, our highway engineers and city planners have helped to destroy the living tissue of the city and to limit the possibilities of creating a larger urban organism on a regional scale. Mass transportation for short distances, under a mile, should rely mainly upon the pedestrian. By discouraging and eliminating the pedestrian, by failing to extend and to perfect mass transportation, our municipal officials and highway engineers have created a situation that calls for extremely low residential densities. Here again the monopoly of private space not merely reduces the social facilities of the city but sacrifices public open space to private.

The absurd belief that space and rapid locomotion are the chief ingredients of a good life has been fostered by the agents of mass suburbia. That habit of low density building is the residual bequest of the original romantic movement, and by now it is one of the chief obstacles to reassembling the parts of the city and uniting them in a new pattern that shall offer much richer resources for living than either the congested and disordered central metropolis or the outlying areas reached by its expressways. The *reductio ad absurdum* of this myth is, notoriously, Los Angeles. Here the suburban standard of open space, with free standing houses, often as few as five houses to the acre, has been maintained: likewise the private motor car, as the major means of transportation, has supplanted what was only a generation or so ago an extremely efficient system of public transportation.

Los Angeles has now become an undifferentiated mass of houses, walled off into sectors by many-laned expressways, with ramps and viaducts that create special bottlenecks of their own. These expressways move but a small fraction of the traffic per hour once carried by public transportation, at a much lower rate of speed, in an environment befouled by smog, itself produced by the lethal exhausts of the technologically backward motor cars. More than a third of the Los Angeles area is consumed by these grotesque transportation facilities; *two-thirds* of central Los Angeles are occupied by streets, freeways, parking facilities, garages. This is space-eating with a vengeance. The last stage of the process already beckons truly progressive minds—to evict the remaining inhabitants and turn the entire area over to automatically propelled vehicles, completely emancipated from any rational human purpose.

Even in cities as spacious as Washington, it is only the original central area that has a residential density of ten or more families per acre: on the spreading outskirts, under ten is the rule, and a fast moving tide is putting an even larger tract under a density of settlement less than five per acre. This is ruinous both to urban living and to leisured recreation; for the attempt to service the distant areas with expressways will not merely sterilize more and more of the land, but will scatter social facilities that should be concentrated in new cities, organized so as to diffuse and amplify the central facilities.

The conclusion should be plain. Any attempt to create an adequate transportation system without creating in advance sufficient reserves of public land, without laying down a desirable density for balanced urban occupation *higher than the present suburban level,* without providing for a regional network largely independent of the bigger trunk line highways, will degrade the landscape without bringing any permanent benefits to its new inhabitants.

To keep the advantages first incorporated in the romantic suburb, we must acclimate them to the building of cities. To keep the advantages first discovered in the closed city, we must create a more porous pattern, richer in both social and esthetic variety. Residential densities of about one hundred people per net acre, exclusive of streets and sidewalks, will provide usable private gardens and encourage small public inner parks for meeting and relaxing. This can be achieved without erecting the sterile, space-mangling high-rise slabs that now grimly parade, in both Europe and America, as the ultimate contribution of "modern" architecture. If we are concerned with human values, we can no longer afford either sprawling Suburbia or the congested Metropolis: still less can we afford a congested Suburbia, whose visual openness depends upon the cellular isolation and regimentation of its component families in mass structures.

Families in Space

As it has worked out under the impact of the present religion and myth of the machine, mass Suburbia has done away with most of the freedoms and delights that the original disciples of Rousseau sought to find through their exodus from the city. Instead of centering attention on the child in the garden, we now have the image of "Families in Space." For the wider the scattering of the population, the greater the isolation of the individual household, and the more effort it takes to do privately, even with the aid of many machines and automatic devices, what used to be done in company often with conversation, song, and the enjoyment of the physical presence of others.

The town housewife, who half a century ago knew her butcher, her grocer, her dairyman, her various other local tradesmen, as individual persons, with histories and biographies that impinged on her own, in a daily interchange, now has the benefit of a single weekly expedition to an impersonal supermarket, where only by accident is she likely to encounter a neighbor. If she is well-to-do, she is surrounded with electric or electronic devices that take the place of flesh and blood companions: her real companions, her friends, her mentors, her lovers, her fillers-up of unlived life, are shadows on the television screen, or even less embodied voices. She may answer them, but she cannot make herself heard: as it has worked out, this is a one-way system. The greater the area of expansion, the greater the dependence upon a distant supply center and remote control.

On the fringe of mass Suburbia, even the advantages of the primary neighborhood group disappear. The cost of this detachment in space from other men is out of all proportion to its supposed benefits. The end product is an encapsulated life, spent more and more either in a motor car or within the cabin of darkness before a television set: soon, with a little more automation of traffic, mostly in a motor car, travelling even greater distances, under remote control, so that the one-time driver may occupy himself with a television set, having lost even the freedom of the steering wheel. Every part of this life, indeed, will come through official channels and be under supervision. Untouched by human hand at one end: untouched by human spirit at the other. Those who accept this existence might as well be encased in a rocket hurtling through space, so narrow are their choices, so limited and deficient their permitted responses. Here indeed we find "The Lonely Crowd."

The organizers of the ancient city had something to learn from the new rulers of our society. The former massed their subjects within a walled enclosure, under the surveillance of armed guardians within the smaller citadel, the better to keep them under control. That method is now obsolete. With the present means of long-distance mass communication, sprawling isolation has proved an even more effective method of keeping a population under control. With direct contact and face-to-face association inhibited as far as possible, all knowledge and direction can be monopolized by central agents and conveyed through guarded channels, too costly to be utilized by small groups or private individuals. To exercise free speech in such a scattered, dissociated community one must "buy time" on the air or "buy space" in the newspaper. Each member of Suburbia becomes imprisoned by the very separation that he has prized: he is fed through a narrow opening: a telephone line, a radio band, a television circuit. This is not, it goes without saying, the result of a conscious conspiracy by a cunning minority: it is an organic by-product of an economy that sacrifices human development to mechanical processing.

In a well-organized community, all these technological improvements might admirably widen the scope of social life: in the disorganized communities of today, they narrow the effective range of the person. Under such conditions, nothing can happen spontaneously or autonomously—not without a great deal of mechanical assistance. Does this not explain in some degree the passiveness and docility that has crept into our existence? In the recent Caracas revolution that deposed a brutal dictatorship in Venezuela, the starting signal, I have been told by an eye-witness, was the honking of motor car horns. That honking, growing louder, coming nearer, converging from every quarter of the city upon the palace, struck terror into the hearts of the rulers. That, too, was an urban phenomenon. Suburbia offers poor facilities for meeting, conversation, collective debate, and common action—it favors silent conformity, not rebellion or counter-attack. So Suburbia has become the favored home of a new kind of absolutism: invisible but all-powerful.

I might be uneasy about the validity of this analysis had not the prescient de Tocqueville anticipated it long ago, in "Democracy in America." He sought to "trace the novel features under which despotism may appear in the world." "The first thing that strikes observation," he says, "is an uncountable number of men, all equal and alike, incessantly endeavoring to produce the petty and paltry pleasures with which they glut their lives. Each of them living apart, is a stranger to the fate of all the rest—his children and his private friends constitute to him the whole of mankind; as for the rest of his fellow-citizens, he is close to them, but he sees them not; he touches them, but he feels them not; he exists but in himself and for himself alone; and if his kindred still remain to him, he may be said at any rate to have lost his country."

De Tocqueville was describing in anticipation the temper and habit of life in Suburbia, a habit that has worked back into the city and made even democratic nations submit, with hardly a murmur, to every manner of totalitarian compulsion and corruption. What this great political philosopher foresaw with his inner eye, less gifted observers can now see with their outer eye. This is the last stage in the breakup of the city. The expansion of our technology only quickens the pace of this change. What is left, if no counter-movement takes place, will not be worth saving. For when the container changes as rapidly as its contents nothing can in fact be saved. . . .

The Removal of Limits

Let us now view the situation of the metropolis in more general terms: what some have called the urban explosion is in fact a symptom of a more general state—the removal of quantitative limits. This marks the change from an organic system to a mechanical system, from purposeful growth to purposeless expansion.

Until the nineteenth century the limitations of both local and regional transportation placed a natural restriction upon the growth of cities. Even the biggest centers, Rome, Babylon, Alexandria, Antioch, were forced to respect that limit. But by the middle of the nineteenth century the tendency toward metropolitan monopoly was supplemented with a new factor brought in by the effective utilization of coal and iron and the extension of the railroad: in terms of purely physical requirements the area of settlement coincided with the coal beds, the ore beds, the railroad network. Patrick Geddes, early in the present century, pointed out the significance of the new population maps, which graphically disclosed a general thickening and spreading of the urban mass: he showed that entire provinces and counties were becoming urbanized, and he proposed to differentiate such diffused formations by a name that would distinguish them from the historic city: the "conurbation."

Meanwhile the original forces that created the conurbation were supplemented by the electric power grid, the electric railway, and still later by the motor car and the motor road: so that a movement that was at first confined largely to the area accessible to the railroad now is taking place everywhere. Whereas the first extension of the factory system produced a multitude of new cities and greatly augmented the population of existing centers, the present diffusion of the area of settlement has largely halted this growth and has enormously increased the production of relatively undifferentiated urban tissue, without any relation either to an internally coherent nucleus or an external boundary of any sort.

The result threatens to be a universal conurbation. Those who ignored Geddes's original definition half a century ago have recently re-discovered the phenomenon itself, and treated it as if it were an entirely new development. Some have even misapplied to the conurbation the inappropriate term Megalopolis, though it represents, in fact, the precise opposite of the tendency that brought the original city of this name into existence. The overgrown historic city was still, residually, an entity: the conurbation is a nonentity, and becomes more patently so as it spreads.

What this removal of limits means can perhaps best be grasped by referring to the extension of historic centers. When Rome was surrounded by the Aurelian Wall in A.D. 274, it covered a little more than five square miles. The present area of London is 130 times as great as this; while it is roughly 650 times as big as the area of medieval London, which was 677 acres. The conurbation of New York is even more widespread: it covers something like 2,514 square miles. If no human purposes supervene to halt the blotting out of the countryside and to establish limits for the growth and colonization of cities, the whole coastal strip from Maine to Florida might coalesce into an almost undifferentiated conurbation. But to call this mass a "regional city" or to hold that it represents the new scale of settlement to which modern man must adapt his institutions and his personal needs is to mask the realities of the human situation and allow seemingly automatic forces to become a substitute for human purposes.

These vast urban masses are comparable to a routed and disorganized army, which has lost its leaders, scattered its battalions and companies, torn off its insignia, and is fleeing in every direction. "Sauve qui peut." The first step toward handling this situation, besides establishment of an over-all command, is to re-group in units that can be effectively handled. Until we understand the function of the smaller units and can bring them under discipline we cannot command and deploy the army as a whole over a larger area. The scale of distances has changed, and the "regional city" is a potential reality, indeed a vital necessity. But the condition for success in these endeavors lies in our abilities to recognize and to impose organic limitations. This means the replacement of the machine-oriented metropolitan economy by one directed toward the goods and goals of life.

Though the removal of limits is one of the chief feats of the metropolitan economy, this does not imply any abdication of power on the part of the chiefs in charge: for there is one countervailing condition to this removal, and that is the processing of all operations through the metropolis and its increasingly complicated mechanisms. The metropolis is in fact a processing center, in which a vast variety of goods, material and spiritual, is mechanically sorted and reduced to a limited number of standardized articles, uniformly packaged, and distributed through controlled channels to their destination, bearing the approved metropolitan label.

"Processing" has now become the chief form of metropolitan control; and the need for its constant application has brought into existence a whole range of inventions, mechanical and electronic, from cash registers to electronic computers, which handle every operation from book-keeping to university examinations. Interests and aptitudes that do not lend themselves to processing are automatically rejected. So complicated, so elaborate, so costly are the processing mechanisms that they cannot be employed except on a mass scale: hence they eliminate all activities of a fitful, inconsecutive, or humanly subtle nature—just as "yes" or "no" answers eliminate those more delicate and accurate discriminations that often lie at one point or another in between the spuriously "correct" answer. That which is local, small, personal, autonomous, must be suppressed. Increasingly, he who controls the processing mechanism controls the lives and destinies of those who must consume its products, and who on metropolitan terms cannot seek any others. For processing and packaging do not end on the production line: they finally make over the human personality.

In short the monopoly of power and knowledge that was first established in the citadel has come back, in a highly magnified form, in the final stages of metropolitan culture. In the end every aspect of life must be brought under control: controlled weather, controlled movement, controlled association, controlled production, controlled prices, controlled fantasy, controlled ideas. But the only purpose of control, apart from the profit, power, and prestige of the controllers, is to accelerate the process of mechanical control itself.

The priests of this regime are easy to identify: the whole system, in its final stages, rests on the proliferation of secret, and thus controllable, knowledge; and the very division of labor that makes specialized scientific research possible also restricts the number of people capable of putting the fragments together. But where are the new gods? The nuclear reactor is the seat of their power: radio transmission and rocket flight their angelic means of communication and transportation: but beyond these minor agents of divinity the Control Room itself, with its Cybernetic Deity, giving His lightning-like decisions and His infallible answers: omniscience and omnipotence, triumphantly mated by science. Faced with this electronic monopoly of man's highest powers, the human can come back only at the most primitive level. Sigmund Freud detected the beginnings of creative art in the infant's pride over his bowel movements. We can now detect its ultimate manifestation in paintings and sculpture whose contents betray a similar pride and a similar degree of autonomy—and a similar product.

One of the ancient prerogatives of the gods was to create man out of their flesh, like Atum, or in their own image, like Yahweh. When the accredited scientific priesthood go a little farther with their present activities, the new life-size homunculus will be processed, too: one can already see anticipatory models in our art galleries. He will look remarkably like a man accoutered in a "space-suit": outwardly a huge scaly insect. But the face inside will be incapable of expression, as incapable as that of a corpse. And who will know the difference?

Sprawling Giantism

Circle over London, Buenos Aires, Chicago, Sydney, in an airplane or view the cities schematically by means of an urban map and block plan. What is the shape of the city and how does it define itself? The original container has completely disappeared: the sharp division between city and country no longer exists. As the eye stretches toward the hazy periphery one can pick out no definite shapes except those formed by nature: one beholds rather a continuous shapeless mass, here bulging or ridged with buildings, there broken by a patch of green or an unwinding ribbon of concrete. The shapelessness of the whole is reflected in the individual part, and the nearer the center, the less as a rule can the smaller parts be distinguished.

Failing to divide its social chromosomes and split up into new cells, each bearing some portion of the original inheritance, the city continues to grow inorganically, indeed cancerously, by a continuous breaking down of old tissues, and an overgrowth of formless new tissue. Here the city has absorbed villages and little towns, reducing them to place names, like Manhattanville and Harlem in New York; there it has, more happily, left the organs of local government and the vestiges of an independent life, even assisted their revival, as in Chelsea and Kensington in London; but it has nevertheless enveloped those urban areas in its physical organization and built up the open land that once served to ensure their identity and integrity. Sometimes the expanding street system forms an orderly pattern, sometimes it produces only a crazy network that does not even serve traffic: but the difference between one type of order and another is merely a difference in the degree of sprawl, confusion, de-building.

As one moves away from the center, the urban growth becomes ever more aimless and discontinuous, more diffuse and unfocussed, except where some surviving town has left the original imprint of a more orderly life. Old neighborhoods and precincts, the social cells of the city, still maintaining some measure of the village pattern, become vestigial. No human eye can take in this metropolitan mass at a glance. No single gathering place except the totality of its streets can hold all its citizens. No human mind can comprehend more than a fragment of the complex and minutely specialized activities of its citizens. The loss of form, the loss of autonomy, the constant frustration and harassment of daily activities, to say nothing of gigantic breakdowns and stoppages—all these become normal attributes of the metropolitan regime. There is a special name for power when it is concentrated on such a scale: it is called impotence.

The giantism of the metropolis is not the result of technological progress alone. Contrary to popular belief, the growth of great cities preceded the decisive technical advances of the last two centuries. But the metropolitan phase became universal only when the technical means of congestion had become adequate—and their use profitable to those who manufactured or employed them. The modern metropolis is, rather, an outstanding example of a peculiar cultural lag within the realm of technics itself: namely, the continuation by highly advanced technical means of the obsolete forms and ends of a socially retarded civilization. The machines and utilities that would lend themselves to decentralization in a life-centered order, here become either a means to increase congestion or afford some slight temporary palliation—at a price.

The form of the metropolis, then, is its formlessness, even as its aim is its own aimless expansion. Those who work within the ideological limits of this regime have only a quantitative conception of improvement: they seek to make its buildings higher, its streets broader, its parking lots more ample: they would multiply bridges, highways, tunnels, making it ever easier to get in and out of the city, but constricting the amount of space available within the city for any other purpose than transportation itself. Frank Lloyd Wright's project for a skyscraper a mile high was the ultimate reduction to absurdity of this whole theory of city development. The ultimate form of such a city would be an acre of building to a square mile of expressways and parking lots. In many areas this is rapidly approaching fulfillment.

When both the evil and the remedy are indistinguishable, one may be sure that a deep-seated process is at work. An expanding economy, dedicated to profit, not to the satisfaction of life-needs, necessarily creates a new image of the city, that of a perpetual and ever-widening maw, consuming the output of expanding industrial and agricultural production, in response to the pressures of continued indoctrination and advertising. Two centuries ago the need for such an economy was indisputable, and in many poverty-stricken countries that need still remains, to lift the population above the margin of starvation and helpless depression. But in the countries of the West, particularly in the United States, the problem of scarcity has been solved, apart from distribution and relation to organic needs, only to create a new set of problems just as embarrassing: those of surfeit and satiety. Today, accordingly, expansion has become an end in itself: to make it possible the rulers of this society resort to every possible device of pyramid-building.

For unfortunately, once an economy is geared to expansion, the means rapidly turn into an end, and "the going becomes the goal." Even more unfortunately, the industries that are favored by such expansion must, to maintain their output, be devoted to goods that are readily consumable, either by their nature, or because they are so shoddily fabricated that they must soon be replaced. By fashion and built-in obsolescence the economies of machine production, instead of producing leisure and durable wealth, are duly cancelled out by mandatory consumption on an ever larger scale.

By the same token, the city itself becomes consumable, indeed expendable: the container must change as rapidly as its contents. This latter imperative undermines a main function of the city as an agent of human continuity. The living memory of the city, which once bound together generations and centuries, disappears: its inhabitants live in a self-annihilating moment-to-moment continuum. The poorest Stone Age savage never lived in such a destitute and demoralized community.

Now organic processes are purposeful, goal-seeking, self-limiting: indeed all organisms have built-in controls that serve to co-ordinate action and limit growth. The expanding economy, like the technological system on which it is so largely based, has no such limitations: its stabilization takes the form of multiplying the number of consumers and intensifying their wants. But to ensure continued productivity, it limits these wants to those that can be supplied at a profit by the machine. Thus this economy produces motor cars and refrigerators galore; but has no motive to supply durable works of art, handsome gardens, or untrammelled, nonconsuming leisure. Our economic establishment is better equipped to destroy the product outright than to give it away or to limit the output at source.

The image of modern industrialism that Charlie Chaplin carried over from the past into "Modern Times" is just the opposite of megalopolitan reality. He pictured the worker as an old-fashioned drudge, chained to the machine, mechanically fed while he continued to operate it. That image belongs to Coketown. The new worker, in the metropolis, has been progressively released from the productive process: the grinding, impoverished toil that made the nineteenth-century factory so hideous has been lifted by social services and security, by mechanical aids and by complete automation. Work is no longer so brutal in the light industries: but automation has made it even more boring. The energy and application that once went into the productive process must now be addressed to consumption.

By a thousand cunning attachments and controls, visible and subliminal, the workers in an expanding economy are tied to a consumption mechanism: they are assured of a livelihood provided they devour without undue selectivity all that is offered by the machine—and demand nothing that is not produced by the machine. The whole organization of the metropolitan community is designed to kill spontaneity and self-direction. You stop on the red light and go on the green. You see what you are supposed to see, think what you are supposed to think: your personal contributions, like your income and security taxes, are deductible at source. To choose, to select, to discriminate, to exercise prudence or continence or forethought, to carry self-control to the point of abstinence, to have standards other than those of the market, and to set limits other than those of immediate consumption—these are impious heresies that would challenge the whole megalopolitan myth and deflate its economy. In such a "free" society Henry Thoreau must rank as a greater public enemy than Karl Marx.

The metropolis, in its final stage of development, becomes a collective contrivance for making this irrational system work, and for giving those who are in reality its victims the illusion of power, wealth, and felicity, of standing at the very pinnacle of human achievement. But in actual fact their lives are constantly in peril, their wealth is tasteless and ephemeral, their leisure is sensationally monotonous, and their pathetic felicity is tainted by constant, well-justified anticipations of violence and sudden death. Increasingly they find themselves "strangers and afraid," in a world they never made: a world ever less responsive to direct human command, ever more empty of human meaning.

The Shadows of Success

To believe, therefore, that human culture has reached a marvellous final culmination in the modern metropolis one must avert one's eyes from the grim details of the daily routine. And that is precisely what the metropolitan denizen schools himself to do: he lives, not in the real world, but in a shadow world projected around him at every moment by means of paper and celluloid and adroitly manipulated lights: a world in which he is insulated by glass, cellophane, pliofilm from the mortifications of living. In short, a world of professional illusionists and their credulous victims.

The swish and crackle of paper is the underlying sound of the metropolis. What is visible and real in this world is only what has been transferred to paper or has been even further etherialized on a microfilm or a tape recorder. The essential daily gossip of the metropolis is no longer that of people meeting face to face at a cross-roads, at the dinner table, in the marketplace: a few dozen people writing in the newspapers, a dozen or so more broadcasting over radio and television, provide the daily interpretation of movements and happenings with slick professional adroitness. Thus even the most spontaneous human activities come under professional surveillance and centralized control. The spread of manifolding devices of every sort gives to the most ephemeral and mediocre products of the mind a temporary durability they do not deserve: whole books are printed to justify the loose evacuations of the tape recorder.

All the major activities of the metropolis are directly connected with paper and its plastic substitutes; and printing and packaging are among its principal industries. The activities pursued in the offices of the metropolis are directly connected with paper: the tabulating machines, the journals, the ledgers, the card-catalogs, the deeds, the contracts, the mortgages, the briefs, the trial records: so, too, the prospectuses, the advertisements, the magazines, the newspapers. As early as the eighteenth century Mercier had observed this metropolitan form of the White Plague. Modern methods of manifolding have not lessened the disease: they have only exchanged easygoing slipshod ways, which often sufficed, for a more exact record, whose elaboration and cost are out of all proportion to the value of what is recorded. What was a mere trickle in Mercier's day has now become a ravaging flood of paper.

As the day's routine proceeds the pile of paper mounts higher: the trashbaskets are filled and emptied and filled again. The ticker tape exudes its quotation of stocks and its report of news; the students in the schools and universities fill their notebooks, digest and disgorge the contents of books, as the silkworm feeds on mulberry leaves and manufactures its cocoon, unravelling themselves on examination day. In the theater, in literature, in music, in business, reputations are made—on paper. The scholar with his degrees and publications, the actress with her newspaper clippings, and the financier with his shares and his voting proxies, measure their power and importance by the amount of paper they can command. No wonder the anarchists once invented the grim phrase: "Incinerate the documents!" That would ruin this whole world quicker than universal flood or earthquake, if not as fatally as a shower of hydrogen bombs.

That life is an occasion for living, and not a pretext for supplying items to newspapers, interviews on television, or a spectacle for crowds of otherwise vacant bystanders—these notions do not occur in the metropolitan mind. For them the show is the reality, and "the show must go on!"

This metropolitan world, then, is a world where flesh and blood are less real than paper and ink and celluloid. It is a world where the great masses of people, unable to achieve a more full-bodied and satisfying means of living, take life vicariously, as readers, spectators, listeners, passive observers. Living thus, year in and year out, at second hand, remote from the nature that is outside them, and no less remote from the nature that is within, it is no wonder that they turn more and more of the functions of life, even thought itself, to the machines that their inventors have created. In this disordered environment only machines retain some of the attributes of life, while human beings are progressively reduced to a bundle of reflexes, without self-starting impulses or autonomous goals: "behaviorist man. . . ."

Destiny of Megalopolis

In following the growth of megalopolitan culture to its conclusion we reach a whole series of terminal processes, and it would be simple-minded to believe that they have any prospect of continuing in existence indefinitely. A life that lacks any meaning, value, or purpose, except that of keeping the mechanism of breathing and ingestion going, is little better than life in an iron lung, which is only supportable because the patient still has hope of recovery and escape.

The metropolitan regime now threatens to reach its climax in a meaningless war, one of total extermination, whose only purpose would be to relieve the anxieties and fears produced by the citadels' wholesale commitment to weapons of annihilation and extermination. Thus absolute power has become in fact absolute nihilism. Scientific and technological over-elaboration, unmodified by human values and aims, has committed countries like the United States and Russia to collective mechanisms of destruction so rigid that they cannot be modified or brought under control without being completely dismantled. Even instinctual animal intelligence remains inoperative in this system: the commitment to the machine overthrows all the safeguards to life, including the ancient law of self-preservation. For the sake of rapid locomotion, we in the United States kill some 40,000 people outright every year and fatally maim hundreds of thousands of others. For the sake of wielding absolute nuclear power our leaders are brazenly prepared to sacrifice from fifty to seventy-five million of their own citizens on the first day of an all-out nuclear war, and mutilate, or even possibly in the end eliminate the human race. The illusionist phrase to cover these psychotic plans is "national security," or even, more absurdly, "national survival."

Now, in every organism, the anabolic and the catabolic processes, the creative and the destructive, are constantly at work. Life and growth depend, not on the absence of negative conditions, but on a sufficient degree of equilibrium, and a sufficient surplus of constructive energy to permit continued repair, to absorb novelties, to regulate quantities, and to establish give-and-take relations with all the other organisms and communities needed to maintain balance. The negative factors in metropolitan existence might have provided the conditions for a higher development if the very terms of expansion had not given them the upper hand and tended to make their domination permanent, in ever more destructive processes.

When "The Culture of Cities" was written in the mid-nineteen-thirties, the external forces that threatened metropolitan civilization were clearly visible: so much so that at this stage of the analysis I laid them out in the form of a "Brief Outline of Hell." I then sought to clarify the picture further by giving a résumé of Patrick Geddes's interpretation of the urban cycle of growth, from village (eopolis) to megalopolis and necropolis. That cycle has described the course of all the historic metropolises, including those that arose again out of their own ruins and graveyards. Even in 1938, when the book was published, this characterization seemed to more than one critic unduly pessimistic, indeed perversely exaggerated and morbidly unrealistic. Many were sure, then, that no dangers worse than chronic unemployment threatened the Western World; above all they were certain that war and the total destruction of cities were both highly improbable.

But today the one section of my original chapter on the metropolis that could not be re-published except as an historic curiosity is precisely this "Brief Outline of Hell," just because all its anticipations were abundantly verified. Though a prediction that is fulfilled naturally no longer concerns us, I recall this *fait accompli,* lest the reader dismiss with equal confidence in its unreality the present portrayal of our even more dire condition. I would remind him that, all too soon, the tensions increased and the war came, with the large-scale destruction of Warsaw in 1939 and that of the center of Rotterdam in 1940. In five years far

vaster urban areas were totally destroyed, and large populations were
exterminated from London to Tokyo, from Hamburg to Hiroshima. Besides the
millions of people—six million Jews alone—killed by the Germans in their
suburban extermination camps, by starvation and cremation, whole cities were
turned into extermination camps by the demoralized strategists of democracy.
Random killing and limitless death gave their final stamp to the realities of
megalopolitan expansion.

Though the ruin was widespread, large patches of healthy tissue
fortunately remained. By an immense gathering together of resources, helped in
many countries by the generous initiatives of the Marshall Plan, the enormous
task of rebuilding cities and transportation systems was successfully undertaken.
Sometimes this constituted a sentimental task of imitative restoration, of "Bilder
aus der Vergangenheit," as in so many towns in Germany: sometimes it produced
a bold effort at old-fashioned rationalization, as in the reconstruction of
Cherbourg: sometimes, as in Rotterdam or in Coventry, it became an energetic
effort to achieve a fresh form for the urban core, which would do justice in wholly
contemporary architectual terms to traditional values neglected in the nineteenth
century. In two countries, Sweden and England, an even larger effort was made to
conceive a new urban pattern that would break away from the automatic
concentration and the equally automatic spread of the big city. In the case of
England's New Towns, the feasibility of directing and controlling urban growth in
relatively self-contained and balanced communities, with a sound industrial base,
was amply demonstrated.

Remarkably, the wholesale rehabilitation of the cities of Europe at a
higher level than they had achieved in the past, took place in less than a dozen
years. The almost superhuman mobilization of energies demonstrated that urban
reconstruction and renewal on a far greater scale might be accomplished, within a
single generation, provided the economy was directly oriented to human needs,
and that the major part of the national income was not diverted to the studious
consumptive dissipations and planned destructions demanded by the expanding
metropolitan economy: above all, by ceaseless preparations for collective genocide
and suicide.

Unfortunately, as soon as the economy recovered and returned to the
pursuit of its original ends, all its irrational features likewise came back: to keep
going, an ever larger part of its energies must be dissipated in pyramid-building.
Nowhere have the irrationalities of the current metropolitan myth been more fully
exposed than in the development of so-called "absolute" weapons for limitless
nuclear, bacterial, and chemical genocide. The building up of these weapons
among the "Nuclear Powers" has given the "death-wish" the status of a fixed
national policy, and made a universal extermination camp the ideal terminus of
this whole civilization.

Even if the nations take timely measures to eliminate the stock of such
weapons, it will be long before the vicious moral effects of this policy are
dissipated: adult delinquency, on the scale not merely contemplated but actually

prepared for in detail, requires therapeutic counter-measures that may take a full century to show any positive effect. This is the last and worst bequest of the citadel (read "Pentagon" and "Kremlin") to the culture of cities.

In a few short years our civilization has reached the point that Henry Adams, with uncanny prescience, foresaw more than half a century ago. "At the present rate of progression since 1600," he wrote, "it will not need another century or half a century to tip thought upside down. Law, in that case would disappear as theory or a priori principle and give place to force. Morality would become police. Explosives would reach cosmic violence. Disintegration would overcome integration." Every part of this prophecy has already been fulfilled; and it is useless to speculate about the future of cities until we have reckoned with the forces of annihilation and extermination that now, almost automatically, and at an ever-accelerating rate, are working to bring about a more general breakdown.

Metropolitan civilization thus embodies and carries to its conclusion the radical contradiction we found already embedded in the life course of the city from the moment of its foundation: a contradiction that comes out of the dual origin of the city, and the perpetual ambivalence of its goals. From the village, the city derives its nature as a mothering and life-promoting environment, stable and secure, rooted in man's reciprocal relations with other organisms and communities. From the village, too, it derives the ways and values of an ungraded democracy in which each member plays his appropriate role at each stage in the life cycle.

On the other hand, the city owed its existence, and even more its enlargement, to concentrated attempts at mastering other men and dominating, with collective force, the whole environment. Thus the city became a power-trapping utility, designed by royal agents gathering the dispersed energies of little communities into a mighty reservoir, collectively regulating their accumulation and flow, and directing them into new channels—now favoring the smaller units by beneficently re-molding the landscape, but eventually hurling its energies outward in destructive assaults against other cities. Release and enslavement, freedom and compulsion, have been present from the beginning in urban culture.

Out of this inner tension some of the creative expressions of urban life have come forth: yet only in scattered and occasional instances do we discover political power well distributed in small communities, as in seventeenth-century Holland or Switzerland, or the ideals of life constantly regulating the eccentric manifestations of power. Our present civilization is a gigantic motor car moving along a one-way road at an ever-accelerating speed. Unfortunately as now constructed the car lacks both steering wheel and brakes, and the only form of control the driver exercises consists in making the car go faster, though in his fascination with the machine itself and his commitment to achieving the highest speed possible, he has quite forgotten the purpose of his journey. This state of helpless submission to the economic and technological mechanisms modern man has created is curiously disguised as progress, freedom, and the mastery of man over nature. As a result, every permission has become a morbid compulsion. Modern man has mastered every creature above the level of the viruses and bacteria—except himself.

Never before has the "citadel" exercised such atrocious power over the rest of the human race. Over the greater part of history, the village and the countryside remained a constant reservoir of fresh life, constrained indeed by the ancestral patterns of behavior that had helped make man human, but with a sense of both human limitations and human possibilities. No matter what the errors and aberrations of the rulers of the city, they were still correctible. Even if whole urban populations were destroyed, more than nine-tenths of the human race still remained outside the circle of destruction. Today this factor of safety has gone: the metropolitan explosion has carried both the ideological and the chemical poisons of the metropolis to every part of the earth; and the final damage may be irretrievable.

These terminal possibilities did not, I repeat, first become visible with the use of nuclear weapons: they were plain to alert and able minds, like Burckhardt in the eighteen-sixties, and like Henry Adams at the beginning of the present century.

Adams' contemporary, Henry James, put the human situation in an image that curiously holds today: that of the Happy Family and the Infernal Machine. "The machine so rooted as to defy removal, and the family still so indifferent, while it carries on the family business of buying and selling, of chattering and dancing, to the danger of being blown up." The machine James referred to was the political machine of Philadelphia, then the classic embodiment of corruption and criminality; but only a too-guileless observer can fail to see that it applies to other demoralized mechanisms in our expanding metropolitan civilization. Once-local manifestations of criminality and irrationality now threaten our whole planet, smugly disguised as sound business enterprise, technological progress, communist efficiency, or democratic statesmanship. No wonder the popular existentialists, mirroring our time, equate "reality" with the "absurd." A large portion of the painting and sculpture of the past generation symbolically anticipates the catastrophic end products of this death-oriented culture: total dismemberment and dehumanization in a lifeless, featureless void. Some of the best of this art, like Henry Moore's archaic pinheaded figures, foretells a new beginning at a level so primitive that the mind has hardly yet begun to operate.

Now, if the total picture were as grim as that I have painted in the present chapter, there would be no excuse for writing this book; or rather, it would be just as irrational a contribution as the many other irrationalities and futilities I have touched on. If I have duly emphasized the disintegrations of the metropolitan stage, it has been for but one reason: only those who are aware of them will be capable of directing our collective energies into more constructive processes. It was not the die-hard Romans of the fifth century A.D., still boasting of Rome's achievements and looking forward to another thousand years of them, who understood what the situation required: on the contrary, it was those who rejected the Roman premises and set their lives on a new foundation who built up a new civilization that in the end surpassed Rome's best achievements, even in engineering and government.

And so today: those who work within the metropolitan myth, treating its cancerous tumors as normal manifestations of growth, will continue to apply poultices, salves, advertising incantations, public relations magic, and quack mechanical remedies until the patient dies before their own failing eyes. No small part of the urban reform and correction that has gone on these last hundred years, and not least this last generation—slum demolition, model housing, civic architectural embellishment, suburban extension, "urban renewal"—has only continued in superficially new forms the same purposeless concentration and organic de-building that prompted the remedy.

Yet in the midst of all this disintegration fresh nodules of growth have appeared and, even more significantly, a new pattern of life has begun to emerge. This pattern necessarily is based on radically different premises from those of the ancient citadel builders or those of their modern counterparts, the rocket-constructors and nuclear exterminators. If we can distinguish the main outlines of this multi-dimensional, life-oriented economy we should also be able to describe the nature and the functions of the emerging city and the future pattern of human settlement. Above all, we should anticipate the next act in the human drama, provided mankind escapes the death-trap our blind commitment to a lopsided, power-oriented, anti-organic technology has set for it.

From **Sick Cities**
MITCHELL GORDON

Help, Police!

There was a time in the past, not too long ago, when the average citizen could expect to go through life suffering no more serious act of unlawfulness than a picked pocket or, perhaps, a stolen purse. Though radio communications, the automobile, and other scientific and technological advances have tended to favor the law more than the lawbreaker, this is no longer true. Anyone living to age 60 or beyond these days can expect, according to statistical averages, to fall victim at least once in his life to some serious crime ranging from the theft of property valued at over $50 to aggravated assault, rape, or even murder. And, as the years pass, unless the trend is suddenly reversed, the law of the jungle will continue to stage its comeback in this space-age civilization.

The surge in crime in recent years has, in fact, assumed such proportions as to make public complacency itself almost criminal negligence.

According to the Uniform Crime Reports issued by the Federal Bureau of Investigation, the number of serious crimes committed in the United States in

1960 was at a record high—up 98 percent from 1950 to nearly 1.9 million at a time when the nation's population, according to the United States Bureau of the Census, was rising just 12 percent, from 151 million to 179 million. The increase in crime from the previous year alone amounted to 14 percent! According to the FBI report, someone was being murdered in the United States every 58 minutes throughout 1960, raped every 38 minutes, robbed every 6 minutes, and burgled every 39 seconds; every minute a car was stolen and every fourth minute someone was undergoing a beating that would later be described as "aggravated assault."

Public indifference in the light of these facts needs some explaining. In part, perhaps, it results from the nature of crime itself; its victims are individuals and not, directly, society as a whole, so that the tendency is to regard the act as someone else's uncommon misfortune. Another lulling element may be found in the public-relations policy of police departments, which are understandably more interested in conveying an image of police efficiency than in depicting the alarming growth of lawlessness. A third factor may lie in the community's own adaptation to rising crime rates in the form of insurance coverage designed to cushion property losses arising from illegal acts.

A fourth factor may likewise be at work in causing the public to accommodate itself to a high and rising rate of crime: a certain resignation to its inevitability, the belief that little can be done about it anyway.

FBI crime statistics are not reassuring in this respect. They almost suggest that it is safer, these days, to be a criminal in fear of the law than a law-abiding citizen in fear of the criminal—certainly, at least, when it comes to certain types of crimes. According to the FBI's 1960 crime statistics, over 60 percent of all reported robberies and over 70 percent of reported burglaries resulted in no arrests at all—and only one-third of those that did resulted in convictions. The proportion who go unpunished is even higher for lesser crimes. Indeed, even these statistics do not portray the situation fully since they are compiled from official police records, which, for one reason or another, may not contain all the crimes reported to those agencies and do not, of course, include the many crimes which are not reported to the police at all. The federal agency until recent years did not accept the crime statistics of the New York City Police Department at all because it believed the department's figures so understated. Chicago's new police chief, when he took over in 1960, declined to make comparisons of the city's crime statistics with earlier periods because he was not satisfied with their accuracy, even though the Chicago figures had been used by the FBI.

Though the federal and state governments in the last half-century have taken on a number of policing functions, responsibility for keeping the peace falls primarily on local police departments. And, as crime mounts, population increases, valuables accumulate, and more cars take to more roads, that responsibility assumes the form of an immense financial burden as well—one which very few municipalities manage to carry adequately. That burden becomes heavier still when it is compounded by the rising wave of juvenile delinquency, stemming from a breakdown in family relationships and increased ethnic mobility that puts low-income groups into areas unaccustomed to assimilating them in such numbers.

Even automation, as desirable as it may be from other points of view, has contributed to police problems. Among other things, it has opened new opportunities for the criminal and the pervert. The self-service elevator and the automatic subway train, for example, lend rapists, muggers, and other lawbreakers a free hand for their molestations in the late hours of the night, particularly. Even the coin-operated phone box makes things easier for the thief; a foggy night in Los Angeles has been known to veil the raiding of several miles of such installations along a single thoroughfare. Ultimately, the combating of crime connected with automation may have to be fought with the same means: automated surveillance in the form of television cameras mounted at such strategic places as the ledges of high buildings over deserted streets, inside commuter trains, and even in the lobbies of public housing or other buildings fraught with crime.

Municipalities are not spending anywhere near as much on law enforcement as they should be spending, but these expenditures are greater than all outlays of local government except education, the construction and maintenance of streets and highways, and, by a 4 percent whisker, treatment and conveyance of sewage. The nearly $1.3 billion spent on city police departments in 1960 was 33 percent above the 1956 figure. Yet it represented only a small percentage of what crime and its prevention were costing the nation. According to FBI Director J. Edgar Hoover, the cost to the United States of crime and its prevention, counting such items as prison maintenance, police budgets, and the volume of stolen property itself, may have approached $22 billion in 1961. No one knows exactly what the figure is, of course, but Mr. Hoover's educated guess at least suggests the magnitude of crime's measurable costs. In terms of human suffering and anguish, crime's toll cannot begin to be tallied.

Police capabilities for coping with this toughening assignment leave much to be desired. The likelihood, therefore, is that crime will continue to outpace both law enforcement expenditures and population growth in the years ahead. With few exceptions, police management is not keeping pace either with the increase in police personnel or with the greater complexities of law enforcement in urban areas any more than the law enforcement bodies themselves are keeping pace with lawlessness. Inadequate procedures for self-policing, outmoded recruitment practices which create artificial manpower shortages and prejudice the hiring of more capable personnel, the lack or complete absence of satisfactory training methods, the poor allocation of manpower and facilities, meager or nonexistent research efforts, and a general failure to summon or heed outside professional advice are just a few of the maladies presently endemic at police headquarters generally around the nation.

Not all police departments, needless to say, are guilty of all of these management crimes. St. Louis and Chicago are notable examples of cities which have made great strides in recent years in reshaping their departments, while Los

Angeles has long been known for its use of modern techniques and manning procedures. But the progressive, well-trained, efficient department, authorities agree, is exceptional. "We're still in the horse-and-buggy days when it comes to the policing that is supposed to make life and property safe," declares a leading police consultant.

There is no dearth of evidence to back up that conclusion, either. Take training. Quinn Tamm, Director of the Field Service Division of the International Association of Chiefs of Police in Washington, D.C., notes: "A large number of communities in the United States, particularly smaller ones, have no training requirements for their police and there wasn't a single state, before 1960, that required any. By 1961 one did so: New York." Recently, two municipalities in New Jersey were held responsible by the courts for injuries to children sustained from guns which went off in the hands of policemen later deemed to have been inadequately trained in the use of firearms.

Police pay has improved considerably in recent years, but many authorities contend it still is not adequate to attract enough men of intelligence and integrity in most cities. Los Angeles, one of the better-paying cities, was starting its policemen at $6,540 a year early in 1962 compared with $3,828 a decade earlier. New York, whose wage scales are also considerably above the national average, paid its top-ranking patrolmen (those with at least three years' experience) $7,276 a year in 1962; its ceiling was only $4,150 in 1952.

A good number of cities, however, still pay their police substandard salaries. Despite two raises granted in rapid succession, a police chief with 30 years' experience who headed up a force of some 154 men in the capital city of one of the larger eastern states received less than $6,000 in 1961. The starting wage for patrolmen in the biggest cities of the nation averaged out to less than $100 a week in the beginning of 1961.

The executive officer of the police department in Burlington, Vermont, which was hit by scandals of police thefts early in 1962, was himself receiving $5,400 a year at the time—$1,200 less than a privately-employed plant security patrolman with no responsibility other than that of checking signal boxes.

The reluctance of municipalities to hike police pay stems more from a desire to keep the cost of government down than from a lack of recognition of the need for raises. Personnel costs account for approximately 80 percent to 95 percent of police department budgets, with the biggest cities showing the highest percentages. Police budgets, furthermore, have risen sharply in recent years as police work-weeks have been reduced, in some instances from as much as 76 hours in 1945 to 40 hours at present.

"The reduction in the work week was largely responsible for the doubling of police budgets across the nation in the fifteen years following World War II," notes Donal E. J. MacNamara, Dean of the New York Institute of Criminology and a consultant in the field of police administration. More holidays, longer vacations, and other fringe benefits, such as better disability coverage and improved uniform allowances, have also hiked police personnel costs without fattening dollar sums on individual paychecks.

Taxpayers had best brace themselves for still higher personnel expenditures. Chicago's Police Superintendent and former head of the School of Criminology at the University of California in Berkeley, Orlando W. Wilson, argues: "Quality is influenced by price. If we're going to raise police standards, we're going to have to raise police salaries as well."

Chief Wilson, who came to Chicago to overhaul a scandal-ridden department in 1960, says he'd "like" to have his recruits with at least two years of college but he does not think that is "nearly as vital as character and intelligence." It is going to take money, he argues, to snare such prospects from jobs in government or private industry.

To supplement their income, policemen often hold down second jobs. A good many authorities are highly critical of that practice. Chief of Police Robert V. Murray of Washington, D.C., believes the two-job policeman comes to work tired and tends to avoid making arrests the day before his day off so he won't have to appear in court when he is supposed to be on another job. Chief Murray is also disturbed by the possible conflict between enforcement of the law and loyalty to an outside employer. And he is afraid of losing desirable men: "The better men who take part-time jobs often do well enough to develop these jobs into full-time positions and then they quit the force altogether," says he.

A good many police departments prohibit "moonlighting," as the practice is called, but few enforce the ban lest they lose too much of their force. A top official of the Policeman's Benevolent Association in New York City recently estimated 60 percent to 70 percent of that city's policemen were holding down other jobs despite the fact the department is among those prohibiting the practice. Former Police Commissioner Stephen P. Kennedy aroused considerable wrath among the rank and file when he tried to enforce the ban. His successor, Michael J. Murphy, did not press the issue.

Police dishonesty has often been blamed, in part at least, on moral erosion from substandard pay scales. It has been said low pay makes police officers susceptible to offers of free meals, cigarettes, and other small favors from local merchants and that such practices tend to be followed by more generous gifts later. Then, when they are not forthcoming, there is the dropped hint and, finally, the outright request for gratuities. Whatever truth there may be in this contention, when the "shakedown" is standard procedure throughout a department, as it was revealed in 1961 to have been for years in Denver, it is more reflective of a serious neglect of discipline within the department than of the level of police pay.

"The police service reminds me of George Bernard Shaw's comment on marriage," says the youthful Planning Director of Chicago's Police Department, Richard E. McDonnell. "The reason it's popular, he said, is that it combines a maximum amount of temptation with a maximum amount of opportunity. The absence of internal controls over police conduct makes for the same condition."

The tendency of police management to ignore or show too much leniency toward erring members of the force has been documented repeatedly in various departments around the country, albeit seldom for public eyes. Failure to institute procedures which might more readily bring police malpractices to light have likewise been noted. Many of the more than forty policemen implicated in Denver's 1961 police scandal were found to have been cracking safes for at least a decade; police authorities contend the most rudimentary controls would long before have indicated something was awry with so many members of the force involved.

One reason disciplinary procedures are not more common in police departments is that police supervisors want a maximum of discretionary authority to deal with situations in their departments as they see fit. And they do not want their decisions in this realm questioned, which fixed procedures would make easier. The desire is understandable, but the facility with which it is realized is a luxury in laxity communities can ill afford.

Among the most important innovations Chief Wilson made in the Chicago force when he began to reorganize the department in 1960 was the institution of an Internal Investigation Division consisting of some 90 plainclothesmen. Since the entire department had 10,800 men at the time, that meant assigning the equivalent of nearly 1 percent of the force to police the police. Among other things, the division was to be responsible for recording and investigating every complaint filed against a policeman. It was also to do some investigating on its own. For example, its personnel were instructed to deliberately exceed speed limits on various streets and thoroughfares and then attempt to get out of the ticket by flashing a five-dollar bill, long considered the going rate for a ticket "fix" in Chicago. More than one police officer has been trapped in this manner and dismissed from the force.

The detection of police dishonesty is self-defeating if prosecution is not swift and certain. Chicago resorted to wholesale dismissals of suspect policemen as a result of Chief Wilson's cleanup efforts, but leniency rather than severity has been the rule in many departments in the past. The late Bruce Smith, one of the nation's foremost police experts, in a little-publicized and exceedingly illuminating study of the New York Police Department completed in 1952, cites the case of a police officer who got drunk off duty and used his weapon to take a man's life. He drew a five-day sentence for the act.

Another officer, brought to trial 40 times for various offenses in the course of 20 years, and found guilty 36 times, received penalties totaling less than 33 days' pay, according to Mr. Smith. In all, of eight police officers who were tried and found guilty on at least 20 different accounts, only two were finally dismissed from the force, he notes. "Very few charges," he stated, "are brought against sergeants and almost none against lieutenants or officers of higher rank, unless and until criminal proceedings are initiated against them by other public agencies. Such puny efforts toward discipline," he declared, stood in "unhealthy contrast" to the sentences that would have been imposed by a criminal court on members of the general public had they committed the identical acts.

Just as police authorities have sought to protect their men in the past, regardless of wrongdoing, so have they frequently been guilty of understating the occurrence of crime for the purpose of preserving "community confidence" in their performance. In his book *The Trouble with Cops,* published in 1955, the late Albert Deutsch noted the effect of an overhaul in New York City's crime-reporting which had been too lax for the FBI to include in its Uniform Crime Reports. "When the record system was improved," said he, "the number of known burglaries reported was multiplied 13 times and the number of robberies fivefold as compared with the last previous period for which figures were available."

St. Louis, a model among record keepers, submits its crime statistics to regular audit by the Governmental Research Institute, a nonprofit business-supported organization which strives for better local government. The agency, inspired for many years by a hard-working dedicated public servant, the scholarly Dr. Victor D. Brannon, has helped institute many modern management techniques in its police force as well as in other local government bodies.

Police officials in many cities have long complained of their inability to hire qualified personnel needed to bring their forces up to authorized strength. However, one retired police consultant, Edwin O. Griffenhagen, of Lake Geneva, Wisconsin, who headed his own firm for forty-five years prior to his retirement in 1959, is "not so sure it is as difficult to get good men as police officials frequently make out."

Many cities, authorities agree, needlessly hamstring themselves by barring the hiring of nonresidents or otherwise limiting the geographical scope of their recruitment. The Police Department of New York City, until late 1961 when it stepped up its recruitment efforts in nearby Connecticut and announced it would also seek men farther afield, was among those most frequently bemoaning its hiring difficulties. The practice has only one purpose: to dispense political patronage within a given voting area. Departments that adhere to it and then blame personnel shortages on the community's niggardliness in paying its police apparently don't trust truth too far.

Reports the District of Columbia's Chief Murray: "We had always been short of our authorized strength until November, 1960, when we sent four teams of two men each into 101 communities in the East and Midwest designated by the Labor Department as high-unemployment areas. Shortly thereafter we had not only filled every one of the 180 vacancies we had at the time, but we developed a backlog of men waiting for jobs." The International Association of Chiefs of Police, for its part, has been a vigorous critic of residence requirements in the recruitment of police personnel. Many communities and departments persist in applying them nevertheless.

The recruitment of detectives comes in for special criticism. Too much emphasis, it is said, is often placed on physical attributes and too little on tested aptitude for analysis and problem-solving. "We might clear more of our crimes with convictions if we were more selective about mental abilities among our detectives," maintains one consultant.

Police department officials can stretch police manpower by employing more civilians to handle clerical and other tasks which don't require the capabilities of a patrolman for their performance. The Los Angeles Police

Department figures that in the decade from 1951 to 1961 it freed over 400 police personnel for enforcement duties—and saved the city up to $500,000 a year in the process—by taking them off typewriters, switchboards, filing, stenographic work, and even photography and fingerprinting, and giving those chores largely to clerk-typists. The clerk-typists were paid $246 less per month, and, of course, their qualifications weren't nearly so difficult to come by. According to the city's law-trained Police Chief, William H. Parker, 23 percent of the department's 6,100-person mid-1961 payroll was made up of civilians, compared with only 13 percent of the 4,757 persons the department employed on December 31, 1950.

In Oakland, California, Police Chief Edward M. Toothman recently replaced police personnel with civilians in 30 jail positions and in 18 of the 20 posts in the department's radio room. Civilian personnel already accounted for nearly 25 percent of the department's total employment by 1962. Colonel H. Sam Priest, President of the St. Louis Board of Police Commissioners, reports that even his Research and Planning Division is 100 percent civilian-manned and has been ever since it was established in 1957; the department's training director is also a civilian.

In contrast, only 227 of the 2,973 persons working for the Boston Police Department on the same date, or 7 percent of its total employment, were civilians. New York City's percentage at the time was even lower: approximately 1,250, or 5 percent of its total payroll. Jacob S. Katz, Deputy Police Commissioner in Charge of Administration, notes the proportion of civilians to total department personnel in the city's force has been almost unchanged for "20 years or longer." A visitor to the department in 1961 could have found police personnel performing a wide variety of clerical tasks, including the issuance of licenses for the operation of dance halls, secondhand stores, taxicabs, and other enterprises whose activities are supervised by the department. Deputy Katz blames the scarcity of civilian employees on poor civilian pay for police department positions and undesirable working hours and conditions.

New York Police Commissioner Michael J. Murphy says he "tried to get the Civil Service Commission to provide a differential for civilians working in the department at night, but I haven't gotten anywhere so far." The department at the time had authorization for 24,590 sworn personnel, however, nearly 25 percent more than the 20,000 it had seven years earlier.

A number of departments are easing their manpower problems at low cost and helping to meet future personnel needs as well through the use of police cadets. The system provides for the hiring of young men between the ages of 17 and 21, too young to qualify as police officers. For the most part, they are assigned to clerical and other nonenforcement tasks. The theory is that police aspirants too young for service may thus become better acquainted with it, and it with them, for mutual benefit on future application to the force. The program has a further advantage to the department: its cost is exceedingly modest. The city of Buffalo, New York, launched its cadet program in mid-1961 with a going wage of $2,400 a year; it aimed to have 40 in the corps within four years. Detroit at the time boasted a police cadet corps of 55. A new program in Fresno, California, had cadets experimentally replacing "meter maids" in tabbing overparked cars; the cadets were expected to prove less susceptible to illness, bad weather, and the abuse of motorists than the female meter corps had been.

Some police authorities argue women could be employed to a far greater extent in police work, particularly in certain aspects of detective work, in laboratory and identification assignments, as desk and communications officers, in traffic control and in other roles where personal safety is not in jeopardy.

Another device for stretching manpower, whether the department is utilizing the cadet system or not, consists in the cultivation of an auxiliary or volunteer force. Such forces are being created increasingly by broadening the role of civil defense units. Comprised essentially of males, though conceivably women could be used as well, the auxiliary is expected to purchase its own uniforms and generally is not paid. Candidates are customarily screened first for character. Denver, which turned to the idea in mid-1959 when it had about as much trouble recruiting cadets as recruiting policemen, boasts an auxiliary of approximately 150 members previously organized as a civil defense unit; the group meets monthly for training purposes. It supplements the regular police force in disasters and parades, directs traffic from ball games and other special events, and helps out on such community chores as the posting of Christmas lights. An official of the Denver department finds some of the city's volunteer police "better trained and more enthusiastic than some of our regular officers." They are also taking some of the load off the department from increased traffic, which forced the assignment of 120 men to that function in 1962, twice as many as in 1950.

The International City Managers Association, in a report published not long ago, notes the "widespread organization and use of civilian auxiliary police since World War II." Many of these units, it adds, remain principally "civil defense" in character.

Facilities, as well as manpower, are not being used anywhere near as efficiently as they should be. Bruce Smith, who has followed in his father's footsteps as a police consultant from a base in Norfolk, Virginia, maintains: "Most police station locations in our older cities were laid out before the day of the automobile and the telephone, when they had to be within walking distance for public and patrolman alike. But advances in transportation and communications since that time, which cause the public to phone rather than personally visit stations when they need help and which also permit the dispersal of patrolmen by bus or squad car, make many stations obsolete and unnecessary."

The elder Mr. Smith in 1953 suggested New York City did not need more than 75 stations—but it was still operating five more than that nearly a decade later. In mid-1961, the so-called Blyth-Zellerbach Committee reported that San Francisco could be effectively protected with just four stations; it had nine at the time. In Boston, one of the most heavily-policed cities in the nation in relation to population, City Councilman Gabriel F. Piemonte not long ago pointed to four police stations from the window of his office, all within a five-minute walk from one point. The four, he insisted, could be consolidated into one to cut custodial services, heat and light bills, and eventually the salaries of three of their four captains simply by failing to fill their positions when they retired. The need for lieutenants, sergeants, and clerks to man these stations would similarly be reduced. The elder Smith called for the closing of seven Boston police stations, but not a single one had been shut down thirteen years later.

Police chiefs generally agree on the desirability of operating fewer stations, but they often argue as Washington, D.C., Chief Murray does: "We tried consolidating some stations a few years back, and the people who were losing their station howled from the rooftops. We had to give them back their stations again." To save money on the real estate investment, and communications equipment as well, a small number of cities are housing some police stations with fire companies, a joint tenancy not altogether unknown in the past.

As cities grow together, the principle of local control, which was devised to prevent the concentration of police power in too few hands, tends also to foster conflict, confusion, duplication, and waste. A woman who stopped overnight at a motel in El Portal, near Miami, recalls she had to phone three different police departments to report a suspected prowler outside her door before she got through to the right department; fortunately, she was either mistaken or he moved on, since there was ample time for anyone nearby to fulfill any suspected intentions and move on before the police arrived. In Shelby County, Tennessee, sheriff's cars were having to drive 13 miles to get outside the city of Memphis to begin their patrol but, says Memphis Mayor Henry Loeb, "they would be even less centrally-located if they were headquartered in the county itself." An estate owner summoning police aid in an eastern metropolitan area one day found two squad cars pulling into his driveway; one, it turned out, was a county car with jurisdiction over that particular address and the other was a city car which normally patrolled the area and therefore knew it better. In Los Angeles, not long ago, a speeding motorist managed to accumulate police cars from seven different municipalities before he was finally caught.

A recent study by the Northwestern University Law School found 90 law-enforcement agencies in Chicago's 954-square-mile Cook County. Writing in the *Journal of Criminal Law, Criminology and Political Science,* Gordon Linkon noted these separate agencies "operate for the most part without coordination and many times without knowledge of what other forces in the County are doing or attempting to do. The combined strength of law enforcement in Cook County is so weakened by the discoordinated structure that the process of law enforcement is seriously impeded."

According to the *Municipal Yearbook,* published by the International City Managers Association in Chicago, there were over 40,000 autonomous police jurisdictions operating in the United States in the beginning of 1961. "The political design of law enforcement in this country," says Los Angeles' Chief Parker, "is a tragedy in view of our modern mode of living. We are trying to maintain village-type autonomous law enforcement in areas which have long since outgrown it." Retired consultant Earle W. Garrett, one of the nation's leading police authorities, observes that local municipalities "cling to the police service they know they can control, even though such service is far less efficient than one that would result from a coordination of police departments."

After investigating the highly fragmented metropolitan regions of Cook County, Illinois, in which Chicago is located, Bergen County, New Jersey, and Los Angeles County, the United States Senate Crime Committee, otherwise known as the Kefauver Committee, declared in 1951 it found "no centralized direction of control and no centralized responsibility for seeing that a uniform law-enforcement policy is applied over the entire geographic area of a county. The situation," it went on to state, "lends itself to buck-passing and evasion of responsibility which can only inure to the advantage of gangsters and racketeers. It makes it possible for hoodlums to find those cities and towns where law enforcement is low and to concentrate their operations there."

Widespread agreements calling for mutual aid between police departments, authorities say, are pitiful counter-measures against vice and syndicated crime which know no municipal boundaries. They can also present legal problems for police departments which are parties to such agreements. In Santa Monica, California, a policeman who was shot answering a call for help on the Los Angeles side of a street forfeited his workmen's compensation because he was not legally a ward of the City of Santa Monica when he answered the call outside Santa Monica. The situation has since been remedied by an exchange of benefits between the two cities, but a good many other areas in the country have no such reciprocal arrangements.

Feuding or jealous departments which hide evidence from one another or don't call for assistance until it is too late, needless duplication of records and other facilities, and a thinning of resources which might otherwise be used for better service are just a few of the consequences of fragmented police authority.

Few police experts believe the solution lies in the creation of a single police force for the entire nation. Such an organization would probably be too big even for efficiency, not to say anything of the dangers it might pose to the nation through its concentration of power. A good many police authorities, however, argue the police function would be better served through the consolidation of several departments in a given metropolitan area or at least through the combination of certain of their functions, criminal identification and recordkeeping, for instance.

The lack of communication between departments becomes rather surprising at times. For instance, the Police Department of Oakland, California, in 1956 came up with a system for getting a patrolman's routine reports into the station without his having to come to the station to type them himself or even dictate them by phone, which often leads to errors. The periodic report is one of the big consumers of patrolmen's time in many cities even today. One police authority has estimated patrolmen spend up to 20 percent of their time on reports when they have to type them in the station. The Oakland Police Department simply had its men write their reports on the street in longhand and leave them in the police callbox where a patrol car or wagon picked them up on its regular rounds. "We tried everything," Chief Toothman recalls, "even having the reports phoned in to a tape for transcription by a stenographer later, but nothing has been as cheap or as foolproof as this system." Yet, he admitted, the system had never been written up or otherwise reported to the profession, and, so far as he knew, no one outside the Bay Area had much knowledge of it. A police chief of one of the biggest cities in the area whose own men were still coming into the station to type out their reports five years after the Oakland innovation began, confessed recently to having "heard" about the Oakland system but not being "too familiar" with how it was working out.

Because manpower accounts for so large a portion of the police budget and because its more effective use is crucial in the combat of crime, new techniques and devices for increasing its effectiveness are vital. Some of the new techniques appear to offer some promise. In mid-1961, for example, the St. Louis Police Department launched its Special Deployment Squads. Two, each consisting of twelve men and women dressed in civilian clothes, roamed high-crime areas night and day as decoys for muggings, purse snatching, holdups, and other crimes. Concealed miniature two-way radios kept them in touch with "cover" cars positioned ahead and behind them. In their first month of operation, the two squads apprehended more than half-a-dozen persons. The squads proved so effective, Police Chief Curtis Brostron decided to place two more just like them on the city's streets only two months after the first two began operating.

St. Louis has also established a special "Mobile Reserve" to saturate heavy crime areas with speedily dispatched forces. The unit in 1961 consisted of 65 men and some 30 cars. It is generally on duty from 7:00 P.M. to 3:00 A.M., though the shift varies as the situation warrants.

San Francisco's "Operation S," created in 1958, goes into action when the crime load becomes too great for its special 12-man night Crime Prevention Squad to handle. In 1961 some 72 officers and 36 squad cars were assigned to the unit. When they're not needed, the men and cars of "Operation S" serve on routine patrol.

Radio communications and recordkeeping leave much to be desired in a great many police departments around the land. Boston claims the distinction of having placed into operation the first police radio system in the United States as far back as 1932. It was still operating the same system in 1962. Recently, when it made a pitch to the city for $250,000 for a new radio network, the department produced a technical report which showed the new unit would pay for itself in five years in gasoline savings alone, since patrol cars would no longer have to race their motors to maintain transmitting power.

New York City's Police Department was unable as late as 1962 to broadcast simultaneously to all patrol cars. It had to relay these calls from one borough to the next. Its radio network was also burdened with some 300,000 ambulance calls yearly. Because of the network's limited capacity, emergency calls may not be taken for several minutes during periods of particularly heavy traffic.

Identification procedures likewise are often cumbersome and slow. St. Louis recently completed the installation of electrically powered card-filing machines which helped reduce its clerical force substantially while also reducing to a matter of minutes identification procedures which previously took half an hour or more. The new automated record room, however, is highly unusual among police departments. Most continue to hobble along with facilities and procedures outdated decades ago.

The weakness of management science in police administration would seem to be further demonstrated by the accumulation of controversy, rather than thoroughly researched evidence, in a surprising number of techniques that are no longer new. Nowhere does that controversy rage more heatedly than around the polygraph, or the lie detector, as it is more commonly known. Essentially, the lie detector is only an instrument for measuring such physiological phenomena as respiration and blood pressure. Its use in crime detection is based on the theory that most people are afraid of getting caught in a lie and show that fear by altering their normal patterns of respiration and blood pressure. The device, however, is not infallible. Some persons just aren't that afraid of being caught or of the instrument's ability to betray them. Others, though innocent, behave as if they are telling a lie when they really aren't. For these reasons, the lie detector is not admissible as evidence in most courts.

But its value as an investigative tool has been proved over and over again. A Los Angeles police official relates how the instrument was used to find a murder weapon: a series of Yes and No questions was put to the suspect until the place where the weapon was hidden was narrowed down sufficiently to permit a search. A gun was subsequently found within feet of the location where the polygraph indicated it might be.

The Police Department of Evanston, Illinois, recently hired the services of a polygraph specialist to screen police candidates who had passed all other qualifying exams. Through use of the device one aspirant who admitted to no crime record was discovered to have committed eight burglaries. Another, who went similarly undetected through interviews and written procedures, was found to have participated in five armed robberies. Still another, who qualified on all other accounts and who might otherwise have been appointed to the force, was identified as a sexual pervert.

Impressed with Evanston's results, the St. Louis Police Department in 1961 hired the same polygraph specialists to screen 50 of its applicants. At $150 a day for an examiner capable of handling 8 applicants in his 8 working hours, the department considered it a bargain: an investment of $16 to $18 per applicant, it figured, might be saving many times that cost in terms of training, equipment, and the betrayal of public trust which might otherwise ensue if due precautions weren't taken. St. Louis, along with other cities, is also submitting applicants to psychiatric examination to reduce chances of hiring sadistic persons or persons otherwise unsuited to the responsibility who may not have betrayed that fact on a crime report. Psychologists have long noted the tendency of police work to attract a certain percentage of maladjusted individuals, but it is still the exceptional force that tries to weed them out with every means at its command.

Indeed, some police forces turn their back even on the polygraph, for this or any other purpose. The New York Police Department is among those who ban its use. New York Police Chief Murphy explains the policy by stating simply that "they're not admissible as evidence in court, so we don't use them." A number of critics contend the use of the polygraph is sometimes prohibited by departments who fear it may be turned against their own police to discredit testimony or for other purposes.

Another practice still debated among police authorities which is not exactly new is the use of dogs in police work. Baltimore, for example, has used German shepherds for searching dark warehouses, controlling unruly gangs, and for other purposes, since 1956. Police Commissioner James H. Hepbron had read of their use in London and dispatched representatives of the department to study the value of dogs in police work firsthand. Within four years, Baltimore had a K-9 corps of 39 dogs. A number of other cities, including Pittsburgh, Houston, St. Louis, and Minneapolis, followed suit with K-9 corps of their own. The dogs are useful, the contention goes, as a deterrent to such crimes as burglaries and robberies and for flushing suspects out of hideaways. They are not trained, however, to kill. The first sign of viciousness generally brings a canine elimination from the force.

Some police authorities, however, remain skeptical of the value of dogs in police work. One consultant argues that "their main use is to produce newspaper stories for publicity-minded chiefs," though he concedes they may have such limited application as routing perverts from parks. "In crime patrols," says he, "they're more of a nuisance than a help."

What about the two-man patrol car: is it really necessary or can the community get more mileage out of its patrol dollar by splitting its men up and giving them a car apiece? This debate, too, has been raging for years without any thoroughgoing effort to investigate scientifically its pros and cons, its dangers and possible means for lessening them. Practices, possibly as a result, vary sharply. Except for a single squad car which is manned by two men only during hours of darkness, the city of Oakland, for example, has been using one-man cars exclusively with no apparent ill effects. New York City, on the other hand, was not operating a single one-man patrol car anywhere in the city in 1961. A top executive contended this was because "driving in New York City occupies all of the driver's attention and one-man patrol cars are anyway unsafe in criminal situations."

Proponents of the one-man car are critical of flat bans against it, arguing that foot patrolmen generally walk their beats alone without even the benefit of a radio, which a man in a squad car has. As for the contention that the driver's time is fully occupied with driving in a city like New York, critics argue that there are sections of the city, residential areas in Queens, for instance, which are no more difficult to drive in nor any more dangerous from the standpoint of crime than the suburbs of many another municipality which does use one-man cars. They further justify the use of one-man cars on the grounds that the mere presence of a police car is reassuring to the public and serves as a deterrent to crime.

The issue of the marked versus the unmarked patrol car is similarly unresolved, and likewise a subject of highly divergent practice. The use of unmarked patrol cars, that is, cars which look like any other on the road, is common in such states as Colorado and Connecticut. The theory, of course, is that the unmarked car is more likely to catch violators and discourage others from speeding. Police authorities in other locales, Los Angeles for one, argue the presence of the law should be made as conspicuous as possible as a means of deterring violations of the law which, they argue, is after all their principal function. The same philosophy gives rise to the removal of motorcycle cops from behind billboards and their making themselves conspicuous even to the extent of moving along with traffic, if at a slightly slower pace.

While police experts go on debating such basic issues as the unmarked car, the one- and two-man patrol, the use of dogs, and the pitfalls of the polygraph, they generally agree on one point: that more research is needed on these and other aspects of police administration and that very little research of this nature is being conducted at present simply because no one department is large or rich enough to finance it, and even if one was, the application of its findings to other cities might be questioned. They agree on the need for—but don't yet foresee—the creation of a national agency which might carry on these functions independent of individual departments.

Whether police departments generally would follow the findings of such an agency or continue to go on their own ways as they see fit is another question. Few departments even now bother to call in outside help for advice or scrutiny. One organization particularly well qualified to provide it, as it often does, is the International Association of Chiefs of Police, with headquarters in Washington and a field staff roaming the nation. The organization, however, will make only those investigations requested of it by a department's chief of police. If he does not care for its advice on a particular subject, for one reason or another, it makes little difference who exhorts it to do so, the I.A.C.P. will not investigate. Boston officials found that out recently when they attempted to get the I.A.C.P. to make a study of the city's police department at a time when former Boston Police Commissioner Leo J. Sullivan was being asked for his resignation by Governor John A. Volpe following a television show which depicted as many as ten Boston policemen entering and leaving a bookmaking establishment.

Police departments which will go out and hire outside consultants of their own accord are rare. Again, St. Louis stands out in this respect. That city's Board of Police Commissioners in 1957 authorized the independent Governmental Research Institute to do whatever consulting work it considered necessary, including the hiring of other outside authorities at the Department's expense; G.R.I. hired the services in 1957 and 1958 of Orlando Wilson while he was still at the University of California, and subsequently of Sanford Shoults, who had gone from a high-ranking post with the Detroit Police Department to the faculty of the School of Police Administration at Michigan State University and then to the University of Arizona to develop courses in police administration.

Mr. MacNamara, of New York's Institute of Criminology, however, figures: "There are over 40,000 police jurisdictions in the country, but I doubt if more than 20 of them a year hire consultants to look into the way their departments are run and to make recommendations."

Not too many, it might be added, want the looking glass lifted before them. Until they do, however, the growing burdens of mounting crime and spreading urbanization will continue to catch them off balance.

A Word on Juvenile Delinquency

One factor which is likely to aggravate policing problems in the years ahead is the persisting rise in juvenile delinquency. The number of youngsters in the critical 14- to 17-year-old age group will swell nearly 50 percent in the decade to 1971. Because the jobless rate is about three times as high among unskilled youth as it is among adults, unemployment could strike hard at those failing to pursue their education into higher institutions of learning. Climbing divorce rates and the deterioration of family relationships that previously nourished respect and compassion for others are also likely to contribute to the rise in youthful lawbreaking in the future.

A great many efforts—federal, state, and local—are being directed against the surge in juvenile crime, and some may yet be successful. But they probably will not be found in the bargain basement. Keenly aware of that probability, the Congress in 1961 passed an act authorizing the expenditure of $10 million yearly for a period of at least three years to stimulate local efforts in combating juvenile delinquency. The first project to gain its support, $1.9 million to be provided over a three-year period, was a massive effort aimed at reforming the entire Lower East Side of New York City at a total cost to local, state, federal, and private agencies over the period of some $12.6 million. The area's 107,000 population at the time had an average family income of $69 a week; only 15 percent of its adults had ever finished high school. The program, which got under way in the summer of 1962, was fashioned by an organization known as Mobilization for Youth, Inc. It was designed, in the words of then Attorney General Robert F. Kennedy, to give the area's youth "a stake in conformity."

The project, a sort of Golden Gate of social engineering, ran the gamut from organizing the play of seven-year-olds to providing jobs for 16- to 21-year-olds in an Urban Service Corps, repairing tenements, beautifying the neighborhood, and otherwise dressing up the cityscape and enhancing municipal services. An "adventure corps" on para-military lines was to be provided for boys 9 to 13. In addition to a host of special facilities, including three "cool and jazzy" coffee shops featuring art and folk music, 300 "homework-helpers" were to tutor failing pupils, teachers' home visits were to be stepped up, educational and cultural efforts were to be aimed at adults as well as their offspring, and welfare programs tailored to troubled families, addicted youth, and other social diseases were also to be provided.

The task nevertheless was awesome: delinquency rates among those 7 to 20 years of age had risen from 28.7 per 1,000 in 1951 to 62.8 in 1960.

In the past, combatants of juvenile delinquency have produced almost as much confusion as they have practical results, and sometimes more. So many organizations have become involved in the battle and so much has been written on the subject, that two new libraries were created recently to specialize in this field alone: one, by the National Institute of Mental Health, and the other by the National Research and Information Center on Crime and Delinquency. In Los Angeles County, over 90 autonomous community groups are estimated to be working on the problem.

Some of the techniques for combating juvenile delinquency appear to be working in some areas, at least for the time being. Plainclothes patrolmen in Jersey City who get their leads from school authorities have proved effective in getting problem youngsters in for medical and psychological treatment before they end up in court. Clubs organized by businessmen and other public-minded citizens in such cities as St. Louis and Columbus have succeeded in directing the interest of youths toward athletics and the arts and away from diversions that lead to violence and destruction. Supervised recreation in parks and community centers has also helped direct youthful energies into healthier channels. Work programs and efforts to keep youngsters from dropping out of high school also apparently are achieving results.

Despite these efforts, expenditures, and occasional accomplishments, however, the wave of juvenile delinquency is on a sharp upgrade. According to the Children's Bureau in Washington, 1960 was the twelfth consecutive year in which juvenile crime rose to a new peak—up 6 percent from 1959. According to California Probation Officer Karl Holton, the number of San Quentin inmates under 25 years of age rose 40 percent in the 15 years to 1962; the California Youth Authority, he notes further, had 5,000 boys and girls in its correctional schools compared to 1,200 in 1941. Former Attorney General Kennedy repeatedly warned that the problem of juvenile delinquency would be "unbeatable" if it were not licked before the 1960's were out. He figures that by 1970, some 7 million high school dropouts will be entering the labor market—2 million of them without ever having finished the eighth grade.

The rise in juvenile delinquency is not only making vast sections of the nation's larger cities unsafe, it is rapidly spilling over into the suburbs as well. A Senate Judiciary Subcommittee late in 1961 reported juvenile crime was rising considerably faster in suburban and rural areas than in central cities. The Family Service Association of Nassau County, one of metropolitan New York's richer counties, was getting a hundred calls a month in 1961 from parents seeking help in controlling delinquent youngsters.

Juvenile delinquents rarely grow up to become good husbands, wives, and parents, though they marry and have children like everyone else. With their own flock of problem children to add to those society is already producing, the problem is one that could multiply many times over.

As with so many of its other urban ills, the nation could do worse than to look to foreign lands for a clue to the solution of its problems, in this area as in others. In this respect, Switzerland, particularly, bears study. That mountain land under the social microscope reveals not only close family ties but also a severity that prohibits youngsters under 16 from entering motion picture houses and those under 18 from obtaining drivers' licenses. The nation has succeeded in producing generation after generation of youngsters dedicated to hard work, the vigorous pursuit of sports, and a healthy respect for their elders and the law.

The nation, it should be noted, also has one of the lowest divorce rates in the world, has traditionally placed its teachers in high financial and communal regard, encourages thrift through small allowances, and fosters discipline through a brief period of military service required annually of all youths from ages 21 to 33.

Whether these phenomena are responsible for the remarkably high state of social health among Switzerland's youth, of course, has yet to be proved. It would be surprising, however, if delinquency rates rise in that country in the future while these stanchions still stand.

It is hardly likely that similar measures could be widely adopted in this country, but there is no reason why the vein cannot be mined for some useful ore.

SIX

The Emerging Sensibility

PHOTOGRAPH BY
Fred W. McDarrah.

Norman O. Brown's rereading of Freud, his call
for an end to repression, his praise of play
and childhood have opened vistas that have
profound moral implications. The inner animal,
he seems to say, is not necessarily a beast.
In any case, it is time to free this inner animal
if life is to be asserted.
Similarly, Marshall McLuhan, by recognizing
the interrelationship of man and the tools with

which he communicates, revitalizes an old
question: Do the ends justify the means? What if
the ends and the means *are* each other? McLuhan's
provocative suggestion that electronic
communication has produced an end to what he
calls "linear experience" has been used to
explain—as well as to praise— much recent
fragmentary expression.
Timothy Leary and Aldous Huxley, in quite
different ways, prepared the ground
for the psychedelic revolution.
The selections here reflect on the one hand
the unbridled enthusiasm of the convert (Leary)
to a religion that has not yet been entirely invented,
and on the other what happens when a thoughtful
and highly informed mind (Huxley's) tries to make
sense of an unheard-of experience.
In Tom Wolfe's saga of Ken Kesey and the
Merry Pranksters, his literary style *and* his subject
matter together present a glittering example of the
new sensibility almost fully emerged. Wolfe has
what John Donne would have called a
"hydroptic thirst" for experience to which his prose
responds at a pitch just below unbearable
amazement.

From **"The Doors of Perception"**
ALDOUS HUXLEY

If the doors of perception were cleansed every thing would appear to man as it is, infinite.

William Blake

It was in 1886 that the German pharmacologist, Ludwig Lewin, published the first systematic study of the cactus, to which his own name was subsequently given. *Anhalonium Lewinii* was new to science. To primitive religion and the Indians of Mexico and the American Southwest it was a friend of immemorially long standing. Indeed, it was much more than a friend. In the words of one of the early Spanish visitors to the New World, "they eat a root which they call peyote, and which they venerate as though it were a deity."

Why they should have venerated it as a deity became apparent when such eminent psychologists as Jaensch, Havelock Ellis and Weir Mitchell began their experiments with mescalin, the active principle of peyote. True, they stopped short at a point well this side of idolatry; but all concurred in assigning to mescalin a position among drugs of unique distinction. Administered in suitable doses, it changes the quality of consciousness more profoundly and yet is less toxic than any other substance in the pharmacologist's repertory.

Mescalin research has been going on sporadically ever since the days of Lewin and Havelock Ellis. Chemists have not merely isolated the alkaloid; they have learned how to synthesize it, so that the supply no longer depends on the sparse and intermittent crop of a desert cactus. Alienists have dosed themselves with mescalin in the hope thereby of coming to a better, a first-hand, understanding of their patients' mental processes. Working unfortunately upon too few subjects within too narrow a range of circumstances, psychologists have observed and catalogued some of the drug's more striking effects. Neurologists and physiologists have found out something about the mechanism of its action upon the central nervous system. And at least one professional philosopher has taken mescalin for the light it may throw on such ancient, unsolved riddles as the place of mind in nature and the relationship between brain and consciousness.

There matters rested until, two or three years ago, a new and perhaps highly significant fact was observed.* Actually the fact had been staring everyone

---

* See the following papers: "Schizophrenia. A New Approach." By Humphry Osmond and John Smythies. *Journal of Mental Science.* Vol. XCVIII. April, 1952.

"On Being Mad." By Humphry Osmond. *Saskatchewan Psychiatric Services Journal.* Vol. I. No. 2. September, 1952.

"The Mescalin Phenomena." By John Smythies. *The British Journal of the Philosophy of Science.* Vol. III. February, 1953.

in the face for several decades; but nobody, as it happened, had noticed it until a young English psychiatrist, at present working in Canada, was struck by the close similarity, in chemical composition, between mescalin and adrenalin. Further research revealed that lysergic acid, an extremely potent hallucinogen derived from ergot, has a structural biochemical relationship to the others. Then came the discovery that adrenochrome, which is a product of the decomposition of adrenalin, can produce many of the symptoms observed in mescalin intoxication. But adrenochrome probably occurs spontaneously in the human body. In other words, each one of us may be capable of manufacturing a chemical, minute doses of which are known to cause profound changes in consciousness. Certain of these changes are similar to those which occur in that most characteristic plague of the twentieth century, schizophrenia. Is the mental disorder due to a chemical disorder? And is the chemical disorder due, in its turn, to psychological distresses affecting the adrenals? It would be rash and premature to affirm it. The most we can say is that some kind of a *prima facie* case has been made out. Meanwhile the clue is being systematically followed, the sleuths—biochemists, psychiatrists, psychologists—are on the trail.

By a series of, for me, extremely fortunate circumstances I found myself, in the spring of 1953, squarely athwart that trail. One of the sleuths had come on business to California. In spite of seventy years of mescalin research, the psychological material at his disposal was still absurdly inadequate, and he was anxious to add to it. I was on the spot and willing, indeed eager, to be a guinea pig. Thus it came about that, one bright May morning, I swallowed four-tenths of a gram of mescalin dissolved in half a glass of water and sat down to wait for the results.

We live together, we act on, and react to, one another; but always and in all circumstances we are by ourselves. The martyrs go hand in hand into the arena; they are crucified alone. Embraced, the lovers desperately try to fuse their insulated ecstasies into a single self-transcendence; in vain. By its very nature every embodied spirit is doomed to suffer and enjoy in solitude. Sensations, feelings, insights, fancies—all these are private and, except through symbols and at second hand, incommunicable. We can pool information about experiences, but never the experiences themselves. From family to nation, every human group is a society of island universes.

Most island universes are sufficiently like one another to permit of inferential understanding or even of mutual empathy or "feeling into." Thus, remembering our own bereavements and humiliations, we can condole with others in analogous circumstances, can put ourselves (always, of course, in a slightly Pickwickian sense) in their places. But in certain cases communication between universes is incomplete or even nonexistent. The mind is its own place, and the places inhabited by the insane and the exceptionally gifted are so different from the places where ordinary men and women live, that there is little or no common

"Schizophrenia: A New Approach." By Abram Hoffer, Humphry Osmond and John Smythies. *Journal of Mental Science.* Vol. C. No. 418. January, 1954.

Numerous other papers on the biochemistry, pharmacology, psychology and neurophysiology of schizophrenia and the mescalin phenomena are in preparation.

ground of memory to serve as a basis for understanding or fellow feeling. Words are uttered, but fail to enlighten. The things and events to which the symbols refer belong to mutually exclusive realms of experience.

To see ourselves as others see us is a most salutary gift. Hardly less important is the capacity to see others as they see themselves. But what if these others belong to a different species and inhabit a radically alien universe? For example, how can the sane get to know what it actually feels like to be mad? Or, short of being born again as a visionary, a medium, or a musical genius, how can we ever visit the worlds which, to Blake, to Swedenborg, to Johann Sebastian Bach, were home? And how can a man at the extreme limits of ectomorphy and cerebrotonia ever put himself in the place of one at the limits of endomorphy and viscerotonia, or, except within certain circumscribed areas, share the feelings of one who stands at the limits of mesomorphy and somatotonia? To the unmitigated behaviorist such questions, I suppose, are meaningless. But for those who theoretically believe what in practice they know to be true—namely, that there is an inside to experience as well as an outside—the problems posed are real problems, all the more grave for being, some completely insoluble, some soluble only in exceptional circumstances and by methods not available to everyone. Thus, it seems virtually certain that I shall never know what it feels like to be Sir John Falstaff or Joe Louis. On the other hand, it had always seemed to me possible that, through hypnosis, for example, or autohypnosis, by means of systematic meditation, or else by taking the appropriate drug, I might so change my ordinary mode of consciousness as to be able to know, from the inside, what the visionary, the medium, even the mystic were talking about.

From what I had read of the mescalin experience I was convinced in advance that the drug would admit me, at least for a few hours, into the kind of inner world described by Blake and Æ. But what I had expected did not happen. I had expected to lie with my eyes shut, looking at visions of many-colored geometries, of animated architectures, rich with gems and fabulously lovely, of landscapes with heroic figures, of symbolic dramas trembling perpetually on the verge of the ultimate revelation. But I had not reckoned, it was evident, with the idiosyncrasies of my mental make-up, the facts of my temperament, training and habits.

I am and, for as long as I can remember, I have always been a poor visualizer. Words, even the pregnant words of poets, do not evoke pictures in my mind. No hypnagogic visions greet me on the verge of sleep. When I recall something, the memory does not present itself to me as a vividly seen event or object. By an effort of the will, I can evoke a not very vivid image of what happened yesterday afternoon, of how the Lungarno used to look before the bridges were destroyed, of the Bayswater Road when the only buses were green and tiny and drawn by aged horses at three and a half miles an hour. But such images have little substance and absolutely no autonomous life of their own. They stand to real, perceived objects in the same relation as Homer's ghosts stood to the men of flesh and blood, who came to visit them in the shades. Only when I have a high temperature do my mental images come to independent life. To those in whom the faculty of visualization is strong my inner world must seem curiously drab, limited and uninteresting. This was the world—a poor thing but my own—which I expected to see transformed into something completely unlike itself.

The change which actually took place in that world was in no sense revolutionary. Half an hour after swallowing the drug I became aware of a slow dance of golden lights. A little later there were sumptuous red surfaces swelling and expanding from bright nodes of energy that vibrated with a continuously changing, patterned life. At another time the closing of my eyes revealed a complex of gray structures, within which pale bluish spheres kept emerging into intense solidity and, having emerged, would slide noiselessly upwards, out of sight. But at no time were there faces or forms of men or animals. I saw no landscapes, no enormous spaces, no magical growth and metamorphosis of buildings, nothing remotely like a drama or a parable. The other world to which mescalin admitted me was not the world of visions; it existed out there, in what I could see with my eyes open. The great change was in the realm of objective fact. What had happened to my subjective universe was relatively unimportant.

I took my pill at eleven. An hour and a half later, I was sitting in my study, looking intently at a small glass vase. The vase contained only three flowers—a full-blown Belle of Portugal rose, shell pink with a hint at every petal's base of a hotter, flamier hue; a large magenta and cream-colored carnation; and, pale purple at the end of its broken stalk, the bold heraldic blossom of an iris. Fortuitous and provisional, the little nosegay broke all the rules of traditional good taste. At breakfast that morning I had been struck by the lively dissonance of its colors. But that was no longer the point. I was not looking now at an unusual flower arrangement. I was seeing what Adam had seen on the morning of his creation—the miracle, moment by moment, of naked existence.

"Is it agreeable?" somebody asked. (During this part of the experiment, all conversations were recorded on a dictating machine, and it has been possible for me to refresh my memory of what was said.)

"Neither agreeable nor disagreeable," I answered. "It just *is*."

Istigkeit—wasn't that the word Meister Eckhart liked to use? "Is-ness." The Being of Platonic philosophy—except that Plato seems to have made the enormous, the grotesque mistake of separating Being from becoming and identifying it with the mathematical abstraction of the Idea. He could never, poor fellow, have seen a bunch of flowers shining with their own inner light and all but quivering under the pressure of the significance with which they were charged; could never have perceived that what rose and iris and carnation so intensely signified was nothing more, and nothing less, than what they were—a transience that was yet eternal life, a perpetual perishing that was at the same time pure Being, a bundle of minute, unique particulars in which, by some unspeakable and yet self-evident paradox, was to be seen the divine source of all existence.

I continued to look at the flowers, and in their living light I seemed to detect the qualitative equivalent of breathing—but of a breathing without returns to a starting point, with no recurrent ebbs but only a repeated flow from beauty to heightened beauty, from deeper to ever deeper meaning. Words like "grace" and "transfiguration" came to mind, and this, of course, was what, among other things, they stood for. My eyes traveled from the rose to the carnation, and from that feathery incandescence to the smooth scrolls of sentient amethyst which were the iris. The Beatific Vision, *Sat Chit Ananda,* Being-Awareness-Bliss—for the first time I understood, not on the verbal level, not by inchoate hints or at a distance, but precisely and completely what those prodigious syllables referred to. And then I remembered a passage I had read in one of Suzuki's essays. "What is the Dharma-Body of the Buddha?" ("The Dharma-Body of the Buddha" is another way of saying, Mind, Suchness, the Void, The Godhead.) The question is asked in a Zen monastery by an earnest and bewildered novice. And with the prompt irrelevance of one of the Marx Brothers, the Master answers, "The hedge at the bottom of the garden." "And the man who realizes this truth," the novice dubiously inquires, "what, may I ask, is he?" Groucho gives him a whack over the shoulders with his staff and answers, "A golden-haired lion."

It had been, when I read it, only a vaguely pregnant piece of nonsense. Now it was all as clear as day, as evident as Euclid. Of course the Dharma-Body of the Buddha was the hedge at the bottom of the garden. At the same time, and no less obviously, it was these flowers, it was anything that I—or rather the blessed Not-I, released for a moment from my throttling embrace—cared to look at. The books, for example, with which my study walls were lined. Like the flowers, they glowed, when I looked at them, with brighter colors, a profounder significance. Red books, like rubies; emerald books; books bound in white jade; books of agate; of aquamarine, of yellow topaz; lapis lazuli books whose color was so intense, so intrinsically meaningful, that they seemed to be on the point of leaving the shelves to thrust themselves more insistently on my attention.

"What about spatial relationships?" the investigator inquired, as I was looking at the books.

It was difficult to answer. True, the perspective looked rather odd, and the walls of the room no longer seemed to meet in right angles. But these were not the really important facts. The really important facts were that spatial relationships had ceased to matter very much and that my mind was perceiving the world in terms of other than spatial categories. At ordinary times the eye concerns itself with such problems as *Where?—How far?—How situated in relation to what?* In the mescalin experience the implied questions to which the eye responds are of another order. Place and distance cease to be of much interest. The mind does its perceiving in terms of intensity of existence, profundity of significance, relationships within a pattern. I saw the books, but was not at all concerned with their positions in space. What I noticed, what impressed itself upon my mind was the fact that all of them glowed with living light and that in some the glory was more manifest than in others. In this context position and the three dimensions were beside the point. Not, of course, that the category of space had been abolished. When I got up and walked about, I could do so quite normally, without misjudging the whereabouts of objects. Space was still there; but it had lost its predominance. The mind was primarily concerned, not with measures and locations, but with being and meaning.

And along with indifference to space there went an even more complete indifference to time.

"There seems to be plenty of it," was all I would answer, when the investigator asked me to say what I felt about time.

Plenty of it, but exactly how much was entirely irrelevant. I could, of course, have looked at my watch; but my watch, I knew, was in another universe. My actual experience had been, was still, of an indefinite duration or alternatively of a perpetual present made up of one continually changing apocalypse.

From the books the investigator directed my attention to the furniture. A small typing table stood in the center of the room; beyond it, from my point of view, was a wicker chair and beyond that a desk. The three pieces formed an intricate pattern of horizontals, uprights and diagonals—a pattern all the more interesting for not being interpreted in terms of spatial relationships. Table, chair and desk came together in a composition that was like something by Braque or Juan Gris, a still life recognizably related to the objective world, but rendered without depth, without any attempt at photographic realism. I was looking at my furniture, not as the utilitarian who has to sit on chairs, to write at desks and tables, and not as the cameraman or scientific recorder, but as the pure aesthete whose concern is only with forms and their relationships within the field of vision or the picture space. But as I looked, this purely aesthetic, Cubist's-eye view gave place to what I can only describe as the sacramental vision of reality. I was back where I had been when I was looking at the flowers—back in a world where everything shone with the Inner Light, and was infinite in its significance. The legs, for example, of that chair—how miraculous their tubularity, how supernatural their polished smoothness! I spent several minutes—or was it several centuries?—not merely gazing at those bamboo legs, but actually *being* them—or rather being myself in them; or, to be still more accurate (for "I" was not involved in the case, nor in a certain sense were "they") being my Not-self in the Not-self which was the chair.

Reflecting on my experience, I find myself agreeing with the eminent Cambridge philosopher, Dr. C. D. Broad, "that we should do well to consider much more seriously than we have hitherto been inclined to do the type of theory which Bergson put forward in connection with memory and sense perception. The suggestion is that the function of the brain and nervous system and sense organs is in the main *eliminative* and not productive. Each person is at each moment capable of remembering all that has ever happened to him and of perceiving everything that is happening everywhere in the universe. The function of the brain and nervous system is to protect us from being overwhelmed and confused by this mass of largely useless and irrelvant knowledge, by shutting out most of what we should otherwise perceive or remember at any moment, and leaving only that very small and special selection which is likely to be practically useful." According to such a theory, each one of us is potentially Mind at Large. But in so far as we are animals, our business is at all costs to survive. To make biological survival possible, Mind at Large has to be funneled through the reducing valve of the brain and nervous system. What comes out at the other end is a measly trickle of the kind of consciousness which will help us to stay alive on the surface of this particular planet. To formulate and express the contents of this reduced awareness, man has invented and endlessly elaborated those symbol-systems and implicit philosophies which we call languages. Every individual is at once the beneficiary and the victim of the linguistic tradition into which he has been born—the beneficiary inasmuch as language gives access to the accumulated records of other people's experience, the victim in so far as it confirms him in the belief that reduced awareness is the only awareness and as it bedevils his sense of reality, so that he is all too apt to take his concepts for data, his words for actual things. That which, in the language of religion, is called "this world" is the universe of reduced awareness, expressed, and, as it were, petrified by language. The various "other worlds," with which human beings erratically make contact are so many elements in the totality of the awareness belonging to Mind at Large. Most people, most of the time, know only what comes through the reducing valve and is consecrated as genuinely real by the local language. Certain persons, however, seem to be born with a kind of by-pass that circumvents the reducing valve. In others temporary by-passes may be acquired either spontaneously, or as the result of deliberate "spiritual exercises," or through hypnosis, or by means of drugs. Through these permanent or temporary by-passes there flows, not indeed the perception "of everything that is happening everywhere in the universe" (for the by-pass does not abolish the reducing valve, which still excludes the total content of Mind at Large), but something more than, and above all something different from, the carefully selected utilitarian material which our narrowed, individual minds regard as a complete, or at least sufficient, picture of reality.

The brain is provided with a number of enzyme systems which serve to co-ordinate its workings. Some of these enzymes regulate the supply of glucose to the brain cells. Mescalin inhibits the production of these enzymes and thus lowers the amount of glucose available to an organ that is in constant need of sugar. When mescalin reduces the brain's normal ration of sugar what happens? Too few cases have been observed, and therefore a comprehensive answer cannot yet be given. But what happens to the majority of the few who have taken mescalin under supervision can be summarized as follows.

1 The ability to remember and to "think straight" is little if at all reduced. (Listening to the recordings of my conversation under the influence of the drug, I cannot discover that I was then any stupider than I am at ordinary times.)

2 Visual impressions are greatly intensified and the eye recovers some of the perceptual innocence of childhood, when the sensum was not immediately and automatically subordinated to the concept. Interest in space is diminished and interest in time falls almost to zero.

3 Though the intellect remains unimpaired and though perception is enormously improved, the will suffers a profound change for the worse.

The mescalin taker sees no reason for doing anything in particular and finds most of the causes for which, at ordinary times, he was prepared to act and suffer, profoundly uninteresting. He can't be bothered with them, for the good reason that he has better things to think about.

4 These better things may be experienced (as I experienced them) "out there," or "in here," or in both worlds, the inner and the outer, simultaneously or successively. That they *are* better seems to be self-evident to all mescalin takers who come to the drug with a sound liver and an untroubled mind.

These effects of mescalin are the sort of effects you could expect to follow the administration of a drug having the power to impair the efficiency of the cerebral reducing valve. When the brain runs out of sugar, the undernourished ego grows weak, can't be bothered to undertake the necessary chores, and loses all interest in those spatial and temporal relationships which mean so much to an organism bent on getting on in the world. As Mind at Large seeps past the no longer watertight valve, all kinds of biologically useless things start to happen. In some cases there may be extra-sensory perceptions. Other persons discover a world of visionary beauty. To others again is revealed the glory, the infinite value and meaningfulness of naked existence, of the given, unconceptualized event. In the final stage of egolessness there is an "obscure knowledge" that All is in all—that All is actually each. This is as near, I take it, as a finite mind can ever come to "perceiving everything that is happening everywhere in the universe."

In this context, how significant is the enormous heightening, under mescalin, of the perception of color! For certain animals it is biologically very important to be able to distinguish certain hues. But beyond the limits of their utilitarian spectrum, most creatures are completely color blind. Bees, for example, spend most of their time "deflowering the fresh virgins of the spring"; but, as Von Frisch has shown, they can recognize only a very few colors. Man's highly developed color sense is a biological luxury—inestimably precious to him as an intellectual and spiritual being, but unnecessary to his survival as an animal. To judge by the adjectives which Homer puts into théir mouths, the heroes of the Trojan War hardly excelled the bees in their capacity to distinguish colors. In this respect, at least, mankind's advance has been prodigious.

Mescalin raises all colors to a higher power and makes the percipient aware of innumerable fine shades of difference, to which, at ordinary times, he is completely blind. It would seem that, for Mind at Large, the so-called secondary characters of things are primary. Unlike Locke, it evidently feels that colors are more important, better worth attending to, than masses, positions and dimensions. Like mescalin takers, many mystics perceive supernaturally brilliant colors, not only with the inward eye, but even in the objective world around them. Similar reports are made by psychics and sensitives. There are certain mediums to whom the mescalin taker's brief revelation is a matter, during long periods, of daily and hourly experience.

From this long but indispensable excursion into the realm of theory, we may now return to the miraculous facts—four bamboo chair legs in the middle of a room. Like Wordsworth's daffodils, they brought all manner of wealth—the gift, beyond price, of a new direct insight into the very Nature of Things, together with a more modest treasure of understanding in the field, especially, of the arts.

A rose is a rose is a rose. But these chair legs were chair legs were St. Michael and all angels. Four or five hours after the event, when the effects of a cerebral sugar shortage were wearing off, I was taken for a little tour of the city, which included a visit, towards sundown, to what is modestly claimed to be the World's Biggest Drug Store. At the back of the W.B.D.S., among the toys, the greeting cards and the comics, stood a row, surprisingly enough, of art books. I picked up the first volume that came to hand. It was on Van Gogh, and the picture at which the book opened was "The Chair"—that astounding portrait of a *Ding an Sich,* which the mad painter saw, with a kind of adoring terror, and tried to render on his canvas. But it was a task to which the power even of genius proved wholly inadequate. The chair Van Gogh had seen was obviously the same in essence as the chair I had seen. But, though incomparably more real that the chairs of ordinary perception, the chair in his picture remained no more than an unusually expressive symbol of the fact. The fact had been manifested Suchness; this was only an emblem. Such emblems are sources of true knowledge about the Nature of Things, and this true knowledge may serve to prepare the mind which accepts it for immediate insights on its own account. But that is all. However expressive, symbols can never be the things they stand for.

It would be interesting, in this context, to make a study of the works of art available to the great knowers of Suchness. What sort of pictures did Eckhart look at? What sculptures and paintings played a part in the religious experience of St. John of the Cross, of Hakuin, of Hui-neng, of William Law? The questions are beyond my power to answer; but I strongly suspect that most of the great knowers of Suchness paid very little attention to art—some refusing to have anything to do with it at all, others being content with what a critical eye would regard as second-rate, or even tenth-rate, works. (To a person whose transfigured and transfiguring mind can see the All in every *this,* the first-rateness or tenth-rateness of even a religious painting will be a matter of the most sovereign indifference.) Art, I suppose, is only for beginners, or else for those resolute dead-enders, who have made up their minds to be content with the *ersatz* of Suchness, with symbols rather than with what they signify, with the elegantly composed recipe in lieu of actual dinner.

I returned the Van Gogh to its rack and picked up the volume standing next to it. It was a book on Botticelli. I turned the pages. "The Birth of Venus"—never one of my favorites. "Mars and Venus," that loveliness so passionately denounced by poor Ruskin at the height of his long-drawn sexual tragedy. The marvelously rich and intricate "Calumny of Apelles." And then a somewhat less familiar and not very good picture, "Judith." My attention was arrested and I gazed in fascination, not at the pale neurotic heroine or her attendant, not at the victim's hairy head or the vernal landscape in the background, but at the purplish silk of Judith's pleated bodice and long wind-blown skirts.

This was something I had seen before—seen that very morning, between the flowers and the furniture, when I looked down by chance, and went on passionately staring by choice, at my own crossed legs. Those folds in the trousers—what a labyrinth of endlessly significant complexity! And the texture of the gray flannel—how rich, how deeply, mysteriously sumptuous! And here they were again, in Botticelli's picture.

Civilized human beings wear clothes, therefore there can be no portraiture, no mythological or historical story-telling without representations of folded textiles. But though it may account for the origins, mere tailoring can never explain the luxuriant development of drapery as a major theme of all the plastic arts. Artists, it is obvious, have always loved drapery for its own sake—or, rather, for their own. When you paint or carve drapery, you are painting or carving forms which, for all practical purposes, are non-representational—the kind of unconditioned forms on which artists even in the most naturalistic tradition like to let themselves go. In the average Madonna or Apostle the strictly human, fully representational element accounts for about ten per cent of the whole. All the rest consists of many colored variations on the inexhaustible theme of crumpled wool or linen. And these non-representational nine-tenths of a Madonna or an Apostle may be just as important qualitatively as they are in quantity. Very often they set the tone of the whole work of art, they state the key in which the theme is being rendered, they express the mood, the temperament, the attitude to life of the artist. Stoical serenity reveals itself in the smooth surfaces, the broad untortured folds of Piero's draperies. Torn between fact and wish, between cynicism and idealism, Bernini tempers the all but caricatural verisimilitude of his faces with enormous sartorial abstractions, which are the embodiment, in stone or bronze, of the everlasting commonplaces of rhetoric—the heroism, the holiness, the sublimity to which mankind perpetually aspires, for the most part in vain. And here are El Greco's disquietingly visceral skirts and mantles; here are the sharp, twisting, flame-like folds in which Cosimo Tura clothes his figures: in the first, traditional spirituality breaks down into a nameless physiological yearning; in the second, there writhes an agonized sense of the world's essential strangeness and hostility. Or consider Watteau; his men and women play lutes, get ready for balls and harlequinades, embark, on velvet lawns and under noble trees, for the Cythera of every lover's dream; their enormous melancholy and the flayed, excruciating sensibility of their creator find expression, not in the actions recorded, not in the gestures, and the faces portrayed, but in the relief and texture of their taffeta skirts, their satin capes and doublets. Not an inch of smooth surface here, not a moment of peace or confidence, only a silken wilderness of countless tiny pleats and wrinkles, with an incessant modulation—inner uncertainty rendered with the perfect assurance of a master hand—of tone into tone, of one indeterminate color into another. In life, man proposes, God disposes. In the plastic arts the proposing is done by the subject matter; that which disposes is ultimately the artist's temperament, proximately (at least in portraiture, history and genre) the carved or painted drapery. Between them, these two may decree that a *fête galante* shall move to tears, that a crucifixion shall be serene to the point of cheerfulness, that a stigmatization shall be almost intolerably sexy, that the likeness of a prodigy of female brainlessness (I am thinking now of Ingres' incomparable Mme. Moitessier) shall express the austerest, the most uncompromising intellectuality.

But this is not the whole story. Draperies, as I had now discovered, are much more than devices for the introduction of non-representational forms into naturalistic paintings and sculptures. What the rest of us see only under the influence of mescalin, the artist is congenitally equipped to see all the time. His perception is not limited to what is biologically or socially useful. A little of the knowledge belonging to Mind at Large oozes past the reducing valve of brain and ego, into his consciousness. It is a knowledge of the intrinsic significance of every existent. For the artist as for the mescalin taker draperies are living hieroglyphs that stand in some peculiarly expressive way for the unfathomable mystery of pure being. More even than the chair, though less perhaps than those wholly supernatural flowers, the folds of my gray flannel trousers were charged with "is-ness." To what they owed this privileged status, I cannot say. Is it, perhaps, because the forms of folded drapery are so strange and dramatic that they catch the eye and in this way force the miraculous fact of sheer existence upon the attention? Who knows? What is important is less the reason for the experience than the experience itself. Poring over Judith's skirts, there in the World's Biggest Drug Store, I knew that Botticelli—and not Botticelli alone, but many others too—had looked at draperies with the same transfigured and transfiguring eyes as had been mine that morning. They had seen the *Istigkeit,* the Allness and Infinity of folded cloth and had done their best to render it in paint or stone. Necessarily, of course, without success. For the glory and the wonder of pure existence belong to another order, beyond the power of even the highest art to express. But in Judith's skirt I could clearly see what, if I had been a painter of genius, I might have made of my old gray flannels. Not much, heaven knows, in comparison with the reality; but enough to delight generation after generation of beholders, enough to make them understand at least a little of the true significance of what, in our pathetic imbecility, we call "mere things" and disregard in favor of television.

"This is how one ought to see," I kept saying as I looked down at my trousers, or glanced at the jeweled books in the shelves, at the legs of my infinitely more that Van-Goghian chair. "This is how one ought to see, how things really are." And yet there were reservations. For if one always saw like this, one would never want to do anything else. Just looking, just being the divine Not-self of flower, of book, of chair, of flannel. That would be enough. But in that case what about other people? What about human relations? In the recording of that morning's conversations I find the question constantly repeated, "What about human relations?" How could one reconcile this timeless bliss of seeing as one ought to see with the temporal duties of doing what one ought to do and feeling as one ought to feel? "One ought to be able," I said, "to see these trousers as infinitely important and human beings as still more infinitely important." One ought—but in practice it seemed to be impossible. This participation in the manifest glory of things left no room, so to speak, for the ordinary, the necessary concerns of human existence, above all for concerns involving persons. For persons are selves and, in one respect at least, I was now a Not-self, simultaneously perceiving and being the Not-self of the things around me. To this new-born Not-self, the behavior, the appearance, the very thought of the self it had momentarily ceased to be, and of other selves, its one-time fellows, seemed not indeed distasteful (for distastefulness was not one of the categories in terms of which I was thinking), but enormously irrelevant. Compelled by the investigator to analyze and report on what I was doing (and how I longed to be left alone with Eternity in a flower, Infinity in four chair legs and the Absolute in the folds of a pair of flannel trousers!), I realized that I was deliberately avoiding the eyes of those who were with me in the room, deliberately refraining from being too much aware of them. One was my wife, the other a man I respected and greatly liked; but both belonged to the world from which, for the moment, mescalin had delivered me—the world of selves, of time, of moral judgments and utilitarian considerations, the world (and it was this aspect of human life which I wished, above all else, to forget) of self-assertion, of cocksureness, of overvalued words and idolatrously worshiped notions.

At this stage of the proceedings I was handed a large colored reproduction of the well-known self-portrait by Cézanne—the head and shoulders of a man in a large straw hat, red-cheeked, red-lipped, with rich black whiskers and a dark unfriendly eye. It is a magnificent painting; but it was not as a painting that I now saw it. For the head promptly took on a third dimension and came to life as a small goblin-like man looking out through a window in the page before me. I started to laugh. And when they asked me why, "What pretensions!" I kept repeating. "Who on earth does he think he is?" The question was not addressed to Cézanne in particular, but to the human species at large. Who did they all think they were?

"It's like Arnold Bennett in the Dolomites," I said, suddenly remembering a scene, happily immortalized in a snapshot, of A.B., some four or five years before his death, toddling along a wintry road at Cortina d'Ampezzo. Around him lay the virgin snow; in the background was a more than gothic aspiration of red crags. And there was dear, kind, unhappy A.B., consciously overacting the role of his favorite character in fiction, himself, the Card in person. There he went, toddling slowly in the bright Alpine sunshine, his thumbs in the armholes of a yellow waistcoat which bulged, a little lower down, with the graceful curve of a Regency bow window at Brighton—his head thrown back as though to aim some stammered utterance, howitzer-like, at the blue dome of heaven. What he actually said, I have forgotten; but what his whole manner, air and posture fairly shouted was, "I'm as good as those damned mountains." And in some ways, of course, he was infinitely better; but not, as he knew very well, in the way his favorite character in fiction liked to imagine.

Successfully (whatever that may mean) or unsuccessfully, we all overact the part of our favorite character in fiction. And the fact, the almost infinitely unlikely fact, of actually being Cézanne makes no difference. For the consummate painter, with his little pipeline to Mind at Large by-passing the brain valve and ego-filter, was also and just as genuinely this whiskered goblin with the unfriendly eye.

For relief I turned back to the folds in my trousers. "This is how one ought to see," I repeated yet again. And I might have added, "These are the sort of things one ought to look at." Things without pretensions, satisfied to be merely themselves, sufficient in their Suchness, not acting a part, not trying, insanely, to go it alone, in isolation from the Dharma-Body, in Luciferian defiance of the grace of God.

"The nearest approach to this," I said, "would be a Vermeer."

Yes, a Vermeer. For that mysterious artist was trebly gifted—with the vision that perceives the Dharma-Body as the hedge at the bottom of the garden, with the talent to render as much of that vision as the limitations of human capacity permit, and with the prudence to confine himself in his paintings to the more manageable aspects of reality; for though Vermeer represented human beings, he was always a painter of still life. Cézanne, who told his female sitters to do their best to look like apples, tried to paint portraits in the same spirit. But his pippin-like women are more nearly related to Plato's Ideas than to the Dharma-Body in the hedge. They are Eternity and Infinity seen, not in sand or flower, but in the abstractions of some very superior brand of geometry. Vermeer never asked his girls to look like apples. On the contrary, he insisted on their being girls to the very limit—but always with the proviso that they refrain from behaving girlishly. They might sit or quietly stand but never giggle, never display self-consciousness, never say their prayers or pine for absent sweethearts, never gossip, never gaze enviously at other women's babies, never flirt, never love or hate or work. In the act of doing any of these things they would doubtless become more intensely themselves, but would cease, for that very reason, to manifest their divine essential Not-self. In Blake's phrase, the doors of Vermeer's perception were only partially cleansed. A single panel had become almost perfectly transparent; the rest of the door was still muddy. The essential Not-self could be perceived very clearly in things and in living creatures on the hither side of good and evil. In human beings it was visible only when they were in repose, their minds untroubled, their bodies motionless. In these circumstances Vermeer could see Suchness in all its heavenly beauty—could see and, in some small measure, render it in a subtle and sumptuous still life. Vermeer is undoubtedly the greatest painter of human still lives. But there have been others, for example, Vermeer's French contemporaries, the Le Nain brothers. They set out, I suppose, to be genre painters; but what they actually produced was a series of human still lives, in which their cleansed perception of the infinite significance of all things is rendered not, as with Vermeer, by subtle enrichment of color and texture, but by a heightened clarity, an obsessive distinctness of form, within an austere, almost monochromatic tonality. In our own day we have had Vuillard, the painter, at his

best, of unforgettably splendid pictures of the Dharma-Body manifested in a
bourgeois bedroom, of the Absolute blazing away in the midst of some
stockbroker's family in a suburban garden, taking tea.

> Ce qui fait que l'ancien bandagiste renie
> Le comptoir dont le faste alléchait les passants,
> C'est son jardin d'Auteuil, où, veufs de tout encens,
> Les Zinnias ont l'air d'être en tôle vernie.

For Laurent Tailhade the spectacle was merely obscene. But if the retired rubber
goods merchant had sat still enough, Vuillard would have seen in him only the
Dharma-Body, would have painted, in the zinnias, the goldfish pool, the villa's
Moorish tower and Chinese lanterns, a corner of Eden before the Fall.

But meanwhile my question remained unanswered. How was this
cleansed perception to be reconciled with a proper concern with human relations,
with the necessary chores and duties, to say nothing of charity and practical
compassion? The age-old debate between the actives and the contemplatives was
being renewed—renewed, so far as I was concerned, with an unprecedented
poignancy. For until this morning I had known contemplation only in its humbler,
its more ordinary forms—as discursive thinking; as a rapt absorption in poetry or
painting or music; as a patient waiting upon those inspirations, without which
even the prosiest writer cannot hope to accomplish anything; as occasional
glimpses, in Nature, of Wordsworth's "something far more deeply interfused"; as
systematic silence leading, sometimes, to hints of an "obscure knowledge." But
now I knew contemplation at its height. At its height, but not yet in its fullness.
For in its fullness the way of Mary includes the way of Martha and raises it, so to
speak, to its own higher power. Mescalin opens up the way of Mary, but shuts the
door on that of Martha. It gives access to contemplation—but to a contemplation
that is incompatible with action and even with the will to action, the very thought
of action. In the intervals between his revelations the mescalin taker is apt to feel
that, though in one way everything is supremely as it should be, in another there is
something wrong. His problem is essentially the same as that which confronts the
quietist, the *arhat* and, on another level, the landscape painter and the painter of
human still lives. Mescalin can never solve that problem; it can only pose it,
apocalyptically, for those to whom it had never before presented itself. The full
and final solution can be found only by those who are prepared to implement the
right kind of *Weltanschauung* by means of the right kind of behavior and the right
kind of constant and unstrained alertness. Over against the quietist stands the
active-contemplative, the saint, the man who, in Eckhart's phrase, is ready to
come down from the seventh heaven in order to bring a cup of water to his sick
brother. Over against the *arhat,* retreating from appearances into an entirely
transcendental Nirvana, stands the Bodhisattva, for whom Suchness and the
world of contingencies are one, and for whose boundless compassion every one of
those contingencies is an occasion not only for transfiguring insight, but also for
the most practical charity. And in the universe of art, over against Vermeer and
the other painters of human still lives, over against the masters of Chinese and

Japanese landscape painting, over against Constable and Turner, against Sisley and Seurat and Cézanne, stands the all-inclusive art of Rembrandt. These are enormous names, inaccessible eminences. For myself, on this memorable May morning, I could only be grateful for an experience which had shown me, more clearly than I had ever seen it before, the true nature of the challenge and the completely liberating response.

Let me add, before we leave this subject, that there is no form of contemplation, even the most quietistic, which is without its ethical values. Half at least of all morality is negative and consists in keeping out of mischief. The Lord's Prayer is less than fifty words long, and six of those words are devoted to asking God not to lead us into temptation. The one-sided contemplative leaves undone many things that he ought to do; but to make up for it, he refrains from doing a host of things he ought not to do. The sum of evil, Pascal remarked, would be much diminished if men could only learn to sit quietly in their rooms. The contemplative whose perception has been cleansed does not have to stay in his room. He can go about his business, so completely satisfied to see and be a part of the divine Order of Things that he will never even be tempted to indulge in what Traherne called "the dirty Devices of the world." When we feel ourselves to be sole heirs of the universe, when "the sea flows in our veins . . . and the stars are our jewels," when all things are perceived as infinite and holy, what motive can we have for covetousness or self-assertion, for the pursuit of power or the drearier forms of pleasure? Contemplatives are not likely to become gamblers, or procurers, or drunkards; they do not as a rule preach intolerance, or make war; do not find it necessary to rob, swindle or grind the faces of the poor. And to these enormous negative virtues we may add another which, though hard to define, is both positive and important. The *arhat* and the quietist may not practice contemplation in its fullness; but if they practice it at all, they may bring back enlightening reports of another, a transcendent country of the mind; and if they practice it in the height, they will become conduits through which some beneficent influence can flow out of that other country into a world of darkened selves, chronically dying for lack of it . . . .

From **Life Against Death**
NORMAN O. BROWN

Sexuality and Childhood

As we saw in the first chapter, it is in our unconscious repressed desires that we shall find the essence of our being, the clue to our neurosis (as long as reality is repressive), and the clue to what we might become if reality ceased to repress. The results of Freud's exploration of the unconscious can be summarized in two formulae: Our repressed desires are the desires we had, unrepressed, in childhood; and they are sexual desires.

In analyzing neurotic symptoms and dreams, Freud found that they invariably contained a nucleus representing a return or regression to the experiences of early childhood. But, according to the whole hypothesis of repression, the consciousness which comes into conflict with the unconscious is the product of education. It follows that children are in some sense unrepressed. Or, to put it another way, in the child the conscious and the unconscious are not yet separated. It was therefore natural to infer that the adult, in flight from repressive reality in dreams and neurosis, regresses to his own childhood because it represents a period of happier days before repression took place. Furthermore, Freud found that the analysis of neurotic symptoms invariably led not only to the patient's childhood but also to his sexual life. The symptom is not merely a substitute for a pleasure denied by reality, but more specifically a substitute for sexual satisfaction denied by reality. But the repressed sexual desires whose presence was indicated were for the most part of the kind labeled "abnormal" or "perverse." Thus the analysis of neurosis required the construction of a theory of sexuality which would account for perverted as well as normal sexuality and would trace both to their origins in childhood.

The axiom on which Freud constructed this extension of his basic hypothesis is that the pattern of normal adult sexuality is not a natural (biological) necessity but a cultural phenomenon. The pattern of normal adult sexuality—the mutual love of man and woman and all the variations of the pattern—represents a particular organization of certain possibilities given in the human organism. This sexual organization is made possible by the social organization which marks the transition from ape to man, and simultaneously it makes the social organization possible. Man's sexual organization and his social organization are so deeply interconnected that we cannot say which came first, but can only assume a simultaneous evolution (whether sudden or gradual) of both.

The critical institution in the transition from ape to man, the link between man's sexual and social organization, is parenthood, with the prolonged maintenance of children in a condition of helpless dependence. That parenthood implies family organization of some sort or another, and that family organization is the nucleus of all social organization, are anthropological axioms which Freud accepted and built into his structure. Freud's originality consists in drawing attention to the consequences of prolonged parenthood and prolonged infantile dependence on the sexual life of both parents and children. As far as the parents are concerned, it is clear that while adult sexuality serves the socially useful purpose of breeding children, it is for the individual in some sense an end in itself as a source of pleasure—according to Freud, the highest pleasure. Adult sexuality, in so far as it is restricted by rules designed to maintain the institution of the family and in so far as the desire for sexual satisfaction is diverted and exploited for the purpose of maintaining a socially useful institution, is a clear instance of that subordination of the pleasure-principle to the reality-principle which is repression; as such it is rejected by the unconscious essence of the human being and therefore leads to neurosis.

Prolonged infancy has even more far-reaching consequences. On the one hand, infancy is protected from the harshness of reality by parental care; it represents a period of privileged irresponsibility and freedom from the domination of the reality-principle. This privileged irresponsibility permits and promotes an early blossoming of the essential desires of the human being, without repression and under the sign of the pleasure-principle. On the other hand, the infant's objective dependence on parental, especially maternal, care promotes a dependent attitude toward reality and inculcates a passive (dependent) need to be loved, which colors all subsequent interpersonal relationships. This psychological vulnerability is subsequently exploited to extract submission to social authority and to the reality-principle in general.

Thus prolonged infancy shapes human desires in two contradictory directions: on the one hand, on the subjective side, toward omnipotent indulgence in pleasure freed from the limitations of reality; on the other hand, on the objective side, toward powerless dependence on other people. The two tendencies come into conflict because the early experience of freedom and absorption in pleasure must succumb to the recognition of the reality-principle, in a capitulation enforced by parental authority under the threat of loss of parental love. And since the pleasure-principle is forced to capitulate against its will and for reasons which the child does not understand, under circumstances which reproduce its primal experiences of helpless dependence (anxiety), the capitulation can be accomplished only by repression. Hence it constitutes a trauma from which the individual never recovers psychologically. But in the unconscious the repressed dreams of omnipotent indulgence in pleasure persist, as the nucleus of man's universal neurosis and his restless discontent, the *cor irrequietum* of St. Augustine. The infantile conflict between actual impotence and dreams of omnipotence is also the basic theme of the universal history of mankind. And in both conflicts—in the history of the individual and the history of the race—the stakes are the meaning of love.

With his rude, persistent demand for the bodily origin of spiritual things, Freud starts not with love but with sexuality. But the man who discussed what he called the sexual life of children, and who insisted on the sexual character of thumbsucking, must have had a special definition of sexuality. In fact, Freud's definition of the sexual instinct shows that he means something very general. It is the energy or desire with which the human being pursues pleasure, with the further specification that the pleasure sought is the pleasurable activity of an organ of the human body. He attributed the capacity of yielding such pleasure (an erotogenic quality, he calls it) to all parts of the surface of the human body and also to the internal organs. The organ in question may be the genital, or it may be the mouth, as in thumb-sucking, or it may be the eyes, as in the delight of seeing. If sex is so defined, there will surely be little disposition to deny that infants do have a sexual life, or even that sex in this sense is their chief aim. Infants are naturally absorbed in themselves and in their own bodies; they are in love with themselves; in Freudian terminology, their orientation is narcissistic. Infants are ignorant of the serious business of life (the reality-principle) and therefore know no guide except the pleasure-principle, making pleasurable activity of their own body their sole aim. And since childhood is a period of real immunity from the serious business of life, children are really in a position to obtain pleasure from the activity of their bodies to an extent which the adult is not. So Freud's definition of sexuality entails the proposition that infants have a richer sexual life than adults.

If we grant that children pursue pleasurable activity of their bodies, we ask why this must be called sexual. The answer is that Freud is offering a genetic, historical explanation of adult sexuality, tracing it to its origin in childhood. On general grounds, because of his general notion of the individual psyche as a historically evolving and historically determined organization, Freud could only reject the idea that the powerful adult sexual drive appeared suddenly from nowhere at the age of puberty. And the evidence of dreams and neurotic symptoms pointed unmistakably to the childhood origin of the repressed sexuality of the adult. Now to say that the infantile pattern of seeking pleasurable activity of the body is sexual is equivalent to saying that this is the infantile pattern which develops into adult sexuality. Freud then found that this hypothesis not only explained the prominence of sexual themes in the repressed unconscious (in dreams and symptoms) but also accounted for the adult sexual perversions, thus satisfying the basic desiderata for an adequate theory of sexuality.

If normal adult sexuality is a pattern which has grown out of the infantile delight in the pleasurable activity of all parts of the human body, then what was originally a much wider capacity for pleasure in the body has been narrowed in range, concentrated on one particular (the genital) organ, and subordinated to an aim derived not from the pleasure-principle but from the reality-principle, namely, propagation (in Freudian terminology, the genital function). Then the pattern of normal adult sexuality (in Freud's terminology, genital organization) is a tyranny of one component in infantile sexuality, a tyranny which suppresses some of the other components altogether and subordinates the rest to itself. (We shall see later that genital organization is constructed not by the sexual instinct but by the death instinct.) But the pattern of normal adult sexuality can exist only on condition that the discared pattern of infantile sexuality continues to exist side by side with it, and in conflict with it, in the repressed unconscious.

The discarded elements of infantile sexuality are, judged by the standard of normal adult sexuality, perverse. The adult sexual perversions, like normal adult sexuality, are well-organized tyrannies: they too represent an exaggerated concentration on one of the many erotic potentialities present in the human body, which are all actively explored in infancy. The manner of this tyranny, as well as the close connection between normal and perverted sexuality, is illustrated by the fact that various erotic activities, which are called perversions if they are pursued as substitutes for the normal sexual act, are called legitimate if they are subordinated as preliminaries to the normal sexual aim. Children, on the other hand, explore in indiscriminate and anarchistic fashion all the erotic potentialities of the human body. In Freudian terms, children are polymorphously perverse. But if infantile sexuality, judged by the standard of normal adult sexuality, is perverse, by the same token normal adult sexuality, judged by the standard of infantile sexuality, is an unnatural restriction of the erotic potentialities of the human body.

Freud's notion of normal adult sexuality (genital organization) as an unnatural tyranny is so contrary to our usual way of thinking that it needs to be elaborated. We usually think of the pattern of normal adult sexuality as given by nature, as a biological necessity. In other words, we accept the subordination of sexual activity to the purpose of reproduction as a natural state of affairs. In what sense, then, does Freud call it unnatural? Is not subordination to the reproductive function characteristic of sexuality wherever it appears, not only in human beings but also in animals and even plants? Adult animals seem to have what Freud calls genital organization. Will Freud say that in their case genital organization is an unnatural tyranny?

These objections take us to the root problem of the distinction between men and animals. Psychoanalysis must maintain that there is a qualitative distinction between men and animals; but the distinction is based on what is perhaps only a quantitative phenomenon, namely, the peculiar prolongation of infancy in the human species. In the case of man, the prolongation of infancy and the postponement of puberty give infantile sexuality a longer period in which to mature, and at the same time parental care shelters it from the reality-principle. Under these conditions infantile sexuality achieves a full bloom to which there can be no parallel in other species of animals. Hence there is a conflict in the sexual life of man, as there is not in other animals. In man infantile sexuality is repressed and never outgrown; repression (and consequently neurosis) distinguishes man from the other animals. The result is that genital organization is a tyranny in man because his peculiar infancy has left him with a lifelong allegiance (i.e., fixation) to the pattern of infantile sexuality.

Thus Freud's theory of infantile sexuality is an essential part of his theory of neurosis, so that he puts this concept on the same level of importance as his concept of repression and the unconscious, and says that psychoanalysis stands or falls by the expansion of the idea of the "sexual function" as opposed to the narrower one of a "genital function." The therapeutic value of the concept of infantile sexuality as an aid in the psychiatric treatment of those individuals whose neurosis has reached the point of incapacitating them for practical living is not the issue here. What matters is the flood of light which the concept of infantile sexuality throws on the universal neurosis of mankind and on his ultimate nature and destiny.

In Freud's theory of infantile sexuality there is first of all a critique of the genital function and an implied rejection of genital intercourse—"free love" and the orgasm—as a solution to the sexual problem. Not only is there an implied critique of D. H. Lawrence; there is an implied critique of superficial followers of Freud himself, and even some great ones (Abraham, Reich, Fenichel), who have idealized the "genital character" as a way out of the human neurosis. Thus Fenichel: "The ability to obtain full satisfaction through genital orgasm makes the physiological regulation of sexuality possible and thus puts an end to the damming up of instinctual energies, with its unfortunate effects on the person's behavior." This appearance of finding the solution to the world's problems in the genital has done much to discredit psychoanalysis: mankind, from history and from personal experience, knows better. How perilous the pitfalls are that lie on both sides of the psychoanalytical path can be seen in the sad career of Wilhelm Reich. A man with keen insight into the sociological implications of psychoanalysis, he foundered on the theory of infantile sexuality (as do the neo-Freudians) and ended up in a glorification of the orgasm as the solution to all social and bodily ailments.

Freud sees conflict—in his earlier theory, between the pleasure-principle and the reality-principle; in his later theory, between Eros and Death—in the genital act itself. He distinguishes fore-pleasure and end-pleasure in sexual intercourse. The fore-pleasure is the preliminary play with all parts of the body, and represents a perpetuation of the pure polymorphous perverse play of infantile sexuality. The end-pleasure in the orgasm is purely genital and post-pubertal.

From the Freudian point of view the subordination of fore-pleasure to end-pleasure in sexual intercourse is a compromise concealing a conflict between the desire of the immortal child in us for pure polymorphous play and the reality-principle which imposes genital organization on us. This conflict explains the fact that while it is not true, as the Church father said, that *post coitum omne animal triste,* it is true of the human animal: the immortal child in us is frustrated, even in the sexual act, by the tyranny of genital organization. Hence the attempt to overthrow genital organization in certain practices of mysticism—mysticism being able, as Freud said, "to grasp certain relations in the deeper layers of the ego and the id which would otherwise be inaccessible." The heretical Christian sect known as Adamites, who sought to recapture in this life the innocent eroticism of Adam before the Fall, practiced *coitus reservatus,* intercourse without orgasm, that is to say, pure fore-pleasure. If he knew psychoanalysis, Needham would not be so puzzled that in Taoist mysticism "*coitus reservatus* should have been considered so valuable for mental health."

For Freud, the clue not only to normal adult sexuality but to our whole repressed and hidden ultimate essence lies in infantile sexuality. This is not a proposition to which we take kindly. Ignorance and fear, both of them the results of repression, together with the noble illusion, fostered by our higher aspirations, that we are all soul and no body, set in motion one or another of a number of mechanisms of intellectual flight whenever the topic of sexuality is taken seriously. If deference to the scientific attitude has induced a certain broad- or open-mindedness toward the general topic, the specific details are more than we can take, and we slip into the evasion of abhorrence or amusement. We are likely to withdraw our willingness to listen when we are told that infantile sexuality is polymorphously perverse. And Freud must mean that polymorphous perversity is the pattern of our deepest desires. How can this proposition be taken seriously?

If we divest ourselves of the prejudice surrounding the "perverse," if we try to be objective and analyze what infantile sexuality is in itself, we must return again to the definition. Infantile sexuality is the pursuit of pleasure obtained through the activity of any and all organs of the human body. So defined, the ultimate essence of our desires and our being is nothing more or less than delight in the active life of all the human body. That this is Freud's notion becomes abundantly clear if we examine the specific nature of the "perverse" components in infantile sexuality. They include the pleasure of touching, of seeing, of muscular activity, and even the passion for pain. It is therefore perfectly consistent, and implies no change of view, when in his later writings Freud added the term "life instinct" as synonymous with what he in other contexts called "the sexual instinct," "Eros," or "libido." And there is no difference between Freud's notion of the ultimate essence of the human being and William Blake's when he said, "Energy is the only life, and is from the Body. . . . Energy is Eternal Delight." As with the concept of repression and the unconscious, so in his concept of the libido Freud appears less as an inventor of unheard-of novelties than as one who grasped irrational and scientific form intuitions which have haunted the imagination of poets and philosophers throughout the modern or Romantic period of our intellectual history.

Freud and Blake are asserting that the ultimate essence of our being remains in our unconscious secretly faithful to the principle of pleasure, or, as Blake calls it, delight. To say this is to call in question the psychological assumptions upon which our Western morality has been built. For two thousand years or more man has been subjected to a systematic effort to transform him into an ascetic animal. He remains a pleasure-seeking animal. Parental discipline, religious denunciation of bodily pleasure, and philosophic exaltation of the life of reason have all left man overtly docile, but secretly in his unconscious unconvinced, and therefore neurotic. Man remains unconvinced because in infancy he tasted the fruit of the tree of life, and knows, that it is good, and never forgets.

Freud is also asserting that in spite of two thousand years of higher education based on the notion that man is essentially a soul for mysterious accidental reasons imprisoned in a body, man remains incurably obtuse and still secretly thinks of himself as first and foremost a body. Our repressed desires are not just for delight, but specifically for delight in the fulfillment of the life of our own bodies. Children, at the stage of early infancy which Freud thinks critical, are unable to distinguish between their souls and their bodies; in Freudian terminology, they are their own ideal. Children are also unable to make the distinction—fundamental for culture, the reality-principle, and the serious business of life—between higher and lower functions and parts of the body. They have not acquired that sense of shame which, according to the Biblical story, expelled mankind from Paradise, and which, presumably, would be discarded if paradise were regained. Neurotic symptoms, with their fixation on perversions and obscenities, demonstrate the refusal of the unconscious essence of our being to acquiesce in the dualism of flesh and spirit, higher and lower.

Thus Freud's doctrine of infantile sexuality, rightly understood, is essentially a scientific reformulation and reaffirmation of the religious and poetical theme of the innocence of childhood. Freud of course neither advocates nor thinks possible a return to a state of innocence; he is simply saying that childhood remains man's indestructible goal. His pessimism is ultimately based on his inability to see how this goal is reconcilable with man's equally deep commitment to culture and cultural progress. With this qualification, it is true to say that Freud takes with absolute seriousness the proposition of Jesus: "Except ye become as little children, ye can in no wise enter the kingdom of heaven." As a religious ideal, the innocence of childhood has turned out to resist assimilation into the rational-theological tradition. Only mystics and heretics like St. Francis and Jacob Boehme have made Christ's ideal their own. Poets like Blake and Rilke have affirmed its secular validity. Rousseau attempted to grasp it in philosophic-rational terms. Freud formulated it as an indispensable axiom of scientific psychology.

This concept of childhood enabled Freud to grasp a fundamental form of human activity in the world over and beyond the economic activity and struggle for existence dictated by the reality-principle. For children on the one hand pursue pleasure: on the other hand they are active; their pleasure is in the active life of the human body. Then what is the pattern of activity, free from work, the serious business of life, and the reality-principle, which is adumbrated in the life of children? The answer is that children play.

Freud is not merely referring to all the activities conventionally recognized as children's play; he is also making a structural analysis of the infantile activities which he insisted were sexual and perverse, of which thumb-sucking is the prototype. In early infancy the child, according to Freud, inevitably takes his own body as his sexual object; in doing so, he plays with it. Play is the essential character of activity governed by the pleasure-principle rather than the reality-principle. Play is "purposeless yet in some sense meaningful." It is the same thing if we say that play is the erotic mode of activity. Play is that activity which, in the delight of life, unites man with the objects of his love, as is indeed evident from the role of play in normal adult genital activity. But according to Freud, the ultimate essence of our being is erotic and demands activity according to the pleasure-principle.

Freud has thus put into his science the famous conclusion of Schiller's *Letters on the Aesthetic Education of Man:* "Man only plays when in the full meaning of the word he is a man, and he is only completely a man when he plays." And, from another point of view, Sartre says: "As soon as a man apprehends himself as free and wishes to use his freedom . . . then his activity is play." Sartre appreciates the concept of play because of his concern with the problem of existential freedom: Schiller appreciated it because of his concern with the aesthetic nature of man. But the same notion of play can be and has been reached by minds operating within the Christian religious tradition, and taking the Christian notion of redemption and regeneration of the flesh seriously: for example, the fountainhead of Protestant mystical theology, Jacob Boehme. I quote from H. H. Brinton:

In giving the will primacy over the intellect Boehme's system makes it supremely difficult to define the nature of the *summum bonum,* which is the end of all action. The essence of will is purposeful activity yet such activity is generated by want. How then can we have activity as a final goal? Boehme answers by calling the perfect state "play." In "play" life expresses itself in its fullness; therefore play as an end means that life itself has intrinsic value. . . . When Boehme is speaking of God's life as it is in itself he refers to it as "play." . . . Adam ought to have been content to play with nature in Paradise. "As God plays with the time of this outward world, so also should the inward divine man play with the outward in the revealed wonders of God in this world, and open the Divine Wisdom in all creatures, each according to its property." Adam fell when this play became serious business.

Boehme had the divine naïveté to take the Christian promise of the regeneration of the flesh, the perfection of man in the flesh, seriously. As Brinton says, "Boehme hears the divine melody, not from a choir of Protestant angels, nor in the Gregorian chant of the Church. It is for him *'das Freudenspiel der ewigen Gebärung'*—'the joyful play of eternal generation.' " In other words, Boehme placed man's perfection and bliss not in a Protestant future life nor in Catholic sacraments, but in the transformation of this bodily life into joyful play.

Heretical mystics of the type of Jacob Boehme deserve more honor than they have received from secular humanists. For modern secular humanist intellectuals have in the main followed Plato and Descartes over the abyss into the insane delusion that the true essence of man lies in disembodied mental activity. The philosopher's efforts to overcome the mind-body dualism in theory are betrayed by the philosophers' own practical commitment to the pure life of the mind. The rationalism of the philosophers has only led them further astray, and the irrationality of the mystics has enabled them to hold fast to a truth for which the time was not ripe. Perhaps the time is now ripe when the mystic can break the glass through which he sees all things darkly, and the rationalist can break the glass through which he sees all things clearly, and both together can enter the kingdom of psychological reality.

The doctrine that play is the essential mode of activity of a free or of a perfected or of a satisfied humanity has obvious implications for social reform. Over a hundred years ago the utopian socialist Fourier tried to work out the structure of a society in which work had been transformed into play; his influence can be seen in some of the early writings of Marx, which call for the abolition of labor as a necessary precondition for the emancipation of genuinely free and genuinely human self-activity. These utopian speculations have been laughed out of serious consideration by the realists, who apparently are made happy if they can prove, by their special interpretation of the doctrine of original sin, that their children and their children's children are condemned to be as unhappy as they are. But history is transforming the question of reorganizing human society and human nature in the spirit of play from a speculative possibility to a realistic necessity. The most realistic observers are emphasizing man's increasing alienation from his work; the possibility of mass unemployment—i.e., liberation from work—given by modern technology; and the utter incapacity of human nature as it is today to make genuinely free use of leisure—to play.

The crisis of our time was diagnosed by one of the greatest and most realistic of twentieth-century economists, John Maynard Keynes, in an essay written in 1930 and called "Economic Possibilities for Our Grandchildren." Keynes takes as his premise the proposition that, because of modern technological advances, mankind is solving the economic problem, which "always has been hitherto the primary, most pressing problem of the human race—not only of the human race, but of the whole of the biological kingdom from the beginnings of life in its most primitive forms." Keynes' reflections on this situation are follows:

> Thus we have been expressly evolved by nature—with all our impulses and deepest instincts—for the purpose of solving the economic problem. If the economic problem is solved, mankind will be deprived of its traditional purpose.
>
> Will this be a benefit? If one believes at all in the real values of life, the prospect at least opens up the possibility of benefit. Yet I think with dread of the readjustment of the habits and instincts of the ordinary man, bred into him for countless generations, which he may be asked to discard within a few decades.
>
> To use the language of today—must we not expect a general "nervous breakdown"? We already have a little experience of what I mean—a nervous breakdown of the sort which is already common enough in England and the United States amongst the wives of the well-to-do classes, unfortunate women, many of them, who have been deprived by their wealth of their traditional tasks and occupations—who cannot find it sufficiently amusing, when deprived of the spur of economic necessity, to cook and clean and mend, yet are quite unable to find anything more amusing.
>
> To those who sweat for their daily bread leisure is a longed-for sweet—until they get it.
>
> There is the traditional epitaph written for herself by the old charwoman:
>
> > Don't mourn for me, friends, don't weep for me never,
> > For I'm going to do nothing for ever and ever.
>
> This was her heaven. Like others who look forward to leisure she conceived how nice it would be to spend her time listening-in—for there was another couplet which occurred in her poem:
>
> > With psalms and sweet music the heavens'll be ringing,
> > But I shall have nothing to do with the singing.
>
> Yet it will only be for those who have to do with the singing that life will be tolerable—and how few of us can sing!

These reflections generate in Keynes a mood of anxious foreboding. "There is no country and no people," he writes, "who can look forward to the age of leisure and abundance without a dread."

From the Freudian point of view the necessary readjustment of the habits and instincts of the ordinary man appears no less formidable, but there are grounds for optimism not accessible to Keynes. For Keynes the art of life itself, which in an age of abundance and leisure will have to replace the art of accumulating the means of life, is a difficult art requiring refined sensitivity of the kind possessed by the Bloomsbury group and immortalized in the work of

Virginia Woolf. So Keynes looks with dread at the prospect of the ordinary man's emancipation from work. But from the Freudian point of view, every ordinary man has tasted the paradise of play in his own childhood. Underneath the habits of work in every man lies the immortal instinct for play. The foundation on which the man of the future will be built is already there, in the repressed unconscious; the foundation does not have to be created out of nothing, but recovered. Nature—or history—is not setting us a goal without endowing us with the equipment to reach it.

But the concept of play is not simply a tool for eschatological prophecy and social criticism; it has, like all valuable eschatological concepts, analytical applications to history and anthropology. Huizinga in *Homo Ludens* elaborated Frobenius' definition of human culture as *eines aus dem natürlichen Sein aufgestiegenen Spieles.* He shows the presence of an irreducible nonfunctional element of play in all the basic categories of human cultural activity—religion, art, war, law, economics. Huizinga suggests that the advance of civilization has repressed the play element in culture; the implication is that, since play is the distinctively human mode of activity, the advance of civilization has dehumanized culture.

Take, for example, economic behavior. The element of play in primitive economics—in potlatch contests of prestige, in the merry-go-round circuits of gift-exchange—is obvious. Perhaps primitive economics can be distinguished from civilized economics as that pattern of economic behavior in which play and the pleasure-principle have primacy over the ostensibly rational calculus of maximum gains—that is to say, over the reality-principle. Perhaps, more generally, the two levels of culture which sociology has distinguished under various labels—primitive and civilized, *Gemeinschaft* and *Gesellschaft,* folk and urban—can be distinguished psychoanalytically. Primitive is that level of culture in which the rhythm of what Freud calls the primary process—the rhythm of dreams and childhood play—is predominant. Civilized is that level of culture which effectively represses the rhythm of the primary process in favor of rationality and the reality-principle. The exploration of this hypothesis is part of a psychoanalytical anthropology.

And is there no element of play in that triumph of utilitarian rationalism and the reality-principle, modern economic behavior? Fifty years ago Thorstein Veblen, in *The Theory of the Leisure Class,* exposed the irrational psychological springs of pecuniary emulation and showed that economic competition, not the theory but the practice, psychologically considered, is a "game of ownership" lineally descended from the barbarian game of predatory war. Quite recently economic theorists, abandoning the notion that the model of a rational-utilitarian man can explain the actualities of economic behavior, have found their most fruitful alternative model in the theory of gambling and games.

What then does psychoanalysis have to add to Huizinga and Veblen? The play element in culture provides a prima facie justification for the psychoanalytical doctrine of sublimation, which views "higher" cultural activities as substitutes for lost infantile pleasures. Thus Ferenczi's psychoanalytical study of money as a sublimation concludes with the proposition that the pursuit of money is governed not only by the reality-principle but also by the pleasure-principle; Ferenczi is vindicated by the *Theory of Games and Economic Behavior.*

Furthermore, the psychoanalytical notion of the repressed unconscious seems necessary in order to define the play element in culture. It seems to be an essential feature of the play element in culture, for example the "game of ownership," that it must not be perceived or enjoyed as such, it is unconscious play, and at the same time it is never pure play. In other words, it has the same psychic structure as a neurotic symptom. According to basic Freudian theory, a repressed instinct is bound to return in the form of neurotic symptoms, compromises between the pleasure-principle and the reality-principle which are not recognized as such. And the neurotic symptoms are "substitute-gratifications"; they provide pleasure, but only neurotic pleasure. Further psychoanalytical light on culture as neurotic play depends on the difficult and paradoxical concept of sublimation, to which we shall return later in this book. In the meantime, we should also warn the reader that to analyze culture or economic activity or even games as play, as a manifestation of Eros, without also taking account of Freud's aggressive instinct (Veblen's "predatory instinct"), is, to put it mildly, one-sided.

Our indestructible unconscious desire for a return to childhood, our deep childhood-fixation, is a desire for a return to the pleasure-principle, for a recovery of the body from which culture alienates us, and for play instead of work. And yet, on the other hand, childhood cannot be recovered and paradise cannot be regained. For the infantile experience of freedom and absorption in pleasure has a fatal flaw. It has not come to terms with the reality-principle. . . . The infant's world of pleasure and play is built out of wishes uninhibited by the reality-principle and satisfied by unreal, hallucinatory fulfillment. Through an elementary mechanism, wish-fulfillment thinking, which survives also in the daydreaming and fantasy of adults, the child is able to create a world where dreams come true and wishes are omnipotent. And by the same token this early blossoming of the erotic life of man remains basically subjective. It fails to reach the objective world; the child takes himself and his own body as the object of his love. In Freudian terminology, infantile sexuality is fundamentally autoerotic or narcissistic. Freud is too realistic to follow the mystics or romantics who wish to ignore the demands of the reality-principle. Infantilism, however glorified, is no solution.

Hence there is for Freud a final contradiction between the reality-principle and our unconscious desires. Here is the source of Freud's pessimism, and the central problem for anyone who takes Freud seriously. Hence anyone who takes Freud seriously must follow him into the closest anatomy of the desires of childhood—in his terminology, infantile sexuality. Even in childhood, according to Freud, human love can be seen going out beyond itself and finding its first object in the world, the mother. Our analysis of Eros, even infantile Eros, is incomplete until we have analyzed this love of objects in the world, how it originates, and what its aim is. . . .

The Resurrection of the Body

The path of sublimation, which mankind has religiously followed at least since the foundation of the first cities, is no way out of the human neurosis, but, on the contrary, leads to its aggravation. Psychoanalytical theory and the bitter facts of contemporary history suggest that mankind is reaching the end of this road. Psychoanalytical theory declares that the end of the road is the dominion of death-in-life. History has brought mankind to that pinnacle on which the total obliteration of mankind is at last a practical possibility. At this moment of history the friends of the life instinct must warn that the victory of death is by no means impossible; the malignant death instinct can unleash those hydrogen bombs. For if we discard our fond illusion that the human race has a privileged or providential status in the life of the universe, it seems plain that the malignant death instinct is a built-in guarantee that the human experiment, if it fails to attain its possible perfection, will cancel itself out, as the dinosaur experiment canceled itself out. But jeremiads are useless unless we can point to a better way. Therefore the question confronting mankind is the abolition of repression—in traditional Christian language, the resurrection of the body.

We have already done what we could to extract from psychoanalytical theory a model of what the ressurrected body would be like. The life instinct, or sexual instinct, demands activity of a kind that, in contrast to our current mode of activity, can only be called play. The life instinct also demands a union with others and with the world around us based not on anxiety and aggression but on narcissism and erotic exuberance.

But the death instinct also demands satisfaction; as Hegel says in the *Penomenology,* "The life and knowledge of God may doubtless be described as love playing with itself; but this idea sinks into triviality, if the seriousness, the pain, the patience and the labor of the Negative are omitted." The death instinct is reconciled with the life instinct only in a life which is not repressed, which leaves no "unlived lines" in the human body, the death instinct then being affirmed in a body which is willing to die. And, because the body is satisfied, the death instinct no longer drives it to change itself and make history, and therefore, as Christian theology divined, its activity is in eternity.

At the same time—and here again Christian theology and psychoanalysis agree—the resurrected body is the transfigured body. The abolition of repression would abolish the unnatural concentrations of libido in certain particular bodily organs—concentrations engineered by the negativity of the morbid death instinct, and constituting the bodily base of the neurotic character disorders in the human ego. In the words of Thoreau: "We need pray for no higher heaven than the pure senses can furnish, a purely sensuous life. Our present senses are but rudiments of what they are destined to become." The human body would become polymorphously perverse, delighting in that full life of all the body which it now fears. The consciousness strong enough to endure full life would be no longer Apollonian but Dionysian—consciousness which does not observe the limit, but overflows; consciousness which *does not negate any more.*

If the question facing mankind is the abolition of repression, psychoanalysis is not the only point of view from which the question can and should be raised. We have already indicated that the question is intrinsic to Christian theology. The time has come to ask Christian theologians, especially the neo-orthodox, what they mean by the resurrection of the body and by eternal life. Is this a promise of immortality after death? In other words, is the psychological premise of Christianity the impossibility of reconciling life and death either in "this" world or the "next," so that flight from death—with all its morbid consequences—is our eternal fate in "this world" and in "the next"? For we have seen that the perfect body, promised by Christian theology, enjoying that perfect felicity promised by Christian theology, is a body reconciled with death.

In the last analysis Christian theology must either accept death as part of life or abandon the body. For two thousand years Christianity has kept alive the mystical hope of an ultimate victory of Life over Death, during a phase of human history when Life was at war with Death and hope could only be mystical. But if we are approaching the last days, Christian theology might ask itself whether it is only the religion of fallen humanity, or whether it might be asleep when the bridegroom comes. Certain it is that if Christianity wishes to help mankind toward the erasure of the traces of original sin which Baudelaire said was the true definition of progress, there are priceless insights in its tradition—insights which have to be transformed into a system of practical therapy, something like psychoanalysis, before they are useful or even meaningful.

The specialty of Christian eschatology lies precisely in its rejection of the Platonic hostility to the human body and to "matter," its refusal to identify the Platonic path of sublimation with ultimate salvation, and its affirmation that eternal life can only be life in a body. Christian asceticism can carry punishment of the fallen body to heights inconceivable to Plato; but Christian hope is for the redemption of that fallen body. Hence the affirmation of Tertullian: *Resurget igitur caro, et quidem omnis, et quidem ipsa, et quidem integra*—The body will rise again, all of the body, the identical body, the entire body. The medieval Catholic synthesis between Christianity and Greek philosophy, with its notion of an immortal soul, compromised and confused the issue; only Protestantism carries the full burden of the peculiar Christian faith. Luther's break with the doctrine of sublimation (good works) is decisive; but the theologian of the resurrected body is the cobbler of Görlitz, Jacob Boehme. When Tillich and Barth finally get round to the substance of things hoped for, their eschatology, they will have to reckon with Boehme. Meanwhile, as neo-orthodox theology plunges deeper into the nature of sin and death, Boehme's *theologia ex idea vitae deducta* is neglected except by the lonely mystic and revolutionary Berdyaev.

Whatever the Christian churches do with him, Boehme's position in the Western tradition of mystic hope of better things is central and assured. Backward he is linked, through Paracelsus and alchemy, to the tradition of Christian gnosticism and Jewish cabalism; forward he is linked, through his influence on the romantics Blake, Novalis, and Hegel, with Freud. We have argued that psychoanalysis has not psychoanalyzed itself until it places itself inside the history of Western thought—inside the general neurosis of mankind. So seen, psychoanalysis is the heir to a mystical tradition which it must affirm.

Mysticism, in the mind of the general public, is identified with that flight from the material world and from life preached by such popularizers as Evelyn Underhill and Aldous Huxley—which, from the psychoanalytical point of view, may be termed Apollonian or sublimation mysticism. But there is in the Western tradition another kind of mysticism, which can be called Dionysian or body mysticism, which stays with life, which is the body, and seeks to transform and perfect it. Western body mysticism—a tradition which urgently needs re-examination—contains three main strands: the Christian (Pauline) notion of the "spiritual" body, the Jewish (cabalistic) notion of Adam's perfect body before the Fall, and the alchemical notion of the subtle body. All of these strands unite in Boehme, and even a little knowledge of the real Boehme—for example Ernst Benz' first-rate book, not available in English—makes it plain that Boehme and Freud have too much in common to be able to dispense with each other.

Boehme, like Freud, understands death not as a mere nothing but as a positive force either in dialectical conflict with life (in fallen man), or dialectically unified with life (in God's perfection). Thus, says Benz, "Our life remains a struggle between life and death, and as long as this conflict lasts, anxiety lasts also." In Boehme's concept of life, the concept of play, or love-play, is as central as it is in Freud's and his concept of the spiritual or paradisical body of Adam before the Fall recognizes the potent demand in our unconscious both for an androgynous mode of being and for a narcissistic mode of self-expression, as well as the corruption in our current use of the oral, anal, and genital functions. It is true that Boehme does not yet accept the brutal death of the individual physical body, and therefore makes his paradisical body ambiguously immaterial, without oral, anal, and genital organs; and yet he clings obstinately to the body and to bodily pleasure, and therefore says that Adam was "magically" able to eat and enjoy the "essence" of things, and "magically" able to reproduce and to have sexual pleasure in the act of reproduction. Boehme is caught in these dilemmas because of his insight into the corruption of the human body, his insight that all life is life in the body, and, on the other hand, his inability to accept a body which dies. No Protestant theologian has gone further; or rather, later Protestantism has preferred to repress the problem and to repress Boehme.

Oriental mysticism also, to judge from Needham's survey of Taoism or Eliade's study of Yoga, has reached the same point. Needham (quoting Maspéro) is right in stressing that the Taoist quest for a more perfect body transcends the Platonic dualism of soul and matter. But Needham's enthusiasm for Taoism as a human and organismic response to life in the world must be qualified by recognizing that the Taoist perfect body is immortal: Taoism does not accept death as part of life. (In an earlier chapter we argued that there is the same defect in Needham's other enthusiasm, Whitehead's philosophy of nature.)

Psychoanalysis accepts the death of the body; but psychoanalysis has something to learn from body mysticism, occidental and oriental, over and above the wealth of psychoanalytical insights contained in it. For these mystics take seriously, and traditional psychoanalysis does not, the possibility of human perfectibility and the hope of finding a way out of the human neurosis into that simple health that animals enjoy, but not man.

As Protestantism degenerated from Luther and Boehme, it abandoned its religious function of criticizing the existing order and keeping alive the mystical hope of better things; in psychoanalytical terminology, it lost contact with the unconscious and with the immortal repressed desires of the unconscious. The torch passed to the poets and philosophers of the romantic movement. The heirs of Boehme are Blake, Novalis, Hegel, and, as Professor Gray has recently shown, Goethe. These are the poets whom Freud credited with being the real discoverers of the unconscious.

Not only toward the mystics but also toward the poets psychoanalysis must quit its pretension of supramundane superiority. Instead of exposing the neuroses of the poets, the psychoanalysts might learn from them, and abandon the naïve idea that there is an immense gap, in mental health and intellectual objectivity, between themselves and the rest of the world. In the world's opinion, in the eyes of common sense, Novalis is crazy, and Ferenczi also: the world will find it easier to believe that we are all mad than to believe that the psychoanalysts are not. And further, it does not seem to be the case that the psychoanalytical mode of reaching the unconscious has superannuated the poetic, or artistic, mode of attaining the same objective. Anyone conversant both with modern literature and with psychoanalysis knows that modern literature is full of psychoanalytical insights not yet grasped, or not so clearly grasped, by "scientific" psychoanalysis. And anyone who loves art knows that psychoanalysis has no monopoly on the power to heal. What the times call for is an end to the war between psychoanalysis and art—a war kept alive by the sterile "debunking" approach of psychoanalysis to art—and the beginning of cooperation between the two in the work of therapy and in the task of making the unconscious conscious. A little more Eros and less strife.

Modern poetry, like psychoanalysis and Protestant theology, faces the problem of the resurrection of the body. Art and poetry have always been altering our ways of sensing and feeling—that is to say, altering the human body. And Whitehead rightly discerns as the essence of the "Romantic Reaction" a revulsion against abstraction (in psychoanalytical terms, sublimation) in favor of the concrete sensual organism, the human body. "Energy is the only life, and is from the Body. . . . Energy is Eternal Delight," says Blake.

A young critic, whose first book represents a new mode of criticism—a criticism for which poetry is an experience both mystical and bodily—has traced the persistent quest in modern poetry for the resurrection of the body and the perfection of the body. Wordsworth, in contrast with the sublime (and sublimating) tendency of Milton, "considers that his revelation can be expressed in the forms and symbols of daily life" and "sees Paradise possible in any sweet though bare nook of the earth." Hopkins "is engaged on a theodicy, and has taken for his province the stubborn senses and the neglected physical world"; "no one has gone further than Hopkins in presenting Christ as the direct and omnipresent object of perception, so deeply ingrained in the eyes, the flesh, and the bone (and the personal sense of having eyes, flesh, and bone), that the sense of self and the sense of being in Christ can no longer be distinguished." Rilke's plaint throughout his career is that "we do not know the body any more than we know nature": Rilke believes (in his own words) that "the qualities are to be taken away from God, the no longer utterable, and returned to creation, to love and death"; so that the outcome of his poetry is that "for Rilke, the body becomes a spiritual fact." Valéry's poetry "may be considered as the Odyssey of Consciousness in search of its true body"; and "the intellectual pursuit of Valéry is to this end, that the body may be seen as what it virtually is, a magnificent revelation and instrument of the soul. Could it be viewed as such, the eyes would not be symbol, but reality."

The "magical" body which the poet seeks is the "subtle" or "spiritual" or "translucent" body of occidental mysticism, and the "diamond" body of oriental mysticism, and, in psychoanalysis, the polymorphously perverse body of childhood. Thus, for example, psychoanalysis declares the fundamentally bisexual character of human nature; Boehme insists on the androgynous character of human perfection; Taoist mysticism invokes feminine passivity to counteract masculine aggressivity; and Rilke's poetic quest is a quest for a hermaphroditic body. There is an urgent need for elucidation of the interrelations between these disparate modes of articulating the desires of the unconscious. Jung is aware of these interrelations, and orthodox psychoanalysts have not been aware of them. But no elucidation results from incorporation of the data into the Jungian system, not so much because of the intellectual disorder in the system, but rather because of the fundamental orientation of Jung, which is flight from the problem of the body, flight from the concept of repression, and a return to the path of sublimation. Freudianism must face the issue, and Freud himself said: "Certain practices of the mystics may succeed in upsetting the normal relations between the different regions of the mind, so that, for example, the perceptual system becomes able to grasp relations in the deeper layers of the ego and in the id which would otherwise be inaccessible to it."

Joseph Needham's interest in what we have called body mysticism, an interest which underlies his epoch-making work *Science and Civilization in China,* reminds us that the resurrection of the body has been placed on the agenda not only by psychoanalysis, mysticism, and poetry, but also by the philosophical criticism of modern science. Whitehead's criticism of scientific abstraction is, in psychoanalytical terms, a criticism of sublimation. His protest against "The Fallacy of Misplaced Concreteness" is a protest on behalf of the living body as a whole: "But the living organ of experience is the living body as a whole"; and his protest "on behalf of value" insists that the real structure of the human body, of human cognition, and of the events cognized is both sensuous and erotic, "self-enjoyment." Whitehead himself recognized the affinity between himself and the romantic poets; and Needham of course recognized the affinity between the philosophy of organism and mysticism. Actually Needham may be exaggerating the uniqueness of Taoism. The whole Western alchemical tradition, which urgently needs re-examination, is surely "Whiteheadian" in spirit, and Goethe, the last of the alchemists, in his "Essay on the Metamorphosis of Plants" produced the last, or the first, Whiteheadian scientific treatise. Goethe, says a modern biologist, "reached out to the reconciliation of the antithesis between the senses and the intellect, an antithesis with which traditional science does not attempt to cope."

Needham has recognized the crucial role of psychology in the philosophy of science. The refutation of Descartes, he has said, will come from psychology, not biology. And yet he seems to be unaware of the profound affinities between the Tao, which he so much admires, and psychoanalysis. He seems to be unaware of Ferenczi's brilliant essay attempting to reorganize the whole theory of biological evolution in the light of psychoanalysis. But the function of psychoanalysis in relation to Whitehead and Needham's critique of science is not that of supplementing their ideology with sympathetic support; rather it is indispensable if their critique of science is to amount to more than mere ideology. For what they are calling in question is the subjective attitude of the scientist, and if their critique is to amount to more than mere dislike, it must be supplemented by a psychoanalysis of the subject. In fact a psychoanalysis of the subject (the "observer") seems necessary if science is to remain "objective." The essential point has been seen by Ferenczi, who coined the term "utraquism" to indicate the required combination of analysis of the subject and analysis of the object: "If science is really to remain objective, it must work alternately as pure psychology and pure natural science, and must verify both our inner and outer experience by analogies taken from both points of view. . . . I called this the 'utraquism' of all true scientific work."

Frenczi's formulations date from 1923–1926: today we would presumably think of "integration" rather than alternation. Ferenczi saw psychoanalysis as marking a significant step forward in general scientific methodology, a step which he defined as "a return to a certain extent to the methods of ancient animistic science" and "the re-establishment of an animism no longer anthropomorphic." But the re-establishment of an animism is precisely the outcome of Whitehead and Needham's line of thought. And Ferenczi argues that psychoanalysis is necessary in order to differentiate the new "purified" animism from the old naïve animism:

> Insofar as Freud attempts to solve problems of biology as well as of sexual activity by means of psychoanalytic experience, he returns to a certain extent to the methods of ancient animistic science. There is a safeguard, however, against the psychoanalyst falling into the error of such naïve animism. Naïve animism transferred human psychic life *en bloc* without analysis onto natural objects. Psychoanalysis, however, dissected human psychic activity, pursued it to the limit where psychic and physical came into contact, down to the instincts, and thus freed psychology from anthropocentrism, and only then did it trust itself to evaluate this purified animism in terms of biology. To have been the first in the history of science to make this attempt is the achievement of Freud.

We therefore conclude with a plea for "utraquistic" integration between psychoanalysis and the philosophy of science. Ferenczi, in his important analysis of Ernst Mach entitled "The Psychogenesis of Mechanism," put it this way:

"When will the physicist, who finds the soul in the mechanism, and the psychoanalyst, who perceives mechanisms in the soul, join hands and work with united forces at a *Weltanschauung* free from one-sidedness and 'idealizations'?"

Perhaps there are even deeper issues raised by the confrontation between psychoanalysis and the philosophy of organism. Whitehead and Needham are protesting against the inhuman attitude of modern science; in psychoanalytical terms, they are calling for a science based on an erotic sense of reality, rather than an aggressive dominating attitude toward reality. From this point of view alchemy (and Goethe's essay on plants) might be said to be the last effort of Western man to produce a science based on an erotic sense of reality. And conversely, modern science, as criticized by Whitehead, is one aspect of a total cultural situation which may be described as the dominion of death-in-life. The mentality which was able to reduce nature to "a dull affair, soundless, scentless, colourless; merely the hurrying of material endlessly, meaninglessly"—Whitehead's description—is lethal. It is an awe-inspiring attack on the life of the universe; in more technical psychoanalytical terms, its anal-sadistic intent is plain. And further, the only historian of science who uses psychoanalysis, Gaston Bachelard, concludes that it is of the essence of the scientific spirit to be mercilessly ascetic, to eliminate human enjoyment from our relation to nature, to eliminate the human senses, and finally to eliminate the human brain:

> It does indeed seem that with the twentieth century there begins a kind of scientific thought in opposition to the senses, and that it is necessary to construct a theory of objectivity *in opposition to* the object. . . . It follows that the entire use of the brain is being called into question. From now on the brain is strictly no longer adequate as an instrument for scientific thought; that is to say, the brain is the *obstacle* to scientific thought. It is an obstacle in the sense that it is the coordinating center for human movements and appetites. It is necessary to think *in opposition to* the brain.

Thus modern science confirms Ferenczi's aphorism: "*Pure intelligence* is thus a product of dying, or at least of becoming mentally insensitive, and is therefore *in principle madness.*"

What Whitehead and Needham are combating is not an error but a disease in consciousness. In more technical psychoanalytical terms, the issue is not the conscious structure of science, but the unconscious premises of science; the trouble is in the unconscious strata of the scientific ego, in the scientific character-structure. Whitehead called the modern scientific point of view, in spite of its world-conquering successes, "quite unbelievable." Psychoanalysis adds the crucial point: it is insane. Hence there is unlikely to be any smooth transition from the "mechanistic" point of view to the "organismic" point of view. It is unlikely that problems generated in the mechanistic system will lead to organismic solutions. The two points of view represent different instinctual orientations, different fusions of life and death. It is even doubtful that the adoption of an organismic point of view under present conditions would be a gain; it might be a relapse into naïve animism. Thus the kind of thinking which Needham hails as Taoist wisdom (alchemy, etc.), is attacked by Bachelard as unconscious projection, dreaming, and naïve mythologizing; he sees science (and psychoanalysis) as sternly committed to the task of demythologizing our view of nature. It would seem, therefore, in line with Ferenczi's argument, that Taoist ideology without psychoanalytical consciousness could be a relapse into naïve animism. And psychoanalytical consciousness means psychoanalytical therapy also. Psychoanalytical therapy involves a solution to the problem of repression; what is needed is not an organismic ideology, but to change the human body so that it can become for the first time an organism—the resurrection of the body. An organism whose own sexual life is as disordered as man's is in no position to construct objective theories about the Yin and Yang and the sex life of the universe.

The resurrection of the body is a social project facing mankind as a whole, and it will become a practical political problem when the statesmen of the world are called upon to deliver happiness instead of power, when political economy becomes a science of use-values instead of exchange-values—a science of enjoyment instead of a science of accumulation. In the face of this tremendous human problem, contemporary social theory, both capitalist and socialist, has nothing to say. Contemporary social theory (again we must honor Veblen as an exception) has been completely taken in by the inhuman abstractions of the path of sublimation, and has no contact with concrete human beings, with their concrete bodies, their concrete though repressed desires, and their concrete neuroses.

To find social theorists who are thinking about the real problem of our age, we have to go back to the Marx of 1844, or even to the philosophers influencing Marx in 1844, Fourier and Feuerbach. From Fourier's psychological analysis of the antithesis of work and pleasure Marx obtained the concept of play, and used it, in a halfhearted way to be sure, in some of his early utopian speculations. From Feuerbach Marx learned the necessity of moving from Hegelian abstractions to the concrete senses and the concrete human body. Marx' "philosophic-economic manuscripts" of 1844 contain remarkable formulations calling for the resurrection of human nature, the appropriation of the human body, the transformation of the human senses, and the realization of a state of self-enjoyment. Thus, for example, "Man appropriates himself as an all-sided being in an all-sided way, hence as total man. [This appropriation lies in] every one of his human relationships to the world—seeing, hearing, smell, taste, feeling, thought, perception, experience, wishing, activity, loving, in short, all organs of his individuality." The human physical senses must be emancipated from the sense of possession, and then the humanity of the senses and the human enjoyment of the senses will be achieved for the first time. Here is the point of contact between Marx and Freud: I do not see how the profundities and obscurities of the "philosophic-economic manuscripts" can be elucidated except with the aid of psychoanalysis.

Psychoanalysis, mysticism, poetry, the philosophy of organism, Feuerbach, and Marx—this is a miscellaneous assemblage; but, as Heraclitus said, the unseen harmony is stronger than the seen. Common to all of them is a mode of consciousness that can be called—although the term causes fresh difficulties—the dialectical imagination. By "dialectical" I mean an activity of consciousness struggling to circumvent the limitations imposed by the formal-logical law of contradiction. Marxism, of course, has no monopoly of "dialectics." Needham has shown the dialectical character of Whitehead's philosophy, and he constantly draws attention to dialectical patterns in mystical thought. The goal of Indian body mysticism, according to Eliade, is the "conjunction of contrarieties" *(coincidentia oppositorum)*. Scholem, in his survey of Jewish mysticism, says, "Mysticism, intent on formulating the paradoxes of religious experience, uses the instrument of dialectics to express its meaning. The Kabbalists are by no means the only witnesses to this affinity between mystical and dialectical thinking."

As for poetry, are not those basic poetic devices emphasized by recent criticism—paradox, ambiguity, irony, tension—devices whereby the poetic imagination subverts the "reasonableness" of language, the chains it imposes? (Compare Valéry's theory of poetry. . . .) And from the psychoanalytical point of view, if we, with Trilling. . . , accept the substantial identity between poetic logic (with its symbolism, condensation of meaning, and displacement of accent) and dream logic, then the connection between poetry and dialectics, as defined, is more substantially grounded. Dreams are certainly an activity of the mind struggling to circumvent the formal-logical law of contradiction.

Psychoanalytical thinking has a double relation to the dialectical imagination. It is, on the one hand (actually or potentially), a mode of dialectical consciousness; on the other hand, it contains, or ought to contain, a theory about the nature of the dialectical imagination. I say "actually or potentially" because psychoanalysis, either as a body of doctrine or an experience of the analysand, is no total revelation of the unconscious repressed. The struggle of consciousness to circumvent the limitations of formal logic, of language, and of "common sense" is under conditions of general repression never ending (see Freud's essay, "Analysis Terminable and Interminable"). "Dialectical" are those psychoanalysts who continue this struggle; for the rest, psychoanalytical terminology can be a prison house of Byzantine scholasticism in which "word-consciousness" is substituting for consciousness of the unconscious. . . .

And even if we take Freud as the model of psychoanalytical consciousness, we have argued that at such crucial points as the relation between the two instincts and the relation between humanity and animality, Freud is trapped because he is not sufficiently "dialectical." Nevertheless, the basic structure of Freud's thought is committed to dialectics, because it is committed to the vision of mental life as basically an arena of conflict; and his finest insights (for example, that when the patient denies something, he affirms it) are incurably "dialectical." Hence the attempt to make psychoanalysis out to be "scientific" (in the positivist sense) is not only vain but destructive. Empirical verification, the positivist test of science, can apply only to that which is fully in consciousness; but psychoanalysis is a mode of contracting the unconscious under conditions of general repression, when the unconscious remains in some sense repressed. To put the matter another way, the "poetry" in Freud's thought cannot be purged away, or rather such an expurgation is exactly what is accomplished in "scientific" textbooks of psychology; but Freud's writings remain unexpurgatable. The same "poetical" imagination marks the work of Róheim and Ferenczi as superior, and explains why they are neglected by "scientific" anthropologists and psychoanalysts. The whole nature of the "dialectical" or "poetical" imagination is another problem urgently needing examination; and there is a particular need for psychoanalysis, as part of the psychoanalysis of psychoanalysis, to become conscious of the dialectical, poetical, mystical stream that runs in its blood.

The key to the nature of dialectical thinking may lie in psychoanalysis, more specifically in Freud's psychoanalysis of negation. There is first the theorem that "there is nothing in the id which can be compared to negation," and that the law of contradiction does not hold in the id. Similarly, the dream does not seem to recognize the word "no." Instead of the law of contradiction we find a unity of opposites: "Dreams show a special tendency to reduce two opposites to a unity"; "Any thing in a dream may mean its opposite." We must therefore entertain the hypothesis that there is an important connection between being "dialectical" and dreaming, just as there is between dreaming and poetry or mysticism. Furthermore, in his essay "The Antithetical Sense of Primal Words" Freud compares the linguistic phenomenon of a hidden (in the etymological root) identity between words with antithetical meanings; he reveals the significant fact that it was the linguistic phenomenon that gave him the clue to the dream phenomenon, and not vice versa. It is plain that both psychoanalysis and the study of language (philosophical and philological) need a marriage or at least a meeting.

And, on the other hand, Freud's essay "On Negation" may throw light on the nature of the "dialectical" dissatisfaction with formal logic. Negation is the primal act of repression; but it at the same time liberates the mind to think about the repressed under the general condition that it is denied and thus remains essentially repressed. With Spinoza's formula *omnis determinatio est negatio* in mind, examine the following formulations of Freud: "A negative judgment is the intellectual substitute for repression; the 'No' in which it is expressed is the hall-mark of repression. . . . By the help of the symbol of negation, the thinking process frees itself from the limitations of repression and enriches itself with the subject-matter without which it could not work efficiently." But: "Negation only assists in undoing one of the consequences of repression—the fact that the subject-matter of the image in question is unable to enter consciousness. The result is a kind of intellectual acceptance of what is repressed, though in all essentials the repression persists."

We may therefore entertain the hypothesis that formal logic and the law of contradiction are the rules whereby the mind submits to operate under general conditions of repression. As with the concept of time, Kant's categories of rationality would then turn out to be the categories of repression. And conversely, "dialectical" would be the struggle of the mind to circumvent repression and make the unconscious conscious. But by the same token, it would be the struggle of the mind to overcome the split and conflict within itself. It could then be identified with that "synthesizing" tendency in the ego of which Freud spoke, and with that attempt to cure, inside the neurosis itself, on which Freud came finally to place his hope for therapy. As an attempt to unify and to cure, the "dialectical" consciousness would be a manifestation of Eros. And, as consciousness trying to throw off the fetters of negation, the "dialectical" consciousness would be a step toward that Dionysian ego which does not negate any more.

What the great world needs, of course, is a little more Eros and less strife; but the intellectual world needs it just as much. A little more Eros would make conscious the unconscious harmony between "dialectical" dreamers of all kinds—psychoanalysts, political idealists, mystics, poets, philosophers—and abate the sterile and ignorant polemics. Since the ignorance seems to be mostly a matter of self-ignorance, a little more psychoanalytical consciousness on all sides (including the psychoanalysts) might help—a little more self-knowledge, humility, humanity, and Eros. We may therefore conclude with the concluding words of Freud's *Civilization and Its Discontents:*

> Men have brought their powers of subduing the forces of nature to such a pitch that by using them they could now very easily exterminate one another to the last man. They know this—hence arises a great part of their current unrest, their dejection, their mood of apprehension. And now it may be expected that the other of the two "heavenly forces," eternal Eros, will put forth his strength so as to maintain himself alongside of his equally immortal adversary.

And perhaps our children will live to live a full life, and so see what Freud could not see—in the old adversary, a friend.

From Understanding Media: The Extension of Man
MARSHALL McLUHAN

The Medium Is the Message

In a culture like ours, long accustomed to splitting and dividing all things as a means of control, it is sometimes a bit of a shock to be reminded that, in operational and practical fact, the medium is the message. This is merely to say that the personal and social consequences of any medium—that is, of any extension of ourselves—result from the new scale that is introduced into our affairs by each extension of ourselves, or by any new technology. Thus, with automation, for example, the new patterns of human association tend to eliminate jobs, it is true. That is the negative result. Positively, automation creates roles for people, which is to say depth of involvement in their work and human association that our preceding mechanical technology had destroyed. Many people would be disposed to say that it was not the machine, but what one did with the machine, that was its meaning or message. In terms of the ways in which the machine altered our relations to one another and to ourselves, it mattered not in the least whether it turned out cornflakes or Cadillacs. The restructuring of human work and association was shaped by the technique of fragmentation that is the essence of machine technology. The essence of automation technology is the opposite. It is integral and decentralist in depth, just as the machine was fragmentary, centralist, and superficial in its patterning of human relationships.

The instance of the electric light may prove illuminating in this connection. The electric light is pure information. It is a medium without a message, as it were, unless it is used to spell out some verbal ad or name. This fact, characteristic of all media, means that the "content" of any medium is always another medium. The content of writing is speech, just as the written word is the content of print, and print is the content of the telegraph. If it is asked, "What is the content of speech?," it is necessary to say, "It is an actual process of thought, which is in itself nonverbal." An abstract painting represents direct manifestation of creative thought processes as they might appear in computer designs. What we are considering here, however, are the psychic and social consequences of the designs or patterns as they amplify or accelerate existing processes. For the "message" of any medium or technology is the change of scale or pace or pattern that it introduces into human affairs. The railway did not introduce movement or transportation or wheel or road into human society, but it accelerated and enlarged the scale of previous human functions, creating totally new kinds of cities and new kinds of work and leisure. This happened whether the railway functioned in a tropical or a northern environment, and is quite independent of the freight or content of the railway medium. The airplane, on the other hand, by accelerating the rate of transportation, tends to dissolve the railway form of city, politics, and association, quite independently of what the airplane is used for.

Let us return to the electric light. Whether the light is being used for brain surgery or night baseball is a matter of indifference. It could be argued that these activities are in some way the "content" of the electric light, since they could not exist without the electric light. This fact merely underlines the point that "the medium is the message" because it is the medium that shapes and controls the scale and form of human association and action. The content or uses of such media are as diverse as they are ineffectual in shaping the form of human association. Indeed, it is only too typical that the "content" of any medium blinds us to the character of the medium. It is only today that industries have become aware of the various kinds of business in which they are engaged. When IBM discovered that it was not in the business of making office equipment or business machines, but that it was in the business of processing information, then it began to navigate with clear vision. The General Electric Company makes a considerable portion of its profits from electric light bulbs and lighting systems. It has not yet discovered that, quite as much as A.T.&T., it is in the business of moving information.

The electric light escapes attention as a communication medium just because it has no "content." And this makes it an invaluable instance of how people fail to study media at all. For it is not till the electric light is used to spell out some brand name that it is noticed as a medium. Then it is not the light but the "content" (or what is really another medium) that is noticed. The message of the electric light is like the message of electric power in industry, totally radical, pervasive, and decentralized. For electric light and power are separate from their uses, yet they eliminate time and space factors in human association exactly as do radio, telegraph, telephone, and TV, creating involvement in depth.

A fairly complete handbook for studying the extensions of man could be made up from selections from Shakespeare. Some might quibble about whether or not he was referring to TV in these familiar lines from *Romeo and Juliet:*

> But soft! what light through yonder window breaks?
> It speaks, and yet says nothing.

In *Othello,* which, as much as *King Lear,* is concerned with the torment of people transformed by illusions, there are these lines that bespeak Shakespeare's intuition of the transforming powers of new media:

> Is there not charms
> By which the property of youth and maidhood
> May be abus'd? Have you not read,
> Roderigo,
> Of some such thing?

In Shakespeare's *Troilus and Cressida,* which is almost completely devoted to both a psychic and social study of communication, Shakespeare states his awareness that true social and political navigation depend upon anticipating the consequences of innovation:

> The providence that's in a watchful state
> Knows almost every grain of Plutus' gold,
> Finds bottom in the uncomprehensive deeps,
> Keeps place with thought, and almost like the gods
> Does thoughts unveil in their dumb cradles

The increasing awareness of the action of media, quite independently of their "content" or programming, was indicated in the annoyed and anonymous stanza:

> In modern thought, (if not in fact)
> Nothing is that doesn't act,
> So that is reckoned wisdom which
> Describes the scratch but not the itch.

The same kind of total, configurational awareness that reveals why the medium is socially the message has occurred in the most recent and radical medical theories. In his *Stress of Life,* Hans Selye tells of the dismay of a research colleague on hearing of Selye's theory:

> When he saw me thus launched on yet another enraptured description of what I
> had observed in animals treated with this or that impure, toxic material, he

looked at me with desperately sad eyes and said in obvious despair: "But Selye, try to realize what you are doing before it is too late! You have now decided to spend your entire life studying the pharmacology of dirt!"

Hans Selye, The Stress of Life

As Selye deals with the total environmental situation in his "stress" theory of disease, so the latest approach to media study considers not only the "content" but the medium and the cultural matrix within which the particular medium operates. The older unawareness of the psychic and social effects of media can be illustrated from almost any of the conventional pronouncements.

In accepting an honorary degree from the University of Notre Dame a few years ago, General David Sarnoff made this statement: "We are too prone to make technological instruments the scapegoats for the sins of those who wield them. The products of modern science are not in themselves good or bad; it is the way they are used that determines their value." That is the voice of the current somnambulism. Suppose we were to say, "Apple pie is in itself neither good nor bad; it is the way it is used that determines its value." Or, "The smallpox virus is in itself neither good nor bad; it is the way it is used that determines its value." Again, "Firearms are in themselves neither good nor bad; it is the way they are used that determines their value." That is, if the slugs reach the right people firearms are good. If the TV tube fires the right ammunition at the right people it is good. I am not being perverse. There is simply nothing in the Sarnoff statement that will bear scrutiny, for it ignores the nature of the medium, of any and all media, in the true Narcissus style of one hypnotized by the amputation and extension of his own being in a new technical form. General Sarnoff went on to explain his attitude to the technology of print, saying that it was true that print caused much trash to circulate, but it had also disseminated the Bible and the thoughts of seers and philosophers. It has never occurred to General Sarnoff that any technology could do anything but *add* itself on to what we already are.

Such economists as Robert Theobald, W. W. Rostow, and John Kenneth Galbraith have been explaining for years how it is that "classical economics" cannot explain change or growth. And the paradox of mechanization is that although it is itself the cause of maximal growth and change, the principle of mechanization excludes the very possibility of growth or the understanding of change. For mechanization is achieved by fragmentation of any process and by putting the fragmented parts in a series. Yet, as David Hume showed in the eighteenth century, there is no principle of causality in a mere sequence. That one thing follows another accounts for nothing. Nothing follows from following, except change. So the greatest of all reversals occurred with electricity, that ended sequence by making things instant. With instant speed the causes of things began to emerge to awareness again, as they had not done with things in sequence and in concatenation accordingly. Instead of asking which came first, the chicken or the egg, it suddenly seemed that a chicken was an egg's idea for getting more eggs.

Just before an airplane breaks the sound barrier, sound waves become visible on the wings of the plane. The sudden visibility of sound just as sound ends is an apt instance of that great pattern of being that reveals new and opposite forms just as the earlier forms reach their peak performance. Mechanization was never so vividly fragmented or sequential as in the birth of the movies, the moment that translated us beyond mechanism into the world of growth and organic interrelation. The movie, by sheer speeding up the mechanical, carried us from the world of sequence and connections into the world of creative configuration and structure. The message of the movie medium is that of transition from lineal connections to configurations. It is the transition that produced the now quite correct observation: "If it works, it's obsolete." When electric speed further takes over from mechanical movie sequences, then the lines of force in structures and in media become loud and clear. We return to the inclusive form of the icon.

To a highly literate and mechanized culture the movie appeared as a world of triumphant illusions and dreams that money could buy. It was at this moment of the movie that cubism occurred, and it has been described by E. H. Gombrich *(Art and Illusion)* as "the most radical attempt to stamp out ambiguity and to enforce one reading of the picture—that of a man-made construction, a colored canvas." For cubism substitutes all facets of an object simultaneously for the "point of view" or facet of perspective illusion. Instead of the specialized illusion of the third dimension on canvas, cubism sets up an interplay of planes and contradiction or dramatic conflict of patterns, lights, textures that "drives home the message" by involvement. This is held by many to be an exercise in painting, not in illusion.

In other words, cubism, by giving the inside and outside, the top, bottom, back, and front and the rest, in two dimensions, drops the illusion of perspective in favor of instant sensory awareness of the whole. Cubism, by seizing on instant total awareness, suddenly announced that *the medium is the message.* Is it not evident that the moment that sequence yields to the simultaneous, one is in the world of the structure and of configuration? Is that not what has happened in physics as in painting, poetry, and in communication? Specialized segments of attention have shifted to total field, and we can now say, "The medium is the message" quite naturally. Before the electric speed and total field, it was not obvious that the medium is the message. The message, it seemed, was the "content," as people used to ask what a painting was *about.* Yet they never thought to ask what a melody was about, nor what a house or a dress was about. In such matters, people retained some sense of the whole pattern, of form and function as a unity. But in the electric age this integral idea of structure and configuration has become so prevalent that educational theory has taken up the matter. Instead of working with specialized "problems" in arithmetic, the structural approach now follows the linea of force in the field of number and has small children meditating about number theory and "sets."

Cardinal Newman said of Napoleon, "He understood the grammar of gunpowder." Napoleon had paid some attention to other media as well, especially the semaphore telegraph that gave him a great advantage over his enemies. He is on record for saying that "Three hostile newspapers are more to be feared than a thousand bayonets."

Alexis de Tocqueville was the first to master the grammar of print and typography. He was thus able to read off the message of coming change in France and America as if he were reading aloud from a text that had been handed to him. In fact, the nineteenth century in France and in America was just such an open book to de Tocqueville because he had learned the grammar of print. So he, also, knew when that grammar did not apply. He was asked why he did not write a book on England, since he knew and admired England. He replied:

> One would have to have an unusual degree of philosophical folly to believe oneself able to judge England in six months. A year always seemed to me too short a time in which to appreciate the United States properly, and it is much easier to acquire clear and precise notions about the American Union than about Great Britain. In America all laws derive in a sense from the same line of thought. The whole of society, so to speak, is founded upon a single fact; everything springs from a simple principle. One could compare America to a forest pierced by a multitude of straight roads all converging on the same point. One has only to find the center and everything is revealed at a glance. But in England the paths run criss-cross, and it is only by travelling down each one of them that one can build up a picture of the whole.

De Tocqueville, in earlier work on the French Revolution, had explained how it was printed word that, achieving cultural saturation in the eighteenth century, had homogenized the French nation. Frenchmen were the same kind of people from north to south. The typographic principles of uniformity, continuity, and lineality had overlaid the complexities of ancient feudal and oral society. The Revolution was carried out by the new literati and lawyers.

In England, however, such was the power of the ancient oral traditions of common law, backed by the medieval institution of Parliament, that no uniformity or continuity of the new visual print culture could take complete hold. The result was that the most important event in English history has never taken place; namely, the English Revolution on the lines of the French Revolution. The American Revolution had no medieval legal institutions to discard or to root out, apart from monarchy. And many have held that the American Presidency has become very much more personal and monarchical than any European monarch ever could be.

De Tocqueville's contrast between England and America is clearly based on the fact of typography and of print culture creating uniformity and continuity. England, he says, has rejected this principle and clung to the dynamic or oral common-law tradition. Hence the discontinuity and unpredictable quality of English culture. The grammar of print cannot help to construe the message of oral and nonwritten culture and institutions. The English aristocracy was properly classified as barbarian by Matthew Arnold because its power and status had nothing to do with literacy or with the cultural forms of typography. Said the Duke of Gloucester to Edward Gibbon upon the publication of his *Decline and Fall*: "Another damned fat book, eh, Mr. Gibbon? Scribble, scribble, scribble, eh, Mr. Gibbon?" De Tocqueville was a highly literate aristocrat who was quite able to be detached from the values and assumptions of typography. That is why he alone understood the grammar of typography. And it is only on those terms, standing aside from any structure or medium, that its principles and lines of force can be discerned. For any medium has the power of imposing its own assumption on the unwary. Prediction and control consist in avoiding this subliminal state of Narcissus trance. But the greatest aid to this end is simply in knowing that the spell can occur immediately upon contact, as in the first bars of a melody.

A Passage to India by E. M. Forster is a dramatic study of the inability of oral and intuitive oriental culture to meet with the rational, visual European patterns of experience. "Rational," of course, has for the West long meant "uniform and continuous and sequential." In other words, we have confused reason with literacy, and rationalism with a single technology. Thus in the electric age man seems to the conventional West to become irrational. In Forster's novel the moment of truth and dislocation from the typographic trance of the West comes in the Marabar Caves. Adela Quested's reasoning powers cannot cope with the total inclusive field of resonance that is India. After the Caves: "Life went on as usual, but had no consequences, that is to say, sounds did not echo nor thought develop. Everything seemed cut off at its root and therefore infected with illusion."

A Passage to India (the phrase is from Whitman, who saw America headed Eastward) is a parable of Western man in the electric age, and is only incidentally related to Europe or the Orient. The ultimate conflict between sight and sound, between written and oral kinds of perception and organization of existence is upon us. Since understanding stops action, as Nietzsche observed, we can moderate the fierceness of this conflict by understanding the media that extend us and raise these wars within and without us.

Detribalization by literacy and its traumatic effects on tribal man is the theme of a book by the psychiatrist J. C. Carothers, *The African Mind in Health and Disease* (World Health Organization, Geneva, 1953). Much of his material appeared in an article in *Psychiatry* magazine, November, 1959: "The Culture, Psychiatry, and the Written Word." Again, it is electric speed that has revealed the lines of force operating from Western technology in the remotest areas of bush, savannah, and desert. One example is the Bedouin with his battery radio on board the camel. Submerging natives with floods of concepts for which nothing has prepared them is the normal action of all of our technology. But with electric media Western man himself experiences exactly the same inundation as the remote native. We are no more prepared to encounter radio and TV in our literate milieu than the native of Ghana is able to cope with the literacy that takes him out of his collective tribal world and beaches him in individual isolation. We are as numb in our new electric world as the native involved in our literate and mechanical culture.

Electric speed mingles the cultures of prehistory with the dregs of industrial marketeers, the nonliterate with semi-literate and the post-literate. Mental breakdown of varying degrees is the very common result of uprooting and inundation with new information and endless new patterns of information. Wyndham Lewis made this a theme of his group of novels called *The Human Age.* The first of these, *The Childermass,* is concerned precisely with accelerated media change as a kind of massacre of the innocents. In our own world as we become more aware of the effects of technology on psychic formation and manifestation, we are losing all confidence in our right to assign guilt. Ancient prehistoric societies regard violent crime as pathetic. The killer is regarded as we do a cancer victim. "How terrible it must be to feel like that," they say. J. M. Synge took up this idea very effectively in his *Playboy of the Western World.*

If the criminal appears as a nonconformist who is unable to meet the demand of technology that we behave in uniform and continuous patterns, literate man is quite inclined to see others who cannot conform as somewhat pathetic. Especially the child, the cripple, the woman, and the colored person appear in a world of visual and typographic technology as victims of injustice. On the other hand, in a culture that assigns roles instead of jobs to people—the dwarf, the skew, the child create their own spaces. They are not expected to fit into some uniform and repeatable niche that is not their size anyway. Consider the phrase "It's a man's world." As a quantitative observation endlessly repeated from within a homogenized culture, this phrase refers to the men in such a culture who have to be homogenized Dagwoods in order to belong at all. It is in our I.Q. testing that we have produced the greatest flood of misbegotten standards. Unaware of our typographic cultural bias, our testers assume that uniform and continuous habits are a sign of intelligence, thus eliminating the ear man and the tactile man.

C. P. Snow, reviewing a book of A. L. Rowse (*The New York Times Book Review,* December 24, 1961) on *Appeasement* and the road to Munich, describes the top level of British brains and experience in the 1930s. "Their I.Q.'s were much higher than usual among political bosses. Why were they such a disaster?" The view of Rowse, Snow approves: "They would not listen to warnings because they did not wish to hear." Being anti-Red made it impossible for them to read the message of Hitler. But their failure was as nothing compared to our present one. The American stake in literacy as a technology or uniformity applied to every level of education, government, industry, and social life is totally threatened by the electric technology. The threat of Stalin or Hitler was external. The electric technology is within the gates, and we are numb, deaf, blind, and mute about its encounter with the Gutenberg technology, on and through which the American way of life was formed. It is, however, no time to suggest strategies when the threat has not even been acknowledged to exist. I am in the position of Louis Pasteur telling doctors that their greatest enemy was quite invisible, and quite unrecognized by them. Our conventional response to all media, namely that is how they are used that counts, is the numb stance of the technological idiot. For the "content" of a medium is like the juicy piece of meat carried by the burglar to distract the watchdog of the mind. The effect of the medium is made strong and intense just because it is given another medium as "content." The content of a movie is a novel or a play or an opera. The effect of the movie form is not related to its program content. The "content" of writing or print is speech, but the reader is almost entirely unaware either of print or of speech.

Arnold Toynbee is innocent of any understanding of media as they have shaped history, but he is full of examples that the student of media can use. At one moment he can seriously suggest that adult education, such as the Workers Educational Association in Britain, is a useful counterforce to the popular press. Toynbee considers that although all of the oriental societies have in our time accepted the industrial technology and its political consequences: "On the cultural plane, however, there is no uniform corresponding tendency." (Somervell, I. 267) This is like the voice of the literate man, floundering in a milieu of ads, who boasts, "Personally, I pay no attention to ads." The spiritual and cultural reservations that the oriental peoples may have toward our technology will avail them not at all. The effects of technology do not occur at the level of opinions or concepts, but alter sense ratios or patterns of perception steadily and without any resistance. The serious artist is the only person able to encounter technology with impunity, just because he is an expert aware of the changes in sense perception.

The operation of the money medium in seventeenth century Japan had effects not unlike the operation of typography in the West. The penetration of the money economy, wrote G. B. Sansom (in *Japan,* Cresset Press, London, 1931) "caused a slow but irresistible revolution, culminating in the breakdown of feudal government and the resumption of intercourse with foreign countries after more than two hundred years of seclusion." Money has reorganized the sense life of peoples just because it is an *extension* of our sense lives. This change does not depend upon approval or disapproval of those living in the society.

Arnold Toynbee made one approach to the transforming power of media in his concept of "etherialization," which he holds to be the principle of progressive simplification and efficiency in any organization or technology. Typically, he is ignoring the *effect* of the challenge of these forms upon the response of our senses. He imagines that it is the response of our opinions that is relevant to the effect of media and technology in society, a "point of view" that is plainly the result of the typographic spell. For the man in a literate and homogenized society ceases to be sensitive to the diverse and discontinuous life of forms. He acquires the illusion of the third dimension and the "private point of view" as part of his Narcissus fixation, and is quite shut off from Blake's awareness or that of the Psalmist, that we become what we behold.

Today when we want to get our bearings in our own culture, and have need to stand aside from the bias and pressure exerted by any technical form of human expression, we have only to visit a society where that particular form has not been felt, or a historical period in which it was unknown. Professor Wilbur Schramm made such a tactical move in studying *Television in the Lives of Our Children.* He found areas where TV had not penetrated at all and ran some tests. Since he had made no study of the peculiar nature of the TV image, his tests were of "content" preferences, viewing time, and vocabulary counts. In a word, his approach to the problem was a literary one, albeit unconsciously so. Consequently, he had nothing to report. Had his methods been employed in 1500 A. D. to discover the effects of the printed book in the lives of children or adults, he could have found out nothing of the changes in human and social psychology resulting from typography. Print created individualism and nationalism in the sixteenth century. Program and "content" analysis offer no clues to the magic of these media or to their subliminal charge.

Leonard Doob, in his report *Communication in Africa,* tells of one African who took great pains to listen each evening to the BBC news, even though he could understand nothing of it. Just to be in the presence of those sounds at 7 P.M.

each day was important for him. His attitude to speech was like ours to melody—the resonant intonation was meaning enough. In the seventeenth century our ancestors still shared this native's attitude to the forms of media, as is plain in the following sentiment of the Frenchman Bernard Lam expressed in *The Art of Speaking* (London, 1696):

> 'Tis an effect of the Wisdom of God, who created Man to be happy, that whatever is useful to his conversation (way of life) is agreeable to him . . . because all victual that conduces to nourishment is relishable, whereas other things that cannot be assimilated and be turned into our substance are insipid. A Discourse cannot be pleasant to the Hearer that is not easie to the Speaker; nor can it be easily pronounced unless it be heard with delight.

Here is an equilibrium theory of human diet and expression such as even now we are only striving to work out again for media after centuries of fragmentation and specialism.

Pope Pius XII was deeply concerned that there be serious study of the media today. On February 17, 1950, he said:

> It is not an exaggeration to say that the future of modern society and the stability of its inner life depend in large part on the maintenance of an equilibrium between the strength of the techniques of communication and the capacity of the individual's own reaction

Failure in this respect has for centuries been typical and total for mankind. Subliminal and docile acceptance of media impact has made them prisons without walls for their human users. As A. J. Liebling remarked in his book *The Press,* a man is not free if he cannot see where he is going, even if he has a gun to help him get there. For each of the media is also a powerful weapon with which to clobber other media and other groups. The result is that the present age has been one of multiple civil wars that are not limited to the world of art and entertainment. In *War and Human Progress,* Professor J. U. Nef declared: "The total wars of our time have been the result of a series of intellectual mistakes . . ."

If the formative power in the media are the media themselves, that raises a host of large matters that can only be mentioned here, although they deserve volumes. Namely, that technological media are staples or natural resources, exactly as are coal and cotton and oil. Anybody will concede that society whose economy is dependent upon one or two major staples like cotton, or grain, or lumber, or fish, or cattle is going to have some obvious social patterns of organization as a result. Stress on a few major staples creates extreme instability in the economy but great endurance in the population. The pathos and humor of the American South are embedded in such an economy of limited staples. For a society configured by reliance on a few commodities accepts them as a social bond quite as much as the metropolis does the press. Cotton and oil, like radio and TV, become "fixed charges" on the entire psychic life of the community. And this pervasive fact creates the unique cultural flavor of any society. It pays through the nose and all its other senses for each staple that shapes its life.

That our human senses, of which all media are extensions, are also fixed charges on our personal energies, and that they also configure the awareness and experience of each one of us, may be perceived in another connection mentioned by the psychologist C. G. Jung:

> Every Roman was surrounded by slaves. The slave and his psychology flooded ancient Italy, and every Roman became inwardly, and of course unwittingly, a slave. Because living constantly in the atmosphere of slaves, he became infected through the unconscious with their psychology. No one can shield himself from such an influence.
>
> Contributions to Analytical Psychology, *London, 1928.*

Media Hot and Cold

"The rise of the waltz," explained Curt Sachs in the *World History of the Dance,* "was a result of that longing for truth, simplicity, closeness to nature, and primitivism, which the last two-thirds of the eighteenth century fulfilled." In the century of jazz we are likely to overlook the emergence of the waltz as a hot and explosive human expression that broke through the formal feudal barriers of courtly and choral dance styles.

There is a basic principle that distinguishes a hot medium like radio from a cool one like the telephone, or a hot medium like the movie from a cool one like TV. A hot medium is one that extends one single sense in "high definition." High definition is the state of being well filled with data. A photograph is, visually, "high definition." A cartoon is "low definition," simply because very little visual information is provided. Telephone is a cool medium, or one of low definition, because the ear is given a meager amount of information. And speech is a cool medium of low definition because so little is given and so much has to be filled in by the listener. On the other hand, hot media do not leave so much to be filled in or completed by the audience. Hot media are, therefore, low in participation, and cool media are high in participation or completion by the audience. Naturally, therefore, a hot medium like radio has very different effects on the user from a cool medium like the telephone.

A cool medium like hieroglyphic or ideogrammic written characters has very different effects from the hot and explosive medium of the phonetic alphabet. The alphabet, when pushed to a high degree of abstract visual intensity, became typography. The printed word with its specialist intensity burst the bonds of medieval corporate guilds and monasteries, creating extreme individualist patterns of enterprise and monopoly. But the typical reversal occurred when extremes of monopoly brought back the corporation, with its impersonal empire over many lives. The hotting-up of the medium of writing to repeatable print intensity led to nationalism and the religious wars of the sixteenth century. The heavy and unwieldy media, such as stone, are time binders. Used for writing, they are very cool indeed, and serve to unify the ages; whereas paper is a hot medium that serves to unify spaces horizontally, both in political and entertainment empires.

Any hot medium allows of less participation than a cool one, as a lecture makes for less participation than a seminar, and a book for less than dialogue.

With print many earlier forms were excluded from life and art, and many were given strange new intensity. But our own time is crowded with examples of the principle that the hot form excludes, and the cool one includes. When ballerinas began to dance on their toes a century ago, it was felt that the art of the ballet had acquired a new "spirituality." With this new intensity, male figures were excluded from ballet. The role of woman had also become fragmented with the advent of industrial specialism and the explosion of home functions into laundries, bakeries, and hospitals on the periphery of the community. Intensity or high definition engenders specialism and fragmentation in living as in entertainment, which explains why any intense experience must be "forgotten," "censored," and reduced to a very cool state before it can be "learned" or assimilated. The Freudian "censor" is less of a moral function that an indispensable condition of learning. Were we to accept fully and directly every shock to our various structures of awareness, we would soon be nervous wrecks, doing double-takes and pressing panic buttons every minute. The "censor" protects our central system of values, as it does our physical nervous system by simply cooling off the onset of experience a great deal. For many people, this cooling system brings on a lifelong state of psychic *rigor mortis,* or of somnambulism, particularly observable in periods of new technology.

An example of the disruptive impact of a hot technology succeeding a cool one is given by Robert Theobald in *The Rich and the Poor.* When Australian natives were given steel axes by the missionaries, their culture, based on the stone axe, collapsed. The stone axe had not only been scarce but had always been a basic status symbol of male importance. The missionaries provided quantities of sharp steel axes and gave them to women and children. The men had even to borrow these from the women, causing a collapse of male dignity. A tribal and feudal hierarchy of traditional kind collapses quickly when it meets any hot medium of the mechanical, uniform, and repetitive kind. The medium of money or wheel or writing, or any other form of specialist speedup of exchange and information, will serve to fragment a tribal structure. Similarly, a very much greater speed-up, such as occurs with electricity, may serve to restore a tribal pattern of intense involvement such as took place with the introduction of radio in Europe, and is now tending to happen as a result of TV in America. Specialist technologies detribalize. The nonspecialist electric technology retribalizes. The process of upset resulting from a new distribution of skills is accompanied by much culture lag in which people feel compelled to look at new situations as if they were old ones, and come up with ideas of "population explosion" in an age of implosion. Newton, in an age of clocks, managed to present the physical universe in the image of a clock. But poets like Blake were far ahead of Newton in their response to the challenge of the clock. Blake spoke of the need to be delivered "from single vision and Newton's sleep," knowing very well that Newton's response to the challenge of the new mechanism was itself merely a mechanical repetition of the challenge. Blake saw Newton and Locke and others as hypnotized Narcissus types quite unable to meet the challenge of mechanism.

W. B. Yeats gave the full Blakean version of Newton and Locke in a famous epigram:

> Locke sank into a swoon;
> The garden dies;
> God took the spinning jenny
> Out of his side

Yeats presents Locke, the philosopher of mechanical and lineal associationism, as hypnotized by his own image. The "garden," or unified consciousness, ended. Eighteenth-century man got an extension of himself in the form of the spinning machine that Yeats endows with its full sexual significance. Woman, herself, is thus seen as a technological extension of man's being.

Blake's counterstrategy for his age was to meet mechanism with organic myth. Today, deep in the electric age, organic myth is itself a simple and automatic response capable of mathematical formulation and expression, without any of the imaginative perception of Blake about it. Had he encountered the electric age, Blake would not have met its challenge with a mere repetition of electric form. For myth *is* the instant vision of a complex process that ordinarily extends over a long period. Myth is contraction or implosion of any process, and the instant speed of electricity confers the mythic dimension on ordinary industrial and social action today. We *live* mythically but continue to think fragmentarily and on single planes.

Scholars today are acutely aware of a discrepancy between their ways of treating subjects and the subject itself. Scriptural scholars of both the Old and New Testaments frequently say that while their treatment must be linear, the subject is not. The subject treats of the relations between God and man, and between God and the world, and of the relations between man and his neighbor—all these subsist together, and act and react upon one another at the same time. The Hebrew and Eastern mode of thought tackles problem and resolution, at the outset of a discussion, in a way typical of oral societies in general. The entire message is then traced and retraced, again and again, on the rounds of a concentric spiral with seeming redundancy. One can stop anywhere after the first few sentences and have the full message, if one is prepared to "dig" it. This kind of plan seems to have inspired Frank Lloyd Wright in designing the Guggenheim Art Gallery on a spiral, concentric basis. It is a redundant form inevitable to the electric age, in which the concentric pattern is imposed by the instant quality, and overlay in depth, of electric speed. But the concentric with its endless intersection of planes is necessary for insight. In fact, it is the technique of insight, and as such is necessary for media study, since no medium has its meaning or existence alone, but only in constant interplay with other media.

The new electric structuring and configuring of life more and more encounters the old lineal and fragmentary procedures and tools of analysis from the mechanical age. More and more we turn from the content of messages to study total effect. Kenneth Boulding put this matter in *The Image* by saying, "The meaning of a message is the change which it produces in the image." Concern with *effect* rather than *meaning* is a basic change of our electric time, for effect involves the total situation, and not a single level of information movement. Strangely, there is recognition of this matter of effect rather than information in the British idea of libel: "The greater the truth, the greater the libel."

The effect of electric technology had at first been anxiety. Now it appears to create boredom. We have been through the three stages of alarm, resistance, and exhaustion that occur in every disease or stress of life, whether individual or collective. At least, our exhausted slump after the first encounter with the electric has inclined us to expect new problems. However, backward countries that have experienced little permeation with our own mechanical and specialist culture are much better able to confront and to understand electric technology. Not only have backward and nonindustrial cultures no specialist habits to overcome in their encounter with electromagnetism, but they have still much of their traditional oral culture that has the total, unified "field" character of our new electromagnetism. Our old industrialized areas, having eroded their oral traditions automatically, are in the position of having to rediscover them in order to cope with the electric age.

In terms of the theme of media hot and cold, backward countries are cool, and we are hot. The "city slicker" is hot, and the rustic is cool. But in terms of the reversal of procedures and values in the electric age, the past mechanical time was hot, and we of the TV age are cool. The waltz was a hot, fast mechanical dance suited to the industrial time in its moods of pomp and circumstance. In contrast, the Twist is a cool, involved and chatty form of improvised gesture. The jazz of the period of the hot new media of movie and radio was hot jazz. Yet jazz of itself tends to be a casual dialogue form of dance quite lacking in the repetitive and mechanical forms of the waltz. Cool jazz came in quite naturally after the first impact of radio and movie had been absorbed.

In the special Russian issue of *Life* magazine for September 13, 1963, it is mentioned that in Russian restaurants and night clubs, "though the Charleston is tolerated, the Twist is taboo." All this is to say that a country in the process of industrialization is inclined to regard hot jazz as consistent with its developing programs. The cool and involved form of the Twist, on the other hand, would strike such a culture at once as retrograde and incompatible with its new mechanical stress. The Charleston, with its aspect of a mechanical doll agitated by strings, appears in Russia as an avant-garde form. We, on the other hand, find the *avant-garde* in the cool and the primitive, with its promise of depth involvement and integral expression.

The "hard" sell and the "hot" line become mere comedy in the TV age, and the death of all the salesmen at one stroke of the TV axe has turned the hot American culture into a cool one that is quite unacquainted with itself. America, in fact, would seem to be living through the reverse process that Margaret Mead described in *Time* magazine (September 4, 1954): "There are too many complaints about society having to move too fast to keep up with the machine. There is great advantage in moving fast if you move completely, if social, educational, and recreational changes keep pace. You must change the whole pattern at once and the whole group together—and the people themselves must decide to move."

Margaret Mead is thinking here of change as uniform speed-up of motion or a uniform hotting-up of temperatures in backward societies. We are certainly coming within conceivable range of a world automatically controlled to the point where we could say, "Six hours less radio in Indonesia next week or there will be a great falling off in literary attention." Or, "We can program twenty more hours of TV in South Africa next week to cool down the tribal temperature raised by radio last week." Whole cultures could now be programmed to keep their emotional climate stable in the same way that we have begun to know something about maintaining equilibrium in the commercial economies of the world.

In the merely personal and private sphere we are often reminded of how changes of tone and attitude are demanded of different times and seasons in order to keep situations in hand. British clubmen, for the sake of companionship and amiability, have long excluded the hot topics of religion and politics from mention inside the highly participational club. In the same vein, W. H. Auden wrote, ". . . this season the man of goodwill will wear his heart up his sleeve, not on it. . . . the honest manly style is today suited only to Iago" (Introduction to John Betjeman's *Slick But Not Streamlined*). In the Renaissance, as print technology hotted up the social *milieu* to a very high point, the gentleman and the courtier (Hamlet-Mercutio style) adopted, in contrast, the casual and cool nonchalance of the playful and superior being. The Iago allusion of Auden reminds us that Iago was the *alter ego* and assistant of the intensely earnest and very non-nonchalant General Othello. In imitation of the earnest and forthright general, Iago hotted up his own image and wore his heart on his sleeve, until General Othello read him loud and clear as "honest Iago," a man after his own grimly earnest heart.

Throughout *The City in History,* Lewis Mumford favors the cool or casually structured towns over the hot and intensely filled-in cities. The great period of Athens, he feels, was one during which most of the democratic habits of village life and participation still obtained. Then burst forth the full variety of human expression and exploration such as was later impossible in highly developed urban centers. For the highly developed situation is, by definition, low in opportunities of participation, and rigorous in its demands of specialist fragmentation from those who would control it. For example, what is known as "job enlargement" today in business and in management consists in allowing the employee more freedom to discover and define his function. Likewise, in reading a detective story the reader participates as co-author simply because so much has been left out of the narrative. The open-mesh silk stocking is far more sensuous than the smooth nylon, just because the eye must act as hand in filling in and completing the image, exactly as in the mosaic of the TV image.

Douglas Cater in *The Fourth Branch of Government* tells how the men of the Washington press bureaus delighted to complete or fill in the blank of Calvin Coolidge's personality. Because he was so like a mere cartoon, they felt the urge to complete his image for him and his public. It is instructive that the press applied the word "cool" to Cal. In the very sense of a cool medium, Calvin Coolidge was word for him. He was real cool. In the hot 1920s, the hot press medium found Cal very cool and rejoiced in his lack of image, since it compelled the participation of the press in filling in an image of him for the public. By contrast F.D.R. was a hot press agent, himself a rival of the newspaper medium and one who delighted in scoring off the press on the rival hot medium of radio. Quite in contrast, Jack Paar ran a cool show for the cool TV medium, and became a rival for the patrons of the night spots and their allies in the gossip columns. Jack Paar's war with the gossip columnists was a weird example of clash between a hot and cold medium such as had occurred with the "scandal of the rigged TV quiz shows." The rivalry between the hot press and radio media, on one hand, and TV on the other, for the hot ad buck, served to confuse and to overheat the issues in the affair that pointlessly involved Charles Van Doren.

An Associated Press story from Santa Monica, California, August 9, 1962, reported how

> Nearly 100 traffic violators watched a police traffic accident film today to atone for their violations. Two had to be treated for nausea and shock. . . .
> Viewers were offered a $5.00 reduction in fines if they agreed to see the movie, *Signal* 30, made by Ohio State police.
> It showed twisted wreckage and mangled bodies and recorded the screams of accident victims.

Whether the hot film medium using hot content would cool off the hot drivers is a moot point. But it does concern any understanding of media. The effect of hot media treatment cannot include much empathy or participation at any time. In this connection an insurance ad that featured Dad in an iron lung surrounded by a joyful family group did more to strike terror into the reader than all the warning wisdom in the world. It is a question that arises in connection with capital punishment. Is a severe penalty the best deterrent to serious crime? With regard to the bomb and the cold war, is the threat of massive retaliation the most effective means to peace? Is it not evident in every human situation that is pushed to a point of saturation that some precipitation occurs? When all the available resources and energies have been played up in an organism or in any structure there is some kind of reversal of pattern. The spectacle of brutality used as deterrent can brutalize. Brutality used in sports may humanize under some conditions, at least. But with regard to the bomb and retaliation as deterrent, it is obvious that numbness is the result of any prolonged terror, a fact that was discovered when the fallout shelter program was broached. The price of eternal vigilance is indifference.

Nevertheless, it makes all the difference whether a hot medium is used in a hot or cool culture. The hot radio medium used in cool or nonliterate cultures has a violent effect, quite unlike its effect, say in England or America, where radio is felt as entertainment. A cool or low literacy culture cannot accept hot media like movies or radio as entertainment. They are, at least, as radically upsetting for them as the cool TV medium has proved to be for our high literacy world.

And as for the cool war and the hot bomb scare, the cultural strategy that is desperately needed is humor and play. It is play that cools off the hot situations of actual life by miming them. Competitive sports between Russia and the West will hardly serve that purpose of relaxation. Such sports are inflammatory, it is plain. And what we consider entertainment or fun in our media inevitably appears as violent political agitation to a cool culture.

One way to spot the basic difference between hot and cold media uses is to compare and contrast a broadcast of a symphony performance with a broadcast of a symphony rehearsal. Two of the finest shows ever released by the CBC were of Glenn Gould's procedure in recording piano recitals, and Igor Stravinsky's rehearsing the Toronto symphony in some of his new work. A cool medium like TV, when really used, demands this involvement in process. The neat tight package is suited to hot media, like radio and gramophone. Francis Bacon never tired of contrasting hot and cool prose. Writing in "methods" or complete packages, he contrasted with writing in aphorisms, or single observations such as "Revenge is a kind of wild justice." The passive consumer wants packages, but those, he suggested, who are concerned in pursuing knowledge and in seeking causes will resort to aphorisms, just because they are incomplete and require participation in depth.

The principle that distinguishes hot and cold media is perfectly embodied in the folk wisdom: "Men seldom make passes at girls who wear glasses." Glasses intensify the outward going vision, and fill in the feminine image exceedingly, Marion the Librarian notwithstanding. Dark glasses, on the other hand, create the inscrutable and inaccessible image that invites a great deal of participation and completion.

Again, in a visual and highly literate culture, when we meet a person for the first time his visual appearance dims out the sound of the name, so that in self-defense we add: "How do you spell your name?" Whereas, in an ear culture, the *sound* of a man's name is the overwhelming fact, as Joyce knew when he said in *Finnegans Wake,* "Who gave you that numb?" For the name of a man is a numbing blow from which he never recovers.

Another vantage point from which to test the difference between hot and cold media is the practical joke. The hot literary medium excludes the practical and participant aspect of the joke so completely that Constance Rourke, in her *American Humor,* considers it as no joke at all. To literary people, the practical joke with its total physical involvement is as distasteful as the pun that derails us from the smooth and uniform progress that is typographic order. Indeed, to the literary person who is quite unaware of the intensely abstract nature of the typographic medium, it is the grosser and participant forms of art that seem "hot," and the abstract and intensely literary form that seems "cool." "You may perceive, Madam," said Dr. Johnson, with a pugilistic smile, "that I am well-bred to a degree of needless scrupulosity." And Dr. Johnson was right in supposing that "well-bred" had come to mean a white-shirted stress on attire that rivaled the rigor of the printed page. "Comfort" consists in abandoning a visual arrangement in favor on one that permits casual participation of the senses, a state that is excluded when any one sense, but especially the visual sense, is hotted up to the point of dominant command of a situation.

On the other hand, in experiments in which all outer sensation is withdrawn, the subject begins a furious fill-in or completion of senses that is sheer hallucination. So the hotting-up of one sense tends to result in hallucination.

From **The Psychedelic Experience**
TIMOTHY LEARY

General Introduction

A psychedelic experience is a journey to new realms of consciousness. The scope and content of the experience is limitless, but its characteristic features are the transcendence of verbal concepts, of space-time dimensions, and of the ego or identity. Such experiences of enlarged consciousness can occur in a variety of ways: sensory deprivation, yoga exercises, disciplined meditation, religious or aesthetic ecstasies, or spontaneously. Most recently they have become available to anyone through the ingestion of psychedelic drugs such as LSD, psilocybin, mescaline, DMT, etc.*

Of course, the drug does not produce the transcendent experience. It merely acts as a chemical key—it opens the mind, frees the nervous system of its ordinary patterns and structures. The nature of the experience depends almost entirely on set and setting. Set denotes the preparation of the individual, including his personality structure and his mood at the time. Setting is physical—the weather, the room's atmosphere; social—feelings of persons present towards one another; and cultural—prevailing views as to what is real. It is for this reason that manuals or guide-books are necessary. Their purpose is to enable a person to understand the new realities of the expanded consciousness, to serve as road maps for new interior territories which modern science has made accessible.

Different explorers draw different maps. Other manuals are to be written based on different models—scientific, aesthetic, therapeutic. The Tibetan model, on which this manual is based, is designed to teach the person to direct and control awareness in such a way as to reach that level of understanding variously called liberation, illumination, or enlightenment. If the manual is read several times before a session is attempted, and if a trusted person is there to remind and refresh the memory of the voyager during the experience, the consciousness will be freed from the games which comprise "personality" and from positive-negative

---

* This is the statement of an ideal, not an actual situation, in 1964. The psychedelic drugs are in the United States classified as "experimental" drugs. That is, they are not available on a prescription basis, but only to "qualified investigators." The Federal Food and Drug Administration has defined "qualified investigators" to mean psychiatrists working in a mental hospital setting, whose research is sponsored by either state or federal agencies.

hallucinations which often accompany states of expanded awareness. *The Tibetan* over that the free consciousness has only to hear and remember the teachings in order to be liberated.

The Tibetan Book of the Dead is ostensibly a book describing the experiences to be expected at the moment of death, during an intermediate phase lasting forty-nine (seven times seven) days, and during rebirth into another bodily frame. This however is merely the exoteric framework which the Tibetan Buddhists used to cloak their mystical teachings. The language and symbolism of death rituals of Bonism, the traditional pre-Buddhist Tibetan religion, were skillfully blended with Buddhist conceptions. The esoteric meaning, as it has been interpreted in this manual, is that it is death and rebirth of the ego that is described, not of the body. Lama Govinda indicates this clearly in his introduction when he writes: "It is a book for the living as well as for the dying." The book's esoteric meaning is often concealed beneath many layers of symbolism. It was not intended for general reading. It was designed to be understood only by one who was to be initiated personally by a *guru* into the Buddhist mystical doctrines, into the premortem-death-rebirth experience. These doctrines have been kept a closely guarded secret for many centuries, for fear that naive or careless application would do harm. In translating such an esoteric text, therefore, there are two steps: one, the rendering of the original text into English; and two, the practical interpretation of the text for its uses. In publishing this practical interpretation for use in the psychedelic drug session, we are in a sense breaking with the tradition of secrecy and thus contravening the teachings of the *lama-gurus.*

However, this step is justified on the grounds that the manual will not be understood by anyone who has not had a consciousness-expanding experience and that there are signs that the *lamas* themselves, after their recent diaspora, wish to make their teachings available to a wider public.

Following the Tibetan model then, we distinguish three phases of the psychedelic experience. The first period *(Chikhai Bardo)* is that of complete transcendence—beyond words, beyond space-time, beyond self. There are no visions, no sense of self, no thoughts. There are only pure awareness and ecstatic freedom from all game (and biological) involvements. *The second lengthy period involves self, or external game reality *(Chönyid Bardo)*—in sharp exquisite clarity or in the form of hallucinations (karmic apparitions). The final period *(Sidpa Bardo)* involves the return to routine game reality and the self. For most persons the second (aesthetic or hallucinatory) stage is the longest. For the initiated the first stage of illumination lasts longer. For the unprepared, the heavy game players, those who anxiously cling to their egos, and for those who take the drug in a non-supportive setting, the struggle to regain reality begins early and usually lasts to the end of their session.

---

* "Games" are behavioral sequences defined by roles, rules, rituals, goals, strategies, values, language, characteristic space-time locations and characteristic patterns of movement. Any behavior not having these nine features is non-game: this includes physiological reflexes, spontaneous play, and transcendent awareness.

Words like these are static, whereas the psychedelic experience is fluid and ever-changing. Typically the subject's consciousness flicks in and out of these three levels with rapid oscillations. One purpose of this manual is to enable the person to regain the transcendence of the First Bardo and to avoid prolonged entrapments in hallucinatory or ego-dominated game patterns.

The Basic Trusts and Beliefs

You must be ready to accept the possibility that there is a limitless range of awarenesses for which we now have no words; that awareness can expand beyond the range of your ego, your self, your familiar identity, beyond everything you have learned, beyond your notions of space and time, beyond the differences which usually separate people from each other and from the world around them.

You must remember that throughout human history, millions have made this voyage. A few (whom we call mystics, saints or buddhas) have made this experience endure and have communicated it to their fellow men. You must remember, too, that the experience is safe (at the very worst, you will end up the same person who entered the experience), and that all of the dangers which you have feared are unnecessary productions of your mind. Whether you experience heaven or hell, remember that it is your mind which creates them. Avoid grasping the one or fleeing the other. Avoid imposing the ego game on the experience.

You must try to maintain faith and trust in the potentiality of your own brain and the billion-year old life process. With your ego left behind you, the brain can't go wrong.

Try to keep the memory of a trusted friend or a respected person whose name can serve as guide and protection.

Trust your divinity, trust your brain, trust your companions.

Whenever in doubt, turn off your mind, relax, float downstream.

After reading this guide, the prepared person should be able, at the very beginning of his experience, to move directly to a state of non-game ecstasy and deep revelation. But if you are not well prepared, or if there is game distraction around you, you will find yourself dropping back. . . .

> Liberation in this context does not necessarily imply (especially in the case of the average person) the Liberation of Nirvana, but chiefly a liberation of the 'life-flux' from the ego, in such manner as will afford the greatest possible consciousness and consequent happy rebirth. Yet for the very experienced and very highly efficient person, the [same] esoteric process of Transference can be, according to the *lama-gurus,* so employed as to prevent any break in the flow of the stream of consciousness, from the moment of the ego-loss to the moment of a conscious rebirth (eight hours later). Judging from the translation made by the late Lama Kazi Dawa-Samdup, of an old Tibetan manuscript containing practical directions for ego-loss states, the ability to maintain a non-game ecstasy throughout the entire experience is possessed only by persons trained in mental concentration, or one-pointedness of mind, to such a high degree of proficiency as to be able to control all the mental functions and to shut out the distractions of the outside world.

Evans-Wentz, p. 86, note 2

This manual is divided into four parts. The first part is introductory. The second is a step-by-step description of a psychedelic experience based directly on the Tibetan Book of the Dead. The third part contains practical suggestions on how to prepare for and conduct a psychedelic session. The fourth part contains instructive passages adapted from the *Bardo Thödol,* which may be read to the voyager during the session, to facilitate the movement of consciousness.

In the remainder of this introductory section, we review three commentaries on the Tibetan Book of the Dead, published with the Evans-Wentz edition. These are the introduction by Evans-Wentz himself, the distinguished translator-editor of four treatises on Tibetan mysticism; the commentary by Carl Jung, the Swiss psychoanalyst; and by Lama Govinda, an initiate of one of the principal Buddhist orders of Tibet. . . .

A Tribute to Lama Anagarika Govinda

. . . Eastern philosophy and psychology—poetic, indeterministic, experiential, inward-looking, vaguely evolutionary, open-ended—is more easily adapted to the findings of modern science than the syllogistic, certain, experimental, externalizing logic of western psychology. The latter imitates the irrelevant rituals of the energy sciences but ignores the data of physics and genetics, the meanings and implications.

Even Carl Jung, the most penetrating of the western psychologists, failed to understand the basic philosophy of the *Bardo Thödol.*

Quite in contrast are the comments on the Tibetan manual by Lama Anagarika Govinda.

His opening statement at first glance would cause a Judaeo-Christian psychologist to snort in impatience. But a close look at these phrases reveals that they are the poetic statement of the genetic situation as currently described by biochemists and DNA researchers.

> It may be argued that nobody can talk about death with authority who has not died; and since nobody, apparently, has ever returned from death, how can anybody know what death is, or what happens after it?
>   The Tibetan will answer: "There is not *one* person, indeed, not *one* living being, that has *not* returned from death. In fact, we all have died many deaths, before we came into this incarnation. And what we call birth is merely the reverse side of death, like one of the two sides of a coin, or like a door which we call 'entrance' from outside and 'exit' from inside a room."

The *lama* then goes on to make a second poetic comment about the potentialities of the nervous system, the complexity of the human cortical computer.

> It is much more astonishing that not everybody remembers his or her previous death; and, because of this lack of remembering, most persons do not believe there was a previous death. But, likewise, they do not remember their recent

birth—and yet they do not doubt that they were recently born. They forget the active memory is only a small part of our normal consciousness, and that our subconscious memory registers and preserves every past impression and experience which our waking mind fails to recall.

The *lama* then proceeds to slice directly to the esoteric meaning of the *Bardo Thödol*—that core meaning which Jung and indeed most European Orientalists have failed to grasp.

> For this reason, the *Bardo Thödol,* the Tibetan book vouchsafing liberation from the intermediate state between life and re-birth,—which state men call death,—has been couched in symbolical language. It is a book which is sealed with the seven seals of silence,—not because its knowledge should be withheld from the uninitiated, but because its knowledge would be misunderstood, and, therefore, would tend to mislead and harm those who are unfitted to receive it. But the time has come to break the seals of silence; for the human race has come to the juncture where is must decide whether to be content with the subjugation of the material world, or to strive after the conquest of the spiritual world, by subjugating selfish desires and transcending self-imposed limitations.

The *lama* next describes the effects of consciousness-expansion techniques. He is talking here about the method he knows—the Yogic—but his words are equally applicable to psychedelic experience.

> There are those who, in virtue of concentration and other *yogic* practices, are able to bring the subconscious into the realm of discriminative consciousness and, thereby, to draw upon the unrestricted treasury of subconscious memory, wherein are stored the records not only of our past lives but the records of the past of our race, the past of humanity, and all pre-human forms of life, if not of the very consciousness that makes life possible in this universe.
>   If, through some trick of nature, the gates of an individual's subconsciousness were suddenly to spring open, the unprepared mind would be overwhelmed and crushed. Therefore, the gates of the subconscious are guarded, by all initiates, and hidden behind the veil of mysteries and symbols.

In a later section of his foreword the *lama* present a more detailed elaboration of the inner meaning of the *Thödol.*

> If the *Bardo Thödol* were to be regarded as being based merely upon folklore, or as consisting of religious speculation about death and a hypothetical after-death state, it would be of interest only to anthropologists and students of religion. But the *Bardo Thödol* is far more. It is a key to the innermost recesses of the human mind, and a guide for initiates, and for those who are seeking the spiritual path of liberation.
>   Although the *Bardo Thödol* is at present time widely used in Tibet as a breviary, and read or recited on the occasion of death,—for which reason it has been aptly called "The Tibetan Book of the Dead"—one should not forget that it was originally conceived to serve as a guide not only for the dying and the dead, but for the living as well. And herein lies the justification for having made *The Tibetan Book of the Dead* accessible to a wider public.
>   Notwithstanding the popular customs and beliefs which, under the influence of age-old traditions of pre-Buddhist origin, have grown around the profound revelations of the *Bardo Thödol,* it has value only for those who practise and realize its teaching during their life-time.

There are two things which have caused misunderstanding. One is that the teachings seem to be addressed to the dead or the dying; the other that the title contains the expression "Liberation through Hearing" (in Tibetan, *Thos-grol*). As a result, there has arisen the belief that it is sufficient to read or to recite the *Bardo Thödol* in the presence of a dying person, or even of a person who has just died, in order to effect his or her liberation.

Such misunderstanding could only have arisen among those who do not know that it is one of the oldest and most universal practices for the initiate to go through the experience of death before he can be spiritually reborn. Symbolically he must die to his past, and to his old ego, before he can take his place in the new spiritual life into which he has been initiated.

The dead or the dying person is addressed in the *Bardo Thödol* mainly for three reasons: (1) the earnest practitioner of these teachings should regard every moment of his or her life as if it were the last; (2) when a follower of these teachings is actually dying, he or she should be reminded of the experiences at the time of initiation, or of the words (or *mantra*) of the *guru,* especially if the dying one's mind lacks alertness during the critical moments; and (3) one who is still incarnate should try to surround the person dying, or just dead, with loving and helpful thoughts during the first stages of the new, or afterdeath, state of existence, without allowing emotional attachment to interfere or to give rise to a state of morbid mental depression. Accordingly, one function of the *Bardo Thödol* appears to be more to help those who have been left behind to adopt the right attitude towards the dead and towards the fact of death than to assist the dead, who, according to Buddhist belief, will not deviate from their own *karmic* path. . . .

This proves that we have to do here with life itself and not merely with a mass for the dead, to which the *Bardo Thödol* was reduced in later times. . . .

Under the guise of a science of death, the *Bardo Thödol* reveals the secret of life; and therein lies its spiritual value and its universal appeal.

Here then is the key to a mystery which has been passed down for over 2,500 years—the consciousness-expansion experience—the pre-mortem death and rebirth rite. The Vedic sages knew the secret; the Eleusinian initiates knew it; the Tantrics knew it. In all their esoteric writings they whisper the message: it is possible to cut beyond ego-consciousness, to tune in on neurological processes which flash by at the speed of light, and to become aware of the enormous treasury of ancient racial knowledge welded into the nucleus of every cell in your body.

Modern psychedelic chemicals provide a key to this forgotten realm of awareness. But just as this manual without the psychedelic awareness is nothing but an exercise in academic Tibetology, so, too, the potent chemical key is of little value without the guidance and the teachings.

Westerners do not accept the existence of conscious processes for which they have no operational term. The attitude which is prevalent is:—if you can't label it, and if it is beyond current notions of space-time and personality, then it is not open for investigation. Thus we see the ego-loss experience confused with schizophrenia. Thus we see present-day psychiatrists solemnly pronouncing the psychedelic keys as psychosis-producing and dangerous.

The new visionary chemicals and the pre-mortem-death-rebirth experience may be pushed once again into the shadows of history. Looking back, we remember that every middle-eastern and European administrator (with the exception of certain periods in Greece and Persia) has, during the last three thousand years, rushed to pass laws against any emerging transcendental process, the pre-mortem-death-rebirth session, its adepts, and any new method of consciousness-expansion.

The present moment in human history (as Lama Govinda points out) is critical. Now, for the first time, we possess the means of providing the enlightenment to any prepared volunteer. (The enlightenment always comes, we remember, in the form of a new energy process, a physical, neurological event.) For these reasons we have prepared this psychedelic version of *The Tibetan Book of the Dead.* The secret is released once again, in a new dialect, and we sit back quietly to observe whether man is ready to move ahead and to make use of the new tools provided by modern science. . . .

First Bardo; The Period of Ego-loss or Non-game Ecstasy

Part 1: The Primary Clear Light Seen At the Moment of Ego-Loss.

All individuals who have received the practical teachings of this manual will, if the text be remembered, be set face to face with the ecstatic radiance and will win illumination instantaneously, without entering upon hallucinatory struggles and without further suffering on the age-long pathway of normal evolution which traverses the various worlds of game existence.

This doctrine underlies the whole of the Tibetan model. Faith is the first step on the "Secret Pathway." Then comes illumination and with it certainty; and when the goal is won, emancipation. Success implies very unusual preparation in consciousness expansion, as well as much calm, compassionate game playing (good *karma*) on the part of the participant. If the participant can be made to see and to grasp the idea of the empty mind as soon as the guide reveals it—that is to say, if he has the power to die consciously—and, at the supreme moment of quitting the ego, can recognize the ecstasy which will dawn upon him then, and become one with it, all game bonds of illusion are broken asunder immediately: the dreamer is awakened into reality simultaneously with the mighty achievement of recognition.

It is best if the *guru* (spiritual teacher), from whom the participant received guiding instructions, is present, but if the *guru* cannot be present, then another experienced person; or if the latter is also unavailable, then a person whom the participant trusts should be available to read this manual without imposing any of his own games. Thereby the participant will be put in mind of what he had previously heard of the experience and will at once come to recognize the fundamental Light and undoubtedly obtain liberation.

Liberation is the nervous system devoid of mental-conceptual activity. The mind in its conditioned state, that is to say, when limited to words and ego games, is continuously in thought-formation activity. The nervous system in a state of quiescence, alert, awake but not active is comparable to what Buddhists call the highest state of *dhyāna* (deep meditation) when still united to a human body. The conscious recognition of the Clear Light induces an ecstatic condition of consciousness such as saints and mystics of the West have called illumination.

The first sign is the glimpsing of the "Clear Light of Reality," "the infallible mind of the pure mystic state." This is the awareness of energy transformations with no imposition of mental categories.

The duration of this state varies with the individual. It depends upon experience, security, trust, preparation and the surroundings. In those who have had even a little practical experience of the tranquil state of non-game awareness, and in those who have happy games, this state can last from thirty minutes to several hours.

In this state, realization of what mystics call the "Ultimate Truth" is possible, provided that sufficient preparation has been made by the person beforehand. Otherwise he cannot benefit now, and must wander on into lower and lower conditions of hallucinations, as determined by his past games, until he drops back to routine reality.

It is important to remember that the consciousness-expansion process is the reverse of the birth process, birth being the beginning of game life and the ego-loss experience being a temporary ending of game life. But in both there is a passing from one state of consciousness into another. And just as an infant must wake up and learn from experience the nature of this world, so likewise a person at the moment of consciousness expansion must wake up in this new brilliant world and become familiar with its own peculiar conditions.

In those who are heavily dependent on their ego games, and who dread giving up their control, the illuminated state endures only so long as it would take to snap a finger. In some, it lasts as long as the time taken for eating a meal.

If the subject is prepared to diagnose the symptoms of ego loss, he needs no outside help at this point. Not only should the person about to give up his ego be able to diagnose the symptoms as they come, one by one, but he should also be able to recognize the Clear Light without being set face to face with it by another person. If the person fails to recognize and accept the onset of ego loss, he may complain of strange bodily symptoms. This shows that he has not reached a liberated state. Then the guide or friend should explain the symptoms as indicating the onset of ego loss.

Here is a list of commonly reported physical sensations:

1 Bodily pressure, which the Tibetans call earth-sinking-into-water;

2 Clammy coldness, followed by feverish heat, which the Tibetans call water-sinking-into-fire;

3 Body disintegrating or blown to atoms, called fire-sinking-into-air;

4 Pressure on head and ears, which Americans call rocket-launching-into-space;

5 Tingling in extremities;

6 Feelings of body melting or flowing as if wax;

7 Nausea;

8 Trembling or shaking, beginning in pelvic regions and spreading up torso.

These physical reactions should be recognized as signs heralding transcendence. Avoid treating them as symptoms of illness, accept them, merge with them, enjoy them.

Mild nausea occurs often with the ingestion of morning-glory seeds or peyote, rarely with mescaline and infrequently with LSD or psilocybin. If the subject experiences stomach messages, they should be hailed as a sign that consciousness is moving around in the body. The symptoms are mental; the mind controls the sensation, and the subject should merge with the sensation, experience it fully, enjoy it and having enjoyed it, let consciousness flow on to the next phase. It is usually more natural to let consciousness stay in the body—the subject's attention can move from the stomach and concentrate on breathing, heart beat. If this does not free him from nausea, the guide should move the consciousness to external events—music, walking in the garden, etc.

The appearance of physical symptoms of ego-loss, recognized and understood, should result in peaceful attainment of illumination. If ecstatic acceptance does not occur (or when the period of peaceful silence seems to be ending), the relevant sections of the instructions can be spoken in a low tone of voice in the ear. It is often useful to repeat them distinctly, clearly impressing them upon the person so as to prevent his mind from wandering. Another method of guiding the experience with a minimum of activity is to have the instructions previously recorded in the subject's own voice and to flip the tape on at the appropriate moment. The reading will recall to the mind of the voyager the former preparation; it will cause the naked consciousness to be recognized as the "Clear Light of the Beginning;" it will remind the subject of his unity with this state of perfect enlightenment and help him maintain it.

If, when undergoing ego-loss, one is familiar with this state, by virtue of previous experience and preparation, the Wheel of Rebirth (i.e., all game playing) is stopped, and liberation instantaneously is achieved. But such spiritual efficiency is so very rare, that the normal mental condition of the person is unequal to the supreme feat of holding on to the state in which the Clear Light shines; and there follows a progressive descent into lower and lower states of the Bardo existence, and then rebirth. The simile of a needle balanced and set rolling on a thread is used by the *lamas* to elucidate this condition. So long as the needle retains its balance, it remains on the thread. Eventually, however, the law of gravitation (the pull of the ego or external stimulation) affects it, and it falls. In the realm of the Clear Light, similarly, the mentality of a person in the ego-transcendent state momentarily enjoys a condition of balance, of perfect equilibrium, and of oneness.

Unfamiliar with such a state, which is an ecstatic state of non-ego, the consciousness of the average human being lacks the power to function in it. *Karmic* (i.e., game) propensities becloud the consciousness-principle with thoughts of personality, of individualized being, of dualism. Thus, losing equilibrium, consciousness falls away from the Clear Light. It is thought processes which prevent the realization of *Nirvāna* (which is the "blowing out of the flame" of selfish game desire); and so the Wheel of Life continues to turn.

All or some of the appropriate passages in the instructions may be read to the voyager during the period of waiting for the drug to take effect, and when the first symptoms of ego-loss appear. When the voyager is clearly in a profound ego-transcendent ecstasy, the wise guide will remain silent. . . .

Second Bardo; The Period of Hallucinations

Introduction

If the Primary Clear Light is not recognized, there remains the possibility of maintaining the Secondary Clear Light. If that is lost, then comes the *Chönyid Bardo,* the period of *karmic* illusions or intense hallucinatory mixtures of game reality. It is very important that the instructions be remembered—they can have great influence and effect.

During this period, the flow of consciousness, microscopically clear and intense, is interrupted by fleeting attempts to rationalize and interpret. But the normal game-playing ego is not functioning effectively. There exist, therefore, unlimited possibilities for, on the one hand, delightful sensuous, intellectual and emotional novelties if one floats with the current; and, on the other hand, fearful ambuscades of confusion and terror if one tries to impose his will on the experience.

The purpose of this part of the manual is to prepare the person for the choice points which arise during this stage. Strange sounds, weird sights and disturbed visions may occur. These can awe, frighten and terrify unless one is prepared.

The experienced person will be able to maintain the recognition that all perceptions come from within and will be able to sit quietly, controlling his expanded awareness like a phantasmagoric multi-dimensional television set: the most acute and sensitive hallucinations—visual, auditory, touch, smell, physical and bodily; the most exquisite reactions, compassionate insight into the self, the world. The key is *inaction:* passive integration with all that occurs around you. If you try to impose your will, use your mind, rationalize, seek explanations, you will get caught in hallucinatory whirlpools.

The motto: peace, acceptance. It is all an ever-changing panorama. You are temporarily removed from the world of game. Enjoy it.

The inexperienced and those to whom ego control is important may find this passivity impossible. If you cannot remain inactive and subdue your will, then the one certain activity which can reduce panic and pull you out of hallucinatory mind-games is physical contact with another person. Go to the guide or to another participant and put your head on his lap or chest; put your face next to his and concentrate on the movement and sound of his inspiration. Breathe deeply and feel the air rush in and the sighing release. This is the oldest form of living communication; the brotherhood of breath. The guide's hand on your forehead may add to the relaxation.

Contact with another participant may be misunderstood and provoke sexual hallucinations. For this reason, helping contact should be made explicit by prearrangement. Unprepared participants may impose sexual fears or fantasies on the contact. Turn them off; they are *karmic* illusory productions.

The tender, gentle, supportive huddling together of participants is a natural development during the second phase. Do not try to rationalize this contact. Human beings and, for that matter, most all mobile terrestrial creatures have been huddling together during long, dark confused nights for several hundred thousand years.

Breathe in and breathe out with your companions. We are all one! That's what your breath is telling you.

Explanation of the Second Bardo

The underlying problem of the Second Bardo is that any and every shape—human, divine, diabolical, heroic, evil, animal, thing—which the human brain conjures up or the past life recalls, can present itself to consciousness: shapes and forms and sounds whirling by endlessly.

The underlying solution—repeated again and again—is to recognize that your brain is producing the visions. They do not exist. Nothing exists except as your consciousness gives it life.

You are standing on the threshold of recognizing the truth: there is no reality behind any of the phenomena of the ego-loss state, save the illusions stored up in your own mind either as accretions from game *(Sangsāric)* experience or as gifts from organic physical nature and its billion-year-old past history. Recognition of this truth gives liberation.

There is, of course, no way of classifying the infinite permutations and combinations of visionary elements. The cortex contains file-cards for billions of images from the history of the person, of the race, and of living forms. Any of these, at the rate of a hundred million per second (according to neurophysiologists), can flood into awareness. Bobbing around in this brilliant, symphonic sea of imagery is the remnant of the conceptual mind. On the endless watery turbulence of the Pacific Ocean bobs a tiny open mouth shouting (between saline mouthfuls), "Order! System! Explain all this!"

One cannot predict what visions will occur, nor their sequence. One can only urge the participants to shut the mouth, breathe through the nose, and turn off the fidgety, rationalizing mind. But only the experienced person of mystical bent can do this (and thus remain in serene enlightenment). The unprepared person will be confused or, worse, panicky: the intellectual struggle to control the ocean. . . .

Vision 3: The Fire-Flow of Internal Unity

EYES CLOSED, EXTERNAL STIMULI IGNORED, EMOTIONAL ASPECTS

The First Bardo instructions should keep you face-to-face with the void-ecstasy. Yet there are classes of men who, having carried over *karmic* conflict about feeling-inhibition, prove unable to hold the pure experience beyond all feelings, and slip into emotionally toned visions. The undifferentiated energy of the First Bardo is woven into visionary games in the form of intense feelings. Exquisite, intense, pulsating sensations of unity and love will be felt; the negative counterpart is feelings of attachment, greed, isolation and bodily concerns.

It comes about this way: the pure flow of energy loses its white void quality and becomes sensed as intense feelings. An emotional game is imposed. Incredible new physical sensations pulse through the body. The glow of life is felt flooding along veins. One merges into a unitive ocean of orgastic, fluid electricity, the endless flow of shared-life, of love.

Visions related to the circulatory system are common. The subject tumbles down through his own arterial network. The motor of the heart reverberates as one with the pulsing of all life. The heart then breaks, and red fire bleeds out to merge with all living beings. All living organisms are throbbing together. One is joyfully aware of the two-billion-year-old electric sexual dance; one is at last divested of robot clothes and limbs and undulates in the endless chain of living forms.

Dominating this ecstatic state is the feeling of intense love. You are a joyful part of all life. The memory of former delusions of self-hood and differentiation invokes exultant laughter.

All the harsh, dry, brittle angularity of game life is melted. You drift off—soft, rounded, moist, warm. Merged with all life. You may feel yourself floating out and down into a warm sea. Your individuality and autonomy of movement are moistly disappearing. Your control is surrendered to the total organism. Blissful passivity. Ecstatic, orgiastic, undulating unity. All worries and concerns wash away. All is gained as everything is given up. There is organic revelation. Every cell in your body is singing its song of freedom—the entire biological universe is in harmony, liberated from the censorship and control of you and your restricted ambitions.

But wait! You, YOU, are disappearing into the unity. You are being swallowed up by the ecstatic undulation. Your ego, that one tiny remaining strand of self, screams STOP! You are terrified by the pull of the glorious, dazzling, transparent, radiant red light. You wrench yourself out of the life-flow, drawn by your intense attachment to your old desires. There is a terrible rending as your roots tear out of the life matrix—a ripping of your fibres and veins away from the greater body to which you were attached. And when you have cut yourself off from the fire-flow of life the throbbing stops, the ecstasy ceases, your limbs harden and stiffen into angular forms, your plastic doll body has regained its orientation. There you sit, isolated from the stream of life, impotent master of your desires and appetites, miserable.

While you are floating down the evolutionary river, there comes a sense of limitless self-less power. The delight of flowing cosmic belongingness. The astounding discovery that consciousness can tune in to an infinite number of organic levels. There are billions of cellular processes in your body, each with its universe of experience—an endless variety of ecstasies. The simple joys and pains and burdens of your ego represent one set of experiences—a repetitious, dusty set. As you slip into the fire-flow of biological energy, series after series of experiential sets flash by. You are no longer encapsulated in the structure of ego and tribe.

But through panic and a desire to latch on to the familiar, you shut off the flow, open your eyes; then the flowingness is lost. The potentiality to move from one level of consciousness to another is gone. Your fear and desire to control have driven you to settle for one static site of consciousness. To use the Eastern or genetic metaphor, you have frozen the dance of energy and committed yourself to one incarnation, and you have done it out of fear.

When this happens, there are several steps which can take you back to the biological flow (and from there to the First Bardo). First, close your eyes. Lie on your stomach and let your body sink through the floor, merge with the surroundings. Feel the hard, square edges of your body soften and start to move in the bloodstream. Let the rhythm of breathing become tide flow. Bodily contact is probably the most effective method of softening hardened surfaces. No movement. No body games. Close physical contact with another invariably brings about the unity of fire-flow. Your blood begins to flow into the other's body. His breathing pours into your lungs. You both drift down the capillary river.

Another form of life process images is the flow of auditory sensations. The endless series of abstract sounds (described in the preceding vision) bounce through awareness. The emotional reaction to these can be neutral or can involve intense feelings of unity, or of annoyed fear.

The positive reaction occurs when the subject merges with the sound flow. The thudding drum of the heart is sensed as the basic anthem of humanity. The whooshing sough of the breath as the rushing river of all life. Overwhelming feelings of love, gratitude and oneness funnel into the moment of sound, into each note of the biological concerto.

But, as always, the voyager may intrude his personality with its wants and opinions. He may not "like" the noise. His judgmental ego may be aesthetically offended by the sounds of life. The heart thud is, after all, monotonous; the natural music of the inner ear, with its clicks and hums and whistles, lacks the romantic symmetries of Beethoven. The terrible separation of "me" from my body occurs. Horrible. Out of my control. Turn it off. . . .

Vision 4:   The Wave-Vibration Structure of External Forms

EYES OPEN OR RAPT INVOLVEMENT WITH EXTERNAL STIMULI; INTELLECTUAL ASPECTS

The pure, content-free light of the First Bardo probably involves basic electrical wave energy. This is nameless, indescribable, because it is far beyond any concepts which we now possess. Some future atomic physicist may be able to classify this energy. Perhaps it will always be ineffable for a nervous system such as that of *homo sapiens.* Can an organic system "comprehend" the vastly more efficient inorganic? At any event, most persons, even the most illuminated, find it impossible to maintain experiential contact with this void-light and slip back to imposing mental structures, hallucinatory and revelatory, upon the flow.

Thus we are brought to another frequent vision which involves intense, rapt, unitive awareness of external stimuli. If the eyes are open, this super-reality effect can be visual. The penetrating impact of other stimuli can also set off revelatory imagery.

It comes about this way. The subject's awareness is suddenly invaded by an outside stimulus. His attention is captured, but his old conceptual mind is not functioning. But other sensitivities are engaged. He experiences direct sensation. The raw "is-ness." He sees, not objects, but patterns of light waves. He hears, not "music" or "meaningful" sound, but acoustic waves. He is struck with the sudden revelation that all sensation and perception are based on wave vibrations. That the world around him which heretofore had an illusory solidity, is nothing more than a play of physical waves. That he is involved in a cosmic television show which has no more substantiality that the images on his TV picture tube.

The atomic structure of matter is, of course, known to us intellectually, but never experienced by the adult except in states of intense altered consciousness. Learning from a physics textbook about the wave structure of matter is one thing. Experiencing it—being in it—with the old, familiar, gross, hallucinatory comfort of "solid" things gone and unavailable, is quite another matter.

If these super-real visions involve wave phenomena, then the external world takes on a radiance and a revelation that is staggeringly clear. The experienced insight that the world of phenomena exists in the form of waves, electronic images, can produce a sense of illuminated power. Everything is experienced as consciousness.

These exultant radiations should be recognized as productions of your own internal processes. You should not attempt to control or conceptualize. This can come later. There is the danger of hallucinatory freezing. The subject rushes back (sometimes literally) to the three-dimensional reality, convinced of the fixed "truth" of one experienced revelation. Many misguided mystics and many persons called insane have fallen into this ambuscade. This is like making a still photograph of a television pattern and shouting that one has finally seized the truth. All is ecstatic electric *Māyā* the two-billion-year dance of waves. No one part of it is more real than another. Everything at all moments is shimmering with all the meaning.

So far we have considered the positive radiance of clarity; but there are fearful negative aspects of the fourth vision. When the subject senses that his "world" is fragmenting into waves, he may become terrified. "He," "me," "I" are dissolving! The world around me is supposed to sit, static and dead, quietly awaiting my manipulation. But these passive things have changed into a shimmering dance of living energy! The *Māyā* nature of phenomena creates panic. Where is the solid base? Every thing, every concept, every form upon which one rests one's mind collapses into electrical vibrations lacking solidity.

The face of the guide or of one's beloved friend becomes a dancing mosaic of impulses on one's cortex. "My consciousness" has created everything of which I am conscious. I have kinescoped my world, my loved ones, myself. All are just shimmering energy patterns. Instead of clarity and exultant power, there is confusion. The subject staggers around, grasping at electron-patterns, striving to freeze them back into the familiar robot forms.

All solidity is gone. All phenomena are paper images pasted on the glass screen of consciousness. For the unprepared, or for the person whose *karmic* residue stresses control, the discovery of the wave-nature of all structure, the *Māyā* revelation, is a disastrous web of uncertainty.

We have discussed only the visual aspects of the fourth vision. Auditory phenomena are of equal importance. Here the solid, labelled nature of auditory patterns is lost, and the mechanical impact of sound hitting the eardrum is registered. In some cases, sound becomes converted into pure sensation, and synesthesia (mixture of sense modalities) occurs. Sounds are experienced as colors. External sensations hitting the cortex are recorded as molecular events, ineffable.

The most dramatic auditory visions occur with music. Just as any object radiates a pattern of electrons and can become the essence of all energy, so can any note of music be sensed as naked energy trembling in space, timeless. The movement of notes, like the shuttling of oscillograph beams. Each capturing all energy, the electric core of the universe. Nothing existing except the needle-clear resonance on the tympanic membrane. Unforgettable revelations about the nature of reality occur at these moments.

But the hellish interpretation is also possible. As the learned structure of sound collapses, the direct impact of waves can be sensed as noise. For one who is compelled to institute order, his order, on the world around him, it is at least annoying and often disturbing to have the raw tatoo of sound resonating in consciousness.

Noise! What an irreverent concept. Is not everything noise; all sensation the divine pattern of wave energy, meaningless only to those who insist on imposing their own meaning?

Preparation is the key to a serene passage through this visionary territory. The subject who has studied this manual will be able, when face to face with the phenomenon, to recognize and flow with it. . . .

Vision 5: The Vibratory Waves of External Unity

EYES OPEN, OR RAPT INVOLVEMENT WITH EXTERNAL STIMULI; EMOTIONAL ASPECTS

As the learned perceptions disappear and the structure of the external world disintegrates into direct wave phenomena, the aim is to maintain a pure, content-free awareness (First Bardo). Despite the preparations, one is likely to be led backwards by one's own mental inclinations into two hallucinatory or revelatory interpretations of reality. One reaction leads to the intellectual clarity or frightened confusion of the fourth vision (just described). Another interpretation is the emotional reaction to the fragmentation of differentiated forms. One can be engulfed in ecstatic unity, or one can slip into isolated egotism. The *Bardol Thödol* calls the former the "Wisdom of Equality" and the latter the "quagmire of worldly existence accruing from violent egotism." In the state of radiant unity, one senses that there is only one network of energy in the universe and that all things and all sentient beings are momentary manifestations of the single pattern. When egotistic interpretations are imposed on the fifth vision, the "plastic doll" phenomena are experienced. Differentiated forms are seen as inorganic, dull, mass-produced, shabby, plastic, and all persons (including self) are seen as lifeless mannequins isolated from the vibrant dance of energy, which has been lost.

The experiential data of this vision are similar to that of the fourth vision. All artifactual learned structure collapses back to energy vibrations. The awareness is dominated not by revelatory clarity but by shimmering unity. The subject is entranced by the silent, whirling play of forces. Exquisite forms dance by him, all surrounding objects radiate energy, brilliant emanations. His own body is seen as a play of forces. If he looks in a mirror, he sees a shining mosaic of particles. The sense of his own wave structure becomes stronger. A feeling of melting, floating off. The body is no longer a separate unit but a cluster of vibrations sending and receiving energy—a phase of the dance of energy which has been going on for millennia.

A sense of profound one-ness, a feeling of the unity of all energy. Superficial differences of role, cast, status, sex, species, form, power, size, beauty, even the distinctions between inorganic and living energy, disappear before the ecstatic union of all in one. All gestures, words, acts and events are equivalent in value—all are manifestations of the one consciousness which pervades everything. "You," "I" and "he" are gone, "my" thoughts are "ours," "your" feelings are "mine." Communication is unnecessary, since complete communion exists. A person can sense another's feeling and mood directly, as if they were his own. By a glance, whole lifetimes and words can be transmitted. If all are at peace, the vibrations are "in phase." If there is discord, "out of phase" vibrations will be set up which will be felt like discordant music. Bodies melt into waves. Objects in the environment—lights, trees, plants, flowers—seem to open and welcome you: they are part of you. You are both simply different pulses of the same vibrations. A pure feeling of ecstatic harmony with all beings is the keynote of this vision.

But as before, terrors can occur. Unity requires ecstatic self-sacrifice. Loss of ego brings fright to the unprepared. The fragmentation of form into waves can bring the most terrible fear known to man: the ultimate epistemological revelation.

The fact of the matter is that all apparent forms of matter and body are momentary clusters of energy. We are little more than flickers on a multidimensional television screen. This realization directly experienced can be delightful. You suddenly wake up from the delusion of separate form and hook up to the cosmic dance. Consciousness slides along the wave matrices, silently at the speed of light.

The terror comes with the discovery of transience. Nothing is fixed, no form solid. Everything you can experience is "nothing but" electrical waves. You feel ultimately tricked. A victim of the great television producer. Distrust. The people around you are lifeless television robots. The world around you is a facade, a stage set. You are a helpless marionette, a plastic doll in a plastic world.

If others attempt to help, they are seen as wooden, waxen, feelingless, cold, grotesque, maniacal, space-fiction monsters. You are unable to feel. "I am dead. I will never live and feel again." In wild panic you may attempt to force feeling back—by action, by shouting. You will then enter the Third Bardo stage and be reborn in an unpleasant way.

The best method to escape from fifth vision terrors is to remember this manual, relax, and swing with the wave dance. Or to communicate to the guide that you are in a plastic doll phase, and he will guide you back.

Another solution is to move to the internal biological flow. Follow the instructions given in the third vision: close your eyes, lie prone, seek bodily contact, float down into your bodily stream. In so doing, you are recapitulating the evolutionary sequence. For billions of years, inorganic energy danced the cosmic round before the biological rhythm began. Don't rush it. . . .

Vision 6: "The Retinal Circus"

Each of the Second Bardo visions thus far described was one aspect of the "experiencing of reality." The inner fire or outer waves, apprehended intellectually or emotionally—each vision with its correspondent traps. Each of the "Peaceful Deities" appears with its attendant "Wrathful Deities." To maintain any of these visions for any length of time requires a certain degree of concentration or "one-pointedness" of mind, as well as the ability to recognize them and not to be afraid. Thus, for most persons, the experience may pass through one or more of these phases without the voyager being able to hold them or stay with them. He may open and close his eyes, he may become alternately absorbed in internal sensations and external forms. The experience may be chaotic, beautiful, thrilling, incomprehensible, magical, ever-changing.

He will travel freely through many worlds of experience—from direct contact with life-process forms and images, he may pass to visions of human game-forms. He may see and understand with unimagined clarity and brilliance various social and self-games that he and others play. His own struggles in *karmic* (game) existence will appear pitiful and laughable. Ecstatic freedom of consciousness is the keynote of this vision. Exploration of unimagined realms. Theatrical adventures. Plays within plays within plays. Symbols change into things symbolized and vice versa. Words become things, thoughts are music, music is smelled, sounds are touched, complete interchangeability of the senses.

All things are possible. All feelings are possible. A person may "try on" various moods like so many pieces of clothing. Subjects and objects whirl, transform, change into each other, merge, fuse, disperse again. External objects dance and sing. The mind plays upon them as upon a musical instrument. They assume any form, significance or quality upon command. They are admired, adored, analyzed, examined, changed, made beautiful or ugly, large or small, important or trivial, useful, dangerous, magical or incomprehensible. They may be reacted to with wonder, amazement, humor, veneration, love, disgust, fascination, horror, delight, fear, ecstasy.

Like a computer with unlimited access to any programs, the mind roams freely. Personal and racial memories bubble up to the surface of consciousness, inter-play with fantasies, wishes, dreams and external objects. A present event becomes charged with profound emotional significance, a cosmic phenomenon becomes identical with some personal quirk. Meta-physical problems are juggled and bounced around. Pure "primary process," spontaneous outpouring of association, opposites merging, images fusing, condensing, shifting, collapsing, expanding, merging, connecting.

This kaleidoscopic vision of game-reality may be frightening and confusing to an ill-prepared subject. Instead of exquisite clarity of many-levelled perception, he will experience a confused chaos of uncontrollable, meaningless forms. Instead of delight at the playful acrobatics of the free intellect, there will be anxious clinging to an elusive order. Morbid and scatological hallucinations may occur, evoking disgust and shame.

As before, this negative vision occurs only if the person attempts to control or rationalize the magic panorama. Relax and accept whatever comes. Remember that all visions are created by your mind, the happy and the unhappy, the beautiful and the ugly, the delightful and the horrifying. Your consciousness is creator, performer and spectator of the "retinal circus . . . ."

Vision 7: "The Magic Theatre"

If the voyager was unable to maintain the passive serenity necessary for the contemplation of the previous visions (the peaceful deities), he moves now into a more dramatic and active phase. The play of forms and things becomes the play of heroic figures, superhuman spirits and demi-gods. You may see radiating figures in human forms. The "Lotus Lord of Dance": the supreme image of a demi-god who perceives the effects of all actions. The prince of movement, dancing in an ecstatic embrace with his female counterpart. Heroes, heroines, celestial warriors, male and female demi-gods, angels, fairies—the exact form of these figures will depend on the person's background and tradition. Archetypal figures in the forms of characters from Greek, Egyptian, Nordic, Celtic, Aztec, Persian, Indian, Chinese mythology. The shapes differ, the source is the same: they are the concrete embodiments of aspects of the person's own psyche. Archetypal forces below verbal awareness and expressible only in symbolic form. The figures are often extremely colorful and accompanied by a variety of awe-inspiring sounds. If the voyager is prepared and in a relaxed, detached frame of mind, he is exposed to a fascinating and dazzling display of dramatic creativity. The Cosmic Theatre. The Divine Comedy. If his eyes are open, he may visualize the other voyagers as representing these figures. The face of a friend may turn into that of young boy, a baby, the child-god; into a heroic statue, a wise old man; a woman, animal, goddess, sea-mother, young girl, nymph, elf, goblin, leprechaun. Images of the great painters arise as the familiar representations of these spirits. The images are inexhaustible and manifold. An illuminating voyage into the areas where the personal consciousness merges with the supra-individual.

The danger is that the voyager becomes frightened by or unduly attracted to these powerful figures. The forces represented by them may be more intense than he was prepared for. Inability or unwillingness to recognize them as products of one's own mind, leads to escape into animalistic pursuits. The person may become involved in the pursuit of power, lust, wealth and descend into Third Bardo rebirth struggles. . . .

From **The Electric Kool-Aid Acid Test**
TOM WOLFE

The Bus

I couldn't tell you for sure which of the Merry Pranksters got the idea for the bus, but it had the Babbs touch. It was a superprank, in any case. The original fantasy, here in the spring of 1964, had been that Kesey and four or five others would get a station wagon and drive to New York for the New York World's Fair. On the way they could shoot some film, make some tapes, freak out on the Fair and see what happened. They would also be on hand, in New York, for the publication of Kesey's second novel, *Sometimes a Great Notion,* early in July. So went the original fantasy.

Then somebody—Babbs?—saw a classified ad for a 1939 International Harvester school bus. The bus belonged to a man in Menlo Park. He had a big house and a lot of grounds and a nice set of tweeds and flannels and eleven children. He had rigged out the bus for the children. It had bunks and benches and a refrigerator and a sink for washing dishes and cabinets and shelves and a lot of other nice features for living on the road. Kesey bought it for $1,500—in the name of Intrepid Trips, Inc.

Kesey gave the word and the Pranksters set upon it one afternoon. They started painting it and wiring it for sound and cutting a hole in the roof and fixing up the top of the bus so you could sit up there in the open air and play music, even a set of drums and electric guitars and electric bass and so forth, or just ride. Sandy went to work on the wiring and rigged up a system with which they could broadcast from inside the bus, with tapes or over microphones, and it would blast outside over powerful speakers on top of the bus. There were also microphones outside that would pick up sounds along the road and broadcast them inside the bus. There was also a sound system inside the bus so you could broadcast to one another over the roar of the engine and the road. You could also broadcast over a tape mechanism so that you said something, then heard your own voice a second later in variable lag and could rap off of that if you wanted to. Or you could put on earphones and rap simultaneously off sounds from outside, coming in one ear, and sounds from inside, your own sounds, coming in the other ear. There was going to be no goddamn sound on that whole trip, outside the bus, inside the bus, or inside your own freaking larynx, that you couldn't tune in on and rap off of.

The painting job, meanwhile, with everybody pitching in in a frenzy of primary colors, yellows, oranges, blues, reds, was sloppy as hell, except for the parts Roy Seburn did, which were nice manic mandalas. Well, it was sloppy, but one thing you had to say for it; it was freaking lurid. The manifest, the destination sign in the front, read: "Furthur," with two *u*'s.

They took a test run up into northern California and right away this wild-looking thing with wild-looking people was great for stirring up consternation and vague befuddling resentment among the citizens. The Pranksters were now out among them, and it was exhilarating—look at the mothers staring!—and there was going to be holy terror in the land. But there would also be people who would look up out of their poor work-a-daddy lives in some town, some old guy, somebody's stenographer, and see this bus and register . . . delight, or just pure open-invitation wonder. Either way, the Intrepid Travelers figured, there was hope for these people. They weren't totally turned off. The bus also had great possibilities for altering the usual order of things. For example, there were the cops.

One afternoon the Pranksters were on a test run in the bus going through the woods up north and a forest fire had started. There was smoke beginning to pour out of the woods and everything. Everybody on the bus had taken acid and they were zonked. The acid was in some orange juice in the refrigerator and you drank a paper cup full of it and you were zonked. Cassady was driving and barreling through the burning woods wrenching the steering wheel this way and that way to his inner-wired beat, with a siren wailing and sailing through the rhythm.

A *siren?* It's a highway patrolman, which immediately seems like the funniest thing in the history of the world. Smoke is pouring out of the woods and they are all sailing through leaf explosions in the sky, but the cop is bugged about this freaking bus. The cop yanks the bus over to the side and he starts going

through a kind of traffic-safety inspection of the big gross bus, while more and more of the smoke is billowing out of the woods. Man, the license plate is on wrong and there's no light over the license plate and this turn signal looks bad and how about the brakes, let's see that hand brake there. Cassady, the driver, is already into a long monologue for the guy, only he is throwing in all kinds of sirs: "Well, yes sir, this is a Hammond bi-valve serrated brake, you understand, sir, had it put on in a truck ro-de-o in Springfield, Oregon, had to back through a slalom course of baby's bottles and yellow nappies, in the existential culmination of Oregon, lots of outhouse freaks up there, you understand, sir, a punctual sort of a state, sir, yes, sir, holds to 28,000 pounds, 28,000 pounds, you just look right here, sir, tested by a pure-blooded Shell Station attendant in Springfield, Oregon, winter of '62, his gumball boots never froze, you understand, sir, 28,000 pounds hold, right here—" Whereupon he yanks back on the hand-brake handle as if it's attached to something, which it isn't, it is just dangling there, and jams his foot on the regular brake, and the bus shudders as if the hand brake has a hell of a bite, but the cop is thoroughly befuddled now, anyway, because Cassady's monologue has confused him, for one thing, and what the hell are these . . . *people* doing. By this time everybody is off the bus rolling in the brown grass by the shoulder, laughing, giggling, yahooing, zonked to the skies on acid, because, mon, the woods are burning, the whole world is on fire, and a Cassady monologue on automotive safety is rising up from out of his throat like weenie smoke, as if the great god Speed were frying in his innards, and the cop, representative of the people of California in this total freaking situation, is all hung up on a hand brake that doesn't exist in the first place. And the cop, all he can see is a bunch of crazies in screaming orange and green costumes, masks, boys and girls, men and women, twelve or fourteen of them, lying in the grass and making hideously crazy sounds—christ almighty, why the hell does he have to contend with . . .
So he wheels around and says, "What are you, uh—show people?"

"That's right, officer," Kesey says. "We're show people. It's been a long row to hoe, I can tell you, and it's *gonna* be a long row to hoe, but that's the business."

"Well," says the cop, "you fix up those things and. . . ."
He starts backing off toward his car, cutting one last look at the crazies. ". . . And watch it next time. . . ." And he guns on off.

That was it! How can you give a traffic ticket to a bunch of people rolling in the brown grass wearing Day-Glo masks, practically Greek masques, only with Rat phosphorescent *élan,* giggling, keening in their costumes and private world while the god Speed sizzles like a short-order French fry in the gut of some guy who doesn't even stop talking to breathe. A traffic ticket? The Pranksters felt more immune than ever. There was no more reason for them to remain in isolation while the ovoid eyes of La Honda supurated. They could go through the face of America muddling people's minds, but it's a momentary high, and the bus would be gone, and all the Fab foam in their heads would settle back down into their brain pans.

So the Hieronymus Bosch bus headed out of Kesey's place with the destination sign in front reading "Furthur" and a sign in the back saying "Caution: Weird Load." It was weird, all right, but it was euphoria on board, barreling through all that warm California sun in July, on the road, and everything they had been working on at Kesey's was on board and heading on Furthur. Besides, the joints were going around, and it was nice and high out here on the road in America. As they headed out, Cassady was at the wheel, and there was Kesey, Babbs, Page Browning, George Walker, Sandy, Jane Burton, Mike Hagen, Hassler, Kesey's brother Chuck and his cousin Dale, a guy known as Brother John, and three newcomers who were just along for the ride or just wanted to go to New York.

One of them was a young, quite handsome kid—looked sort of like the early, thin Michael Caine in *Zulu*—named Steve Lambrecht. He was the brother-in-law of Kesey's lawyer, Paul Robertson, and he was just riding to New York to see a girl he knew named Kathy. Another was a girl named Paula Sundsten. She was young, plump, ebullient, and very sexy. Kesey knew her from Oregon. Another one was some girl Hagen of the Screw Shack had picked up in San Francisco, on North Beach. She was the opposite of Paula Sundsten. She was thin, had long dark hair, and would be moody and silent one minute and nervous and carrying on the next. She was good-looking like a TV witch.

By the time they hit San Jose, barely 30 miles down the road, a lot of the atmosphere of the trip was already established. It was nighttime and many souls were high and the bus had broken down. They pulled into a service station and pretty soon one of the help has his nose down in under the hood looking at the engine which Cassady races the motor and the fluorescent stanchion lights around the station hit the bus in weird phosphorescent splashes, the car lights stream by on the highway, Cassady guns the engine some more, and from out of the bus comes a lot of weird wailing, over the speakers or just out the windows. Paula Sundsten has gotten hold of a microphone with the variable-lag setup and has found out she can make weird radio-spook laughing ghoul sounds with it, wailing like a banshee and screaming "How was your stay-ay-ay-ay . . . in San Ho-zay-ay-ay-ay-ay," with the variable lag picking up the ay-ay-ay-ays and doubling them, quadrupling them, octupling them. An endless richocheting echo—and all the while this weird, slightly hysterical laugh and a desperate little plunking mandolin sail through it all, coming from Hagen's girl friend, who is lying back on a bench inside, plunking a mandolin and laughing—in what way . . .

Outside, some character, some local, has come over to the bus, but the trouble is, he is not at all impressed with the bus, he just has to do the American Man thing of when somebody's car is broken down you got to come over and make your diagnosis.

And he is saying to Kesey and Cassady, "You know what I'd say you need? I'd say you need a good mechanic. Now, I'm not a good mechanic, but I—" And naturally he proceeds to give his diagnosis, while Paula wails, making spook-house effects, and the Beauty Witch keens and goons—and—

"—like I say, what you need is a good mechanic, and I'm not a good mechanic, but—"

And—of course!—the Non-people. The whole freaking world was full of people who were bound to tell you they weren't qualified to do this or that but they were determined to go ahead and do just that thing anyway. Kesey decided he was the Non-navigator. Babbs was the Non-doctor. The bus trip was already becoming an allegory of life.

Before heading east, out across the country, they stopped at Babb's place in San Juan Capistrano, down below Los Angeles. Babbs and his wife Anita had a place down there. They pulled the bus into Babb's garage and sat around for one final big briefing before taking off to the east.

Kesey starts talking in the old soft Oregon drawl and everybody is quiet.

"Here's what I hope will happen on this trip," he says. "What I hope will continue to happen, because it's already starting to happen. All of us are beginning to do our thing, and we're going to keep doing it, right out front, and none of us are going to deny what other people are doing."

"Bullshit," says Jane Burton.

This brings Kesey up short for a moment, but he just rolls with it.

"That's Jane," he says. "And she's doing her thing. Bullshit. That's her thing and she's doing it."

"None of us are going to deny what other people are doing. If saying bullshit is somebody's thing, then he says bullshit. If somebody is an ass-kicker, then that's what he's going to do on this trip, kick asses. He's going to do it right out front and nobody is going to have anything to get pissed off about. He can just say, 'I'm sorry I kicked you in the ass, but I'm not sorry I'm an ass-kicker. That's what I do, I kick people in the ass.' Everybody is going to be what they are, and whatever they are, there's not going to be anything to apologize about. What we are, we're going to wail with on this whole trip. . . ."

Cloud

A hulking great sign on the gate out front

> The Merry Pranksters Welcome the Beatles

The Beatles were going to be at the Cow Palace outside of San Francisco on the evening of September 2. The papers, the radio, the TV could talk of nothing else. Kesey's idea, the current fantasy, is that after the show the Beatles will come to La Honda for a good freaking rout with the Merry Pranksters. Now as to how this is to all come about. . . .

But one has to admit the sign creates an effect.

> The Merry Pranksters Welcome the Beatles

Out on Route 84, Mom&Dad&Buddy&Sis in their Ocelot Rabies 400 hardtop sedans, they slow down and stop and stare. The last sign, the one reading THE

MERRY PRANKSTERS WELCOME THE HELL'S ANGELS, for that one they mainly just slowed down. After all, it didn't say *when.* It might be 30 seconds from now—hundreds of the beasts, coming 'round the mountain in a shower of spirochetes and crab lice, spitting out bone marrow from the last cannibal rape job up the road.

Well, it worked with the Hell's Angels. They put up the sign THE MERRY PRANKSTERS WELCOME THE HELL'S ANGELS, and sure enough the Angels came, these unbelievable bogeymen for the middle class, in the flesh, and they became part of the Prankster movie, in the rich ripe cheesy Angel flesh. So they put up the sign THE MERRY PRANKSTERS WELCOME THE BEATLES and maybe the Beatles will come. There is this one small difference of course. Kesey *knew* the Hell's Angels. He invited them, face to face. Ah, but comes a time to put a few professed beliefs to the test. Control, Attention, Imagine the little freaks into the movie . . .

Kesey raps on to Mountain Girl out in the backhouse. They lie there on the mattresses, with Kesey rapping on and on and Mountain Girl trying to absorb it. Ever since Asillomar, Kesey has been deep into the religion thing. Miracles—Control—*Now*—The Movie—on and on he talks to Mountain Girl out in the backhouse and very deep and far-out stuff it is, too. Mountain Girl tries to concentrate, but the words swim by like great waves of . . . The words swim by and she hears the sound but it is like her cerebral cortex is tuned out to the content of it. Her mind keeps rolling and spinning over another set of data, always the same. Like—the eternal desperate calculation. In short, Mountain Girl is pregnant.

And yet with all this desperation rolling and spinning going on, something he says will catch hold. They are that bizarre, but that plausible, Kesey's dreams are. It's a matter of imagining them into the movie. The Beatles. It is like an experiment in everything the Pranksters have learned up to now. We can't *make* the Beatles come out here to our place. We can't *cause* them to do it in the usual sense. But we can imagine them into the movie and work them into the great flow of acausal connection and then it will happen of its own accord. This sign starts the movie going, THE MERRY PRANKSTERS WELCOME THE BEATLES, and our movie becomes their movie, Mom's and Dad's and Buddy's and Sis's and all the Berkeley kids' and all the heads' and proto-heads' of the San Francisco peninsula, until our fantasy becomes the Beatles' fantasy. . . . Wonder when they will first feel it. . . . Despite the rolling and spinning and all, Mountain Girl can't hardly help but marvel at the current fantasy because there has already been so much . . . weird shit . . . that worked. Bringing the Angels in, like Kesey did, the most feared demons in America . . . and finding Good People like Buzzard and Sonny and Tiny and Frank and Terry the Tramp, who Done Well, and Beautiful people like Gut. . . . And the poor tortured intellectual angels at Asillomar, from Watermelon Henry to freaking Rachel—for a week Kesey had mystified, like *mystified,* and taken over the whole Unitarian Church of California. They would never be the same again, which was just as well. A true Miracle, in fact, since they had been the same for so goddamn long. Control :::: and it was so plausible the way it sounded in Kesey's certain Oregon drawl. So few humans have the *hubris* to exert their wills upon the flow, maybe not more than forty on the whole planet at any given time. The world *is* flat, it *is* supported by forty, or maybe four men, one at each corner, like the cosmic turtles and elephants in the mythology books, because no one else dares. Mountain Girl is 18 and she is pregnant, but this is Kesey . . . And *Miracles?* You haven't seen miracles yet, Job, until you see the Pranksters draw the Beatles into their movie.

September 2. Faye's sewing machine is the first thing everyone hears as they wake up. Faye and Gretch pull out the big costume chest, full of all sorts of ungainly theatrical shit, swashbuckle swords and plumed hats and Errol Flynn dueling shirts and Robin Hood boots and quivers and quail masks and Day-Glo roadworker vests and sashes and medals and saris and sarongs and shades and beaks and bells and steelworker hard hats and World War I aviator helmets and Dr. Strange capes and cutlasses and codpieces and jumpsuits and football jerseys and aprons and ascots and wigs and warlock rattles and Jungle Jim jodhpurs and Captain Easy epaulets and Fearless Four tights—and Merry Prankster Page Browning special face paints. The Merry Pranksters are getting ready to head bombed out into the mightiest crazed throng in San Francisco history, come to see the Beatles at the Cow Palace.

One of the Pranksters' outer circle, so to speak, a fellow called C———, from Palo Alto—C———had worked out some kind of a deal and gotten thirty tickets to the Beatles concert for the Pranksters, even though tickets were supposed to be impossible to get. C———was one of the Pranksters' acid sources. Another was an old guy known as the Mad Chemist, an amateur chemistry genius who was also a gun freak. Anyway, this C——— worked out some kind of deal and he also got enough acid for everybody for the trip. Just before the Pranksters, inner and outer circle, and kids, climbed on the bus, Kesey grinned and passed out the acid. It was in capsules, but it was such high concentration it just coated part of the inside of the capsules, so it looked like there was nothing in there. The Pranksters called it acid gas. So they all took acid gas and got on the bus. Cassady was off somewhere, so Babbs drove. Kesey was up on top of the bus, directing the movie. Well, it was colorful enough, this movie. The bus was super-rigged, all the sound equipment, two big speakers up top, records and tapes, plus the whole Prankster band up top of the bus, George Walker's drums, and basses and guitars and trombones and plumes spilling out the windows and flashes of Day-Glo and flapping epaulets, freaking flashing epaulets, and the Beatles album from the movie *Help!* screaming out the speakers, and up on top, Kesey and Sandy, Mountain Girl, Walker, Zonker, and a new Prankster, a little girl called Mary Microgram, and guitars and drums—*He-e-e-elp I ne-e-e-ed somebody*—the whole flapping whooing carnival of a bus bouncing and jouncing and grinding up over Skylonda, Cahill Ridge, and down through Palo Alto and out onto the Harbor Freeway heading toward San Francisco, a goddamn rolling circus once again. Everybody was getting kind of high on acid, *wasted,* in fact, and starting, one by one, Mountain Girl and Sandy and Norman, who was inside the bus, to have that thing where the motion and the roar of the bus and the beat of the music and the sound of it are all one thing rolling together, and like Babbs is driving to the exact tempo and speed of the Beatles music, since they are all one thing together, growing high as baboons down through the freaking motels and electric signs and gull lights in Burlingame, near the airport, the Hyatt House super-America motel spires aloft—pitching and rolling and gunning along in *exact* time to the Beatle music, that being the soundtrack of this movie, you understand—and then off the expressway at the Cow Palace exit and down the swerving—*ne-e-e-ed some-body*—ramp, down an incline, down a hill, toward dusk, with the fever millions of cars streaming south on the freeway and the sun a low bomb over the hills, zonked, in fact. And grinding down to the stop light, thunk, and the brakes sound like a cast-iron flute A below high C—and at that very moment, that very moment of bus stop—the Beatles song *Help!* ends, in that very moment, and weird music starts, from the part of the movie *Help!* where the Arab is sneaking up behind Ringo, and in that weird moment the wind rises over the freeway and to the right there is an abandoned factory, all brick and glass, mostly glass, great 1920s factory glass panes and all of them bending weird in the wind and flashing sheets of that huge afternoon sun like a huge thousand-eyed thing pulsing explosions of sunlight in *exact* time to the weird Arab music—and in that very moment Kesey, Mountain Girl, Sandy, Zonker, all of them—no one even has to look at another because they not only *know* that everyone else is seeing it at once, they *feel,* they feel it flowing through one brain, Atman and Brahman, all one on the bus and all one with the writhing mass sun reflector ripple sun bomb prisms, the bricks, the glass, the whole hulk of it, Pranksters and Beatles and sun bombs flashing Arab music—and then in *that* very moment, they all, the all in one, the one brain flow, see the mouldering sign silhouetted against the sky above the building:

Cloud

Suddenly it seemed like the Pranksters could draw the whole universe into . . .the movie . . .

And then, curiously, being as it is, so freaking high out here—Mountain Girl thinks what the fuck is this. It looks like a slaughterhouse. In fact, it is the Cow Palace. She can't even focus on the big hulking building itself for the miles and endless rings of slaughterhouse fences around it, fences and barbed wire and a million cars jamming in and being jammed in the cold fag end of the dusk. Curiously, it isn't terrifying to Mountain Girl, however. It is just a slaughterhouse, that's all.

But to other Pranksters—a concentration camp. We're going to jail, for the rest of our lives only. Everybody scrambling down off the bus, all still in motion with the ground and the concentration-camp fences flailing in the gruesome gloaming while billions of teeny freaks rush by them, screaming and freaking. They have their tickets in their hand like it is the last corner of salvation extant but they can't even read the mothers. They are wasted. The letters on the ticket curdle and freak off into the teeny freak flow. Thirty Pranksters in full flapping epaulets and plumes desperately staring at the minute disappearing tickets in their hands in the barby ante-pens of the concentration camp. They are going to arrest us and lock us away for the rest of our lives. That seems very certain, almost like well, that's why we came. Thirty acid heads, with innocent children in tow, in full Prankster regalia, bombed out of their gourds on the dread LSD, veering, careening in delirium sun pulse, In public, stoned out of their skulls on LSD, not only in public but in this momentous heaving Beatles throng amid 2,000 red dog forensic cops, in full go-to-hell costume—*exterminate the monsters*— . . . but . . . no one lays a hand on them or says the first word, thousands of cops and not even one hassle . . . because we're *too* obvious. Suddenly it couldn't be clearer to Norman. We're too obvious and we've blown their brains. They can't focus on us—or—we've sucked them into the movie and *dissolved* the bastids—

Inside the Cow Palace it is very roaring hell. Somehow Kesey and Babbs lead the Day-Glo crazies up to their seats. The Pranksters are sitting in a great clump, a wacky perch up high in precipitous pitch high up pitching down to the stage and millions of the screaming teeny freaks. The teeny freaks, tens of thousands of little girls, have gone raving mad already, even though the Beatles have not come on. Other groups, preliminaries, keep trooping on, *And now—Martha and the Vandellas* and the electrified throb and brang vibrates up your aorta and picks your bones like a sonic cleaner, and the teeny freaks scream—great sheets of scream like sheets of rain in a squall—and *kheew, kheew, pow, pow, pow*—how very marvelous, how very clever, figures Norman. From up out of the Cow Palace horde of sheet scream teeny freaks comes this very marvelous clever light display, hundreds of exploding lights throughout the high intensity lights, ricocheting off everything, what a marvelous clever thing they've rigged up here for our . . .

—Mountain Girl smiles . . . the incredible exploding lights explode out in front of her, a great sea of them, and they they explode on her retina in great sunburst retinal sulphur rockets, images and after-images that she will never forget as long as she lives, in truth—

. . . for our entertainment, and it is twenty or thirty minutes before Norman, stoned, realizes that they are flashbulbs, hundreds, thousands of teeny freaks with flashbulb cameras, aimed at the stage or just shot off in optic orgasm. Sheets of screams, rock 'n' roll, *blam blam*, a sea of flashbulbs—perfect madness, of course.

—Mountain Girl grins and takes it all in—

Other Pranksters, stoned, are slowly getting up tight, however, including Kesey and Babbs. The vibrations are very bad, a poison madness in the air—

Each group of musicians that goes off the stage—the horde thinks *now* the Beatles, but the Beatles don't come, some other group appears, and the sea of girls gets more and more intense and impatient and the screaming gets higher, and the thought slips into Norman's flailing flash-frayed brain stem ::: the human lung cannot go beyond this ::::: and yet when the voice says *And now—the Beatles*—what else could he say?—and out they come on stage—*them*—John and George and Ringo and uh the other one—it might as well have been four imported vinyl dolls for all it was going to matter—that sound he thinks cannot get higher, it doubles, his eardrums ring like stamped metal with it and suddenly *Ghhhhhhwoooooooooowwwwww,* it is like the whole thing has snapped, and the whole front section of the arena becomes a writhing, seething mass of little girls waving their arms in the air, this mass of pink arms, it is all you can see, it is like a single colonial animal with a thousand waving pink tentacles—it *is* a single colonial animal with a thousand waving pink tentacles,

    —vibrating poison madness and filling the universe with the teeny agony torn out of them. It dawns on Kesey: it is *one being.* They have all been transformed into one being

    —Mountain Girl grins and urges them on—its scream does not subside for a moment, during after or between numbers, the Beatles could be miming it for all it matters. But something else . . . does . . . matter . . . and Kesey sees it. One of the Beatles, John, George, Paul, dips his long electric guitar handle in one direction and the whole teeny horde ripples precisely along the line of energy he set off—and then in the other direction, precisely along that line. It causes them to grin, John and Paul and George and Ringo, rippling the poor huge freaked teeny beast this way and that—

    Control—it is perfectly obvious—they have brought this whole mass of human beings to the point where they are one, out of their skulls, one psyche, and they have utter control over them—but they don't know what in the hell to do with it, they haven't the first idea, and they will lose it. In Kesey the vibration is an awful anticipation of the snap—

    Ghhhhhhwoooooooooowwwwww, thousands of teeny bodies hurtling toward the stage and a fence there and a solid line of cops, fighting to hurl the assault back, while the Beatles keep moving their chops and switching their hips around sunk like a dumb show under the universal scream. In that surge, just when you would have thought not another sound in the universe could break through, it starts—*thwaaaack—thwaaack—*the sound of the folding chairs on the arena floor collapsing and smashing down on the floor, and the remains are down there amid the pink tentacles, crushed to a pulp, little bits and splinters that used to be folding chairs, debris being passed out from hand to hand traveling over the pink tentacles from one to the other like some hideously diseased lurching monster cockroaches. And then the girls start fainting, like suffocation, and getting tromped on, and they start handing out their bodies, cockroach chair debris and the bodies of little teeny freaks being shuttled out over the pitched sea like squashed lice picked off the beast, screaming and fainting and *Ghhhhhhwooooooowwwwww* again up against the cop fence while the Beatles cheese and mince at them in the dumb show, utterly helpless to ripple them or anything else now, with no control left—

    CANCER—Kesey has only to look and it is perfectly obvious—all of them, the teeny freaks and the Beatles, are one creature, caught in a state of sheer poison mad cancer. The Beatles are the creature's head. The teeny freaks are the body. But the head has lost control of the body and the body rebels and goes amok and that is what cancer is. The vibrations of it hit the Pranksters, in a clump, stoned out of their gourds, in sickening waves. Kesey—Babbs—they all feel it at once, and Norman.

—Mountain Girl looks very surprised. She wants to see the rest of it. But Kesey and Babbs have decided they should all leave—before the Monster Snap occurs, the big cancer wrapup of the whole process.

—Wait a minute, says Mountain Girl.

But the Pranksters get up in a clump and a rustle of plumes and epaulets and Day-Glo, zonked out of their heads on acid, and all sorts of people start getting up—but like, *concrete.* The more headway they make toward the exits, the more it becomes a claustrophobia of pens, an endless series of pens. They head down long corridors, all concrete, and already hundreds are jammed in the corridors, all looking kind of raggy—because—They get the total vibration from them—everybody has the one same feeling: suppose this thing snaps *now* and there is a panic and everybody makes a rush for it, the exit, but there is no exit, only concrete walls and concrete ceilings weighing down like a thousand tons and ramps—toward nothing—leading down—then up in a great clump of hump—and then down, outside, there is the sky, but it is black, it is nighttime by now and sick ochre floodlights, but they have merely made it to another pen, more Cyclone fences and barbed wire with frantic raggy people —all *fleeing*—milling around in it like rats, trying to get to the exit, which is a turnstile, an upright turnstile with bars, like an iron maiden, and you have to get inside of it, totally, one person at a time, with a frantic crush on both sides, and even then you have only made it to another pen, a parking lot, with more Cyclone fence and barbed wire and now teeny freaks and cars crushed in here, all trying to get out, seven and eight cars at a whack trying to nose through an opening big enough for one. Cages, cages, cages and no end to it. Even out there, beyond, where cars have escaped and they are in a line with their lights on—trapped by the hills, which are another great pen trapping the whole place in . . . in . . . The Pranksters all silent and numb with the apprehension of the Great Cancer Snap to come—

—Except that Mountain Girl says Wait a minute—

—and Zonker, with his huge euphoric Zonker grin on, fraternizing madly with all teeny freaks as they stream out, saying to all who will listen: "The Beatles are going to Kesey's when they leave here . . . the Beatles are going to Kesey's . . ." and the word spreads among the crowd in the most delirious way—

Kesey plunges back in for survivors. See if there are any Pranksters trapped inside. He tells the rest to go to the bus and stay there, and plunges in. The Pranksters touch the bus and their morale revives a bit. They rev up the amplifiers and the speakers and climb up on top in their crazy costumes and start idling over the drums and the electric guitars. The thousands of little raggy girls keep pouring out into the parking lot, still wound up like a motorcycle and no release and of course they see the bus and these strange Day-Glo people. One group of kids is protesting that the music business is rigged and they're carrying placards and screaming and they figure the Pranksters support them—the Pranksters grin and wave back—everybody figures the strange Day-Glo people are for whatever they're for. They start piling around the bus, these little teeny freaks, and start pelting it with jelly beans, the hard kind, the kind they brought to throw at the Beatles. The Pranksters sit on top of the bus with the jelly beans clattering off the side and the flaming little teeny freaks pressed around screaming—So *this* is what the Beatles feel, this mindless amok energy surging at them for—what?

At last Kesey returns with the last to be rescued, Mary Microgram, looking like a countryside after a long and fierce war, and Kesey says let's haul ass out of here. Babbs starts the bus up and they pull out, bulling their way slowly out toward freedom.

Cancer! We saw it. It was there. Bad vibrations, say all. Endless cages. They all rock and sway, stoned on acid.

"Hell," thinks Mountain Girl. "I have to come here with a bunch of old men who never saw a rock 'n' roll show before. . . ."

The Young

The selections from C. Wright Mills, Irving Howe,
Mario Savio, Peter Berg, and Richard Goldstein
form a brief historical silhouette of the origins
and progress of the New Left movement
and its encounter with hippie attitudes.
Mills is credited with fathering the New Left,
while Howe's critical (in the constructive sense)
interest in it helped early to validate it as a
political entity. But that was the work of older men
acknowledging the presence of the young.
Savio, Berg, and Goldstein literally embodied
and then defined some of the forms of rebellion
to which youth was attracted. The momentum of
that energy is still with us and will no doubt
shape forms of activism still to come.

PHOTOGRAPH BY *Joe Molnar.*

On the New Left
C. WRIGHT MILLS

It is no exaggeration to say that since the end of World War II, smug conservatives, tired liberals and disillusioned radicals in Britain and the United States have carried on a weary discourse in which issues are blurred and potential debate muted; the sickness of complacency has prevailed, the bipartisan banality flourished. There is no need to explain again why all this has come about among "people in general" in the NATO countries;* but it may be worthwhile to examine one style of cultural work that is in effect an intellectual celebration of apathy.

Many intellectual fashions, of course, do just that; they stand in the way of a release of the imagination—about the Cold War, the Soviet bloc, the politics of peace, about any new beginnings at home and abroad. But the fashion I have in mind is the weariness of many NATO intellectuals with what they call "ideology," and their proclamation of "the end of ideology." So far as I know, this fashion began in the mid-fifties, mainly in intellectual circles more or less associated with the Congress for Cultural Freedom and the magazine *Encounter*. Reports on the Milan Conference of 1955 heralded it; since then, many cultural gossips have taken it up as a posture and an unexamined slogan. Does it amount to anything?

I

Its common denominator is not liberalism as a political philosophy, but the liberal rhetoric, become formal and sophisticated and used as an uncriticized weapon with which to attack Marxism. In the approved style, various elements of this rhetoric appear simply as snobbish assumptions. Its sophistication is one of tone rather than of ideas: in it, the *New Yorker* style of reportage has become politically triumphant. The disclosure of fact—set forth in a bright-faced or in a deadpan manner—is the rule. The facts are duly weighed, carefully balanced, always hedged. Their power to outrage, their power truly to enlighten in a political way, their power to aid decision, even their power to clarify some situation—all that is blunted or destroyed.

So reasoning collapses into reasonableness. By the more naïve and snobbish celebrants of complacency, arguments and facts of a displeasing kind are simply ignored; by the more knowing, they are duly recognized, but they are neither connected with one another nor related to any general view.

---

* See, for example, E. P. Thompson, ed., *Out of Apathy* (London: Stevens and Son, 1960).

Acknowledged in a scattered way, they are never put together: to do so is to risk being called, curiously enough, "one-sided."

This refusal to relate isolated facts and fragmentary comment to the changing institutions of society makes it impossible to understand the structural realities which these facts might reveal or the longer-run trends of which they might be tokens. In brief, fact and idea are isolated, so the real questions are not even raised, analysis of the meanings of facts not even begun.

Practitioners of the no-more-ideology school do, of course, smuggle in general ideas under the guise of reportage, by intellectual gossip, and by their selection of the notions they handle. Ultimately, the-end-of-ideology is based upon a disillusionment with any real commitment to socialism in any recognizable form. *That* is the only "ideology" that has really ended for these writers. But with its ending, *all* ideology, they think, has ended. *That* ideology they talk about; their own ideological assumptions, they do not. Yet these assumptions, which they snobbishly take for granted, provide the terms of their rejection of "all ideology"; and upon these assumptions, they themselves stand.

Underneath this style of observation and comment there is the assumption that in the West there are no more real issues or even problems of great seriousness. The mixed economy plus the welfare state plus prosperity—that is the formula. U.S. capitalism will continue to be workable; the welfare state will continue along the road to ever greater justice. In the meantime, things everywhere are very complex; let us not be careless; there are great risks.

This posture—one of "false consciousness" if there ever was one—stands in the way, I think, of considering with any chances of success what may be happening in the world.

First and above all, this posture rests upon a simple provincialism. If the phrase "the end of ideology" has any meaning at all, it pertains to self-selected circles of intellectuals in the richer countries. It is in fact merely their own self-image. The total population of these countries is a fraction of mankind; the period during which such a posture has been assumed is very short indeed. To speak in such terms of much of Latin America, Africa, Asia, the Soviet bloc is merely ludicrous. Anyone who stands in front of audiences—intellectual or mass—in any of these places and talks in such terms will merely be shrugged off (if the audience is polite) or laughed at out loud (if the audience is more candid and knowledgeable). The end-of-ideology is a slogan of complacency, circulating among the prematurely middle-aged, centered in the present, and in the rich Western societies. In the final analysis, it also rests upon a disbelief in the shaping by men of their own futures—as history and as biography. It is a consensus of a few provincials about their own immediate and provincial position.

Second, the end-of-ideology is of course itself an ideology—a fragmentary one, to be sure, and perhaps more a mood. The end-of-ideology is in reality the ideology of an ending: the ending of political reflection itself as a public fact. It is a weary know-it-all justification, by tone of voice rather than by explicit argument, of the cultural and political default of the NATO intellectuals.

II

All this is just the sort of thing that I at least have always objected to, and do object to, in the "socialist realism" of the Soviet Union.

There too, criticisms of milieux are of course permitted, but they are not to be connected with criticism of the structure itself: one may not question "the system." There are no "antagonistic contradictions."

There too, in novels and plays, criticisms of characters, even of party members, are permitted, but they must be displayed as "shocking exceptions"; they must be seen as survivals from the old order, not as systematic products of the new.

There too, pessimism is permitted, but only episodically and only within the context of the big optimism; the tendency is to confuse any systematic or structural criticism with pessimism itself. So they admit criticisms, first of this and then of that, but engulf them all by the long-run historical optimism about the system as a whole and the goals proclaimed by its leaders.

I neither want nor need to overstress the parallel, yet in a recent series of interviews in the Soviet Union concerning socialist realism I was very much struck by it. In Uzbekistan and Georgia, as well as in Russia, I kept writing notes to myself at the end of recorded interviews: "This man talks in a style just like Arthur Schlesinger, Jr." "Surely this fellow is the counterpart of Daniel Bell, except not so—what shall I say?—so gossipy; and certainly neither so petty nor so vulgar as the more envious status-climbers. Perhaps this is because here they are not thrown into such a competitive status-panic about the ancient and obfuscating British models of prestige." "The would-be enders of ideology," I kept thinking, "are they not the self-coordinated or, better, the fashion-coordinated, socialist realists of the NATO world?" And: "Check this carefully with the files of *Encounter* and *The Reporter*." I have now done so; it is the same kind of thing.

Certainly there are many differences: above all, the fact that socialist realism is part of an official line, while the end of ideology is self-managed. But the differences one knows. It is more useful to stress the parallels, and the generic fact that both of these postures stand opposed to radical criticisms of their respective societies.

In the Soviet Union, only political authorities at the top, or securely on their way up there, can seriously tamper with structural questions and ideological lines. These authorities, of course, are much more likely to be intellectuals (in one or another sense of the word—say a man who actually writes his own speeches) than are American politicians. Moreover, since the death of Stalin, such Soviet authorities *have* begun to tamper quite seriously with structural questions and basic ideology, although for reasons peculiar to the tight and official joining of culture and politics in their set-up, they must try to disguise this fact.

The end-of-ideology is very largely a mechanical reaction, not a creative response, to the ideology of Stalinism. As such it takes from its opponent something of its inner quality. What it all means is that these people have become aware of the uselessness of vulgar Marxism, but are not yet aware of the uselessness of the liberal rhetoric.

III

But the most immediately important thing about the "end of ideology" is that it *is* merely a fashion, and fashions change. Already this one is on its way out. Even a few diehard anti-Stalinists are showing signs of a reappraisal of their own past views; some are even beginning to recognize publicly that Stalin himself no longer runs the Soviet party and state. They begin to see the poverty of their comfortable ideas as they come to confront Khrushchev's Russia.

We who have been, in moral terms, consistently radical in our work throughout the postwar period are often amused nowadays that various writers, sensing another shift in fashion, are beginning to call upon intellectuals to work once more in ways that are politically explicit. But we should not be merely amused; we ought to try to make their shift more than a fashion change.

The end-of-ideology is on the decline because it stands for the refusal to work out an explicit political philosophy. And alert men everywhere today do feel the need for such a philosophy. What we should do is to continue directly to confront this need. In doing so, it may be useful to keep in mind that to have a working political philosophy means to have a philosophy that enables you to work, and that at least four kinds of work are needed, each of them at once intellectual and political.

In these terms, think for a moment longer of the end-of-ideology:

1 It is a kindergarten fact that any political reflection that is of possible public significance is *ideological;* in its terms policies, institutions, and men of power are criticized or approved. In this respect, the end-of-ideology stands, negatively, for the attempt to withdraw oneself and one's work from political relevance; positively, it is an ideology of political complacency which seems the only way now open for many writers to acquiesce in or to justify the status quo.

2 So far as orienting *theories* of society and of history are concerned, the end-of-ideology stands for, and presumably stands upon, a fetishism of empiricism: more academically, upon a pretentious methodology used to state trivialities about unimportant social areas; more essayistically, upon a naïve journalistic empiricism—which I have already characterized above—and upon a cultural gossip in which "answers" to the vital and pivotal issues are merely assumed. Thus political bias masquerades as epistomological excellence, and there are no orienting theories.

3 So far as the *historic agency of change* is concerned, the end-of-ideology rests upon the identification of such agencies with going institutions, perhaps upon their piecemeal reform, but never upon the search for agencies that might be used for, or that might themselves operate toward, a structural change of society. The problem of agency is never posed as a problem to solve, as "our problem." Instead there is endless talk of the need to be pragmatic, flexible, open. Surely all this has already been adequately dealt with: such a view makes sense politically only if the blind drift of human affairs is in general beneficent.

4 So far as political and human *ideals* are concerned, the end-of-ideology stands for a denial of their relevance, except as abstract ikons. Merely to hold such ideals seriously is in this view "utopian."

IV

But enough. Where do *we* stand on each of these four aspects of political philosophy? Various of us are of course at work on each of them, and all of us are generally aware of our needs in regard to each. As for the articulation of ideals, there I think your magazines have done their best work so far.* That is *your* meaning—is it not?—of the emphasis upon cultural affairs. As for ideological analysis and the rhetoric with which to carry it out, I do not think any of us is nearly good enough. But that will come with further advance on the two fronts where we are weakest: theories of society, history, and human nature, and—the major problem—ideas about the historical agencies of structural change.

We have frequently been told by an assorted variety of dead-end people that the meanings of left and of right are now liquidated, by history and by reason. I think we should answer them in some such way as this:

The *Right,* among other things, means what you are doing: celebrating society as it is, a going concern. *Left* means, or ought to mean, just the opposite. It means structural criticism and reportage and theories of society, which at some point or another are focussed politically as demands and programs. These criticisms, demands, theories, programs are guided morally by the humanist and secular ideals of Western civilization—above all, the ideals of reason, freedom and justice. To be "left" means to connect up cultural with political criticism, and both with demands and programs. And it means all this inside *every* country of the world.

Only one more point of definition: absence of public issues there may well be, but this is not due to any absence of problems or of contradictions, antagonistic and otherwise. Impersonal and structural changes have not eliminated problems or issues. Their absence from many discussions is an ideological condition, regulated in the first place by whether or not intellectuals detect and state problems as potential *issues* for probable publics, and as *troubles* for a variety of individuals. One indispensable means of such work on these central tasks is what can only be described as ideological analysis. To be actively left, among other things, is to carry on just such analysis.

* This refers to *The New Left Review, The New Reasoner,* and *Universities & Left Review,* all of Great Britain.—Eds.

    To take seriously the problem of the need for a political orientation is not, of course, to seek for A Fanatical and Apocalyptic Vision, for An Infallible and Monolithic Lever of Change, for Dogmatic Ideology, for A Startling New Rhetoric, for Treacherous Abstractions, and all the other bogeymen of the dead-enders. These are, of course, "the extremes," the straw men, the red herrings used by our political enemies to characterize the polar opposite of where they think they stand.

    They tell us, for example, that ordinary men cannot always be political "heroes." Who said they could? But keep looking around you; and why not search out the conditions of such heroism as men do and might display? They tell us that we are too "impatient," that our "pretentious" theories are not well enough grounded. That is true, but neither are our theories trivial. Why don't they get to work to refute or ground them? They tell us we "do not really understand" Russia and China today. That is true; we don't; neither do they. We at least are studying the question. They tell us we are "ominous" in our formulations. That is true: we do have enough imagination to be frightened, and we don't have to hide it. We are not afraid we'll panic. They tell us we are "grinding axes." Of course we are: we do have, among other points of view, morally grounded ones, and we are aware of them. They tell us, in their wisdom, that we do not understand that The Struggle is Without End. True: we want to change its form, its focus, its object.

    We are frequently accused of being "utopian" in our criticisms and in our proposals and, along with this, of basing our hopes for a new left *politics* "merely on reason," or more concretely, upon the intelligentsia in its broadest sense.

    There is truth in these charges. But must we not ask: What now is really meant by *utopian?* And is not our utopianism a major source of our strength? *Utopian* nowadays, I think, refers to any criticism or proposal that transcends the up-close milieux of a scatter of individuals, the milieux which men and women can understand directly and which they can reasonably hope directly to change. In this exact sense, our theoretical work is indeed utopian—in my own case, at least, deliberately so. What needs to be understood, and what needs to be changed, is not merely first this and then that detail of some institution or policy. If there is to be a politics of a new left, what needs to be analyzed is the *structure* of institutions, the *foundation* of policies. In this sense, both in its criticisms and in its proposals, our work is necessarily structural, and so—*for us,* just now—utopian.

    This brings us face to face with the most important issue of political reflection and of political action in our time: the problem of the historical agency of change, of the social and institutional means of structural change. There are several points about this problem I would like to put to you.

V

First, the historic agencies of change for liberals of the capitalist societies have been an array of voluntary associations, coming to a political climax in a parliamentary or congressional system. For socialists of almost all varieties, the

historic agency has been the working class—and later the peasantry, or parties
and unions composed of members of the working class, or (to blur, for now, a
great problem) of political parties acting in its name, "representing its interests."

I cannot avoid the view that both these forms of historic agency have
either collapsed or become most ambiguous. So far as structural change is
concerned, neither seems to be at once available and effective as *our* agency any
more. I know this is a debatable point among us, and among many others as well;
I am by no means certain about it. But surely, if it is true, it ought not to be taken
as an excuse for moaning and withdrawal (as it is by some of those who have
become involved with the end-of-ideology); and it ought not to be bypassed (as it
is by many Soviet scholars and publicists, who in their reflections upon the course
of advanced capitalist societies simply refuse to admit the political condition and
attitudes of the working class).

Is anything more certain than that in 1970—indeed, at this time next
year—our situation will be quite different, and—the chances are high—decisively
so? But of course, that isn't saying much. The seeming collapse of our historic
agencies of change ought to be taken as a problem, an issue, a trouble—in fact, as
the political problem which *we* must turn into issue and trouble.

Second, it is obvious that when we talk about the collapse of agencies of
change, we cannot seriously mean that such agencies do not exist. On the
contrary, the means of history-making—of decision and of the enforcement of
decision—have never in world history been so enlarged and so available to such
small circles of men on both sides of The Curtains as they now are. My own
conception of the shape of power, the theory of the power elite, I feel no need to
argue here. This theory has been fortunate in its critics, from the most diverse
political view-points, and I have learned from several of these critics. But I have
not seen, as of this date, an analysis of the idea that causes me to modify any of its
essential features.

The point that is immediately relevant does seem obvious: what is
utopian for us, is not at all utopian for the presidium of the Central Committee in
Moscow, or the higher circles of the Presidency in Washington, or, recent events
make evident, for the men of SAC and CIA. The historic agencies of change that
have collapsed are those which were at least thought to be open to *the left* inside
the advanced Western nations, to those who have wished for structural changes of
these societies. Many things follow from this obvious fact; of many of them, I am
sure, we are not yet adequately aware.

Third, what I do not quite understand about some new-left writers is why
they cling so mightily to "the working class" of the advanced capitalist societies as
the historic agency, or even as the most important agency, in the face of the really
impressive historical evidence that now stands against this expectation.

Such a labor metaphysic, I think, is a legacy from Victorian Marxism that
is now quite unrealistic.

It is an historically specific idea that has been turned into an historical
and unspecific hope.

The social and historical conditions under which industrial workers tend
to become a-class-for-themselves, and a decisive political force, must be fully and

precisely elaborated. There have been, there are, there will be such conditions. These conditions vary according to national social structure and the exact phase of their economic and political development. Of course we cannot "write off the working class." But we must *study* all that, and freshly. Where labor exists as an agency, of course we must work with it, but we must not treat it as The Necessary Lever, as nice old Labour Gentlemen in Britain and elsewhere tend to do.

Although I have not yet completed my own comparative studies of working classes, generally it would seem that only at certain (earlier) stages of industrialization, and in a political context of autocracy, *etc.,* do wage-workers tend to become a-class-for-themselves, *etc.* The *etceteras* mean that I can here merely raise the question.

VI

It is with this problem of agency in mind that I have been studying, for several years now, the cultural apparatus, the intellectuals, as a possible, immediate, radical agency of change. For a long time, I was not much happier with this idea than were many of you; but it turns out now, at the beginning of the 1960s, that it may be a very relevant idea indeed.

In the first place, is it not clear that if we try to be realistic in our utopianism—and that is no fruitless contradiction—a writer in our countries on the left today *must* begin with the intellectuals? For that is what we are, that is where we stand.

In the second place, the problem of the intelligentsia is an extremely complicated set of problems on which rather little factual work has been done. In doing this work, we must, above all, not confuse the problems of the intellectuals of West Europe and North America with those of the Soviet bloc or with those of the underdeveloped worlds. In each of the three major components of the world's social structure today, the character and the role of the intelligentsia is distinct and historically specific. Only by detailed comparative studies of them in all their human variety can we hope to understand any one of them.

In the third place, who is it that is getting fed up? Who is it that is getting disgusted with what Marx called "all the old crap?" Who is it that is thinking and acting in radical ways? All over the world—in the bloc, outside the bloc and in between—the answer is the same: it is the young intelligentsia.

I cannot resist copying out for you, with a few changes, some materials I recently prepared for a 1960 paperback edition of a book of mine on war:

"In the spring and early summer of 1960, more of the returns from the American decision and default are coming in. In Turkey, after student riots, a military junta takes over the state, of late run by Communist Container Menderes. In South Korea, too, students and others knock over the corrupt American-puppet regime of Syngman Rhee. In Cuba, a genuinely left-wing revolution begins full-scale economic reorganization, without the domination of U.S. corporations. Average age of its leaders: about 30—and certainly a revolution without Labor As Agency. On Taiwan, the eight million Taiwanese under the American-imposed dictatorship of Chiang Kai-shek, with his two million Chinese, grow increasingly restive. On Okinawa, a U.S. military base, the people get their first chance since World War II ended to demonstrate against U.S. seizure of their island; and some students take that chance, snake-dancing and chanting angrily to the visiting President: 'Go home, go home—take away your missiles.' (Don't worry, 12,000 U.S. troops easily handle the generally grateful crowds; also the President is 'spirited out the rear end of the United States compound'—and so by helicopter to the airport.) In Japan, weeks of student rioting succeed in rejecting the President's visit, jeopardizing a new treaty with the U.S.A., and displacing the big-business, pro-American Prime Minister, Kishi. And even in our own pleasant Southland, Negro and white students are—but let us keep that quiet: it really *is* disgraceful.

"That is by no means the complete list; that was yesterday; see today's newspaper. Tomorrow, in varying degree, the returns will be more evident. Will they be evident enough? They will have to be very obvious to attract real American attention: sweet complaints and the voice of reason—these are not enough. In the slum countries of the world today, what are they saying? The rich Americans, they pay attention only to violence—and to money. You don't care what they say, American? Good for you. Still, they may insist; things are no longer under the old control; you're not getting it straight, American: your country—it would seem—may well become the target of a world hatred the like of which the easy-going Americans have never dreamed. Neutralists and Pacifists and Unilateralists and that confusing variety of Leftists around the world—all those tens of millions of people, of course they are misguided, absolutely controlled by small conspiratorial groups of trouble-makers, under direct orders from Moscow and Peking. Diabolically omnipotent, it is *they* who create all this messy unrest. It is *they* who have given the tens of millions the absurd idea that they shouldn't want to remain, or to become, the seat of American nuclear bases—those gay little outposts of American civilization. So now they don't want U-2's on their territory; so now they want to contract out of the American military machine; they want to be neutral among the crazy big antagonists. And they don't want their own societies to be militarized.

"But take heart, American: you won't have time to get really bored with your friends abroad: they won't be your friends much longer. You don't need *them;* it will all go away; don't let them confuse you."

Add to that: In the Soviet bloc, who is it that has been breaking out of apathy? It has been students and young professors and writers; it has been the young intelligentsia of Poland and Hungary, and of Russia, too. Never mind that they have not won; never mind that there are other social and moral types among them. First of all, it has been these types. But the point is clear, isn't it?

That is why we have got to study these new generations of intellectuals around the world as real live agencies of historic change. Forget Victorian Marxism, except when you need it; and read Lenin again (be careful)—Rosa Luxemburg, too.

"But it is just some kind of moral upsurge, isn't it?" Correct. But under it: no apathy. Much of it is direct non-violent action, and it seems to be working, here and there. Now we must learn from the practice of these young intellectuals and with them work out new forms of action.

"But it's all so ambiguous—Cuba, for instance." Of course it is; history-making is always ambiguous. Wait a bit; in the meantime, help them to focus their moral upsurge in less ambiguous political ways. Work out with them the ideologies, the strategies, the theories that will help them consolidate their efforts: new theories of structural changes of and by human societies in our epoch.

"But it is utopian, after all, isn't it?" No, not in the sense you mean. Whatever else it may be, it's not that. Tell it to the students of Japan. Tell it to the Negro sit-ins. Tell it to the Cuban Revolutionaries. Tell it to the people of the hungry-nation bloc.

New Styles in Leftism
IRVING HOWE

I propose to describe a political style or outlook before it has become hardened into an ideology or the property of an organization. This outlook is visible along limited portions of the political scene; for the sake of exposition I will make it seem more precise and structured than it really is. . . .

II Ideologues and Desperadoes

   A Ideologues, white

      The disintegration of American radicalism these last few decades left a
      good many ideologues emotionally unemployed: people accustomed to
      grand theorizing who have had their theories shot out from under them;
      people still looking for some belated evidence that they were "right" all
      along; people with unexpended social energy and idealism of a sort, who
      desperately needed new arenas in which to function.

     1 The remains of Stalinism. The American Communist Party was broken
      first by McCarthyite and government persecution, and second by an
      inner crisis following Khrushchev's revelations and the Hungarian
      Revolution. Those who left out of disillusionment were heartsick people,
      their convictions and sometimes their lives shattered. But those who left
      the party or its supporting organizations because they feared government
      attack were often people who kept, semi-privately, their earlier
      convictions. Many of them had a good deal of political experience; some
      remained significantly placed in the network of what might be called

conscience organizations. Naturally enough, they continued to keep in touch with one another, forming a kind of reserve apparatus based on common opinions, feelings, memories. As soon as some ferment began a few years ago in the civil rights movement and the peace groups, these people were present, ready and eager; they needed no directives from the CP to which, in any case, they no longer (or may never have) belonged; they were quite capable of working on their own *as if they were working together,* through a variety of groups and periodicals like *The National Guardian.* Organizational Stalinism declined, but a good part of its heritage remained: people who could offer political advice, raise money, write leaflets, sit patiently at meetings, put up in a pleasant New York apartment visitors from a distant state, who, by chance, had been recommended by an old friend.

2 *True believers.* On the far left there remains a scatter of groups still convinced that Marxism-Leninism, in one or another version, is "correct." What has failed them, however, is the historical motor provided by Marxist theory: the proletariat, which has not shown the "revolutionary potential" or fulfilled the "historical mission" to which it was assigned. Though the veteran Marxists cannot, for fear of shattering their whole structure of belief, give up the *idea* of the proletariat, they can hardly act, day by day, as if the American working class were indeed satisfying Marxist expectations or were the actual center of revolutionary ferment. Thus, in somewhat schizoid fashion, they have clung to their traditional faith in the proletariat as the revolutionary class, while in practice searching for a new embodiment of it which might provide the social energy they desire. And in the Negro movement they seem to have found it.

        That this movement, with great creative flair, has worked out an indigenous strategy of its own; that it has developed nonviolent resistance into an enormously powerful weapon; that the Negro clergy, in apparent disregard of Leninist formulas, plays a leading and often militant role—all this does not sit well with the old Marxists. They must therefore develop new theories, by means of which the Negroes become the vanguard of the working class or perhaps the "true" (not yet "bought-off") working class. And, clustering around the Negro movement, they contribute a mite of wisdom here and there: scoffing at nonviolence, employing the shibboleth of "militancy" as if it were a magical device for satisfying the needs of the Negro poor, etc. They are experienced in "deepening the struggle," usually other people's struggles: which means to scorn the leadership of Dr. King without considering that the "revolutionary" course they propose for the Negro movement could, if adopted, lead it into a *cul de sac* of isolation, exhaustion and heroic blood. Understandably, they find allies in Negro nationalists who want not so much to deepen as to divert the struggle, and among young militants who dislike the idea that Negroes might, if successful in their struggle, come to share some of the American affluence and thus become "middle-class."

3 *Authoritarian leftists.* In figures like Isaac Deutscher and Paul Sweezey we find the true intellectual progenitors of at least part of the "new leftism"; the influence they exert has been indirect, since they are not involved in immediate struggles, but it has nevertheless been there.

Sweezey's *Monthly Review* is the main spokesman in this country for the view that authoritarianism is inherent or necessary in the so-called socialist countries; that what makes them "socialist" is simply the nationalization of the means of production; that democracy, while perhaps desirable in some long-range calculation, is not crucial for judging the socialist character of a society; that the claim that workers must be in a position to exercise political power if the state can in any sense be called "theirs," is a utopian fallacy. At times this technological determinism, put to the service of brutal dictatorship, has been given a more subtle reading by Sweezey: namely, that when the conditions supposedly causing the Communist dictatorship—economic backwardness and international insecurity—have been overcome, the Soviet regime would in some unspecified way democratize itself. In November 1957, after the Khrushchev revelations, *Monthly Review* printed a notably frank editorial:

> The conditions which produced the [Soviet] dictatorship have been overcome. . . . Our theory is being put to the crucial test of practise. And so far—let us face it frankly—there is precious little evidence to confirm it. In all that has happened since Stalin's death we can find nothing to indicate that the Communist Party of any of its competing factions, has changed in the slightest degree its view of the proper relation between the people and their leadership . . . there is apparently no thought that the Soviet people will ever grow up enough to decide for itself who knows best and hence who should make and administer the policies which determine its fate.

And finally from Sweezey: "forty years is too long for a dictatorship to remain temporary"—surely the understatement of the Christian Era!

One might suppose that if "our theory is being put to the crucial test" and there "is precious little evidence to confirm it," honest men would proceed to look for another theory, provided, that is, they continued to believe that freedom is desirable.

Eight years have passed since the above passage appeared in *Monthly Review,* the "precious little evidence" remains precious little, and Sweezey, once apparently dismayed over the lack of democracy in Russia, has moved not to Titoism or "revisionism." No, he has moved toward Maoist China, where presumably one does not have to worry about "the proper relation between the people and their leadership. . . ."

Writing in December 1964 the *MR* editors declared with satisfaction that "there could be no question of the moral ascendency of Peking over Moscow in the underdeveloped world." They agreed with the Chinese that Khrushchev's fall was "a good thing" and they wrote further:

> The Chinese possession of a nuclear potential does not increase the danger of nuclear war. Quite the contrary. The Chinese have solemnly pledged never to be the first to use nuclear weapons . . . and their revolutionary record of devotion to the cause of socialism and progress entitles them to full trust and confidence.

The logic is clear: begin with theoretical inquiry and concern over the perpetuation of dictatorship in Russia and end with "full trust and confidence" in China, where the dictatorship is more severe.

There is an aphorism by a recent Polish writer: "The dispensing of injustice is always in the right hands." And so is its defense.

B Ideologues, Negro

1 *Black nationalism.* Here is a creed that speaks or appears to speak totally against compromise, against negotiating with "the white power structure," against the falsities of white liberals, indeed, against anything but an indulgence of verbal violence. Shortly before his tragic murder Malcolm X spoke at a Trotskyist-sponsored meeting and listening to him, I felt, as did others, that he was in a state of internal struggle, reaching out for an ideology he did not yet have. For the Negroes in his audience he offered the relief of articulating subterranean feelings of hatred, contempt, defiance, feelings that did not have to be held in check because there was a tacit compact that the talk about violence would remain talk. Malcolm declared that he would go, not unarmed, to Mississippi, *if* the Negroes there would ask him to come: a condition that could only leave him safely North, since the last thing the Negroes of Mississippi needed or wanted was Malcolm's military aid. For both the Negroes and whites in the audience there was an apparent feeling that Malcolm and Malcolm alone among the Negro spokesmen was authentic because . . . well, because finally he spoke for nothing but his rage, for no proposal, no plan, no program, just a sheer outpouring of anger and pain. And that they could understand. The formidable sterility of his speech, so impressive in its relation to a deep personal suffering, touched something in their hearts. For Malcolm, intransigent in words and nihilistic in reality, never invoked the possibility or temptations of immediate struggle; he never posed the problems, confusions and risks of maneuver, compromise, retreat. Brilliantly Malcolm spoke for a rejection so complete it transformed him into an apolitical spectator, or in the language his admirers are more inclined to use than I am, a pure "cop-out."

2 *Caricature.* If, nevertheless, there was something about Malcolm which commands our respect, that is because we know his life-struggle, his rise

from the depths, his conquest of thought and speech. LeRoi Jones, by contrast, stands as a burlesque double of whatever is significant in Malcolm.

In his success as both a New School lecturer and prophet of "guerrilla warfare" in the U.S.; in his badgering of white liberal audiences; in his orgies of verbal violence committed, to be sure, not in Selma, Alabama, but Sheridan Square, New York; in his fantasies of an international race war in which the whites will be slaughtered, Jones speaks for a contemporary sensibility. But he speaks for it in a special way: as a distinctively American success, the pop-art guerrilla warrior.

He speaks at that center of revolutionary upsurge, the Village Vanguard. He explains that the murder of Negroes in the South does not arouse the kind of horror and indignation that the murder of white civil rights workers does. *He is absolutely right,* the point cannot be made too often. But Jones cannot stop there: it would be too sensible, too humane, and it would not yield pages in the *Village Voice.* Instead, responding to a question, "What about Goodman and Schwerner, the two white boys killed in Mississippi, don't you care about them?" Jones continues, as quoted in the *Voice;*

> "Absolutely not," rapped out Jones. "Those boys were just artifacts, artifacts, man. They weren't real. If they want to assuage their leaking consciences, that's their business. I won't mourn for them. I have my own dead to mourn for."

Is this not exactly the attitude Jones had a moment earlier condemned in regard to killings in the South, but the same attitude in reverse? And is it really impossible for the human heart to mourn for *both* Negro and white victims? Not, to be sure, for ordinary whites, since they, we all know, are "white devils"; but at least for those who have given their lives in the struggle?

The essential point about Jones' racist buffoonery has been made by George Dennison in a recent review of Jones' plays:

> Just as he mis-labels the victims *black,* he mis-labels the authority *white.* Certainly he knows, or should know, that the authority which in fact pertains is not the authority of race . . . but an authority of property and arms; and certainly he knows, or should know, that the life-destroying evil inheres in the nature of the authority, not in the color of those who wield it. But if Jones wanted change, he would speak change. He speaks, instead, for the greatest possible rejection, a rejection so absolute, so confined to fantasy, that it amounts to nothing more than hands-off-the-status-quo. . . . Point by point his is an upside down version of the most genteel, middle-class, liberal position. And I think that the liberals see him as one of their own, albeit a Dropout. He addresses every word to them and is confined to their systems of values because he is in the business of denying no other values but those. That spurious anger, so resonant with career, can be trusted not to upset the apple-cart.

3 *Desperadoes, white.* In effect, I have already described this group, so let me here confine myself to a few remarks about one of its central battle cries, "alienation."

The trouble with the current use of alienation as a mode of social analysis is that it explains almost everything, and thereby almost nothing. The term has become impossibly loose (like those other handy tags, "the Establishment" and "the Power Structure"). As used by Marx, alienation had a rather precise reference: it pointed to the condition of the worker in the capitalist productive process, a condition in which "the worker's deed becomes an alien power . . . forcing him to develop some specialized dexterity at the cost of a world of productive impulses." This kind of analysis focuses upon the place of the proletarian within the social structure, and not upon the sediment of malaise among those outside it.

Since Marx wrote, the term has acquired an impossible load of signification. During most of the bourgeois era, the European intellectuals grew increasingly estranged from the social community because the very ideals that had animated the bourgeois revolution were now being violated by bourgeois society; their "alienation" was prompted not by Bohemian wilfullness but by a loyalty to Liberty, Fraternity, Equality, or to an induced vision of pre-industrial society which, by a twist of history, came pretty much to resemble Liberty, Fraternity, Equality. Just as it was the triumph of capitalism which largely caused this sense of estrangement, so it was the expansion of capitalism which allowed the intellectuals enough freedom to release it. During the greater part of the bourgeois era, intellectuals preferred alienation from the community to alienation from themselves. Precisely this choice made possible their boldness and strength, precisely this "lack of roots" gave them their speculative power.

By now the term "alienation" frequently carries with it a curious reversal of moral and emotional stress. For where intellectuals had once used it as a banner of pride and self-assertion, today it tends to become a complaint, a token of self-pity, a rationale for a degree of estrangement from the society which connotes not an active rebellion against—nor even any active relation to—it, but rather a justification for marginality and withdrawal.

Somewhere amid the current talk about "alienation" an important reality *is* being touched upon or pointed to. There *is,* in our society, a profound estrangement from the sources of self-hood, the possibilities of human growth and social cohesion. But simply to proclaim this estrangement can be a way of preserving it. Alienation is not some metaphysical equivalent of the bubonic plague which constitutes an irrevocable doom; it is the powerlessness deriving from human failure to act. It is neither a substitute for thought, nor a dissolvent of human will, nor even a roadblock in the way of useful work. To enter into the society which in part causes this estrangement and by establishing bonds with other men to transform the society, is one way of partially overcoming alienation. Each time the civil rights movement brings previously mute Negroes into active political life, each time a trade union extends its power of decision within a factory, the boundaries of alienation are shrunk.

Meanwhile, there is truth in Harold Rosenberg's remark that

> The sentiment of diminution of personality ["alienation"] is an historical hypothesis upon which writers have constructed a set of literary conventions by this time richly equipped with theatrical machinery and symbolic allusions. . . . By all evidence, the hollow-man tradition has completely captured our "serious" prose [and some of our serious youth]. . . . Once vanguardist, this tradition . . . has lately come to dominate popular literature and feeling. The individual's emptiness and inability to act have become an irrefrangible cliche, untiringly supported by an immense phalanx of latecomers to modernism. In this manifestation, the notion of the void has lost its critical edge and is thoroughly reactionary.

4 *Desperadoes, Negro.* A new kind of young Negro militant has appeared in the last few years, and he is a figure far more authentic and impressive than any of those I have thus far mentioned. He is fed up with white promises. He is proud to be estranged from white society. He has strong, if vague, "nationalist" inclinations. He is desperate—impatient with the tactics of gradualism, nonviolence and passive resistance. He sees few, if any, allies upon whom he can count; few, if any, positive forces in society that might stir people into action. In effect, he decides that he must "go it alone," scornful of the white liberal and labor groups, as well as of those Negro leaders who choose to work with them. He seeks to substitute for a stagnant history his own desire and sacrifice.

Let me suggest a very limited comparison. This kind of young Negro militant, though not of course interested in any kind of individual terrorism, acts out of social motives somewhat like those of the late-nineteenth-century Russian terrorists, who also tried to substitute their intransigent will for the sluggishness of history. And the consequences may be similar: the best cadres exhausted in isolation and defeat.

Such a response may well be the inevitable result of an abrupt and painful coming-to-awareness on the part of young Negro militants who had previously suppressed their suffering simply in order to survive but now feel somewhat freer to release it. Their devotion is beyond doubt, as their heroism is beyond praise; yet what I'm here tempted to call kamikaze radicalism, or what Bayard Rustin calls the "no win" outlook, can become self-defeating in political life. . . .

III The "New Leftist"—A Sketch

A Cultural style

The "new leftist" appears, at times, as a figure embodying a style of speech, dress, work and culture. Often, especially if white, the son of the middle class—and sometimes the son of middle-class parents nursing radical memories—he asserts his rebellion against the deceit and hollowness of American society. Very good; there is plenty to rebel against. But in the course of his rebellion he tends to reject not merely the middle-class ethos but a good many other things he too hastily associates with it: the intellectual heritage of the West, the tradition of liberalism at its most serious, the commitment to democracy as an indispensable part of civilized life. He tends to think of style as the very substance of his revolt, and while he may, on one side of himself, engage in valuable activities in behalf of civil rights, student freedom, etc., he nevertheless tacitly accepts the "givenness" of American society, has little hope or expectation of changing it, and thereby, in effect, settles for a mode of personal differentiation.

Primarily that means the wish to shock, the wish to assault the sensibilities of a world he cannot overcome. If he cannot change it, then at least he can outrage it. He searches in the limited repertoire of sensation and shock: for sick comics who will say "fuck" in nightclubs; for drugs that will vault him beyond the perimeters of the suburbs; for varieties, perversities, and publicities of sex so as perhaps to create an inner, private revolution that will accompany—or replace?—the outer, public revolution.

But "the new leftist" is frequently trapped in a symbiotic relationship with the very middle class he rejects, dependent upon it for his self-definition: quite as the professional anti-Communist of a few years ago was caught up with the Communist Party which, had it not existed, he would have had to invent—as indeed at times he did invent. So that for all its humor and charm, the style of the "new leftist" tends to become a rigid anti-style, dependent for its survival on the enemy it is supposed to panic. To *épater le bourgeois*—in this case, perhaps, to *épater le père*—is to acquiesce in a basic assumption of at least the more sophisticated segments of the middle class; that values can be inferred from, or are resident in, the externals of dress, appearance, furnishings and hair-dos.

Shock as he will, disaffiliate as he may choose, the "new leftist" discovers after a while that nothing has greatly changed. The relations of power remain as before, the Man still hovers over the scene, the "power structure" is unshaken. A few old ladies in California may grow indignant, a DA occasionally arrest someone, a *Village Voice* reporter arrange an interview; but surely that is all small change. And soon the "new leftist" must recognize that even he has not been greatly transformed. For in his personal manner he is acting out the dilemmas of a utopian community, and just as Brook Farm had to remain subject to the laws of the market despite its internal ethic of cooperation, so must he remain subject to the impress of the dominant institutions despite his desire to be totally different.

Victimized by a lack of the historical sense, the "new leftist" does not realize that the desire to shock and create sensations has itself a long and largely disastrous history. The notion, as Meyer Schapiro has remarked, that opium is the revolution of the people has been luring powerless intellectuals and semi-intellectuals for a long time. But the damnable thing is that for an almost equally long time the more sophisticated and urban sectors of the middle class have refused to be shocked. They know the repertoire of sensationalism quite as well as the "new leftist"; and if he is to succeed in shocking them or even himself, he must keep raising the ante. The very rebel who believes himself devoted to an absolute of freedom and looks with contempt upon any mode of compromise, is thereby caught up in the compulsiveness of his escalation: a compulsiveness inherently bad enough, but rendered still more difficult, and sometimes pathetic, by the fact that, alas, each year he gets a year older.

Let me amend this somewhat. To say that the urban middle class has become jaded and can no longer be shocked, is not quite correct. No; a kind of complicity is set up between the outraged and/or amused urban middle class and the rebels of sensation. Their mutual dependency requires that each shock, to provide the pleasures of indignation, must be a little stronger (like a larger dose . . .) than the previous one. For the point is not so much that the urban middle class can no longer be shocked as that it positively yearns for and comes to depend upon the titillating assaults of its cultural enemies. So that when a new sensation (be it literary violence, sexual fashion, intellectual outrage, high-toned pornography, or sadistic denunciation) is provided by the shock troops of culture, the sophisticated middle class responds with outrage, resistance and anger—*for upon these initial responses its pleasure depends.* But then, a little later, it rolls over like a happy puppy on its back, moaning, "Oh, baby, *épater* me again, harder this time, tell me what a sterile impotent louse I am and how you are so tough and virile, how you're planning to murder me, *épater* me again, baby. . . ."

Thus a fire-eating character like LeRoi Jones becomes an adjunct of middle-class amusement and, to take an enormous leap upward in talent and seriousness, a writer like Norman Mailer becomes enmeshed in his public conduct with popular journalism and publicity.

The whole problem was anticipated many years ago by Trotsky when, writing about the Russian poet Yesenin, he remarked that the poet thought to frighten the bourgeoisie by making scenes but as it turned out, the bourgeoisie was delighted, it adored scenes.

One thing alone will not delight the bourgeoisie: a decrease in income, a loss in social power, a threat to its property.

There is another sense in which cultural style dominates the behavior of the "new leftists." Some of them display a tendency to regard political—and perhaps all of—life as a Hemingwayesque contest in courage and rectitude. People are constantly being tested for endurance, bravery, resistance to temptation, and if found inadequate, are denounced for having "copped out." Personal endurance thus becomes the substance of, and perhaps even a replacement for, political ideas.

Now this can be a valid and serious way of looking at things, especially in extreme situations: which is, of course, what Hemingway had in mind. Among civil rights workers in the Deep South such a vision of life reflects the ordeal they must constantly face; they *are* under extreme pressure and their courage *is* constantly being tested. Yet their situation cannot be taken as a model for the political life of the country as a whole. If one wants to do more than create a tiny group of the heroic, the tested and the martyred, their style of work will not suffice. If one wants to build a movement in which not everyone need give "the whole of their lives," then the suspicion and hostility such an outlook is bound to engender toward the somewhat less active and somewhat less committed can only be damaging. For in effect, if not intent, it is a strategy of exclusion, leaving no place for anyone but the vanguard of the scarred.

It is, at times, a strategy of exclusion in a still more troubling sense: it reduces differences of opinions to grades of moral rectitude. If, for example, you think Martin Luther King or Bayard Rustin was wrong in regard to certain tactical matters; if you disagree with what Rustin proposed at the Democratic National Convention and what King did in Selma, then you call into question their loyalty and commitment: you may even charge them with "copping-out" or "fooling with the power structure." This approach makes it impossible to build a movement and, in the long run, even to maintain a sect. . . .

C Politics and Freedom

The "new leftists" feel little attachment to Russia. Precisely as it has turned away from the more extreme and terroristic version of totalitarianism, so have they begun to find it unsatisfactory as a model: too Victorian, even "bourgeois." Nor are they interested in distinguishing among kinds of anti-Communism, whether of the right or left.

When they turn to politics, they have little concern for precise or complex thought. (By contrast, the more reflective among the younger radicals, such as some leaders of Students for a Democratic Society, have made a serious effort to develop their intellectual and political views; they understand the sterility to which a mere "activism" can lead, in fact, the way it must sooner or later undermine the possibilities even for activity). A few years ago the "new leftists" were likely to be drawn to Communist China, which then seemed bolder than Khrushchev's Russia. But though the Mao regime has kept the loyalty of a small group of students, most of the "new leftists" seem to find it too grim and repressive. They tend to look for their new heroes and models among the leaders of underdeveloped countries. Figures like Lumumba, Nasser, Sukarno, Babu and above all Castro attract them, suggesting the possibility of a politics not yet bureaucratized and rationalized. But meanwhile they neglect to notice, or do not care, that totalitarian and authoritarian dictatorship can set in even before a society has become fully modernized. They have been drawn to charismatic figures like Lumumba and Castro out of a distaste for the mania of industrial production which the Soviet Union shares with the United States; but they fail to see that such leaders of the underdeveloped countries, who in their eyes represent spontaneity and anarchic freedom, are themselves—perhaps unavoidably—infused with the same mania for industrial production.

Let me specify a few more of the characteristic attitudes among the "new leftists":

1 An extreme, sometimes unwarranted, hostility toward liberalism. . . .

2 An impatience with the problems that concerned an older generation of radicals. . . .

3 A vicarious indulgence in violence, often merely theoretic and thereby all the more irresponsible. . . .

4 An unconsidered enmity toward something vaguely called the Establishment. . . .

5 An equally unreflective belief in "the decline of the West". . . .

6 A crude, unqualified anti-Americanism, drawing from every possible source, even if one contradicts another: the aristocratic bias of Eliot and Ortega, Communist propaganda, the speculations of Tocqueville, the resentment of post-war Europe, etc.

7 An increasing identification with that sector of the "third world" in which "radical" nationalism and Communist authoritarianism merge. . . .

The authoritarians find political tendencies and representative men with whom to identify in the Communist world; but so do we. We identify with the people who have died for freedom, like Imre Nagy, or who rot in prison, like Djilas. We identify with the "revisionists," those political *maranoes* who, forced to employ Communist jargon, yet spoke out for a socialism democratic in character and distinct from both Communism and capitalism. As it happens, our friends in the Communist world are not in power; but since when has that mattered to socialists?

In 1957, at the height of the Polish ferment, the young philosopher Leszek Kolakowski wrote a brief article entitled "What Is Socialism?" It consisted of a series of epigrammatic sentences describing what socialism is not (at the moment perhaps the more immediate concern), but tacitly indicating as well what socialism should be. The article was banned by the Gomulka regime but copies reached Western periodicals. Here are a few sentences:

Socialism is not

A society in which a person who has committed a crime sits at home waiting for the police.

A society in which one person is unhappy because he says what he thinks, and another happy because he does not say what is in his mind.

A society in which a person lives better because he does not think at all.

A state whose neighbors curse geography.

A state which wants all its citizens to have the same opinions in philosophy, foreign policy, economics, literature and ethics.

A state whose government defines its citizens' rights, but whose citizens do not define the government's rights.

A state in which there is private ownership of the means of production.

A state which considers itself solidly socialist because it has liquidated private ownership of the means of production.

A state which always knows the will of the people before it asks them.

A state in which the philosophers and writers always say the same as the generals and ministers, but always after them.

A state in which the returns of parliamentary elections are always predictable.

A state which does not like to see its citizens read back numbers of newspapers.

These negatives imply a positive, and that positive is the greatest lesson of contemporary history: the unity of socialism and democracy. To preserve democracy as a political mode without extending it into every crevice of social and economic life is to make it increasingly sterile, formal, ceremonial. To nationalize an economy without enlarging democratic freedoms is to create a new kind of social exploitation. Radicals may properly and fraternally disagree about many things; but upon this single axiom, this conviction wrung from the tragedy of our age, politics must rest.

From **Berkeley:**
The New Student Revolt
MARIO SAVIO

Introduction

There are many things that happened at Berkeley which will not be of interest to people elsewhere, and need not be; it is to be hoped that others will have their own problems to contend with, and will have interesting things of their own to do. Others should not have to get their experience second hand. But there are certain things that happened at Berkeley which it would be useful for people in other places to know about, as an aid in understanding themselves, as help to them in preparing revolts of their own.

There were some things which made the Berkeley revolt peculiarly Berkeley's, but other things made it a revolt among white middle-class youth that could happen at any state university. And it is the second set of factors which will probably be of most importance to people outside Berkeley.

Why did it happen in Berkeley? The important question to ask, rather, is: why did it happen in Berkeley *first?*—because there are several universities in the East and Midwest where, since last semester, little home-grown revolts have flared up.

Asking why it happened in Berkeley first is like asking why Negroes, and not Americans generally, are involved in securing access for all, to the good which America could provide for her people. This may seem strange to those who imagine America to be a virtual paradise except for certain groups, notably Negroes, who have been excluded. But this is a distortion. What oppresses the American Negro community is merely an exaggerated, grotesque version of what oppresses the rest of the country—and this is eminently true of the middle class, despite its affluence. In important ways the situation of students at Berkeley is an exaggerated representation of what is wrong with American higher education.

The forces influencing students at Berkeley—not merely those resulting from participation in the university itself, but also those deriving from student involvement in politics—these forces are likewise exaggerations of the forces to which society subjects other university students in other parts of the country. So probably the reason it could happen here first is this: while the same influences are present elsewhere, there is no university (none that I know of, at all events) where these influences are present in as extreme a form as here in Berkeley.

The influences upon students are of three main kinds: those deriving from personal history; "internal" problems resulting directly from being a student; and "external" problems deriving from after-class political activities. The external influences on students result primarily from involvement in the civil-rights movement, both in the Bay Area and in the South. The internal derive primarily from the style of the factory-like mass miseducation of which Clark Kerr is the leading ideologist. There are many impersonal universities in America; there is probably none more impersonal in its treatment of students than the University of California. There are students at many Northern universities deeply involved in the civil-rights movement; but there probably is no university outside the South where the effect of such involvement has been as great as it has been at Berkeley.

One factor which helps explain the importance of civil rights here is the political character of the Bay Area. This is one of the few places left in the United States where a personal history of involvement in radical politics is not a form of social leprosy. And, of course, there are geographical considerations. The Berkeley campus is very close to the urban problems of Oakland and San Francisco, but not right in either city. On campus it is virtually impossible for the thoughtful to banish social problems from active consideration. Many students here find it impossible not to be in some sense *engagé*. The shame of urban America (just south of campus or across the bay) forces itself upon the conscience of the community. At the same time it is possible to think about political questions by retreating from their immediate, physical, constant presence. Thus, at Columbia or CCNY it is difficult to tell where the city ends and the university begins, whereas at Berkeley there is a clearly demarcated university community, with places where students and faculty members can enjoy a certain sense of retreat and apartness. At Berkeley we are both close enough to gross injustice not to forget; but far enough away, and set well enough apart, so as neither to despair nor simply to merge into the common blight. Furthermore, ours is not a commuter school; the students live here at least part of the year. This makes possible a continuing community such as would be impossible at UCLA for example. This community, with a great deal of internal communication, has been essential to the development of political consciousness. And there is a good deal for the students to communicate to one another. Over ten per cent of the student body has taken part *directly* in civil-rights activity, in the South or in the Bay Area. These three thousand, all of whom have at least walked picket lines, are a leaven for the campus. And many more can be said to have participated vicariously: there is great and widespread interest in what those who "go South" have done and experienced. Of course, there is a natural receptivity for politics at Berkeley simply because this is a state-supported university: a good percentage of the student body comes from lower-middle-class or working-class homes; many who can afford to pay more for education go, for example, to Stanford.

Now for those problems which have their origin within the university: the tale which follows is strictly true only for undergraduates in their first two years; there are some improvements during the second two years; but only graduate students can expect to be treated tolerably well.

It is surprising at first, after taking a semester of undergraduate courses here—except in the natural sciences or mathematics—to realize how little you have learned. It is alarming at the same time to recognize how much busy work you have done: so many papers hastily thrown together, superficially read by some graduate-student teaching assistant. Even if you want to work carefully, it is difficult to do so in each of five courses, which often have unrealistically long reading lists—courses with little or no logical relationship to one another. Perhaps in the same semester, the student will "take" a superficial survey of all the major (and many minor) principles of biology, *and* a language course a good part of which is spent in a language "laboratory" very poorly integrated into the grammar and reading part of the course, a laboratory which requires its full hour of outside preparation but which benefits the student very little in terms of speaking ability in the foreign language. Perhaps, ironically, the semester's fare will include a sociology course in which you are sure to learn, in inscrutably "scientific" language, just what is so good and only marginally improvable in today's pluralistic, democratic America.

If you are an undergraduate still taking non-major courses, at least one of your subjects will be a "big" lecture in which, with field glasses and some good luck, you should be able, a few times a week, to glimpse that famous profile giving those four- or five-year-old lectures, which have been very conveniently written up for sale by the Fybate Company anyway. The lectures in the flesh will not contain much more than is already in the Fybate notes, and generally no more than will be necessary to do well on the examinations. Naturally, it will be these examinations which determine whether or not you pass the course. Such an education is conceived as something readily quantifiable: 120 units constitute a bachelor's degree. It is rather like the outside world—the "real" world—where values are quantified in terms of the dollar: at the university we use play money, course units. The teacher whom you will have to strain to see while he lectures will be very seldom available for discussion with his students; there is usually an hour set aside, in the course of each week, during which all of the students who want to speak with him will have to arrange to do so. In the face of physical impossibility, there are generally few such brave souls. If more came, it would make little difference; this system is rarely responsive to individual needs. There are too few teachers, and too little time. Indeed, if the professor is one of those really famous scholars of whom the university is understandably proud, then the primary reason there is not enough time for the problems of individual undergraduates is that the bulk of the professor's time (other than the six or eight hours spent in the classroom each week) is devoted to "research" or spent with graduate students. The moral of the piece is: if you want to get an education, you will have to get it yourself. This is true in any case, but it is not usually intended to be true in the sense that getting it yourself means *in spite* of the work at school. There are just too many nonsense hours spent by American students, hours to "do" much as one "does" time in prison.

In the course of one semester, doubtless, there will be several opportunities for each unlucky student to come into contact with the administration of the university. This may be to request an exception from some university requirement. However formal the requirement may be, invariably at least once a semester, the student finds he cannot be excepted, not because the requirement is important but simply because it happens to be a *requirement.* Well, that is a problem common to bureaucracies of various kinds, but one wonders if this is the sort of thing that should be regularly encountered at a university. Yet this ordeal is what a large part of American college-age youth have to endure. We should ask not whether such intellectual cacophony and bureaucratic harassment are appropriate at universities—for certainly they are not—but rather, whether these local "plants" in what Clark Kerr calls the "knowledge industry" deserve the name university at all.

This is a somewhat overdrawn picture of life at Berkeley. The students are aware of meaningful activity going on outside the university. For there is some meaningful activity going on in America today—in the civil-rights movement, certainly. At the same time, but much more dimly, each student is aware of how barren of essential meaning and direction is the activity in which he is primarily involved, as a card-carrying student. I write "each student is aware" but I realize that this is to express more hope than fact. In less than a tenth of the students is this "awareness" a "consciousness." This consciousness of the poverty of one's immediate environment is a difficult thing to come by. In most it must remain a dim awareness. It is far easier to become aware of (and angry at) the victimization of others than to perceive one's own victimization. It is far easier to become angry when others are hurt. This is so for a number of reasons. Fighting for others' rights cannot engender nearly so great a guilt as striking rebelliously at one's own immediate environment. Also, it is simply easier to see the injustice done others—it's "out there." Many of us came to college with what we later acknowledge were rather romantic expectations, perhaps mostly unexpressed at first, about what a delight and adventure learning would be. We really did have unanswered questions searching for words, though to say so sounds almost corny. But once at college we quickly lose much of the romantic vision; although, fortunately, some never give in to the disappointment. Discovering that college is really high school grown up and not significantly more challenging, many console themselves with the realization that it is not much more difficult either.

The revolt began in the fall semester of 1964 as an extension of either vicarious or actual involvement in the struggle for civil rights. It was easy to draw upon this reservoir of outrage at the wrongs done to other people; but such action usually masks the venting, by a more acceptable channel, of outrage at the wrongs done to oneself. I am far from propounding a psychoanalytic theory of politics, yet most people whom I have met who are committed to radical political innovation are people who have experienced a good deal of personal pain, who have felt strong frustration in their own lives. This mechanism made possible the *beginning* of one pint-sized revolution on the Berkeley campus. The university set about denying students access to those facilities and rights on campus which had made possible student involvement in the civil-rights movement in the previous few years. Yet very rapidly the concern of the movement shifted from Mississippi to much closer to home; we soon began doing an awful lot of talking and thinking about the limitations of the university, the "Multiversity," the "knowledge industry"—these metaphors became ever more a part of the rhetoric of the movement. Civil rights was central in our fight because of business-community pressure on the university to crack down on campus-launched campaigns into the surrounding community—which had proven all too effective. University spokesmen have acknowledged that the need to respond to such pressures was the only "justification" for the ban on political activity. Nevertheless, the focus of our attention shifted from our deep concern with the victimization of others to outrage at the injustices done to ourselves. These injustices we came to perceive more and more clearly with each new attack upon us by the university bureaucracy as we sought to secure our own rights to political advocacy. The political consciousness of the Berkeley community has been quickened by this fight. The Berkeley students now demand what hopefully the rest of an oppressed white middle class will some day demand: freedom for all Americans, not just for Negroes!

"Everybody Turns When the Tide Turns"
PETER BERG

Q: What do you see happening?

PETER: What's happening is the question of the generation. What's happening is exactly the question of the generation.

Q: What is that question?

PETER: What's happening?

Q: Tell me what you think is happening.

PETER: People are beginning to tell it. The foundation of a civilization is growing here. . . built on people who are really very wishful. . . . Hope is the shot. Walking around with empty baskets. Hope . . . people with empty flour bins . . . hope. Hope [is the] handle. That's the foundation of it. Then the forms it takes are the wishful forms that are either overdue or are the best that can be made.

Something is coming that is going to make the most of what we are doing. . . . Y'know, the mark of history on a thing dates it, makes it anachronistic. . . . Talkin' about the French Revolution, about changing the names of the months, well, any historian would write, "In the flush of revolutionary fervor, they even felt [that] they must change the names of the months." That isn't what the people felt. I don't think the people felt they had to change the names of the months. I think that they had a distinctly different vision of the universe. They started there—popped open. Freedom, revolution, liberation pops the cork of imagination, just lets it out. And they were full out. In the flush of liberation spring those roots. Take things up in the Haight-Ashbury. There are forms of a civilization to come, after this deal goes down.

Q: What is this deal that's going to go down?

PETER: Roughly the same position as the Soviet Union in 1917. It was the only country which hadn't had a democracy—1848 settled the hash for all the European countries, and there was Russia, sitting there with every

accommodating gesture suddenly being made. . . . And what the serfs were
doing was roaming in bands of thirty to three hundred going from
mansion to mansion burning down aristocrats' estates, raping the women,
cutting up the cats and quartering 'em, killing the animals and roasting
'em, pulling out the booze and drinking it, tearing down the drapes,
dancing on the pianos, using them for firewood, waking up in the morning
with a hangover with the smell of burning flesh and ruins around them,
and going on to the next town to do it again. They did that from 1915 to
1917—they were doing it all over Russia. Finely tuned, precise intellectual
abstractions about revolution didn't make any difference. And this is what
the people were actually doing—they were doing it to accommodate their
desire. The desire was to kill the aristocrats, break down the drapes, eat
the food, and get on someplace quick.

Q: You think we're in a situation like that in this country?

PETER: It's exactly what it's like.

Q: What do you suppose produced this particular kind of moment? What
happened to make all these kids suddenly appear on this scene? Why
1965?

PETER: I don't think it happened in '65. Notice most of the people that are
involved are from before '65. They say it's the failures of the fifties . . .
what sometimes has been called the ideology of failure was developed in
the fifties. It became the basis of life for people thereafter. When I read
Howl, I knew I didn't have anything to lose. That's what did it. That's
what sent people out in search of experience. Ex-per-i-ence. Expedient
experience. 'Cause it kept 'em busy durin' Korea—Korea was something
nobody wanted to think about too much. During that time, people sought
out the junkies, con-men, hard-living jailbirds, down-and-outers, and gave
them credence. . . . When the people followed this—followed the line of
failure in the fifties—and gave credence to where it would go, credence to
junkies, the hardest-hit junkies, mainlining people, hop-heads. In love
with something a hustler could tell you more about than you'd be able to
pick up from Mom or Tab Hunter—Mom and Tab Hunter almost the
same thing. They are the same thing.

Q: Where were you born, Peter?

PETER: New York.

Q: When?

PETER: '37.

Q: Quick, how old does that make you?

PETER: Twenty-nine.

Q: Did you grow up in New York?

PETER: Till I was about seven.

Q: Then where?

PETER: Florida, northern Florida is southern Georgia. Call the rednecks there
"Florida crackers." And that gets outcast. [I was] cast out of that
society—nigger-lovin', motherfuckin', New York Yankee Jew.

Q: Is that what you are?

PETER: Well, I wasn't, but I became all those things.

Q: Where did you have your adolescence? In Florida?

PETER: Dade County—Miami. I was a car-hiker in Miami Beach. When I was sixteen, worked a club called the Beachcomber, and that's where I learned to drive. Used to drag-race Cadillacs . . . put a nice little Lincoln in the seawall. . . . It's a bizarre kinda world. It's like . . . Nathanael West kind of reality going down. It's a place like Biscayne Bay and "Lots for Sale" signs. Imperial Sunshine Parkway Village signs floating at low tide with rubber tires and condoms with sailor's choice, come in and get hit by the barracuda in moonlight. This tide is a netherworld. It's a spaced-out kind of reality. Hillbilly kids that went to war with shotguns, bicycle chains, brass knucks. . . . I was with the hillbilly kids.

Q: How'd you get in with them if you were from New York?

PETER: Protection, adventure, beauty, sex—

Q: How old were you?

PETER: The girls fucked a lot. I was fifteen. When you're fifteen you want to fuck a lot, there were girls that fucked a lot at fifteen. No, I'm just sayin' that like crying over somebody's virginal bedroom fantasy is not where those chicks were at.

Q: Did you resent being lower-middle-class as you grew up? Were you a gang kid just because it was beautiful?

PETER: Do you know what Miami is? What an incredible potpourri Miami is? . . . Well, Miami . . . They have bridges that go across the bay, y'know, and on these islands that support these bridges are these drive-ins, and there's sports cars with Cuban émigrés, hot rods, hillbilly kids in 'em, pale green Chevrolet sedans . . . motorcycles, Navy personnel. . . . You know, Miami was built in 1927. That's when the city started. That means it's thirty-nine years old. That's Miami, and that thing's just Pow! Pow! Pow! Pow! . . . They had a club out in Hallandale called the Palms where Little Willy was singin' "Fever." . . . That was the music that we heard. We heard "Fever" . . . and these Hank Williams songs that you wouldn't believe, man! Things like, "You live on a mansion on a hill, / and I live in the valley down below / And your daddy won't lemme see you." And a song called "Window Shopping"—you ever hear a hillbilly song called "Window Shopping"? [singing]: "Window shopping. You're only lookin' around."

Window shopping is new to hillbillies, man—window shopping, c'mon—now we're going to go window shopping. Winder shoppin', hah-hah! Dey went winder shoppin', dey goan gotta shoppin' dem winders, boy. . . . You know those brokenhearted people didn't know why they were in the city any more. . . . And those cats were like fourteen-fifteen-year-old hillbilly boys that used to stand in Levi's and boots with thunderbird belts and kind of like denim or, y'know, a shirt with whaddaya-call-it, a Western shirt, pearl buttons on the things, drunk,

drunk, and going like this and looking like Montgomery Clift in that flick he made with Arthur Miller's script and lookin' like that, y'know, with brass knuckles. When I was fifteen, I took a hit right here with a wolf ring. A wolf ring is a ring that comes out with the head of a wolf on it—it's silver-plated, and it sticks out about an inch and a half from your fist. And I get tapped on the shoulder—tap 'im on the shoulder, make 'im turn around. And pingo *Pow!* with that thing right here . . . just missed killin' me. I would have been happily middle-class, I supposed, I wasn't given the opportunity, baby. Just flied out. . . .

Q: Someone tells me you were a Quiz Kid.

PETER: Yep.

Q: Where?

PETER: In Miami.

Q: Then you were a genius kid?

PETER: Yeah, that's what they kept sayin'.

Q: Got any notion what your I.Q. is?

PETER: Yeah, 160.

Q: What did you do after high school?

PETER: Well, there was no money to send me to college, and I was able to send in for scholarships, for work scholarships at the University of Florida. Graduated from high school when I was sixteen. I'd just turned sixteen. Actually, I graduated when I was fifteen. Turned sixteen in my freshman year at college. And so that's when I left my people and went away to college.

Q: Where was your father?

PETER: In New Jersey.

Q: Where did you go?

PETER: Go when?

Q: When you left.

PETER: University of Florida.

Q: Did you stay there any length of time?

PETER: Yeah. I graduated from the university.

Q: So you put in four years. . . . Where is the university?

PETER: Gainesville, northern Florida, southern Alabama.

Q: Did you have to work after school?

PETER: Yeah, that's right. That's the way I went to college.

Q: What'd you do?

PETER: Washed dishes, uh, used to wash the tables in the pool halls in the Student Union, used to knock down about five dollars a night out there . . . swept, used to get up mornings at seven o'clock to put coffee and doughnuts . . . outside the guest room at the Student Union; gave tests, IBM test instrument. . . . [At this point, Peter objected to my probing about his college years.] . . . All this nostalgia may fit like some strange image of yours. It seems to me that it flatters an illusion of adolescence that you may have concerning me or someone else.

Q: No. I had an adolescence too.

PETER: That's very good of you. . . . I grew up bein' called "boy." You know, really, I feel very strong about that shit. Don't you know to what degree people are kept impotent in this society? . . . There're only certain roles that you can play, saying certain kinds of things. You can be queer, you can be a character, you can be an entertainer or an artist, you can be an adolescent, you can be a woman—you can't be a man. I don't think you can be a man in the power sense of the society. . . . I grew up in the South. The South is full of naked power. The power's made very obvious. When I wasn't a nigger-lover—or when I *was* a nigger-lover—the society I grew up in checked me one way or the other. "How'd you like one to go to bed with your sister?" was a mystique. It kept your urinal cigar-straight.

Q: When you were growing up, you didn't know any Negroes?

PETER: There was no access, there was no access for me. I mean, there were several things that kept me from it, one was my mind.

Q: You were . . . ?

PETER: I mean, my mind was a white mind.

Q: When did you really get to know black people?

PETER: As soon as I got out of the South. I made it a point to—

Q: I want to get back to the college scene, because—

PETER: Ain't no black people in the college I went to. I was brought to the dean for putting up signs that said "Integrate in '58."

Q: When was that?

PETER: In '57. . . . We were all called into the dean's office. . . .

Q: Did you pick up a political orientation in college?

PETER: I picked up a political orientation as a child, man! . . . My father was—through frustration or anguish or an image of his own intellect, I don't know which, because I only saw him right before he died . . . —he was a politically conscious man, described as everything from a paranoid alcoholic to a street teacher. He used to go in bars with a copy of the *Decline of the West* and lecture to the people. . . . These are the stories about my father, and they're true. He was an H. G. Wells *Outline of History* libertarian. . . . Steinbeck, when I was eleven-twelve years old, *Grapes of Wrath* turned me on. The kinds of books that were in the house were *Grapes of Wrath*, books by Defoe, Dickens . . . and the Russians were good people. . . . [Also] no matter how middle-class or suburban a high school might be, there's gonna be some contact with poor people. If there's contact with poor people, then credence has to be given to the gangs that are in the school, because if you don't give 'em credence, they're gonna beat the shit out of you. High-school politicos are the kinds of guys who've had their neckties grabbed a couple a times and been shoved up against the lockers once or twice, kneed in the nuts on the football field—that kinda thing. And so credence is taken of that, and gangs—you should know that gangs in the United States, urban gangs even in Miami, Florida, are politically conscious and are political power.

It's fourteen- or fifteen-year-old black kids that are gonna lead their revolutions—they're leading it now. . . . It would be utterly square to assume that gangs aren't politically conscious. . . .

Q: But you didn't join a group like the Young People's Socialist League?

PETER: There wasn't any of it around.

Q: What was your major?

PETER: I was seventeen, hadn't straightened it out. The last year they wanted some information so that they could sort the credits out. So I told 'em. They said which one would be best for you, and I said psychology. [They said,] "But the degree you'll get in psychology'll be worthless." And I said great, yeah. So I started going more for literature, took a course in modern drama; a senior-level course with the drama department and tore it apart. I was the only one that got an A at the end of the thing. I guess that was enough of an education, y'know; that's what I was interested in, and what I was interested in I would do. . . . That's what happened, I drifted, drifted, and the drift was toward myself.

Q: But you did graduate?

PETER: Yeah, I was in San Francisco in 1958. I decided to drop out of college. I went to San Francisco to meet Allen Ginsberg, who had just written *Howl,* which I read in a bar and I read on peyote and understood very clearly. I wanted to come meet these wondrous old men, Henry Miller and Kenneth Rexroth. . . . So I came out to meet them and hung around and got lost and wasn't ready—

Q: Did you run with Ginsberg at all?

PETER: No. . . . I wasn't a part of any of the establishment cabals, y'know. I belonged to a cabal. The fifties were cabalistic times, man, that's when people belonged to cabals. I can tell you a great deal about Dick and Marvin—I can't tell you that much about Jack and Gary. I want you to understand . . . that the thing the beat people established was the reality of small groups of kindred turned-on people. So it doesn't matter to me whether Kerouac was writing about Gary Snyder. It could be me writing about Marvin, or Marvin writing about me. Because that's what they were doing. They were celebrating their cabal. I say cabal because it was the only form—life-affirming form—that was available at the time. Ginsberg is a veteran of several million cabals, I suppose. Universal cabals. And now he's gotten into the biggest cabal of all—the man cabal.

Q: Had you any sense that you were joining the Beat Generation?

PETER: I don't think anybody joined. That's what I was tryin' to tell you. I took peyote when I was seventeen years old, the first thing I ever took in my life—

Q: Where?

PETER: University of Florida. Sent away to Texas for peyote buttons, five dollars for fifty in a crate. I didn't even know what to do—

Q: You mean you could do it by mail?

PETER: Sure you could do it by mail. Texas Cactus Company in some small Texas town. . . . Don't you know that all this is drugs? All this is the revolution, did you know that? Drug consciousness is the key to it. Drugs . . . because of their properties invited the distance that was necessary for us to find out who we really were. That to undertake the sexual explorations that were paraded in front of our consciousness by the "daddies" of the thirties and the bent-up twisted beauties; we had to get that kind of separation to be able to do it and survive. We had to sever feed-back, status-gains off the culture we were born into. Severing it . . . and in that was our beauty. . . .

   In Rock Creek Park in Washington, D.C., in a graveyard with a bottle of Pernod, smoking reefers, balling a beautiful girl named Sandy . . . We got into a crypt . . . and erosion was carrying those graves into a creek. We walked through the high grass and saw that shit . . . mausoleum with sprung door; we looked inside, where the casket had been canted at an angle, and we just had to go make it in there. We made it and came out with mold and cobwebs all over our clothes and smelling of this musty stuff. We ran down to the creek and waded up to our waists, then read Chinese poetry, Li Po, squatting on the rock near that creek.

Q: Did she like it?

PETER: She liked everything. Blonde hair, blue-eyed Jewish girl from Virginia who didn't know what *schmaltz* meant. Her father was a Socialist candidate for governor of Virginia. He got a thousand votes, all from Norfolk. . . . Kicks. Hard kicks. Hard kicks became the way out, became the way. My parents, man, I came from what you call a "broken home"—in television tragedy language. . . . And it was like: "Broken-home-booby-baby-you-never-had-a-break." It sounds like a song, a song from the fifties. But that's where it really is and how those people fucked themselves up so bad. . . . People in [their] forties were wreckage, nothing but wreckage, complete syndromic wreckage. . . . Don't you know that thing when you're walking on the surface of the world, you're walking on the surface of the world, and you bring your broken mind, broken spirit, into a linoleum hospital, a hospital for linoleum, a linoleum hospital for people, for linoleum people, a hospital, broken hospital for linoleum people, linoleum hospital, where it's more important to keep the linoleum clean than to keep the people, to keep the linoleum clean, linoleum hospital people, linoleum hospital people . . . well, that's where it was.

   It was walking on the surface and linoleum, on aluminum, on a cellophane surface of the world. It's not advertising, it's to walk that way as though, if you can just keep your linoleum straight, you'd be all right, just keep up your linoleum, baby, just wrap it up in linoleum, man, eat that linoleum, I used to eat that linoleum, linoleum pie, linoleum soul and that's what it was about. And the fact is that gods didn't make it through . . . nobody ever made it through there. . . . [And] what I was tryin' to tell you, is that hard kicks is the only impetus to reality. . . .

   These hard-livers paid dues. [You can't] have the beauty of being a hard-liver without payin' those dues. You're not gonna do it. You try it, you're not gonna do it.

Why are hard-livers beautiful? It's what they said, y'know. To have a pair of balls! For a man to stand up and scream, "There's nothing but anguish." Allen Ginsberg really incorporated the dead man of the thirties—he really got the dead man of the thirties in the strong homosexual of the fifties that he was. He captured the dead man of the thirties soul and stood up with a pair of balls and started bellowing and saying, "Oh, what! Say who! Fuck what, man!" That was the thing. . . .

Before I was talkin' about black people actually being picked up as slaves [and] that's why they are the black mirror. We see our dark image in black people. We'll always stand for the hypocrisy of this civilization, in the same way the white Southerners were sold an illusion of freedom so complete that it effectively castrated them all. Had to, because, baby, when the governor of Florida comes into Palatka, he comes in with fifty black-and-white highway patrol cars, ten motorcycle escorts, there's a lotta heat on the street that day. A tremendous amount. There's a lot of flexin' and rubbin' legs against motorcycles, there's an awful lot of masturbating billy-clubs goes down that day; and the cats crouch and mouth and make that platform secure for their Good Governor, their Good Old Boy, their Good Old Mistah-Governah-Man. Now that little sweet piece of castration happened a long time ago, and you just say about the governor that he's a good old boy. You say about that sheriff, "He's a good old boy," and he'll say back, he'll say, "These niggers, they just good old boys, we just good old boys. Boy, we're just good old boys." I'm trying to tell you, it's a mystique, it's a fascism of the United States, it's explicit. Then you'd be able to see that General Motors is a Nazi symbol.

What keeps you from seeing General Motors as a Nazi symbol, if anything keeps you, is the "good old boys." We're all good old boys, good old white boys. All of us are good old boys, sure, old Rockefeller he just hit it rich, anybody can hit it rich. Just a good old boy. And if it turns out that we can't hit it rich without hitting somebody else in the head from 50,000 feet with a 500-pound bomb, well then we'll do it that way. We're all supposed to hit it rich because we're all supposed to be good old boys, a democratic country club there, boy. Good old boy. You're all gonna get in that good old country club, boy. . . .

Q: Did you go to New York after Florida?

PETER: Yeah, sure.

Q: How long did you stay in New York?

PETER: Long enough to get awful blue there.

Q: What are the blues like?

PETER: The blues life is a mystique. When I was over the blues-life mystique, I left New York. . . . And the blues-life mystique is that if you want to do anything, you have to lose your left arm. You have to pay a lot of dues . . . to live full out—full out, not far out—as you can, if the cost is in dues. The only people that can do it are oppressed . . . the hard-kick seekers who laid down the patterns of extreme beauty for this civilization . . . like the blues singers and John Dillinger, Willie Sutton and Billie Holiday. . . . They're all people who got burned for what they did . . . being repressed beyond recourse. . . . Don't you know what that means? . . . People who lived it were essentially oppressed beyond action, oppressed beyond action. To be oppressed without recourse is blues life. . . .

Q: Oppressed beyond recourse?

PETER: The beauty of being oppressed beyond recourse—don't you know what that means?

Q: I'm trying to understand.

PETER: Nobody wants to be ugly, nobody wants to be plastic except Andy Asshole, who *wants* to be a plastic man. . . . One wants to be real, to feel that one's being is actually there. . . . The thing about hard kicks. Hard kicks is a way of acquiring life, y'know, breaking into life, so the masters of hard kicks became the wizards of a few years ago. Now hard kicks is available to anyone because LSD is really, y'know, like the hardest kick that was ever discovered. Now maybe STP gonna be harder. It's going to be the mind-cracking motherfucking drugs that gonna be the hard kicks. Hard kicks is a way of looking at your existence, not like mistreating your body or throwing your mind to the crows. It's a way of extending yourself [so that] something spectacular and beautiful can be available to you. But you gotta reach through linoleum to get it—that's the thing. You gotta push past the crap of recognition. You know: "Yes-sir-no-sir-thank-you." . . . There's an edge of non-living, non-being that is pushed on you fuckin' hard, man. . . . We live in the most manipulated society ever created by man. It's an economic, psychological, cultural, manipulation of such a high order and such a degree—because of this thing about individualist pigs that the thing becomes rapacious. Hard kicks and then drugs, drugs, distance, then hard kicks is the extension of the spine, is the extension of individual spirit, to be able to comprehend a large shot that's going down. This is history. This is time. This is moment. This is grand. It is mean. . . .

The common reaction of people who get high the first time is, "Wow! is that real! Is that really what's happening? Wow! did you see it? It's real! "Not a specimen world anymore. It's not consumer-conveyor, consumer-conveyor-sit-in-a-slot-boom-boom-boom-boom-boom-boom-boom-boom-boom-boom-FEED-boom-boom-boom-SHIT-boom-boom-SLEE-p-boom-boom-boom . . . it's not that. It's like sentences don't have so many periods, it's like getting more dashes and colons and commas and involutions.

Q: How is a hard kick more real than a soft kick?

PETER: I'm not saying it's *more* real. I'm saying hard kicks are the perimeters of existence. A being.

Q: Is there a special value in being at the perimeter instead of, say, at the center?

PETER: It's called life. I'd rather shiver when it rains than not. Pure lightning, mental or otherwise. Fantastic sky-break—

Q: Being struck by it really blows your mind.

PETER: The Hopi have a struck-by-lightning fraternity. You can only get in if you've been struck by lightning. People that have survived lightning bolts belong to it. They're considered special seers.

Q: People in the community talk about acid as being the key to insight. Is this of any interest to you?

PETER: Insight, sight-in what? In what sight?

Q: They look inside, they claim to see their hangups.

PETER: And then what?

Q: That's what I'm asking. . . .

PETER: That's where we start, man. Now, do it. Now, do it, shit, now, go ahead, drop out now. What, now what, what now, now, what, whatever you want, go ahead, do it, do it. . . . You doin' what you want to? Uh-huh? *Sure* it's what you want to do? Do what you want to do, right? Can't do what you want to do? Uh-oh. Now things get very real. . . . Go do what you want to do. You tell me you're free, you tell me you're free, man. Tell me you're free, man, you do whatever you want to do, you tell me that. Now what. What happens now? Got busted? Did what? Free store, free food, wow, beautiful! Free theater, free poems, like that, we got busted! Yeah. You assume freedom? *Assume* freedom. Now what? It's pure intuition, man. Come on, we're talking about freedom. . . . You sit on the floor. You tell me what you can do tomorrow. You tell me what you can do, what you can get away with. . . . And then we find it's necessary to bail each other out.

There are internal contradictions in the society that have been heightened to such a degree that the country has become the equivalent of fascist. It's General Motors fascism. That's out front. Our lives are in fact revolutionary within the context of General Motors fascism. We expect to live our lives and to defend them. We have been cultural outsiders in this civilization. We will become the political dynamic of the new society because we are *living* a new civilization. My life is now political, it's ultimately political. . . .

The internal contradictions in this country are creating a void that one would have to be blind not to see. The void is rushing at us so fast now that Zen is breakfast. Within a short time, the general cultural movement will become more social. The issue is being forced by the black people. . . . We are in the middle, we people, and we find our vanity can no longer be a shield. So we have to adopt the state of mind that's proper to the world that's opening for us. Our life style is the mode of existence for free men, a new vision of freedom that is bought at the price that freedom has always been bought. Our people are in jails. What we do now will be called treason. . . . It is necessary to take the responsibility for being. . . . There is no escape; there can only be confrontation. . . . And there's every chance that we won't be allowed the opportunity to carry it out without an interim period where there's going to be a great deal of death. We've passed the meridian. . . . We're passing now into a time of death, and we have to confront death with the vision of life.

Q: What do you foresee?

PETER: Civil war. Civil war with some attendant trips.

Q: Like what?

PETER: Well, psychedelic celebration . . . hand-holding, candle-watching, high-on-acid-trust-and-hope routine. That's attendant. LSD hand-holding is not the end. Civil war with these things: the life-affirming banners. We're going to view what we're doing as the best we could come up with. It's only the best, scratch it. Scratch sixty-seven. Summer in San Francisco has been the first be-together. Summer in San Francisco '67 First Be-Together for Escapees and Refugees. . . . Our part now coming up is to communicate in direct spinal language. Nothing said that can't be done. . . . To push as hard as we can . . . to move past the Civil War in the United States to our planetary concerns, the forms and modes of which we are developing now . . . to get those models out and to prepare ourselves to carry them out. . . . The U.S. goes down. . . . The world *has* to get past. . . . The species on the planet has to get past the non-living of the last century, that most barren sterile time. The time when men died for wages, when lives were counted against profit-sharing coupons . . . when coupons and clip-outs became days and nights, when sunup was time to go to work and sundown was exhausted relief, or an alcoholic night out. . . . When grass was lunch outside the office, when flowers were passed on the way to work or grown on the weekend . . . ol' lady lawn, ol' lady lawn. . . .

It's the moment . . . and the thing moves, and the moment moves. . . .

Y'know, when people are high, man, they're talking music—and music was to Plato the highest form of art, because music imitates the harmony of the spheres. And we're trying to move our minds as sensuous instruments . . . to bring the species and ourselves . . . to move the school of fish we swim in. . . . To move onto the next place that we've got to go because if we don't move from where we are now, the barracuda are going to hit us. And they do. Every time the tide turns, the barracuda turns. Everybody turns when the tide turns.

"Theatre of Fear: One on the Aisle"
RICHARD GOLDSTEIN

I brought the Fear out with me from New York, in a white plastic helmet and a bottle of Vaseline. The same fear that built the fences, and erected the barricades, and brought all those soldiers in from Texas. Touch-fear: the kind that burns when you tap its roots. And this fear was worse than paranoia, because it involved no element of persecution, but only a gnawing awareness of inner dread.

I invoke these anxiety-obsessions now, under the pretext of relevance. If you want to experience the ecstacy of street-turmoil, you must first understand the reality of fear. Because no one could have come to Chicago without first fighting in his head the battle he would later fight in the streets.

I made lists. Weeks before my first whiff of tear gas, I spent a night dissecting my motives and expectations, in two neat columns. On one side, I wrote: adventure, good copy, and historical imperative. On the other: danger, loneliness, and cost. The word commitment didn't appear on either side. Not since college, the New Frontier, and the White Castle riot in the Bronx, had I been able to associate that word with politics. I simply re-directed my radicalism toward aesthetics. At Columbia, last spring, I realized that I had become a white liberal. I never saw the stirring of revolution on College Walk, and while I agreed with their goals, I felt distinct from the student-radicals, and enraged by their style. My cynic's streak flowed river-deep when I witnessed the martyrdom of Mimi (one of two girls who served short terms in the Women's House of Detention and inspired the chant, "Free Huey . . . Free Mimi.") If these people couldn't take punishment, did they really deserve to be free?

Not long after that, I had lunch with a Broadway producer who wanted me to help write the script for a protest-musical. Eyes aglow, he related his opening scene. Thirty kids march onstage, carrying signs. A voice screams: Up against the Wall, and the ensemble breaks into a chorus of "We Protest," to the tune of the 1812 Overture. There has been an undeclared alliance in my mind between that scenario and the tweedy revolutionaries at Columbia. Before Chicago, I couldn't perceive the difference between the guerrilla theatre on Morningside Heights and the realpolitik of Broadway.

"You afraid?" I asked a kid from California. He zipped his army jacket up to his neck, and filled his palm with a wad of Vaseline. "I dunno," he answered. "My toes feel cold, but my ears are burning."

We were standing together in Lincoln Park, not long after curfew on Tuesday night, watching an unbroken line of police. Around us were 1000 insurgents: hippies, Marxists, tourists, reporters, Panthers, Angels, and a phalanx of concerned ministers, gathered around a 12-foot cross. Occasionally a cluster of kids would break away from the rally to watch the formation in the distance. They spoke quietly, rubbing cream on their faces, and knotting dampened undershirts around their mouths. Not all their accoutrements were defensive. I saw saps and smoke bombs, steel-tipped boots and fistfuls of tacks. My friend pulled out a small canister from his pocket. "Liquid pepper," he explained.

Watching these kids gather sticks and stones, I realized how far we have come from that mythical summer when everyone dropped acid, sat under a tree, and communed. If there were any flower children left in America, they had heeded the underground press, and stayed home. Those who came fully anticipated confrontation. There were few virgins to violence in the crowd tonight. Most had seen—if not shed—blood, and that baptism had given them a determination of sorts. The spirit of Lincoln Park was to make revolution the way you make love—ambivalently, perhaps, but for real.

The cops advanced at 12:40 a.m., behind two massive floodlight-trucks. They also had the fear; you could see it in their eyes (wide and wet) and their mouths. All week, you watched them cruise the city—never alone, and never unarmed. At night, you heard their sirens in the streets, and all day, their helicopters in the sky. On duty, the average Chicago cop was a walking arsenal—with a shotgun in one hand, a riot baton (long and heavy with steel tips) in the other, and an assortment of pistols, nightsticks, and ominous canisters in his belt. At first, all that equipment seemed flattering. But then you saw under the helmets, and the phallic weaponry, and you felt the fear again. Immigrant to stranger, cop to civilian, old man to kid. The fear that brought the people of Chicago out into the streets during Martin Luther King's open housing march, now reflected in the fists of these cops. The fear that made the people of Gage Park spit at priests, and throw stones at nuns, now authorized to kill. And you realized that the cops weren't putting on that display for you; no—a cop's gun is his security blanket, just as Vaseline was yours.

Then the lights shone brilliant orange and the tear gas guns exploded putt—putt—puttutt, and the ministers dipped their cross into a halo of smothering fog. The gas hit like a great wall of pepper and you ran coughing into the streets, where you knew there would be rocks to throw and windows to smash and something to feel besides fear.

The soldiers stood on all the bridges, sealing off Grant Park from the city streets. The kids couldn't be gassed anymore, because the wind was blowing fumes across the guarded bridges and into every open pore of the Conrad Hilton, and the hotel was filled with good people who had tears in their eyes. So the soldiers just stood with their empty guns poised against the tide. And they were frowning at the kids who shouted "put down your guns; join us." A few hid flowers in their uniforms, and some smiled, but mostly, they stood posing for their own death masks.

"Wouldn't you rather hold a girl than a gun?" asked one kid with his arm around two willing chicks.

"You don't understand," the soldier stammered, moving his tongue across his lips. "It's orders. We have to be here."

That was Wednesday—nomination day—and the city was braced for escalation. At the afternoon rally, an American flag was hauled down, and the police responded by wading into the center of the crowd, with clubs flying. The kids built barricades of vacated benches, pelted the police with branches, and tossed plastic bags of cow's blood over their heads.

I stood in the shade applying Vaseline. I had my route mapped out in advance; across the northmost bridge and into the free Loop. With every semblance of press identification I owned pinned to my shirt, I set out across the mall. But most of the crowd had the same idea. Across on Michigan Avenue, I could hear the shouts of demonstrators who were re-grouping at the Hilton. I stopped to wet my undershirt in a fountain and ran down the street. My hands were shaking with anticipation and I could no longer close my eyes without seeing helmets and hearing chants. So my body was committed, but my head remained aloof.

It brought me back to the Columbia uprising, because I learned something then about why I am a journalist, and it has stayed with me since. Near Fayerwether Hall, I came face to face with a bloodied Liberator. He looked up at the press card on my jacket, and muttered: "That keeps you safe, huh?"

He was right. I demand that distance; it's part of my psyche. And I wasn't yet prepared to smash the tape recorder in my brain, which retains impressions without actually experiencing them. For me, the Chicago fear amounted to going up against the wall without that little card which reads, "Police Please Pass."

But now, I found myself swept up in the crowd around the Hilton. Rolls of toliet paper fell from the windows above. Floodlights flashed, cameras snapped, and somewhere, a glass pane shattered. That was enough. The cops turned on the crowd, and shoved us against the hotel's wall. People shrieked with one breath, and apologized for stepping on toes with the other. Then the cops rushed in two directions, and I fell on someone's back. A window broke behind me, and I saw people falling into the hotel pharmacy. Ahead, the police were clubbing in wide circles. Up close, and frozen into place, I saw their fists move in slow motion. I thought, no invective can capture this moment, because I could hear the stockyard around me then—the sound of slaughter, and I looked up at a kid whose arms were twisted behind in the crush, and I felt the Guernica in his eyes; the same expression on the big horse was on his lips. And I knew where it had come from and why.

I slipped out and walked across the street, shaking. I sat for 10 minutes with a girl who had been unconscious. We watched the medical crews covering their faces. And when the tear gas came, we ran away.

On Michigan Avenue, I sat in the street, and ripped away the remnants of my press cards. I whooped the way they did in "The Battle of Algiers," and chanted the way they did in "La Chinoise," and I raised my hands in a television "V" at the flag they had lowered to half mast. When the sirens came closer, I ran by rote up the steps of the Art Institute. Behind a pillar, I started to cry. You blew your cool, I thought, but it was like watching someone else's headache. I had found the other side of fear, which is not heroism, but rage. My eyes burned with it, and my hands shook with it. Behind me, a cop fired over my head, and I ran forward shouting "Pigs eat shit," not so he could hear, but so I could. In the street, I saw a straight kid in a crew-neck sweater heave a rock through the window of a police car. "The first one's hard," he said, as we ran toward State Street, "but after that, it's easy."

Which is where it's at, with America, and me.